Oracle® Performance Survival Guide

A Systematic Approach
to Database Optimization

Guy Harrison

Prentice Hall

Upper Saddle River, NJ • Boston • Indianapolis • San Francisco
New York • Toronto • Montreal • London • Munich • Paris • Madrid
Cape Town • Sydney • Tokyo • Singapore • Mexico City

Many of the designations used by manufacturers and sellers to distinguish their products are claimed as trademarks. Where those designations appear in this book, and the publisher was aware of a trademark claim, the designations have been printed with initial capital letters or in all capitals.

The author and publisher have taken care in the preparation of this book, but make no expressed or implied warranty of any kind and assume no responsibility for errors or omissions. No liability is assumed for incidental or consequential damages in connection with or arising out of the use of the information or programs contained herein.

The publisher offers excellent discounts on this book when ordered in quantity for bulk purchases or special sales, which may include electronic versions and/or custom covers and content particular to your business, training goals, marketing focus, and branding interests. For more information, please contact:

U.S. Corporate and Government Sales
(800) 382-3419
corpsales@pearsontechgroup.com

For sales outside the United States please contact:

International Sales
international@pearson.com

Visit us on the Web: informit.com/ph

Library of Congress Cataloging-in-Publication Data:
Harrison, Guy.
  Oracle performance survival guide : a systematic approach to database optimization / Guy Harrison.
    p. cm.
  Includes bibliographical references and index.
  ISBN 978-0-13-701195-7 (pbk. : alk. paper) 1. Oracle. 2. Database management. 3. Databases. I. Title.
  QA76.9.D3H3651536 2009
  005.75'75—dc22

                        2009036481

Pearson Education, Inc.
Rights and Contracts Department
501 Boylston Street, Suite 900
Boston, MA 02116
Fax (617) 671-3447

ISBN-13: 978-0-13-701195-7
ISBN-10: 0-13-70119-54
Text printed in the United States on recycled paper at Edwards Brothers, Ann Arbor, Michigan.

First printing October 2009

Editor-in-Chief *Mark Taub*
Acquisitions Editor *Trina MacDonald*
Development Editor *Michael Thurston*
Managing Editor *Patrick Kanouse*
Senior Project Editor *Tonya Simpson*
Copy Editor *Apostrophe Editing Services*
Indexer *WordWise Publishing Services*
Proofreader *Leslie Joseph*
Publishing Coordinator *Olivia Basegio*
Cover Designer *Anne Jones*
Compositor *Laserwords*

To my family

CONTENTS

TABLE OF CONTENTS

PREFACE

Performance has always been a major issue for databases, and Oracle is no exception. As the part of the application that performs the most disk IO and data crunching, databases are often the limiting factor on application throughput and the determining factor in application response time. Performance management of databases and tuning of database code is and always will be a high priority for database professionals.

In recent years the significance of database performance optimization has increased. Performance tuning has traditionally been mainly about meeting business service-level objectives: application throughput and transaction response time. During the Internet boom years, we had more money than time and throwing money at a performance problem—usually by adding hardware—often seemed the quickest route to improved performance. Today, however, the situation is very different:

❏ The economy, both in general and in terms of IT budgets, has changed. Business looks to reduce the total cost of ownership of IT whenever possible, including hardware expenditure, software licensing, IT payroll, and power consumption costs. It might not be possible to buy your way out of a performance problem at all, and it certainly doesn't make business sense.

❏ There's an increasing social imperative to reduce energy consumption, and electricity in particular. Electricity to run busy database servers not only costs money, but also exacts an environmental cost. A badly tuned database is like a poorly tuned car that backfires and belches smoke: It might get you from A to B, but it costs you more in gas and exacts a heavier toll on the environment.

❏ Grid and utility computing are becoming a reality. Prior to grid and virtualization technologies IO, memory or CPU saved from one database could not easily be recycled to other databases. Today it is increasingly possible to take saved resources from one database and recycle them to another database or to a non-database server.

So although it's still correct to focus performance tuning efforts on business service-level objectives, performance tuning also contributes to business profitability by reducing power consumption and has the added benefit of being socially and environmentally responsible. We have both a business and social responsibility to ensure that our databases run at peak efficiency.

As a book-lover and a committed Oracle technologist, I've bought dozens of wonderful Oracle technical books. Some of my favorites are listed in the bibliography. With so many great books already available, why write another?

It seems to me there's still a need for a book that presents a systematic, comprehensive, and accessible approach to Oracle tuning, covering all aspects of Oracle performance management. A book that covers the essentials of Oracle tuning, suitable for all levels of expertise and across all relevant disciplines: A "survival guide" that can guide you through the majority of performance management challenges and opportunities.

Therefore, in writing this book, I set out with the following objectives:

❏ To provide a structured methodology for Oracle performance tuning that addresses performance issues in the most systematic and efficient manner possible.
❏ To address all aspects of Oracle performance management: from application and database design, through SQL tuning, contention management, and on to memory and physical IO management.
❏ To maintain a strong focus on tuning *fundamentals*, while providing technical depth and breadth. Fundamentals are usually where the biggest performance gains can be found and—if not addressed—usually limit the benefits gained through the application of advanced techniques.
❏ To provide content that is accessible both to those with limited Oracle tuning expertise and to the experienced practitioner.

WHO SHOULD READ THIS BOOK

This book is written for anyone who is interested in improving the performance of an Oracle database or database application. This includes application architects, developers, and Oracle database administrators. Not all sections of the book will necessarily appeal to application architects and developers who rarely have an opportunity to (for example) determine the layout of Oracle data files on a disk storage array. Similarly, DBAs are often involved in all aspects of performance, but just as often have no input into the application design. Each of these groups might choose to skip sections of the book covering aspects of performance in which they have no control. However, I emphasize that the philosophy of this book advocates addressing the root causes of performance issues before alleviating symptoms. It's assumed in later chapters (disk IO tuning, for instance) that you have addressed the activities outlined in preceding chapters (tuning SQLs, for instance).

This book is intended to be accessible to those who are relatively new to the Oracle database, so I briefly explain and define key concepts and Oracle architecture. Some familiarity with Oracle and the SQL language is assumed, however.

HOW THIS BOOK IS STRUCTURED

In Chapter 1, "Oracle Performance Tuning: A Methodical Approach," I provide an introduction to a tuning methodology based around the concept of tuning by layers. This methodology provides an efficient and systematic approach to Oracle performance optimization that concentrates on optimizing root causes before symptoms, and which maximizes performance return on your tuning investment. This book is broadly organized around this methodology and contains the following major sections:

❏ **Part I: "Methods, Concepts, and Tools"**—In Chapters 1–3 I describe the performance tuning methodologies that provide the most effective means of tuning Oracle databases. We also look at the fundamental tools and techniques for tracing, monitoring, and diagnosing Oracle database performance and provide an overview of the Oracle database architecture.

❏ **Part II: "Application and Database Design"**—These chapters (4–6) cover application and database design. Here we cover database logical and physical design, indexing, transaction design, and optimal use of the Oracle APIs.

❏ **Part III: "SQL and PL/SQL Tuning"**—This part, composed of Chapters 7–14, covers the optimization of SQL statements. SQL statement tuning usually offers the most-significant database performance opportunities and should be addressed prior to database server tuning. We also look at ways to leverage parallel SQL and the tuning of PL/SQL code.

❏ **Part IV: "Minimizing Contention"**—These chapters (15–17) discuss various aspects of contention. Contention for Oracle database resources such as locks, latches, and shared memory limits the capability of the database to process the requests created by the application. By reducing contention we increase the amount of application demand that the database can service.

❏ **Part V: "Optimizing Memory"**—Chapters 18–20 look at improving performance through optimal memory configuration. Memory optimization reduces the amount of logical IO that becomes physical IO. Optimizing memory is therefore a fundamental factor in database server performance.

❏ **Part VI: "IO Tuning and Clustering"**—Chapters 21–22 discuss physical disk IO. We've gone to all possible lengths to avoid disk IO; now it's time to optimize the disk IO that remains. In this section we look at how to configure Oracle and the disk IO subsystem to reduce IO overhead and improve IO throughput.

Chapters 1–22 are applicable to both Real Application Clusters (RAC) databases and single-instance Oracle. However, RAC does introduce some unique considerations that we address in Chapter 23, "Optimizing RAC."

ABOUT THE EXAMPLES AND THE SAMPLE DATA

Discussions in the book frequently use various scripts to report on aspects of database performance. You can download these scripts from this book's Web site http://www.informit.com/store/product.aspx?isbn=0137011954. You can also visit my Web site at http://www.guyharrison.net where you can find other materials and my blog.

Throughout the book, you'll also see examples of SQL statements and PL/SQL programs that illustrate various tuning principles. Wherever possible, these examples were written against the standard Oracle Database Sample Schemas that can be installed when the database is created, or manually installed later. Oracle has fully documented these schemas in the book B10771-01 (Oracle 10g) or B28328-01 (Oracle 11g), available on line at http://technet.oracle.com.

In some cases, the row counts in some of the sample tables were too low to effectively illustrate certain SQL tuning or other scenarios. For this reason, I wrote a routine to increase the sizes of key tables such as CUSTOMERS and SALES. The PL/SQL package written to achieve this is included in this book's scripts package available at this book's Web site.

ORACLE VERSIONS COVERED

This book comprehensively covers Oracle versions 10g and 11g, including version 11g Release 2. Some reference occasionally is made to earlier versions of Oracle, but all the examples shown in the book are from Oracle 10g or Oracle 11g databases.

Oracle 11g Release 2 was still in beta as this book went to press. Some minor changes in behavior in the production release of Oracle 11g Release 2 are possible. I'll note these at the book's Web site and at my personal Web site if they occur.

ABOUT QUEST SOFTWARE AND SPOTLIGHT

I've worked at Quest Software for roughly half of my 21-year involvement with Oracle technology. At Quest, I've been heavily involved in the development of many Oracle development and administration tools, but most notably Spotlight on Oracle and Spotlight on Oracle RAC. Where I've felt that an aspect of Oracle performance management is particularly well covered by Spotlight, I've mentioned the feature and sometimes provided a screenshot. Because I'm both the architect of Spotlight and the author of this book, you can assume that Spotlight embodies many of the principles and practices outlined in this book, and I certainly encourage you to download and evaluate Spotlight. However, be aware that Spotlight is "my baby," and I'm hardly unbiased when it comes to Spotlight or any Quest Software product.

FOR READERS OF ORACLE SQL HIGH PERFORMANCE TUNING

It's been almost eight years since the second edition of *Oracle SQL High Performance Tuning*, but I still receive regular requests for a third edition. Those that found *Oracle SQL High Performance Tuning* useful should find this book a more than adequate substitute for a third edition. In this book I continue the empirical and pragmatic approach of *Oracle SQL High Performance Tuning* and extend it to a wider discipline of Oracle performance management. In this book, the key emphasis on SQL tuning remains, but within a wider scope that includes application and database design and database server configuration and optimization.

ACKNOWLEDGMENTS

I'd like to thank acquisitions editor Trina McDonald for encouraging me to take on this project and for overseeing the process. Also at Pearson I'd particularly like to thank Olivia Basegio, Michael Thurston, and Tonya Simpson.

Many thanks to technical reviewers Patrick O'Keeffe, Bert Scalzo, and Oleg Voskoboynikov. This book covers a wide range of material, and I'm so grateful to have had their technical support and feedback. Steven Feuerstein also contributed some great feedback on Chapters 6 and 12. Thanks all!

Thanks to those in the Oracle community who continually share their experiences with and insights into Oracle technology. I really couldn't have written this book without this wealth of freely shared wisdom. The appendix lists some of the blogs and bloggers that I am most grateful for.

Finally—but most important——thanks as always to my wife Jenni and children Chris, Kate, Mike, and William. Your love and support made this book possible, and I'm sorry you had to put up with me during this and my other writing projects. KahPlah!

About the Author

Guy Harrison has worked with Oracle databases as a developer, administrator, and performance expert for more than two decades. He is the author of many articles and several books on database technology, including *Oracle SQL High Performance Tuning* (Prentice Hall) and *MySql Stored Procedure Programming* (with Steven Feuerstein, O'Reilly). Guy is currently a director of development at Quest Software and is the chief architect of Quest's popular Spotlight product family. He lives in Melbourne, Australia, with his wife Jenni and children Chris, Kate, Mike, and William. You can find Guy on the Web at http://www.guyharrison.net

Oracle Performance Tuning: A Methodical Approach

Oracle performance tuning has come a long way over the years, but it is too often still approached in a haphazard or inefficient manner. Consider the following cautionary tale:

A mission-critical application system is experiencing unsatisfactory performance. As an experienced Oracle performance specialist, you are called in to diagnose the problem. The first - you do is examine the database wait times to see where the database is spending the majority of execution time. As we'll see later, this information can easily be found by looking in the V$SYSTEM_EVENT and V$SYS_TIME_MODEL views.

Looking at these views, two things stand out. First, the vast majority of database time is spent reading from disk devices. Second, the average time to read a single block from disk is much higher than you would expect given the capabilities of the disk hardware involved.

You suspect that the disk array might have insufficient IO bandwidth to support the application's demands. In other words, not enough physical disks are in the disk array to support the IO rate required. After a quick calculation, you recommend increasing the number of disk devices in the array by a factor of four. The dollar cost is substantial, as is the downtime required to redistribute data across the new disks within the array.[1] Nevertheless, something needs to be done, so management approves the expense and the downtime. Following the

---

[1]With some technologies, this downtime can be avoided; however, an extended period of degraded performance would still be required.

implementation, users report they are satisfied with performance, and you modestly take all the credit.

A successful outcome? You think so, until . . .

❑ Within a few months performance is again a problem and disk IO is again the culprit.

❑ Another Oracle performance expert is called in and reports that a single indexing change would have fixed the original problem with no dollar cost and no downtime.

❑ The new index is implemented, following which the IO rate is reduced to one-tenth of that observed during your original engagement. Management prepares to sell the now-surplus disk devices on eBay and marks your consulting record with a "do not reengage" stamp.

❑ Your significant other leaves you for an Oracle salesperson, and you end up shaving your head and becoming a monk.

After years of silent mediation, you realize that while your tuning efforts correctly focused on the activities consuming the most time within the database, they failed to differentiate between *causes* and *effects*. Consequently, you mistakenly dealt with an *effect*—the high disk IO rate—while neglecting the *cause* (a missing index).

In this chapter we consider a methodology that ensures that you focus on the root causes of Oracle performance problems. This approach avoids the repetitive trial-and-error process that is characteristic of a lot of performance-tuning efforts and ensures that you get the biggest performance gains for your tuning efforts.

A BRIEF HISTORY OF ORACLE PERFORMANCE TUNING

In the early '90s, the discipline of tuning an Oracle server was nowhere near as well established as today. In fact, performance tuning was mostly limited to a couple of well-known "rules of thumb."

The most notorious of these guidelines was that you should tune the *Buffer Cache Hit Ratio*: the ratio that describes the proportion of blocks of data requested by a SQL that are found in memory. If ten blocks of data are requested, and nine of them are found in memory, the hit ratio is 90 percent. Increasing the buffer cache size until the ratio reached 90 percent to 95 percent was often suggested. Similar target values were suggested for other ratios, such as the latch hit ratio.

The problem with these "ratio-based" techniques was that although the ratios usually reflected some measure of internal Oracle efficiency, they were often only loosely associated with the performance experienced by an application using the database. For example, although it is obviously better for a block of data to be found in memory—resulting in a high hit rate—SQL statements that inefficiently read the same data over and over again would often result in a high hit rate. Indeed, a *very* high hit ratio is often a symptom of badly tuned SQL.

The emergence of wait information in Oracle version 7.1 provided an alternative method of approaching tuning. This wait information showed the amount of time Oracle sessions spent waiting for various events, such as a lock becoming available or a disk IO completing. By concentrating on the wait events that accounted for the greatest amount of total wait time, Oracle performance tuners could target their tuning efforts more effectively.

Pioneers of systematic Oracle performance tuning, such as Anjo Kolk, author of the famous "Yet Another Performance Profiling" (YAPP) methodology, promoted this technique vigorously.

Wait-based tuning took a surprisingly long time to reach the mainstream: 5–10 years passed between the original release of the wait information and widespread acceptance of the technique; however, today almost all Oracle professionals are familiar with wait-based tuning.

MOVING BEYOND A SYMPTOMATIC APPROACH

The shift from ratio-based to wait-based tuning has resulted in radical improvements in our ability to diagnose and tune Oracle-based applications. However, as noted previously, simplistically focusing on the largest component of response time can have several undesirable consequences:

❏ We might treat the symptoms rather than the causes of poor performance.
❏ We might be tempted to seek hardware-based solutions when configuration or application changes would be more cost-effective.
❏ We might deal with today's pain but fail to achieve a permanent or scalable solution.

To avoid the pitfalls of a narrow wait-based analysis, we need our tuning activities to follow a number of well-defined stages. These stages are dictated by the reality of how applications, databases, and operating systems interact. At a high level, database processing occurs in *layers*, as follows:

1. Applications send requests to the database in the form of SQL statements (including PL/SQL requests). The database responds to these requests with return codes and result sets.
2. To deal with an application request, the database must parse the SQL and perform various overhead operations (security, scheduling, and transaction

management) before finally executing the SQL. These operations use operating system resources (CPU and memory) and might be subject to contention between concurrently executing database sessions.

3. Eventually, the database request needs to process (create, read, or change) some of the data in the database. The exact amount of data that needs to be processed can vary depending on the database design (indexing, for example) and the application (wording of the SQL, for example).

    Some of the required data will be in memory. The chance that a block will be in memory will be determined mainly by the frequency with which the data is requested and the amount of memory available to *cache* the data. When we access database data in memory, it's called a *logical IO*. Memory is also used to perform sorting and hashing operations.

4. If the block is not in memory, it must be accessed from disk, resulting in real physical IO. Physical IO is by far the most expensive of all operations, and consequently the database goes to a lot of effort to avoid performing unnecessary IO operations. However, some disk activity is inevitable. Disk IO also occurs when sorting and hashing operations are too large to complete in memory.

Activity in each of these layers influences the demand placed on the subsequent layer. For instance, if an SQL statement is submitted that somehow fails to exploit an index, it will require an excessive number of logical reads, which in turn will increase contention and eventually involve a lot of physical IO. It's tempting when you see a lot of IO or contention to deal with the symptom directly by tuning the disk layout. However, if you sequence your tuning efforts so as to work through the layers in order, you have a much better chance of fixing root causes and relieving performance at lower layers.

Here's the tuning by layers approach in a nutshell:

Problems in one database layer can be caused or cured by configuration in the higher layer. The logical steps in Oracle tuning are therefore

1. **Reduce application demand to its logical minimum by tuning SQL and PL/SQL and optimizing physical design (partitioning, indexing, and so on).**
2. **Maximize concurrency by minimizing contention for locks, latches, buffers, and other resources in the Oracle code layer.**
3. **Having normalized logical IO demand by the preceding steps, minimize the resulting physical IO by optimizing Oracle memory.**
4. **Now that the physical IO demand is realistic, configure the IO subsystem to meet that demand by providing adequate IO bandwidth and evenly distributing the resulting load.**

The tuning procedures in this book are organized according to the tuning by layers approach.[2] In the remainder of this chapter, we will examine each of these steps, as shown in Figure 1-1, in turn.

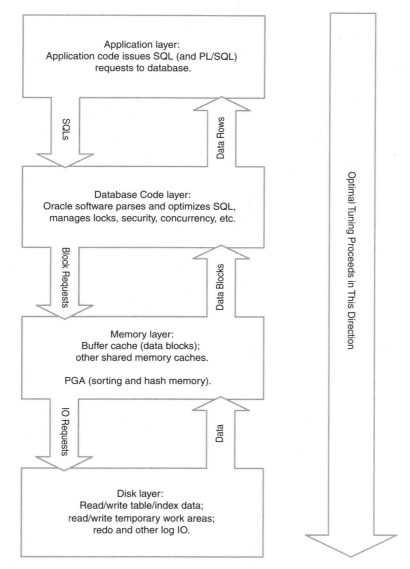

FIGURE 1-1 The four major "layers" of the Oracle database.

---

[2] The general concept of "tuning by layers" for Oracle was first proposed by Steve Adams (http://www.ixora.com.au/tips/layers.zip).

STAGE 1: MINIMIZING THE APPLICATION WORKLOAD

Our first objective is to minimize the application's demands on the database. We want the database to satisfy the application's data requirements with the least possible processing. In other words, we want Oracle to work smarter, not harder.

Broadly speaking, we use two main techniques to reduce application workload:

❏ **Tuning the application code**—This might involve changing application code—C#, Ruby or Java—so that it issues fewer requests to the database (by using a client-side cache, for instance). However, more often this will involve rewriting application SQL and/or PL/SQL.

❏ **Modifying the physical implementation of the application's databases**— This might involve indexing, denormalization, or partitioning.

Chapters 4 through 14 cover in detail the various techniques we can use to minimize application workload. Specifically

❏ **Structuring an application to avoid overloading the database**—Applications can avoid making needless requests of the database and can be architected to minimize lock and other contention.

❏ **Using best practices when communicating with the Oracle server**—The programs that communicate with Oracle can be designed and implemented to minimize database round trips and unnecessary requests.

❏ **Optimizing the physical database design**—This includes indexing, denormalization, partitioning, and other ways of physically structuring data to reduce the work required to execute SQL requests.

❏ **Optimizing the Oracle query optimizer**—By correctly configuring the collection of optimizer statistics, over-riding optimizer plans when necessary, and instituting ongoing monitoring of SQL performance.

❏ **Tuning the performance of individual SQL statements**—This might involve changing the SQL execution plan using hints, stored outlines, profiles, and SQL rewrites.

❏ **Using parallel SQL capabilities**—This allows you to apply multiple processes to the SQL execution.

❏ **Tuning and using PL/SQL programs**—You can use PL/SQL used in certain circumstances to improve application performance, and PL/SQL programs present unique tuning issues and opportunities.

These techniques not only represent the logical place to start in our tuning efforts, but they also represent the techniques that provide the most dramatic performance improvements. It's not at all uncommon for SQL tuning to result in performance improvements of 100 or even 1,000 times: improvements that you rarely see when tuning contention, optimizing memory, or adjusting physical disk layout.

STAGE 2: REDUCING CONTENTION AND BOTTLENECKS

After we adjust the application workload demand to a sensible minimum, we are ready to tackle contention within the Oracle server. Contention occurs when two or more sessions want simultaneous access to a resource, such as a lock or memory buffer.

When the application demand hits the database, contention—the proverbial "bottleneck"—limits the amount of work that can be done. From the applications perspective, the database appears slow or stalled. At lower levels—the disk subsystem, for instance—the demand appears to be lower than it really is. The contention bottleneck prevents the demand from getting through the database code into the IO subsystem. Figure 1-2 illustrates the phenomenon.

The two most prevalent forms of contention observed in Oracle-based applications are contention for rows within tables—generally showing up as waits for locks—and contention for areas of shared memory—showing up as waits for latches, memory buffers, and so on.

Lock contention is largely a factor of application design: Oracle's locking model allows for high concurrency because readers never wait for locks, writers never wait for readers, and locks are applied at the row level only. Typically, lock contention is caused by an application design that involves high simultaneous updates against a single row or in which locks are held for an excessive length of time, perhaps due to a pessimistic locking model. This sort of contention is

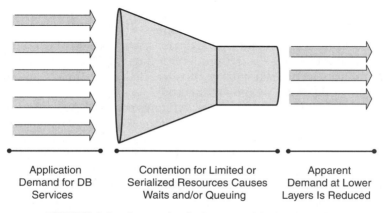

| Application
Demand for DB
Services | Contention for Limited or
Serialized Resources Causes
Waits and/or Queuing | Apparent
Demand at Lower
Layers Is Reduced |

FIGURE 1-2   Contention is the proverbial bottleneck.

almost impossible to eliminate without application logic changes—changes that we address in the first stage of tuning. However, there are scenarios in which excessive lock contention is caused by database or schema configuration problems, or by Oracle internal mechanisms.

Contention for shared memory occurs when sessions want to read or write to shared memory in the SGA concurrently. All shared memory is protected by *latches* (or *mutexes*), which are similar to locks except that they prevent concurrent access to data in shared memory rather than data in tables. If a session needs to modify some data in memory, it acquires the relevant latch, or mutex, and if another session wants to read or modify the same data, a latch, or mutex, wait might occur. Contention for data blocks in the buffer cache can occur for other reasons as well: A variety of *buffer* waits can occur when a block of memory is unavailable due to conflicting processing demands between sessions.

Chapters 15–17 address the techniques for eliminating Oracle contention. Specifically

❏ Detecting and dealing with lock contention, including Oracle internal locks
❏ Optimizing Oracle latching mechanisms that protect Oracle shared memory
❏ Identifying and correcting contention for shared memory itself

STAGE 3: REDUCING PHYSICAL IO

Now that the application demand has been minimized, and contention that might otherwise mask that demand eliminated, we turn our attention to reducing the time spent waiting for IO. In other words, before trying to reduce the time taken for *each* IO (IO latency), we try to reduce the *amount* of IO. As it turns out, reducing the amount of IO almost always reduces the IO latency, so attacking the volume of IO first is doubly effective. Having reduced application demand through SQL tuning and other means, we now try to further reduce IO by configuring memory to cache and buffer IO requests.

Most physical IO in an Oracle database occurs either because an application session requests data to satisfy a query or data modification request, because the session must sort or hash data, or must create a temporary segment to support a large join, ORDER BY, or similar operation.

Oracle's shared memory (the SGA) stores copies of data blocks in memory and eliminates the need to perform a disk IO if the requested data block is in that memory. Correctly allocating this memory goes a long way toward minimizing disk IO.

In the past, allocating SGA memory was a hit-and-miss affair. Luckily, in modern Oracle the server can automatically adjust memory allocations for you, or you can measure the effect of adjusting the size of the various memory pools by examining *advisories*, which accurately predict the effect of changing the sizes of those pools.

Oracle enables you to set up separate memory areas to cache blocks of different size and also enables you to nominate specific areas to cache data that might need to be kept in memory. Not all these memory areas will be automatically and dynamically resized by Oracle, and Oracle will not automatically allocate the areas in the first place, or assign specific data segments to these areas; those tasks are left to the DBA.

In addition to disk reads when accessing data not in the shared memory, Oracle might perform substantial IO when sorting or hashing data during ordering, grouping, or join operations. Where possible, Oracle performs a sort or hash operation in memory within the area of memory allocated for program use—the Program Global Area (PGA). However, if sufficient memory is not available, Oracle writes to—and reads from—temporary segments on disk to complete the sort or hash operation.

Oracle has improved its capability to automatically manage these memory areas in most recent releases. As of 10g, Oracle automatically resizes allocations *within* the PGA and the SGA, but will not shift memory *between* these areas. In 11g Oracle can move memory between the PGA and SGA as required—or at least, as Oracle calculates is required.

Despite the progress in automatic memory management, there's still a lot for the Oracle administrator to do to ensure optimal performance. These tasks include

- ❑ Determining whether the correct amount of OS memory is available to Oracle
- ❑ Determining the correct division of memory between the PGA and SGA, or—in 11g—allowing Oracle's Automatic Memory Management to make that determination
- ❑ Fine-tuning the allocation of segments to specific memory areas
- ❑ Fine-tuning the parameters controlling sorting and joining
- ❑ Monitoring Oracle's memory allocations and over-riding if necessary

Chapters 18–20 cover these memory optimization techniques.

STAGE 4: OPTIMIZING DISK IO

At this point, we've normalized the application workload—in particular the amount of logical IO demanded by the application. We've eliminated contention that might be blocking—and therefore masking—those logical IO requests. Finally, we've configured available memory to minimize the amount of logical IO that ends up causing physical IO. Now—and only now—it makes sense to make sure that our disk IO subsystem is up to the challenge.

To be sure, optimizing disk IO subsystems can be a complex and specialized task, but the basic principles are straightforward:

❑   Ensure the IO subsystem has enough bandwidth to cope with the physical
    IO demand. This is primarily determined by the number of distinct disk de-
    vices you have allocated. Disks vary in performance, but the average disk
    device might be able to perform approximately 100 random IOs per second
    before becoming saturated. Good response time usually requires that the
    disk be less than 100 percent utilized—say 50 percent to 75 percent. For
    most databases, meeting IO requirements means acquiring much more disk
    than simple storage requirements dictate. You need to acquire enough disks
    to sustain your IO rate with acceptable response time, not just enough disks
    to store all your data.

❑   Spread your load evenly across the disks you have allocated. The best way
    to do this is RAID 0 (Striping). The worst way—for most databases—is
    RAID 5, which incurs a heavy penalty on write IO.

The obvious symptom of an overly stressed IO subsystem is excessive delays responding to IO requests. The expected delay—called *service time*—varies
from disk to disk, but even on the slowest disks should not exceed approximately
10ms. Disk arrays boasting large memory caches and Solid State Disk (SSD) devices might provide much lower latencies. Network Attached Storage (NAS) devices might also have a high network-related component to the service time.

Spreading the load across spindles is best done by hardware or software
striping. Oracle's ASM technology provides a simple and universally available
method of doing this for ordinary disk devices. Alternating datafiles across multiple disks is usually less effective, though still better than no striping at all. Most
high-end databases employ the striping capabilities of a hardware disk array.

For most databases, optimizing the datafiles for read activity makes the
most sense because Oracle sessions do not normally wait for datafile writes; the
database writer process (DBWR) writes to disk asynchronously. However, if
the DBWR cannot keep up with database activity, sessions need to wait for the
DBWR to catch up. Likewise, we need to ensure that the flashback and redo log
writer processes can keep up; otherwise, user sessions need to wait for these
processes as well.

Chapters 21 and 22 covers the issues associated with optimizing disk IO:

❑   Understanding the Oracle IO mechanisms—buffered IO and direct IO, redo
    and archive log IO, flashback IO, and other mechanisms.

❑   Measuring IO performance and calculating optimal disk configurations.

❑   Using mechanisms for striping data, including RAID levels.

❑   Utilizing specific IO-related technologies such as ASM and SSD.

SUMMARY

When faced with an obviously IO-bound database, it's tempting to deal with the most obvious symptom—the IO subsystem—immediately. Unfortunately, this usually results in treating the symptom rather than the cause, is often expensive, and is often ultimately futile. Because problems in one database layer can be caused or cured by configuration in the higher layer, the most efficient and effective way to optimize an Oracle database is to tune higher layers before tuning lower layers:

1. Reduce application demand to its logical minimum by tuning SQL, optimizing physical design (partitioning, indexing), and tuning PL/SQL.
2. Maximize concurrency by minimizing contention for locks, latches, buffers, and other resources in the Oracle code layer.
3. Having normalized logical IO demand by the preceding steps, minimize the resulting physical IO by optimizing Oracle memory.
4. Now that the physical IO demand is realistic, configure the IO subsystem to meet that demand by providing adequate bandwidth and evenly distributing the resulting load.

ORACLE ARCHITECTURE AND CONCEPTS

In this chapter we review aspects of the Oracle database architecture that become important when reading the chapters to come, and that are particularly relevant to Oracle performance.

You need to be broadly familiar with these aspects of Oracle database technology:

❑ The way in which programs interact with the Oracle database server through the APIs implemented within various programming languages

❑ The Oracle optimizer, which is the software layer concerned with maximizing the performance of SQL statements

❑ The Oracle server architecture, including the memory, processes, and files that interact to provide database services

❑ Oracle schema objects, including tables, indexes, partitions, and other segments that implement an application's data model

If you are thoroughly familiar with these matters, you might want to skim or skip this chapter. However, subsequent chapters assume that you are familiar with the concepts presented in this chapter.

THE ORACLE APIs

Almost every programming language has an application programming interface (API) for dealing with the Oracle database. Here are some of the more widely used APIs:

❑ The Oracle Call Interface (OCI) is the C language API that forms the basis for many of the higher-level interfaces.

❑ Java DataBase Connectivity (JDBC) is a generic API that enables Java programs to interact with various databases and data sources. Oracle provides a "thin" 100 percent Java driver and an OCI driver that is based on the OCI libraries.

❑ .NET programs use the generic ADO.NET libraries to communicate with databases. Microsoft provides a basic—but recently depreciated—Oracle adaptor, while Oracle provides a more fully fledged adaptor known as Oracle Data Provider for .NET (ODP.NET).

❑ Open source languages such as Perl, Python, PHP, and Ruby all provide generic APIs for database access, and each of these are associated with an Oracle adaptor, generally implemented on top of the OCI interface.

❑ PL/SQL executes inside the database and requires no explicit API to communicate with Oracle. However, PL/SQL itself uses programming patterns similar to those of external languages, especially when executing dynamic SQL.

Each of these APIs exhibits a similar sequence of interactions with Oracle.

Each SQL statement is represented in the client—behind the scenes if not explicitly—as a *context area* or *cursor*. Figure 2-1 provides an overview of the life-cycle of a SQL statement cursor.

We discuss each of these stages in detail, but here is a brief overview of each step:

1. Create the cursor. The cursor is the area in memory that holds the definition of a currently open SQL statement.

2. Check for a cached copy of the SQL statement inside Oracle shared memory.

3. Parse the SQL. Parsing SQL involves checking the SQL for syntax and object references and invoking the Oracle optimizer to determine a query plan.

4. Assign bind variables. Before the SQL statement can be executed, the values of any bind variables—placeholders that represent values to be supplied by the calling program—must be attached to the SQL.

5. Execute the SQL. If the SQL statement is not a query, executing the SQL involves processing the DML or DDL statement in its entirety. If the SQL statement is a query, executing the SQL prepares the statement for fetch operations.

6. Fetch the rows. For queries, fetching involves retrieving one or more rows from the result set.

7. Close the cursor. This involves releasing all the memory and resources associated with the cursor. (Although a shared representation of the cursor might be retained in Oracle shared memory.)

The following sections look at each of these stages in detail.

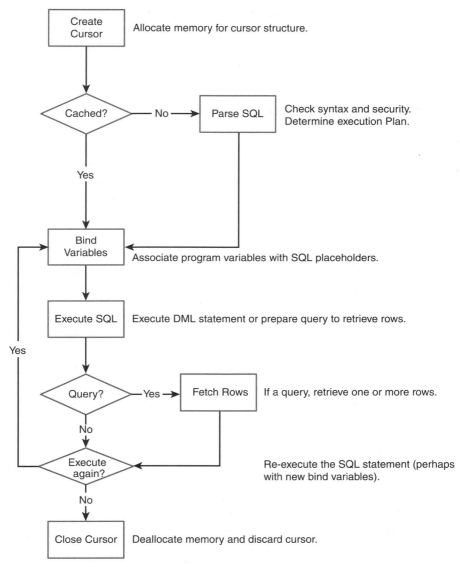

FIGURE 2-1 SQL Statement processing overview.

CREATING THE CURSOR

A cursor—or *context area*—is an area in memory in which Oracle stores your SQL statement and associated information. This includes the parsed and unparsed representation of your SQL statement, the execution plan, and a pointer to the current row.

When SQL statement execution is complete, the memory associated with the cursor can be freed for other purposes or can be saved for re-execution.

In most programming languages, a cursor corresponds to a SQL object or statement handle. In Java JDBC, a cursor is equivalent to a *Statement* or *PreparedStatement* object.

CHECKING FOR CACHED SQL STATEMENTS

To avoid unnecessary parsing, Oracle maintains a cache of recently executed SQL statements together with their execution plans. This cache is maintained in an area of shared memory: the *SQL Area* of the *Shared pool*. Whenever a request to execute a SQL statement is issued, Oracle looks for a matching statement in this cache. If a matching statement is found, Oracle uses the execution plan stored in the cache and avoids most of the overhead involved in parsing.

PARSING THE SQL

Parsing is the process of preparing your SQL statement for execution. The parse process

❑ Checks that the SQL statement is syntactically valid, that the SQL conforms to the rules of the SQL language, and that all keywords and operators are valid and correctly used.
❑ Checks that the SQL is semantically valid. With this means that all references to database objects (that is, tables and columns) are valid.
❑ Checks so that the user has security permissions to perform the specified SQL operations on the objects involved.
❑ Determines an execution plan for the SQL statement. The execution plan describes the series of steps that Oracle performs to access and update the data involved. This is done by the Oracle *optimizer* that is discussed in detail later in this chapter.

Parsing can be an expensive operation, although often its overhead is masked by the greater overhead of high IO requirements. However, eliminating unnecessary parsing is always desirable.

ASSOCIATING BIND VARIABLES

A SQL statement can contain variables that change from execution to execution. These variables are typically parameters to the SQL statement that define the rows to be processed or new values to be inserted or updated. We can specify these variables either as literals or as *bind variables*.

For instance, using literals, we can retrieve details for employee 206 with the following SQL statement:

```
SQL> SELECT first_name, last_name
  2    FROM hr.employees
  3   WHERE employee_id = 206
```

The next time we want to select an employee, we would change the "206" literal to the new value and re-execute. This works, of course, but remember that the SQL statement must be absolutely identical if a match is to be found in the shared pool. Because the EMPLOYEE_ID is likely to be different for every execution, we will almost never find a matching statement in the shared pool, and consequently the statement needs to be reparsed every time.

An alternative approach is to specify these variable portions with bind variables. Bind variables are fixed references to variables defined elsewhere in the programming language or query tool. Within most languages or tools, bind variables are recognizable because they are prefixed by a colon. For instance, in the following SQL*PLUS example, the value of EMPLOYEE_ID is stored in a bind variable (the SQL*PLUS VARIABLE command allows us to define a bind variable):

```
SQL> VARIABLE bind_employee_number NUMBER
SQL> BEGIN
  2      :bind_employee_number := 206;
  3   END;
  4   /

PL/SQL procedure successfully completed.

SQL> SELECT first_name, last_name
  2    FROM hr.employees
  3   WHERE employee_id = :bind_employee_number
  4   /

FIRST_NAME           LAST_NAME
-------------------- --------------------------
William              Gietz
```

There are at least two compelling reasons for using bind variables. First, if the value of the bind variable changes, you don't need to create a new cursor or reparse the SQL statement when re-executing the SQL. Second, if another session executes the same SQL statement, it finds a match in the shared pool because the name of the bind variable does not change from execution to execution.

Conversely, if you use literals instead of bind variables, you'll suffer from the following problems:

❏ Every time you change the value of a literal, you (or your software tool) will have to request that the SQL be reparsed.

❏ When you do request the parse, the chance of finding a match in the shared pool will be negligible.

❏ The SQL cache will fill up with "one-off" SQL and might need to be bigger than it otherwise would be.

❏ When an Oracle session wants to place a new SQL statement in the shared pool, it has to acquire an Oracle internal lock (a *latch* or *mutex*). Under extreme circumstances, contention for these latches or mutexes can result in a performance bottleneck at best or dramatic performance problems at worst. We look at latches and mutexes in detail in Chapter 16, "Latch and Mutex Contention."

Oracle can automatically substitute bind variables for literals if the parameter CURSOR_SHARING is set to TRUE or SIMILAR. This topic is covered in Chapter 6, "Application Design and Implementation."

EXECUTING THE SQL

When the SQL statement is parsed and all variables are bound, Oracle is ready to execute the statement. In the case of DML (INSERT, UPDATE, MERGE, DELETE), executing the statement results in the SQL being processed immediately, although the changes do not become permanent until a COMMIT is issued.

In the case of a SELECT statement, the execute call readies the cursor for fetch operations. In the case of certain queries (for example, where the rows must be sorted or locked), opening the cursor makes Oracle retrieve all the rows to be returned. In other cases, opening the cursor simply locates the record pointer at the first row.

FETCHING ROWS

Regardless of whether the open call must access all rows to be returned, it is the fetch call that returns data to the client environment. The fetch call retrieves one or more rows from the database and stores the results in host variables that can be manipulated by the program.

From the program's point of view, each fetch call simply returns one or more rows. Under the hood, Oracle might fetch the rows from disk or from the buffer cache—an area in shared memory that caches data blocks. In 11g, Oracle might return the entire result set from either the client-side result set cache or from the server-side result set cache. The client-side result set cache is described in Chapter 6, whereas the server-side cache is described in Chapter 20, "Other Memory Management Topics."

USING ARRAY FETCH

Each fetch request can return more than one row. When a fetch returns a batch of rows in this manner, it is known as an *array fetch*. Array fetches are much more efficient than fetching single rows at a time.

Often your client tool (for instance, SQL*PLUS) automatically performs array fetches. Other tools might require that you explicitly perform an array fetch. We look at the performance implications of array processing in Chapter 6 and Chapter 9, "Tuning Table Access."

PROCESSING RESULT SETS

The output from a SQL query is referred to as a result set. A result set consists of rows and columns and can be thought of as a temporary table containing the query's results. Result sets are also created during intermediate operations. For instance, in a join of tables A, B, and C, table A is first joined to B, creating an intermediate result set. This result set is then joined to table C to create the final result set that is returned to your program.

CLOSING THE CURSOR

Closing the cursor releases all the memory associated with the cursor. If you need to re-execute the SQL, you will need to create a new cursor. Oracle does, however, sometimes transparently keep a copy of the cursor in memory in case you re-execute the SQL. This behavior is controlled by the SESSION_CACHED_CURSORS configuration parameter.

OPTIMIZING ORACLE API CALLS

When writing code that interfaces with an Oracle server—aside from the SQL statements themselves—there are three main keys to optimal performance:

❏ Ensure that SQL statements, or cursors, are reused within the application. This reduces the number of parse calls to Oracle and thus reduces CPU overhead and database contention.
❏ Use bind variables to ensure that SQL is sharable across and within sessions. This reduces parse overhead by increasing the chance that a matching SQL statement will be found in the shared pool.
❏ Enable array fetch to improve query and insert performance. Using the array fetch facility reduces the number of calls to Oracle and also reduces network traffic—especially in the client server environment.

We discuss each of these principles in detail in Chapter 4, "Logical and Physical Database Design."

THE ORACLE QUERY OPTIMIZER

SQL is a nonprocedural language: You define the data you want, not how to get it. Although the nonprocedural nature of SQL results in significant productivity gains for the programmer, the RDBMS must support a set of sophisticated algorithms to determine the optimal method of retrieving the results or processing updates. In Oracle, these algorithms are collectively referred to as *the optimizer*.

For almost all SQL statements, there will be more than one way for Oracle to retrieve the rows required. When Oracle parses a SQL statement, it must decide which approach will be fastest. The process of determining this optimal path to the data is referred to as *query optimization*.[1]

As of 10g, Oracle supports only the *cost based* optimization (CBO) approach. This means that the optimizer tries to calculate algorithmically the cost of each alternative SQL execution approach and chooses the one that is cheaper. Prior to 10g, the *rule based* optimizer (RBO) was also available. The rule based optimizer would not try to calculate costs but would instead use a relatively simple and predictable—but not always correct—set of rules (indexes are better than table scans, for example).

Because SQL is a nonprocedural language, the SQL itself does not include instructions for retrieving the data. It is up to Oracle to devise a means of retrieving the data, and the resulting scheme is referred to as the *execution plan*.

For instance, consider the following SQL:

```
SELECT DISTINCT cust_first_name, cust_last_name
  FROM oe.customers c
  JOIN oe.orders o USING (customer_id)
  JOIN hr.employees e ON (o.sales_rep_id = e.employee_id)
 WHERE o.order_date > (SYSDATE - INTERVAL '10' YEAR)
   AND e.last_name = 'Olsen'
   AND e.first_name = 'Christopher'
```

In English, this query might be stated as "give me the names of all customers who bought something from sales representative Christopher Olsen in the past 10 years."

The optimizer has to work out the best way to get the data. Some possible approaches are

❑ Get all orders for the past 10 years. Then get the names of all the customers matching those sales. Then filter out any customers who aren't handled by Mr. Olsen.

---

[1] Of course, the *query* optimizer also optimizes the performance of DML statements such as UPDATE, DELETE, INSERT, and so on.

❏ Get Mr. Olsen's EMPLOYEE_ID. Using that EMPLOYEE_ID, get all orders handled by Olsen. Then filter out any orders more than 10 years old, and then get the customers for those orders.

❏ Get all the orders, and then get all the customers for those orders. Then filter out those more than 10 years old. Then filter out those not handled by Olsen.

It is clear that the approach taken will have a significant impact on the amount of time taken to retrieve the results. It might also be obvious that the last approach is likely to be the worst, because *all* order records would need to be read and joined to *all* the customer records before any rows are eliminated—so we hope the optimizer won't pick that path.

COST BASED OPTIMIZATION

The Cost Based Optimizer (CBO) considers the cost of all or many of the possible access paths for the query and tries to estimate the "cost" that would be required to satisfy each execution plan. The execution plan with the lowest cost is selected.

The calculation of cost is based on a number of factors, including

❏ Estimated number of database reads required
❏ Requirements for sorting and the amount of memory available
❏ Relative cost weightings for CPU and IO
❏ Availability of the parallel query option

The optimizer might not consider all possible plans because that might take too long. The higher the cost of the SQL statement, the more plans the optimizer will consider. The algorithms for cost are extremely sophisticated, and there are a relatively small number of people in the world who have a comprehensive understanding of how the CBO works.[2] Luckily, you don't need to understand all the optimizer's algorithms to exploit its capabilities.

Despite the improvements Oracle has made to the optimizer, some SQL statements receive execution plans that are far from perfect. Reducing the number of these imperfect SQL plans—and dealing with imperfect plans when they do arise—will probably always require human intervention.

OPTIMIZER GOAL

The OPTIMIZER_GOAL (or OPTIMIZER_MODE) configuration parameter controls how the optimizer calculates cost:

---

[2] Jonathan Lewis is probably the best-known independent expert on CBO. His book *Cost Based Oracle Fundamentals* (Apress, 2006) is essential reading for anyone who wants to understand CBO internals.

ALL_ROWS   Instructs the CBO to minimize the cost of processing *all* the rows returned by the SQL statement. This is the default behavior for the CBO. It is most suitable for batch processing and reporting queries.

FIRST_ROWS_*N*   Instructs the CBO to choose an execution plan that will minimize the cost of retrieving the first "N" rows, where "N" is one of 1, 10, 100, or 1,000. This setting can be useful for interactive applications because the critical performance measure might be the time taken to display the first row or page of information.

These optimizer goal settings can lead to different execution plans: ALL_ROWS tends to favor plans that employ full table scans and nonindexed joins. FIRST_ROWS plans are more likely to favor index-based approaches.

OPTIMIZER STATISTICS

To make informed decisions, the optimizer needs to have a good understanding of table data: both volumes and distributions. To this end, Oracle maintains *optimizer statistics* that include the following:

❏ For a table, the number of rows, number of blocks used and empty, average row length, and average amount of used space within each block.

❏ For columns, the number of distinct values, low and high values, and some information about the selectivity of the column.

❏ Optionally, a *histogram* recording the distribution of values within a column. This can be useful when a column includes both frequently and infrequently encountered values and where an index is, therefore, only sometimes effective. The histogram enables Oracle to decide when to use the index based on the value of the search criteria.

BIND VARIABLE PEEKING AND ADAPTIVE CURSOR SHARING

In older versions of Oracle, column histograms and bind variables were mutually exclusive. To use the histogram, the optimizer needed to know the value of variables at parse time, but bind variables "hid" the value until execute time.

In 10g, the *bind variable peeking* method was introduced, in which Oracle "peeked" at the first bind variable provided before deciding on an execution plan. Although this often led to better plans, it also introduced a randomness into query execution that caused a lot of headaches. Some SQLs would randomly use an index depending on which bind variable happened to be the first one supplied by the application.

Oracle 11g attempts to overcome this problem by employing *adaptive cursor sharing*. This involves generating a separate execution plan for a SQL statement where the different values of a bind variable might justify different plans. Such a SQL is called *bind sensitive*. Bind sensitive SQLs might be represented by multiple cursors with separate plans. The appropriate plan is chosen when the SQL is executed with new bind variables.

HINTS

Hints are instructions that you can include in your SQL statement to instruct or "guide" the optimizer. Using hints you can specify join orders, type of access paths, indexes to be used, the optimization goal, and other instructions.

An optimizer hint appears as a comment following the first word of the SQL statement, such as SELECT, INSERT, UPDATE, MERGE, or DELETE. A hint is differentiated from other comments by the presence of the plus sign (+) following the opening comment delimiter (/*). For example, the FULL hint in the following SQL instructs the optimizer to resolve this statement via a full table scan, even if the optimizer calculates that an index lookup would be more optimal.

```
SELECT /*+ FULL(orders) */ *
  FROM oe.orders
 WHERE order_date < (SYSDATE - INTERVAL '5' YEAR )
```

We look at hints in detail in Chapter 8, "Execution Plan Management."

OUTLINES, PROFILES, AND BASELINES

Adding hints—or otherwise changing SQL statement syntax to get a desired execution plan—is okay if you're developing new SQL but not useful if you are trying to tune SQL in a live system. You usually cannot change the SQL quickly and often cannot change the SQL text at all. Partly for this reason, Oracle provides the *stored outline* facility that instructs Oracle how a given SQL should be executed. Essentially, stored outlines are sets of hints that you can apply to a SQL statement without editing it. Stored outlines are a way of achieving *plan stability*—the assurance that a plan will not change over time as statistics or Oracle software versions change.

Stabilizing a plan is often a good idea in an OLTP environment, in which predictable SQL statements should result in predictable performance. But in data warehousing, we can't always predict the SQL that will be issued, and therefore, we are more interested in *optimizer flexibility*. To achieve this, SQL Profiles were introduced in 10g. SQL Profiles include additional statistics about SQL statement execution that are intended to help the optimizer make better decisions.

Normal optimizer statistics are collected against specific tables and indexes. SQL profile statistics, on the other hand, are collected against a specific SQL statement and include data unique to the optimization of that SQL.

SQL baselines were introduced in Oracle 11g. Baselines store both plans and execution statistics for a SQL statement. When a new plan is generated, it is compared to the baseline and implemented only if deemed to be an improvement. The improvement is usually determined by a mini-benchmark conducted automatically during the maintenance window. Baselines reduce the possibility that SQL statements will exhibit performance regressions (for example, run slower) as new statistics are collected.

We look at how to use outlines, profiles, and baselines in detail in Chapter 8.

TRANSACTIONS AND LOCKING

A *transaction* is a set of one or more SQL statements that are logically grouped together and that must be either applied to the database in their entirety or not applied at all. Transactions are often described as ACID—Atomic, Consistent, Independent, and Durable.

The ACID properties of a transaction can be guaranteed only by restricting simultaneous changes to the database. This is achieved by placing locks on modified data. These locks persist until the transaction issues a COMMIT or ROLLBACK statement.

Oracle usually applies locks at the row level. For instance, when a row is updated, only that row will be locked; other rows in the table can still be updated without restriction.

Locks can also be placed manually on a row or table. This is commonly done to ensure that a row is not modified between the time it is read and the time it is later updated.

The most important factor influencing lock contention is application design—in particular the choice between the "optimistic" and "pessimistic" locking patterns. These issues are discussed in Chapter 6.

Row-level locking usually works well, but in some cases locks can be inadvertently applied at the table or block level. Additionally, Oracle internal locks can sometimes become an issue. These issues—locking problems independent of application design—are addressed in Chapter 15, "Lock Contention."

ORACLE SERVER ARCHITECTURE

In this section we review the architecture of the Oracle database server.

Figure 2-2 represents the major memory areas, processes, disk files, and data flows involved in this architecture. We discuss each aspect of this diagram in the remainder of this chapter.

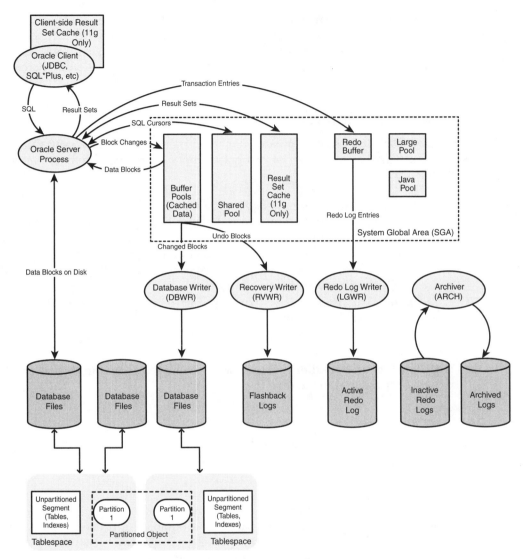

FIGURE 2-2   Overview of Oracle architecture.

INSTANCES AND DATABASES

An Oracle *database* is composed of a logical set of data *schemas*, all of which are stored on a specific set of database files. Each schema typically represents an application's data model.

An Oracle *instance* is a single occurrence of the running Oracle software, composed of an area of shared memory and various Oracle background processes.

Most of the time there is a one-to-one relationship between instances and databases, and as a result a lot of us tend to use the terms interchangeably. However, with the increasing popularity of Real Application Clusters (RAC)—in which a database is comprised of multiple instances—the distinction is increasingly significant.

THE SYSTEM GLOBAL AREA

The *System Global Area (SGA)* is an area of shared memory available to all Oracle sessions. The SGA has a number of distinct memory segments, the most important of which are

❑ **Buffer pools**—Also known as *buffer caches*, store copies of datafile blocks. SQL statements that want to access data from disk can often find the data they need in the buffer cache.
❑ **Shared pool**—This stores cached SQL and PL/SQL statements and shared meta-data. Shared SQL improves performance by avoiding the need to parse a SQL on every execution.
❑ **Large pool**—This pool caches shared server session state, large PL/SQL blocks, and parallel execution message buffers.
❑ **Java Pool**—This cache contains Java stored procedures and other stored Java programs.
❑ **Redo buffers and smaller *redo strands***—Cache redo log entries that have not yet been written to the redo logs on disk.

DATA CACHING

Oracle provides multiple levels of data caching. Traditionally (prior to 11g), data was cached only in the buffer cache. However, in 11g a SQL statement might find the data it needs in any of three memory locations:

❑ A client-side result set cache maintained by the Oracle 11g client libraries. This cache helps avoid a round trip to the database if a client issues the same SQL statement in rapid succession. This cache can be exploited only by 11g database clients using the OCI-based drivers.
❑ A server-side result set cache that stores complete result sets for selected queries. Like the client-side equivalent, this cache stores all the results for a specific query; a query either finds all of its results here or nothing at all. This cache exists only in 11g databases.
❑ Multiple buffer pools that store data blocks. Blocks "age out" of these caches, and typically a query finds only some of the data it needs in this cache. Blocks that cannot be found here must be read from disk.

THE PROGRAM GLOBAL AREA

The Program Global Area (PGA) represents memory that is local to a specific *process*. Be aware that this is not the same as session-specific data: Memory for a session (*User Global Area* or UGA) most often resides in the PGA—for a *dedicated server* connection—but sometimes lives in the SGA when you have a *shared server* connection. We discuss the difference between the two models later in this chapter. The PGA is the memory available for the running program and is independent of the session that is currently using the process.

The biggest part of the PGA is composed of work areas for sorts and temporary result sets. These work areas are created in the following circumstances:

❑ A temporary result set is created as an intermediate step in a SQL operation, most typically a join or subquery. For instance, in a complex join, each join creates a temporary result set that is then joined to the next table in the join sequence.

❑ Memory is required to sort data in a sort-merge join, an ORDER BY, or a GROUP BY operation.

❑ Memory is required to create the hash structure to satisfy a hash join or other hash operation. In a hash join, a temporary hash table is created for one of the tables in the join; that hash structure is used as a sort of temporary index to perform the join. Some other operations, such as a GROUP BY, might also employ hash areas.

If these temporary segments and work areas are too large to fit into the PGA, data will be written and read back from temporary segments in temporary tablespaces; the resulting IO can have a significant effect on performance. These issues are further discussed in Chapter 11, "Sorting, Grouping, and Set Operations," and in Chapter 19, "Optimizing PGA Memory."

MEMORY MANAGEMENT

Each component of the SGA and PGA can be manually sized, but the consistent trend in each release of Oracle since 9i has been to improve on the automatic sizing of these areas. In 10g memory *within* the SGA and PGA can be automatically allocated, and in 11g memory can be shifted *between* the SGA and PGA automatically.

It remains critically important to ensure that memory allocated to these areas is sufficient to meet demand, and there are a wide variety of configuration options that can be considered. Chapters 18 through 20 discuss these issues in detail.

SEGMENTS AND FILES

The data stored in the database, and various configuration data and other information, are stored as files on disk. Within the database, segments represent the logical containers for various types of data.

TABLES

Tables are the fundamental logical unit of database storage, corresponding to an *entity* in the relational model. A table normally consists of a two-dimensional structure of columns and rows, although some of the Oracle object-relational structures stretch or break this definition.

Oracle offers a wide variety of table types, each of which has distinct logical or physical storage characteristics:

❏ **Heap organized table**—This is the default table type; if you use CREATE TABLE without any specific options, you end up with a heap table. The term *heap* signifies that rows will be stored in no particular order. Every row in a heap table is identified by a ROWID, which can be used to locate the row on disk.

❏ **Hash clustered table**—This is a table in which the physical location of a row is determined by the primary key. This allows a row to be retrieved rapidly via the primary key without requiring an index lookup. A *sorted hash cluster* is a variation in which rows for a particular hash value are retrieved in a specific sort sequence.

❏ **Index organized table**—This is structured like a B-tree index in which the "leaf" block contains the row itself rather than—as in a real B-tree index—a pointer to the row.

❏ **Index cluster**—The index cluster stores multiple tables in the same segment, with rows that share a common key stored together. You might think of it as "prejoined" data.

❏ **Object tables**—These are based on Oracle object types. They are identified by object REFs rather than primary key and can have more complex internal structure than a normal table.

❏ **Nested table**—This is an object type that has the characteristics of a relational table and that can be "nested" inside a column of a heap table. Each master row in the table can have detail rows stored within the nested table column.

❏ **External tables**—These are tables that map to files stored outside the database. They are most typically used for accessing files that need to be loaded into the database without the intermediate step of loading into a staging table.

❏ **Temporary tables**—A temporary table can be explicitly or implicitly created to store data that will not persist beyond the current session or transaction.

This wide range of table types can be daunting, and the permutations for performance tuning can be great. However, the vast majority of database activity is based around the traditional heap organized tables.

INDEXES

Indexes exist primarily to improve SQL statement and database performance. It's therefore essential that the Oracle performance practitioner have a sound understanding of indexing principles and practices.

Here we provide a quick overview of indexing options. More detail can be found in Chapter 5, "Indexing and Clustering."

❏ **B*-Tree index**—This is Oracle's default index type. A B*-Tree consists of a hierarchical tree in which each level contains pointers to a subsequent level. The final level (the leaf blocks) points to the data entries themselves. B*-Tree indexes are flexible and time-proven and are the most common type of index for almost all applications.

❏ **Bitmap index**—A bitmap index consists of a map of bits for each value assumed by a column. These compact structures can be scanned quickly and multiple bitmaps can be merged effectively, making them far more efficient for quick lookups and index merges than B-trees. However, bitmap indexes can increase lock contention and cannot be used for range scans. Consequently, bitmap indexes are most commonly found in data warehousing databases where most access is read-only.

❏ **Functional index**—This is an index constructed against an expression rather than a column name. These indexes can optimize queries in which such an expression appears in the WHERE clause, but must be comprised from deterministic expressions, in which the same inputs always result in the same outputs.

❏ **Virtual index**—Virtual indexes are index definitions without a physical index. Such definitions are useful when tuning because they enable you to determine how a plan would change if certain indexes were to be created.

BLOCKS, EXTENTS, SEGMENTS, AND PARTITIONS

Tables and indexes are composed of individual units of storage known as *extents*. Extents in turn are composed of very small units of storage referred to as *blocks*, which are typically in the range of 8K–32K in size. When a table or index grows, additional extents will be added as required to support the growth. The size of the extents can be specified in the table definition, but best practice in modern Oracle is to allow for automatic allocation (using Automatic Segment Storage Management [ASSM]).

For nonpartitioned tables and indexes, extents will be part of a single *segment* that represents the physical storage of the table or index. A partitioned table or index, however, will consist of multiple segments—each segment representing a *partition*. Tables and indexes can also consist of multiple segments when they have a LOB (embedded large object), a nested table, or are index organized.

TABLESPACES AND DATA FILES

Segments must belong to a specific *tablespace* that might define the storage characteristics—block size, for example—of the segment. Tablespaces are composed of multiple *datafiles* that can be represented as operating system files, raw disk partitions, or as Automatic Storage Management (ASM) files. The tablespace to which a segment belongs determines which datafiles contain the extents that comprise the segment. Segments can be housed in multiple datafiles, but each extent will be in a specific datafile.

UNDO SEGMENTS

To allow for the ROLLBACK statement, which cancels a transaction that has not yet been committed, Oracle keeps "before image" copies of modified data blocks in structures known as *rollback* or *undo segments*. These segments are also used to implement *consistent read* that ensures that changes made to a table during a query are not reflected in the query result.

REDO LOGS AND ARCHIVE LOGS

Because transactions must be durable (the D in the "ACID" transaction definition), the commit of a transaction must be associated with a write of the transaction information to disk. Otherwise, transactions might be lost if the database crashed suddenly with transaction information in memory. To minimize this necessary IO, almost all database systems use a transaction log to record transaction information on commit. In Oracle, this log is called the redo log (because you can use it to *redo* a transaction).

There are multiple online redo logs that Oracle reuses in a circular fashion. An online log can be reused providing all the information in the log has been written to database files and the log has been archived if necessary.

Archived redo logs are copies of the online logs used to allow point in time recovery after disk failure. After an online backup is restored, archived logs can be used to apply transactions until the database is back up to date.

FLASHBACK LOGS

"Rolling forward" a backup using redo logs allows for complete recovery but can be time-consuming, especially if the backup is not recent. Oracle flashback logs provide an alternative mechanism. Flashback logs store undo information—similar to that stored in rollback segments. If a logical corruption occurs, this information can be used to "roll back" the database. Oracle supports other flashback technologies as well: Flashback query allows for queries to be executed as at previous points in time, and flashback data archive allows flashback information to be stored for long-term archive and auditing purposes.

SERVER PROCESSES

The processes that perform activities on behalf of clients—that is, the processes that actually execute the user's SQL statements—are referred to as *server processes*. When a client program wants to execute a SQL, it relies on a server process to execute the SQL and return the results.

- ❏ **Dedicated servers**—A dedicated server performs activities on behalf of only one client. This sort of server is started when the client connects and is destroyed when the client disconnects. Dedicated servers are usually the default.
- ❏ **Shared servers**—Shared servers perform tasks on behalf of multiple clients. This is often referred to, somewhat misleadingly, as a Multi Threaded Server (MTS) configuration.[3] In an MTS connection, SQL statements issued by a client are allocated to the next available shared server.
- ❏ **Parallel Query servers**—Oracle can employ multiple parallel threads or processes to execute a single SQL statement. A pool of parallel query servers is available to be deployed for this parallel processing.
- ❏ **Job and Scheduler servers**—PL/SQL programs (or OS commands in 11g) can be submitted for background or periodic processing. The Job and Scheduler servers execute these commands in the background or on schedule as required.

BACKGROUND PROCESSES

The processes (or threads in the Windows OS) that perform tasks on behalf of all sessions or that perform Oracle internal activities are called the *background processes*. There are a couple of dozen of these processes even in a desktop database. Here are some of the more significant background processes:

---

[3] Misleading because operating system threads are not involved; the servers are supporting multiple sessions, but only one session is active on a server at any time.

❑ **Listener**—One or more listener processes will be active on every host that contains a database server. The listener accepts requests for connection and, in the case of a dedicated server connection, creates a server process to manage that connection. In the case of a shared server connection, the listener passes the request to a *dispatcher* process that mediates between sessions and shared servers.

❑ **Database writer (DBWR)**—Server processes read from database files, but most of the time it's the Database Writer process that writes changes to these files. The database writer is a "lazy" writer. Instead of writing changes out immediately, it writes the changes at some convenient later time. As a result, database sessions do not normally need to wait for writes to disk, although there are "direct" IO modes in which sessions will write directly to the database files. Database Writer IO is described in more detail in Chapter 17, "Shared Memory Contention."

❑ **Log writer (LGWR)**—The Log writer writes redo log entries from a redo log buffer in memory to the redo logs. The LGWR writes these entries periodically and almost always when a COMMIT statement is issued. In certain circumstances these writes can be asynchronous or batched. (See Chapter 14 for more details.)

❑ **Log Archiver (ARCH)**—The Log Archiver copies modified redo logs to archived logs that recover the database if a disk failure occurs.

❑ **Recovery writer (RVWR)**—The Recovery writer writes "undo" information, similar to rollback segment information, to the flashback log files.

REAL APPLICATION CLUSTERS

A Real Application Clusters (RAC) database is a shared-disk clustered database. Each member of the RAC database is a separate instance of Oracle, with its own shared memory, processes, and sessions. All instances share a common set of database files, which are made available via a clustered file system, typically Oracle's own Oracle Clustered File System (OCFS) or the Automatic Storage Management (ASM) facility.

A private high-speed network, called the *cluster interconnect*, connects all members of the cluster and enables a global cache, allowing instances to exploit data cached in other instances and to ensure consistency between instances. Figure 2-3 illustrates the Oracle RAC architecture.

Most Oracle tuning principles apply equally to RAC and single-instance Oracle. However, there are some RAC-specific considerations, which are discussed in Chapter 23, "Optimizing RAC."

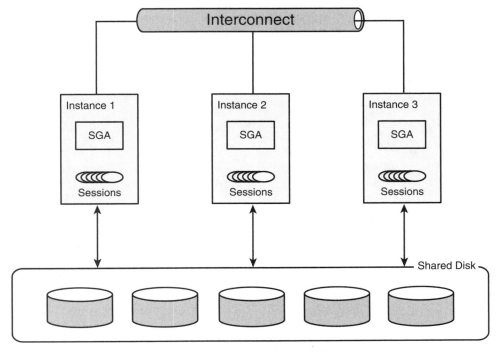

FIGURE 2-3   RAC database architecture.

SUMMARY

This chapter provided a brief overview of essential Oracle concepts and architectures. Oracle is a complex system, and it's impossible to cover it completely in a chapter of this size. However, hopefully you will end this chapter with some understanding of the following critical architectural components:

❑ Oracle API procedures, in particular the process of parsing, binding, and executing SQL statements including the use of array fetch and insert interfaces

❑ The Oracle cost based query optimizer, the concept of the execution plan, the role of statistics, and the general purpose of outlines, profiles, and baselines

❑ The Oracle server architecture: the tablespaces, segments, files, processes, and memory structures that comprise an Oracle database

TOOLS OF THE TRADE

In this chapter we'll look at the core tools for assessing and improving Oracle database performance.

A wide variety of tuning tools are available both from Oracle and from third parties.[1] However, in this chapter we concentrate on core tools that are available with the base Oracle server that require no special licensing.[2]

EXPLAINING SQL STATEMENTS

In the previous chapter we described the concept of the *execution plan*: the sequence of steps that the optimizer determines it will use to execute a SQL statement. Without knowledge of this execution plan, you have only a vague understanding of how your SQL is being processed. You might know if it is "running

---

[1] Full disclosure: I have worked for Quest Software, where I contributed to the design and implementation of a range of Quest's Oracle tuning and administration products, most notably the Spotlight on Oracle and Spotlight on RAC products.

[2] Oracle ships with a lot of functionality that requires licensing if you make use of it. In particular, the Active Workload Repository (AWR), Automatic Database Diagnostic Monitor (ADDM), Active Session History (ASH), and certain other packages, views, and OEM screens require a diagnostic and/or tuning pack licenses. See http://tinyurl.com/cgkofc for more information.

fast" or "running slow," but you will probably not know why, and you will be in a poor position to predict how it might behave if data volumes change or if indexing is changed.

The EXPLAIN PLAN command is one of the ways you can determine the execution plan Oracle applies to a particular SQL statement. EXPLAIN PLAN inserts the execution plan into a plan table that you can query to extract the execution plan.

The EXPLAIN PLAN command has the following syntax:

```
EXPLAIN PLAN
  [SET STATEMENT_ID = 'statement_id'}
  [INTO table_name ]
    FOR sql_statement
```

The options for EXPLAIN PLAN follow:

STATEMENT_ID	A unique identifier for your SQL statement. By using a statement identifier, you can store multiple SQL statements in one plan table.
TABLE_NAME	The name of the plan table you want to use to store the execution plan. This table must already exist and must conform to the standard structure of a plan table. If you don't specify a plan table, EXPLAIN PLAN attempts to use the name PLAN_TABLE.
SQL_STATEMENT	The SQL for which you want to determine the execution plan. The SQL must be valid, and you must have sufficient privileges to run the SQL. The SQL can contain bind variables.

THE PLAN TABLE

By default, Oracle inserts the execution plan into a table called PLAN_TABLE. You can create your own plan table using the script *utlxplan.sql*, which you can find in the $ORACLE_HOME/rdbms/admin subdirectory of the Oracle software distribution. However, from Oracle 10g forward, Oracle creates a global temporary PLAN_TABLE that is available to all users, so you won't normally need to create your own. As this default plan table is a global temporary table, you cannot see the plans inserted by other sessions, and your plans disappear when your session ends.

The EXPLAIN PLAN command inserts a row into the plan table for every step of the execution plan. Below we see the columns in the plan table for Oracle 10g and 11g. (Not all columns are present in earlier versions.)

STATEMENT_ID	The statement identifier provided by the SET STATEMENT_ID clause of the EXPLAIN PLAN.
PLAN_ID	A unique identifier for the plan in the global PLAN_TABLE. Populated by the sequence ORA_PLAN_ID_SEQ$.
TIMESTAMP	The date and time the EXPLAIN PLAN statement was executed.

REMARKS	Not populated by the EXPLAIN PLAN command.
ID	A unique identifier for the step.
PARENT_ID	The parent of this step. The output of a step is fed into its parent step.
POSITION	If two steps have the same parent, the step with the lowest position will be executed first.
OPERATION	The type of operation being performed; for example, TABLE ACCESS or SORT.
OPTIONS	Additional information about the operation. For example, in the case of TABLE SCAN, the option might be FULL or BY ROWID.
OBJECT_NODE	If this is a distributed query, this column indicates the database link used to reference the object. For a parallel query, it might nominate a temporary result set.
OBJECT_OWNER	Owner of the object.
OBJECT_NAME	Name of the object.
OBJECT_INSTANCE	Location of the object in the SQL statement.
OBJECT_TYPE	Type of object (TABLE, INDEX, and so on).
OPTIMIZER	Optimizer goal in effect when the statement was explained.
SEARCH_COLUMNS	Unused.
OTHER	For a distributed query, this might contain the text of the SQL sent to the remote database. For a parallel query, it indicates the SQL statement executed by the parallel slave processes.
OTHER_XML	Contains additional other information in an XML document. This includes version information, SQL Profile or outlines used, dynamic sampling, and plan hash value.
OTHER_TAG	Indicates the type of value in the OTHER column. This can denote whether the step is being executed remotely in a distributed SQL statement or the nature of parallel execution.
COST	The relative cost of the operation as estimated by the optimizer.
CARDINALITY	The number of rows that the optimizer expects will be returned by the step.
BYTES	The number of bytes expected to be returned by the step.
PARTITION_START	If partition elimination is to be performed, this column indicates the start of the range of partitions that will be accessed. It might also contain the keywords KEY or ROW LOCATION, which indicates that the partitions to be accessed will be determined at run time.
PARTITION_END	Indicates the end of the range of partitions to be accessed.
PARTITION_ID	This column lists the execution plan ID (as indicated in the ID column) for the execution plan step that determined the partitions identified by PARTITION_START and PARTITION_END.
DISTRIBUTION	This column describes how rows from one set of parallel query slaves—the "producers"—are allocated the subsequent "consumer" slaves. Possible values are PARTITION (ROWID), PARTITION (KEY), HASH, RANGE, ROUND-ROBIN, BROADCAST, QC (ORDER), and QC (RANDOM). These options are discussed further in Chapter 13, "Parallel SQL."
CPU_COST	Estimated CPU cost of the operation.

IO_COST	Estimated IO cost of the operation.
TEMP_SPACE	Estimated amount of temporary storage (such as memory or disk for sorting) used by the step.
ACCESS _PREDICATES	The clauses in the SQL statement that determine how rows will be retrieved in the current step; this might include clauses that will be used to feed an index lookup or join.
FILTER _PREDICATES	Clauses in the SQL statement that determine how rows will be filtered, such as WHERE clause conditions on nonindexed columns.
PROJECTION	Clauses that determine rows that will be returned, usually SELECT list columns.
TIME	Elapsed time estimated by the optimizer for the step execution.
QBLOCK_NAME	A unique identifier for the query block, usually system-generated or set by the QB_NAME hint.

One way to make sense of the PLAN_TABLE data is to execute a hierarchical query against the table. The PARENT_ID and ID columns allow for a self-join, which can be implemented using the CONNECT BY clause of the SELECT statement.

Here is a common representation of such a query:

```
SELECT RTRIM (LPAD (' ', 2 * LEVEL) ||
       RTRIM (operation) || ' ' ||
       RTRIM (options) || ' ' ||
           object_name) query_plan,
       cost,
       cardinality
  FROM plan_table
CONNECT BY PRIOR id = parent_id
START WITH id = 0
```

This query produces the typical nested representation of an explain plan. For instance, if we EXPLAIN a statement and issue the preceding query afterward:

```
SQL> EXPLAIN PLAN FOR
  2  SELECT *
  3    FROM hr.employees JOIN hr.departments USING (department_id);

Explained.

SQL>
SQL> SELECT RTRIM (LPAD (' ', 2 * LEVEL) ||
  2         RTRIM (operation) || ' ' ||
  3         RTRIM (options) || ' ' ||
```

```
4                    object_name) query_plan,
5           cost, cardinality
6      FROM plan_table
7      CONNECT BY PRIOR id = parent_id
8      START WITH id = 0 ;
```

We produce the following output:

```
QUERY_PLAN                                           COST CARDINALITY
------------------------------------------------ ------ -----------
  SELECT STATEMENT                                   4        106
    NESTED LOOPS                                     4        106
      TABLE ACCESS FULL EMPLOYEES                    3        107
      TABLE ACCESS BY INDEX ROWID DEPARTMENTS        1          1
        INDEX UNIQUE SCAN DEPT_ID_PK                 0          1
```

You might want to modify the SELECT statement to retrieve additional columns depending on your specific circumstances. For instance, if explaining a parallel query, you might want to see the OTHER_TAG columns; if explaining a query against a partitioned table, you might want to see the PARTITON_START and PARTITION_STOP columns.

Another—usually better—way to see the execution plan is to use the DBMS_XPLAN package, as in the following example:

```
SQL> SELECT * FROM TABLE(dbms_xplan.display());

PLAN_TABLE_OUTPUT
--------------------------------------------------------------------------------
Plan hash value: 4201152682


--------------------------------------------------------------------------------
| Id  | Operation                     | Name        | Rows  | Bytes | Cost (%CPU)|
--------------------------------------------------------------------------------
|   0 | SELECT STATEMENT              |             |   106 |  9328 |     4   (0)|
|   1 |  NESTED LOOPS                 |             |   106 |  9328 |     4   (0)|
|   2 |   TABLE ACCESS FULL           |EMPLOYEES    |   107 |  7276 |     3   (0)|
|   3 |   TABLE ACCESS BY INDEX ROWID |DEPARTMENTS  |     1 |    20 |     1   (0)|
|*  4 |    INDEX UNIQUE SCAN          |DEPT_ID_PK   |     1 |       |     0   (0)|
--------------------------------------------------------------------------------

Predicate Information (identified by operation id):
---------------------------------------------------

   4 - access("EMPLOYEES"."DEPARTMENT_ID"="DEPARTMENTS"."DEPARTMENT_ID").
```

DBMS_XPLAN is usually more convenient than writing your own PLAN_TABLE query, though there will be times that DBMS_XPLAN fails to show you all the information you need. We examine DBMS_XPLAN in detail a bit later.

EXPLOITING CACHED SQL

There are a number of ways to identify SQL that might need tuning, but since time immemorial (well, since Oracle 7 anyway) the easiest way has been to examine the cached SQL information held in the V$SQL view. This view contains information about the SQL statements that are stored in the shared pool. Provided SQL statements are sharable—usually meaning that they use bind variables appropriately or that the CURSOR_SHARING option is in effect—most of the interesting SQL for an application will be found in the cache and hence appear in this view. Figure 3-1 summarizes the structure of V$SQL and related views.

Although SQL statements that consume the most logical IO or have the highest elapsed times are often good targets for tuning, it's often only the examination of individual steps that will pinpoint the best tuning opportunities. In

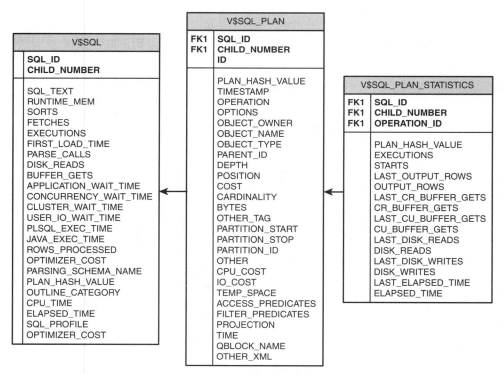

FIGURE 3-1   V$SQL and related views (not all columns shown).

Oracle Database 10g, we can use cached query plan statistics to pinpoint individual steps within an SQL execution that might warrant attention. The view V$SQL_PLAN shows the execution plan for all cached SQL statements, whereas V$SQL_PLAN_STATISTICS shows execution counts, IO, and rows processed by each step in the plan. You might need to increase your STATISTICS_LEVEL from TYPICAL to ALL to populate the rows in V$SQL_PLAN_STATISTICS.

By mining V$SQL, we can identify SQL statements that have high elapsed times, CPU, or IO requirements. Using the V$SQL_PLAN and V$SQL_PLAN_STATISTICS, we can find SQLs that perform actions that might be undesirable, such as table scans of large tables. We can also see the "real" execution plan and even get information about which steps in the plan are most troublesome.

For example, the following SQL finds us the top ten SQL statements with the greatest aggregate elapsed time:

```
SQL> SELECT sql_id,child_number,sql_text, elapsed_time
  2     FROM (SELECT sql_id, child_number, sql_text, elapsed_time,
  3                    cpu_time,disk_reads,
  4           RANK () OVER (ORDER BY elapsed_time DESC) AS elapsed_rank
  5              FROM v$sql)
  6     WHERE elapsed_rank <= 10
  7   /


SQL_ID          CHILD_NUMBER SQL_TEXT                        ELAPSED_TIME
-------------   ------------ ------------------------------  ------------
6v7n0y2bq89n8             0  BEGIN EMDW_LOG.set_context(MGM    3527151847
                             T_JOB_ENGINE.MODULE_NAME, :1);
                             MGMT_JOB_ENGINE.get_scheduled
                             _steps(:2, :3, :4, :5); EMDW_L
                             OG.set_context; END;

2b064ybzkwf1y             3  BEGIN EMD_NOTIFICATION.QUEUE_R    1848364405
                             EADY(:1, :2, :3); END;

6gvch1xu9ca3g             0  DECLARE job BINARY_INTEGER :=     1157137564
                             :job; next_date DATE := :mydat
```

We can write more complex statements to retrieve and format the cached SQL plan information from V$SQL_PLAN and V$SQL_PLAN_TEXT, but luckily this is not usually necessary. DBMS_XPLAN has a method that can retrieve and format the plan, provided we know the SQL_ID and CHILD_NUMBER.[3]

---

[3] The SQL_ID uniquely references SQL statement text; if there is SQL with the same text but with different plans (perhaps it is executed in another schema or with different run time options), it will have a different CHILD_NUMBER.

```
SQL> SELECT *  FROM TABLE (DBMS_XPLAN.display_cursor ('at6ss8tmxm5xz', '0',
'TYPICAL -BYTES'));


PLAN_TABLE_OUTPUT
--------------------------------------------------------------------------------
SQL_ID  at6ss8tmxm5xz, child number 0
------------------------------------
SELECT   department_name, last_name, job_title     FROM hr.employees JOIN
hr.departments USING (department_id)         JOIN hr.jobs USING (job_id)
ORDER BY department_name, job_title

Plan hash value: 3225241925


--------------------------------------------------------------------------------
| Id | Operation                       | Name        | Rows |Cost (%CPU)| Time     |
--------------------------------------------------------------------------------
|  0 | SELECT STATEMENT                |             |      |  26 (100)|          |
|  1 |  SORT ORDER BY                  |             | 106  |  26   (8)| 00:00:01 |
|  2 |   NESTED LOOPS                  |             | 106  |  25   (4)| 00:00:01 |
|  3 |    MERGE JOIN                   |             | 107  |  24   (5)| 00:00:01 |
|  4 |     TABLE ACCESS BY INDEX ROWID| EMPLOYEES   | 107  |  20   (0)| 00:00:01 |
|  5 |      INDEX FULL SCAN            | EMP_JOB_IX  | 107  |  12   (0)| 00:00:01 |
|* 6 |     SORT JOIN                   |             |  19  |   4  (25)| 00:00:01 |
|  7 |      TABLE ACCESS FULL          | JOBS        |  19  |   3   (0)| 00:00:01 |
|  8 |    TABLE ACCESS BY INDEX ROWID | DEPARTMENTS|   1  |   1   (0)| 00:00:01 |
|* 9 |     INDEX UNIQUE SCAN           | DEPT_ID_PK  |   1  |   0   (0)|          |
--------------------------------------------------------------------------------


Predicate Information (identified by operation id):
---------------------------------------------------

   6 - access("EMPLOYEES"."JOB_ID"="JOBS"."JOB_ID")
       filter("EMPLOYEES"."JOB_ID"="JOBS"."JOB_ID")
   9 - access("EMPLOYEES"."DEPARTMENT_ID"="DEPARTMENTS"."DEPARTMENT_ID")
```

DBMS_XPLAN

We've seen a few examples of DBMS_XPLAN, so now let's look at this valuable tool in more detail.

DBMS_XPLAN usually yields better results than manually issuing queries against the plan table because it has a less complex syntax, provides many useful output formats, and exploits the cached plan statistics.

The DBMS_XPLAN functions are most easily invoked using the SELECT * FROM TABLE() syntax, as in

```
SELECT * FROM TABLE (DBMS_XPLAN.function (options));
```

The two DBMS_XPLAN functions used most often are

```
DBMS_XPLAN.display (
    table_name      VARCHAR2 DEFAULT 'PLAN_TABLE',
    statement_id    VARCHAR2 DEFAULT NULL,
    format          VARCHAR2 DEFAULT 'TYPICAL',
    filter_preds    VARCHAR2 DEFAULT NULL
)

DBMS_XPLAN.display_cursor (
    sql_id          VARCHAR2 DEFAULT NULL,
    cursor_child_no INTEGER  DEFAULT 0,
    format          VARCHAR2 DEFAULT 'TYPICAL'
)
```

The DISPLAY function shows an explain plan from the PLAN_TABLE, whereas the DISPLAY_CURSOR function shows the explain plan from the cached plan information in V$SQL_PLAN. The arguments for these functions follow:

TABLE_NAME	The name of the plan table that contains the execution plan, by default PLAN_TABLE.
STATEMENT_ID	The unique identifier for a plan as set by the STATEMENT_ID argument to EXPLAIN PLAN. If absent, the most recent plan is displayed.
FORMAT	A set of keywords that control output formats. These include the high-level keywords BASIC, TYPICAL, and ALL, plus other keywords that fine-tune the output. The FORMAT parameter is described in more detail later.
FILTER_PREDS	This keyword allows you to insert modifiers into the WHERE clause that runs against the plan table. You can use this to find a plan in the plan table that contains a certain step or has other characteristics.
SQL_ID	Specifies a SQL_ID that identifies a cached SQL in V$SQL.
CURSOR_CHILD_NO	Specifies a particular child cursor in V$SQL. The combination of SQL_ID and CURSOR_CHILD_NUMBER specifies a specific row in V$SQL.

The FORMAT parameter controls the amount of information displayed in the execution plan. There are three major formats:

TYPICAL	The default display setting. Most relevant information is displayed but details of distributed SQL, projection information (see below), and other information will be shown only if the DBMS_XPLAN considers them directly relevant to the plan.
BASIC	Only the execution plan will be shown.
ALL	All information will be shown.

Individual elements can be tailored by using the following modifiers. A modifier is prefixed by the + or − operator to indicate that the item should be included or suppressed.

BYTES	The estimated number of bytes processed in the plan step.
COST	The estimated optimizer cost for the plan step.
PARTITION	Information relating to partition elimination and pruning.
PARALLEL	Information about parallel processing.
PREDICATE	Predicate information (join and WHERE clause filters).
PROJECTION	Projection information. This includes the columns processed in sorts, selects, and so on.
ALIAS	Shows query block aliases that include cross references used in interpreting remote SQL and parallel query SQL.
REMOTE	Shows remote SQL (SQL sent to external databases to satisfy a distributed SQL).
NOTE	Miscellaneous notes.
IOSTATS	IO statistics associated with the cached SQL plan. These will be present only if STATISTICS_LEVEL=ALL or the query contains the GATHER_PLAN_STATS hint.
MEMSTATS	Show information about memory and disk usage for sorts and hash joins.
ALLSTATS	Same as +IOSTATS +MEMSTATS.
LAST	Shows cached plan statistics for the most recent execution, rather than for all SQL statement executions.

The ability to add or subtract information from the high-level formats gives you a lot of control over your output. For example, if you are uninterested in IO, you might choose ALL – IOSTATS; if you are specifically tuning a parallel query, you might choose BASIC +PARALLEL.

DBMS_XPLAN provides more detail and flexible output than "traditional" queries against the PLAN_TABLE.

Here's a sample of DBMS_XPLAN output:

```
SQL> EXPLAIN PLAN FOR
  2  SELECT    department_name, last_name, job_title
  3    FROM hr.employees JOIN hr.departments USING (department_id)
  4        JOIN hr.jobs USING (job_id)
  5  ORDER BY department_name, job_title;

Explained.
```

```
SQL> SELECT * FROM TABLE(DBMS_XPLAN.DISPLAY(null,null,
                        'TYPICAL -BYTES'));


PLAN_TABLE_OUTPUT
------------------------------------------------------------------------
Plan hash value: 3225241925[1]
```

Id[2]	Operation[3]	Name[4]	Rows[5]	Cost(%CPU)[6]	Time[7]	
0	SELECT STATEMENT		106	26 (8)	00:00:01	
1	SORT ORDER BY		106	26 (8)	00:00:01	
2	NESTED LOOPS		106	25 (4)	00:00:01	
3	MERGE JOIN		107	24 (5)	00:00:01	
4	TABLE ACCESS BY INDEX ROWID	EMPLOYEES	107	20 (0)	00:00:01	
5	INDEX FULL SCAN	EMP_JOB_IX	107	12 (0)	00:00:01	
* 6	SORT JOIN		19	4 (25)	00:00:01	
7	TABLE ACCESS FULL	JOBS	19	3 (0)	00:00:01	
8	TABLE ACCESS BY INDEX ROWID	DEPARTMENTS	1	1 (0)	00:00:01	
* 9	INDEX UNIQUE SCAN	DEPT_ID_PK	1	0 (0)	00:00:01	

```
Predicate Information (identified by operation id)[8]:
---------------------------------------------------

   6 - access("EMPLOYEES"."JOB_ID"="JOBS"."JOB_ID")
       filter("EMPLOYEES"."JOB_ID"="JOBS"."JOB_ID")
   9 - access("EMPLOYEES"."DEPARTMENT_ID"="DEPARTMENTS"."DEPARTMENT_ID")
```

Let's step through this DBMS_XPLAN output. I've added some highlighted superscripts to the output, which are referred to below:

1. First we see the plan hash value (1) that corresponds to the column PLAN_HASH_VALUE in V$SQL and V$SQL_PLAN.
2. Next the execution plan is displayed in a grid. The step ID (2), operation (3), and Name (4) are always shown. Other columns might be shown depending on the nature of the SQL and on the FORMAT options provided. In this case we show estimated rows (5), Cost (6), and Elapsed time (7) for each step. Other columns that can appear in the DBMS_XPLAN table output are listed in the following table.
3. Finally, the access and filter predicates are shown (8). These are the clauses in the SQL that are driving various join, filter, or access operations.

Here are the DBMS_XPLAN column descriptions:

Operation	Operation undertaken by the step; for example, TABLE ACCESS FULL.
Name	Name of the object processed by the step. Can be a table name or index name, or a temporary result set indicator.
Rows	Number of rows expected to be processed by this step.
Bytes	Bytes of data expected to be processed by this step.
Cost (%CPU)	Total optimizer cost and—in brackets—the percentage of that cost which is attributed to CPU.[4]
Time	Elapsed time estimated for the step.
TmpSpc	Temporary space estimated for the operation, perhaps to perform a sort or hash join.
TQ	For parallel execution, shows the table queue information. This can be used to interpret which stream and sequence of parallel processing is involved. See Chapter 13 for more details.
IN-OUT	For parallel execution identifies the step as being Parallel->Parallel (P->P), Parallel to Serial (P->S), Parallel combined with Parent (PCWP), Parallel combined with Child (PCWC), or Serial to Parallel (S->P). See Chapter 13 for more details.
PQ Distrib	Describes the nature of the parallel execution, typically for coordination activities; for example, QC (master query coordinator) or RANGE (assigning parallel streams of data). See Chapter 13 for more details.
Starts	For IOSTATS, the number of times the step has been started.
E-Rows	For IOSTATS, the estimated number of rows that will be processed by the step.
A-Rows	For IOSTATS, the actual number of rows processed by the step.
Buffers	For IOSTATS, the number of buffer gets (logical reads) for the step.
Reads	For IOSTATS, the number of physical disk reads for the step.
OMem	For MEMSTATS, the estimated optimal memory size for the operation. The optimal size is that which enables the operation to proceed completely in memory.
1Mem	For MEMSTATS, the estimated memory size required to enable the operation to proceed with only a single pass temporary segment. See Chapter 11, "Sorting, Grouping, and Set Operations," for more details.
O/1/M	The number of Optimal Executions/One Pass Executions/Multi-pass executions. These record the number of times the operation had to perform temporary segment IO, and whether the IO was single-pass or multi-pass (see Chapter 11).
Pstart	For partitioned operations, lowest partition number processed by the step.
Pstop	For partitioned operations, highest partition number processed by the step.

---

[4] Apparently calculated as **round**((**cost**-io_cost)*100/**cost**)

INTERPRETING THE EXECUTION PLAN

Interpreting a formatted execution plan, such as that shown in the previous section, requires practice and some judgment. However, the following principles should guide the interpretation:

❏ The more heavily indented an access path is, the earlier it is executed.
❏ If two steps are indented at the same level, the uppermost statement is executed first.

With these principles in mind, let's interpret the following execution plan:

```
SQL> EXPLAIN PLAN FOR
  2  SELECT   department_name, last_name
  3      FROM hr.employees JOIN hr.departments using (department_id)
  4  /

SQL> SELECT * FROM TABLE(DBMS_XPLAN.DISPLAY(null,null,
                      'BASIC +PREDICATE'));
-----------------------------------------------------------
| Id  | Operation                    | Name              |
-----------------------------------------------------------
|   0 | SELECT STATEMENT             |                   |
|   1 |  TABLE ACCESS BY INDEX ROWID | EMPLOYEES         |
|   2 |   NESTED LOOPS               |                   |
|   3 |    TABLE ACCESS FULL         | DEPARTMENTS       |
|*  4 |    INDEX RANGE SCAN          | EMP_DEPARTMENT_IX |
-----------------------------------------------------------

Predicate Information (identified by operation id):
---------------------------------------------------

   4 - access("EMPLOYEES"."DEPARTMENT_ID"="DEPARTMENTS"."DEPARTMENT_ID")
```

Here's how this plan would be interpreted:

1. The most heavily indented statements are the full scan of DEPARTMENTS and the index scan of EMP_DEPARTMENT_IX (steps 3 and 4).
2. The table scan of DEPARTMENTS (step 3) is "higher" than the index scan, so the order of operations is DEPARTMENTS scan; then EMP_DEPARTMENT_IX index scan.
3. These steps feed into a NESTED LOOPS join (step 2), indicating that for each row from the full table scan, an index lookup of EMP_DEPARTMENT_IX was executed to find the matching employee.

4. The next step (step 1), is a table access of the EMPLOYEES table, retrieving the EMPLOYEE row found by the index lookup.

5. Finally (step 0), the results are fed into the SELECT statement.

Table 3-1 lists some of the execution plan steps that you might expect to encounter. As you can see, there are a lot! However, you'll soon get used to the most common steps. Oracle documents some of the operations in the "Using EXPLAIN PLAN" chapter of the *Oracle Database Performance Tuning Guide*.

Table 3-1   Common Execution Plan Steps

OPERATION	OPTION	DESCRIPTION
Table Access Paths		
TABLE ACCESS	FULL	The well-known full table scan. This involves reading every row in the table (strictly speaking, every block up to the table's high water mark).
	CLUSTER	Access of data via an index cluster key.
	HASH	A hash key is issued to access one or more rows in a table with a matching hash value.
	BY INDEX ROWID	Access a single row in a table by specifying its ROWID. ROWID access is the fastest way to access a single row. Very often, the ROWID will have been obtained by an associated index lookup.
	BY USER ROWID	Access via a ROWID provided by a bind variable, literal, or WHERE CURRENT OF CURSOR clause.
	BY INDEX ROWID	Access via a ROWID obtained through an index lookup.
	BY GLOBAL INDEX ROWID	Access via a ROWID obtained from a globally partitioned index.
	BY LOCAL INDEX ROWID	Access via a ROWID obtained from a locally partitioned index.
	SAMPLE	A subset of rows are returned as a result of the use of the SAMPLE clause.
EXTERNAL TABLE ACCESS		An access to an external table.
RESULT CACHE		The SQL results might be retrieved from the result set cache; see Chapter 20, "Other Memory Management Topics."
MAT_VIEW REWRITE ACCESS		The SQL statement was rewritten to take advantage of a materialized view.

OPERATION	OPTION	DESCRIPTION
Index Operations		
AND-EQUAL		The results from one or more index scans are combined.
INDEX	UNIQUE SCAN	An index lookup that returns the address (ROWID) of only one row.
	RANGE SCAN	An index lookup that returns the ROWID of more than one row. This can be because the index is nonunique or because a range operator (for example, >) was used.
	FULL SCAN	Scan every entry in the index in key order.
	SKIP SCAN	Index scan that searches nonleading columns in the index key.
	FULL SCAN (MAX/MIN)	Find the highest or lowest index entry.
	FAST FULL SCAN	Scan every entry in the index in block order, possibly using multi-block read.
DOMAIN INDEX		Lookup of a domain index (user defined index type).
Bitmap Operations		
BITMAP	CONVERSION	Convert ROWID to bitmaps or bitmaps to ROWID.
	INDEX	Retrieve a value or range of values from the bitmap.
	MERGE	Merge multiple bitmaps.
	MINUS	Subtract one bitmap from another.
	OR	Create a bit-wise OR of two bitmaps.
Join Operations		
CONNECT BY		A hierarchical self-join is performed on the output of the preceding steps.
MERGE JOIN		A merge join performed on the output of the preceding steps.
NESTED LOOPS		A Nested loops join is performed on the preceding steps. For each row in the upper result set, the lower result set is scanned to find a matching row.
HASH JOIN		A hash join is performed of two row sources.
Any join operation	OUTER	The join is an outer join.
Any join operation	ANTI	The join is an antijoin (see Chapter 10, "Joins and Subqueries").
Any join operation	SEMI	The join is a semijoin (see Chapter 10).
Any join operation	CARTESIAN	Every row in one result set is joined to every row in the other result set.

Table 3-1   Common Execution Plan Steps *(continued)*

OPERATION	OPTION	DESCRIPTION
Set Operations CONCATENATION		Multiple result sets are merged in the same way as in an explicit UNION statement. This typically occurs when an OR statement is used with indexed columns.
INTERSECTION		Two result sets are compared and only rows common to both are returned. This operation usually takes place only as a result of an explicit use of the INTERSECT clause.
MINUS		All result sets in the first result set are returned, except those appearing in the second result set. This occurs as a result of the MINUS set operator.
UNION-ALL		Two result sets are combined and rows from both are returned.
UNION		Two result sets are combined and rows from both are returned. Duplicate rows are not returned.
VIEW		Either a view definition has been accessed or a temporary table has been created to store a result set.
Miscellaneous FOR UPDATE		The rows returned are locked as a result of the FOR UPDATE clause.
COLLECTION ITERATOR	Various	An operation that retrieves rows from a table function (that is, FROM TABLE()).
FAST DUAL		An access to DUAL that avoids reading from the buffer cache.
FILTER		Rows from a result set not matching a selection criterion are eliminated.
REMOTE		An external database is accessed through a database link.
FIRST ROW		Retrieve the first row of a query.
SEQUENCE		An Oracle sequence generator is used to obtain a unique sequence number.
INLIST ITERATOR		Perform the next operation once for each value in an IN list.
LOAD AS SELECT		Denotes a direct path INSERT based on a SELECT statement.
FIXED TABLE		Access of a fixed (X$ or V$) table.
FIXED INDEX		Access of an index on fixed (X$) table.
WINDOW	BUFFER	Internal operation to support an analytic function such as OVER().
WINDOW	SORT [PUSHED] RANK	An analytic function requires a sort to implement the RANK() function.

OPERATION	OPTION	DESCRIPTION
Partition Operations		
PARTITION	SINGLE	Access a single partition.
	ITERATOR	Access multiple partitions.
	ALL	Access all partitions.
	INLIST	Access multiple partitions based on the values contained in an IN list.
Aggregation		
COUNT		Count the rows in the result set to satisfy the COUNT() function.
COUNT	STOPKEY	Count the number of rows returned by a result set and stop processing when a certain number of rows are reached. This is usually the result of a WHERE clause that specifies a maximum ROWNUM (for instance, WHERE ROWNUM <= 10).
BUFFER	SORT	An in-memory sort of a temporary result set.
HASH	GROUP BY	A hash operation is used instead of a sort to implement a GROUP BY.
INLIST	ITERATOR	Implements the child operation once for every value in an IN list
SORT	ORDER BY	A result set is sorted to satisfy an ORDER BY clause.
	AGGREGATE	This occurs when a group function is used on data that is already grouped.
	JOIN	Sort the rows in preparation for a merge join.
	UNIQUE	A sort to eliminate duplicate rows. This typically occurs as a result of using the DISTINCT clause.
	GROUP BY	A sort of a result set to group them for the GROUP BY CLAUSE.
	GROUP BY NOSORT	A group by which does not require a sort operation.
	GROUP BY ROLLUP	A group by which includes the ROLLUP option.
	GROUP BY CUBE	A group by which includes the CUBE option.

VIRTUAL INDEXING

Virtual indexes are definitions for indexes that are not physically created. The purpose of a virtual index is to determine whether an index would be useful in tuning a SQL statement without having to go through the time-consuming CPU, IO, and storage intensive process of actually creating the index.

For instance, consider the following query:

```
SQL> EXPLAIN PLAN FOR
  2      SELECT * FROM sh.sales WHERE quantity_sold > 10000
  3  /

Explained.

SQL> SELECT *
  2      FROM TABLE (DBMS_XPLAN.display (NULL, NULL, 'BASIC +COST'))
  3  /
```

```
---------------------------------------------------
| Id  | Operation              | Name  | Cost (%CPU)|
---------------------------------------------------
|   0 | SELECT STATEMENT       |       |   441  (12)|
|   1 |  PARTITION RANGE ALL|       |   441  (12)|
|   2 |   TABLE ACCESS FULL | SALES |   441  (12)|
---------------------------------------------------
```

We can create a virtual index to see if the optimizer would choose to use an index on QUANTITY_SOLD and what the expected change in cost would be:

```
SQL> ALTER SESSION SET "_use_nosegment_indexes"=TRUE;

Session altered.

SQL> CREATE INDEX sh.sales_vi1 ON sh.sales(quantity_sold) NOSEGMENT;

Index created.
```

The NOSEGMENT option of CREATE INDEX specifies that the index is "virtual"—not associated with an actual index segment. The _USE_NOSEGMENT _INDEXES parameter instructs Oracle to use these indexes in explain plans, if the optimizer determines that such an index would be useful. Now let's see if this index would be used if we create it for real:

```
SQL> EXPLAIN  PLAN FOR
  2      SELECT * FROM sh.sales WHERE quantity_sold > 10000;

Explained.

SQL> SELECT *
  2      FROM TABLE (DBMS_XPLAN.display (NULL, NULL, 'BASIC +COST'));
```

```
-----------------------------------------------------------------
| Id  | Operation                          | Name      | Cost (%CPU)|
-----------------------------------------------------------------
|   0 | SELECT STATEMENT                   |           |    3   (0)|
|   1 |  TABLE ACCESS BY GLOBAL INDEX ROWID| SALES     |    3   (0)|
|   2 |   INDEX RANGE SCAN                  | SALES_VI1 |    2   (0)|
-----------------------------------------------------------------
```

In the preceding example, DBMS_XPLAN shows that the index was indeed deemed useful and that the cost estimate reduced from 441 to 3. If queries like this were going to be common, we'd be well advised to create the index.

You can use virtual indexes to determine whether the optimizer would use an index without having to build the index structure.

TRACING ORACLE EXECUTION

The EXPLAIN PLAN and DBMS_XPLAN utilities are extremely useful, and—provided you leverage both the execution plan and cached statistics—can be your principal SQL tuning tool.

However, Oracle also provides a facility for tracing session activity that can be more effective when tuning a collection of SQLs for a particular transaction or application, and which can also help you collect execution statistics in production environments. Tracing provides all the information provided by EXPLAIN PLAN and DBMS_XPLAN but is more accurate, allows you to focus on the entire transaction rather than individual SQLs, and can reveal details of execution performance that can't be obtained using any other tool.

SQL tracing includes two principle ingredients:

❏ The ability to initiate a trace in your session or in another session; we call this *SQL trace*.
❏ A tool, tkprof, that enables the trace files generated to be formatted in a meaningful way.

The SQL tracing facility and tkprof utility are a powerful tuning combination, but they are somewhat awkward to use, and the output is sometimes difficult to interpret. Consequently, these tools are not used as widely as they should be. However, the SQL tracing facility is one of the most powerful freely available tools for tuning SQL statements.

There's a variety of ways to start SQL trace:

❏ Issuing a command within your application code
❏ Issuing a command to trace another session
❏ Invoking the DBMS_MONITOR package to specify sessions that should automatically be traced
❏ Creating a login trigger that traces based on your individual needs

Let's now look at each method in detail.

TRACING FROM WITHIN YOUR SESSION

The simplest way to start a trace within your own session is to issue the following command:

```
ALTER SESSION SET SQL_TRACE=TRUE;
```

This creates a basic trace, in which SQL statement execution statistics and execution plans are recorded but not the values of bind variables or the time spent waiting for various events. To get a more advanced trace, we can use the DBMS_SESSION package:

```
DBMS_SESSION.session_trace_enable (
        waits       IN    BOOLEAN DEFAULT TRUE,
        binds       IN    BOOLEAN DEFAULT FALSE,
        plan_stat   IN    VARCHAR2 DEFAULT NULL --11g Only
    );
```

Here are the parameters for dbms_session.session_trace_enable:

WAITS   TRUE if wait information is to be collected, FALSE otherwise.
BINDS   TRUE if bind information is to be collected, FALSE otherwise.
PLAN_STAT   For 11g, determines when row counts for individual plan steps are
             collected. Valid values are NEVER, FIRST_EXECUTION, or ALL
             _EXECUTIONS.

For instance, the following command commences tracing, includes wait information, does not include bind information, and includes step row counts aggregated across all executions:

```
BEGIN
    DBMS_SESSION.session_trace_enable (waits       => TRUE,
                                       binds       => FALSE,
                                       plan_stat   => 'all_executions'
                                      );
END;
```

IDENTIFYING YOUR TRACE FILE

As we will soon see, it can be hard to identify individual trace files. One way to make it easier is to specify a trace file identifier for your session. This can be done by setting the TRACEFILE_IDENTIFIER parameter from within your session:

```
ALTER SESSION SET tracefile_identifier=GUY
```

Now when we look in the trace file directory, the tracefile can be identified by the trailing "GUY":[5]

```
$ ls -lt
total 1448
-rw-r-----  1 oracle oinstall  12625 Jul 20 17:09 gh11R1GA_ora_31429_GUY.trc
-rw-r-----  1 oracle oinstall    153 Jul 20 17:09 gh11R1GA_ora_31429_GUY.trm
-rw-r-----  1 oracle oinstall   1940 Jul 20 17:07 gh11R1GA_ora_31429.trc
-rw-r-----  1 oracle oinstall     84 Jul 20 17:07 gh11R1GA_ora_31429.trm
-rw-r-----  1 oracle oinstall  32676 Jul 20 17:07 gh11R1GA_dbrm_4095.trc
-rw-r-----  1 oracle oinstall   1697 Jul 20 17:07 gh11R1GA_dbrm_4095.trm
-rw-r-----  1 oracle oinstall    862 Jul 20 17:03 gh11R1GA_m000_32109.trc
-rw-r-----  1 oracle oinstall     61 Jul 20 17:03 gh11R1GA_m000_32109.trm
-rw-r-----  1 oracle oinstall    861 Jul 20 16:03 gh11R1GA_m000_31979.trc
```

GETTING TRACING STATUS

In V$SESSION, the columns SQL_TRACE, SQL_TRACE_WAITS, and SQL_TRACE_BINDS show the status of tracing for a session, and in V$PROCESS, the columns TRACEID and TRACEFILE (11g only) show the name of the trace file and the TRACEFILE_IDENTIFIER in effect for a given server process.

The following query (11g only) shows the values of these columns for the current session:

```
SQL> SELECT s.sql_trace, s.sql_trace_waits, s.sql_trace_binds,
  2         traceid, tracefile
  3    FROM v$session s JOIN v$process p ON (p.addr = s.paddr)
  4   WHERE audsid = USERENV ('SESSIONID')
  5  /
```

---

[5] The .TRC file contains the trace output. In 11g each file can be associated with a .TRM file that contains metadata in binary format about the .TRC file. The .TRM file appears to be for Oracle internal purposes only.

```
SQL_TRACE   SQL_TRACE_WAITS   SQL_TRACE_BINDS   TRACEID
----------  ----------------  ----------------  ----------
TRACEFILE
--------------------------------------------------------------------
ENABLED     TRUE              FALSE             GUY
/oracle/diag/rdbms/gh11r1ga/gh11R1GA/trace/gh11R1GA_ora_32200_GUY.
```

Remember that for a dedicated server connection, there is a one-to-one match between the session and the server process, but for shared servers a session can be serviced by multiple servers, and a server can perform activities on behalf of multiple clients. As a result, when using shared servers the relevant trace file might change from SQL statement to SQL statement. We discuss this issue and its solution in the "Merging Multiple SQL Trace Files" section later in this chapter.

INVOKING TRACE IN ANOTHER SESSION

The DBMS_MONITOR package includes a number of routines for starting tracing in other sessions. The easiest way to create a trace in another session is to invoke a DBMS_MONITOR.SESSION_TRACE_ENABLE package:

```
DBMS_MONITOR.session_trace_enable (
    session_id   IN    BINARY_INTEGER DEFAULT NULL,
    serial_num   IN    BINARY_INTEGER DEFAULT NULL,
    waits        IN    BOOLEAN DEFAULT TRUE,
    binds        IN    BOOLEAN DEFAULT FALSE,
    plan_stat    IN    VARCHAR2 DEFAULT NULL   -- 11g only
);
```

The parameters SESSION_ID and SERIAL_NUM correspond to the columns SID and SERIAL# in the V$SESSION view. The parameters WAITS, BINDS, and PLAN_STAT are used in the same way as for the DBMS_SESSION .SESSION_TRACE_ENABLE package previously described. You can interrogate the V$SESSION view to identify the sessions that you wanted to trace and then invoke the procedure for each of those sessions. For instance, the following routine turns on a basic trace with bind variable information for every SQL*Plus session:

```
BEGIN
   FOR ROW IN (SELECT SID, serial#
                 FROM v$session
                WHERE LOWER (program) LIKE '%sqlplus%')
```

```
    LOOP
        DBMS_MONITOR.session_trace_enable (session_id => ROW.SID,
                                           serial_num => ROW.serial#,
                                           waits      => FALSE,
                                           binds      => TRUE
                                           );
    END LOOP;
END;
```

Use DBMS_MONITOR to start tracing in other sessions.

TRACING BY MODULE, ACTION, OR SERVICE

Many Oracle-aware applications set module and action attributes through the DBMS_APPLICATION_INFO package. These attributes can be viewed in V$SESSION, enabling you to work out what application a session belongs to and what it is currently doing.

It's also increasingly common—especially in Real Application Clusters (RAC) environments—for services to be used to manage server resources and to allocate sessions to the most appropriate cluster instance.

DBMS_MONITOR enables you to automatically enable tracing for specific module, action, and service combinations. The SERV_MOD_ACT_TRACE _ENABLE method enables you to set the tracing on for sessions matching particular service, module, actions, and (for RAC clusters) instance identifiers.

```
    DBMS_MONITOR.serv_mod_act_trace_enable (
        service_name    IN    VARCHAR2,
        module_name     IN    VARCHAR2 DEFAULT all_modules,
        action_name     IN    VARCHAR2 DEFAULT all_actions,
        waits           IN    BOOLEAN  DEFAULT TRUE,
        binds           IN    BOOLEAN  DEFAULT FALSE,
        instance_name   IN    VARCHAR2 DEFAULT NULL,
        plan_stat       IN    VARCHAR2 DEFAULT NULL  -- 11g Only
        );
```

STARTING A TRACE USING A LOGIN TRIGGER

If you want more fine-grained control over which sessions get traced, or if you also want to specify a TRACEFILE_IDENTIFIER or perform some other session level activity, a login trigger is a good way to go. The login trigger gets executed at session initialization. You can then invoke trace if the session meets your criteria. For instance, the following login trigger sets an appropriate TRACE-FILE_IDENTIFIER and starts a trace for all sessions logged on as the user "GUY":

```
CREATE OR REPLACE TRIGGER trace_login_trigger
    AFTER LOGON ON DATABASE
BEGIN
    IF USER = 'GUY'
    THEN
        EXECUTE IMMEDIATE 'alter session set tracefile_identifier=GUY';

        DBMS_SESSION.session_trace_enable (waits      => TRUE,
                                           binds      => FALSE,
                                           plan_stat  => 'all_executions'
                                           );
    END IF;
END;
```

FINDING THE TRACE FILE

Having enabled SQL_TRACE, your next challenge is often to find the trace file that has been generated. The trace file is written to the location defined by the Oracle configuration parameter USER_DUMP_DEST, as returned by the following query:

```
SELECT VALUE
    FROM v$parameter
  WHERE name = 'user_dump_dest'
```

The name of the trace file is
Sid_procid_pid[_traceid].trc
The components of the trace filename follow:

Sid	The Oracle instance name (as found in V$INSTANCE).
ProcId	Identifies the type of server. For dedicated servers this will be "ora" but for background processes, job servers, shared servers, and the like, it will be a short abbreviation that identifies the type of server (for instance S001, J001, and so on).
Pid	The operating system process or thread id for the server process concerned.
Traceid	The tracefile identifier (if any) specified by the TRACEFILE_IDENTIFIER parameter.

There might be many trace files in the USER_DUMP_DEST directory, and typically they will all be owned by the Oracle account. Here are some of the ways you can determine which trace is yours:

❏ Examine time stamps of the files.
❏ Search for a particular SQL statement. A handy way of tagging your trace file is by issuing a statement such as "SELECT 'Catherines trace file' FROM

dual;"—then you can search among trace files for the string "Catherines trace file."

❏ Have your program tell you where the trace will be written. For instance, in 11g your program could examine the TRACEFILE column of V$PROCESS and report the appropriate value.

❏ Use the TRACEFILE_IDENTIFER parameter to uniquely tag the file.

OTHER SPECIALIZED TRACES

SQL trace creates a general trace that is useful in almost all circumstances for tuning sessions that issue SQL. However, there are some other trace mechanisms that can come in handy in special circumstances:

❏ DBMS_PROFILE tracks execution of PL/SQL packages down to the line of code. When a PL/SQL program needs tuning, this is the tool of choice. We look at DBMS_PROFILE in detail in Chapter 12, "Using and Tuning PL/SQL."

❏ There's a bunch of specialized traces that you can generate, using the ALTER SESSION SET EVENTS command. Most of these are beyond the scope of this book. The Jonathan Lewis blog at http://jonathanlewis .wordpress.com is probably a good place to start reading about these sorts of advanced techniques.

The 10053 trace is probably the most useful of these advanced trace events. We initiate a 10053 trace with the following command:

```
ALTER SESSION SET EVENTS '10053 trace name context forever'
```

This generates a trace file in the USER_DUMP_DEST that contains information about optimizer processing during query optimization. It shows—among other things—any rewrites that might occur, and details of each execution plan considered.

FORMATTING TRACES WITH tkprof

When the trace file is found, the tkprof utility is used to render it into a usable form. The basic syntax for tkprof follows:

```
tkprof trace_file output_file
    explain=connection waits=yes|no sort=(sort keys)
```

The key parameters for tkprof follow:

trace_file	The raw trace file generated by the SQL trace facility.
output_file	The file to which formatted trace information will be written.
Explain=connection	Connect to Oracle using the connection parameters given and issue an explain plan for each statement. This is only necessary if the trace file doesn't have embedded execution plans (if it were truncated, for example) or for older versions of Oracle.
Waits=yes/no	Provide a summary of wait information for each SQL.
sort=(sort keys)	Display the SQL statements in descending values of the sort keys. The sort keys (prsela,exeela,fchela) sort the SQL statements in elapsed time order and are a common choice.

A typical `tkprof` invocation follows:

```
tkprof mysid_ora_31429.trc tkprof_out1.prf explain=opsg/opsg
    sort='(prsela,fchela,exeela)'
```

The preceding command processes the raw trace file *mysid_ora_31429.trc* and writes the output file *tkprof_out1.prf*, generating execution plans using the OPSG account and sorting SQL statements by elapsed time. Note that because this example was created under Linux, the parentheses were enclosed in single quotes; this isn't necessary in Windows.

THE `tkprof` SORT OPTIONS

The `tkprof` sort keys consist of two parts: the first part indicates the type of calls that are to be sorted, the second part indicates the values to be sorted. So `exedsk` indicates statements are to be sorted on disk reads during execute calls. Adding options together causes statements to be sorted by the sum of the options specified: so `prsdsk,exedsk,fchdisk` causes statements to be sorted by overall physical disk reads. A few combinations are not valid:

❑ `mis` can be applied only to `prs`
❑ `row` can apply only to `exe` or `fch`.

Table 3-2 shows the various components of the `tkprof` sort key.

OTHER `tkprof` OPTIONS

The `tkprof` options outlined in the previous examples will usually give you output that contains all the information needed to tune your SQL. The following table describes the other `tkprof` options that might be useful in some circumstances.

| table=owner.tablename | By default, `tkprof` uses the default PLAN_TABLE to generate the execution plans. If you want to use a different PLAN_TABLE, you can specify it with this option. |

Table 3-2 `tkprof` Sort Options

FIRST PART	DESCRIPTION	SECOND PART	DESCRIPTION
prs	Sort on values during parse calls	cnt	Sort on number of calls
exe	Sort on values during execute calls (equivalent to open cursor for a query)	cpu	Sort on CPU consumption
fch	Sort on values during fetch calls (queries only)	ela	Sort on elapsed time
		dsk	Sort on disk reads
		qry	Sort on consistent reads
		cu	Sort on current reads
		mis	Sort on library cache misses
		row	Sort on rows processed

print=number_of_statements	Restricts the number of SQL statements printed.
aggregate=yes/no	If set to yes (the default), SQL statements in the trace file that are identical will be reported only once and execution statistics will be summed. If set to no, each time a SQL statement is parsed, a separate entry will be written to the `tkprof` output, even if the statements are identical to ones encountered previously. This option doesn't appear to be active in recent releases.
sys=no	If set to no, statements executed as the SYS user will not be included in the trace output. These statements are usually recursive SQL that are often not of interest.
record=filename	Generates a file containing all the SQL statements (aside from recursive SQL) in the trace file.
insert=filename	Generates a file that can be run under SQL*PLUS to keep a record of the SQL statements in the trace file and their execution statistics. This facility was introduced to enable you to set and compare SQL statement execution over time, perhaps to establish the effect of increasing data volumes or user load.

MERGING MULTIPLE SQL TRACE FILES

Sometimes the information you need can be spread across multiple SQL trace files. This can happen when

❏ You want to generate a `tkprof` report for a session, but that session connected using shared server connections. Because each SQL statement can be executed by a different shared server, the session's trace information can be spread across the trace files generated by each of the server processes.

❏ You want to generate a `tkprof` report from the output of multiple sessions, all of which have been traced.

❏ You want to report on information specific to a particular module, action, or service and the information is spread across multiple session trace files.

The `trcsess` utility can provide a solution for these scenarios. The `trcsess` utility takes input from multiple trace files, applies various filters, and outputs matching records as a single trace file that you can then process with `tkprof`. Filters can be set for client identifier (set by DBMS_SESSION.SET_IDENTIFIER), service name, module names, or actions.

`trcsess` syntax is fairly straightforward:

```
trcsess [output=<output file name >]  [session=<session ID>]
    [clientid=<clientid>] [service=<service name>]
[action=<action name>] [module=<module name>] <trace file names>
```

> Use `trcsess` to merge multiple trace files if your session trace is spread across multiple files or if you want to analyze traces from multiple sessions.

INTERPRETING `tkprof` OUTPUT

The `tkprof` output can be a little overwhelming at first, so let's step through an example. The following is some sample `tkprof` output. Some highlighted superscripts have been added, which are referenced in the commentary.

```
************************************************************************

SELECT * FROM g_orders[1]
  JOIN g_line_items USING (order_id)
  JOIN g_customers USING (customer_id) WHERE
        g_line_items.book_id=:book_id
```

call	count[2]	cpu[3]	elapsed[4]	disk[5]	query[6]	current[7]	rows[8]
Parse[a]	1[d]	0.00	0.00	0	0	0	0
Execute[b]	2[e]	0.00	0.00	0	0	0	0
Fetch[c]	18[j]	0.87	39.35	18093	18822	0	255[i]
total	21	0.87	39.35	18093[k]	18822[f]	0[g]	255[h]

```
Misses in library cache during parse: 1[m]
Optimizer mode: ALL_ROWS
Parsing user id: 88  (TRANSIM)
```

```
Rows    Row Source Operation[n]
------  ------------------------------------------------------
   255  NESTED LOOPS  (cr=18822 pr=18093 pw=18093 time=39285904 us)
   255   NESTED LOOPS  (cr=18567 pr=17892 pw=17892 time=35072868 us …)
   255    NESTED LOOPS  (cr=18294 pr=17814 pw=17814 time=33429490 us  …)
   255     TABLE ACCESS FULL G_LINE_ITEMS (cr=17511 pr=17490 pw=17490 …)
   255     TABLE ACCESS BY INDEX ROWID G_ORDERS (cr=783 pr=324 pw=324 time=0 …)
   255      INDEX UNIQUE SCAN G_ORDERS_PK (cr=528 pr=83 pw=83 time=0 us …)
   255     INDEX UNIQUE SCAN G_CUSTOMERS_PK (cr=273 pr=78 pw=78 time=0 us … )
   255    TABLE ACCESS BY INDEX ROWID G_CUSTOMERS (cr=255 pr=201 pw=201 time=0 …)
```

```
Rows[1]   Execution Plan[o]
------  ------------------------------------------------------
     0  SELECT STATEMENT    MODE: ALL_ROWS
   255   NESTED LOOPS
   255    NESTED LOOPS
   255     NESTED LOOPS
   255      TABLE ACCESS    MODE: ANALYZED (FULL) OF 'G_LINE_ITEMS'
   255      TABLE ACCESS    MODE: ANALYZED (BY INDEX ROWID) OF 'G_ORDERS'
   255       INDEX MODE:ANALYZED (UNIQUE SCAN) OF 'G_ORDERS_PK' (INDEX (UNIQUE))
   255       INDEX MODE:ANALYZED (UNIQUE SCAN) OF 'G_CUSTOMERS_PK' (INDEX (UNIQUE))
   255      TABLE ACCESS    MODE: ANALYZED (BY INDEX ROWID) OF 'G_CUSTOMERS' (TABLE)
```

```
Elapsed times include waiting on following events:[p]
  Event waited on                       Times   Max. Wait  Total Waited
  ------------------------------------- Waited  ---------- ------------
  SQL*Net message to client                19      0.00          0.00
  SQL*Net message from client              19      0.46          5.30
  direct path read                        309      0.00          0.00
  db file sequential read                 603      0.21         17.58
```

Let's closely examine each item in the tkprof output. Letters in parentheses refer to superscripts in the output.

- ❑ The SQL text is displayed (1).
- ❑ Next is a table containing the execution statistics. Working across the top of the table:
  - ❑ The number of times each category of call was issued (2).
  - ❑ The CPU time required in seconds (3).
  - ❑ The elapsed time required in seconds (4).
  - ❑ Number of disk reads required (5).
  - ❑ Number of buffers read in query (consistent) (6) or current (7) mode. Blocks read in query mode are usually for consistent read queries.

Blocks read in current mode are often for modifications to existing blocks. I don't believe the distinction is particularly important when tuning SQL, so I say add them together and call them "logical reads."

❑ The number of rows processed (8).

❑ Working down the table, we see that each measurement is broken down by the category of Oracle call. The three categories are

   ❑ Parse (a), in which the SQL statement is checked for syntax, valid objects, and security, and in which an execution plan is determined by the optimizer.

   ❑ Execute (b), in which a SQL statement is executed, or in the case of a query, prepared for first fetch. Some queries, such as those that use FOR UPDATE or perform a sort, will actually retrieve every row at this point.

   ❑ Fetch (c), in which rows are returned from a query.

We can tell a great deal about the efficiency of the SQL statement by deriving some ratios from this output. Some of the important ratios are

❑ Blocks read (f+g) to rows processed (h). This is a rough indication of the relative expense of the query. The more blocks that have to be accessed relative to the number of rows returned, the more "expensive" each row is. A similar ratio is blocks read (f+g) to executions (e).

❑ Parse count (d) over execute count (e). Ideally, the parse count should be close to one. If it is high in relation to execute count, the statement has been needlessly reparsed. We discuss this in detail within Chapter 4, "Logical and Physical Database Design."

❑ Rows fetched (i) to fetches (j). This indicates the level to which the array fetch facility has been exercised. (See Chapter 4 for a discussion of array processing.)

❑ Disk reads (k) to logical reads (f+g). This is a measurement of the "miss rate" within the data buffer cache.

EXECUTION PLANS IN `tkprof`

You might notice that in our example, the execution plan is displayed twice. The first execution plan, marked in our example as (n), is based on information stored in the trace file when the statement was closed. This execution plan is not constructed using the output of the EXPLAIN PLAN statement and represents the "real" plan that was used at execution time. The second plan—marked as (o) in our example—is generated if the EXPLAIN option has been specified and is constructed by `tkprof` using the EXPLAIN PLAN command.

If present, this "real" plan is potentially more accurate than that generated by EXPLAIN PLAN. This is because the execution plan might have been affected by session options such as OPTIMIZER_GOAL, PARALLEL DML ENABLED, or SORT_AREA_SIZE that were set in the session when the SQL was executed. The `tkprof` utility cannot take these settings into account when executing EXPLAIN PLAN. Second, if you wait too long before executing `tkprof`, table statistics might change sufficiently to alter the execution plan that EXPLAIN PLAN generates. Finally, the bind variable values that are provided at run time might influence the execution plan—`tkprof` cannot take this into account later when issuing an EXPLAIN PLAN.

Both types of execution plan show both the step (m) and also the number of rows processed by each step. This row count can indicate which step did the most work and hence might be most usefully tuned.

Also shown in `tkprof` are detailed statistics for each step, though in a rather unfriendly format. Each step in the plan might have information similar to the following appended (some of these are truncated in our example):

```
(cr=49754 pr=49749 time=296110 us cost=13766 size=10458 card=747)
```

The abbreviations in these annotations represent the following statistics:

cr   Number of consistent (logical) data block reads processed in this step
pr   Number of physical reads processed by the step
time   Amount of time in microseconds spent processing this step
cost   Optimizer cost of the step
size   Number of bytes processed by the step
card   Number of rows processed by the step

In 11g, the PLAN_STAT options of DBMS_SESSION.SESSION_TRACE _ENABLE or DBMS_MONITOR.SESSION_TRACE_ENABLE determine whether these statistics refer to the first execution or all executions of the SQL within the trace file.

The execution step row counts provided by SQL_TRACE/`tkprof` are an invaluable aid to SQL tuning. All other things being equal, the more rows processed, the more computer resources required. We furthermore have indications of CPU times and elapsed times for each step. You can get similar data from DBMS_XPLAN.DISPLAY_CURSOR() only if the server parameter STATISTICS _LEVEL is set to ALL.

SQL trace and `tkprof` are powerful utilities for examining SQL statement performance and should be tools of choice for tuning SQL statements.

WAIT STATISTICS AND `tkprof`

Oracle sessions often need to relinquish the CPU to wait for a resource, such as a lock, to become available or to wait for IO to complete. The time spent waiting for these resources can be recorded in the trace file and will be shown if you choose the WAITS=YES `tkprof` option.

In our `tkprof` example output, this wait information is marked as (p). Our SQL statement experienced approximately 5.3 seconds of network wait and 17.6 seconds of IO wait. Theoretically, CPU and wait time together should add up to the total elapsed time, but in practice on busy systems, time spent waiting for the CPU and other unaccounted time results in the data not quite adding up.

ALTERNATIVES TO `tkprof`

The SQL trace file contains a lot of information that is not directly exposed by `tkprof`. For instance, the trace file can include the values and execution times for bind variables and contains much more detail of each wait than is exposed in the `tkprof` report. Versions of `tkprof` prior to 10g would not generally expose wait information at all. Consequently, there have been many free and commercial tools developed to help you get more information out of your SQL trace file. In fact, I designed the Analyze Trace facility in Quest Software's Spotlight on Oracle (http://www.quest.com/spotlight-on-oracle/), which provides the ability to explore trace file information in a graphical environment and which exposes details of wait statistics and bind variables.

Other popular trace file utilities include free and commercial profilers from Hotsos (www.hotsos.com) and Oracle's own Trace Analyzer (TRCANLZR) utility (see Oracle support note 224270.1).

USING AUTOTRACE IN SQL*PLUS

The SQL*Plus AUTOTRACE option can generate execution plans and execution statistics for each SQL statement executed. The output is not as definitive or extensive as that provided by SQL Trace but provides a good high level view of SQL performance. When AUTOTRACE is in effect, an explain plan and/or execution statistics will be printed after every SQL statement execution.

The execution plan generated by AUTOTRACE is created by the DBMS_XPLAN utility outlined previously in this chapter. Execution statistics include a number of metrics collected from the V$SESSTAT table including logical and physical reads, sorts, and network statistics.

AUTOTRACE takes the following options:

```
SET AUTOT[RACE] {OFF | ON | TRACE[ONLY]} [EXP[LAIN]] [STAT[ISTICS]]
```

The AUTOTRACE options are as follows:

OFF	Turn off AUTOTRACE output.
ON	Turn on all AUTOTRACE output.
TRACEONLY	Suppress output from queries; display the AUTOTRACE output only.
EXPLAIN	Generate execution plan only.
STATISTICS	Generate execution statistics only.

The following example shows us invoking AUTOTRACE to report the execution plan and statistics but suppressing the query result set:

```
SQL> set AUTOTRACE TRACEONLY

SQL> SELECT * FROM hr.departments JOIN hr.employees
            USING (department_id);

106 rows selected.


Execution Plan
----------------------------------------------------------
Plan hash value: 1343509718
```

Id	Operation	Name	Rows	Bytes
0	SELECT STATEMENT		106	9328
1	MERGE JOIN		106	9328
2	TABLE ACCESS BY INDEX ROWID	DEPARTMENTS	27	540
3	INDEX FULL SCAN	DEPT_ID_PK	27	
* 4	SORT JOIN		107	7276
5	TABLE ACCESS FULL	EMPLOYEES	107	7276

```
Predicate Information (identified by operation id):
---------------------------------------------------

4 - access("DEPARTMENTS"."DEPARTMENT_ID"="EMPLOYEES"."DEPARTMENT_ID")
    filter("DEPARTMENTS"."DEPARTMENT_ID"="EMPLOYEES"."DEPARTMENT_ID")
```

```
Statistics
-----------------------------------------------------------
         0  recursive calls
         0  db block gets
        19  consistent gets
         0  physical reads
         0  redo size
      9001  bytes sent via SQL*Net to client
       493  bytes received via SQL*Net from client
         9  SQL*Net roundtrips to/from client
         1  sorts (memory)
         0  sorts (disk)
       106  rows processed
```

MONITORING THE ORACLE SERVER

In this section we discuss ways in which we can measure Oracle server performance. General server performance metrics help us diagnose contention, memory configuration, and IO performance issues that can affect the performance of all SQLs. Ideally, we concentrate on these issues only after we've done our best to reduce the application workload via SQL tuning. However, having insight into overall server performance is useful at every stage of the tuning process.

THE V$ TABLE INTERFACE

The Oracle kernel developers have always been generous when it comes to exposing internal performance counters. Oracle's approach to exposing performance information revolves around the so-called *V$ views*.[6] V$ views—and the X$ fixed tables upon which they are based—are representations of Oracle internal memory structures and include both information cached in the SGA and the contents of various counters that the Oracle server maintains for automatic and manual tuning.

Some of the more significant V$ views follow:

V$SYSTAT	A table containing a collection of general database performance statistics—approximately 500 in Oracle 11g.
V$SESSION	Contains one row per connected session.
V$SESSTAT	Contains the statistics from V$SYSSTAT for each session.

---

[6] V$ views show data for the current instance. In a RAC cluster GV$ views show data for the cluster as a whole. We use V$ views here because GV$ views can be slower and should be used only when you are explicitly considering performance of a RAC cluster.

V$PROCESS	Contains one row per server process: dedicated server, shared server, background process, and so on.
VSQL, VSQL_PLAN, V$_SQL_PLAN_ STATISTICS	Contains details of cached SQL; we looked at these tables in the previous "Exploiting Cashed SQL" section.

You can argue that Oracle has been too generous with performance information. There are hundreds of V$ tables typically containing millions of individual data items. How are we to make sense of all this data?

WAIT INTERFACE

One set of V$ tables have long stood out as the most useful in tuning practice: the *wait interface* tables.

As Oracle responds to application requests, it spends some of it's time executing Oracle code and thereby consuming CPU. But from time to time Oracle needs to wait for some activity to complete. Most notably, Oracle waits for IO requests to complete and also for internal resources such as locks and latches to become available. When this happens the Oracle process relinquishes the CPU and waits until the request completes or the resource becomes available. The wait interface records the number and duration of these wait times. We first saw the wait data when viewing SQL trace wait statistics previously in this chapter. Wait data is also available from the following V$ tables:

V$SYSTEM_EVENT	Records totals of waits since database startup
V$SESSION_EVENT	Records totals of waits for individual sessions
V$SESSION (or V$SESSION_WAIT)	Shows the current wait for a session (if any)

V$SYSTEM_EVENT gives us a summary of all the waits incurred by the server since startup. It includes the following key columns:

EVENT	Name or short description of the event.
TOTAL_WAITS	Total number of times the wait has occurred.
TIME_WAITED_MICRO	Time spent waiting on the event in microseconds.
TOTAL_WAITS_FG	Total number of times the wait has occurred in *foreground sessions*. Foreground sessions are user sessions that are created as users connect to the database—as opposed to *background sessions*, which are created when the database starts. This column was introduced in Oracle 11g.
TIME_WAITED_MICRO_FG	Time spent waiting on the event in microseconds by foreground sessions.
WAIT_CLASS	The *class* of the wait. *Wait classes* are high-level groupings of event types. In particular, the Idle wait class identifies those waits that occur when session are simply waiting for instructions or sleeping.

Because the waits in the idle wait class are not very useful—they reflect times when processes are awaiting their next SQL request for instance—we normally eliminate them. Therefore, the following query provides a good high-level summary of the waits experienced in a database:

```
SQL> SELECT   wait_class, event, total_waits AS waits,
  2             ROUND (time_waited_micro / 1000) AS total_ms,
  3             ROUND (time_waited_micro * 100 / SUM (time_waited_micro) OVER (),
  4                2
  5                ) AS pct_time,
  6             ROUND ((time_waited_micro / total_waits) / 1000, 2) AS avg_ms
  7        FROM v$system_event
  8       WHERE wait_class <> 'Idle'
  9    ORDER BY time_waited_micro DESC;
```

```
WAIT_CLASS   EVENT                             WAITS   TOTAL_MS PCT_TIME  AVG_MS
----------   ----------------------------  ----------  --------- --------  -------
User I/O     db file sequential read         5948228   40312397    40.40    6.78
System I/O   control file sequential read   86008433   39558569    39.65     .46
User I/O     db file scattered read           770023   11202005    11.23   14.55
User I/O     read by other session             87225    2128471     2.13    24.4
System I/O   control file parallel write     1194484    1239331     1.24    1.04
Network      SQL*Net message to client      96735881     927984      .93     .01
```

Many, but not all, event names that are contained in V$SYSTEM_EVENT are documented in the *Oracle Reference Manual*. Table 3-3 lists some of the more significant wait events.

Table 3-3   Some Commonly Encountered Wait Events

WAIT_CLASS	EVENT	DESCRIPTION
Application	enq: *enqueue name*	An enqueue is a wait for a lock. Each lock type has its own wait event. Lock contention is discussed in Chapter 15, "Lock Contention."
Application	SQL*Net message to client	The server process is sending a message to the client process.
Application	SQL*Net more data to client	The server process is sending data to the client process.
Commit	log file sync	The server is waiting for a redo log record to be written, probably following a commit. See chapter 14, "DML Tuning."
Concurrency	library cache pin	Pins occur when library cache objects (shared SQL and similar) are loaded or modified.

WAIT_CLASS	EVENT	DESCRIPTION
Concurrency	latch: *latch name*	A latch is similar to a lock, but on shared memory rather than on table data. Many latches have their own wait events. Latch contention is discussed in detail in Chapter 16, "Latch and Mutex Contention."
Concurrency	cursor: mutex	The server is waiting for a mutex (similar to a latch) adding or modifying a cached SQL in the shared pool. Mutexes are discussed in Chapter 16.
Concurrency	row cache lock	Waiting for a lock on the cached copies of the data dictionary tables. See Chapter 15.
Concurrency	buffer busy waits	A block in the buffer cache is being accessed by another session. See Chapter 17, "Shared Memory Contention," for more details.
Configuration	log file switch (*reason*)	Waiting for a log file to switch, perhaps because the log is not archived or checkpointed. See Chapter 21, "Disk IO Tuning Fundamentals," for more details.
Configuration	free buffer waits	All the blocks in the buffer cache are dirty. Probably indicates a DBWR bottleneck. See Chapter 17 for more details.
Configuration	write complete waits	Waiting for a block to be written to disk by the DBWR. See Chapter 17 for more details.
System I/O	log file single|parallel write	Waiting for a write to the log file to complete. This is usually a wait recorded by the LGWR process. See Chapter 21 for more details.
System I/O	control file sequential read|write	Waiting for a read from a control file. This usually happens when reading from certain V$ tables or when performing system operations.
User I/O	db file single write	Single block writes to the datafiles, possibly writing the file header. See Chapter 21 for more details.
User I/O	direct path write temp	Writes that were made directly to the temporary datafile, bypassing the buffer cache and not involving the DBWR. See Chapter 21 for more details.
User I/O	direct path read	Reads that bypass the buffer cache. See Chapter 21 for more details.
User I/O	direct path read temp	Reads from the temporary tablespace that bypass the buffer cache. See Chapter 19, "Optimizing PGA Memory," and Chapter 21 for more details.
User I/O	read by other session	Waiting for another session to read data into the buffer cache. Formally recorded as buffer busy waits. See Chapter 17 for more details.
User I/O	db file parallel read	An operation in which multiple blocks are read into the buffer cache in a single operation. See Chapter 21 for more details.
User I/O	db file scattered read	Reading from disk as part of a full table scan or other multiblock read. See Chapter 21 for more details.
User I/O	db file sequential read	Reading a single block from disk, often as a result of an indexed-read. See Chapter 21 for more details.

THE TIME MODEL

Wait interface data has been a mainstay of Oracle tuning going all the way back to Oracle7. However, the wait interface alone has never given a complete picture of Oracle performance. As noted earlier, waits occur only when the session gives up the CPU. To get a complete picture of activity, we need to have some insight into CPU timings. Furthermore, we'd like to get some insight into activities that span wait states and CPU utilization, such as time spent executing PL/SQL code.

The time model introduced in 10g offers a solution. The time model accurately records total elapsed time, CPU time, and time spent on various interesting activities that involve both CPU and wait times.

Time model data is shown for the database as a whole by V$SYS_TIME _MODEL and for individual sessions in V$SESS_TIME_MODEL. Here are some of the statistics recorded in these views:

DB Time	Elapsed time in microseconds spent executing database requests. These requests include all user SQL statements but not activities from background processes.
DB CPU	CPU time in microseconds spent executing database requests. These requests include all user SQL statements but not activities from background processes.
Background elapsed time	Elapsed time in microseconds consumed by background processes.
Background CPU time	CPU time consumed by background processes.
Sequence load elapsed time	Time spent loading sequence numbers into cache. This happens when the application uses up the numbers defined in the CACHE clause of CREATE SEQUENCE.
Parse time elapsed	Total time spent parsing SQL statements.
Hard parse elapsed time	Time spent parsing SQL statements when no match is found in the shared pool; a parse that *can* use the cached information in the shared pool is called a "soft" parse.
SQL execute elapsed time	Total time spent executing SQL statements.
Connection management call elapsed time	Time spent connecting or disconnecting from the database.
Failed parse elapsed time	Amount of time spent on failed parse requests.
Hard parse (sharing criteria) elapsed time	Time spent on hard parsing caused by an inability to share cursors.
Hard parse (bind mismatch) elapsed time	Time spent on hard parsing caused by a mismatch in bind variable data types.
PL/SQL execution elapsed time	Time spent executing PL/SQL.
PL/SQL compilation elapsed time	Time spent compiling PL/SQL.
Inbound PL/SQL rpc elapsed time	Time inbound PL/SQL remote procedure calls have spent executing.
Java execution elapsed time	Time spent executing Java code inside the database.

What makes the time model confusing is that categories are arbitrarily nested and somewhat incomplete. It's "nested" in that some categories incorporate times from other categories. It's incomplete in that wait times contribute to elapsed time but are not shown in the model.

So although the time model is valuable, don't expect it to add up! Below we see how statistics in the time model are nested, and where the data from the wait interface would logically appear.

```
1) background elapsed time
      2) background cpu time
      2) background wait time (from wait interface)
1) DB time
   2) DB CPU
   2) User wait time (from wait interface)
   2) connection management call elapsed time
   2) sequence load elapsed time
   2) sql execute elapsed time
   2) parse time elapsed
         3) hard parse elapsed time
               4) hard parse (sharing criteria) elapsed time
                     5) hard parse (bind mismatch) elapsed time
         3) failed parse elapsed time
               4) failed parse (out of memory) elapsed time
   2) PL/SQL execution elapsed time
   2) inbound PL/SQL rpc elapsed time
   2) PL/SQL compilation elapsed time
   2) Java execution elapsed time
```

INTEGRATING THE TIME MODEL AND WAIT INTERFACE

The most valuable way to use the time model is in conjunction with the wait interface. Joining the two allows us to get a breakdown of CPU and wait time, for instance as in the following query:

```
SQL> SELECT    event, total_waits,
  2            ROUND (time_waited_micro / 1000000) AS time_waited_secs,
  3            ROUND (time_waited_micro * 100 /
  4              SUM (time_waited_micro) OVER (),2) AS pct_time
  5      FROM (SELECT event, total_waits, time_waited_micro
  6              FROM v$system_event
  7             WHERE wait_class <> 'Idle'
  8             UNION
```

```
 9              SELECT stat_name, NULL, VALUE
10                FROM v$sys_time_model
11               WHERE stat_name IN ('DB CPU', 'background cpu time'))
12   ORDER BY 3 DESC
13   /
```

EVENT	TOTAL_WAITS	TIME_WAITED_SECS	PCT_TIME
DB CPU		40893	34.58
db file sequential read	4004509	29442	24.9
background cpu time		19125	16.17
control file sequential read	12898084	18208	15.4
row cache lock	2721680	2519	2.13
enq: WF - contention	8027	1526	1.29

You often need to obtain this sort of breakdown for a specific time period, rather than for the entire uptime of the server. There are plenty of tools that can help you do this, but if you don't have access to any of these, you can use the OPSG_PKG package available from this book's Web site. The package includes a view that when queried within a session reports the time spent in various categories since the last time the query was run from within the session. For instance, in the following example the query was run twice approximately 86 seconds apart. Here we see the output from the second execution, which reports waits and CPU times over the intervening 86 seconds:

```
SQL> SELECT sample_seconds, stat_name, waits_per_second waits_per_sec,
  2         ms_per_second ms_per_sec, pct_of_time pct
  3    FROM opsg_delta_report
  4*  WHERE ms_per_second>0
/
```

SAMPLE _SECONDS	STAT_NAME	WAITS_PER_SEC	MS_PER_SEC	PCT
86	CPU		126.1709	70.14
86	db file sequential read	5.3605	48.862	27.16
86	control file sequential read	4.3256	2.5285	1.41
86	log file sync	1.6163	1.2668	.70
86	SQL*Net message to client	45.9767	.3491	.19
86	control file parallel write	.3256	.2403	.13
86	CGS wait for IPC msg	9.7326	.1577	.09

You can obtain this package and other scripts from this book's Web site; see the preface for details.

ORACLE ENTERPRISE MANAGER

We've avoided relying upon features in Oracle Enterprise Manager (OEM) because many of these rely on add-on packs that require special licensing. However, if you have a Diagnostic pack license, Enterprise Manager offers many useful views. The Enterprise Manager "Average Active Sessions" chart (Figure 3-2) shows the average number of sessions that are in a particular state at a particular time. This is another way of describing the amount of time spent in each state per second by the database as a whole and so is equivalent to "seconds waited per second" in each state.

The breakdowns in the Enterprise Manager chart are based on the WAIT_CLASS column that appears in V$SYSTEM_EVENT; clicking on a particular wait class allows us to see a detail screen that breaks down the category (if appropriate). For instance, clicking on the Application label shows a break down of

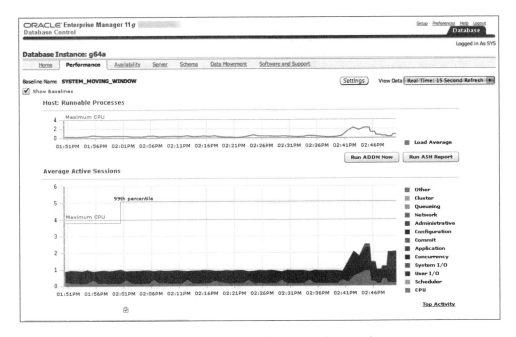

FIGURE 3-2   Enterprise Manager active sessions.

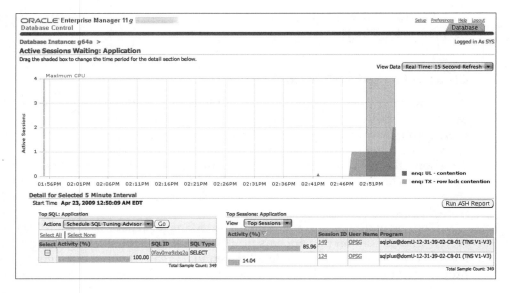

FIGURE 3-3   Enterprise Manager wait detail page.

Application class waits into individual wait categories, and shows sessions and SQLs most associated with the waits. In Figure 3-3 we see that the Application class waits were almost exclusively accounted for by the TX lock, which is a result of row level table lock waits.

We'll look at other Enterprise Manager screens as appropriate throughout the book. Note that the views above, and most Enterprise Manager Performance related pages, require a Diagnostic pack license.

SPOTLIGHT ON ORACLE

There are also a wide variety of third-party tools that provide enhanced access to and interpretation of Oracle performance data. I've personally been heavily involved in designing and developing Quest Software's Spotlight on Oracle product, which aims to provide an intuitive interface to all the facilities outlined in this chapter and provide alerts on performance bottlenecks and tuning opportunities. Figure 3-4 shows the Spotlight on Oracle main page; visit http://www.quest.com/spotlight-on-oracle/ for more details.

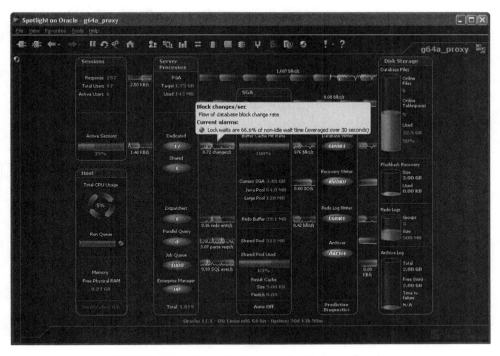

FIGURE 3-4   Quest Software's Spotlight on Oracle.

SUMMARY

In this chapter we've looked at some of the core tools useful in Oracle performance tuning. If you're lucky, you might have access to more advanced tools that
make your life easier and your tuning efforts more efficient. However, regardless
of your Oracle license or third-party tool status, all Oracle tuning practitioners
have the following tools at their disposal:

❏   The EXPLAIN PLAN command and the DBMS_XPLAN utility to format
    and examine SQL execution plans.
❏   The SQL trace and `tkprof` utilities, to trace session execution and to exam-
    ine SQL execution and wait statistics.
❏   The time model and wait interface V$ tables, which can be used to deter-
    mine exactly where the Oracle server spends its time and which can help to
    guide your tuning efforts effectively.

LOGICAL AND PHYSICAL DATABASE DESIGN

In traditional application development, the design of the data model occurs before almost any other design task. All subsequent application design activities build off the data model, and as a result the data model tends to constrain the ultimate performance of the application. Changing the data model in production is typically an expensive or nearly impossible undertaking, requiring coordinated changes to both schema and application code, and potentially expensive and time-consuming database rebuilds. Therefore, optimizing the data model is a critical, early task.

LOGICAL DATA MODELING

Application data models are commonly created in two phases. Establishing the logical data model involves modeling the information that will be stored and processed by the application and ensuring that all necessary data is correctly, completely, and unambiguously represented. For relational database implementations, this usually involves constructing a normalized entity-relationship (ER) model.

The logical data model is then mapped to a physical data model. For a relational database, the physical data model describes the tables, indexes, views, keys, and other characteristics of the database. In traditional methodologies, performance requirements are ignored during the logical modeling process and are first considered during the physical modeling process.

NORMALIZATION AND THIRD NORMAL FORM

A normalized data model is one in which any data redundancy has been elimi-nated and in which data and relationships are uniquely identifiable by primary and foreign keys. Although the normalized data model is rarely the final destina-tion from a performance point of view, the normalized data model is almost al-ways the best starting point. Indeed, failing to normalize your logical model is frequently a recipe for a poorly performing physical model.

Relational theory provides for various levels of normal form, some of which are of academic interest only. Third normal form is the most commonly adopted normalization level, and it has the following characteristics:

❏ All data in an entity (table) is dependent on the primary key.
❏ There should be no repeating groups of attributes (columns).
❏ No data in an entity is dependent on only part of the key.
❏ No data in an entity is dependent on any nonkey attribute.

These characteristics are often remembered through the adage "the key, the whole key, and nothing but the key."

DATA TYPE CHOICES

Logical modeling tools often allow attributes to adopt a wide variety of data types. Typically, you need to choose between the following:

❏ Fixed length and varying length character strings
❏ Integer and floating point numbers
❏ LONGs or LOBs versus character strings
❏ Varieties of date types

There can be some advantages from a documentation and definition per-spective to precisely defining the length, precision, or types of attribute in the logical model. However, over-precise specification can lead to problems later if not all the data matches your preconceptions. Furthermore, Oracle uses gener-ous and flexible internal implementations, and there is often no advantage from a performance or storage perspective from specifying restrictive data types or precisions.

In general, keep the following in mind when assigning attribute data defini-tions:

❏ Regardless of the constraints you place on numeric types, Oracle mostly uses large-magnitude, high precision floating point representations inter-nally.

- Fixed length character strings consume a fixed amount of storage regardless of the size of the data. This results in a more predictable row length that can reduce fragmentation but generally results in longer average row lengths that increase the overhead of full table scans. Varying length character strings (VARCHARs) are, therefore, often preferred unless the data is really invariant in length.
- In Oracle, VARCHARs can store 4000 bytes of information and are capable of storing data that would need to be in a LONG or LOB data type in other databases or in early editions of Oracle. (We might consider anything prior to Oracle 9i as early.)
- The Oracle LONG type has significant limitations and it is almost always preferable to use LOB types.

ARTIFICIAL KEYS

A *natural key* is one constructed from unique attributes that occur normally within the entity. An *artificial*, or *synthetic*, *key* is one that contains no meaningful column information and that exists only to uniquely identify the row. There is a continual debate within the database community regarding the merits of artificial primary keys versus the natural key.

Natural keys can consist of multiple columns and can be composed of any datatypes. In contrast, artificial keys are usually sequential numbers. For instance, the natural key for a CUSTOMER table might be a combination of the government allocated corporation number together with department or address (if we anticipate multiple customers within a single large corporation). An artificial key could be composed of a single numeric column populated by an Oracle sequence.

Without entering into the wider debate of the merits of natural keys from a data modeling and design perspective, it is worth considering the merits of artificial keys from a performance perspective. There is little doubt that artificial keys generally result in superior performance:

- An artificial key usually consists of a single numeric column. If a natural key consists of non-numeric or concatenated columns, the key length will be longer, and joins and index lookups will be less efficient.
- Because an artificial key contains no meaningful information, it should never need to be updated. If a natural primary key is updated, updates to any referencing foreign keys will be required, which can significantly increase IO overhead and lock contention.
- Artificial keys result in smaller indexes and can result in a shallower index tree. This helps optimize index lookups.

Clearly there will often be a requirement for the natural key columns to exist within the table and for these columns to be accessible via an index lookup.

To allow for this, you can simply create an index or unique constraint on these columns.

Where possible, use numeric artificial keys, populated by sequences, in preference to natural keys composed of concatenated or non-numeric columns.

DATA WAREHOUSE DESIGN

Just like any other type of database, a data warehouse design involves logical and physical data modeling phases. However, the requirements of a data warehouse and the known best practices for data warehouse implementation tend to favor certain well-known design patterns. The most common data warehouse models are based on the *star schema*, in which central large *fact* tables are associated with numerous *dimension* tables. When the dimension tables implement a more complex set of foreign key relationships, the schema is referred to as a *snowflake schema*.

These schemas sometimes arise naturally from a traditional ER modeling exercise but more often arise from a hybrid logical/physical modeling in which certain characteristics of data warehouses are assumed.

The choice of a star or snowflake logical design is often associated with certain physical design choices, such as partitioning, bitmap indexes, and materialized views.

Star schema design is discussed in depth later in this chapter.

LOGICAL TO PHYSICAL

Although you might be factoring performance requirements into your logical design decisions, the primary aim of the logical design phase is to create a design that meets the *functional* requirements of your application. By comparison, the physical design phase is primarily about ensuring that the database meets the *performance* requirements of the application.

The biggest mistake that occurs at this stage is to create a physical model that is an exact replica of the logical model. Performing a one-to-one mapping of a logical model to a physical model is usually simple to achieve; perhaps requiring only a single click in your data modeling tool. However, such a translation rarely results in a physical design that supports a high performance application. Invest time in the physical modeling process; the dividend will be a physical model that can support your performance requirements.

Don't create a physical model that is a one-to-one representation of the logical model. Take the time to build a physical model that enables your application to reach its full performance potential. Remember that time spent during physical modeling is likely to be repaid many times during production tuning.

MAPPING ENTITIES OR CLASSES TO TABLES

An entity in a logical model often translates to a table in the physical model. This transformation is usually straightforward except when the entity contains subtypes.

Subtypes categorize or partition a logical entity and help to classify the types of information that is within the entity. A subtype usually has a set of attributes that are held in common with the parent entity (the super-type) and other attributes that are not shared with the super-type or other subtypes. Figure 4-1 shows how a PEOPLE entity could be split into subtypes of CUSTOMERS and EMPLOYEES.

When translating entity subtypes into tables, we have the following options:

❑ Create tables for the super-type and for each subtype. The super-type table contains only columns that are common to both subtypes.
❑ Create a table for the super-type only. Attributes from all subtypes become columns in this super-table. Typically, columns from subtype attributes will be nullable, and a category column indicates the subtype in which a row belongs.
❑ Create separate tables for each subtype without creating a table for the super-type. Attributes from the super-type are duplicated in each table.

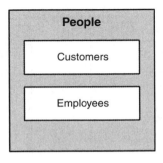

FIGURE 4-1   Representation of subtypes in an entity-relationship diagram.

Figure 4-2 illustrates three options for translating the entities in Figure 4-1 from a logical to physical model.

The three solutions result in very different performance outcomes. In particular, creating tables for the super-type *and* each subtype is likely to reduce performance in most circumstances, except where only the super-type is subject to a full table scan. Table 4-1 compares the performance of each of the three solutions for common database operations.

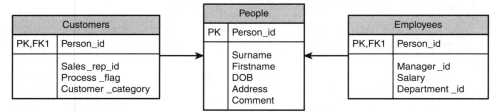

Option1: Implement subtypes as a master table with detail tables for each subtype.

People	
PK	Person_id
	Surname
	Firstname
	DOB
	Address
	Comment
	Person _Type
	Sales_rep_id
	Process_flag
	Customer_category
	Manager_id
	Salary
	Department_id

Option 2: Implement subtypes in a single table.

Customers	
PK	Customer_id
	Surname
	Firstname
	DOB
	Address
	Comment
	Sales_rep_id
	Process _flag
	Customer _category

Employees	
PK	Employee_id
	Surname
	Firstname
	DOB
	Address
	Comment
	Manager _id
	Salary
	Department _id

Option 3: Implement subtypes as two tables.

FIGURE 4-2 Options for physically modeling logical subtypes.

Table 4-1 Performance of Various Subtype/Supertype Implementations

OPERATION	SINGLE TABLE	SEPARATE SUBTYPE AND SUPER-TYPE TABLES	SEPARATE SUBTYPE TABLES ONLY; NO SUPER-TYPE TABLE
Inserting a new row	Single insert only. Uniqueness can be enforced by efficient primary key constraint.	Two inserts will be required. Uniqueness can be enforced by efficient primary key constraint.	Single insert only. Uniqueness must be enforced, if required, by using expensive cross-table trigger or application logic.
Updating a row	Single update only.	Usually a single update. If you need to update super-type and subtype columns, two updates will be required.	Single update only.
Fetching a single row via an index	Single table access.	If you need rows from both subtype and super-type, a join will be required.	Single table access.
Full table scan super-type columns only	Slowest, because row length might be increased by columns from both subtypes.	Fastest, because super-table row length will be short.	Okay. Row length will be greater than for a super-type/subtype split but shorter than for the single table solution.
Full table scan subtype and super-type columns	Good performance—a single table scan only.	Poor, because a join to one or more subtype tables will be required.	Best. No joins are required and no irrelevant columns need be scanned.

> When implementing tables derived from subtypes, avoid implementing both super-type and subtype tables. It is usually preferable to implement a single table for all subtypes or multiple sub-tables without a super-type table.

CHOOSING A TABLE TYPE

We saw in Chapter 2, "Oracle Architecture and Concepts," that Oracle supports a wide range of table types, such as heap, Index-only, clustered, and so on. The default heap table is the most flexible table type, and generally you want to have specific reasons for choosing a more exotic type.

Because clusters and object table types are often used as an alternative to a specific indexing scheme, or to optimize specific access paths such as joins, we discuss the benefits of clusters and various other table types in Chapter 5, "Indexing and Clustering."

But because these options need to be at least considered during the physical design stage, here's a brief summary of why you might look at these nondefault table types:

❏ Hash clusters can be effective in optimizing primary key lookups for tables that are of relatively static size. Hash clusters can also reduce hot block latch contention that can occur with B*-Tree indexes.

❏ Index clusters can be used to optimize joins because rows from multiple tables that share the cluster key value will be stored together. Enhanced join performance comes at the cost of degraded performance when scanning individual tables in the cluster.

❏ Nested tables can optimize the retrieval of detail rows for a specific master row. However, performance when retrieving details across master rows generally suffers.

❏ Index organized tables can be effective when most accesses are through the primary key and the table is too volatile for a hash cluster.

❏ Object tables have rows that are defined as an Oracle object type. Situations in which object tables are required are fairly rare.

If you think any of these considerations might apply, refer to Chapter 5 in which we consider the trade-offs between these options and more traditional indexing schemes for the default heap table type.

DATA TYPES AND PRECISIONS

Numeric and date data types generally pose few complications when converting from the logical to the physical model. As we discussed previously, Oracle usually stores numbers in a flexible large magnitude, flexible precision data type. So although you might choose to supply a NUMBER with a precision, this serves more as a constraint or as documentation than as a performance optimization.

However, one circumstance in which setting a precision might help performance is when there is a possibility of high precision values being accidentally assigned to numbers that do not require such precision.

For example, currency values will often be rounded up to 2 decimal places (dollars and cents) as a matter of course. However, a numeric operation on such a number might result in a high precision number, such as an "irrational" fraction, in which the decimal values repeat endlessly. For example, say we decide to calculate a credit equal to 1/6th of a sales amount for each sale. Many values will not divide evenly. So for instance while $99.99/6 returns $16.665, $100/6 returns $16.66666666666666666666666666666666667. If the column that receives this unnecessary precision has no precision defined (that is, is simply defined as NUMBER), Oracle must allocate storage for all the significant digits after the initial .66. The additional storage results in larger row lengths and some degradation in scan performance. However, if the column has a precision, defined as

NUMBER(*,2) for example, the unnecessary precision will be truncated and row length will be reduced accordingly.

> Setting a precision for numeric columns can sometimes reduce row length when numeric operations result in an unnecessarily high fractional precision.

Oracle does support BINARY_FLOAT and BINARY_DOUBLE data types that map to 32-bit and 64-bit floating point native data types. Using these data types might lead to some computational or storage efficiencies not provided by the NUMBER data type, but for most applications these would not be measurable.

Oracle supports a basic date type that implements a second of precision, and you can use the TIMESTAMP data type if you want subsecond precision: a TIMESTAMP column can be configured up to nanosecond precision and has a default microsecond precision. The INTERVAL data type is available to store time periods.

The choice of string storage requires the most thought. In general:

❑ For a string that will be less than 4000 bytes in length, VARCHAR2 is preferred.

❑ When strings are greater than 4000 bytes, one of the various LOB types is recommended: CLOB for character-based data and BLOB for binary data.

❑ Oracle 11g offers a new, high-performance LOB storage option known as SecureFiles. This is the preferred option for new LOB storage but is not yet the default.

❑ The LONG datatype has significant disadvantages compared to LOB types and exists primary for compatibility with earlier versions of Oracle. There can be only one LONG column per table.

❑ The VARCHAR2 datatype should be used in preference to VARCHAR. VARCHAR is subject to changes to conform to ANSI specifications.

OPTIONAL ATTRIBUTES AND NULL VALUES

Standard modeling guidelines suggest that optional attributes should become NULL columns. However, some key performance factors can influence the decision to allow NULL values:

❑ NULL values are not included in B*-Tree indexes, so it will usually require a full table scan to find NULL values. There are some exceptions to this, including bitmap indexes and partially null values in multicolumn concatenated indexes. See Chapter 5 for more information.

❏ The use of NULL values can reduce average row lengths, thus improving full table scan performance.

❏ If most column values are NULL and queries seek only values that are not NULL, an index on the column will be compact and efficient.

Therefore, when determining the nullability of a column, consider whether it will ever be required to search for a row—using a B*-Tree index—in which the column is NULL. If the answer is yes, don't make the column NULL. Instead, define the column as NOT NULL and apply a default value.

> Don't define a column as NULL if you expect to be searching for those unknown values. Instead, define the column as NOT NULL with a default.

In the case of character data, this default value will usually be a string such as UNKNOWN or N/A. In the case of numeric data, it can be more difficult to determine an appropriate default value. For example, consider a statistical database that contains the column AGE. Index-based scans on age are common, as are queries to find rows where the age is unknown. If we create a default value for such a column, we distort attempts to retrieve average, maximum, or minimum age from the database. In cases such as this, it might be necessary to use NULLs and either accept the consequent difficulty in quickly identifying unknown ages, or use denormalization to create an indexed indicator column (AGE_KNOWN=N) that flags rows where the age is unknown.

Remember that null values *are* included in bitmap indexes. You may or may not choose to use a bitmap index for this reason alone, but if you do have a bitmap index on a column, you can efficiently find null values. See Chapter 5 for more guidance on choosing index types.

COLUMN ORDER

The order of columns in a table can have a minor impact on performance. Unless every column in a table is a fixed-length character string—very unusual—Oracle has no way of knowing exactly where a specific column will be in the row structure. Columns later in the column list require a slightly greater amount of CPU to retrieve than earlier columns, because Oracle must "walk" through the row structure looking for a particular column. For this reason, there can be a slight positive effect on performance if more frequently accessed columns are stored earlier in the column list.

Columns whose value is NULL require a single byte of storage normally, but if all the trailing columns in a row are NULL, Oracle doesn't even need to store these single bytes. If columns that tend to be NULL are stored later in the column list, the row length might be reduced leading to shorter row length and, therefore, better table scan performance.

These column order optimizations are really fairly minor, however, and should there be a logical column order that enables the model to be more readily understood and maintained, you would not normally want to sacrifice that logical order to achieve these slight optimizations.

EXPLOITING ORACLE OBJECT TYPES

We saw an overview of Oracle object types in Chapter 2. These types, such as VARRAYs and object tables, offer an alternative to traditional physical data modeling techniques. For instance, rather than implement a master-detail table configuration with two tables joined by a foreign key, you can implement the detail table using a nested table or possibly even as a set of VARRAY columns. Is this a good idea?

For certain well-defined access patterns, the Oracle object types can offer definite advantages. However, these advantages are rarely decisive. Employing an Oracle object type carries with it the following disadvantages:

❏ The resulting physical model is heavily Oracle-specific. Admittedly, it's rare for applications to swap-out database vendors. However, the Oracle object types are so unusual that they often prevent standard Business Intelligence and data query tools from functioning effectively.

❏ There's a far smaller body of knowledge relating to Oracle object type optimization; you might find yourself attempting to optimize in circumstances in which even the most experienced performance experts would plead ignorance.

❏ Most of the object types involve serious trade-offs; the traditional physical model approaches are generally optimal across a wider range of application designs and types.

❏ The use of Oracle objects can sometimes make the overall data model harder to understand and, therefore, harder to maintain.

DENORMALIZATION

Normalization is the process of eliminating redundancy and repeating groups from the data model and ensuring that key attributes are correctly defined. A normalized data model is the usual output from the logical modeling stage.

Denormalization is the process of reintroducing redundant, repeating, or otherwise non-normalized structures into the physical model—almost always with the intention of improving performance.

Normalized data models tend to be inherently reasonably efficient, and they are certainly easier to maintain. Denormalization—although sometimes desirable—entails certain risks:

❑ Denormalizing might improve the performance of certain key transactions or queries, but might inadvertently make other operations awkward, inefficient, or impossible. For instance, repeating groups often seem to be a useful denormalization because they avoid a join to a detail table. However, producing statistical information, such as averages, from repeating groups might be difficult.

❑ Denormalization almost always leads to higher insert and update overhead. Whenever a row is created or updated, the denormalized data needs to be maintained.

❑ Because denormalization introduces redundant information, it can also allow for inconsistent information. This can occur if the application code that is maintaining the denormalized data contains bugs or if the use of an ad-hoc tool avoids the denormalization routines. These inconsistencies might be difficult to detect and correct. The cost of the inconsistencies might be huge (for instance, if a denormalized aggregate invoice total was inaccurate).

❑ There will be a software development and maintenance cost associated with maintaining the denormalized data. Database triggers and materialized views reduce this cost because the code to maintain any replicated or redundant data can be stored within the database and need not be embedded in the application code. Database triggers also help to avoid inconsistencies arising if data is manipulated from outside of the application (from SQL*PLUS, for instance).

Denormalization is not, therefore, something that should be undertaken lightly. Make sure you have fully determined the costs and benefits of each proposed denormalization. Ideally, you should test the performance gains (and costs!) of each denormalization prior to final implementation.

Do not undertake denormalization lightly; any denormalization involves performance and maintainability trade-offs and increases the risk of data inconsistencies.

REPLICATING COLUMN VALUES TO AVOID JOINS

One common denormalization is the replication of a column from a related table to avoid a join. This is a common form of denormalization and can be effective because joins can multiply the cost of a query considerably. We discuss this in more detail when looking at join performance in Chapter 10, "Joins and Sub-queries."

Consider replicating columns to avoid joins in critical queries. This can be effective when the denormalized data is stored on static lookup tables.

SUMMARY TABLES

Queries that generate totals or aggregations can be expensive and are often too resource-intensive to be run in prime time. One solution is to maintain a *summary table* that allows ready access to this information.

Such a summary table can be maintained in the following ways:

❑ If real-time summary data is required, the summary data can be updated whenever the source data is changed. This can be done manually by using a database trigger or by using materialized views (more on this later). Although this approach allows real-time totals to be accessed without the overhead of aggregation, it has a negative impact on transaction processing. There is also a danger that the heavy update activity on the summary table might lead to unacceptable lock contention.

❑ If real-time summary information is not essential, the summary table can be populated by regularly scheduled jobs—possibly during off-peak processing periods. Oracle's materialized view mechanism provides a convenient means of implementing such an approach. The approach has the advantage of eliminating any overhead during peak transaction processing periods but can result in less accurate summary information.

In some cases, the Oracle 11g result set cache might eliminate the need to create summary tables. A cached result set can act like a dynamically created, in-memory summary table. See Chapter 20, "Other Memory Management Topics," for more details on the 11g result set cache.

Queries that perform aggregate operations can be resource-intensive. Consider maintaining denormalized aggregate information, possibly by using materialized views.

VERTICAL PARTITIONING

We discussed in an earlier section the issues involving the translation of logical subtypes into physical tables. In general, we found that implementation of subtypes as detail tables generally diminished the performance of commonplace SQL operations.

However, if a large table is to be subjected to frequent table scans, but only a small subset of columns are included in these scans, it can be worthwhile splitting the table in two, especially if the infrequently accessed columns are long. Columns that are frequently included in full table scan operations would be kept in the main table and infrequently accessed columns kept in the secondary table. This is sometimes referred to as *vertical partitioning*.

Although a view can be used to maintain the illusion of a single table, this solution usually requires that the application query against subtables to get best performance, which complicates application SQL. However, Oracle will sometimes allow you to split a table into multiple segments while still retaining a single logical table. For instance:

❑ LOB data will usually be stored in a separate segment (see the "Lob Storage" section later in this chapter).

❑ In an index-organized table, some rows can be stored in an overflow segment. See Chapter 5 for more details.

If a large table is expected to be subject to frequent table scans, consider moving long, infrequently accessed columns to a separate subtable to reduce row length and improve table scan performance.

IMPLEMENTING DENORMALIZATION

Denormalization is sometimes implemented within application code, requiring that the application issue DML to maintain redundant columns or aggregates.

Database triggers provide an easier, safer and often more efficient means of maintaining denormalized information. A database trigger fires regardless of the tool used to update the source data, so the risk of inconsistent data is reduced. By using triggers, application logic can be kept simpler and independent of changes to the database schema. See Chapter 12, "Using and Tuning PL/SQL," for an example of such a trigger.

Use database triggers to maintain denormalized data in preference to application code. Database triggers reduce the risk of inconsistent denormalized data, simplify application code, and often perform more efficiently.

STAR SCHEMA DESIGN

Data warehouse design is a big topic and not something we can cover in great depth within this chapter. For a more comprehensive coverage, I suggest *Oracle DBA Guide to Data Warehousing and Star Schemas* by Bert Scalzo (Prentice Hall, 2003). I provide a brief coverage of best practice and common issues here.

STAR SCHEMA BASICS

A star schema is an extremely common design pattern in data warehouses in which a large *fact* table contains detailed business data and includes foreign keys to smaller more static *dimension* tables that categorize the fact items in business terms: things such as time, product, customer, and so on.

Star schemas are a performance and storage efficient way of representing large data sets for Business Intelligence and analytics. Oracle and other commercial databases include significant optimizations to ensure that star schema processing is as efficient as possible.

Figure 4-3 shows an example of a star schema. This diagram is a simplification of the star schema distributed in the Oracle SH sample schema. The central SALES fact table contains sales totals that are aggregated across various time periods, products, customers, and promotions. The detail and explanation of each aggregation can be found by joining to the dimension tables TIMES, PRODUCTS, CUSTOMERS, and PROMOTIONS.

Foreign keys in the fact table are almost always artificial numeric keys populated by sequences. Meaningful foreign keys in the fact table are expensive from a storage point of view: For example, a product *name* probably requires ten times the storage of a product *ID*. Keeping the row length down in the fact table is important because the fact table is often subjected to full table (or partition) scans.

SNOWFLAKES SCHEMAS

Snowflake schemas, in which dimension tables contain foreign keys to other higher-level dimensions or other data, are a common enough occurrence and can be justified by the requirements of the data warehouse. However, snowflakes can also arise from an understandable but unnecessary instinct to normalize the dimensions.

Figure 4-4 shows a simplified snowflake star schema. The PRODUCT_DIM table contains a foreign key to a PRODUCT_CATEGORY table.

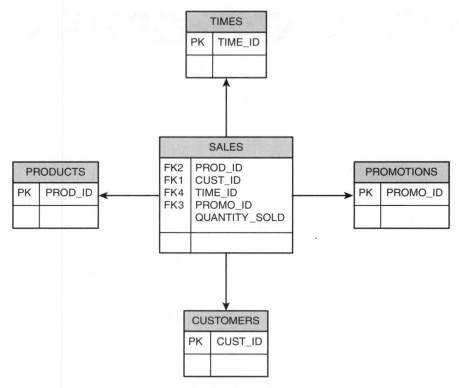

FIGURE 4-3   Star schema.

An alternative to the snowflake design is to denormalize dimensions into a single table. Figure 4-5 shows the denormalized version of the schema; the PRODUCT_DIM dimension is now clearly not the third normal form because PRODUCT_CAT_NAME depends on PRODUCT_CAT_ID that is not part of the primary key. However, queries that aggregate on product category will now be simpler to construct and most likely more efficient.

Snowflakes complicate query construction and can result in reduced query efficiency. In extreme cases, the snowflake joins can prevent the Oracle optimizer from recognizing the schema as being a star schema at all, and result in inappropriate optimization strategies. On the other hand, loading data into a snowflake schema might be more efficient, and there might be a slight reduction in storage requirements.

> Avoid snowflake schemas where possible; query performance is usually optimized when dimensions do not contain foreign keys.

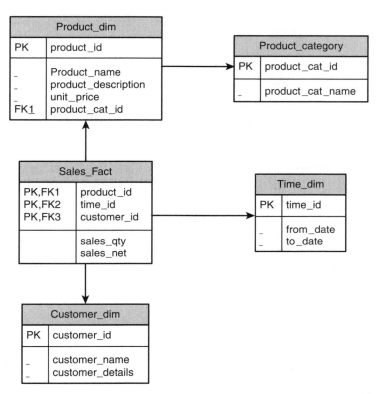

FIGURE 4-4 A snowflake schema: The PRODUCT dimension contains a foreign key to PRODUCT_CATEGORY.

DIMENSION HIERARCHIES

Business analytics often involve queries that aggregate data at various hierarchical levels. For instance, we might seek total sales for the year, for the quarter, or for the month. Depending on business requirements, it might be desirable to precompute these various levels of aggregation and store them in the fact table rather than reaggregating at query time. For instance, we might want to store sales totals for the year, rather than computing sales totals by adding up individual daily sales every time a yearly total is requested.

In a star schema, these hierarchies can be represented within a dimension, and Oracle provides explicit DDL to support this; the CREATE DIMENSION command. Dimension hierarchies are one of the most complex topics in Oracle schema design, and we provide only a broad overview here. You should refer to the Oracle *Database Warehousing Guide* for a more detailed description.

The key concept is that dimension tables can store data at multiple levels of detail. For instance, consider the TIMES dimension in Figure 4-6.

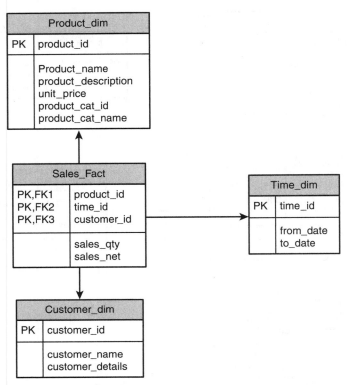

FIGURE 4-5   Removing the snowflake by denormalizing a dimension.

Table 4-2 illustrates the TIMES dimension data for the first few periods within the 2009 year. Depending on the hierarchy level, certain columns will not be included. For instance, for the MONTH level, the day and week identifiers will be NULL; for the YEAR level, all columns but YEAR are null.

The CREATE DIMENSION command provides a means to define the relationships between hierarchical columns. For instance, CREATE DIMENSION can

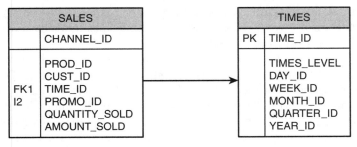

FIGURE 4-6   TIMES dimension with a hierarchy.

Table 4-2 Data in the TIMES Dimension Showing Hierarchy

TIME_ID	TIMES_LEVEL	DAY_ID	WEEK_ID	MONTH_ID	QUARTER_ID	YEAR_ID
1	DAY	1	1	1	1	2009
2	WEEK		1	1	1	2009
3	MONTH			1	1	2009
4	QUARTER				1	2009
5	YEAR					2009
6	DAY	2	1	1	1	2009

be used to tell the database that days belong to weeks, weeks belong to months, months belong to quarters, and so on.

Inside the fact table, data will be stored at multiple levels of aggregation. For instance, the fact table might contain product sales totals aggregated at the year, quarter, month, week, and day. Alternatively, we can create multiple fact tables, each of which contains different levels of aggregations.

AGGREGATIONS AND MATERIALIZED VIEWS

Creating hierarchical dimensions speeds up queries that request data at the higher aggregation levels. For instance, monthly totals will be significantly quicker because it will not be necessary to aggregate individual rows for a particular month. However, this requires that redundant summary information be added to the fact tables that can increase the time for queries that scan across dimensions or which are targeted to the lowest dimensions. Consequently, you can consider multiple fact tables at various levels of aggregation, as shown in Figure 4-7.

Multiple fact tables are a generic data warehousing solution, but Oracle provides a more sophisticated solution with *materialized views*. A materialized view is essentially a physical table that contains the rows that would be returned by the view definition. If you think of normal views as stored *queries*, materialized views are stored *results*.

Materialized views can be automatically maintained by Oracle so that they will always be up to date, or they can be updated periodically. If dimensions have been created, Oracle can perform a transparent *query rewrite* to direct queries made against the fact table to the materialized view. The optimizer will do this if it determines that the rewrite would be more efficient and that the materialized view data is sufficiently current.

An optional *materialized view log* captures updates, deletes, and inserts against the source tables. When the materialized view is rebuilt, this log can be used to apply the changes without having to rescan all the rows in the source tables.

For most data warehouses, materialized views offer a superior solution to manually created aggregate tables. The key advantages are

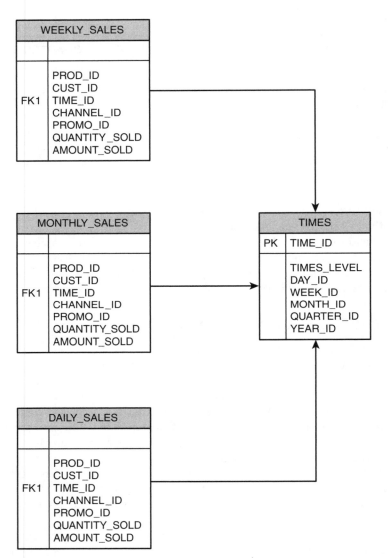

FIGURE 4-7   Implementing multiple fact tables to provide multiple aggregations.

❑ Query rewrite can direct queries to the appropriate materialized view without the end user needing to even be aware of the existence of the materialized views.

❑ Materialized views can be more efficiently rebuilt using materialized view
logs.

The advantages of materialized views are compelling and—unless independence from Oracle is desired—the use of materialized views in preference to manually maintained aggregate tables is recommended.

MATERIALIZED VIEW BEST PRACTICES

As with other data warehousing topics, we can provide only a brief summary here. These are general guidelines to create materialized views:

❏ Create a materialized view log on each of the tables contributing to the materialized view.

❏ Use CREATE DIMENSION statements to identify the hierarchies within your dimensions.

❏ Enable query rewrite by setting QUERY_REWRITE_ENABLED.

❏ Choose an appropriate refresh policy for your materialized view. ON COMMIT refreshes are extremely dangerous unless changes to the underlying fact table are rare (in which case, they are probably both less dangerous and less useful). It's often preferable to choose ON DEMAND refresh and then refresh the materialized view after bulk updates.

❏ Select a QUERY_REWRITE_INTEGRITY setting. This decision determines if query rewrite can be used only when the materialized view is guaranteed to be in sync with the underlying tables. The settings of ENFORCED, TRUSTED, and STALE_TOLERATED control whether data must be in sync, is assumed to be in sync, or can knowingly be out of sync for a query rewrite to be enabled.

❏ Create the appropriate materialized views. Remember that each materialized view adds to database overhead, so make sure each pays off in terms of improved performance for the intended queries. Most data warehousing experts advise that improvements of 10–50 times in query performance should be anticipated. If in doubt, measure the performance of both DML and queries with and without the materialized view to determine if the materialized view overhead offers sufficient performance improvements.

PHYSICAL STORAGE OPTIONS

Oracle provides a diverse range of physical storage options for tables and other segments. Many of these options can have significant performance implications.

MANUAL AND AUTOMATIC SEGMENT STORAGE MANAGEMENT

By default, Oracle 10g and 11g tablespaces use Automatic Segment Storage Management (ASSM) in which the management of many physical storage options are transparently optimized. For a new 10g or 11g database, it's actually quite difficult to avoid using ASSM because if the SYSTEM tablespace is using ASSM, so must all other tablespaces. However, databases that have been upgraded from previous versions might still use the older Manual Segment Storage Management (MSSM). See Chapter 2 for a further discussion of ASSM and MSSM.

CONCURRENT INSERTS AND FREELISTS

When Oracle inserts new rows into a table, it consults a *freelist* that identifies data blocks that contain free space and that are eligible for insert.

Tables that are subjected to concurrent insert activity might need multiple freelists to avoid a specific type of buffer-busy contention. This is handled automatically in ASSM and can easily be adjusted after table creation in MSSM. If using MSSM, you should ensure that the number of freelists matches the expected number of concurrent insert processes. We see an example of MSSM freelist contention in Chapter 17, "Shared Memory Contention."

Using Automatic Segment Storage Management (ASSM) generally avoids a number of potential problems that occur in manual storage management: in particular the issue of freelist management.

PCTFREE AND PCTUSED

PCTFREE and PCTUSED control the circumstances under which new rows can be inserted into a data block and have a direct impact on the number of rows per block, which, in turn, determines how much storage a table consumes.

PCTFREE controls the amount of space reserved in the block for updates that increase the row length. When there is only PCTFREE percent free space in the block, no more rows will be inserted. PCTFREE is relevant both for ASSM and MSSM.

PCTUSED determines the point where a block that has reached PCTFREE becomes re-eligible for inserts when DELETEs reduce the number of rows in the block. When the block is only PCTUSED percent full, new rows can again be inserted into the block. PCTUSED is applicable only to MSSM.

If PCTFREE is set too low and the table is subject to heavy update activity, row migration can occur. This happens when an update causes a row to increase in length. If this increase cannot be accommodated by free space within the block, the row will be relocated to a new block, and a pointer to the new block inserted into the original block. Index entries still contain the address of the original row. This means that an index lookup of the row incurs an additional IO as Oracle accesses the original row, only to find that it must jump to the new row location. Excessive row migration is generally a result of setting PCTFREE too low.

Every time Oracle needs to continue a fetch to a migrated row from the initial row location, the statistic *table fetch continued row* in V$SYSSTAT will be incremented.

If you set PCTFREE too high, space will be wasted in each block, leading to degradation when performing full table scans. In particular, if a table is subject to inserts and deletes but never updates, or if the updates never increase the row length, you can set PCTFREE to near 0.

If a table is subject to frequent table scans, ensure that PCTFREE is no higher than necessary, especially if row-lengthening updates are rare. If the table is subject to frequent row-lengthening updates, make sure PCTFREE is high enough to avoid row migration.

If you set PCTFREE very low, consider increasing the value of the INITRANS setting in the CREATE TABLE statement. This parameter controls the initial number of transaction slots within an Oracle data block. These "slots" comprise the *Interested Transaction List (ITL)*. When a block is created, it will have only two or three ITL entries. When additional transaction slots are required, they are allocated from free space within the block.

If PCTFREE is 0, then it's possible that the block will become completely full before additional transaction slots are allocated. If this occurs, multiple sessions will be unable to update the block concurrently and row level locking will degrade to block level locking. We see this phenomenon in Chapter 15, "Lock Contention."

When setting PCTFREE low for a table with concurrent transactional activity, consider increasing INITRANS to match the expected level of concurrent transactions on each block.

COMPRESSION

We usually think of compression as a trade-off between performance and storage: Compression reduces the amount of storage required, but the overhead of compressing and decompressing makes things slower. However, although there is always some CPU overhead involved in compression, the effect on IO can be favorable because if a table is reduced in size, it requires less IO operations to read it. Therefore, if a table is likely to be subject to frequent full table scans, performance might actually be improved if the table is compressed.

Prior to Oracle 11g, table compression could only be achieved when the table was created, rebuilt, or using direct load operations. However, in 11g, the Advanced Compression option enables data to be compressed when manipulated by normal DML.

Compression provides the best results when the table contains character strings that are highly compressible and which are subject to full table scans. Tables that are mainly accessed by index lookup, or which consist of mostly numeric data, get little or no benefit from compression. Furthermore, table scans that find most of the required blocks in memory get only marginal benefit compared with those that involve significant IO.

Figure 4-8 shows the elapsed time when scanning an uncompressed table, and one that is compressed. The table in question contained a mix of numeric and character data. When none of the data is present in the buffer cache, the performance advantage from compression, due to reduced IO, is remarkable. When all the data is present in the buffer cache, the performance advantage is marginal.

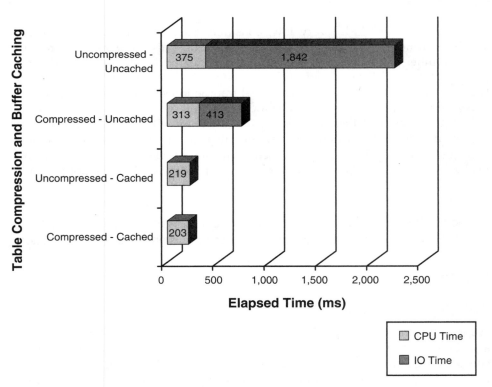

FIGURE 4-8   Effect of compression on table scan performance.

> Consider using table compression if a table is expected to generate significant IO from table scans and contains compressible (typically character) data.

Oracle 11g Release 2 introduces columnar compression that can achieve higher compression rates, and higher overhead in some cases. We look at columnar compression in more detail in Chapter 9, "Tuning Table Access."

LOB STORAGE

Deciding that a column should be defined as a LOB is not in itself a particularly difficult decision; if the column stores text less than 4000 bytes, it probably should be a VARCHAR2. If it is longer than 4000 bytes or stores true binary data, it probably should be a LOB. If it's a LOB and you want the data to be stored outside of the database (in the original files, for example), it's a BFILE. If it contains only text, it's a CLOB, if binary data, it's a BLOB.

Actually that's just where the fun starts! Here are some of the LOB storage issues:

❑ LOBs are not generally stored in the same blocks as the rest of the data in the row. By default, only LOBs less than 4000 bytes will be stored with the row (or *inline*). You can use the ENABLE | DISABLE STORAGE IN ROW clause to ensure that even small LOBs will be stored outside of the table. This can be a good idea if you only occasionally need to access the LOB because it reduces the row length and, therefore, keeps the main part of the table smaller (and quicker to scan). On the other hand, if you almost always retrieve the LOB when you read the row, it's better to keep it inline because out-of-line LOBs require extra IOs to retrieve. (Only inline LOBs will be cached by default in the Oracle buffer cache.)

❑ LOBs are stored in chunks, which is the smallest allocation possible when a LOB is stored outside the row. You can manipulate the size of the chunk with the CHUNK clause. If the chunk size is too small, there will be a large number of chunks that slow down retrieval of the LOB. If the chunk size is too high, you'll waste space when a LOB is smaller than the chunk size, and this might slow performance as well. The chunk size must be a multiple of the tablespace block size.

❑ You can store your LOBs in a separate tablespace from your table data. This tablespace can have a different block size and can be placed on dedicated disk devices designed to maximize LOB IO.

❑ You can explicitly decide whether to cache LOB data in the buffer cache: CACHE, NOCACHE, and CACHE READS subclauses of the LOB STORE AS clause determine under what circumstances caching occurs.

In Oracle 11g, the new SecureFiles LOB format allows for substantial improvements in security, performance, and storage compared to 10g LOBs and is recommended for new applications. The STORE AS SECUREFILE clause results in the LOB being stored in the new format. STORE AS BASICFILE is the default in 11g and results in LOBs being stored in the pre-11g format. The DB_SECURE-FILE database parameter can be used to make SecureFiles a default for all new LOB columns. SecureFiles are expected to become the default in a future version of Oracle.

ORACLE PARTITIONING

Partitioning enables a table or index to be composed of multiple segments. Each of these segments can be manipulated individually, and each can have its own storage characteristic. (Each can be stored in a different tablespace for instance.)

Partitioning can provide a wide range of advantages:

❏ Queries need only read partitions that contain relevant data, reducing the number of logical reads required for a particular query. This *partition elimination* technique is particularly suitable for queries that read too great a portion of the table to be able to leverage an index but that still do not need to read the entire table.

❏ By splitting tables and indexes into multiple segments, parallel processing can be significantly improved. This is true both for data operations, such as queries, inserts, updates, and deletes, and also for maintenance operations, such as index rebuilds.

❏ Deleting old data can sometimes be achieved by deleting old partitions, rather than needing to perform expensive delete operations on large numbers of individual rows.

❏ Splitting up tables and indexes can reduce contention in some circumstances."Hot" block contention can be reduced, which can relieve latch contention generally (see Chapter 16, "Latch and Mutex Contention") and is particularly useful when the database uses the Real Application Clusters (RAC) option.

Partitioning is not available in all Oracle editions: The partitioning option is currently an extra cost option of the Oracle Enterprise Edition.

TYPES OF PARTITIONS

Various partitioning schemes are available to determine which rows are allocated to which partitions. In each case, partitioning is based on the value of nominated columns, known as the *partition key*. These are the mechanisms for allocating rows to partitions:

❑ Range partitioning allows rows to be allocated to partitions based on contiguous ranges of the partition key. Range partitioning on a time-based column is common because it enables us to quickly purge older data by dropping a partition. Interval partitioning is an Oracle 11g extension in which new range partitions are created automatically when data in a new interval (typically month or other time range) is encountered.

❑ Hash partitioning allocates rows based on a mathematical hash function. This helps ensure that each partition is of the same size but tends to reduce the possibility of partition elimination for range scans.

❑ List partitioning enables rows to be allocated to partitions based on nominated lists of values. This is similar but more flexible than range partitioning and enables nonadjacent partition key rows to be stored in the same partition.

Oracle database 11g introduced several other new capabilities in partitioning:

❑ Reference partitioning is an 11g enhancement in which a child table can inherit the partitioning scheme from a parent table.

❑ Virtual column-based partitioning enables the partition key to be a virtual column. A virtual column is based on an expression that is evaluated on demand, so this essentially allows partitioning on expressions.

COMPOSITE PARTITIONS

In addition to the basic types, composite partitions can also be created. In a composite partition, the partitions created by the primary partitioning scheme are each further partitioned by a single additional criterion. These partitions within a partition are called subpartitions. Composite partitioning is often employed to get the advantages of range-based partition elimination and purge with the parallelism and maintenance advantages that accompany hash based partitioning.

For database version 10g, Oracle supports only range-list and range-hash partitioning. However, in 11g extended composite partitioning enables range-range and list-list composite partitioning schemes.

CHOOSING A PARTITIONING STRATEGY

The wide variety of partitioning schemes can be confusing. But if you are licensed for partitioning, you can almost always use partitioning to good effect for databases with nontrivial data volumes or transaction rates.

You should consider range (or list) partitioning if any of the following are true:

❑ You anticipate queries that will access data ranges that are too great to be supported by indexes but that are still only fractions of the total table size.

In this case, you can use range or list partitioning to optimize these queries through partition elimination.

❑ You periodically purge old data from your tables. If your range partition is based on the time-based key that is used for these purges, you can rapidly implement these purges by simply dropping the relevant partition.

You should consider hash-based partitioning if you anticipate any of the following:

❑ You will be performing parallel operations such as parallel DML on large tables or parallelized joins with other large tables.

❑ You expect heavy concurrent OLTP style access to the table, and particularly if you think that there are likely to be "hot blocks" that can become contention points. In this case, hash partitioning might distribute these blocks evenly across multiple segments.

If both range and hash-based partitioning are indicated, you should consider a composite range-hash or list-hash partitioning scheme.

We look at indexing issues for partitions in Chapter 5 and look at the issues relating to parallelism in Chapter 13, "Parallel SQL."

ENTERPRISE MANAGER PARTITIONING ADVISOR

Oracle 11g Enterprise Manager includes a partitioning advisor that can suggest partitioning schemes that might improve the performance of SQL workloads. This advisor is part of the SQL Access Advisor that we examine in more detail in Chapter 8, "Execution Plan Management."

When initiating a standard SQL Access Advisor session, you can select the Partitioning and, if you want, the Materialized View options during the Recommendation Options stage. This is shown in Figure 4-9.

Depending on the workload, the SQL Access Advisor might recommend partitioning schemes and indexing schemes.

For instance, in Figure 4-10, the SQL Access Advisor is attempting to optimize some time-based range scans of the RAW_SALES table (an unpartitioned copy of SH.SALES). The SQL Access Advisor recommends partitioning, a materialized view log, and a materialized view.

Figure 4-11 shows the partitioning recommendation generated. The partitioning advisor recommended 3-month interval partitioning.

Also recommended was a Materialized View that aggregates data by TIME_ID (see Figure 4-12).

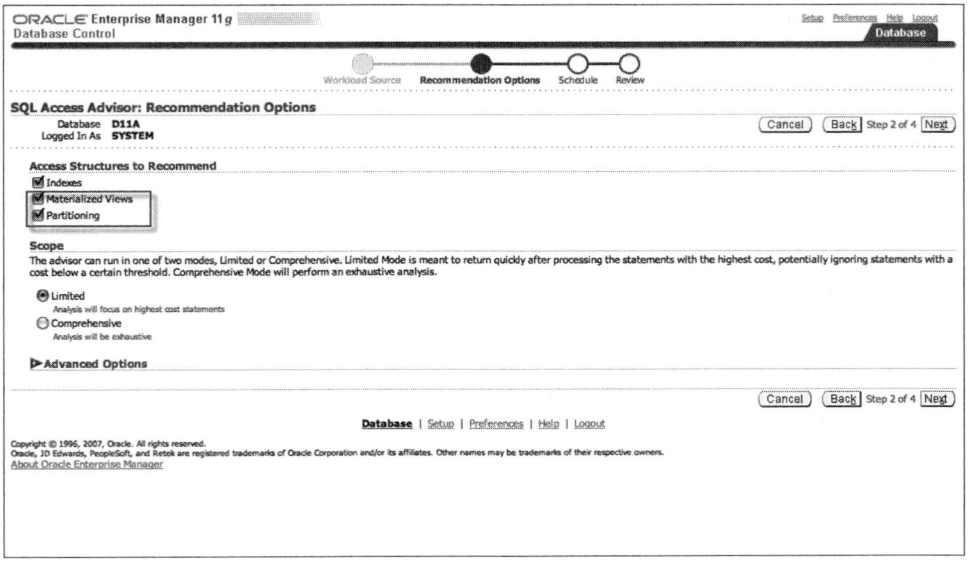

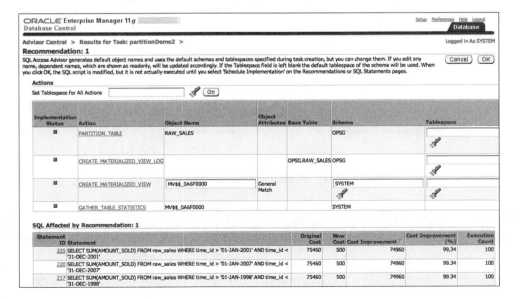

FIGURE 4-9 Choosing Partitioning and Materialized View recommendations in the SQL Access Advisor.

FIGURE 4-10 Partitioning and Materialized View recommendations in the SQL Access Advisor.

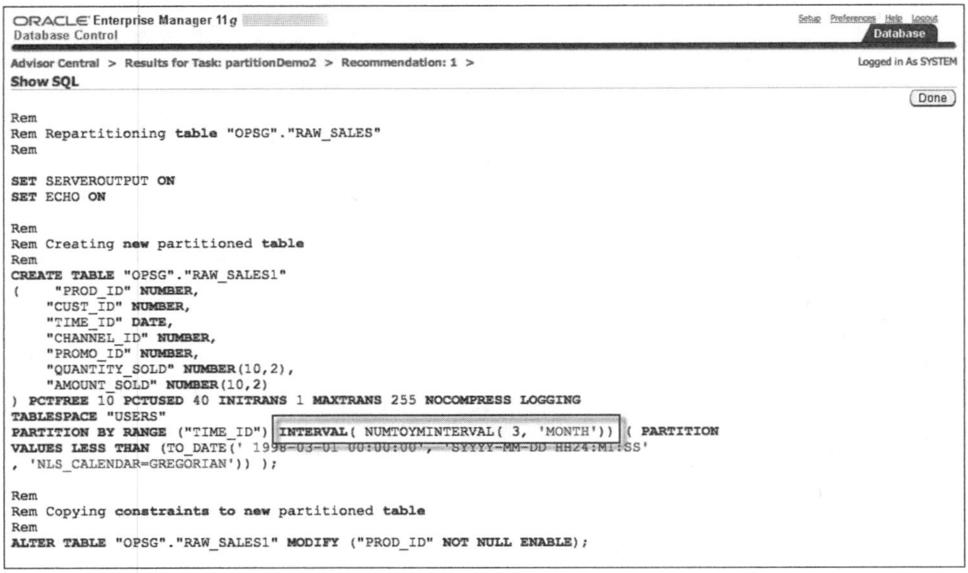

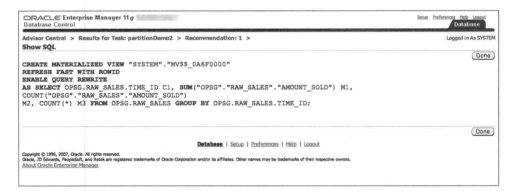

FIGURE 4-11 Interval partitioning recommendation.

FIGURE 4-12 Materialized View recommendation.

SUMMARY

The aim of the logical modeling phase is to identify the data required to implement the application's functional requirements. The physical modeling phase attempts to construct a data model that can meet both functional and performance requirements. The physical model should almost never be a direct copy of the logical model.

During physical modeling the following choices will be made:

❏ Determine the mapping of subtypes and supertypes to tables. An entity with two subtypes can be implemented as one, two, or three tables.
❏ Consider the use of nondefault table types such as index-organized tables or various clustered table types.
❏ Choose data types, lengths, and precisions.
❏ Consider the use of NULL values.

Denormalization involves introducing redundancy into the model to improve targeted SQL performance.

Data warehouse design requires a different mindset and discipline. Data warehouse best practice often involves establishing a denormalized data model that incorporates a star schema, dimensions with hierarchies, and possibly aggregate tables or materialized views.

Oracle offers a wide range of physical storage options, some of which have significant performance impacts. The modern Automated Segment Storage Management (ASSM) option reduces complexity significantly and is recommended.

Partitioning requires specific licensing but offers a great deal in return. Advantages of partitioning include the following:

❏ Enhanced query performance through partition elimination
❏ Improvements to parallel processing capabilities
❏ Fast purges through partition drop
❏ Possible reduction in "hot block" contention

INDEXING AND CLUSTERING

In this chapter, we look at the indexing and clustering facilities provided by Oracle.

An index is an object with its own unique storage that provides a fast access path into a table. A cluster is a means of organizing table data to optimize certain access paths. Indexes and clusters exist primarily to enhance performance, so understanding and using indexes or clusters effectively is of vital importance when optimizing Oracle performance.

OVERVIEW OF ORACLE INDEXING AND CLUSTERING

Oracle provides a variety of indexing and clustering mechanisms. We examine each in detail throughout the chapter, but here is a brief overview:

- ❏ **B*-Tree indexes**—This is Oracle's default index type. It is a highly flexible index with well-understood performance characteristics.
- ❏ **Bitmap indexes**—These are commonly used in data warehouses; they provide a solution for low-cardinality columns and provide efficient index merges. Locking implications normally rule them out for OLTP, however.
- ❏ **Bitmap join indexes**—These are bitmap indexes that are constructed from a join of two tables. Bitmap join indexes are often used in star schemas to join fact and dimension tables.

❑ **Index Organized Table (IOT)**—An IOT is a table structured as a B*-Tree index. The leaf blocks of the index structure contain the table's data.

❑ **Hash clusters**—In a hash cluster the location of a row within the cluster is determined by a hash function of hash key columns. This enables a row to be rapidly located by the hash key without an index.

❑ **Index cluster**—In an index cluster multiple tables are stored in the cluster based on the value of a common cluster key. Rows with the same key are stored close together and might be considered "pre-joined."

❑ **Nested tables**—In a nested table a column contains an object type that effectively embeds detail rows within the master row. Nested tables can provide similar benefits to an index cluster.

B*-TREE INDEXES

The B*-Tree (Balanced Tree) index is Oracle's default index structure. Figure 5-1 shows a high-level overview of B*-Tree index structure.

The B*-Tree index has a hierarchical tree structure. At the top of the tree is the header block. This block contains pointers to the appropriate branch block for a given range of key values. The branch block will usually point to the appropriate leaf block for a more specific range or, for a larger index, point to another branch block. The leaf block contains a list of key values and pointers (ROWIDS) to the appropriate rows in the table.

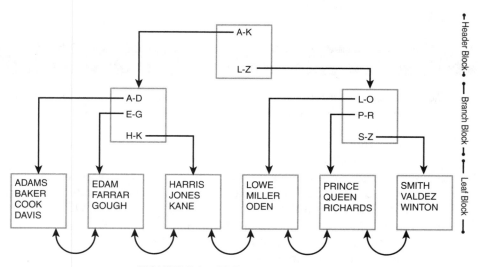

FIGURE 5-1   B*-Tree index structure.

Examining Figure 5-1, let's imagine how Oracle would traverse this index. Should we need to access the record for BAKER, we would first consult the header block. The header block would tell us that key values starting with A through K are stored in the left-most branch block. Accessing this branch block, we find that key values starting with A through D are stored in the left-most leaf block. Consulting this leaf block, we find the value BAKER and its associated ROWID, which we would then use to get to the table row concerned. Figure 5-2 shows how the ROWIDs in a leaf block determine the physical location of the row within the table.

As shown in Figure 5-2, leaf blocks contain links to both the previoius and the next leaf block. This enables us to scan the index in either ascending or descending order and enables range queries using the >, <, or BETWEEN operators to be satisfied using the index.

Each leaf block is at the same depth. This means that from the header block, you always traverse the same number of branch blocks before locating the leaf block.

B*-Tree indexes have the following advantages over older indexing strategies (for instance, the Indexed Sequential Access Method [ISAM]):

❏ Because each leaf node is at the same depth, performance is predictable. Every row in the table requires the same number of index reads to locate.

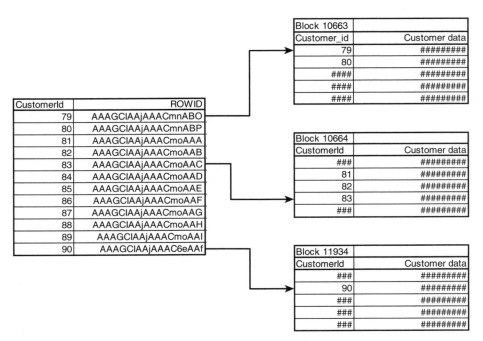

FIGURE 5-2 Leaf blocks contain ROWIDs that point to the physical location of table blocks.

❑   B*-Trees offer good performance for large tables, because the depth is almost never greater than four (one header block, two levels of branch blocks, and one level of leaf block). In fact, because the header block will almost always be already loaded in memory, and branch blocks usually loaded in memory, the actual number of physical disk reads is usually only one or two.

❑   The B*-Tree index supports range queries and exact lookups. This is possible because each leaf block is linked to the previous and next leaf block.

The B*-Tree index provides flexible and efficient query performance. However, maintaining the B*-Tree when changing data can be expensive. For instance, consider inserting a row with the key value NIVEN into the table index diagrammed in Figure 5-1. To insert the row, we must add a new entry into the L–O block. If there is free space within this block, the cost is not excessive. But what happens if there is no free space in the block?

If there is no free space within a leaf block for a new entry, an *index split* is required. A new block must be created and half of the entries in the existing block moved into the new block. Also, there is a requirement to add a new entry to the branch block (to point to the newly created leaf block) and links to the new block added to the adjacent leaf blocks. If there is no free space in the branch block, the branch block must also be split.

INDEX SELECTIVITY

The *selectivity* of a column or group of columns is a common measure of the usefulness of an index on those columns. Columns or indexes are selective if they have a large number of unique values or few duplicate values. For instance, a DATE_OF_BIRTH column will be quite selective whereas a GENDER column will not be selective.

Selective indexes are more efficient than nonselective indexes because they point more directly to specific values. The optimizer determines the selectivity of the various indexes available to it and tries to use the most selective index.

UNIQUE INDEXES

A unique index is one that prevents any duplicate values for the columns that make up the index. If you try to create a unique index on a table that contains such duplicate values, you receive an error. Similarly, you also receive an error if you try to insert a row that contains duplicate unique index key values.

A unique index is often created to prevent duplicate values rather than to improve performance. However, unique index columns are usually efficient—they point to exactly one row and are, therefore, very selective.

IMPLICIT INDEXES

Implicit indexes are created automatically by Oracle to implement either primary key or unique constraints. Implicit indexes can also be created when implementing Oracle object type tables and in other circumstances.

CONCATENATED INDEXES

A concatenated (or composite) index is simply an index composed of more than one column. The advantage of a concatenated key is that it is often more selective than a single key index. The combination of columns points to a smaller number of rows than indexes composed of the individual columns. A concatenated index that contains all the columns referred to in a SQL statement's WHERE clause is usually very effective.

If you frequently query on more than one column within a table, creating a concatenated index for these columns is an excellent idea. For instance, we might query the EMPLOYEES table by LAST_NAME and FIRST_NAME. In that case, we would probably want to create an index on both LAST_NAME and FIRST-NAME. For instance

```
CREATE INDEX emp_name_ix ON employees
   (last_name ,first_name )
```

Using such an index, we could rapidly find all employees matching a given LAST_NAME/FIRST_NAME combination. Such an index will be far more effective than an index on LAST_NAME alone, or separate indexes on LAST_NAME and FIRST_NAME.

If a concatenated index could only be used when all its keys appeared in the WHERE clause, concatenated indexes would probably be of limited use. Luckily, a concatenated index can be used effectively providing any of the initial or leading columns are used. Leading columns are those that are specified earliest in the index definition.

Figure 5-3 shows the improvements gained as columns are added to a concatenated index for the following query:

```
SELECT cust_id
  FROM sh.customers c
 WHERE cust_first_name = 'Connor'
   AND cust_last_name = 'Bishop'
   AND cust_year_of_birth = 1976;
```

A full table scan required 1,459 logical reads. Indexing on CUST_LAST_NAME alone reduced this to 63 logical IOs, but adding further columns to a concatenated index reduced IO to only 4. The final optimization was to add the CUST_ID column

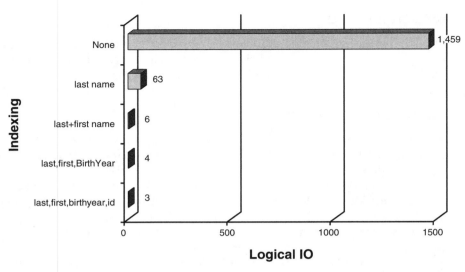

FIGURE 5-3 The effect of adding relevant columns to a concatenated index.

to the index so that the table itself did not need to be read at all. This is sometimes referred to as a *covering* index.

Creating widely applicable and selective concatenated indexes should be a top priority of your indexing strategy.

INDEX SKIP SCANS

If we omit the first column in a concatenated index, Oracle can still use the index by *skip-scanning*. This involves scanning down each leading value for matching values in the nonleading columns. It's kind of like doing a separate index scan for each distinct leading column value, so it works best when the leading value doesn't have too many distinct values.

Figure 5-4 shows how this can work for our query if we didn't specify the CUST_LAST_NAME column in our query. A skip scan on the CUST_LAST_NAME, CUST_FIRST_NAME index is much better than a full table scan but still nowhere near as good as an index that leads with the CUST_LAST_NAME column (shown as Index Range Scan in Figure 5-4).

GUIDELINES FOR CONCATENATED INDEXES

The following guidelines help in deciding when to use concatenated indexes and how to decide which columns should be included and in which order.

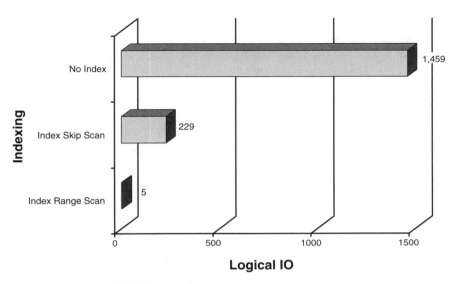

FIGURE 5-4 Skip scan index performance.

❑ Create a concatenated index for columns from a table that appear together in the WHERE clause.

❑ If columns sometimes appear on their own in a WHERE clause, place them at the start of the index.

❑ The more selective a column is, the more useful it will be at the leading end of the index (but keep reading for some important caveats).

❑ Index skip scans can make use of an index even if the leading columns are not specified, but it's a poor second choice to a "normal" index range scan.

If the concatenated index is sometimes going to be used with only the leading columns specified, it makes some sense to put the most selective column first. However, you need to consider all the factors:

❑ A concatenated index is more useful if it also supports queries where not all columns are specified. For instance SURNAME, FIRSTNAME is more useful than FIRSTNAME, SURNAME because queries against SURNAME *only* are more likely to occur than queries against FIRSTNAME only.

❑ Skip-scan queries tend to be more efficient when the leading "skipped" columns are not particularly selective.

❑ Index compression, covered later in this chapter, is more effective when leading columns are less selective.

Don't automatically put the most selective term first in a concatenated index. Consider the queries that can be supported by the leading columns, and the impact of index compression and skip-scan access paths.

INDEX MERGES

If more than one column from a table appears in the WHERE clause and there is no concatenated index that includes all the columns concerned, but there are indexes on the individual columns, Oracle might perform an *index merge*.

To perform an index merge, Oracle retrieves all rows from each index with matching values and then merges these result sets and returns only those rows that appear in each set. For instance, consider the case in which there is an index on CUST_LAST_NAME and another index on CUST_FIRST_NAME. If we issued a query for Ian Smith, we would first retrieve all employees with the surname of Smith, and then retrieve all employees with the first name of Ian. The two sets would be merged, and only employees in both sets (that is, Ian+Smith) would be returned.

Performing B*-Tree index merges is almost always less efficient than the equivalent concatenated index. If you see an index merge, consider creating an appropriate concatenated index. Figure 5-5 illustrates this point. An index merge of CUST_FIRST_NAME, CUST_LAST_NAME, and CUST_YEAR_OF_BIRTH outperformed a full table scan but was not nearly as good as a concatenated index on all three columns.[1]

As we see later, bitmap indexes can be merged much more effectively than the default B*-Tree index.

When no suitable concatenated index exists, Oracle might merge multiple indexes to return results. This can be more efficient than a full table scan but rarely as efficient as the appropriate concatenated index.

NULL VALUES IN INDEXES

When an indexed column is NULL, or when all columns in a concatenated index are NULL, the row concerned will not have entry in a B*-Tree index. This is a fundamental and important concept because it is, therefore, not possible to use a

---

[1] Index merges might be substantially slower in Oracle Standard Edition because the Standard Edition cannot leverage the bitmap conversion approach to index merge used in the Enterprise Edition.

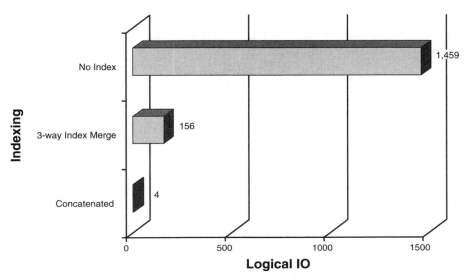

FIGURE 5-5   Index merge performance.

B*-Tree index to find NULL values, although it is possible to find a value that is NOT NULL.

It's therefore usually wise to define the columns that might be referenced in WHERE clauses as NOT NULL so that indexing these columns can be effective. However, it can be worthwhile using NULL values in an indexed column if some or all the following conditions apply:

❑   The column is almost always NULL.
❑   We never want to find rows where the column is NULL.
❑   We do want to search for rows where the column is NOT NULL.
❑   We want to minimize the space required by the index.

Because NULLs are not stored in an index, an index created when the preceding conditions are true will be very compact and can be used to quickly locate rows where the column contains a value.

REVERSE KEY INDEXES

Indexes can be created with a REVERSE keyword, which causes the key value stored in the index to be reversed. So for instance, a REVERSE index would store Smith as htimS.

Reverse key indexes help reduce contention for the leading edge of the index. If you are inserting entries into the table in ascending order (perhaps using a sequence) the leading or right-most block will always be active. Furthermore, space might be wasted if you periodically purge most, but not all, older entries. The old entries that are not purged will remain in blocks that are sparsely populated.

If you use the REVERSE keyword, new index entries will be spread more evenly across existing index blocks, and the blocks might be more tightly packed than would otherwise be the case. However, it will no longer be possible to perform range scans using such an index.

Reverse key indexes might make sense in environments where contention for the leading edge of a standard index might be intense and result in *buffer busy* or *cache buffers chains latch* waits. Real Application Clusters (RAC) databases will also often benefit from a reduction in block contention. We discuss these issues further in Chapter 16, "Latch and Mutex Contention," Chapter 17, "Shared Memory Contention," and Chapter 23, "Optimizing RAC."

INDEX COMPRESSION

Oracle enables index leaf block entries to be compressed. The compression approach used involves removing leading columns of the index key that do not change and storing them in a prefix entry. This leading part of the index entry then can be omitted from the leaf block.

Index compression works best on concatenated indexes where leading parts of the index are repeated. For instance, an index on CUST_LAST_NAME, CUST_FIRST_NAME, CUST_YEAR_OF_BIRTH would be an excellent candidate for compression because we would expect surnames (at least) to be repeated.

The COMPRESS clause specifies the number of columns that should be compressed. For example, the following requests that CUST_LAST_NAME and CUST_FIRST_NAME be compressed:

```
CREATE INDEX cust_i_compr ON sh.customers
(cust_last_name,cust_first_name,cust_year_of_birth) COMPRESS 2;
```

Using COMPRESS in the preceding example reduced the number of index leaf blocks from 224 to 132.

Using compression on suitable indexes has the following beneficial effects:

❑ The storage requirements for the index are reduced.
❑ Because more rows can be stored in each leaf block, range scans will require fewer IO operations.
❑ Because more rows can be stored in each leaf block, the height of the B*-Tree *might* be reduced.

You cannot compress partitioned or bitmap indexes. You also cannot compress a single-column unique index.

Index compression can improve index performance for concatenated indexes that have repeating values for leading columns.

FUNCTIONAL INDEXES

Functional indexes enable you to create an index on a function or an expression. The function or expression must be *deterministic*, which means that if given the same inputs it must always return the same outputs: regardless of changes in the environment, the database, or the date and time.

So for instance, the following is a legal index definition:

```
CREATE INDEX cust_uppr_name_ix ON customers
(UPPER(cust_last_name),UPPER(cust_first_name));
```

However, the following is invalid because the value of the DAYS_LEFT function will change over time:

```
CREATE OR REPLACE FUNCTION days_left(p_eff_date DATE)
    RETURN NUMBER
IS
BEGIN
    RETURN (p_eff_date - SYSDATE);
END;
/
CREATE INDEX cust_i_eff_days ON
        customers ( days_left(cust_eff_to) );
```

The DETERMINISTIC keyword can be used when creating the function to indicate that it will always return the same values. We could apply the DETERMINISTIC keyword to our preceding DAYS_LEFT function and the index would be created. However the index that was created would become invalid over time because index entries would continue to reflect the days left when the index entry was created, whereas in fact the days remaining would decrease over time.

Applying the deterministic clause incorrectly to a function and then using that function in an index can lead to an index that returns incorrect results.

FOREIGN KEYS AND LOCKING

You can declare referential integrity constraints to prevent rows being inserted into detail (or child) tables that do not have a matching row in the master (or parent) table. This facility helps preserves the integrity of your data. For instance, the following statement creates a foreign key constraint between EMPLOYEES and DEPARTMENTS:

```
ALTER TABLE employees
ADD CONSTRAINT emp_dept_fk
FOREIGN KEY (department_id)
REFERENCES departments (department_id)
ON DELETE CASCADE
```

When the constraint is enabled, attempting to create an EMPLOYEE row with an invalid DEPARTMENT_ID will generate an error. However, to prevent inconsistencies during the operation, Oracle applies table level locks (rather than the usual row level locks) to the child table when a parent table primary key is modified or if a parent table row is deleted—unless the foreign key columns are indexed.

These table locks are not required if there is an index on the foreign key in the child table (for instance, an index on EMPLOYEES.DEPARTMENT_ID). Often, you create such an index to optimize joins and queries. However, if you omit such a foreign key index and if the parent table is subject to deletes or primary key updates, you might see heavy lock contention.

Foreign key indexes also support efficient DELETE CASCADE operations. In the preceding example, deleting a department also deletes all employee rows attached to that department (perhaps to support rapid downsizing!). Without the index, all EMPLOYEE rows would need to be scanned to support the operation.

Unindexed foreign keys can lead to increased lock contention if the parent table is subject to primary key updates or deletions while the child table is subject to transactional activity. Furthermore, foreign key indexes optimize DELETE CASCADE operations.

INDEXES AND PARTITIONING

Indexes may be partitioned if the database is licensed for the partitioning option, and of course indexes may be created on partitioned tables. Although it's possible to create a partitioned index on an unpartitioned table, partitioned indexes will more often be created on a table that is itself partitioned.

If an index on a partitioned table is unpartitioned or partitioned on different criteria than the source table, the index is known as a *global index*.

Local indexes are partitioned in the same manner as their source table. If the leading columns of the index are also the columns upon which the index is partitioned (the partition key), the index is known as a *local prefixed index*. Prefixing the index in this way should be done if it makes sense regardless of the partition key, but not as a matter of course. If you want to look for specific values of the partition key, by all means create a prefixed index. But you do not need to prefix the index to achieve *partition elimination*, in which Oracle restricts query processing only to relevant partitions.

Local indexes have some significant management advantages over global indexes. If a partitioned table with a global index has a partition split, merge, or move, the corresponding index partition automatically has the same maintenance operation applied. Furthermore, partitioning often avoids hot-spot contention, and hot spots are even more likely to appear with index blocks than with table blocks. Some partition operations, such as dropping a partition, will invalidate a global index unless the index is rebuilt by specifying the UPDATE GLOBAL INDEXES clause when performing the partition operation.

Despite their disadvantages, global indexes might be required to enforce unique constraints across partition boundaries, or where fast access to a specific row is required and the partitioning scheme doesn't easily identify in which partition the row might be found. For this reason, you tend to see global indexes more commonly in OLTP environments where rapid and predictable response time is required.

Figure 5-6 illustrates a performance comparison between global and local indexes.

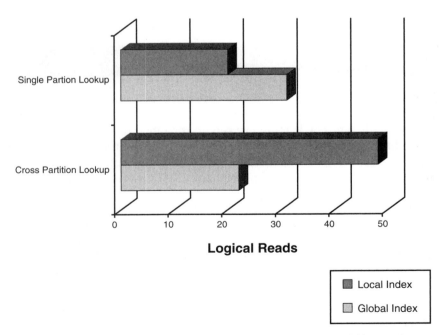

FIGURE 5-6   Global indexes give better performance across partitions, whereas local indexes tend to work better within a partition.

SH.SALES is partitioned by date. For a query that must scan all partitions to return a result, such as the following, a global index is more efficient:

```
SELECT SUM (amount_sold)
  FROM sales s
 WHERE promo_id = 33;
```

But when the WHERE clause supports partition elimination, such as in the following case, the local index wins out because Oracle can determine that it needs to access only local indexes for specific partitions:

```
SELECT SUM (amount_sold)
  FROM sales_int_test s
 WHERE promo_id = 33
   AND time_id < TO_DATE ('01-JAN-1999', 'DD-MON-RRRR')
   AND time_id > TO_DATE ('01-JAN-1998', 'DD-MON-RRRR');
```

Global indexes provide better performance for queries that must span all partitions. Local indexes are more effective in conjunction with partition elimination and also provide many manageability advantages.

BITMAP INDEXES

Bitmap indexes are a feature of Oracle Enterprise Edition. In a bitmap index, Oracle creates a bitmap for each unique value of a single column. Each bitmap contains a single bit (0 or 1) for every row in the table. A 1 indicates that the row has the value specified by the bitmap, and a 0 indicates that it does not. Oracle can rapidly scan these bitmaps to find rows matching specified criteria. Oracle can also rapidly compare multiple bitmaps to find all rows matching multiple criteria. Bitmap indexes are particularly suitable for columns with a limited number of distinct values that are often queried in combination.

Figure 5-7 shows an example of bitmapped indexes on an imaginary table called SURVEY. Bitmapped indexes exist on GENDER, MARITALSTATUS, and HOMEOWNER. To find all single males who own their own home, Oracle extracts the bitmaps for each value provided by the query and finds rows that have a 1 in each of the bitmaps.

FEATURES OF BITMAP INDEXES

Bitmap indexes have the following attractive features:

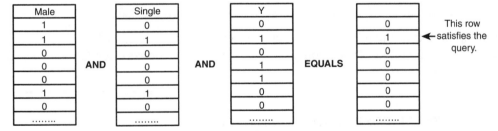

Gender	MaritalStatus	ChildrenYN	Income	HomeOwner
M	Married	N	120000	N
M	Single	N	80000	Y
F	Divorced	Y	75000	N
F	Married	Y	70000	Y
F	Married	Y	130000	Y
M	Single	Y	45000	N
F	Married	N	42000	N
....	....	....	....	....

Male	Female
1	0
1	0
0	1
0	1
0	1
1	0
0	1
....	....

Married	Single	Divorced
1	0	0
0	1	0
0	0	1
1	0	0
1	0	0
0	1	0
1	0	0
....	....	....

Y	N
0	1
1	0
0	1
1	0
1	0
0	1
0	1
....	....

```
SELECT * FROM survey WHERE Gender='Male' AND MaritialStatus='Single' AND
                      HomeOwner='Y'
```

Male		Single		Y			
1		0		0		0	
1		1		1		1	← satisfies the query.
0		0		0		0	
0	AND	0	AND	1	EQUALS	0	
0		0		1		0	
1		1		0		0	
0		0		0		0	
....		....		....		....	

FIGURE 5-7   Example of bitmap index retrieval.

- ❏ Bitmap are more effective than B*-Tree indexes for columns with fewer distinct values—*unselective* columns. For unique or near-unique indexes, B*-Tree indexes will probably be more efficient.
- ❏ Bitmap indexes can be merged far more effectively that B*-Tree indexes. A merge of multiple bitmap indexes is far more efficient than a merge of multiple B*-Tree indexes.
- ❏ Bitmapped indexes are especially suitable for large tables and for aggregate (that is, "how many," "sum of") queries.
- ❏ If used appropriately, bitmapped indexes are very compact—much more compact than the equivalent concatenated index (providing the number of distinct values is not too high).

❑ Contrary to some recommendations, bitmap indexes can be efficient even when there are a large number of distinct values. However, they are less efficient than B*-Tree indexes for unique or nearly unique columns.

❑ Bitmap indexes can be used to implement the star join transformation join (see Chapter 10, "Joins and Subqueries").

❑ Bitmap join indexes are a special type of bitmap index that can optimize queries that would normally require a join.

DRAWBACKS OF BITMAP INDEXES

Against the many advantages of bitmap indexes, a few serious drawbacks restrict their applicability:

❑ Oracle cannot lock a single bit, and consequently, updating a bitmap indexed column can result in locks being applied to a large number of rows. This makes bitmap indexes inappropriate for applications with even moderately high transaction rates.

❑ Bitmap indexes cannot be used to optimize range queries. Use B*-Tree indexes, if necessary, for columns subject to range queries.

Bitmap indexes cause locks to be applied to many large groups of rows, even if only one row is updated. This generally rules out bitmap indexes for tables subject to OLTP-type workloads.

BITMAP INDEXES AND CARDINALITY

At what point should we decide that the column has too many unique values to be suitable for a bitmap index?

Most examples of bitmap indexes (including that in Figure 5-7) show multiple columns of *very* low cardinality, such as gender, marital status, and so on. When we look at those examples we'd be forgiven for thinking that bitmap indexes are not suitable when there are more than a handful of key values.

In fact, bitmap indexes are capable of performing well even when there are many thousands of unique values. Figure 5-8 shows the relative performance of bitmap and B*-Tree-based queries on a million row table for columns varying between 5 and 10,000 distinct values. As we can see, bitmap indexes are still quite effective even when the number of distinct values is very large.

Bitmap indexes can provide good performance even for high cardinality columns, although unique or nearly unique columns will be better served by a B*-Tree index.

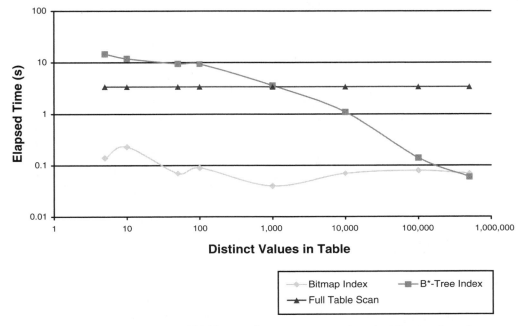

FIGURE 5-8 Bitmap and B*-Tree performance mapped against the number of distinct values in the column.

BITMAP INDEX MERGE

We saw in Figure 5-5 how index merge performance was far inferior to a concatenated index that contained all the columns required. However, for many applications, creating concatenated indexes for every conceivable combination of columns is impractical.

In contrast to B*-Tree indexes, bitmap indexes excel at merge operations. It is quite practical to create a separate bitmap index for every column that might appear in the WHERE clause and then rely on bitmap merging to provide acceptable performance for the widest possible range of queries. Figure 5-9 provides an example; a four-way bitmap merge required only 5 percent of the IO of a four-way B*-Tree index merge, though a concatenated index on all four columns was still superior.

BITMAP JOIN INDEXES

A bitmap join index is a bitmap index that identifies rows in one table that have values matching a value in a second table. This bitmap index can be used to avoid joining the two tables to resolve the results. Figure 5-10 illustrates the concept; the bitmap join index identifies rows in the EMPLOYEES table that are associated with various department names from the DEPARTMENTS table.

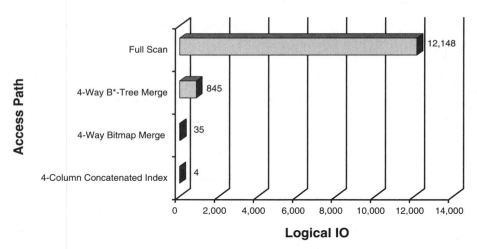

FIGURE 5-9 Bitmap indexes merge more effectively than B*-Tree indexes but concatenated indexes still rule.

Bitmap join indexes can avoid join operations when queries are issued that request rows in the indexed table that have rows matching the value in the other table. For instance, in the SH schema, we might want to find sales for a given customer, identified by email address:

```
SELECT SUM (amount_sold)
  FROM customers JOIN sales s USING (cust_id)
 WHERE cust_email='flint.jeffreys@company2.com';
```

Normally, we would need to perform a join from CUSTOMERS to SALES to resolve this query. We would access CUSTOMERS to retrieve the CUST_ID for the customer concerned, and then use an index on SALES to scan matching rows.

However, by creating a bitmap join index, we effectively allow queries against SALES directly for a specific email address:

```
CREATE  BITMAP INDEX sales_bm_join_i
   ON sales (c.cust_email)
  FROM sales s , customers c
 WHERE s.cust_id=c.cust_id;
```

The resulting execution plan confirms that the CUSTOMERS table is not accessed:

```
SELECT SUM (amount_sold)
  FROM customers JOIN sales s USING (cust_id)
```

```
WHERE cust_email='flint.jeffreys@company2.com';
```

Id	Operation	Name	Rows
0	SELECT STATEMENT		1
1	SORT AGGREGATE		1
2	TABLE ACCESS BY INDEX ROWID	SALES	2052
3	BITMAP CONVERSION TO ROWIDS		
* 4	BITMAP INDEX SINGLE VALUE	SALES_BM_JOIN_I	

In this example, the performance gain is significant because we avoided the scan on the relatively large CUSTOMERS table. Figure 5-11 shows the results for

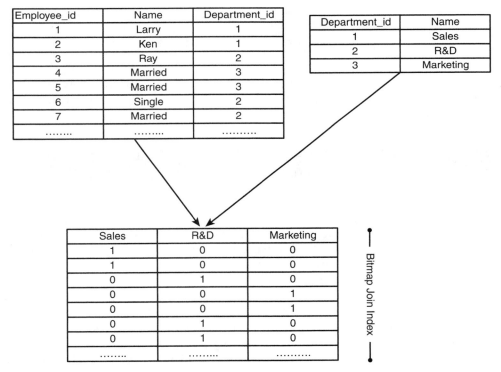

```
CREATE BITMAP INDEX bi_1 ON employees(d.department_name)
    FROM employees e, departments d WHERE d.department_id=e.department_id
```

FIGURE 5-10 A bitmap join index points to rows in one table that have foreign keys that match rows in another table.

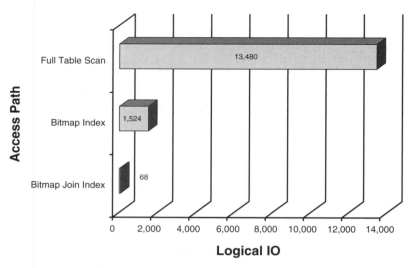

FIGURE 5-11   Bitmap join index performance.

the preceding example query; note that if the CUSTOMERS table were very small or if an index existed on the CUST_EMAIL column, the performance gains would be less significant.

INDEX OVERHEAD

Although indexes can dramatically improve query performance, they do reduce the performance of DML statements such as INSERT, DELETE, UPDATE, and MERGE. All of a table's indexes must normally be updated when a row is inserted or deleted, and an index must also be amended when an update changes any column that appears in the index.

It is, therefore, important that all our indexes contribute to query performance[2] because these indexes will otherwise needlessly degrade DML performance. In particular, you should be especially careful when creating indexes on frequently updated columns. A row can be inserted or deleted only once but can be updated many times. Indexes on heavily updated columns or on tables that have a high insert/delete rate will, therefore, exact a particularly high cost.

The overhead of indexing is critically felt during batch deletes. Whenever a row is deleted, every index entry that contains a reference to that row must be re-

---

[2] An exception can be made for foreign key indexes, which reduce lock contention, and for unique constraint indexes. We might want to keep these even if they don't contribute to query performance.

moved. There's no direct pointer from a row address to an index entry so that often means that a scan of all matching index entries must be performed to find the matching leaf block entries. For instance, if a row with the SURNAME Smith is deleted, we would scan all index entries for Smith and remove any index entries that point to the deleted row.

Figure 5-12 illustrates the overhead of indexes on delete performance. The primary key index adds a relatively small overhead, but each nonunique index adds significant overhead when rows are removed.

> Indexes always add to the overhead of INSERT and DELETE statements and can add to the overhead of UPDATE statements. Avoid over-indexing, especially on columns that are frequently updated.

Because unused indexes add to DML overhead without contributing to query performance, we want a way to identify any indexes that are not being used. There are a couple of ways to do this. First, we can apply the MONITORING

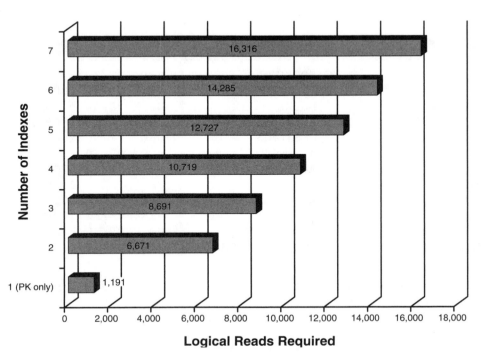

FIGURE 5-12 Effect of indexes on deletes (1,000 rows deleted).

USAGE clause to our indexes. For example, the following PL/SQL applies this clause to all the indexes owned by the current user:

```
BEGIN
    FOR r IN (SELECT index_name
                FROM user_indexes)
    LOOP
        EXECUTE IMMEDIATE 'ALTER INDEX ' || r.index_name ||
          ' MONITORING USAGE';
    END LOOP;
END;
```

When the monitoring clause is applied, we can query V$OBJECT_USAGE, which will indicate whether the index has been used. For instance, in the following we see that two of our indexes have not been used since MONITORING USAGE was applied:

```
SQL> SELECT index_name, table_name, used, start_monitoring
  2    FROM v$object_usage
  3   WHERE MONITORING = 'YES';
```

INDEX_NAME	TABLE_NAME	USED	START_MONITORING
G_BOOKS_PK	G_BOOKS	YES	08/30/2008 22:18:46
SYS_C007815	QSFT_SEQUENCE	YES	08/30/2008 22:18:46
G_BOOKS_I1	G_BOOKS	NO	08/30/2008 22:18:46
G_CUSTOMERS_PK	G_CUSTOMERS	YES	08/30/2008 22:18:46
G_CUSTOMERS_I1	G_CUSTOMERS	YES	08/30/2008 22:18:46
G_AUTHORS_PK	G_AUTHORS	YES	08/30/2008 22:18:46
AUTHOR_NAME_I1	G_AUTHORS	YES	08/30/2008 22:18:46
G_ORDERS_PK	G_ORDERS	YES	08/30/2008 22:18:46
G_LINE_ITEMS_PK	G_LINE_ITEMS	YES	08/30/2008 22:18:46
G_CART_PK	G_CART	YES	08/30/2008 22:18:46
G_BOOK_AUTHORS_PK	G_BOOK_AUTHORS	NO	08/30/2008 22:18:46
BOOK_AUTHOR_I1	G_BOOK_AUTHORS	YES	08/30/2008 22:18:46

Another way to investigate index utilization is by examining the V$SQL_PLAN view. Although this avoids having to apply the MONITORING USAGE clause, there is a chance that some SQL that used an index might have been flushed from the cache.

This query identifies indexes in the current account that are not found in any cached SQL plan:

```
SQL> WITH in_plan_objects AS
  2         (SELECT DISTINCT object_name
  3                   FROM v$sql_plan
  4                  WHERE object_owner = USER)
  5  SELECT table_name, index_name,
  6          CASE WHEN object_name IS NULL
  7               THEN 'NO'
  8               ELSE 'YES'
  9          END AS in_cached_plan
 10    FROM user_indexes LEFT OUTER JOIN in_plan_objects
 11          ON (index_name = object_name);
```

TABLE_NAME	INDEX_NAME	IN_CACHED_PLAN
G_AUTHORS	G_AUTHORS_PK	NO
G_BOOK_AUTHORS	G_BOOK_AUTHORS_PK	NO
G_CART	G_CART_PK	YES
G_BOOKS	G_BOOKS_PK	YES
G_BOOK_AUTHORS	BOOK_AUTHOR_I1	YES
G_ORDERS	G_ORDERS_PK	YES
G_AUTHORS	AUTHOR_NAME_I1	YES
QSFT_SEQUENCE	SYS_C007815	NO
G_LINE_ITEMS	G_LINE_ITEMS_PK	YES
G_CUSTOMERS	G_CUSTOMERS_PK	YES
G_CUSTOMERS	G_CUSTOMERS_I1	NO
G_BOOKS	G_BOOKS_I1	NO

Nonkey indexes that are not used by any query might be candidates for removal. Use monitoring usage or query V$SQL_PLAN to identify such indexes.

Remember that unique, primary key and foreign key indexes can be useful even if they are not used to resolve queries.

INDEX ORGANIZED TABLES

Index Organized Tables (IOT) are tables that you can use in the same way as other tables but are stored internally in a B*-Tree index format. IOTs have the following advantages:

❏   We avoid duplicating storage in both the index and table.

❏   Key lookups are fast because the data required is stored right in the index leaf block.

❏   There is a clustering effect because rows with consecutive key values will be stored together. This can improve the efficiency of range scans and sometimes of foreign key lookups. If the primary key includes a foreign key component, all the rows for a particular foreign key might be stored in the same block.

IOTs are organized as a B*-Tree index constructed against their primary key. The primary key plus the additional columns are stored in the leaf blocks of the B*-Tree. Storing *all* the columns in the leaf block might cause the index structure to degrade because you can store fewer rows in each leaf block. You therefore need more leaf blocks, which will degrade range scans and might increase the depth of the index. To avoid this degradation, you can nominate the columns that will be stored in the leaf block by specifying the INCLUDING clause. Columns that appear after the INCLUDING column in the table definition will be stored in an overflow segment.

The overflow segment can be stored in a separate tablespace if desired, which can allow us to optimize its physical storage separately: perhaps by using a different block size or disk devices with different storage capabilities.

Figure 5-13 compares the layout of a B*-Tree index and table with that of an IOT.

CONFIGURING THE OVERFLOW SEGMENT

The INCLUDING clause determines which columns are stored in the B*-Tree section of the IOT and which are stored in a separate *overflow* segment.

It's not essential to have an overflow segment, but it's almost always desirable unless the number of nonprimary key columns in the table is small. Also, an overflow segment will be created automatically and be mandatory if the size of the row is so large that less than two index entries will fit in a leaf block.

If too many columns are stored in the leaf block, then the number of rows that can be stored in each block will be reduced. This increases the number of entries that must be stored in each branch block, which, in turn, might require that another level of the B*-Tree be provided. By creating an overflow segment, we increase the probability that the height of the B*-Tree will not increase, but we make it more expensive to access the columns in the overflow segment.

The following CREATE TABLE statement creates an Index Organized customers table that stores results of a customer survey. The B*-Tree is created using the CUST_ID and QUESTION_ID primary key columns, and all columns up to and including QUESTION_SCORE are stored in the index leaf blocks, while the remaining column QUESTION_LONG_ANSWER is stored in the overflow tablespace.

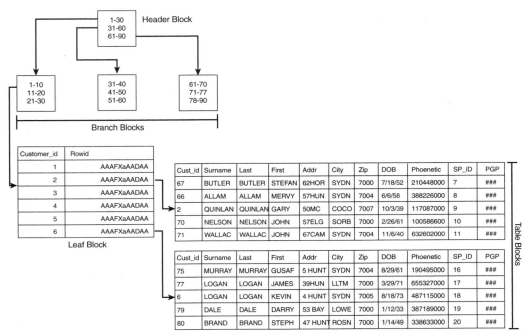

A. B* tree index and associated table blocks

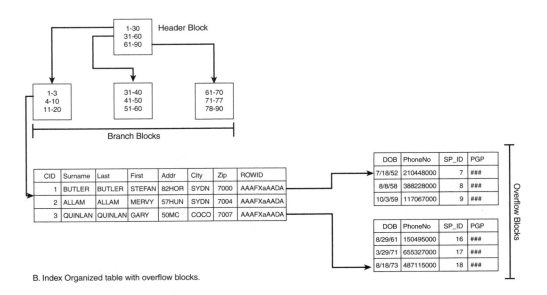

B. Index Organized table with overflow blocks.

FIGURE 5-13 IOT compared with B*-Tree index and table.

```
CREATE TABLE survey_iot_ovrflow
    (cust_id                  NUMBER          NOT NULL ,
    question_id               NUMBER          NOT NULL,
    question_score            NUMBER          NOT NULL,
    question_long_answer      VARCHAR2(1000)  NOT NULL,
    primary key (cust_id,question_id) )
ORGANIZATION INDEX INCLUDING question_score OVERFLOW;
```

Figure 5-14 shows the structure of an IOT that includes an overflow segment.

If we created the table without an overflow segment, all the columns—including relatively long QUESTION_LONG_ANSWER—would need to be stored in the index leaf blocks. This might have meant that only a handful of rows could have been stored in each leaf block. As a result it would have been necessary to have a larger number of leaf blocks and might have been necessary to add an additional level to the B*-Tree. Figure 5-15 illustrates such an outcome. The extra depth degrades index lookups, and the larger number of leaf blocks result in slower range scans across the index key.

Clearly the decision as to which columns are included in the B*-Tree and which are placed in the overflow segment has a tremendous effect on the efficiency of the B*-Tree and on the performance of various queries. Here are the basic considerations:

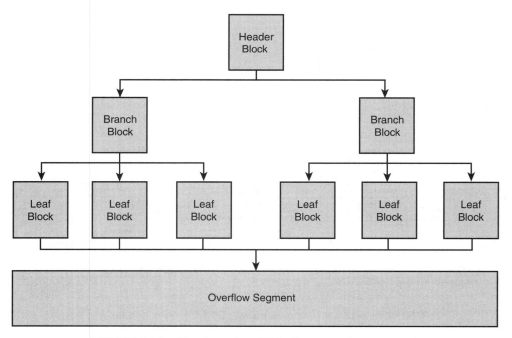

FIGURE 5-14 Structure of an IOT with an overflow segment.

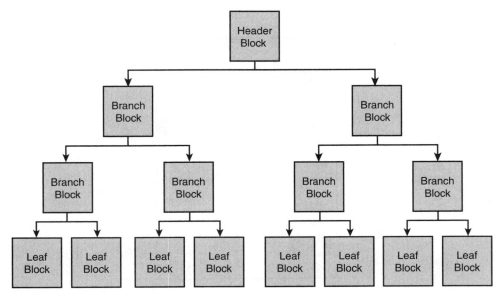

FIGURE 5-15   Structure of an IOT without an overflow segment.

❏ If too many columns are included in the index segment, the height of the
   B*-Tree might increase. This will typically cause every access via the primary key to require an additional IO.

❏ If you retrieve a column by the primary key and that column is in the overflow segment, you will experience an additional IO anyway.

❏ If you access data that is in the B*-Tree segment only via a full table scan,
   the overhead of reading rows from the overflow segment will be avoided.

❏ If you access data that is in the overflow segment, you will need to scan
   both the B*-Tree segment and the overflow segment. This takes longer than
   a full table scan of a traditionally structured table.

Figure 5-16 shows the performance of a query that retrieves survey results
from our CUSTOMER_SURVEY table via index lookup. When we have an overflow segment, queries to the first columns are efficient because we need to simply
access the index structure and find the results in the leaf block. Without an overflow segment, the performance is not so great but still better than a traditional
B*-Tree scan of a heap table. However, when we access data in the overflow segment, we get no performance benefit from the IOT structure; it's just like reading
data from a heap table via an index.

The overflow segment can also play a critical role when performing full
table scans. If our scan needs to access only the columns in the leaf blocks and not
those in the overflow blocks, the table scan will be much quicker. However, if the
scan requires access to both the index structure and to the overflow segment, the

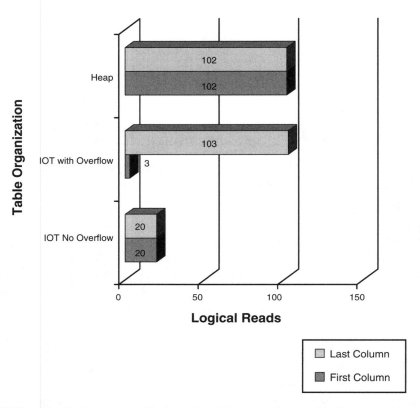

FIGURE 5-16   Performance of index-only table versus heap table for indexed lookup.

full table scan will be worse than that from a heap table. Figure 5-17 illustrates this phenomenon. Performing a full scan on an IOT with an overflow segment was more than ten times more expensive than a HEAP table if the overflow segment was accessed. If overflow segment columns were not required, the table scan required only one-eighth the number of logical IOs.

> Think carefully about how to split your Index Organized table. Data in the index segment will be quicker to access, whereas data in the overflow segment might take much longer to access. However, placing too much data in the index segment can reduce index scan and lookup performance.

PERIODIC REBUILD OF INDEX ONLY TABLES

Indexes tend to become sparse more quickly than tables when rows are deleted because it's not always possible to reuse empty index entries unless a suitable key value occurs. Because in the IOT the index *is* the table, this degradation will also

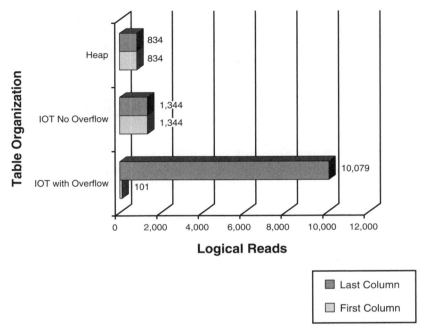

FIGURE 5-17   Full table scan performance for index only tables and heap table.

affect scan performance in a way that doesn't occur in traditional tables. To counter this effect, you might need to rebuild an Index Organized table more frequently than a traditional table.

CLUSTERING

Indexing involves creating a separate structure that enables you to rapidly locate specific data. Clustering, on the other hand, involves physically locating the data in some location that optimizes database access.

Oracle provides two fundamental clustering mechanisms:

❑ An index cluster stores rows with the same key values from multiple tables in close physical proximity. These rows might be thought as having been pre-joined.
❑ A hash cluster stores specific rows in a location that can be deduced from mathematical manipulation of the row's key value.

INDEX CLUSTERS

Index clusters are a mechanism for storing related rows from one or more tables in the same block. Rows that have common cluster key values are stored together.

In theory, this speeds up joins because the rows to be joined are stored in the same block. In practice, multi-table index clusters are of severely limited value and should be used only when the tables are almost always referenced together. Here are some of the disadvantages of index clusters:

❑ Full table scans against only one of the tables in the cluster will be slower because blocks from other tables in the cluster will also need to be scanned.

❑ Inserts can be slower because of the additional effort required to maintain the cluster.

❑ The performance benefit for joins might be minimal.

❑ The internal structure can become degraded if the physical storage is not quite right.

Figure 5-18 shows how an index cluster would be implemented for the PRODUCTS and SALES tables.

Index clusters involve significant drawbacks in well-known circumstances and consequently are rarely used. We look at the performance issues relating to index clusters in Chapter 9, "Tuning Table Access."

HASH CLUSTERS

In a hash cluster, a mathematical transformation translates a key value into a storage address. In Oracle hash clusters, key values are translated into hash keys, and rows with the same hash key are stored together. This means that Oracle can navigate directly to the blocks required without the IO cost of an index lookup.

Hash clusters minimize the number of block reads required to locate a row using the hash key. With a hash cluster, retrieving the row in question might require only one block access—the access of the block containing the row. In comparison, a B*-Tree index requires at least four block reads (index header block, index branch block, index leaf block, and table block).

In addition to this reduction in IO, hash clusters can reduce contention for index hot blocks. As we see in Chapter 17, high levels of index-based lookups can result in latch contention and other contention for index root or branch blocks. Because there's no index involved in a hash cluster lookup, this contention can be reduced or eliminated.

Two significant considerations should be met for a hash cluster:

❑ The cluster key should have a high cardinality (large number of unique values). In fact, unique or primary keys are usually good candidates for the hash key.

❑ The hash key should normally be used to find rows by an exact lookup, rather than by a range or like condition.

> Consider hash clusters when you want to optimize primary key lookups or when you want to reduce index hot-block contention.

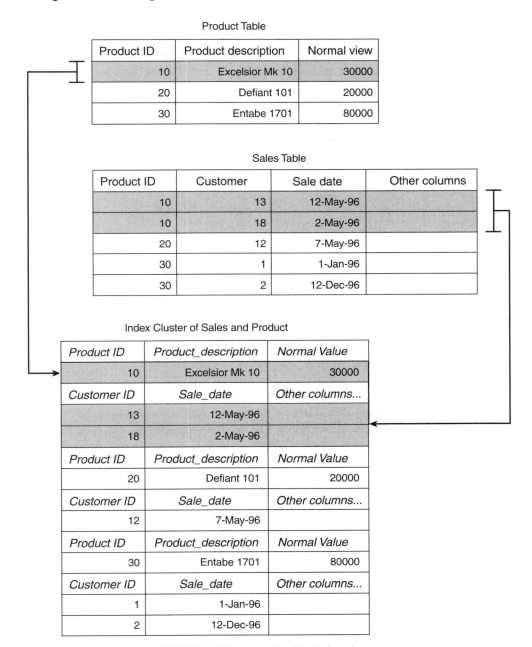

FIGURE 5-18   A multi-table index cluster.

Structure of Hash Clusters   When a hash cluster is created, it is necessary to specify the number of hash key values that are expected; this is done using the HASHKEYS clause of the CREATE CLUSTER statement. The SIZE clause of the CREATE CLUSTER statement determines the number of hash key values stored in each block. The initial size of the hash cluster will, therefore, be dependent on the setting of these two values.

The setting for SIZE and HASHKEYS is critical to the performance of the hash cluster. If HASHKEYS is set too high, the hash cluster becomes sparsely populated, and full table scan performance degrades. On the other hand, if HASHKEYS is set too low, multiple cluster keys will be allocated the same hash key. If too many key values are assigned to the same block, the block can over-flow and additional blocks need be *chained* to the primary block. When chaining occurs, cluster key lookups can require more than one IO to resolve, and the ben-efit of the hash cluster is reduced or eliminated.

By default, Oracle uses an internal algorithm to convert the cluster key into a hash value. This algorithm works well for most circumstances. However, you can also use the cluster key (if it is uniformly distributed), or you can specify your own function (written in PL/SQL).

Figure 5-19 shows an example of a hash cluster. The diagram illustrates some important principles:

❏   The hash key serves as a relative offset into the hash cluster. That is, after Oracle calculates the hash key, it can move directly to the relevant block in the hash cluster.

❏   The same amount of space is allocated for each hash value. If the space allo-cated is too high, space will be wasted, and the cluster will be sparsely pop-ulated—and this will degrade full table scan performance. (For instance, in Figure 5-19 the space allocated for hash key 3 is completely unused.)

❏   If the amount of space allocated for a hash value is too high, additional blocks will have to be chained. This degrades lookup performance because Oracle must perform additional IOs to get to the rows stored in these chained blocks. For instance, in Figure 5-19 the data for employee# 69 is stored in a chained block. Retrieving details for employee# 69 requires an additional IO.

HASHKEYS and SIZE Parameters   The major consideration in optimiz-ing the hash cluster is to accurately determine the SIZE and HASHKEYS settings. You need three pieces of information before you can calculate accurate values for these parameters:

❏   The number of rows in the hash cluster

❏   The number of distinct hash keys (for a unique index, equal to the number of rows in the cluster)

❏   The average length of a row in the hash cluster

Employee Table (unclustered)

Employee_id	Surname	Firstname	Date of Birth
10	Potter	Jean Luc	21/04/23
11	Smith	Ben	23/05/78
12	Thomas	Dianna	5/08/47
15	Jones	Katherine	11/11/34
89	Smith	Montgomery	19/02/20
34	Cane	Beverly	9/09/38
54	Main	Leonard	7/05/30
69	Ryder	William	3/06/40

Cluster key	Hash key
10	0
11	1
12	2
15	0
89	4
34	4
54	4
69	4

Table of conversion from cluster key to hash key

Hash Key	Employee_id	Surname	Firstname	Date of Birth
0	10	Potter	Jean Luc	21/04/23
	15	Jones	Katherine	11/11/34
1	11	Smith	Ben	23/05/78
2	12	Thomas	Dianna	5/08/47
3				
4	89	Smith	Montgomery	19/02/20
	34	Cane	Beverly	9/09/38
	54	Main	Leonard	7/05/30

Hash Cluster of the Employee Table

4	69	Ryder	William	3/06/40

FIGURE 5-19 Structure of a hash cluster.

After this information is obtained, you can calculate approximate values for HASHKEYS and SIZE as follows:

$$HASHKEYS = number\_of\_distinct\_hash\_keys\_values$$

$$SIZE = \frac{total\_rows}{HASHKEYS} \times average\_row\_length \times 1.1$$

In the case of a unique key, set HASHKEYS to the number of rows in the table and SIZE to the average row length plus 10 percent to allow for variation in row sizes. (This is the 1.1 ratio in the preceding formula.)

If the data to be included in the hash table is already in a nonclustered table and the table has been analyzed, you can get an estimate of the average row length and the number of rows in the table with a query like this one:

```
SQL> SELECT avg_row_len, num_rows
  2    FROM all_tables
  3   WHERE owner = 'SH' AND table_name = 'CUSTOMERS'
  4  /

AVG_ROW_LEN    NUM_ROWS
-----------   ----------
        180       55500
```

You can get the number of distinct values for a column with a query such as this:

```
SQL> SELECT num_distinct
  2    FROM all_tab_columns
  3   WHERE owner = 'SH' AND table_name = 'CUSTOMERS'
        AND column_name = 'CUST_LAST_NAME'
  4  /

NUM_DISTINCT
------------
         908
```

So, if we wanted to move the CUSTOMERS table into a hash cluster with CUST_LAST_NAME as the hash key (not that this would necessarily be a good choice for a cluster key), we could set hash keys to a value of approximately 908 (the number of distinct key values) and use the formula below to estimate SIZE:

$$SIZE = \frac{55500}{908} \times 180 \times 1.1 = 12102$$

If the number of rows in the table increases, the preceding calculations cease to be valid and the hash cluster can become de-optimized. Oracle will run out of space in the hash cluster for new rows, and blocks will need to be chained. Rows in these chained blocks will require extra IOs to access, and the hash cluster will lose its advantage over a B*-Tree index. Figure 5-20 shows the effect on I/O when this occurs.

Figure 5-20 and Figure 5-21 illustrate the IO requirements for key lookups and full table scans for an indexed table and for two differently configured hash clusters containing the same data. The hash cluster can offer better performance for a key lookup but only if the cluster is appropriately configured. Table scans of the hash clusters tended to require some additional IO, but the magnitude of the overhead again depends on the configuration of the hash cluster. Ironically, the hash configuration that leads to the best lookup performance resulted in the worst table scan performance.

On the other hand, if we over-configure the SIZE parameter, we risk wasting database space and degrading the performance of full table scans (as shown in Figure 5-21).

If you think this all sounds like too much trouble, most of the time you would be right. The gains from a hash cluster are quite marginal compared to B*-Tree index lookups and can easily go bad if your SIZE and HASHKEYS calculations are out. However, hash clusters can also be effective in reducing *cache buffers chains latch* contention (see Chapter 17).

Ensure that you use only hash clusters for static tables or be prepared to rebuild the hash cluster periodically. When deciding on a hash cluster, ensure that the SIZE and HASHKEYS parameters are correctly configured.

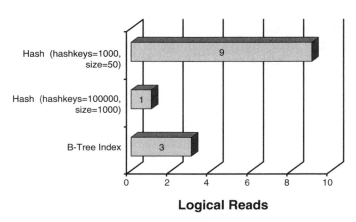

Logical Reads

FIGURE 5-20   Performance of two hash clusters compared to a B*-Tree index lookup.

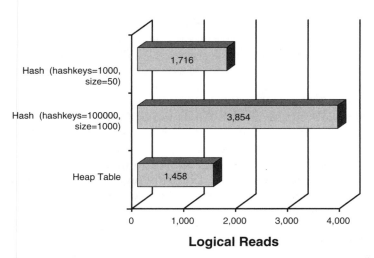

FIGURE 5-21   Full table scan performance for two hash clusters and a normal heap table.

The approach to sizing a hash cluster outlined above assumes that hash keys will be distributed evenly throughout the hash cluster. This assumption is usually a safe one; Oracle's internal hashing algorithm has been designed to evenly distribute values across a wide range of data types and distributions. However, if you know that Oracle's hash function will lead to unevenly distributed hash keys, you can use the HASH IS syntax of the CREATE CLUSTER command to specify the hash function. There are two ways to do this.

❑ If you know that your cluster key will be evenly distributed, you can specify the cluster key. This works only if the cluster key is an integer.
❑ You can specify your own hash function, written in PL/SQL.

Sorted Hash Clusters   In a sorted hash cluster, additional cluster keys are defined that optimize the retrieval of data in a sorted order. For instance, in the following cluster definition, we can use the hash key to lookup customer orders, which will be returned by order date:

```
CREATE CLUSTER ghOrderCluster (
   customer_id NUMBER(8),
   order_date  DATE SORT )
  HASHKEYS 200 HASH IS customer_id
  SIZE 50000 ;

CREATE TABLE g_SORTED_HASH (
   customer_id       NUMBER(8),
   order_date        DATE    SORT,
   order_id          number(8),
```

```
         order_quantity number(10) )
      CLUSTER ghOrderCluster (
      customer_id,order_date );
```

Oracle maintains an internal index that is used to retrieve the rows in sorted order and, at least as far as the execution plan shows, avoids an explicit sort operation. However although there is no sort shown in the explain plan, other statistics do record a sort operation:

```
SQL>   SELECT *
   2     FROM g_SORTED_HASH
   3     WHERE customer_id = 50 order by order_date;

5000 rows selected.

Elapsed: 00:00:01.28

Execution Plan
----------------------------------------------------------
Plan hash value: 1637272916


--------------------------------------------------------------------------
| Id  | Operation          | Name          | Rows  | Bytes | Cost (%CPU)|
--------------------------------------------------------------------------
|   0 | SELECT STATEMENT   |               |  4963 |  189K |    1   (0) |
|*  1 |   TABLE ACCESS HASH| G_SORTED_HASH |  4963 |  189K |    1   (0) |
--------------------------------------------------------------------------

Predicate Information (identified by operation id):
---------------------------------------------------

   1 - access("CUSTOMER_ID"=50)


Statistics
----------------------------------------------------------
         13  recursive calls
          0  db block gets
       4926  consistent gets
         70  physical reads
          0  redo size
     247830  bytes sent via SQL*Net to client
       4044  bytes received via SQL*Net from client
```

```
 335   SQL*Net roundtrips to/from client
   2   sorts (memory)
   0   sorts (disk)
5000   rows processed
```

Sorted hash clusters sound like they should optimize the retrieval of rows for a particular hash key in sorted order, but performance tests have been disappointing. The internal structure of the sorted hash appears to be sparser than that of a normal hash cluster, resulting in degraded full table scan performance. Furthermore, in simple tests the additional IO involved from accessing the hidden index has actually increased the overhead of the actual operations that are supposed to be optimized.

NESTED TABLES

A *nested table* is an object type that has the characteristics of a relational table. You can define a column in another table as being of that object type. The result is that one table appears to be nested within the column of the other. Figure 5-22 shows the logical structure of a nested table.

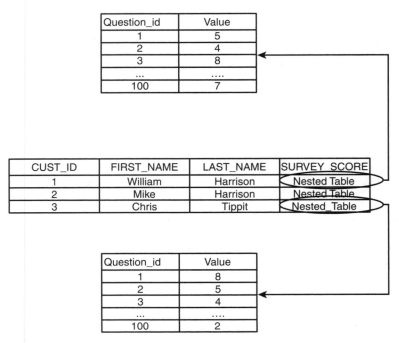

FIGURE 5-22   Nested table logical structure.

A nested table looks like it is clustered with the detail rows stored inside the master rows, but in reality two segments are created: one for the main table and one for all the rows in the nested table. Consequently, there is often little or no performance improvement gained from a nested table. Furthermore, the SQL syntax to deal with nested tables is Oracle-specific at best and downright difficult at worst.

However, if you decide on a nested table solution, be aware that the nested table segment by default is unindexed, and full table scans will be performed whenever you access any of the nested values. One way to avoid this is to define the nested table as an IOT and including the NESTED_TABLE_ID column as part of the primary key. The following code provides an example of doing this with a cluster based on the CUSTOMERS table.

```
-- nested table row structure
CREATE OR REPLACE TYPE survey_ot AS OBJECT (
    item_number    NUMBER,
    score          INT);
/
-- Nested table type
CREATE OR REPLACE TYPE survey_nt_typ AS TABLE OF survey_ot;
/

-- Table containing nested table
CREATE TABLE customers_ntiot_survey
(
    cust_id                NUMBER NOT NULL PRIMARY KEY,
    cust_first_name        VARCHAR2(20) NOT NULL,
    cust_last_name         VARCHAR2(40) NOT NULL,
    cust_gender            CHAR(1) NOT NULL,
    cust_year_of_birth     NUMBER(4,0) NOT NULL,
    cust_marital_status    VARCHAR2(20),
    cust_street_address    VARCHAR2(40) NOT NULL,
    cust_postal_code       VARCHAR2(10) NOT NULL,
    cust_city              VARCHAR2(30) NOT NULL,
    survey                 survey_nt_typ )
  NESTED TABLE survey STORE AS survey_nt_iot
   ((PRIMARY KEY(nested_table_id,item_number) )
    ORGANIZATION INDEX COMPRESS);
```

Nested tables have few performance advantages and have many programmatic drawbacks. However, if you create a nested table, use INDEX organization to avoid unnecessary table scans on the nested segment.

CHOOSING THE BEST INDEXING STRATEGY

We've seen that B*-Tree indexes, Bitmap indexes, and hash clusters each have significant advantages in reasonably familiar scenarios. Index clusters and IOTs might have their uses but are much less widely applicable. Let's review the advantages and disadvantages of our three favorites:

❑ Oracle's default index type—the B*-Tree index—is suitable for improving access for a wide range of queries. B*-Tree indexes can optimize exact lookups and range queries and can sometimes be used to resolve queries without accessing the underlying table.

❑ The hash cluster enables you to store table data in a location that is derived from a mathematical manipulation of a key value. Hash clusters can improve access for exact key lookups but cannot enhance range queries and require careful sizing to prevent degradation of the hash cluster. They can be effective in reducing certain types of latch contention.

❑ Bitmap indexes are useful to optimize queries in which multiple columns of relatively low cardinality (few distinct values) are queried in combination. Unlike B*-Tree indexes, bitmap indexes can work for any combination of columns but increase the chance of lock contention.

Table 5-1 compares the advantages and disadvantages of each strategy for typical processing scenarios.

Table 5-1   Comparison of B*-Tree Indexes, Bitmap Indexes, and Hash Clusters

SITUATION	B*-TREE INDEXES	HASH CLUSTER	BITMAP INDEXES
Exact key lookup on a column with lots of values.	Yes.	Yes.	Yes. Bitmap indexes can still be effective for high-cardinality columns.
Exact key lookups on multiple columns.	Yes.	Yes.	Yes.
Queries on multiple columns in various combinations.	Yes, but you probably need multiple concatenated indexes to support the various combinations.	No. The hash cluster can support only a single combination of values.	Yes. Bitmap indexes can support any combination of columns provided all have a bitmap index.
Queries on ranges of values (>, <, BETWEEN)	Yes.	No. Hash clusters do not support range queries.	Possibly not. It is possible to perform range scans on bitmap indexes, but because it involves accessing multiple bitmaps, it might be less efficient than a B*-Tree index.

SITUATION	B*-TREE INDEXES	HASH CLUSTER	BITMAP INDEXES
Table is subject to high rates on update, insert, or delete.	Yes.	Maybe, but if the over-all size of the table changes markedly you will probably want to rebuild with new HASHKEYS and/or SIZE values.	Probably not. Locking on tables with bitmap indexes is very restric-tive.
You want to enforce UNIQUEness.	Yes.	No.	No.
Table changes in size over time.	Yes.	Only if you can either afford to rebuild the table periodically (to avoid overflows) or can afford to allocate space up front for future growth (degrading table scans).	Yes.
You want to search for null values.	No.	No.	Yes.

If you are in doubt about the most appropriate indexing strategy you will usually be safe using Oracle's default B*-Tree index. The B*-Tree index can be useful across a wide range of circumstances and requires less administration and care than other indexing methods.

SUMMARY

Indexes exist primarily to improve performance, so establishing an optimal in-dexing strategy is critical to database performance.

Oracle's default index is the B*-Tree index, which is applicable across a wide range of circumstances but is not useful for columns that have few distinct values. Creating concatenated, multicolumn B*-Tree indexes to increase selectiv-ity and optimize anticipated multicolumn queries is a fundamental tuning activity.

Indexes add to the overhead of DML—UPDATE, INSERT, MERGE, and DELETE—so every index should pay its way in terms of performance gains.

Bitmap indexes can work more efficiently than B*-Tree indexes for low-cardinality columns (those with few distinct values) and can be merged more effi-ciently than B*-Tree indexes. However, bitmap indexes increase lock contention and should not normally be used in OLTP environments.

Hash clusters can provide faster primary key lookup performance than B*-Tree indexes, providing that the cluster is well configured. Hash clusters also reduce hot block and latch contention under certain circumstances. However, hash clusters can underperform if not carefully configured and might need to be rebuilt from time to time if they change in size.

Index clusters, index only tables, and nested tables can be used in place of traditional indexing in some circumstances. However, each has significant drawbacks and should be chosen only after careful consideration.

APPLICATION DESIGN AND IMPLEMENTATION

In this chapter we look at how to design and implement an application that works efficiently and effectively with the Oracle database server.

Typical optimization efforts focus on tuning SQL statements after the application is built, and we have several chapters devoted to SQL tuning. Overall application design can, however, also make an enormous difference in performance. Poor design can lead to intractable performance issues that can't always be resolved by tuning individual SQLs.

Here are some of the techniques we explore in this chapter:

❑ Reducing the volume of requests from the application to the database server. This can be done by eliminating any unnecessary SQL execution requests and reducing excessive SQL parse requests through the use of bind variables and effective cursor management.

❑ Reducing network overhead and unnecessary network round trips by exploiting the array fetch and insert interface, and by using stored procedures when appropriate.

❑ Reducing application lock contention through sensible transaction design and locking strategies.

SQL STATEMENT MANAGEMENT

Even simple SQL requests are relatively expensive operations; the application must transmit the request to the server, which must parse, prepare, and execute the SQL, possibly incurring physical IO before returning results to the application. An application should, therefore, avoid issuing unnecessary SQL requests. "Unnecessary" requests include

- ❏ Requests to parse a SQL statement that has already been parsed
- ❏ Requests to the database for static (unchanging) data that has recently been requested

OPTIMIZING PARSING

We first discussed *parsing* in Chapter 2, "Oracle Architecture and Concepts." Parsing is the process of preparing a SQL statement for execution and involves checking the syntax, permissions, and object validity and the creation of an *execution plan*, which describes the step-by-step process Oracle undertakes to resolve the SQL statement.

Oracle maintains a cache of SQL statements in the *shared pool*. If a matching SQL is found in the shared pool, most of the parse overhead can be avoided. A parse where a match is found in the shared pool is called a *soft parse*. If no matching SQL is found, a *hard parse* must be performed.

Hard parsing not only consumes CPU but can also create contention when too many sessions try to cache SQLs in the shared pool simultaneously. We are, therefore, strongly motivated to reduce parsing and in particular hard parsing. We achieve this minimization by the use of *bind variables* and through good *cursor management*.

Bind Variables and Cursor Management   The client-side representation of the SQL statement is called a *cursor* (or *context area*). In low-level programming languages such as C++, the Oracle APIs require that you explicitly create the cursor. In higher level languages such as Java or C#, the cursor is represented as a more abstract SQL statement object.

In the following Java snippet, a SQL *statement* object corresponding to a cursor is created, executed, and discarded:

```
Statement s=oracleConnection.createStatement();
s.execute("UPDATE sh.customers SET cust_valid = 'Y'"+
        " WHERE cust_id = 1");
s.close();
```

If your application does nothing but execute a single SQL, this is probably okay. But it's common for a SQL statement to be executed more than once, selecting or modifying different rows with each execution. This next Java snippet issues an UPDATE statement once for every customer ID held in the *custIdList* array:

```
1    for (int custId : custIdList) {
2        Statement stmt = oracleConnection.createStatement();
3        stmt.execute("UPDATE sh.customers SET cust_valid = 'Y'"
4                + " WHERE cust_id = " + custId);
5        stmt.close();
6    }
```

The loop starting on line 1 iterates through an array of CUST_ID values. For each CUST_ID, we create a statement object (line 2) and then construct and execute an UPDATE statement once for each customer in the list. We concatenate the *custId* from the list into the SQL string on line 4.

This works of course, but each UPDATE statement needs to be parsed and executed. This parse overhead can be significant. Furthermore, because each SQL is unique—it includes the hardcoded *custId*—we're unlikely to find a matching SQL in the shared pool. Therefore, a *hard parse*—one in which no matching SQL is found in the shared pool—will be required.

It's far better to create and parse the SQL statement only once and then execute multiple times using *bind variables* to identify the parameters to the SQL statement.

The next example shows this technique in Java. The SQL statement is created as a *PreparedStatement* and includes a *bind variable*—identified as :custId—which acts as a placeholder for the parameters to the SQL. The variable is assigned a value on line 5 prior to the execution on line 6.

```
1    PreparedStatement stmt = oracleConnection.prepare Statement(
2            "UPDATE sh.customers SET cust_valid = 'Y'"
3        + " WHERE cust_id = :custId");
4    for (int custId : custIdList) {
5        stmt.setInt(1, custId);
6        stmt.execute();
7    }
```

Using this technique radically reduces the parse overhead of SQL execution. Figure 6-1 shows the reduction in execution time when the two examples are executed with a list of 1,000 customer IDs; execution time is more than halved by the use of bind variables.

In addition to the reduction in execution time for the individual application, using bind variables reduces the chance of latch or mutex contention for SQL statements in the shared pool. If many sessions are concurrently trying to add new SQL statements to the shared pool, some might need to wait on the *library*

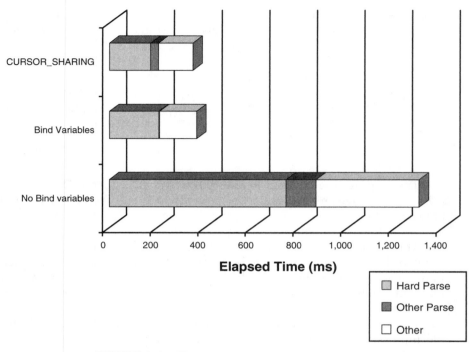

FIGURE 6-1 Elapsed time to execute 1,000 SQLs.

cache mutex (or *latch* prior to Oracle version 10.2). This is a common form of contention that we revisit in Chapter 16 "Latch and Mutex Contention."

> Using bind variables and avoiding unnecessary reparsing radically reduces the parse overhead of SQL statements and reduces latch/mutex contention.

If you need to implement bind variables but can't change existing application code all is not lost. The CURSOR_SHARING parameter can be set to instruct Oracle to transparently replace literals with bind variables. For instance, when CURSOR_SHARING=FORCE, Oracle will transparently replace this SQL statement:

```
UPDATE sh.customers
   SET cust_valid = 'Y'
 WHERE cust_id = 998
```

With this one:

```
UPDATE sh.customers
   SET cust_valid = :"SYS_B_0"
 WHERE cust_id = :"SYS_B_1"
```

Oracle then substitutes the appropriate values into the system generated bind variables as appropriate. Figure 6-1 compares the performance of this approach with the use of bind variables and with literal values. As you can see, using CURSOR_SHARING results in similar performance to the use of bind variables.

CURSOR_SHARING can take the following values:

EXACT   This is the default setting. No substitution of bind variables for literals will occur.

SIMILAR   Bind variables will be substituted for literal values only if this substitution could not change the execution plan. In some cases, different values of literals can result in different execution plans. If the optimizer determines that this is the case, substitution will not occur.

FORCE   Bind variables will be substituted for literal values whenever possible.

If you can't change application code to exploit bind variables, you might be able to use the CURSOR_SHARING parameter to get a similar outcome.

Identifying SQLs Without Bind Variables   You can identify SQLs that might benefit from bind variables or CURSOR_SHARING by exploiting the FORCE_MATCHING_SIGNATURE column in V$SQL. The FORCE_MATCHING_SIGNATURE column will identify SQLs that would have the same signature *if* bind variables or CURSOR_SHARING were implemented. In other words, two SQLs that are identical other than for the values of literals will have the same FORCE_MATCH_SIGNATURE, indicating that these SQLs would be the *same* SQL if bind variables or CURSOR_SHARING was employed.

The following SQL uses the FORCE_MATCH_SIGNATURE to identify such SQLS:

```
SQL> WITH force_matches AS
  2          (SELECT force_matching_signature,
  3                  COUNT( * )  matches,
  4                  MAX(sql_id || child_number) max_sql_child,
  5                  DENSE_RANK() OVER (ORDER BY COUNT( * ) DESC)
  6                      ranking
  7          FROM v$sql
```

```
  8        WHERE force_matching_signature <> 0
  9          AND parsing_schema_name <> 'SYS'
 10        GROUP BY force_matching_signature
 11        HAVING COUNT( * ) > 5)
 12  SELECT sql_id,      matches, parsing_schema_name schema, sql_text
 13    FROM       v$sql JOIN force_matches
 14      ON (sql_id || child_number = max_sql_child)
 15  WHERE ranking <= 10
 16  ORDER BY matches DESC;


SQL_ID              MATCHES SCHEMA
------------     ---------- --------------------
SQL_TEXT
---------------------------------------------------------------------
gzwmz9fzvfkbx        4352 OPSG
select sum(amount_sold)  from sh.sales where cust_id=103215

g1pz6zd253frb          39 OPSG
Select prod_name from sh.products where prod_id=119
```

This query identifies two SQLs that have more than five variations in the Oracle SQL cache. In both instances we can see that literals rather than bind variables have been used (to supply the CUST_ID and PROD_ID values). These SQLs should probably be reworked to use bind variables, or if this is not convenient, perhaps the CURSOR_SHARING parameter should be considered.

AVOIDING UNNECESSARY SQL EXECUTIONS

No matter how well you tune your SQL, each SQL query will involve some overhead. Control must be passed from your application to the Oracle server—often across a network—which must undertake complex processing for even the simplest of SQLs. Any steps you can take to reduce the number of SQL statement executions will be effective in improving the performance of the application and reduce unnecessary load on the database.

Anjo Kolk, the creator of the Yet Another Performance Profiling (YAPP) methodology and pioneer of the Oracle wait interface, sums up this principle as "The best tuned SQL is the SQL you didn't execute."

It's an obvious but easily overlooked point: We can spend a lot of time trying to tune the SQLs that the application sends to the database, but are we sure that all the SQLs are actually necessary? For instance, consider the following PL/SQL code; the SELECT statement on line 4 will be executed once for each EMPLOYEE, although it returns the same value every time.

```
 1 FOR r IN (SELECT *
 2                 FROM hr.employees)
 3    LOOP
 4       SELECT department_name
 5         INTO v_department_name
 6         FROM hr.departments
 7        WHERE department_id = r.department_id;
 8
 9       IF v_department_name = 'MARKETING'
10       THEN
11          -- do something funky to the marketing guys here
12          NULL;
13       END IF;
14    END LOOP;
```

We could improve the preceding example by using a join between EMPLOYEES and DEPARTMENTS, or by pre-fetching the DEPARTMENT_ID that corresponds to the marketing department:

```
 1    SELECT department_id
 2      INTO v_marketing_id
 3      FROM hr.departments
 4     WHERE department_name = 'Marketing';
 5
 6    FOR r IN (SELECT *
 7                 FROM hr.employees)
 8    LOOP
 9       IF r.department_id = v_marketing_id
10       THEN
11          -- do something funky to the marketing guys here
12          NULL;
13       END IF;
14    END LOOP;
```

Applications should avoid issuing unnecessary or redundant SQL statements.

Data Caching   One of the most effective ways of reducing SQL calls is to cache frequently accessed data within your application. This involves allocating an area of local memory—usually an array variable or PL/SQL collection—and storing data items retrieved from the database in this memory. When a new data item is required, the program will first scan the cache to see if it has already been read. If the data is found in the cache, a database access is avoided. If not found, the data item can be retrieved from the database and stored in the cache.

The following code shows a cache created in PL/SQL:

```
CREATE OR REPLACE PACKAGE BODY clientcaching IS

    TYPE prodcachetype IS TABLE
        OF oe.product_information.list_price%TYPE
                            INDEX BY BINARY_INTEGER;
    g_pricecache    prodcachetype;

    FUNCTION getprodprice(p_product_id NUMBER)
        RETURN NUMBER IS
        v_list_value    oe.product_information.list_price%TYPE;
    BEGIN
        --Look in the PL/SQL table for the product_id
        BEGIN
            v_list_value := g_pricecache(p_product_id); --Found!
        EXCEPTION
            WHEN NO_DATA_FOUND THEN
                -- Not found in the cache so get it and
                -- add it to the cache
                SELECT list_price
                  INTO v_list_value
                  FROM oe.product_information
                 WHERE product_id = p_product_id;

                g_pricecache(p_product_id) := v_list_value;
        END;
        RETURN (v_list_value);
    END;

END;
```

The function *getprodprice* is responsible for returning the list price for a given product_id. If the product_id has not been encountered before, the routine fetches it from the table and stores it in the cache. In this way, the application will never fetch the LIST_PRICE for a specific product twice. Of course, this approach should be used only when we are confident that the table data is not going to change during the life of the session. Otherwise we will need complex synchronization logic to ensure that the cache is flushed when the table is subjected to DML. Triggers can form the basis of this synchronization, but because some DML operations bypass triggers, the approach involves some risk.

Caching is particularly suitable for small, frequently accessed tables that contain static lookup values.

Here are some considerations to keep in mind when implementing caching:

❑ Caches consume memory. In PL/SQL the memory will be on the database server;[1] in other languages the memory might be allocated within the application server or on the desktop computer. In many environments, memory is abundant and the memory consumed by caching relatively small. However, for large caches and memory-constrained environments, the implementation of a caching strategy could actually degrade performance by contributing the memory shortages on the database server, the application layer, or on the desktop.

❑ When caches are relatively small, sequential scanning (that is, examining each entry in the cache from the first entry to the last) will probably result in adequate performance. However, if the cache is larger, the sequential scan response time will increase. To maintain good performance, it might be necessary to implement advanced search techniques such as hashing or binary chop. In our preceding example, the cache was effectively indexed by PRODUCT_ID and would, therefore, remain efficient regardless of the number of products involved.

❑ If the table being cached is updated during program execution, the changes might not be reflected in your cache unless you implement some sophisticated synchronization mechanism. For this reason, application caching is best performed on static tables.

> Caching frequently accessed data from small or medium-sized static tables can be very effective in improving program performance. However, beware of memory utilization and program complexity issues.

The 11g Client-Side Result Cache   Oracle 11g enables us to get the benefits from client-side data caching without the need to implement our own caching code. The 11g client-side result set cache—officially known as the *OCI consistent client cache*—stores recently retrieved result sets in the client's memory. If a client program, such as SQL*Plus, Java, C#, or whatever, issues the same query twice within a configurable interval, the client-side cache will return the previously fetched result set without sending the query to the database server.

---

[1] Usually in server process memory (the PGA), but when shared servers (Multi-Threaded Servers or MTS) are involved, the cache consumes shared memory (in the SGA). Chapter 20, "Other Memory Management Topics," discusses the impact of these sorts of memory allocations on the database.

Figure 6-2 compares the performance of the OCI consistent cache against manual caching using the sample PL/SQL code presented in the previous section and against no caching. In this example, the OCI cache compared favorably with the manual cache.

You enable and configure the client result cache as follows:

1. Set a nonzero value for the parameter CLIENT_RESULT_CACHE_SIZE; this is the amount of memory each client program will dedicate to the cache.

2. Enable caching for all or selected SQLs. There are three ways to do this:

   a. Annotate the queries to use the cache with the RESULT_CACHE hint.

   b. From 11g Release 2 forward, you can use the RESULT_CACHE (MODE FORCE) clause in an ALTER TABLE or CREATE TABLE statement. SQL statements that reference these tables will be eligible for inclusion in the cache.

   c. Set the parameter RESULT_CACHE_MODE to FORCE. Setting RESULT_CACHE_MODE to FORCE causes all SQLs to be cached unless the SQL includes a NO_RESULT_CACHE hint. Forced caching should generally not be considered when the server side result set cache is enabled because there is a risk of significant result set cache latch contention. See Chapter 20 for details of the server side result set cache.

3. Consider adjusting CLIENT_RESULT_CACHE_LAG to control how long result sets stay in the cache. The default setting of 3000ms means that results older than 3 seconds will be discarded.

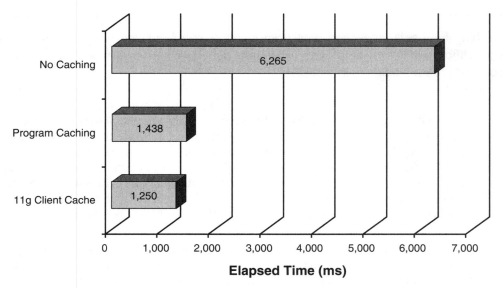

FIGURE 6-2 Performance gains from application data caching.

Although the client result set cache can certainly speed up repetitive SQL executions, you should be cautious about the client cache. In particular

❏ The setting of CLIENT_RESULT_CACHE_LAG is critical; too low and the cache will be ineffective; but set it too high and out-of-date results might be returned.

❏ The RESULT_CACHE_MODE setting affects both the client-side and server-side result set cache. We discuss the server-side cache in Chapter 20. However, note that in the server side cache, results become deactivated when DML renders the results stale, which can result in a better balance between stale data and cache effectiveness.

Consider caching static, frequently referenced data within your application code if possible. The OCI consistent client cache can provide an easy way to enable client-side caching.

Oracle 11g also offers a server-side result set and a PL/SQL function cache that perform a similar function to the client-side cache but which reside within shared pool memory on the server. This cache can store result sets or the results of PL/SQL functions. Effectively using this server-side cache might require application coding changes, such as using the RESULT_CACHE hint or the RESULT CACHE clause in PL/SQL functions. The PL/SQL function cache is covered in detail in Chapter 12, "Using and Tuning PL/SQL," and the Result set cache in Chapter 20.

THE ARRAY INTERFACE

Oracle can retrieve rows from the database one at a time, or it can retrieve rows in batches, sometimes called *arrays*. *Array fetch* refers to the mechanism by which Oracle can retrieve multiple rows in a single fetch operation. Fetching rows in batches reduces the number of calls issued to the database server and can also reduce network traffic and logical IO overhead.

IMPLEMENTING ARRAY FETCH

In some tools, it's necessary to explicitly define the arrays to receive the data. In other tools, the array processing is performed transparently, and the size of the array is established by a configuration parameter. In PL/SQL we use the BULK COLLECT INTO clause to fetch rows into a PL/SQL collection as in this example:

```
DECLARE
   TYPE cust_id_type IS TABLE OF sh.customers.cust_id%TYPE
      INDEX BY BINARY_INTEGER;

   TYPE cust_last_name_type IS TABLE
      OF sh.customers.cust_last_name%TYPE
      INDEX BY BINARY_INTEGER;

   cust_id_list      cust_id_type;
   cust_name_list    cust_last_name_type;
BEGIN
   SELECT cust_id, cust_last_name
      BULK COLLECT INTO cust_id_list, cust_name_list
      FROM sh.customers;
END;
```

The preceding example fetches all the rows from the table into the collection in a single operation. For larger tables you probably will want to employ the LIMIT clause and fetch the data in smaller batches. Chapter 12 provides details on optimizing PL/SQL bulk collect.

In Java, the array fetch size can be set by the *setFetchSize* method:

```
PreparedStatement
stmt=oracleConnection.prepareStatement(sqlText);
stmt.setFetchSize(20);
ResultSet r=stmt.executeQuery();
while (r.next()) {
    //Do something with the results
}
```

Figure 6-3 shows the relationship between the size of the fetch array and the response time for a 55,000-row query. We can see that even relatively small array sizes (less than 20 rows per fetch) can result in significant reductions in processing time. There are diminishing returns as the array size increases.

Use array fetches to retrieve batches of rows from the database in a single call. This will reduce both database and network overhead. In general, array fetch can provide approximately an order of magnitude (10 times) improvement for bulk queries.

Array fetch works in two ways to improve performance: It reduces the number of network round trips between the client and the server, *and* it reduces the number of logical reads on the server. As we reduce the number of fetch calls,

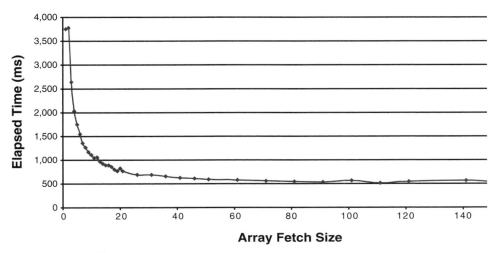

FIGURE 6-3   Effects of increasing array size on table scan performance.

we reduce the network round trips until the point at which each network packet is full of rows. The point at which this occurs depends on the length of the rows we are retrieving.

The reduction in logical reads occurs because each array fetch will usually find that some of the rows it needs are located in the same blocks. Therefore, the larger the array size, the more rows will be piggy-backed on blocks that have already been requested. When the array size is low, the same blocks will be requested over and over again.

Figure 6-4 shows network round trips and logical reads diminishing as the array fetch size is increased.

ARRAY INSERT

Array processing is available for DML as well as for queries. It is most useful for inserts, and performing array inserts results in a throughput improvement similar to that provided by array fetch. The technique varies from language to language. In PL/SQL we use the FORALL command to insert a collection in a single operation:

```
DECLARE
    TYPE xtype IS TABLE OF arrayinserttest.x%TYPE
        INDEX BY BINARY_INTEGER;

    TYPE ytype IS TABLE OF arrayinserttest.y%TYPE
        INDEX BY BINARY_INTEGER;
```

```
   xlist    xtype;
   ylist    ytype;
BEGIN
   FOR i IN 1 .. 100
   LOOP
      xlist (i) := i;
      ylist (i) := 'This is number ' || i;
   END LOOP;

   FORALL i IN 1 .. xlist.COUNT
      INSERT INTO arrayinserttest
                  (x, y)
           VALUES (xlist (i), ylist (i));
END;
```

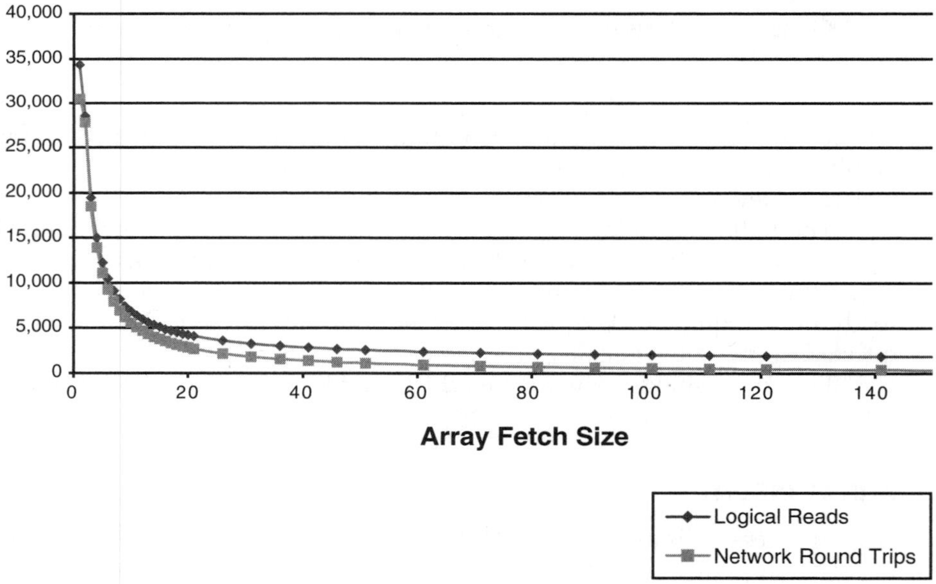

FIGURE 6-4   Higher array fetch sizes reduce network round trips and logical reads.

In Java, the *addBatch* and *executeBatch* methods allow us to insert multiple rows in a single operation. This technique is illustrated in the following code snippet:

```
PreparedStatement InsertStmt = oracleConnection
        .prepareStatement("INSERT INTO arrayInsertTest "
                    + " (x,y)  VALUES (:1,:2)");
```

```
int batchSize = 10;
for (int i = 1; i < 1000; i++) {
     InsertStmt.setInt(1, i);
     InsertStmt.setString(2, "This is number " + i);
     InsertStmt.addBatch();
     if (i % batchSize == 0) {
         InsertStmt.executeBatch();
     }
}
InsertStmt.executeBatch();
```

Array insert and other ways of optimizing DML—INSERT, UPDATE, DELETE, and MERGE—are discussed in Chapter 14, "DML Tuning."

TRANSACTION DESIGN

A *transaction* is a set of one or more SQL statements that are logically grouped together and that must be either applied to the database in their entirety or not applied at all.

We expect database transactions to conform to the ACID principle, which means that transactions should be

❏   **Atomic**—The transaction is indivisible; either all the statements in the transaction are applied to the database or none are.

❏   **Consistent**—The database remains in a consistent state before and after transaction execution.

❏   **Isolated**—Although multiple transactions can be executed by one or more users simultaneously, one transaction should not see the effects of other concurrent transactions.

❏   **Durable**—When a transaction is committed to the database, its changes are expected to *persist*. Even if users turn off their computer or the database server goes down, the changes will be saved. This usually means that the result of the transaction must be written to a nonvolatile form of storage, such as a hard disk. (Alternatively, it could be redundantly stored in multiple memory stores, written to battery-backed memory or solid state disk.)

Locks are an essential mechanism in any transactional multiuser database system: The ACID (Atomic-Consistent-Independent-Durable) properties of a transaction can be implemented only by restricting simultaneous changes to the database. This is achieved by placing locks on modified data. These locks persist until the transaction ends, usually by issuing a COMMIT or ROLLBACK statement. (Although note that DDL statements implicitly issue a COMMIT.)

ISOLATION LEVELS

Isolation levels determine the degree to which transactions in one session can affect the data seen or accessed by another session. All isolation levels are compromises between *concurrency*, the capability of multiple sessions to perform operations on the database at the same time, and *consistency*, the degree to which a session sees a logical and correct view of the data regardless of what activities might be going on in other sessions.

Oracle supports three isolation levels:

❏ **READ COMMITTED**—This is Oracle's default isolation level. At this isolation level, only committed rows can be seen by a transaction. Furthermore, any changes committed after a statement commences cannot be seen by that statement. For example, if you have a long-running SELECT statement in session A that queries from the BOOKS table, and session B inserts a row into BOOKS while A's query is still running, that new row will *not* be visible to the SELECT running in A.

❏ **READ ONLY**—The transaction must not perform any DML. Every read within the transaction is consistent to the time at which the transaction commenced. That is, the transaction will not see the effects of any DML executed in another session that occurred since the READ ONLY transaction commenced.

❏ **SERIALIZABLE**—At this isolation level, every transaction is completely isolated so that transactions behave as if they had executed serially, one after the other. As in the READ ONLY isolation level, the transaction returns results that are consistent with the state of the database at the commencement on the transaction. In addition, if the transaction attempts to update a row that has changed since the start of the transaction, the transaction will fail.

Both READ ONLY and SERIALIZABLE isolation levels place an extra burden on Oracle. To return results that are consistent as at the start of the transaction, Oracle has to read from *undo segment* information (see Chapter 2, "Oracle Architecture and Concepts") to construct the consistent view. This might increase the number of blocks that need to be processed and increase the amount of undo segment storage required.

Figure 6-5 shows the consistent reads required for two identical queries issued under SERIALIZABLE and READ COMMITTED (default) isolation levels. In both cases, a query of SH.CUSTOMERS was conducted after an update against the same table had been issued. The SERIALIZABLE transaction needed to reconstruct the pre-update state of the table using rollback segment data. The READ COMMITED transaction was able to simply read the most recent state and hence required fewer logical reads.

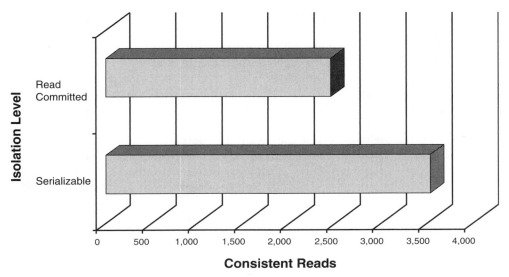

FIGURE 6-5   Serializable or read-only transactions can result in additional logical read overhead.

TRANSACTIONS AND LOCKS

Without locks, a change made by one transaction could be overwritten by another transaction that executes at the same time. Consider, for example, the scenario shown in Figure 6-6. When two different sessions try to update the same account, we encounter some obvious difficulties if locks are not in place.

In this scenario, account number 2 starts with a balance of $2,000. Transaction A reduces the balance of the account by $100. Before transaction A commits,

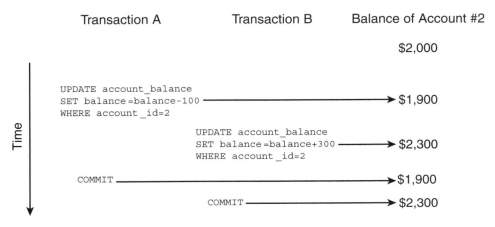

FIGURE 6-6   Transaction without locks.

transaction B increases the account value by $300. Because transaction B cannot see the uncommitted updates made by transaction A, it increases the balance to $2,300. Because we allowed two transactions to simultaneously modify the same row, the database is now in an inconsistent state. The end balance for the account will be the value set by whichever transaction commits last. If transaction B is the last to commit, the owner of account number 2 will have $100 more than she should. On the other hand, if transaction A commits first, the account owner will be $300 out of pocket!

This clearly unacceptable result is completely avoided when locks are placed on rows that have been changed, as is illustrated in Figure 6-7.

Now, when transaction A updates account number 2, the relevant row is locked and cannot be updated by another transaction. Transaction B must wait for transaction A to be committed before its update can proceed. When transaction A commits, transaction B applies its update to the modified account balance, and the integrity of the account balance is maintained.

ROW LEVEL LOCKING IN ORACLE

Oracle was the first commercial database server to implement an effective row level locking strategy. Prior to row level locking, locks would be applied either at the table level or at the block level. Without row level locking, two transactions could experience lock contention even when updating different rows, and

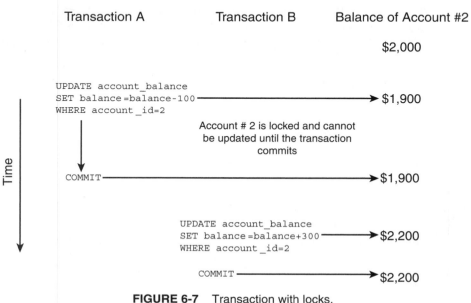

FIGURE 6-7 Transaction with locks.

consequently lock contention would more often be the primary restriction on database throughput.

Most of the time Oracle's row level locking ensures that you experience lock contention only if you are updating or explicitly locking the same row. However, there are some issues relating to foreign key or bitmap indexes that can result in locks being applied to many rows or the entire table. We looked at those index-related locking issues in Chapter 5, "Indexing and Clustering." There's also a few other scenarios in which row level locking can fail, and these are discussed in Chapter 15, "Lock Contention."

APPLICATION LOCKING STRATEGIES

If Oracle locking is working as intended, the nature and degree of Oracle lock contention depends on the application design. Application transaction design should generally aim to hold locks for the least possible amount of time, although you should almost never sacrifice transactional integrity to increase concurrency.

One of the most significant design decisions that affect lock duration will be the decision between employing the *pessimistic locking strategy* and the *optimistic locking strategy*:

❏ **The pessimistic locking strategy** is based on an assumption that it is likely that a row will be updated by another user between the time you fetch it and the time you update it. To avoid any contention, the pessimistic locking strategy requires that you lock the rows as they are retrieved. The application is, therefore, assured that no changes will be made to the row between the time the row is retrieved and the time it is updated.

❏ **The optimistic locking strategy** is based on the assumption that it is unlikely that an update will be applied to a row between the time it is retrieved and the time it is modified. Based on this assumption, the optimistic locking strategy does not require that the row be locked when fetched. However, to avoid the possibility that the row *will* be updated between retrieval and modification, it is necessary to check that the row has not been changed before the transaction finally issues DML against it. This can be done by checking a time-stamp value, by checking that the original selection criteria still applies, or by using the ORA_ROWSCN pseudo-column (more on that later). If it is detected that the row has been modified, it will be necessary to either retry the transaction or return an error to the user.

The optimistic and pessimistic locking strategies are diagrammed in Figure 6-8.

Implementing the Locking Strategy In Oracle 10g, Oracle introduced a pseudo-column ORA_ROWSCN that contains the System Change Number (SCN) for either the row, or—if the table has been created without the

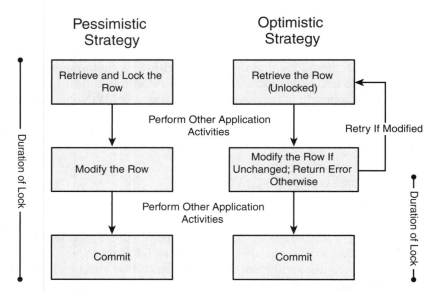

FIGURE 6-8   The optimistic and pessimistic locking strategies.

ROWDEPENDENCIES keyword—the highest SCN in the block that contains the row. Using ORA_ROWSCN is the easiest way to check that a row has not changed, although if ROWDEPENDENCIES is not in force, it can tell you only whether a row *in the same block* has changed.

The following code snippet provides an example of optimistic locking with ORA_ROWSCN:

```
1    CREATE OR REPLACE PROCEDURE optimistic_trans (
2       p_cust_id      NUMBER,
3       p_add_credit   NUMBER
4    )
5    IS
6       v_start_rowscn   NUMBER;
7    BEGIN
8       SELECT ORA_ROWSCN              -- Get the start SCN
9         INTO v_start_rowscn
10        FROM customers_rd
11       WHERE cust_id = p_cust_id;
12
13       credit_check (p_cust_id);     -- Time consuming credit check
14
15       UPDATE customers_rd
16          SET cust_credit_limit = cust_credit_limit + p_add_credit
```

```
17              WHERE cust_id = p_cust_id AND ORA_ROWSCN = v_start_rowscn;
18
19       IF SQL%ROWCOUNT = 0
20       THEN                                -- SCN must have changed
21          ROLLBACK;
22          raise_application_error (-20001,
23                                   'Optimistic transaction failed - please retry'
24                                   );
25       ELSE
26          COMMIT;
27       END IF;
28    END;
```

On line 8 we retrieve the existing ORA_ROWSCN for the row we intend to update. We then call the credit check routine on line 13 that might take some time. After the credit check is complete, we update the row (line 15), but *only* if the ORA_ROWSCN is unchanged. If the SCN has changed, the UPDATE will find no rows to update, and we raise an exception to advise the user to retry the transaction.

If the CUSTOMERS_RD table is created without the ROWDEPENDENCIES clause, the transaction will fail whenever a row in the same block is updated during the credit check. This can be unlikely, but if we want to avoid ever unnecessarily failing the transaction, we might decide either not to use ORA_ROWSCN or to apply ROWDEPENDENCIES to the table. An alternative approach is to check that all relevant columns in the row remained unchanged (probably CREDIT_LIMIT in the above example because that is the column being updated).

The next example shows the same transaction in pessimistic style. The FOR UPDATE clause on line 9 ensures that no one can update this row until our transaction ends, and therefore there is no need for the checking involved in our previous example. However, as a result the duration of our lock has extended and, if the credit check is lengthy, it might be reducing overall application throughput.

```
1    PROCEDURE PESIMISTIC_TRANS (p_cust_id NUMBER, p_add_credit NUMBER)
2    IS
3       v_cust_id   NUMBER;
4    BEGIN
5       SELECT      cust_id
6              INTO v_cust_id                 -- Lock the row
7              FROM customers_rd
8             WHERE cust_id = p_cust_id
9       FOR UPDATE;
10
11       credit_check (p_cust_id);            -- Time consuming credit check
12
```

```
13      UPDATE customers_rd
14         SET cust_credit_limit = cust_credit_limit + p_add_credit
15       WHERE cust_id = p_cust_id;
16
17      COMMIT;
18    END;
```

Choosing Between Locking Strategies   Don't choose between optimistic and pessimistic strategies based on your personality or disposition. Just because your analyst assures you that you are a fairly fun-loving, optimistic guy or gal, that does not mean you should affirm this by always choosing the optimistic locking strategy!

The choice between the two strategies is based on a trade-off between concurrency and robustness: Pessimistic locking is less likely to require transaction retries or failures, whereas optimistic locking minimizes the duration of locks, thus improving concurrency and transaction throughput.

The correct decision will be based on application processing patterns and business requirements. Here are some considerations you should think about when choosing between the two strategies:

❏ What's the chance that two sessions will simultaneously attempt to modify the same data? If the probability is close to zero, optimistic strategy is probably indicated.

❏ In an interactive application, is it acceptable to ask the user to retry a transaction? If it is not, the optimistic strategy is probably unacceptable.

❏ In a batch application, is the overhead of retrying transactions greater than the delay that results from waiting for other sessions to release locks? If so, the pessimistic strategy is probably more efficient.

❏ The optimistic locking strategy tends to hold locks for shorter periods of time, thus reducing the potential for lock contention.

❏ In an interactive application, the pessimistic locking strategy can allow locks to be held indefinitely. This is a common phenomenon in an interactive application that fetches and locks data pending and waits for the user to press the OK button. It's quite possible for the row to remain locked for hours if the user goes to lunch—not realizing that a lock has been placed on the row displayed.

Make an informed choice between optimistic and pessimistic locking strategies when determining your application's transaction handling model.

USING STORED PROCEDURES TO REDUCE NETWORK TRAFFIC

Database stored programs first came to prominence in the late 1980s and early 1990s during what might be called the *client-server* revolution. In the client-server environment of that time, stored programs had some security, performance, and manageability advantages (aspects of which persist in today's multitier and Internet-based architectures).

However, with the emergence of three-tier architectures and web applications, many of the incentives to use stored programs from within applications disappeared. Application clients are now often browser-based; security is predominantly handled by a middle tier; and the middle tier possesses the capability to encapsulate business logic. Most of the purposes for which stored programs were used in client server applications can now be implemented in middle tier code (that is, in PHP, Java, C#, and so on).

However, stored programs, such as PLSQL packages, procedures, triggers, and functions, can still improve application performance by reducing network traffic.

Consider a scenario in which an application accepts input from the end user, reads some data in the database, decides what statement to execute next, retrieves a result, makes a decision, executes some SQL, and so on. If the application code is written entirely outside of the database, each of these steps would require a network round trip between the database and the application. The time taken to perform these network trips can easily dominate overall user response time.

Consider a typical interaction between a bank customer and an Automated Teller Machine (ATM). The user requests a transfer of funds between two accounts. The application must retrieve the balance of each account from the database, check withdrawal limits and possibly other account information, issue the relevant UPDATE statements, and finally issue a commit—all before advising the customer that the transaction has succeeded. Even for this relatively simple interaction, at least six separate database queries must be issued, each with its own network round trip between the application server and the database. Network time could easily become the biggest part of this transactions response time.

Figure 6-9 shows the sequences of interactions that would be required without a stored procedure approach.

On the other hand, if a stored program is used to implement the funds transfer logic, only a single database interaction is required. The stored program takes responsibility for checking balances, withdrawal limits, and so on. Figure 6-10 illustrates the reduction in network round trips that occurs as a result.

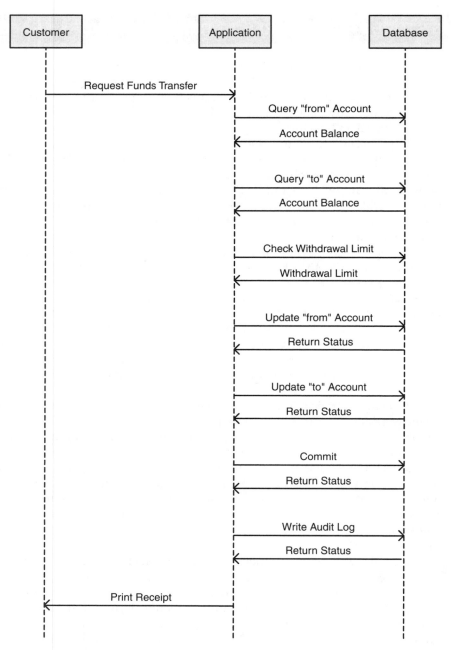

FIGURE 6-9   Network round trips without a stored procedure.

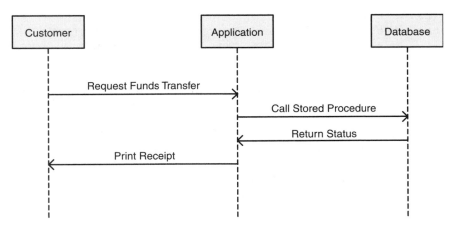

FIGURE 6-10   Network round trips reduced by use of stored procedure.

Transactions that perform multiple database interactions or have many SQL calls can have their network overhead minimized by encapsulating the transaction in a stored procedure or package.

Network round trips can also become significant when an application is required to perform some kind of aggregate processing on large record sets in the database. If the application needs to (for example) retrieve millions of rows to calculate some sort of business metric that cannot easily be computed using native SQL (average time to complete an order, for example), a large number of round trips can result. In such a case, the network delay can again become the dominant factor in application response time. Performing the calculations in a stored program will reduce network overhead, which *might* reduce overall response time. The key determining factor will be the network latency between client and server, and the number of network round trips involved.

For instance, consider the following Java snippet. This code retrieves every sale for a particular customer id and then calculates a discount based on the customer's purchases.

```
String sqlText = "SELECT quantity_sold,amount_sold,prod_id " +
                "FROM sh.sales  WHERE cust_id=:1";
PreparedStatement stmt = oracleConnection.prepareStatement
                (sqlText);
stmt.setInt(1, cust_id);
ResultSet rs = stmt.executeQuery();
```

```
while (rs.next()) {
    totalDisCount += discountCalc(rs.getFloat("QUANTITY_SOLD"),
            rs.getFloat("PROD_ID"), rs.getFloat("AMOUNT_SOLD"));
}
```

The preceding code must fetch every sale row across the network, which might be expensive if there are a lot of sales and the network latency is significant.

Alternatively, we could perform the calculation using a stored function as shown here. The logic is the same, but the network round trips are eliminated.

```
FUNCTION calc_discount (p_cust_id NUMBER)
    RETURN NUMBER
  IS
    CURSOR cust_csr
    IS
      SELECT quantity_sold, amount_sold, prod_id
        FROM sh.sales
       WHERE cust_id = p_cust_id;

    v_total_discount   NUMBER := 0;
  BEGIN
    FOR cust_row IN cust_csr
    LOOP
       v_total_discount :=
            v_total_discount
          + discountcalc (cust_row.quantity_sold,
                          cust_row.prod_id,
                          cust_row.amount_sold
                         );
    END LOOP;
    RETURN(v_total_discount );
  END;
```

If the two approaches are tested on a local database, the performance difference is negligible because the round trips do not need to go across the network. However, if the database is remote and the network latency is significant, the stored procedure is far more efficient. Figure 6-11 compares the performance of the Java client and stored procedure for both local and remote databases.

Stored procedures can be effective in reducing network overhead when you need to calculate a single value from a large number of rows, especially if the database is remote and the network latency is significant.

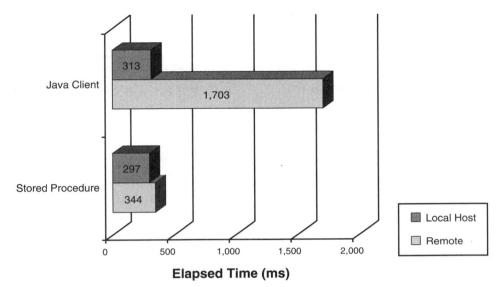

FIGURE 6-11 Using a stored procedure to reduce network overhead is most effective when the database is remote.

SUMMARY

In this chapter we looked at ways to design and implement applications that make efficient and effective use of the Oracle database.

An application should minimize the number of requests it sends to the database by avoiding unnecessary SQL executions and possibly caching frequently accessed but static data.

Parsing is a CPU-intensive operation that can also lead to database contention in some circumstances. The overhead and contention caused by parsing can be minimized by avoiding unnecessary parse requests and using bind variables.

Queries that retrieve multiple rows from the database should do so in batches (or arrays) to reduce network traffic and database overhead. Stored procedures can also be used to reduce the network overhead of transactions that have a large number of individual SQL statements.

Lock contention can be a significant factor on database performance and is most significantly affected by application transaction design. Choose an application locking strategy that attempts to maximize concurrency and that reduces the duration of blocking locks whenever possible.

OPTIMIZING THE OPTIMIZER

This chapter describes how to configure and tune the Oracle optimizer.

SQL is a *nonprocedural* language: You define the data you want, not how to get it. Although the nonprocedural nature of SQL results in improvements in programmer productivity, the RDBMS must support a set of sophisticated algorithms to determine the optimal method of executing the SQL. In Oracle, these algorithms are collectively referred to as the *optimizer*.

The optimizer is one of the most sophisticated parts of the Oracle software stack, and it gets more and more complicated with every release. The optimizer makes good decisions across a wide range of circumstances, but it has not become self-aware yet, and human intervention is often still required.

It's not necessary to understand every nuance of the optimizer or to second guess the optimizer's decisions. Instead, we should seek to assist the optimizer to make the best decisions, identify the SQLs for which poor decisions might have been made, and override or influence the optimizer in those cases.

THE ORACLE OPTIMIZER

For almost all SQL statements, there will be more than one way for Oracle to retrieve the rows required. When Oracle parses a SQL statement, it must decide which approach will be fastest. The process of determining this optimal path to the data is referred to as *query optimization*.

Query optimization is applied to all queries and to any other statements (for example, UPDATE, INSERT, DELETE, MERGE, CREATE TABLE AS statements) that perform data accesses.

Oracle's optimizer is a *cost-based optimizer*[1]: The optimizer calculates a cost value for each execution plan that it considers. The plan with the lowest cost is the plan that is chosen.

WHAT IS COST?

The cost metric reported by the optimizer is a relative value that is hard to translate into a real-world value. It's a composite measure that includes estimates of the time required to perform estimated single-block and multi-block reads plus the amount of estimated CPU time. The end result is divided by the estimated amount of time taken to perform a single-block read.[2] In theory, if you multiply the cost value by this single-block read time, you get the expected elapsed time in milliseconds.

However, you'll be disappointed if you try to use Oracle's cost calculations to try to predict elapsed time. Although Oracle's formula is sophisticated, it doesn't even attempt to account for all components of elapsed time (network time is missing for instance) and in general is useful for comparing the relative cost of competing plans on the same system, rather than for predicting actual elapsed time.

OPTIMIZER GOAL

The OPTIMIZER_GOAL (or OPTIMIZER_MODE) configuration parameter controls how the optimizer calculates cost:

ALL_ROWS   Instructs the optimizer to minimize the cost of processing all rows processed by a SQL statement. This is the default behavior and is most suitable for batch processing and reporting queries.

FIRST_ROWS_*N*   Instructs the optimizer to choose an execution plan that will minimize the cost of retrieving the first N rows, where N is one of 1, 10, 100, or 1000. This setting can be useful for interactive applications because the critical performance measure can be the time taken to display the first row or page of information.

These optimizer goals can lead to different execution plans: ALL_ROWS tends to favor plans that employ full table scans and nonindexed joins. FIRST_ROWS_*N* plans are more inclined to favor index-based approaches.

---

[1] The older *rule-based optimizer* is no longer supported but can still be invoked by using the RULE hint.
[2] Oracle assumes single-block reads take 10ms if *system statistics*—discussed later in this chapter—have not been collected.

SELECTIVITY AND CARDINALITY

Selectivity and cardinality are related concepts, both of which relate to the number of rows that would be returned by an expression. A highly selective expression is one that returns a small proportion of rows from a table. Cardinality refers more specifically to the number of rows returned: A cardinality of 20,000 is simply another way of saying that 20,000 rows would be returned.

A column is regarded as highly selective if it has a large number of distinct values compared to the total number of rows in the table. Primary keys and unique columns are the most highly selective of all columns.

QUERY TRANSFORMATION

Certain SQL statements are transformed into logically equivalent statements.

For instance, a statement that incorporates a subquery involving the IN clause can often be represented as a join. For instance, the statement below selects all employees who work for departments in the city of Seattle:

```
SELECT first_name, last_name
  FROM hr.employees
 WHERE department_id IN
       (SELECT department_id
          FROM hr.departments
         WHERE location_id IN
             (SELECT location_id
                FROM hr.locations
               WHERE city = 'Seattle'))
```

Queries with IN subqueries can usually be expressed as a join, and so Oracle is likely to rewrite this SQL to something like this:

```
SELECT DISTINCT "EMPLOYEES".ROWID "ROWID",
               "DEPARTMENTS"."DEPARTMENT_ID" "$nso_col_1",
               "EMPLOYEES"."FIRST_NAME" "FIRST_NAME",
               "EMPLOYEES"."LAST_NAME" "LAST_NAME"
          FROM "HR"."LOCATIONS" "LOCATIONS",
               "HR"."DEPARTMENTS" "DEPARTMENTS",
               "HR"."EMPLOYEES" "EMPLOYEES"
         WHERE "EMPLOYEES"."DEPARTMENT_ID"
              ="DEPARTMENTS"."DEPARTMENT_ID"
           AND "DEPARTMENTS"."LOCATION_ID"
              ="LOCATIONS"."LOCATION_ID"
           AND "LOCATIONS"."CITY" = 'Seattle';
```

We can see these rewrites using the 10053 trace event: We briefly covered 10053 trace in Chapter 3.

The rewrite above is referred to as *Subquery unnesting*. There's a bunch of other transformations that Oracle might perform including

❑ **View merging**—Taking a view definition and merging it into a SQL statement that calls the view.

❑ **Star transformation**—Rewriting a star join using subqueries to take advantage of bitmap indexes.

❑ **Join elimination**—Eliminating any joins in the SQL statement that are not necessary.

❑ **Join factorization**—Extracting common tables from subselects in union operations and isolating the UNION to an inline view.

❑ **Antijoin and semijoin transformations**—Converting MINUS and INTERSECT operations into antijoins or semijoins.

Most of the time you won't need to worry about the query transformation, although there are a couple of situations, such as view merging and star transformation in particular, which you might want to control with hints or parameters.

COST CALCULATIONS

As noted previously, the optimizer calculates a cost value for each candidate execution plan. To calculate cost, the optimizer needs to make a number of estimates, including

❑ The amount of data from each table that the optimizer determines will be accessed.

❑ An estimate of the amount of that data that might be in memory.

❑ An estimate of the number of physical IOs that might be required.

❑ An estimate of CPU-intensive operations such as sorting or hashing data.

❑ The relative speed of IO operations and of compute operations.

There are three main sets of inputs into these calculations:

❑ Object statistics and histograms, which include things such as the number of data blocks and rows in tables, and the selectivity and distribution of column values within rows. These statistics will normally exist for all the tables, indexes, and partitions that might be involved in the execution plan. Histograms, which contain information about the distribution of values within a column, might be available only for some of the columns.

❑ Database parameters and configuration, which determine how many blocks can be read in a single IO operation, how much memory is available for sorting, the availability of parallel processing, and many other factors. Other parameters determine the assumptions that the optimizer will make about how much data is likely to be in memory and how much benefit to expect from indexes.

❏ System statistics, which enable Oracle to factor in the CPU and IO capacity of the host. These statistics give the optimizer guidance as to the IO rate and latency that can be expected, and the host's CPU processing capability.

Figure 7-1 illustrates the high-level inputs into the cost-based optimization process. Object statistics enable the optimizer to estimate the amount of data that will be processed. Database parameters and configuration help the optimizer translate these data volumes into the CPU and IO operations required. System statistics enable the optimizer to work out a weighted cost based on the CPU and disk performance characteristics of the host.

OBJECT STATISTICS

Object statistics record the volumes and distribution of data within tables, partitions, and indexes. These statistics can be examined in a variety of views, including DBA_IND_STATISTICS, DBA_TAB_STATISTICS, and DBA_TAB _COL_STATISTICS. Some of the key statistics held in these views are outlined in Table 7-1.

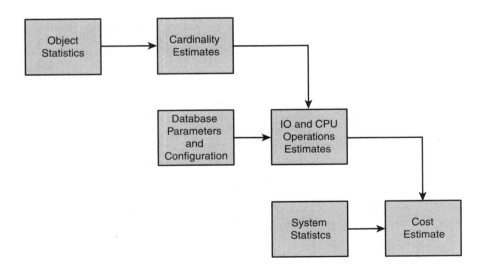

FIGURE 7-1   Inputs to query optimization.

Table 7-1   Key Object Statistics

STATISTIC NAME	APPLIES TO	DESCRIPTION
AVG_CACHE_HIT_RATIO	Tables, partitions, indexes	Average cache hit ratio for the object; how often are blocks for the object found in the buffer cache when sought.
AVG_CACHED_BLOCKS	Tables, partitions, indexes	Average number of blocks of the object found in the buffer cache.
AVG_COL_LEN	Columns	The average length of the column in bytes.
AVG_DATA_BLOCKS_PER_KEY	Indexes	The average number of data blocks per key.
AVG_LEAF_BLOCKS_PER_KEY	Indexes	The average number of leaf blocks per key.
AVG_ROW_LEN	Tables, Partitions	The average row length, including row overhead.
AVG_SPACE	Tables, Partitions, Indexes	The average available free space in the object.
BLEVEL	Indexes	The number of levels in the B*-Tree index.
BLOCKS	Tables, Indexes Partitions	The number of used blocks in the object.
CLUSTERING_FACTOR	Indexes	A measurement of how ordered key values are in the table. If the key values are bunched together, the clustering factor will be low. If the key values are randomly distributed, the clustering factor will be high. The value varies between the number of blocks in the table and the number of rows.
DENSITY	Columns	The density of the column. This is a measure of the selectivity of the column where 0 is very selective and 1 is not at all selective. If there is no histogram, the value will be 1 / (num of distinct values). A much more complex formula is employed when Oracle has histogram data.
EMPTY_BLOCKS	Tables, Partitions	Number of empty blocks in the object.
HIGH_VALUE	Columns	The high value in the column.
LEAF_BLOCKS	Indexes	The number of leaf blocks in the index.
LOW_VALUE	Columns	The low value in the column.
NUM_DISTINCT	Columns	The number of distinct values in the column.
NUM_NULLS	Columns	The number of null values in the column.
NUM_ROWS	Indexes	The number of rows that the index contains (not the same as the number of rows in the table if the column can be NULL).
NUM_ROWS	Tables, Partitions	Number of rows in the table or partition.

HISTOGRAMS

By default, Oracle collects general information about column data, such as high value, low value, number of distinct values, but does not always collect information about the distribution of data within the column. If the data in a column is fairly evenly distributed, the default statistics will be adequate; but if the data is unevenly distributed—*skewed* is another word for this—the optimizer might need a *histogram* to determine the best plan.

For example, consider the distribution of the COUNTRY_ID column in the SH.CUSTOMERS table. The vast majority of customers are in a few well-known countries, and the United States alone accounts for 33 percent of the customers. This skew will, of course, also be reflected in SALES data. Figure 7-2 illustrates this skewed data.

Without the histogram, all the optimizer knows is that there are 19 distinct values in the COUNTRY_ID column. If we seek all the customers for a particular country, the optimizer chooses a full table scan, even if the country code corresponding to Saudi Arabia (.1 percent of customers) is provided:

```
SQL> SELECT MAX (cust_income_level)
  2     FROM customers
  3    WHERE country_id = 52787; /* Saudi Arabia */

Execution Plan
------------------------------------------------------------

------------------------------------------------------------
| Id  | Operation            | Name      | Rows  | Bytes |
------------------------------------------------------------
|   0 | SELECT STATEMENT     |           |     1 |    26 |
|   1 |  SORT AGGREGATE      |           |     1 |    26 |
|*  2 |   TABLE ACCESS FULL| CUSTOMERS  |  2921 | 75946 |
------------------------------------------------------------

Predicate Information (identified by operation id):
---------------------------------------------------

   2 - filter("COUNTRY_ID"=52787)
```

The creation of a column histogram enables Oracle to recognize selective values within otherwise unselective columns and vice versa. The optimizer can then choose to use an index for a selective value (for example, Saudi Arabia) and a full table scan for a nonselective column (in this case, the United States). After a histogram is created, queries for the United States remain unaffected, but queries for Saudi Arabian customers now use the index:

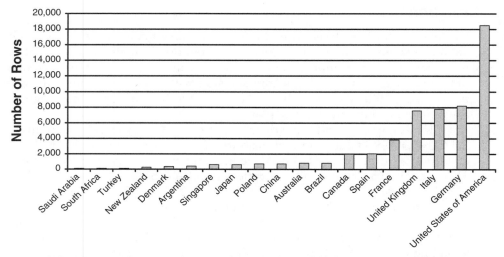

FIGURE 7-2 Skewed distribution of countries in the SH.CUSTOMERS table.

```
-----------------------------------------------------------------
| Id  | Operation                     | Name                | Rows  |
-----------------------------------------------------------------
|   0 | SELECT STATEMENT              |                     |    1 |
|   1 |  SORT AGGREGATE               |                     |    1 |
|   2 |   TABLE ACCESS BY INDEX ROWID | CUSTOMERS           |  153 |
| * 3 |    INDEX RANGE SCAN           | CUSTOMERS_COUNTRY_IX |  153 |
-----------------------------------------------------------------
Predicate Information (identified by operation id):
-------------------------------------------------

  3 - access("COUNTRY_ID"=52787)
```

Figure 7-3 shows how the presence of a histogram can help the optimizer choose a better plan when some values of a column are more selective than others. The presence of histograms can have an enormous impact on the quality of your execution plans.

BIND VARIABLE PEEKING

Prior to Oracle 10g, histograms and bind variables were usually incompatible. To make use of the histogram, the optimizer needed to know the value of the filter value, but the use of bind variables hid that value until the last minute.

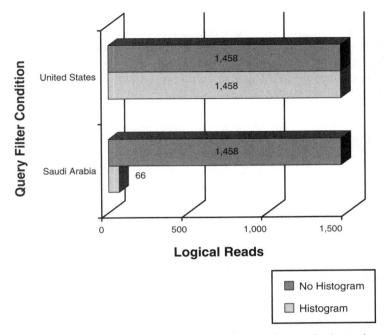

FIGURE 7-3   Histograms can help the optimizer choose the best plan.

Consequently bind variables, which help optimize parse overhead and reduce contention, were incompatible with the histograms that helped the optimizer choose the best access plan.

Oracle 10g introduced *bind variable peeking*, in which Oracle uses the value of the first bind variable provided to determine the execution plan. For instance in the following code, bind variable peeking will result in an index scan because the optimizer sees the selective country id (for Saudi Arabia) during bind variable peeking:

```
VARIABLE v_country_id number;

BEGIN
    :v_country_id := 52787; — Saudi Arabia
END;
/

SELECT MAX (cust_income_level)
  FROM customers
 WHERE country_id = :v_country_id;
```

Unfortunately, this results in every subsequent query using the index scan, even an unselective value—for the United States, for example—is provided. Remember that execution plans are cached in the shared pool, so when the plan is established, it is usually used by all subsequent executions across all sessions.

Bind variable peeking also results in what can seem like random decisions. The first bind variable provided will decide the plan, so after a reboot or a flush of the shared pool, you can't be sure which plan will take effect. For some applications, bind variable peeking would cause SQL tuning issues that could go away following a reboot or flush of the shared pool.

ADAPTIVE CURSOR SHARING

Oracle 11g Adaptive Cursor Sharing attempts to resolve the issues created by bind variable peeking. If the optimizer detects that a SQL might be optimized with different execution plans when provided with different bind variables, it will mark the SQL as *bind sensitive*. When the SQL is executed with different bind variables, multiple copies of the SQL might be cached, each with a different execution plan. Each copy will be assigned the same SQL_ID but will have a different CHILD_NUMBER. We can see all the different plans by scanning V$SQL to find our SQL_IDs and then executing DBMS_XPLAN.DISPLAY_CURSOR to show the various plans.

The following example shows how adaptive cursor sharing results in multiple execution plans for a single statement. The SQL on line 1 of the example finds the SQL_IDs within the V$SQL view. Child number 0 is the parent cursor, and its two children represent different bind sensitive plans. We can view all the plans for a cursor by issuing DBMS_XPLAN.DISPLAY_CURSOR and providing the SQL_ID concerned. In the following example, the plan shown on line 24 shows the plan that will be used for insensitive bind variables, such as the country code for the United States, whereas the plan shown on line 39 is the plan used when selective bind variables, such as the country code for Saudi Arabia, are provided.

```
1    SQL> SELECT sql_id, child_number,
2      2            is_bind_sensitive, is_bind_aware
3      3      FROM v$sql
4      4     WHERE sql_text LIKE 'SELECT MA%v_country_id%';
5
6    SQL_ID          CHILD_NUMBER IS_BIND_SE IS_BIND_AW
7    ------------- ------------- ---------- ----------
8    fru7mqzkt56zr            0 Y          N
9    fru7mqzkt56zr            1 Y          Y
10   fru7mqzkt56zr            2 Y          Y
11
12   SQL> SELECT *
13     2     FROM TABLE (DBMS_XPLAN.display_cursor
```

```
14       3                    ('fru7mqzkt56zr', NULL, 'BASIC'));
15
16
17     <snip>
18
19     EXPLAINED SQL STATEMENT:
20     -----------------------
21     SELECT MAX (cust_income_level)   FROM customers   WHERE country_id =
22     :v_country_id
23
24     Plan hash value: 296924608
25
26     ------------------------------------------
27     | Id | Operation           | Name      |
28     ------------------------------------------
29     |  0 | SELECT STATEMENT    |           |
30     |  1 |  SORT AGGREGATE     |           |
31     |  2 |   TABLE ACCESS FULL | CUSTOMERS |
32     ------------------------------------------
33
34     EXPLAINED SQL STATEMENT:
35     -----------------------
36     SELECT MAX (cust_income_level)   FROM customers   WHERE country_id =
37     :v_country_id
38
39     Plan hash value: 479268801
40
41     -------------------------------------------------------------
42     | Id | Operation                    | Name                 |
43     -------------------------------------------------------------
44     |  0 | SELECT STATEMENT             |                      |
45     |  1 |  SORT AGGREGATE              |                      |
46     |  2 |   TABLE ACCESS BY INDEX ROWID| CUSTOMERS            |
47     |  3 |    INDEX RANGE SCAN          | CUSTOMERS_COUNTRY_IX |
48     -------------------------------------------------------------
```

DATABASE PARAMETERS

Object statistics allow the optimizer to work out how much data is going to have to be retrieved and how much sorting and other operations might need to be done on that data. Database configuration and parameters help the optimizer work out how many machine operations will be required. In particular, the configuration of the database can change how much physical IO might be required.

For instance, if there were an index on the customer year of birth to support age-based queries, normally, the following query declines to use the index:

```
SQL> SELECT MAX (cust_income_level)
  2    FROM customers c
  3    WHERE cust_year_of_birth > 1985;
```

```
Execution Plan
-----------------------------------------------------------------
Plan hash value: 296924608

-----------------------------------------------------------------
| Id  | Operation            | Name      | Rows  | Bytes |
-----------------------------------------------------------------
|   0 | SELECT STATEMENT     |           |     1 |    25 |
|   1 |  SORT AGGREGATE      |           |     1 |    25 |
|*  2 |   TABLE ACCESS FULL  | CUSTOMERS |   762 | 19050 |
-----------------------------------------------------------------
```

The optimizer calculates that using a full table scan will require less work and will "cost" less than using an index. However, if we change the value of DB_FILE_MULTIBLOCK_READ_COUNT to 1, the optimizer calculates the relative costs differently and decides that an index will be more effective:

```
Execution Plan
-----------------------------------------------------------
Plan hash value: 2707785918

------------------------------------------------------------------------
| Id  | Operation                      | Name                 | Rows  |
------------------------------------------------------------------------
|   0 | SELECT STATEMENT               |                      |     1 |
|   1 |  SORT AGGREGATE                |                      |     1 |
|   2 |   TABLE ACCESS BY INDEX ROWID  | CUSTOMERS            |   489 |
|*  3 |    INDEX RANGE SCAN            | CUST_YEAR_OF_BIRTH_IDX |  489 |
------------------------------------------------------------------------
```

DB_FILE_MULTIBLOCK_READ_COUNT controls how many blocks can be read from disk in a single IO operation, typically when performing full table scans. The default, which you normally will not want to change, is set to an operating system–specific value and usually allows between 512K–1M to be read in a single IO. When we set DB_FILE_MULTIBLOCK_READ to 1, the optimizer recalculates the number of IOs that will be required to do the full table scan, making the index lookup more attractive.

The parameters that are most likely to affect query execution plans are those that influence IO behavior and the amount of memory available for various operations. Memory is generally used to avoid IO, so larger memory settings tend to make the optimizer reduce its estimate of IO cost. Parameters such as DB_FILE_MULTIBLOCK_READ_COUNT change the number of physical IOs required to support a given amount of logical IO.

Other statistics directly influence optimizer assumptions, without actually changing run time behaviors. For instance, OPTIMIZER_INDEX_CACHING changes the optimizer's assumptions about how often it will find an index block in the cache. If set to 100, the optimizer will assume that all index blocks will be found in memory, and therefore will reduce the calculated cost of indexed plans. However, the parameter changes only the optimizer's *assumptions*: The actual contents of the buffer cache is unaffected.

The following are some of the other parameters that might affect the optimizers cost calculations:

db_{keep_|recycle_|nK_}cache_size	Size of cache for data buffers. Specific parameters are provided for KEEP, RECYCLE, DEFAULT, and block-size specific caches.
db_block_size	Size of database block in bytes.
db_file_multiblock_read_count	Number of blocks that can be read in a single IO. Higher values result in the optimizer using a lower cost for table scans.
hash_area_size	Size of the in-memory hash work area. Normally relevant only if neither MEMORY_TARGET nor PGA_AGGREGATE target is not set.
memory_target	Target size of Oracle SGA and PGA memory.
optimizer_features_enable	Restricts optimizer features to specific versions of Oracle. Useful when upgrading Oracle and you want to avoid any optimizer upgrade surprises.
optimizer_index_caching	Adjusts the optimizer's assumption of index block caching. Index blocks tend to be retained in cache, whereas table scan blocks tend to be flushed quickly out of the cache. This metric lets the optimizer know how often to expect index blocks to be found in cache. A value of 100 causes the optimizer to assume that 100 percent of the blocks will be found in the cache. The default value is 0.
optimizer_index_cost_adj	Adjusts the relative cost of index paths. You might think of it as a single control to increase or decrease the optimizer's tendency to use an index.
optimizer_mode	Optimizer mode: FIRST_ROWS_*N*, ALL_ROWS, and so on. FIRST_ROWS_*N* tends to favor index-based plans, whereas ALL_ROWS favors full table scans. FIRST_ROWS_*N* (where N is one of 1,10,100,1000) sets the goal to optimize for the first set of rows, not simply the first row.

parallel_threads_per_cpu	Number of parallel execution threads per CPU: See Chapter 13, "Parallel SQL," for more details.
pga_aggregate_target	Target size for the aggregate PGA memory consumed by the instance.
sort_area_size	Size of the in-memory hash work area. Relevant only if neither MEMORY_TARGET nor PGA _AGGREGATE target is not set.
SGA_target	Target size of Oracle SGA.

The views V$SYS_OPTIMIZER_ENV and V$SES_OPTIMIZER_ENV lists many (but not all) of the parameters and settings that affect how the optimizer constructs a plan. The following query shows the values for the current session:

```
SQL> SELECT      NAME, e.isdefault, e.VALUE, p.description
  2      FROM v$ses_optimizer_env e LEFT OUTER
  3          JOIN v$parameter p USING (NAME)
  4          JOIN v$session USING (SID)
  5      WHERE audsid = USERENV ('sessionid')
  6      ORDER BY isdefault, NAME;

NAME                             Default VALUE
-------------------------------- ------- --------------------
DESCRIPTION
-----------------------------------------------------------------
_pga_max_size                    NO      367000 KB


_smm_max_size                    NO      102400 KB


active_instance_count            YES     1
number of active instances in the cluster database

bitmap_merge_area_size           YES     1048576
maximum memory allow for BITMAP MERGE

cell_offload_compaction          YES     ADAPTIVE
Cell packet compaction strategy

cell_offload_plan_display        YES     AUTO
Cell offload explain plan display

cell_offload_processing          YES     true
enable SQL processing offload to cells
```

```
cpu_count                          YES      4
number of CPUs for this instance
  ...                              ...     ...
```

SYSTEM STATISTICS

Object statistics give the optimizer a basis for determining how much data will need to be processed, and database configuration helps work out how much of that work will translate into IO operations. However, to make an informed decision, the optimizer needs to know something about the capacity of the system.

For instance, consider this simple SQL statement:

```
SELECT *
 FROM sh.customers
ORDER BY cust_id
```

There are at least two basic approaches to optimizing this query:

❏ Perform a full table scan of customers and then sort the results.
❏ Retrieve the rows using the primary key index, which return the rows in sorted order.

Using the index requires more IO operations but avoids the sort. If the disk devices attached to the system are fast and the CPUs are relatively slow, this might be the best plan. However, on a system with fast CPUs and slow disks, we prefer to perform the table scan and perform the sort. There's a similar trade off involved between the multiblock reads involved in full table scans and the single-block reads performed by index lookups. The optimizer will make better decisions if it has an accurate idea about the relative overhead of each.

To make better decisions regarding CPU and IO trade-offs, the optimizer leverages *system statistics*. These statistics can be viewed in the table SYS.AUX _STATS$. The statistics concerned are listed below.

Nonworkload statistics: These can be collected in the absence of significant database load:

CPUSPEEDNW	The number of standard operations that each CPU on the system can perform per second. The NW suffix indicates that this is a nonworkload estimate.
IOSEEKTIM	Average time to locate data on disk. Although called seek time, it is actually the total time to retrieve a block from disk, including disk rotational and transfer latency and seek time.
IOTFRSPEED	IO transfer rate from the disk in bytes/ms.

Workload statistics: These measurements are based on actual Oracle database activity, and should be collected during typical database activity:

SREADTIM	Average time to perform a single-block read.
MREADTIM	Average time to perform a multiblock read.
CPUSPEED	The number of standard operations that each CPU on the system can perform per second. Unlike CPUSPEEDNW, this is calculated based on actual Oracle database activity.

Note that the first three statistics above are referred to as *nonworkload* statistics. These are based on simple measurements of system capacity and can in theory be calculated at any time regardless of what work Oracle is doing. Workload statistics measure the system performance for actual Oracle database activities and vary significantly depending on the workload that Oracle encounters.

Immediately after installation, only the nonworkload statistics have values, and these are hardcoded values that are not based on measurements made on the current system. Workload statistics are collected while the database is running and are more reflective of the hardware configuration of the database server. You should collect workload statistics during a period when your workload is most critical or most representative. We'll see how to collect these statistics later in this chapter.

COLLECTING STATISTICS

As we have seen, the optimizer's decisions rely heavily on the object and system statistics that have been collected. Consequently, one of the most important things you can do to optimize performance is to make sure the statistics are as accurate and comprehensive as possible.

Automatic Statistics Gathering   From Oracle 10g forward, object statistics will be collected by default by a system generated task. By default, this task will run every day during the *maintenance window* that is defined when the database is created. You can view or change this collection task in the Automated Maintenance Task Configuration page of the Enterprise manager database control (see Figure 7-4).

Clicking Configure from the Maintenance Task page, as shown in Figure 7-4, enables us to configure the automatic gathering task. Figure 7-5 shows the resulting configuration screen. You can modify the collection to change the default sampling level, degrees of parallelism, and many of the other options that we discuss in detail when we look at manual statistics gathering.

The collection preferences can be adjusted manually by using the DBMS_STATS.SET_GLOBAL_PREFS procedure. You can manually enable or disable the collection using the DBMS_AUTO_TASK_ADMIN package. For instance, the following turns off automatic statistics collections in an 11g database:

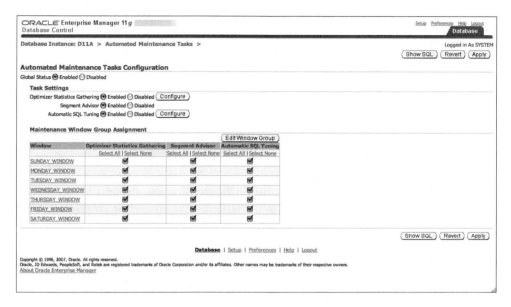

FIGURE 7-4 The optimizer STATISTICS GATHERING job shown in the Scheduler Central page of Enterprise Manager.

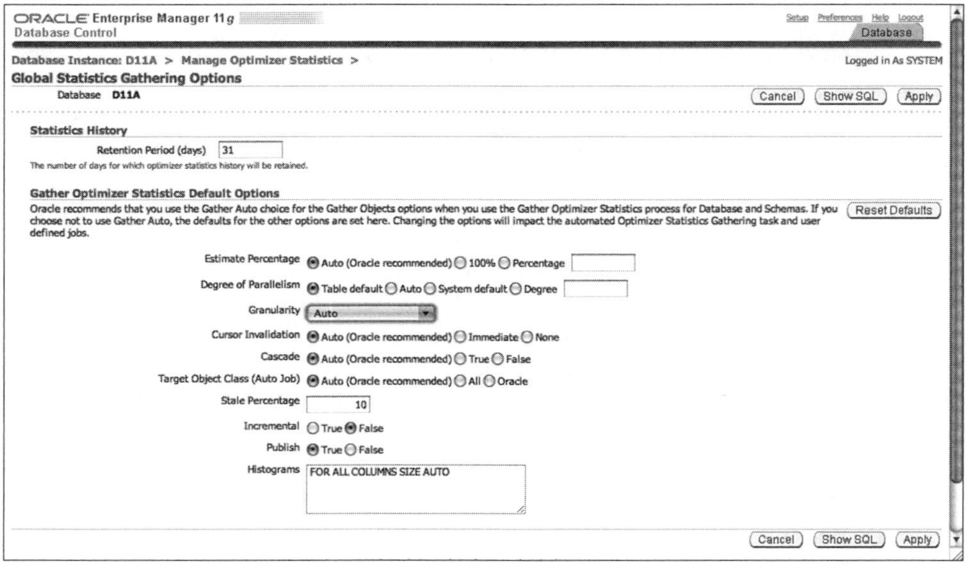

FIGURE 7-5 Configuring automatic statistic collections.

```
BEGIN
   dbms_auto_task_admin.disable
               (client_name=> 'auto optimizer stats collection',
                operation        => NULL,
                window_name      => NULL
               );
END;
```

A similar call to the DBMS_AUTO_TASK_ADMIN.ENABLE routine will reenable automatic collection.

Stale Statistics If the parameter STATISTICS_LEVEL is set to TYPICAL (the default) or ALL, Oracle tracks updates, deletes, inserts, and truncates against all tables. The statistics collected are visible in the ALL_TAB_MODIFICATIONS view. If the number of rows affected exceeds 10 percent of the table row count, then statistics for that table are considered *stale* and will be re-collected by the automatic statistics job, or when_STATS.GATHER_SCHEMA_STATS or DBMS _STATS.GATHER_DATABASE_STATS is run with the OPTIONS parameter set to GATHER STALE or GATHER AUTO. For instance, the following causes statistics to be gathered for all tables in the current schema that have had more than 10 percent of rows modified since the last statistics collection:

```
BEGIN
DBMS_STATS.gather_schema_stats
      (ownname       => USER,
       options       => 'GATHER STALE');
END;
```

Manually Collecting Statistics The automatic collection of statistics goes a long way toward eliminating *missing statistics* as a cause of poor SQL performance. However, you're still likely to want to perform manual collections from time to time. Here are a few of the most common manual collection scenarios:

❑ You have a table that is subject to massive fluctuations in data volumes, and you want to make sure that statistics are collected at the most effective point. For instance, a staging table might be empty from time to time, but subject to large data volumes during a periodic load. You might want to ensure that statistics are collected when the table is loaded.

❑ You want to fine-tune the collection options for particular objects. For instance, you might want to create a histogram with a higher than usual number of buckets. We discuss histograms in detail a bit later on.

❑ You want to collect statistics on SYSTEM objects and/or fixed tables; these are not collected by default.

❑ You want to create extended statistics or expression statistics. Extended statistics can be gathered that record the distribution of multiple columns or the distribution of a column subject to an expression. We discuss this soon.

Dynamic Sampling Oracle can collect statistics on-the-fly at SQL execution time under certain circumstances. This can be beneficial when a table has no statistics, or the estimated elapsed time for the SQL is high enough to suggest that the overhead of sampling is likely to lead to a net reduction in run time.

Dynamic sampling is controlled by the parameter OPTIMIZER _DYNAMIC_SAMPLING, which takes a value from 0 to 10. At 0 no sampling is done, whereas a setting of 10 will read all the blocks in any table referenced in the SQL that has missing or incomplete statistics or where the SQL has filter conditions matching two or more columns.

The default setting for OPTIMIZER_DYNAMIC_SAMPLING is 2, which instructs the optimizer to sample a small number of blocks for unanalyzed tables only.

USING DBMS_STAT

The DBMS_STAT package collects and manages optimizer statistics.[3] It has a wide variety of options that can seem overwhelming at first, but the most common operations have a straight-forward syntax.

To get started, here are some of the most common tasks for DBMS_STAT and their syntax:

❑ Collect statistics for a table with default settings.

```
DBMS_STATS.gather_table_stats
(ownname => USER,
tabname => 'EMPLOYEES');
```

❑ Collect statistics for the entire schema.

```
DBMS_STATS.gather_schema_stats
(ownname => 'HR');
```

❑ Collect statistics for any tables in a schema that are "stale."

```
DBMS_STATS.gather_schema_stats
(ownname      => 'HR'
options      => 'GATHER STALE');
```

❑ Create histograms for all indexed columns.

```
DBMS_STATS.gather_schema_stats
(ownname        => 'HR',
method_opt      =>
'FOR ALL INDEXED COLUMNS SIZE AUTO');
```

---

[3] The ANALYZE command was used to collect statistics in older versions of Oracle. In modern Oracle, DBMS_STATS is the preferred method. However, the ANALYZE command still supports a few unique functions such as listing chained rows or dumping detailed index statistics.

❏ Set the default collection to create histograms for indexed columns only if the column has a skewed distribution.

```
DBMS_STATS.set_database_prefs
(pname         => 'METHOD_OPT',
 pvalue        => 'FOR ALL INDEXED COLUMNS SIZE SKEWONLY');
```

❏ Create and export statistics to a statistics table.

```
DBMS_STATS.create_stat_table
   (ownname => USER,
    stattab => 'GuysStatTab');
DBMS_STATS.export_table_stats
   (ownname        => USER,
    tabname        => 'EMPLOYEES',
    stattab        => 'GuysStatTab',
    statid         => 'Demo1');
```

❏ Import statistics from a statistics table into the current schema.

```
DBMS_STATS.import_table_stats
   (ownname        => USER,
    tabname        => 'EMPLOYEES',
    stattab        => 'GuysStatTab',
    statid         => 'Demo1');
```

DBMS_STATS PROCEDURES AND PARAMETERS

DBMS_STATS provides procedures for gathering, dropping, exporting, and importing statistics. The most commonly used procedures are listed here.

CREATE_STAT_TABLE	Create a statistics table that can be used to store statistics for use in EXPORT or IMPORT operations.
DELETE_{DATABASE| SCHEMA| TABLE| INDEX}_STATS	Remove statistics for the database, schema, table, or index.
EXPORT_ {DATABASE| SCHEMA| TABLE| INDEX}_STATS	Exports statistics from the specified objects and stores them in a statistics table created by CREATE_STAT_TABLE.
GATHER_COLUMN_STATS	Gather statistics for a specific column.
GATHER_DATABASE_STATS	Gather object statistics for all objects in the database.
GATHER_DICTIONARY_STATS	Gather statistics on dictionary tables. These are the tables owned by SYS, SYSTEM and other Oracle internal accounts that contain meta-data relating to segments, tablespaces, and so on.

GATHER_FIXED_OBJECT_STATS	Gather statistics on V$ and GV$ fixed tables. These are the dynamic performance tables that expose Oracle performance counters, the wait interface, and other performance data.
GATHER_INDEX_STATS	Gather statistics for an index.
GATHER_SCHEMA_STATS	Gather statistics for all objects in a schema.
GATHER_TABLE_STATS	Gather statistics for a single table.
IMPORT_ {DATABASE| SCHEMA| TABLE| INDEX}_STATS	Imports statistics from a statistics table created by CREATE_STAT_TABLE.

Many of the DBMS_STATS procedures share a common subset of parameters. Some of these are listed here:

OWNNAME	The owner of the object to be analyzed.
STATTAB	The name of a statistics table to be used as the source or destination of statistics.
STATOWN	Owner of the statistics table.
STATID	An identifier to associate with statistics stored in a statistics table.
NO_INVALIDATE	If TRUE, don't invalidate cursors in the shared pool or open in sessions that might depend on the statistics being modified. If NULL or FALSE, any cursor that is dependent on the statistics will be invalidated and will need to be reparsed.
PARTNAME	Name of a partition to be processed.
TABNAME	Name of a table to be processed.
FORCE	Gather the statistics, even if the object(s) concerned are locked.
CASCADE	If true, cascades the operation to all indexes on the table concerned.
INDNAME	Name of an index to be processed.
ESTIMATE_PERCENT	The percentage of rows to be sampled for an analysis. The constant DBMS_STATS.AUTO_SAMPLE_SIZE enables Oracle to determine the best sample based on the size of the table and possibly other factors.
DEGREE	The degree of parallelism to be employed when sampling data. The default value of DBMS_STATS.AUTO_DEGREE results in Oracle choosing the degree based on object storage and instance configuration.
GRANULARITY	Controls how partition statistics are collected. Valid values are ALL, AUTO, GLOBAL, PARTITION, GLOBAL, AND PARTITION, SUBPARTITION.
BLOCK_SAMPLE	Determines whether to randomly sample blocks rather than rows. It's faster to sample blocks, but if the data is highly clustered, it's not as accurate.
METHOD_OPT	Histogram collection options; see the "Creating Histograms with METHOD_OPT" section.

OPTIONS   Controls which objects will have statistics collected. Possible
                             options are
                                         GATHER (all objects)
                                         GATHER AUTO (Oracle determines which objects may
                                         need statistics)
                                         GATHER STALE
                                         GATHER EMPTY
                             The last three options have equivalent LIST options that list the
                             objects that would be processed. For instance, LIST STALE
                             lists all objects with stale statistics.

SETTING DBMS_STATS DEFAULTS

The default DBMS_STATS options can be adjusted by the SET_GLOBAL_ PREFS,
SET_DATABASE_PREFS, SET_SCHEMA_PREFS, and SET_TABLE_ PREFS procedures or—in 10g—by the SET_PARAMS procedure. Defaults for the following
parameters, which we encountered earlier, can be set. Not all of these are available in Oracle 10g or earlier.

❑   CASCADE
❑   DEGREE
❑   ESTIMATE_PERCENT
❑   METHOD_OPT
❑   NO_INVALIDATE
❑   GRANULARITY
❑   PUBLISH
❑   INCREMENTAL
❑   STALE_PERCENT

For example, the following sets the stale statistics threshold to 20 percent for
the HR schema. Statistics in that schema will now be regarded as stale only if
DML has modified 20 percent of the rows:

```
BEGIN
    DBMS_STATS.set_schema_prefs (ownname       => 'HR',
                                 pname         => 'STALE_PERCENT',
                                 pvalue        => 20
                                );
END;
```

CREATING HISTOGRAMS WITH METHOD_OPT

The METHOD_OPT option controls how column level statistics, in particular histograms, are created. The default value is 'FOR ALL COLUMNS SIZE AUTO',
which enables Oracle to choose the columns that will have a histogram collected
and set the appropriate histogram bucket size.

Oracle bases the decision to create a histogram on the cardinality of the data and the presence of execution plans in the SQL cache that contain a filter or other predicate that is dependent on the data. This approach might work well in many cases, but there are some issues worth mentioning:

❏ Unless all anticipated SQLs are in the cache, there's a risk of missing histograms.

❏ Histograms might be created to optimize infrequently executed SQLs.

❏ Oracle's understanding of data distribution in a column before creating the histogram is imperfect, which can result in the ironic result that Oracle can realize it needs a histogram only if the histogram already exists.

Too many histograms will increase the time it takes to collect statistics and result in greater parse overhead and, in 11g, a larger number of child cursors.

It's therefore not always a good idea to rely on Oracle to decide when a histogram might be useful. You can use the METHOD_OPT parameter to manually determine the histogram collection. METHOD_OPT takes the following syntax:

```
FOR [ALL {INDEXED|HIDDEN}] COLUMNS [column_expression] [size_clause] [,
[column_expression] [size_clause] ]
```

The *column_expression* will usually be a column name, although if you use Oracle 11g extended statistics it could be an expression involving one or more columns. *Size_clause* takes the following syntax:

```
SIZE {bucket_size | REPEAT | AUTO | SKEWONLY}
```

Here are the modifiers to the SIZE clause:

❏ *Bucket_size* defines the number of buckets in the histogram.

❏ REPEAT updates histograms only if one already exists.

❏ AUTO determines whether to create a histogram and sets its bucket size based on indications of column skew, and the presence of cached SQLs that might benefit from the histogram.

❏ SKEWONLY creates a histogram only if there is indication that the column data is skewed. This is the same as AUTO, except that the presence of cached SQL statements is not considered.

Histograms increase the accuracy of the optimizer's cost calculations but increase the overhead of statistics collections. It's usually worth creating histograms for columns where you believe the data will have an irregular distribution, and where the column is involved in WHERE or JOIN expressions.

SAMPLING

Accurate statistics can usually be gathered without having to read every block in a table or index. Although statistics generated from reading every block will be more accurate, the increase in time taken to analyze the table will be much greater than the increase in accuracy. Consequently, by default DBMS_STAT will read only a sample of rows from each table.

This behavior is controlled by the ESTIMATE_PERCENT option, which will determine the percentage of rows to be included in the sample. The default value of DBMS_STATS.AUTO_SAMPLE_SIZE results in Oracle attempting to find a balance between sampling time and accuracy.

PARTITION STATISTICS

The GRANULARITY clause enables statistics for a partitioned table to be global across the entire table or to be collected at the partition or subpartition level. In addition, you can use the DBMS_STATS.SET_TABLE_PREFS procedure to establish an INCREMENTAL collection policy for a partitioned table. If INCREMENTAL is set to TRUE, then statistics are collected only from partitions that have been modified. Because time-range partitioned objects often have only a single active partition, this can lead to significant savings in sampling time.

EXTENDED STATISTICS

Extended statistics are statistics that go beyond the raw data in a single column. Extended statistics can be gathered for columns in combination, or for column values manipulated by functions or expressions.

Multicolumn Extended Statistics   *Multicolumn extended statistics* can be collected to calculate the selectivity of multicolumn expressions. For some columns, you can calculate selectivity of multiple columns by multiplying the selectivity of each. For instance, if 50 percent of the customers are male, and 10 percent of customers are from Australia, then it's probably reasonable to estimate that 5 percent (10 percent of 50 percent) of customers are Australian men. However, sometimes the data in two columns will have a dependency. For instance if 50 percent of the customers are female and 5 percent are named John, it's *not* reasonable to assume that 2.5 percent of the customers are women named John!

Multicolumn extended statistics allow the optimizer to recognize these column dependencies. Multicolumn extended statistics can be collected by supplying the column combinations to be collected in the METHOD_OPT parameter. For example, the following DBMS_STATS call gathers statistics on every individual column and also on the combination of gender and first name:

```
BEGIN
    DBMS_STATS.gather_table_stats
        (ownname            => 'SH',
         tabname            => 'CUSTOMERS',
         method_opt         =>
         'FOR ALL COLUMNS FOR COLUMNS (CUST_GENDER,CUST_FIRST_NAME)'
        );

END;
```

Expression Extended Statistics You can also gather extended statistics on an expression, which can help the optimizer calculate query cost when that expression appears in a SQL. For example, consider the following query, which includes a function in the WHERE clause for which a functional index exists:

```
SQL> SELECT COUNT (*), SUM (amount_sold)
  2      FROM sales
  3    WHERE sale_category (amount_sold) = 1;

  COUNT(*) SUM(AMOUNT_SOLD)
---------- ----------------
   2393655        161110431
```

```
-------------------------------------------------
| Id | Operation          | Name  | Rows  |
-------------------------------------------------
|  0 | SELECT STATEMENT   |       |     1 |
|  1 |  SORT AGGREGATE    |       |     1 |
|* 2 |   TABLE ACCESS FULL| SALES | 1238K |
-------------------------------------------------
```

The optimizer makes an attempt to estimate the number of rows that would match the function definition but can't do a particularly good job because it can't know in advance what the output of the function would be for every input value. We can collect statistics for the function using the following syntax:

```
BEGIN
    DBMS_STATS.gather_table_stats
        (ownname            => USER,
         tabname            => 'SALES',
         method_opt         => 'FOR ALL COLUMNS FOR COLUMNS
         (sale_category(amount_sold))'
        );
END;
```

Now that the extended statistics are created, the optimizer's estimate is far more accurate:

```
SQL> SELECT COUNT (*), SUM (amount_sold)
  2    FROM sales
  3    WHERE sale_category (amount_sold) = 1;

  COUNT(*) SUM(AMOUNT_SOLD)
---------- ----------------
   2393655         161110431
```

```
-------------------------------------------------
| Id | Operation          | Name  | Rows  |
-------------------------------------------------
|  0 | SELECT STATEMENT   |       |     1 |
|  1 |  SORT AGGREGATE    |       |     1 |
|* 2 |   TABLE ACCESS FULL| SALES | 2395K |
-------------------------------------------------
```

> In 11g, consider collecting *extended* statistics in which columns that are queried together have data dependencies, for functional indexes or for expressions commonly used in the WHERE clause.

Oracle 11g also allows you to create *virtual columns*, which can be queried as a regular column, but which are defined as an expression. A virtual column can provide the same benefit as using extended statistics because collecting statistics on the virtual column is logically equivalent to collecting extended statistics on the column's expression. For instance, instead of defining the extended statistics collection as previously shown, we can instead create the following virtual column:

```
ALTER TABLE products ADD rounded_list_price GENERATED
     ALWAYS AS (ROUND(prod_list_price,-2))
```

Queries that access the virtual column by name—or use the exact expression that defines the virtual column—can use statistics that the optimizer collects against the virtual column. Creating virtual columns changes the logical structure of the table however, which might not be permissible in a production environment.

Viewing and Managing Extended Statistics Extended statistics are stored in ALL_TAB_COL_STATISTICS with a system generated column alias that matches the EXTENSION_NAME column in ALL_STAT_EXTENSIONS. So we can join those two tables to see details about the statistics collected for our expressions or multicolumn sets:

```
SQL> SELECT extension_name, extension, density, num_distinct
  2    FROM all_stat_extensions e JOIN all_tab_col_statistics s
  3       ON (     e.owner = s.owner
  4             AND e.table_name = s.table_name
  5             AND e.extension_name = s.column_name
  6          )
  7    WHERE e.owner = 'SH' AND e.table_name IN ('CUSTOMERS', 'PRODUCTS')
  8  /

EXTENSION_NAME                   EXTENSION                 DENSITY NUM_DISTINCT
------------------------------   -----------------------   -------  ------------
SYS_STUR$_K1P2O6502N12AT4Z6P$#   (ROUND("PROD_LIST_PR     .006944444           10
                                 ICE",(-2)))

SYS_STUMAWKDOFYUW_WWNZ3OGING0N   ("CUST_GENDER","CUST     .00122549          1449
                                 _FIRST_NAME")
```

We can drop extended statistics using the DROP_EXTENDED_STATS function.

In the preceding examples, we inserted our multicolumn or expression specifications directly in the METHOD_OPT parameter. However, if you want to arrange for these statistics to be collected by default—for instance by the automated statistics collection job—you can use the CREATE_EXTENDED_STATS call. For instance, the following call ensures that whenever column statistics are collected on PRODUCTS, we will collect statistics on the PROD_LIST_PRICE rounded to the nearest $100:

```
DECLARE
    v_extension_name all_stat_extensions.extension_name%TYPE;
BEGIN
  v_extension_name:=DBMS_STATS.create_extended_stats
                    (ownname    => 'SH',
                     tabname    => 'PRODUCTS',
                     extension  => '(ROUND(prod_list_price,-2))'
                               );
END;
```

LOCKING STATISTICS

If you've carefully collected manual statistics with just the right DBMS_STATS options and at just the right time, it can be upsetting if an automatic statistics collection overwrites these statistics. It might be that you've determined that the current set of statistics results in the execution plan you want, and so you'd prefer that they not change. In these circumstances, you can lock statistics for a table or a schema with LOCK_SCHEMA_STATS or LOCK_TABLE_STATS. When locked, the statistics will not be replaced until unlocked with UNLOCK_SCHEMA _STATS or UNLOCK_TABLE_STATS.

SYSTEM STATISTICS

DBMS_STATS can also be used to collect system statistics. As discussed earlier in this chapter, System statistics give the optimizer data regarding the relative performance of the CPU and IO subsystems. System statistics are not gathered by default during the scheduled automatic statistics collection.

Nonworkload statistics, which essentially measure native IO and CPU speeds for trivial test operations, can be gathered with the following call:

```
BEGIN
    DBMS_STATS.gather_system_stats (
            gathering_mode => 'NOWORKLOAD');
END;
```

Workload statistics should be gathered during a period of realistic activity because they are based on real measurements of Oracle activity. These statistics can be collected either by calling GATHER_SYSTEM_STATS with a GATHERING_MODE of 'START' and then later with 'STOP', or by specifying the INTERVAL parameter. INTERVAL creates a background job that collects statistics over the specified number of minutes. For instance, the following call collects workload statistics for the next hour:

```
BEGIN
    DBMS_STATS.gather_system_stats
      (gathering_mode       => 'INTERVAL',
       interval             => 60);
END;
```

> Where possible, collect system statistics with the GATHER_SYSTEM_STATS procedure to give the optimizer information about the relative CPU and IO capabilities of the database server.

EXPORTING AND IMPORTING STATISTICS

The ability to save statistics to a statistics table that we create with CREATE_STAT_TABLE and to export to or import from that table enables us to keep copies of statistics if we want to revert to previous values.

One of the other reasons for using this functionality is to take a copy of statistics from a production or benchmark system and copy them to a test or development environment so that execution plans in these environments are more likely to reflect those that would occur in the production environment.

MANIPULATING STATISTICS

DBMS_STATS provides mechanisms that allow specific statistic values to be set manually. You can, if you want, manipulate table statistics to convince the optimizer that a table is larger than it is, or to directly manipulate the values for column density, number of distinct values, and so on.

It's particularly tempting to manipulate statistics in this way to determine how optimizer plans might change as tables grow. For instance, we might set the size of the employees table to 10,000 and ensure than the MANAGER_ID column reflects our anticipated 200 managers with the following DBMS_STATS calls:

```
BEGIN

    DBMS_STATS.set_table_stats (ownname       => USER,
                                tabname       => 'EMPLOYEES',
                                numrows       => 10000,
                                numblks       =>500
                               );
    DBMS_STATS.set_column_stats (ownname       => USER,
                                 tabname       => 'EMPLOYEES',
                                 colname       => 'MANAGER_ID',
                                 distcnt       => 200,
                                 density       => 0.005
                                );
END;
```

There are some valid reasons for manipulating statistics in this way, but there are usually better ways to achieve your objectives. It's difficult or impossible to accurately set all possible statistic values, and you might end up with inconsistent statistics. If you are trying to create a test or development environment with production level statistics, exporting and importing statistics is probably a better idea. If you are trying to get the optimizer to use a particular execution plan, hints or stored outlines as discussed in the next chapter are probably a better idea.

SUMMARY

The optimizer is the software layer that Oracle employs to determine how best to execute a SQL statement. In this chapter we looked at the Oracle optimizer in some depth, and we have seen how we can help the optimizer make the best decisions.

The optimizer goal determines whether the optimizer seeks to improve performance for the retrieval of all rows from a query, or only from the first row or first set of rows. ALL_ROWS optimization is most suitable for data warehousing and OLTP systems. FIRST_ROWS_*N* modes are most suitable for OLTP systems.

One of the key aspects of optimization is the determination of *selectivity*; the relative number of rows returned by an expression. Highly selective clauses are best served by index-based paths, whereas less selective expressions might require a table scan.

The determination of selectivity, together with other statistical information, allows the optimizer to calculate a cost for each possible plan. Object statistics include information about the size of table and the distribution of data within columns. System statistics help Oracle determine relative costs of various IO operations compared with CPU operations. Some configuration parameters also affect the optimizer's assumptions and its decisions.

Histograms include information about the distribution of data within a column. Oracle collects some histograms by default, but you should consider fine-tuning histogram collection to help optimize queries on columns with uneven data distributions.

Oracle automatically collects statistics using a background task, but you will often want to collect statistics manually or change collection defaults. Manual statistics can be gathered using the DBMS_STATS package.

In Oracle 11g, you can use DBMS_STATS to collect *extended* statistics for multiple columns or for functions or complex expressions. Creating virtual columns on these expressions can sometimes achieve the same outcome.

EXECUTION PLAN MANAGEMENT

As Robert Burns famously said, "The best-laid plans of mice and men often go awry."[1] No matter how thoroughly the optimizer works to find the best plan, it's inevitable that some plans will be less than perfect. When we don't agree with the default decision of the optimizer, we need a way to impose our own plan. Furthermore, sometimes we simply want to ensure that the plan that exists today will not be overridden in the future. Finally, we want to do our best to make sure that if the optimizer makes a change to the plan in the future, that change is for the better.

In the previous chapter, we looked at collecting the information and establishing the configuration that the optimizer uses to make its determinations. In this chapter we look at some specific techniques for overriding the optimizer or for further improving the optimizer's decision-making capabilities. The specific techniques we discuss in this chapter include

❏ Applying hints to SQL statements
❏ Assigning a stored outline to a SQL statement, either to prevent the plan from changing in the future or to apply a new plan
❏ Creating profiles that assist the optimizer to select the best plan now and in the future
❏ Utilizing 11g baselines to ensure that optimizer plans evolve in the direction of greater efficiency in the future

---

[1] As comedian Eddie Izzard asks, "Does this imply that some of the less well-thought-out mice plans do quite well?"

HINTS

Hints are instructions that you can include in your SQL statement to instruct or guide the optimizer. Using hints you can specify join orders, type of access paths, indexes to be used, the optimization goal, and other instructions.

The word *hint* implies that these are merely suggestions that the optimizer can choose to ignore. In reality, the optimizer is obliged to obey optimizer hints if at all possible. You should therefore be careful when using hints because the optimizer will attempt to obey the hint even if doing so results in disastrous performance. In general, you should consider a hint only after you have exhausted less-direct methods—collecting statistics, creating histograms, setting configuration parameters, and so on.

An optimizer hint appears as a comment following the first word of the SQL statement (usually SELECT, MERGE, INSERT, DELETE, or UPDATE). A hint is differentiated from other comments by the presence of the plus sign (+) following the opening comment delimiter (/*). For example, the hint in the following statement will result in the CUSTOMERS table being accessed by a full table scan, even if the optimizer would normally choose an indexed retrieval:

```
SELECT /*+ FULL(customers) */ *
  FROM sh.customers
 WHERE cust_year_of_birth = 1976
   AND cust_gender = 'M'
   AND cust_marital_status = 'single'
```

Here are some of the more commonly used hints. A more complete list can be found in the *Oracle SQL Language Reference*.

ALL_ROWS	Use the ALL_ROWS optimizer goal.
AND_EQUALS(*table_name index_name index_name index_name* ....)	This hint instructs the optimizer to merge the specified indexes when retrieving rows for the specified table. Similar to INDEX_COMBINE but does not use the bitmap conversion strategy that requires Enterprise Edition.
APPEND	Use direct mode inserts (see Chapter 14, "DML Tuning").
CACHE(*table_name*)	When performing a full table scan, encourage the caching of the table within Oracle shared memory. NOCACHE has the opposite effect.
FACT(*table_name*)	Consider the nominated table to be a star schema Fact table (see Chapter 4, "Logical and Physical Database Design").
FIRST_ROWS(*N*)	Use the FIRST_ROWS optimizer goal, optimizing for retrieval of the first *N* rows.

FULL(*table_name*)	Use a full table scan to access the nominated table, even if there is an appropriate index path to the data.
HASH(*table_name*)	Use hash cluster based retrieval on the specified table. (This will obviously work only if the table is in a hash cluster.)
INDEX(*table_name* [*index_name*])	Use the specified index on the specified table. If no index is specified, use the index that results in the lowest cost.
INDEX_COMBINE(*table_name index_name index_name index_name ....*)	This hint instructs the optimizer to merge the specified indexes when retrieving rows for the specified table. Similar to AND_EQUALS but uses a bitmap conversion strategy that requires Enterprise Edition.
INDEX_SS(*table_name index_name*)	Use an index "skip scan" access path (see Chapter 5, "Indexing and Clustering").
LEADING(*table_name ...*)	The specified tables should be the first in the join order and joined in the order specified.
NOPARALLEL(*table_name*)	Don't use parallel query, even if table or database default would normally result in parallel processing.
ORDERED	Use the order of tables in the FROM clause as the join order. This overrides normal preference for an alternative join order based on cost calculations.
PARALLEL(*table_name degree_ of_parallelism*)	This hint directs that the table should be accessed via parallel table scan. The parallelism parameter determines how many query processes should be used. See Chapter 13, "Parallel SQL," for more information.
USE_HASH(*table_name*)	Use the hash join technique when joining this table.
USE_MERGE(*table_name*)	This hint specifies that when the table is joined, the sort-merge join approach should be used.
USE_NL(*table_name*)	This hint specifies that when this table is joined, the nested loops approach should be used.

Multiple hints can appear in the same comment, separated by a space. For instance, the following hint requests a full table scan on both DEPARTMENT and EMPLOYEES:

```
SELECT /*+ FULL(E) FULL(D) */ *
  FROM hr.employees e JOIN
       hr.departments d USING (department_id)
 WHERE department_name='Executive'
```

USING HINTS TO CHANGE THE ACCESS PATH

One of the most frequent uses of hints is to request a particular access path, such as requesting a specific index.

The simplest hint for requesting an index is the rather appropriately named INDEX hint. For instance, the following requests the use of the EMP_MANAGER _IX index:

```
SELECT /*+ index(e emp_manager_ix) */
       employee_id, first_name, last_name,
  FROM hr.employees e
 WHERE manager_id = 100 AND department_id = 90
```

However, you can also instruct the optimizer to choose between a subset of indexes by specifying multiple index names:

```
SELECT /*+ index(e emp_manager_ix emp_department_ix) */ *
  FROM hr.employees e
 WHERE manager_id = 100 AND department_id = 90
```

And you can simply specify that you want an index to be used but leave it up to the optimizer to choose the appropriate index:

```
SELECT /*+  index(e) */ *
  FROM hr.employees e
 WHERE manager_id >0
```

You can also specify that you would like multiple indexes to be merged using the AND_EQUAL or INDEX_COMBINE hint, although this might suggest that you are missing an appropriate concatenated index:

```
SELECT /*+  and_equal(e emp_manager_ix emp_department_ix) */ *
  FROM hr.employees e
where manager_id=100 and department_id=90
```

If you don't want to use an index, you can use the FULL hint. It might be that the optimizer is incorrectly deciding that the indexed based path is superior, but you get a better outcome from the full scan. If this is the case, you should also review your use of histograms, database configuration, and system statistics because all these can influence the optimizer's preference for full table scans over indexed lookups.

```
SELECT /*+  FULL(e) */ *
  FROM hr.employees e
 WHERE department_id = 90 AND manager_id = 100
```

USING HINTS TO CHANGE THE JOIN ORDER

Another common reason for using hints is to change the join order, or to change the type of joins performed.

The ORDERED hint instructs the optimizer to join tables in the order in which they appear in the FROM clause:

```
SELECT /*+ ORDERED*/    *
  FROM hr.departments d JOIN hr.employees e
  USING (department_id)
```

The LEADING hint can achieve the same result without requiring any particular table order in the FROM clause. Tables listed in the LEADING hint should be first in the join order and joined in the same order as is specified in the hint. For instance, the LEADING hint here requests that the join start with the EMPLOYEES table:

```
SELECT /*+ LEADING(e) */    *
  FROM hr.departments d  JOIN hr.employees e
  USING (department_id)
```

We can select the join method (nested-loops, sort-merge, or hash) by using the USE_NL, USE_HASH, or USE_MERGE hints. This example forces a hash join:

```
SELECT /*+ ORDERED USE_HASH(e) */    *
  FROM hr.departments d JOIN hr.employees e
  USING (department_id)
```

ERRORS IN HINT SPECIFICATIONS

If you make an error in a hint specification—for instance, forgetting the plus sign or specifying an invalid hint—Oracle ignores the hint without generating an error or warning. Therefore, it is important that you validate that your hint worked (using the DBMS_XLPAN or tkprof utilities documented in Chapter 3, "Tools of the Trade").

It's particularly easy to make mistakes when specifying table names. If the table name is given an alias in the FROM clause, you must specify this alias in the hint. However, you must not specify an owner (or schema) name, even if it appears in the FROM clause.

For instance, assume this is the query:

```
SELECT *
  FROM hr.employees e
 WHERE e.department_id > 0
```

The following are some valid and invalid hints:

`/*+ INDEX(E EMP_DEPARTMENT_IX ) */`	Correct usage. The index *EMP _DEPARTMENT_IX* will be used.
`/* INDEX(E EMP_DEPARTMENT_IX ) */`	Invalid because the + is missing after the opening comment marker.
`/*+INDEX(Employees EMP_DEPARTMENT_IX)*/`	Invalid because employees is given a table alias in the FROM clause but not in the hint.
`/*+ INDEX(E, EMP_DEPARTMENT_IX */`	Invalid because the ending bracket is missing.
`/*+ INDEX(E, EMP_DEPARTMENT_IX )*/`	Valid, although the comma following the table alias is not necessary.
`/*+ INDEEX(E, EMP_DEPARTMENT_IX )*/`	Invalid because the hint is misspelled.

STORED OUTLINES

As new statistics are collected, the relative costs for various execution plans might change, and consequently the optimizer might decide to change the plan of a SQL statement. Usually, these execution plan changes will be for the best. However, if you have determined that a specific plan is the one you want, you might want to be sure that the optimizer will not "change its mind" in the future. This is when *plan stability* using *stored outlines* is useful.

A stored outline is a way of recording the execution plan for a specific SQL statement at a specific point in time. You can then activate the stored outline to ensure that the specific execution plan is used in the future even if statistics change.

Oracle has announced that stored outlines will be depreciated in favor of SQL plan management based mechanisms, such as baselines, in the future. SQL baselines offer some unique advantages, but they do not yet provide all the capabilities currently provided by outlines. Furthermore, not all the new facilities (baselines in particular) are available in Oracle 10g, and some aspects require a Tuning Pack license. Stored outlines, on the other hand, are fully supported in standard edition Oracle 10g and 11g.

CREATING AN OUTLINE TO STABILIZE A PLAN

It's not unusual for a SQL statement to be positioned on the edge between two plans that have similar cost values. If statistics or database parameters change the plans for these SQL statements, plans might also change.

If two plans with similar costs always have similar performance characteristics, this would be fine. Unfortunately, Oracle's cost estimates are only approximations of performance, and it might be that the change in execution plan is undesirable.

We could, of course, lock the statistics involved, but this would prevent other SQLs from benefiting from possibly highly desirable plan changes. What we typically want in these circumstances is to lock the execution plan. Stored outlines enable us to do this fairly easily.

For example, a small change in the average age of customers can cause the execution plan for the following statement to change from a full table scan to an indexed lookup:

```
SQL> SELECT MAX (cust_income_level)
  2     FROM customers c
  3    WHERE cust_year_of_birth > 1985;
```

If we are happy with the execution plan that exists today, we can create an outline for it as follows:

```
SQL> CREATE OUTLINE customer_yob_qry FOR CATEGORY outlines2 ON
  2   SELECT MAX (cust_income_level)
  3     FROM customers c
  4    WHERE cust_year_of_birth > 1985;

Outline created.
```

Every outline belongs to a specific category; the outline created above belongs to the category "outlines2." A single category can be activated by using the USE_STORED_OUTLINES parameter at the session or system level. To enable the preceding outline (and any others in the same category), we issue the following statement:

```
SQL> ALTER SESSION SET use_stored_outlines=outlines2;

Session altered.
```

Running DBMS_XPLAN, or viewing AUTOTRACE output, confirms that the outline was used, and we can be confident that the execution plan will not change while the outline is active:

```
SQL> SELECT MAX (cust_income_level)
  2     FROM customers c
  3    WHERE cust_year_of_birth > 1985;

Execution Plan
----------------------------------------------------------
Plan hash value: 296924608
```

```
----------------------------------------------------------------------
| Id | Operation          | Name      | Rows | Bytes | Cost (%CPU)| Time     |
----------------------------------------------------------------------
|  0 | SELECT STATEMENT   |           |    1 |    21 | 1488   (1)| 00:00:25 |
|  1 |  SORT AGGREGATE    |           |    1 |    21 |           |          |
|* 2 |   TABLE ACCESS FULL| CUSTOMERS |  661 | 13881 | 1488   (1)| 00:00:25 |
----------------------------------------------------------------------

Predicate Information (identified by operation id):
-----------------------------------------------

   2 - filter("CUST_YEAR_OF_BIRTH">1985)

Note
-----

   - outline "CUSTOMER_YOB_QRY" used for this statement
```

> Stored outlines can be used to "pin" a SQL statement's execution plan, ensuring that it will not change as a result of changes in statistics or database configuration.

HACKING AN OUTLINE

Stabilizing the plan using an outline is all very well, but often what you actually want to do is to force the SQL to take a different plan even though you don't have the ability to edit the SQL text. It's possible to use outlines for this purpose, though it requires a bit of mild hacking.[2]

Let's say we want to change the SQL statement from the previous section so that it always uses an index, but we can't modify the SQL text to insert the index hint. One approach would be to change object statistics or database configuration until we had the plan we wanted, and then create the outline. However, this is not practical for every type of hint we want to apply. Here's how we can create an outline that effectively allows us to apply whatever hints we want.

First, we create an outline on the unchanged SQL statement:

```
SQL> CREATE  OUTLINE cust_yob_otln FOR CATEGORY outlines2 ON
  2    SELECT MIN(cust_income_level)
  3      FROM customers c
  4     WHERE cust_year_of_birth > 1985;
```

---

[2] These techniques are described in Oracle support note 730062.1 and so have the implicit approval of Oracle support.

Next, we create a *private* outline from this public outline. A private outline exists only within our current session:

```
SQL> CREATE PRIVATE OUTLINE original_oln FROM cust_yob_otln;
```

Now we create another private outline; this one is for the same SQL but with whatever hints we want to apply specified:

```
SQL> CREATE  PRIVATE OUTLINE hinted_oln  ON
  2   SELECT /*+ INDEX(C) */ MIN(cust_income_level)
  3    FROM customers c
  4   WHERE cust_year_of_birth > 1985;
```

We now have two private outlines, one matching the public outline for the SQL, another reflecting the outline we'd like to have. If we look in the global temporary table OL$HINTS, which holds the private outline definitions, we can see the hints applied in each outline. Notice that the ORIGINAL_OLN outline has a FULL hint, whereas the HINTED_OLN has an INDEX hint.

```
SQL> SELECT ol_name, hint_text
  2    FROM ol$hints;
```

OL_NAME	HINT_TEXT
ORIGINAL_OLN	OUTLINE_LEAF(@"SEL$1")
ORIGINAL_OLN	ALL_ROWS
ORIGINAL_OLN	OPTIMIZER_FEATURES_ENABLE('10.2.0.1')
ORIGINAL_OLN	IGNORE_OPTIM_EMBEDDED_HINTS
ORIGINAL_OLN	**FULL**(@"SEL$1" "C"@"SEL$1")
HINTED_OLN	**INDEX**(@"SEL$1" "C"@"SEL$1("CUSTOMERS". "CUST_YEAR_OF_BIRTH"))
HINTED_OLN	OUTLINE_LEAF(@"SEL$1")
HINTED_OLN	ALL_ROWS
HINTED_OLN	OPTIMIZER_FEATURES_ENABLE('10.2.0.1')
HINTED_OLN	IGNORE_OPTIM_EMBEDDED_HINTS

What we want to do now is to copy the hints from HINTED_OLN to ORIGINAL_OLN. The OL$HINTS table contains the hints whereas its parent table OL$ contains a hint count that must also be updated. The following SQLs swap the outlines:

```
SQL> UPDATE ol$hints
  2    SET ol_name =
  3         CASE ol_name
```

```
  4                    WHEN 'HINTED_OLN'
  5                        THEN 'ORIGINAL_OLN'
  6                    WHEN 'ORIGINAL_OLN'
  7                        THEN 'HINTED_OLN'
  8                    ELSE ol_name
  9                 END
 10     WHERE ol_name IN ('HINTED_OLN', 'ORIGINAL_OLN');

10 rows updated.

SQL>
SQL> UPDATE ol$ ol1
  2     SET hintcount =
  3              (SELECT hintcount
  4                 FROM ol$ ol2
  5                WHERE ol2.ol_name IN ('HINTED_OLN', 'ORIGINAL_OLN')
  6                  AND ol2.ol_name != ol1.ol_name)
  7     WHERE ol1.ol_name IN ('HINTED_OLN', 'ORIGINAL_OLN');

2 rows updated.
```

Now, if we activate the private outlines by setting USE_PRIVATE
_OUTLINES, we can see that the private outline is used and successfully forces
our original SQL to use the index.

```
SQL> ALTER SESSION SET use_private_outlines=TRUE;

Session altered.

SQL> SELECT MIN (cust_income_level)
  2     FROM customers c
  3    WHERE cust_year_of_birth > 1985;
```

Id	Operation	Name	Rows
0	SELECT STATEMENT		1
1	SORT AGGREGATE		1
2	TABLE ACCESS BY INDEX ROWID	CUSTOMERS	540
* 3	**INDEX RANGE SCAN**	CUST_YEAR_OF_BIRTH_IDX	540

```
Note
-----
   - outline "ORIGINAL_OLN" used for this statement
```

The final thing for us to do is to copy the private outline back into the original public outline:

```
SQL> CREATE OR REPLACE OUTLINE cust_yob_otln FROM PRIVATE
original_oln FOR CATEGORY outlines2 ;
```

Now, if the outline category OUTLINES2 is activated, the SQL uses the index just as if the SQL included the index hint.

Using private outlines, it's possible to edit or copy outlines to apply hints to statements that you cannot edit.

SQL TUNING SETS

Oracle 10g introduced the concept of the SQL Tuning set, which is a group of SQL statements that can be processed as a group by Oracle's SQL Tuning and Plan management facilities. We can load SQL tuning sets with currently cached SQLs, with SQLs from Active Workload Repository (AWR) snapshots, or from a manual workload.

We can use either the DBMS_SQLTUNE package or Oracle Enterprise Manager to create and manage SQL tuning sets. Remember that you need to be licensed for the Tuning Pack to take advantage of these features.

MANUALLY CREATING A TUNING SET

Let's start by creating a SQL tuning set manually:

```
1    DECLARE
2       sqlset_csr    DBMS_SQLTUNE.sqlset_cursor;
3    BEGIN
4
5       DBMS_SQLTUNE.create_sqlset (sqlset_name      => 'MySqlSet',
6           description      => 'SQL Tuning set demonstration');
7
8       OPEN sqlset_csr FOR
9         SELECT VALUE (cache_sqls)
10          FROM TABLE
11           (DBMS_SQLTUNE.select_cursor_cache
12             (basic_filter     => 'parsing_schema_name=''TRANSIM''',
13              ranking_measure1=> 'buffer_gets',
14              result_limit    => 10)) cache_sqls;
```

```
15
16        DBMS_SQLTUNE.load_sqlset (sqlset_name              => 'MySqlSet',
17                                  populate_cursor          => sqlset_csr);
18
19        CLOSE sqlset_csr;
20     END;
```

On line 5 we create the SQL tuning set. On lines 8–14 we select the SQLs to be included in the tuning set from the active cursor cache. The SELECT_CURSOR _CACHE procedure returns a structure similar to the structure of V$SQL and the BASIC_FILTER condition acts like a WHERE clause against V$SQL.

SELECT_CURSOR_CACHE provides additional sorting and filtering criteria. In this example, we've specified that we want only 10 SQLs by specifying the RESULT_LIMIT on line 14; RANKING_MEASURE1 on line 13 determines that those 10 will be the ones with the highest buffer gets.

Having opened a cursor against SELECT_CURSOR_CACHE, we now add the SQLs returned by the cursor into the tuning set using the LOAD_SQLSET procedure on line 16.

We can continue to add SQLs to the tuning set, and we can retrieve the SQLs from a variety of sources. In the next example, we add SQLs from AWR snapshots to the SQL set using the SELECT_WORKLOAD_REPOSITORY procedure:

```
1      DECLARE
2         min_snap_id    NUMBER;
3         max_snap_id    NUMBER;
4         sqlset_csr     DBMS_SQLTUNE.sqlset_cursor;
5      BEGIN
6         SELECT MIN (snap_id), MAX (snap_id)
7           INTO min_snap_id, max_snap_id
8           FROM dba_hist_snapshot;
9
10        OPEN sqlset_csr FOR
11          SELECT VALUE (workload_sqls)
12            FROM TABLE
13                    (DBMS_SQLTUNE.select_workload_repository
14                      (min_snap_id,
15                       max_snap_id,
16                       basic_filter  =>  'parsing_schema_name=''TRANSIM''')
17                    ) workload_sqls;
18
19        DBMS_SQLTUNE.load_sqlset (sqlset_name              => 'MySqlSet',
20                                  populate_cursor          => sqlset_csr,
21                                  load_option              => 'MERGE' );
22
```

```
23        CLOSE sqlset_csr;
24     END;


SQL> SELECT SUBSTR (vs.sql_text, 1, 65) AS sql_text, dss.buffer_gets
  2    FROM dba_sqlset_statements dss JOIN v$sql vs USING (sql_id)
  3    WHERE sqlset_name = 'MySqlSet'
  4    /


SQL_TEXT                                                          BUFFER_GETS
------------------------------------------------------------------------------
SELECT SUM(QUANTITY) FROM g_orders     JOIN g_line_items USI         571455
SELECT /*+INDEX(o) INDEX(b) ORDERED */       *     FROM g_o          384739
SELECT * FROM g_orders    JOIN g_line_items USING (order_id          254936
SELECT title,SUM(quantity) AS quantity     from G_BOOKS join         248902
SELECT * FROM G_ORDERS O              JOIN G_LINE_ITEMS LI USI        247974
SELECT   author_id, fullname, SUM (quantity)    FROM g_autho         246036
SELECT COUNT(*) FROM G_CUSTOMERS WHERE DOB > :1                       77385
```

Other DBMS_SQLTUNE procedures—and the Oracle 11g DBMS_SPM procedure—can take as parameters either individual SQL statement identifiers or SQL tuning sets.

CREATING TUNING SETS IN ENTERPRISE MANAGER

It's straightforward to create SQL tuning sets in Oracle Enterprise Manager. Figure 8-1 shows us creating a SQL tuning set by invoking the *SQL Tuning Sets* link in the *Additional Monitoring Options* section of the *Performance* tab. This page essentially implements the options of the DBMS_SQLTUNE.CREATE_SQLSET procedure.

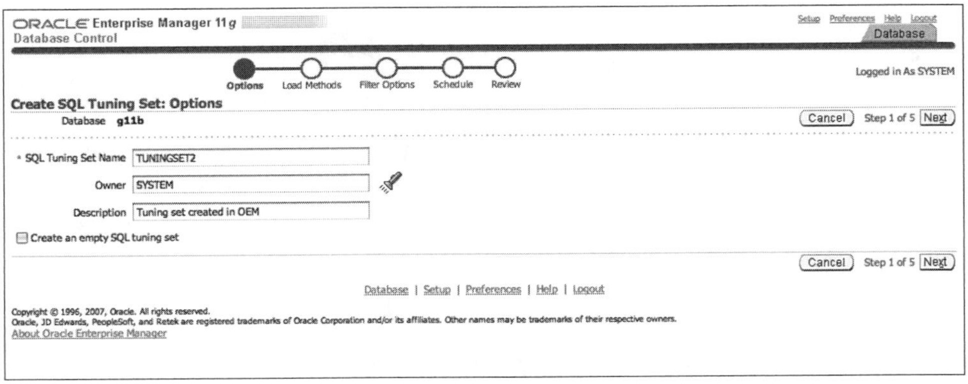

FIGURE 8-1   Creating a SQL tuning set in ENTERPRISE MANAGER.

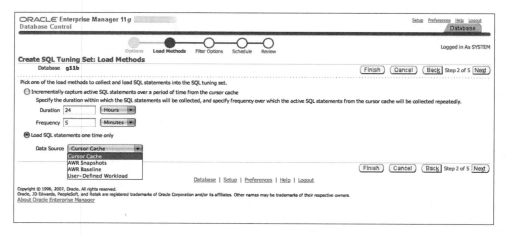

FIGURE 8-2   Choosing SQLs to load into the SQL tuning set.

In Figure 8-2 we choose the method for loading SQLs. We can load directly from cache, from AWR, or from a table created by the user that contains SQL statements and statistics. We can even instruct Oracle to periodically capture SQL statements from the cursor cache: this will create a scheduled task to run SELECT_CURSOR_CACHE and LOAD_SQL_SET procedures periodically.

Figure 8-3 shows us adding filters to the SQL Set we are creating. This screen exposes the parameters of the DBMS_SQLTUNE.SELECT_CURSOR _CACHE procedure.

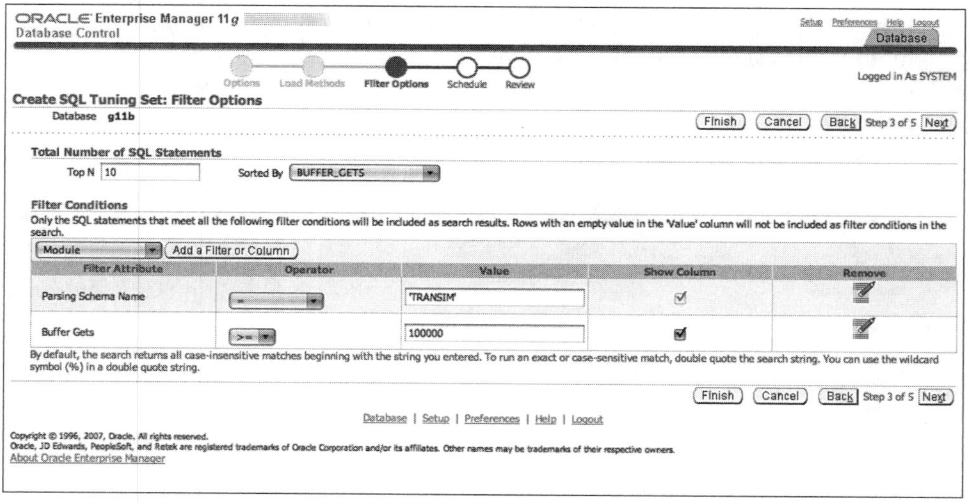

FIGURE 8-3   Specifying filter conditions for the SQL Set.

SQL PROFILES AND THE SQL TUNING ADVISOR

Stored outlines are generally used to fix an execution plan and provide plan stability: The guarantee that a plan will not change if database configuration or statistics are modified. Stored outlines were originally introduced in Oracle 8i time frame and were partly intended to soothe those who were nervous about plan instability when migrating from the predictable rule based optimizer (RBO) to the more powerful but less predictable cost based optimizer (CBO).

SQL Profiles have a slightly different objective: Rather than aiming for optimizer *stability*, they are intended to increase optimizer *flexibility*—the ability to create better plans for new SQLs when circumstances change. SQL Profiles and the associated SQL Tuning Advisor were introduced in Oracle 10g and require an Oracle Tuning Pack license.

A SQL Profile is a collection of statistics specific to the SQL that are created by a SQL tuning task and which can then be used by the SQL tuning advisor to determine an optimum plan. You can think of the SQL tuning advisor as an *off-line optimizer*.

The SQL tuning advisor has a number of unique advantages over the default *run-time optimizer*:

❑ It can spend more time optimizing the SQL statement than is available to the run time optimizer.
❑ It can run the SQL—at least partially—before deciding on a final approach.
❑ It can advise when indexes are missing.
❑ It can create a profile to help the optimizer make better decisions in the future.
❑ Its benefits can be shared between statements that are logically similar, even if they do not have exactly matching text.

The profile contains information collected during the SQL tuning task and which is specific to the SQL Statement. It can include statistics regarding the SQL statement execution that the optimizer can use to refine its estimates of cost, cardinality, or data volumes.

USING DBMS_SQLTUNE

Let's examine the SQL tuning package API first and then the graphical interface within Enterprise Manager.

We use the following SQL statement as the target of our tuning efforts:

```
SQL> SELECT /* OPSG Profile example */ *
  2     FROM customers JOIN countries USING (country_id)
  3    WHERE cust_marital_status = 'Mar-AF'
  4      AND country_name = 'United States of America'
  5      AND cust_year_of_birth > 1960;
```

We start by using the DBMS_SQLTUNE.CREATE_TUNING_TASK package to create a tuning task. This procedure can create a task for supplied SQL text, a SQL_ID as found in V$SQL, or a SQL Tuning Set. In our example, we use a SQL_ID, which we first find in V$SQL. We then supply this SQL_ID to DBMS_SQLTUNE.CREATE_TUNING_TASK and then execute the task with DBMS_SQLTUNE.EXECUTE_TUNING_TASK:

```
SQL> VAR v_sql_id    VARCHAR2(13)
SQL> VAR v_task_name VARCHAR2

SQL> BEGIN
  2     SELECT sql_id
  3       INTO :v_sql_id
  4       FROM v$sql
  5      WHERE sql_text LIKE 'SELECT /* OPSG Profile example%';
  6  END  ;
/
SQL> BEGIN
  2     :v_task_name := DBMS_SQLTUNE.create_tuning_task
(sql_id => :v_sql_id);
  3     DBMS_OUTPUT.put_line (:v_task_name);
  4     DBMS_SQLTUNE.execute_tuning_task (:v_task_name);
  5     COMMIT;
  6  END;
```

The SQL tuning task might take awhile to run, though for a single SQL like the one in our example, it finishes almost immediately. You can track its progress through the DBA_ADVISOR_LOG view.

When finished, we can get a tuning report from DBMS_SQLTUNE .REPORT_TUNING_TASK and an implementation script from DBMS_SQLTUNE .SCRIPT_TUNING_TASK. Both routines return a CLOB. Next we see the output from the tuning task for our example. The tuning advisor recommends implementing a SQL profile that results in an execution plan change with an estimated 97 percent improvement:

```
SQL>SELECT dbms_sqltune.report_tuning_task('TASK_7281') FROM dual;

DBMS_SQLTUNE.REPORT_TUNING_TASK('TASK_7281')
---------------------------------------------------------------------------
```

```
GENERAL INFORMATION SECTION
-------------------------------------------------------------------
Tuning Task Name            : TASK_7281
Tuning Task Owner           : OPSG
Scope                       : COMPREHENSIVE
Time Limit(seconds)         : 1800
Completion Status           : COMPLETED
Started at                  : 09/11/2008 22:56:32
Completed at                : 09/11/2008 22:56:32
Number of SQL Profile Findings  : 1


-------------------------------------------------------------------
Schema Name: OPSG
SQL ID      : f1z71bhu6dybz
SQL Text    : SELECT /* OPSG Profile example */ *
                 FROM customers JOIN countries USING (country_id)
              WHERE cust_marital_status = 'Mar-AF'
                AND country_name = 'United States of America'
                AND cust_year_of_birth > 1960


-------------------------------------------------------------------
FINDINGS SECTION (1 finding)
-------------------------------------------------------------------


1- SQL Profile Finding (see explain plans section below)
-------------------------------------------------------------------
  A potentially better execution plan was found for this statement.

  Recommendation (estimated benefit: 97%)
  --------------------------------------
  - Consider accepting the recommended SQL profile.
    execute dbms_sqltune.accept_sql_profile(task_name => 'TASK_7281',
          replace => TRUE);
-------------------------------------------------------------------
EXPLAIN PLANS SECTION
-------------------------------------------------------------------


1- Original With Adjusted Cost
------------------------------
Plan hash value: 2453622998

 <<original explain plan here>>

2- Using SQL Profile
--------------------
```

```
Plan hash value: 624745445

-----------------------------------------------------------------------
| Id | Operation                        | Name                 | Rows |
-----------------------------------------------------------------------
|  0 | SELECT STATEMENT                 |                      |    2 |
|* 1 |  TABLE ACCESS BY INDEX ROWID     | CUSTOMERS            |    1 |
|  2 |   NESTED LOOPS                   |                      |    2 |
|  3 |    TABLE ACCESS BY INDEX ROWID|   COUNTRIES           |    1 |
|* 4 |     INDEX RANGE SCAN             | COUNTRY_NAME_IDX     |    1 |
|* 5 |     INDEX RANGE SCAN             | CUST_MARITAL_YEAR_IDX|    2 |
-----------------------------------------------------------------------
```

If we accept the profile (using the ACCEPT_SQL_PROFILE command provided in the "Recommendation" section), entries will be created in the DBA _SQL_PROFILE and DBMSHSXP_SQL_PROFILE_ATTR views that we can interrogate to see what's in the profile. As the following output shows, the profile contains plan-specific statistics relating to the expected cardinality of each step. These don't lock the optimizer into a fixed plan but allow it to make better decisions.

```
SQL> SELECT attr_value
  2    FROM dba_sql_profiles p JOIN dbmshsxp_sql_profile_attr a
  3         ON (a.profile_name = p.NAME)
  4   WHERE p.NAME = 'SYS_SQLPROF_0147146e15ff0000';

ATTR_VALUE
-------------------------------------------------------------
OPT_ESTIMATE(@"SEL$58A6D7F6", TABLE, "CUSTOMERS"@"SEL$1",
SCALE_ROWS=0.001204853424)

OPT_ESTIMATE(@"SEL$58A6D7F6", INDEX_SCAN, "CUSTOMERS"@
"SEL$1", CUST_MARITAL_YEAR_IDX, SCALE_ROWS=0.001298158571)

OPT_ESTIMATE(@"SEL$58A6D7F6", JOIN, ("COUNTRIES"@"SEL$1",
"CUSTOMERS"@"SEL$1"), SCALE_ROWS=2)
```

INDEXING ADVICE

DBMS_SQLTUNE provides indexing advice if it determines that an index might be beneficial in optimizing the SQL statements provided. For instance, next we see DBMS_SQLTUNE recommending an index on CUST_MARITAL_STATUS and CUST_YEAR_OF_BIRTH to optimize a query:

```
-------------------------------------------------------------------
FINDINGS SECTION (1 finding)
-------------------------------------------------------------------


1- Index Finding (see explain plans section below)
---------------------------------------------------
  The execution plan of this statement can be improved by creating
  one or more indices.

  Recommendation     (estimated benefit: 100%)
  -------------------------------------------
  - Consider running the Access Advisor to improve the physical schema
    design or creating the recommended index.
    create index OPSG.IDX$$_1CAD0001 on OPSG.CUSTOMERS
     ('CUST_MARITAL_STATUS','CUST_YEAR_OF_BIRTH');
```

SQL TUNING IN ENTERPRISE MANAGER

Most of the facilities provided by DBMS_SQLTUNE can be invoked from within Oracle Enterprise Manager. These features can be invoked from the *SQL Tuning Advisor* link within the *Advisor Central* page, as shown in Figure 8-4.

There are several ways to identify SQLs for tuning advice, including Automatic Workload Repository (AWR) snapshots, a SQL Tuning Set, or SQLs in the SQL cache. In Figure 8-5, we scan for SQL queries accessing the CUSTOMERS table.

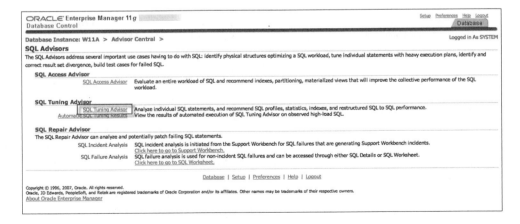

FIGURE 8-4   SQL Tuning Advisor within Enterprise Manager.

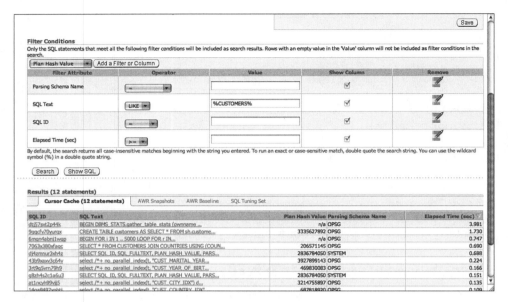

FIGURE 8-5   Finding SQLs in the cache for tuning.

The SQL we select can be examined in the SQL Details screen, as shown in Figure 8-6, in which we can examine its current plan and execution statistics. The *Schedule SQL Tuning Advisor* button enables us to create a SQL tuning analysis either immediately or at a scheduled time of our choosing. This is equivalent to creating and executing a SQL tuning task using DBMS_SQLTUNE.CREATE _TUNING_TASK.

When the tuning task is completed, we can view the results. Figure 8-7 shows the summary of recommendations from the tuning task. This corresponds to the Findings part of the report generated by DBMS_SQLTUNE.REPORT _TUNING_TASK. From here we can view the new explain plan, compare the two plans, or implement the recommendations.

CROSS-SQL TUNING WITH THE SQL ACCESS ADVISOR

The SQL Tuning advisor provides detailed advice for a single SQL statement. Where the advice is in respect of a SQL profile, this makes perfect sense because profiles are indeed specific to a particular SQL. However, because indexes potentially affect many SQL statements, it also makes sense to consider indexing in the light of an entire workload. The same argument can be made for other schema changes such as materialized views and partitioning.

The SQL access advisor enables you to generate indexing and materialized view recommendations that support a workload consisting of multiple SQL statements. In Oracle 11g, the advisor can also advise on partitioning options.

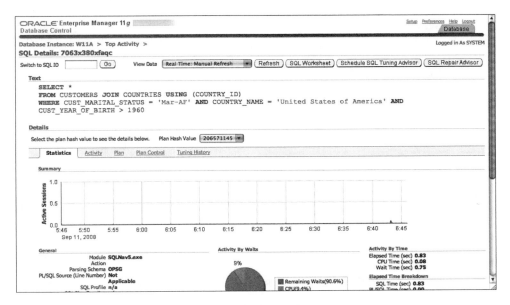

FIGURE 8-6   SQL Details screen.

The advisor can be accessed by selecting the *SQL Access Advisor* link on the *Advisor Central* page. You then select the types of objects for which you want advice and select either Comprehensive mode—considering the impact on all known SQLs—or Limited mode in which only the impact on the highest resource SQLs will be considered. Figure 8-8 shows an example of invoking the access advisor to generate indexing recommendations.

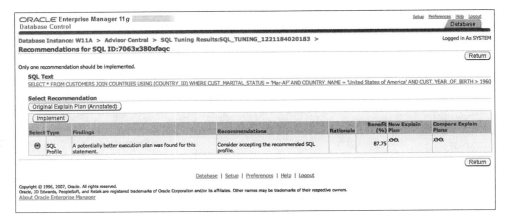

FIGURE 8-7   SQL Tuning summary screen.

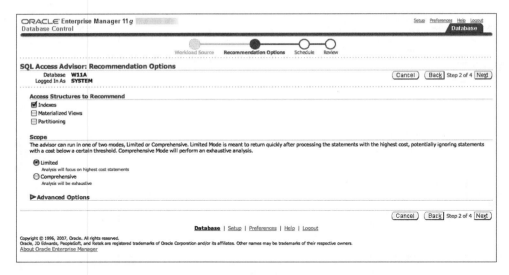

FIGURE 8-8   Invoking the SQL Access Advisor.

When the SQL Access advisor job is complete, we can view summary and detail recommendations. The summary screen, as shown in Figure 8-9, shows the total expected cost impact of the recommendations and the number of SQLs expected to be affected.

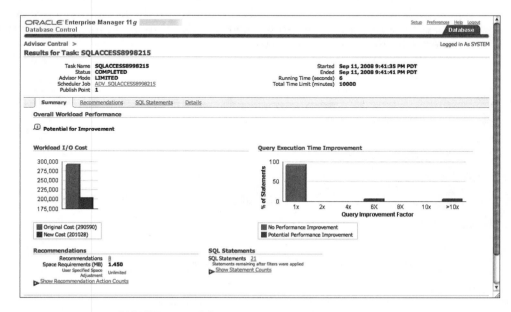

FIGURE 8-9   SQL Access advisor summary screen.

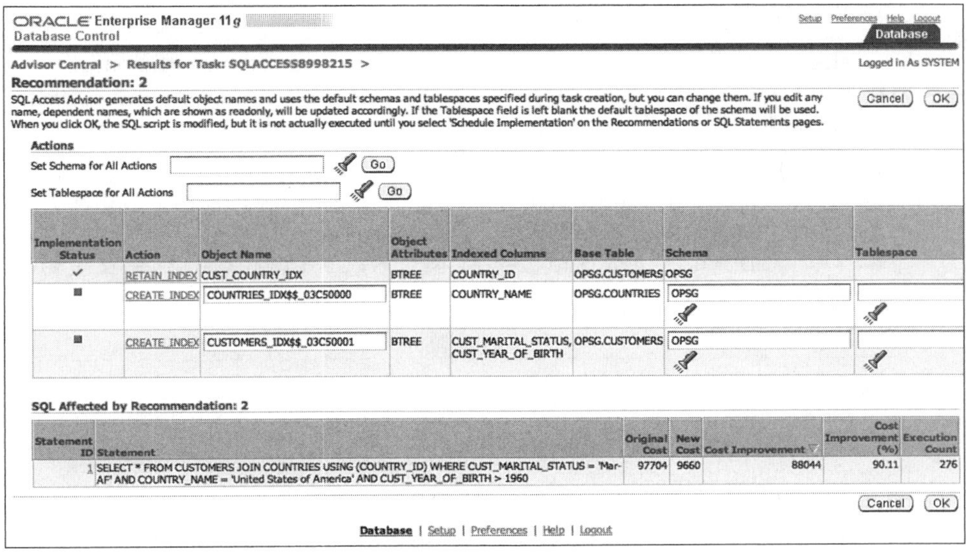

ORACLE Enterprise Manager 11*g*
Database Control

Setup Preferences Help Logout

Database

Advisor Central > Results for Task: SQLACCESS8998215 >   Logged In As SYSTEM

Recommendation: 2

SQL Access Advisor generates default object names and uses the default schemas and tablespaces specified during task creation, but you can change them. If you edit any name, dependent names, which are shown as readonly, will be updated accordingly. If the Tablespace field is left blank the default tablespace of the schema will be used. When you click OK, the SQL script is modified, but it is not actually executed until you select 'Schedule Implementation' on the Recommendations or SQL Statements pages.

Cancel OK

Actions

Set Schema for All Actions _____ Go

Set Tablespace for All Actions _____ Go

Implementation Status	Action	Object Name	Object Attributes	Indexed Columns	Base Table	Schema	Tablespace
✓	RETAIN INDEX	CUST_COUNTRY_IDX	BTREE	COUNTRY_ID	OPSG.CUSTOMERS	OPSG	
■	CREATE INDEX	COUNTRIES_IDX$$_03C50000	BTREE	COUNTRY_NAME	OPSG.COUNTRIES	OPSG	
■	CREATE INDEX	CUSTOMERS_IDX$$_03C50001	BTREE	CUST_MARITAL_STATUS, CUST_YEAR_OF_BIRTH	OPSG.CUSTOMERS	OPSG	

SQL Affected by Recommendation: 2

Statement ID	Statement	Original Cost	New Cost	Cost Improvement	Cost Improvement (%)	Execution Count
1	SELECT * FROM CUSTOMERS JOIN COUNTRIES USING (COUNTRY_ID) WHERE CUST_MARITAL_STATUS = 'Mar-AF' AND COUNTRY_NAME = 'United States of America' AND CUST_YEAR_OF_BIRTH > 1960	97704	9660	88044	90.11	276

Cancel OK

Database | Setup | Preferences | Help | Logout

FIGURE 8-10   An indexing recommendation from the SQL Access advisor.

Detailed recommendations show exactly what objects changes are recommended and which SQL statements will be affected. For instance, in Figure 8-10 we see a recommendation to create two new indexes to optimize a specific SQL statement. The optimizer estimates a cost savings of 90 percent if those indexes are created.

SQL BASELINES

SQL baselines were introduced in Oracle 11g and are intended to supplement SQL profiles and eventually replace stored outlines.

As we've seen, SQL profiles collect statistics from a specific SQL execution and create statistical information that helps the optimizer make better decisions. This makes the optimizer more flexible, which is definitely an advantage, especially in environments where ad-hoc SQL is common or where data volumes are fluid.

This flexibility is all very well, but what we actually want is a mix of *flexibility* and *stability*. We don't mind if the optimizer picks a new plan if circumstances change, providing that the plan is always for the better. Baselines provide a mechanism that enables plans to change, but only after they have proven to be better than any existing plans. Baselines attempt to provide a best-of-both-worlds solution offering both optimizer flexibility and stability.

CREATING THE BASELINE

Let's start by looking at how to create a baseline and see how the baseline works to prevent undesirable changes to an execution plan.

Consider this SQL:

```
SQL> SELECT /*GHBaseLines1*/ COUNT (*)
  2    FROM customers JOIN countries USING (country_id)
  3   WHERE country_name = 'New Zealand'
  4     AND cust_income_level = 'G: 130,000 - 149,999'
  5     AND cust_year_of_birth < 1952;
```

```
---------------------------------------------------------------
| Id  | Operation                      | Name              |
---------------------------------------------------------------
|   0 | SELECT STATEMENT               |                   |
|   1 |  SORT AGGREGATE                |                   |
|   2 |   HASH JOIN                    |                   |
|   3 |    TABLE ACCESS BY INDEX ROWID | COUNTRIES         |
|   4 |     INDEX RANGE SCAN           | COUNTRY_NAME_IDX  |
|   5 |    TABLE ACCESS FULL           | CUSTOMERS         |
---------------------------------------------------------------
```

Although the plan clearly isn't optimal—the index uses only the COUNTRY_NAME and not the other filter predicates—it's not too bad, and we want to ensure that this plan doesn't get replaced by an inferior plan should database configuration or statistics change. To do this we can create a baseline. One way to do that is to find the SQL_ID in the V$SQL view and load the baseline directly from the cached plan. The DBMS_SPM.LOAD_PLANS_FROM_CURSOR _CACHE procedure enables us to do just that. Here we find the SQL_ID for our example SQL and create a baseline:

```
SQL> DECLARE
  2     v_sql_id        v$sql.sql_id%TYPE;
  3     v_plan_count    NUMBER;
  4  BEGIN
  5     SELECT sql_id
  6       INTO v_sql_id
  7       FROM v$sql
  8      WHERE sql_text LIKE 'SELECT /*GHBaseLines1*/%';
  9
 10     v_plan_count := dbms_spm.load_plans_from_cursor_cache
 11                       (sql_id => v_sql_id);
 12     DBMS_OUTPUT.put_line (v_plan_count || ' plans loaded');
 13  END;
 14  /
1 plans loaded
```

The DBMS_SPM package also allows baselines to be created from SQL tuning sets.

The DBA_SQL_PLAN_BASELINES view lists the baselines that have been created. Here we see the baseline entry that we created in the previous example:

```
SQL> SELECT sql_handle, plan_name, origin,  accepted,
  2          optimizer_cost AS COST
  3     FROM dba_sql_plan_baselines
  4    WHERE sql_text LIKE 'SELECT /*GHBaseLines1*/%';

SQL_HANDLE        PLAN_NAME         ORIGIN         ACCEPTED   COST
----------------  ----------------  -------------  ---------- ----
SYS_SQL_94e29f5a  SYS_SQL_PLAN_b2e  MANUAL-LOAD    YES         408
b2ed56a2          d56a27509bcad
```

The SQL_HANDLE identifies the specific SQL concerned, whereas the PLAN_NAME identifies a specific baseline for that SQL. The SQL_HANDLE is particularly important because we'll need this to get more details about the baseline and to perform maintenance tasks. Note that the baseline we create has a YES in the ACCEPTED column: This baseline has been activated and will be used by the optimizer when determining execution plans.

To view the plan attached to the baseline, use the DBMS_ XPLAN.DISPLAY_ SQL_PLAN_BASELINE procedure:

```
SQL> SELECT *
  2     FROM TABLE (DBMS_XPLAN.display_sql_plan_baseline
  3          (:v_sql_handle, NULL, 'BASIC' ) );

PLAN_TABLE_OUTPUT
-----------------------------------------------------------------------
SQL handle: SYS_SQL_94e29f5ab2ed56a2

SQL text: SELECT /*GHBaseLines1*/ COUNT (*)   FROM customers
            JOIN countries USING
            (country_id)  WHERE country_name = 'New Zealand'    AND
            cust_income_level = 'G: 130,000 - 149,999'    AND
            cust_year_of_birth < 1952
-----------------------------------------------------------------------
Plan name: SYS_SQL_PLAN_b2ed56a27509bcad
Enabled: YES    Fixed: NO      Accepted: YES     Origin: MANUAL-LOAD
-----------------------------------------------------------------------
Plan hash value: 4135079021
```

```
-----------------------------------------------------------
| Id | Operation                        | Name              |
-----------------------------------------------------------
|  0 | SELECT STATEMENT                 |                   |
|  1 |  SORT AGGREGATE                  |                   |
|  2 |   HASH JOIN                      |                   |
|  3 |    TABLE ACCESS BY INDEX ROWID|  COUNTRIES        |
|  4 |     INDEX RANGE SCAN             | COUNTRY_NAME_IDX  |
|  5 |    TABLE ACCESS FULL             | CUSTOMERS         |
-----------------------------------------------------------
```

EVOLVING THE BASELINE

Now that the baseline has been created, the optimizer continues to use that plan unless a new baseline is *evolved*. For example, let's suppose that a configuration change occurs that would normally result in a plan change. Perhaps an index is created that would better support the WHERE clause for the query:

```
SQL> CREATE INDEX cust_country_index_dob_ix ON
  2
customers(country_id,cust_income_level,cust_year_of_birth);

Index created.
```

This index is a far better choice for the query than the existing COUNTRY _NAME_IDX index. However, if we examine the query after the index has been created, we clearly see that the new index is not used. Furthermore, DBMS_XPLAN notes that the baseline is in effect:

```
SQL> EXPLAIN PLAN FOR
  2  SELECT /*GHBaseLines1*/ COUNT (*)
  3    FROM customers JOIN countries USING (country_id)
  4   WHERE country_name = 'New Zealand'
  5     AND cust_income_level = 'G: 130,000 - 149,999'
  6     AND cust_year_of_birth < 1952;


PLAN_TABLE_OUTPUT
-----------------------------------------------------------
Plan hash value: 4135079021


-----------------------------------------------------------
| Id  | Operation          | Name              |           |
-----------------------------------------------------------
|   0 | SELECT STATEMENT   |                   |           |
```

```
|   1 |   SORT AGGREGATE                    |                    |
|   2 |    HASH JOIN                        |                    |
|   3 |     TABLE ACCESS BY INDEX ROWID| COUNTRIES          |
|   4 |      INDEX RANGE SCAN               | COUNTRY_NAME_IDX   |
|   5 |     TABLE ACCESS FULL               | CUSTOMERS          |
---------------------------------------------------------------------
```

```
Note
-----
   - SQL plan baseline "SYS_SQL_PLAN_b2ed56a27509bcad" used
for this statement
```

After the index was created, the optimizer generated a new plan but did not use it. Instead, the new plan is stored as an *unaccepted* baseline. We can see the new baseline in the DBA_SQL_PLAN_BASELINES table:

```
SQL> SELECT sql_handle, plan_name,origin,accepted,
  2          optimizer_cost AS COST
  3     FROM dba_sql_plan_baselines
  4    WHERE sql_text LIKE 'SELECT /*GHBaseLines1*/%';
```

SQL_HANDLE	PLAN_NAME	ORIGIN	ACCEPTED	COST
SYS_SQL_94e29f5a b2ed56a2	SYS_SQL_PLAN_b2e d56a27509bcad	MANUAL-LOAD	YES	408
SYS_SQL_94e29f5a b2ed56a2	SYS_SQL_PLAN_b2e d56a2eb21bdae	AUTO-CAPTURE	**NO**	4

The new plan is created but is not yet accepted. This is true even though the cost estimate for the new plan is so much lower than that of the currently active baseline. (The new cost is 4; the existing cost 408.) The optimizer won't apply a baseline just because it has a lower cost; the new plan must be *verified* first.

The optimizer will create new baselines as new execution plans are discovered with lower costs. However a new baseline will not be accepted until it has been *verified.*

The process of verifying new plans and accepting them is called *evolving* the baseline. DBMS_SPM.EVOLVE_SQL_PLAN_BASELINE can be called to evolve baselines for a specific SQL or can evolve all nonaccepted plans currently defined. Here we evolve the baselines for our test SQL:

```
SQL> BEGIN
  2      :v_report :=
  3         dbms_spm.evolve_sql_plan_baseline
  4          (sql_handle      => :v_sql_handle,
  5           verify          => 'YES',
  6           COMMIT          => 'YES' );
  7  END;
  8  /
```

The VERIFY parameter of EVOLVE_SQL_PLAN_BASELINE controls the verification process. If set to YES, unaccepted plans will be moved to accepted plans only if they result in a significant improvement. If NO, all unaccepted plans will be accepted. The COMMIT parameter controls whether we will actually accept eligible baselines or merely report on whether the baseline meets the acceptance criteria.

DBMS_SPM returns a CLOB that contains a report of actual or possible baseline changes. Here is an example of a baseline report:

```
-------------------------------------------------------------------------
                       Evolve SQL Plan Baseline Report
-------------------------------------------------------------------------

Inputs:
-------
  SQL_HANDLE = SYS_SQL_94e29f5ab2ed56a2
  PLAN_NAME  =
  TIME_LIMIT = DBMS_SPM.AUTO_LIMIT
  VERIFY     = YES
  COMMIT     = YES


Plan: SYS_SQL_PLAN_b2ed56a2eb21bdae
-----------------------------------
  Plan was verified: Time used .062 seconds.
  Passed performance criterion: Compound improvement ratio >= 292.
  Plan was changed to an accepted plan.

                        Baseline Plan      Test Plan     Improv. Ratio
                        -------------      ---------     -------------
  Execution Status:       COMPLETE         COMPLETE
  Rows Processed:            1                1
  Elapsed Time(ms):         11               14               .79
  CPU Time(ms):              0                0
  Buffer Gets:            1460                5               292
  Disk Reads:                0                2                0
```

```
Direct Writes:                 0              0
Fetches:                       0              2              0
Executions:                    1              1
```

```
-------------------------------------------------------------------------
                            Report Summary
-------------------------------------------------------------------------
Number of SQL plan baselines verified: 1.
Number of SQL plan baselines evolved: 1.
```

After a plan is changed to an accepted plan, we expect to see it used in future execution. And indeed, DBMS_XPLAN now shows that a new baseline is in effect and that the new index is in use:

```
SQL> EXPLAIN PLAN FOR
  2  SELECT /*GHBaseLines1*/ COUNT (*)
  3    FROM customers JOIN countries USING (country_id)
  4   WHERE country_name = 'New Zealand'
  5     AND cust_income_level = 'G: 130,000 - 149,999'
  6     AND cust_year_of_birth < 1952;
```

```
Explained.
```

```
SQL>
SQL> select * from TABLE(dbms_xplan.display(null,null,'BASIC +NOTE'));
```

```
PLAN_TABLE_OUTPUT
-------------------------------------------------------------------------
Plan hash value: 3013126077
```

```
-------------------------------------------------------------------------
| Id  | Operation                       | Name                          |
-------------------------------------------------------------------------
|   0 | SELECT STATEMENT                |                               |
|   1 |  SORT AGGREGATE                 |                               |
|   2 |   NESTED LOOPS                  |                               |
|   3 |    TABLE ACCESS BY INDEX ROWID| COUNTRIES                       |
|   4 |     INDEX RANGE SCAN            | COUNTRY_NAME_IDX              |
|   5 |     INDEX RANGE SCAN            | CUST_COUNTRY_INDEX_DOB_IX     |
-------------------------------------------------------------------------
```

```
Note
-----
   - SQL plan baseline "SYS_SQL_PLAN_b2ed56a2eb21bdae" used for
     this statement
```

AUTOMATING AND CONFIGURING BASELINES

The use of baselines is controlled primarily by two database parameters:

OPTIMIZER_CAPTURE_SQL_ PLAN_BASELINES	This parameter controls the automatic collection of baselines. The default setting is FALSE. When set to TRUE, baselines are automatically created when SQL statements are first executed. This avoids the necessity of creating baselines manually using the DBMS_SPM package.
OPTIMIZER_USE_SQL_ PLAN_BASELINES	This parameter controls the optimizer's use of baselines. When FALSE, baselines are not considered when the optimizer determines execution plans. The default value is TRUE.

FIXED BASELINES

The DBMS_SPM procedures that create baselines allow a baseline to be defined as FIXED, as in this example:

```
DECLARE
    v_sql_id        v$sql.sql_id%TYPE;
    v_plan_count    NUMBER;
BEGIN
    SELECT sql_id
      INTO v_sql_id
      FROM v$sql
     WHERE sql_text LIKE 'SELECT /*GHBaseLines1*/%';

    v_plan_count := dbms_spm.load_plans_from_cursor_cache
                        (sql_id => v_sql_id, fixed=>'YES');
    DBMS_OUTPUT.put_line (v_plan_count || ' plans loaded');
END;
```

When a fixed baseline exists, the optimizer will not add new baselines for the SQL statement, even if changes occur that would normally lead to a plan change. If other baselines exist for the SQL statement—perhaps they existed before the fixed baseline was created or perhaps they were loaded manually—they will *not* be used in preference to the fixed baseline, even if they have a lower cost or are verified.

Fixed baselines, therefore, operate similarly to stored outlines. In fact, Oracle recommends that you use fixed baselines in preference to outlines and advises that outlines might be depreciated in a future release.

FIGURE 8-11 Baseline support within Oracle Enterprise Manager.

A fixed baseline operates similarly to a stored outline; it prevents an execution plan from changing as a result of optimizer statistics or configuration changes.

BASELINE MANAGEMENT IN ORACLE ENTERPRISE MANAGER

Baselines can be managed using Enterprise Manager: Most of the facilities of the DBMS_SPM package are exposed in Enterprise Manager pages. Baseline management can be found in the *SQL Plan Control* link within the Server tab. Figure 8-11 shows the SQL Plan Baseline page; from here you can create, evolve, and otherwise manage SQL baselines.

SUMMARY

The Oracle optimizer gets more sophisticated with every release, but—short of becoming self-aware and developing human judgment—will never be able to come up with a perfect plan for every SQL. Consequently, Oracle provides methods for influencing or controlling SQL execution plans:

❑ Hints are directives that are embedded within SQL statements and which request specific access methods or optimizer options.

❑ Stored outlines enable SQL execution plans to be stabilized, preventing execution plans changing even when statistics or other circumstances change.

❑ With a bit of mild hacking, a stored outline can be used to change an execution plan for a SQL statement that you cannot edit.

❑ SQL profiles include statistics that are collected during SQL statement execution and that are specific to the SQL statement. These statistics go beyond the statistics that Oracle maintains against schema objects and can lead to improved optimizer plans.

❑ The SQL Tuning advisor works in concert with SQL profiles to create tuning advice including indexing advice and cross-SQL tuning.

❑ A SQL baseline represents a sort of known-good execution plan that will be replaced only if a new plan is proven to result in a better outcome. A *fixed baseline* freezes an execution plan, providing similar functionality to stored outlines. SQL baselines are new in Oracle 11g.

Chapter 9

TUNING TABLE ACCESS

In this chapter, we look at ways to improve the performance of SQL statements that access a single table. The single table query is the building block of more complex SQL queries, so understanding how to optimize the single table access is a prerequisite for improving the performance of more elaborate queries.

There are usually a number of possible access methods for any given table access. A full table scan is always an option and, depending on physical data model, there may be a number of index, partition, or cluster-based retrieval options.

The optimizer will not always choose the best access path, and you need to be able to evaluate the optimizer's choice and sometimes encourage the use of a different access path. Furthermore, you need to make the best possible access paths available to the optimizer by creating appropriate indexes or clusters and perhaps by partitioning the table.

SINGLE VALUE LOOKUPS

Next to the process of reading every row in a table, the most common single table operation is probably to look up one or more rows that match a specific column value. For instance, in this query we retrieve all the customers born in a particular year:

```
SELECT *
  FROM customers_sv c
 WHERE cust_year_of_birth = :year_of_birth
```

There are two main approaches to resolving such a query: to read all rows in the table looking for matching values, or to use some form of indexing or clustering to more directly identify the matching rows. The most efficient approach will depend on the selectivity of the WHERE clause condition.

Recall from Chapter 7, "Optimizing the Optimizer," that a highly selective column or condition is one that returns a low proportion of total rows. Primary keys and unique columns are the most selective, whereas columns with only a few distinct values, gender for instance, have low selectivity.

Programmers learning SQL are usually initially advised to avoid the full table scan. However, table scans sometimes consume fewer resources than the equivalent index lookup: this will usually be true when the selection criteria references a large proportion of the table data. Table scans are also more able to take advantage of the parallel processing capabilities outlined in Chapter 13, "Parallel SQL."

Indexed retrieval requires reading both the index blocks and (usually) table blocks. Furthermore, during an index scan Oracle might need to alternate between index blocks and table blocks and will quite possibly read an individual index block many times. If a large portion of the table is being accessed, the overhead of using the index might be greater than the overhead of scanning the entire table.

In general, full table scans will be the most appropriate retrieval path when the WHERE clause condition is *not* very selective. An index or clustered approach will be more appropriate when the condition *is* very selective.

CHOOSING BETWEEN TABLE AND INDEX SCAN

At what point does index-based retrieval outperform a full table scan?

Rules of thumb to help you decide whether to use a full table scan or an index lookup are commonplace. Here are some of the suggestions that you might encounter:

❏ Use a full table scan if accessing more than 2 percent, 5 percent, or 25 percent of the table data (depending who you ask).
❏ Use a full table scan if accessing more than 8 or 16 (or some other number) of data blocks.
❏ Use a full table scan if it is faster than an index lookup.

The reason why these rules of thumb vary so much is because it is not possible to generalize across all types of SQL statements, hardware platforms, and data distributions.

Some of the factors that affect the break-even point for indexed retrieval follow:

❏ **The hit rate in the buffer cache**—Index retrievals tend to get good hit rates in Oracle's buffer cache, whereas full table scans generally get a much poorer hit rate. This can help improve index performance.

❏ **Row size**—Each index access costs about the same in terms of IO regardless of the size of the row. However, the longer the row, the greater the number of blocks that must be read by a full table scan.

❏ **Data distribution**—If rows in the table are stored in approximately the order of the indexed column (which can happen if rows are inserted in primary key order), the index might have less blocks to visit and experience a much lower logical IO overhead.

Figure 9-1 shows the elapsed time for indexed and full table scan accesses under various conditions. In one case the data was loaded into the table in sorted order, favoring an index lookup. We also compare performance when data was cached in the buffer cache against performance when the buffer cache was flushed (empty). Depending on the circumstances, the break-even point between index and full scan varied from approximately 1 percent to 12 percent and even to 40 percent if the table was cached in memory and the data was loaded in sorted order.

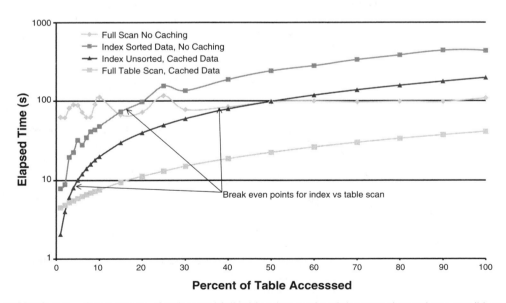

FIGURE 9-1 Comparison of index and full table scan retrieval times under various conditions.

Although it's not possible to provide a one-size-fits-all cutoff point for index retrieval, the following statements are indisputable:

❑ If all rows or a large proportion of rows in the table need to be accessed, a full table scan will be the quickest way to do this.

❑ If a single row is to be retrieved from a large table, an index based on that column will offer the quicker retrieval path.

❑ Between these two extremes, it might be difficult to predict which access path will be quicker.

In many cases, you are either selecting a small number of rows from a table to satisfy a transaction processing (OLTP) type query, or selecting a large number of rows to satisfy a decision support (OLAP) type query. In these circumstances, your decision will be an easy one—use the index or hash for the OLTP query and use a full table scan for the OLAP query.

There is no one-size-fits-all break-even point for indexed versus table scan access. If only a few rows are being accessed, the index will be preferred. If almost all the rows are being accessed, the full table scan will be preferred. In between these two extremes, your "mileage" will vary.

How the Optimizer Chooses Between Indexes and Full Table Scan

The optimizer attempts to calculate the relative cost of retrieving data by an index versus retrieving it by full table scan. The factors influencing the optimizer's decisions include

❑ The number of blocks that would need to be read to perform a full table scan.

❑ The number of blocks that would need to be read to perform an index lookup. This in primarily based on an estimate of the number of rows returned by the WHERE clause predicates.

❑ The relative cost of multiblock reads, as are performed during full table scans, and single block reads used to satisfy index lookups.

❑ Assumptions regarding the likelihood of index blocks and table blocks being cached in memory.

We saw in Chapter 7 how object statistics, database parameters, and system statistics bear on these calculations. However, the most significant factor is the optimizer's estimate of the number of rows that would be returned by the query.

For instance, in the CUSTOMERS table, the customer date of birth varies between 1913 and 1990, and there are 75 distinct values:

```
SQL> SELECT num_distinct, UTL_RAW.cast_to_number (low_value) low_value,
  2          UTL_RAW.cast_to_number (high_value) high_value
  3     FROM all_tab_col_statistics
  4    WHERE table_name = 'CUSTOMERS_CT'
         AND column_name = 'CUST_YEAR_OF_BIRTH';

NUM_DISTINCT   LOW_VALUE  HIGH_VALUE
------------ ----------- -----------
          75        1913        1990
```

In the absence of a histogram (see Chapter 7), the optimizer will calculate the number of rows returned by a query using the number of distinct values. Because there are 55,500 rows, and 75 distinct values, the optimizer expects a single value lookup to return 55500 / 75 = 740 rows:

```
SQL> SELECT MAX (cust_credit_limit), COUNT (*)
  2     FROM customers_c
  3    WHERE cust_year_of_birth =1913;

MAX(CUST_CREDIT_LIMIT)   COUNT(*)
---------------------- ----------
                 15000          5
```

```
-----------------------------------------------------
| Id  | Operation         | Name        | Rows  |
-----------------------------------------------------
|   0 | SELECT STATEMENT  |             |     1 |
|   1 |  SORT AGGREGATE   |             |     1 |
|*  2 |   TABLE ACCESS FULL| CUSTOMERS_C |   740 |
-----------------------------------------------------
```

Of course, 1913 was a long time ago, and we actually have only 5 customers born in that year. Our customer base is heavily skewed toward people born in the latter half of the twentieth century. With a histogram in place, the optimizer makes a much better estimate—now estimating that 10 rows will be returned—and switches the plan from one using a full table scan to one using an index:

```
SQL> SELECT MAX (cust_credit_limit), COUNT (*)
  2     FROM customers_c
  3    WHERE cust_year_of_birth =1913;

MAX(CUST_CREDIT_LIMIT)   COUNT(*)
---------------------- ----------
                 15000          5
```

```
------------------------------------------------------------------
| Id  | Operation                    | Name          | Rows  |
------------------------------------------------------------------
|   0 | SELECT STATEMENT             |               |    1  |
|   1 |  SORT AGGREGATE              |               |    1  |
|   2 |   TABLE ACCESS BY INDEX ROWID| CUSTOMERS_C   |   10  |
| * 3 |    INDEX RANGE SCAN          | CUSTOMERS_C_IX1 | 10  |
------------------------------------------------------------------
```

> Make sure histograms exist on columns with uneven data distributions to ensure that the optimizer makes the best choice between indexes and table scans.

Prior to Oracle 10g, Oracle could not normally make use of histograms when bind variables were used because the bind variable placeholders hid the values of the bind variable at parse time. However, from Oracle 10g forward, Oracle can combine bind variables and histograms, although not necessarily as immediately or accurately. In Oracle 10g, the optimizer "peeks" at the value of the first bind variables supplied to the statement, whereas in Oracle 11g *adaptive cursor sharing* will result in multiple plans being created to suit bind variables with different selectivity. Both of these concepts were introduced in Chapter 7.

Helping the Optimizer   Aside from skewed data in the absence of histograms, other circumstances can cause the optimizer to make a poor index versus table scan decision:

❑   The optimizer goal might be set to ALL_ROWS, whereas the requirement is actually for response time. A full table scan might result in the best response time to retrieve all the rows, but an index will usually be quicker when retrieving only the first row or the first few rows. In this case, you might be well advised to change the OPTIMIZER_MODE parameter to FIRST_ROWS or FIRST_ROWS_*N* (where *N* is 1,10,100 or 1000).

❑   Indexed based plans tend to benefit more from caching of blocks in the buffer cache. The parameter OPTIMIZER_INDEX_CACHING can be used to change the way the optimizer accounts for this. High values can cause the optimizer to reduce the estimated IO cost of index reads.

❑   Index-based lookups also benefit more from data distribution; if all rows for a range of values are in the same block, an index range scan will be more efficient. We saw evidence of that effect back in Figure 9-1. The parameter OPTIMIZER_INDEX_COST_ADJ can be used to change the optimizer's assumptions about index costs to take this into account.

❑   Table scans tend to read multiple blocks from disk in a single operation, whereas index lookups read a single block at a time. The relative cost of each of these operations varies from system to system. System statistics, described in Chapter 7, can help the optimizer make a better informed decision.

Help the optimizer choose between indexes and table scans by maintaining accurate object statistics, including histograms, and collecting system statistics. Parameters such as OPTIMIZER_MODE and OPTIMIZER_INDEX_CACHING have a strong influence on the optimizers' decisions to use indexes.

No matter how good your statistics, you might want to override the optimizer by forcing a particular index or a table scan approach. This is particularly likely if you are working on SQL for an OLTP style system in which predictable access times trump the desire to have flexible optimizer plans.

If you are writing the SQL, you might want to use a FULL or INDEX hint. For instance, to request a full table scan based query plan, we can use the FULL hint:

```
SELECT /*+ FULL(s) */ SUM (amount_sold)
  FROM sh.sales s
 WHERE cust_id = :cust_id
```

Likewise, you might use an INDEX hint to indicate your preference for an index-based query plan. We did not specify a specific index, so the optimizer will try to pick the most selective one:

```
SELECT /*+ INDEX(s) */ SUM (amount_sold)
  FROM sh.sales s
 WHERE cust_id = :cust_id
```

If you want to change the plan for an existing SQL without modifying the SQL source code, you can use stored outlines or fixed baselines as described in Chapter 8, "Execution Plan Management.

BITMAP INDEXES AND SINGLE VALUE LOOKUPS

It's clear that we don't want to use bitmap indexes in a transaction processing environment due to the overhead of locking the bitmaps. (This was discussed in more depth in Chapter 5, "Indexing and Clustering.") But if all other conditions suit bitmap indexes, at what point should we decide that the column has too many unique values to be suitable for a bitmap?

Most examples of bitmap indexes (including those shown in Chapter 5) show multiple columns of *very* low cardinality, such as sex, marital status, and so on. When we look at those examples we'd be forgiven for thinking that bitmap indexes are not suitable when there are more than a handful of key values. However, as we saw in Chapter 5, bitmap indexes can perform well even when there are many thousands of unique values. Figure 9-2 shows how bitmap indexes perform as the number of distinct values increases. The performance of the bitmap retrieval is similar to the B*-Tree index for high cardinality columns, and much better than the B*-Tree index for low cardinality columns.

> Bitmap indexes can still perform well even when a column has many thousand distinct values. However, bitmap indexes outperform B*-Tree indexes only when the number of distinct values is relatively low.

HASH CLUSTERS AND SINGLE VALUE LOOKUPS

We looked at the performance characteristics of hash clusters in Chapter 5. Although they are most suitable for primary key lookups, they can also be used for any single value lookup.

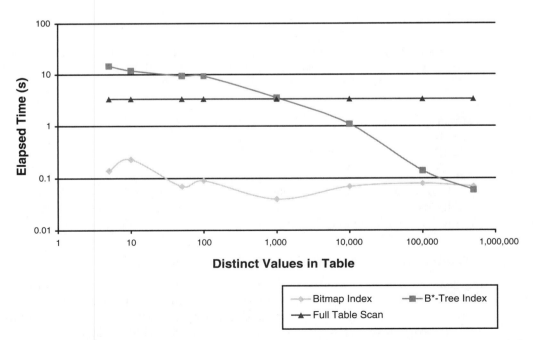

FIGURE 9-2   Relative performance of bitmap versus B*-Tree index depends on the number of distinct values in the indexed column (note logarithmic scale).

In theory, Oracle can determine the location of any value in the hash cluster through the value of the cluster key, regardless of the number of matching values for that value. However, if a large number of rows match the key value, not all of them will fit in the storage specified by the SIZE parameter. Additional blocks will become chained to the first matching block, and additional IOs will be required to fetch those rows.

Figure 9-3 illustrates this principle. As the number of matching rows increase, the hash lookup performance degrades and eventually a hash lookup takes longer than a B*-Tree index or a full table scan. How quickly the hash lookup degrades depends on the value of the SIZE parameter. If the SIZE value is too small, the cluster degrades rapidly as the number of matching values increase. A higher SIZE value reduces—but does not eliminate—the performance penalty that occurs as the number of matching values increase.

You might be forgiven for thinking that a large value for the SIZE parameter will make the hash cluster effective for a wider range of queries. But remember that setting SIZE too large will result in a sparsely populated table that results in longer full table scan times. In general, hash clusters are suitable for queries in which only a few rows ever match the cluster key value.

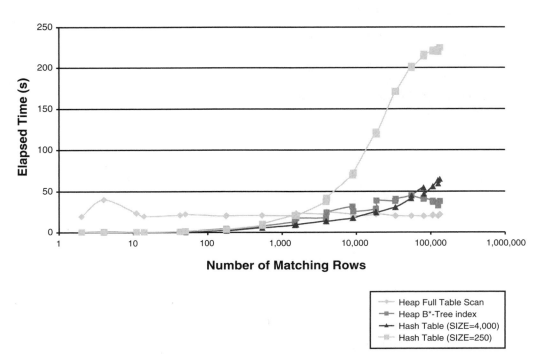

FIGURE 9-3 Hash table lookups degrade as the number of matching rows increase.

Hash clusters can offer superior performance to both table scans and B*-Tree index for single value lookups if the number of matching values is relatively small and the SIZE parameter is set appropriately. Remember that as SIZE increases, full table scan time increases proportionally.

AVOIDING "ACCIDENTAL" TABLE SCANS

Even if an appropriate index or hash retrieval path is available, the optimizer might not be able to take advantage of the access path because of the wording of the SQL statement. Some of the query constructions that prevent indexes from being used follow:

- ❑ Queries involving a NOT EQUALS (<>) condition
- ❑ Searching for NULL values
- ❑ Accidentally disabling an index with a function

NOT EQUALS CONDITIONS

Oracle will normally not employ an index if the NOT EQUALS operator (<>, !=, ^=) is employed. This is generally sensible because when retrieving all rows except for those matching a single value, a full table scan will usually be the fastest way to get the data. However, if the value in question accounts for the majority of the rows in the database, an index based retrieval of the minority of rows (which don't match the value) might be preferable.

For instance, let's say that in the CUSTOMERS table the majority of customers are status "I":

```
SQL> SELECT    cust_valid, COUNT (*)
  2       FROM customers_ne
  3  GROUP BY cust_valid;

C    COUNT(*)
-  ----------
I       54945
A         555
```

The histogram on CUST_VALID allows Oracle to determine that an index is the best option when retrieving all customers whose CUST_VALID value is 'A':

```
SQL> SELECT MAX (cust_income_level), COUNT (*)
  2      FROM customers_ne c
  3      WHERE cust_valid = 'A';


MAX(CUST_INCOME_LEVEL)            COUNT(*)
--------------------------- ----------
L: 300,000 and above                555
```

```
---------------------------------------------------------------
| Id  | Operation                    | Name             | Rows   |
---------------------------------------------------------------
|   0 | SELECT STATEMENT             |                  |      1 |
|   1 |  SORT AGGREGATE              |                  |      1 |
|   2 |   TABLE ACCESS BY INDEX ROWID| CUSTOMERS_NE     |    620 |
| * 3 |    INDEX RANGE SCAN          | CUSTOMERS_NE_IX1 |    620 |
---------------------------------------------------------------
```

However if we look for all customers who have any status but I, which returns exactly the same results, we see that Oracle declines to use the index:

```
SQL> SELECT MAX (cust_income_level), COUNT (*)
  2      FROM customers_ne c
  3      WHERE cust_valid <> 'I';
```

```
Execution Plan
----------------------------------------------------
Plan hash value: 3963802310
```

```
----------------------------------------------------
| Id  | Operation         | Name         | Rows   |
----------------------------------------------------
|   0 | SELECT STATEMENT  |              |      1 |
|   1 |  SORT AGGREGATE   |              |      1 |
| * 2 |   TABLE ACCESS FULL| CUSTOMERS_NE |    625 |
----------------------------------------------------
```

You might be tempted to use an INDEX hint to force a table access, and a
brief glance at the execution plan might convince you that this approach has
worked. For instance, if we add an INDEX hint to the previous statement:

```
SQL> SELECT /*+ INDEX(c) */ MAX (cust_income_level), COUNT (*)
  2      FROM customers_ne c
  3      WHERE cust_valid <> 'I';
```

```
MAX(CUST_INCOME_LEVEL)                COUNT(*)
----------------------------- ----------
L: 300,000 and above                       555
```

```
-------------------------------------------------------------
| Id  | Operation                    | Name            | Rows  |
-------------------------------------------------------------
|  0  | SELECT STATEMENT             |                 |    1 |
|  1  |  SORT AGGREGATE              |                 |    1 |
|  2  |   TABLE ACCESS BY INDEX ROWID| CUSTOMERS_NE    |  625 |
|* 3  |    INDEX FULL SCAN           | CUSTOMERS_NE_IX1|  625 |
-------------------------------------------------------------
```

At first glance the hint seems to work; an index lookup is occurring. However, if you look carefully you'll note that the hint is causing an INDEX FULL SCAN rather than an INDEX RANGE SCAN as in our optimal query. The INDEX FULL SCAN means that every single index entry was read rather than only those that matched our criteria and can actually be worse than a full table scan. Figure 9-4 shows the relative execution time of each approach.

Of course, if the data were different, it might be that the full table scan was the more appropriate approach. But you still need to be aware that by using not-equals you might be ruling out an indexed solution.

Oracle will not usually use an index if the query condition is not equals (!=). If you think the query could benefit from an indexed approach, reword the query using IN, OR, or >. You might still need to use hints or a column histogram to encourage Oracle to use the appropriate index.

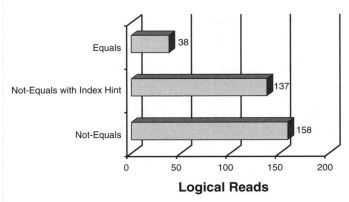

FIGURE 9-4 Performance of a not-equals query and its equivalent equals query.

SEARCHING FOR NULLS

As we discussed in Chapter 5, B*-Tree index entries are not created when all the columns in the index have the NULL value. As a result, you can't use a B*-Tree index on a column to search for a NULL value. For instance, let's suppose the CUSTOMERS.CUST_VALID column might contain NULL values (perhaps prior to the customer being fully registered). We might have a query to find these customers, as follows:

```
SQL> SELECT MAX (cust_income_level), COUNT (*)
  2    FROM customers_nl c
  3   WHERE cust_valid IS NULL;

MAX(CUST_INCOME_LEVEL)            COUNT(*)
------------------------------   ----------
L: 300,000 and above                   56
```

```
-----------------------------------------------------
| Id  | Operation           | Name         | Rows  |
-----------------------------------------------------
|   0 | SELECT STATEMENT    |              |     1 |
|   1 |  SORT AGGREGATE     |              |     1 |
|*  2 |   TABLE ACCESS FULL | CUSTOMERS_NL |    56 |
-----------------------------------------------------
```

To find customers with the NULL status, we can't use the B*-Tree index and must perform a full table scan. If we redefine the column so that it is not NULL and has a default value of 'U' (Unknown), we get

```
SQL> ALTER TABLE customers_nl MODIFY cust_valid
  2    DEFAULT 'U';

SQL> UPDATE customers_nl
  2      SET cust_valid  = 'U'
  3    WHERE cust_valid  IS NULL;
```

Now we can then use the index to find these formally NULL values:

```
SQL> SELECT MAX (cust_income_level), COUNT (*)
  2    FROM customers_nl c
  3   WHERE cust_valid = 'U';

MAX(CUST_INCOME_LEVEL)            COUNT(*)
------------------------------   ----------
L: 300,000 and above                   56
```

```
-------------------------------------------------------------------------
| Id  | Operation                      | Name             | Rows  |
-------------------------------------------------------------------------
|   0 | SELECT STATEMENT               |                  |     1 |
|   1 |  SORT AGGREGATE                |                  |     1 |
|   2 |   TABLE ACCESS BY INDEX ROWID  | CUSTOMERS_NL     |     1 |
| * 3 |    INDEX RANGE SCAN            | CUSTOMERS_NL_IX1 |     1 |
-------------------------------------------------------------------------
```

In this example, using the index reduced logical IO by approximately 97 percent (see Figure 9-5). For bigger tables, the improvement can be even more pronounced although it clearly depends on what proportion of rows contains the NULL value. Note that, as in the not-equals example, it might be necessary to use a hint or define a histogram if the number of unique values is low.

Also remember that bitmaps indexes *do* include NULL values and *can* be used to search for NULLs. However, bitmap indexes should generally not be used in OLTP-type environments and are, therefore, not a general purpose solution when searching for NULLs.

Avoid searching for NULL values in an indexed column. Instead, define the column as NOT NULL with a default value and then search for that default.

SEARCHING FOR VALUES THAT ARE NOT NULL

Although Oracle *cannot* use an index to search for NULL values, it *can* use the index to find those values that are NOT NULL. The optimizer chooses to do this only if it calculates that the combined cost of accessing the table and the relevant index will

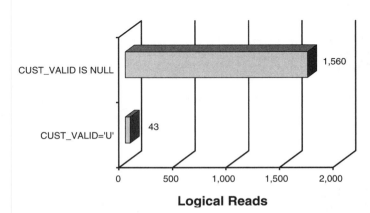

FIGURE 9-5 Searching for NULL values compared with searching for a default value.

be less than the cost of performing a full table scan. For instance, in the following example only 0.1 percent of the rows have a value for PROCESS_FLAG, and consequently the optimizer chooses to use the index to find NOT NULL values:

```
SQL> SELECT MAX (cust_income_level), COUNT (*)
  2     FROM customers_nl c
  3     WHERE process_flag  IS NOT NULL;


MAX(CUST_INCOME_LEVEL)                COUNT(*)
----------------------------------  ----------
L: 300,000 and above                       55
```

Id	Operation	Name	Rows
0	SELECT STATEMENT		1
1	SORT AGGREGATE		1
2	TABLE ACCESS BY INDEX ROWID	CUSTOMERS_NL	55
* 3	**INDEX FULL SCAN**	CUSTOMERS_NL_IX1	55

Note that Oracle scans the entire index. Because NULL values are not indexed, this is equivalent to looking up only those values that are NOT NULL.

You can use an index to find values that are NOT NULL. If most values are NULL, the index will be very small and efficient because NULL values are not indexed.

CREATING INDEXES ON NULLABLE COLUMNS

It's often wise to define the columns referenced in the where clause as NOT NULL so that B*-Tree indexing on these columns can be effective. However, it can be worthwhile using NULL values in a B*-Tree indexed column if the following conditions apply:

❑ The column is almost always NULL.
❑ We never want to find rows where the column is NULL.
❑ We do want to search for rows where the column is NOT NULL.
❑ We want to minimize the space required by the index.

Because NULLs are not stored in an index, an index created when the preceding conditions are true will be very compact and can be used to quickly locate rows where the column contains a value.

UNINTENTIONALLY DISABLING AN INDEX WITH A FUNCTION

The optimizer can't use an index on a column if the column is manipulated by a function or an expression. For instance, in the following example TIME_ID is indexed, but because we incorporated TIME_ID within an expression, the index could not be used:

```
SQL> SELECT SUM (amount_sold)
  2    FROM sales_f
  3    WHERE (SYSDATE - time_id) < 10;
```

Id	Operation	Name	Rows
0	SELECT STATEMENT		1
1	SORT AGGREGATE		1
* 2	**TABLE ACCESS FULL**	SALES_F	123K

However, if we rewrite the query so as to avoid manipulating the indexed column, the index can be used:

```
SQL> SELECT SUM (amount_sold)
  2    FROM sales_f
  3    WHERE time_id > (sysdate-10) ;
```

Id	Operation	Name	Rows
0	SELECT STATEMENT		1
1	SORT AGGREGATE		1
2	TABLE ACCESS BY INDEX ROWID	SALES_F	55121
* 3	**INDEX RANGE SCAN**	SALES_F_I1	55121

> Avoid applying functions or operations to indexed columns in the WHERE clause. Instead, apply functions or operations to the values against which the indexed column is being compared.

FUNCTIONAL INDEXES

Sometimes, it's simply not possible to avoid applying a function to an indexed column. For instance, consider the following query to get customer details:

```
SELECT cust_id, cust_main_phone_number
  FROM customers_fi
 WHERE cust_last_name = :cust_last_name
   AND cust_first_name = :cust_first_name;
```

We can use an index on CUST_LAST_NAME and CUST_FIRST_NAME to satisfy this query with only a couple of IOs. However, let's suppose we make the search ignore distinctions between uppercase and lowercase by rewording the query as follows:

```
SELECT cust_id, cust_main_phone_number
  FROM customers_fi
 WHERE UPPER (cust_last_name) = UPPER (:cust_last_name)
   AND UPPER (cust_first_name) = UPPER (:cust_first_name);
```

Of course, by placing a function around the indexed columns, we prevent the column from being used. One obvious solution is to create a *functional index*. Functional indexes are simply indexes that might include functions or expressions within their definition; as in the following example:

```
CREATE INDEX customers_fi_funcidx_1 ON
customers_fi(UPPER(cust_last_name),UPPER(cust_first_name));
```

After the index is created, queries that use the same functions that are used in the index definition can be used in the WHERE clause, and the functional index will be used to retrieve the results:

```
SQL> SELECT cust_id, cust_main_phone_number
  2    FROM customers_fi
  3   WHERE UPPER (cust_last_name) = UPPER (:cust_last_name)
  4     AND UPPER (cust_first_name) = UPPER (:cust_first_name);
```

```
----------------------------------------------------------------------
| Id  | Operation                    | Name                   | Rows |
----------------------------------------------------------------------
|   0 | SELECT STATEMENT             |                        |  10  |
|   1 |  TABLE ACCESS BY INDEX ROWID | CUSTOMERS_FI           |  10  |
| * 2 |   INDEX RANGE SCAN           | CUSTOMERS_FI_FUNCIDX_1 |  10  |
----------------------------------------------------------------------
```

> When you can't avoid applying functions or expressions to indexed columns in the WHERE clause, consider using functional indexes based on the same functions or expressions.

The expressions that define the functional index might use user-defined functions or built in functions. If user-defined functions are used, they must be created with the DETERMINISTIC keyword. This declaration requires that the function return the same outputs whenever it is supplied with the same inputs. This is necessary to avoid the functional index from becoming invalid if the values of the expression change. The most common cause of indeterminacy is to incorporate an expression whose value changes over time. For instance the following is invalid:

```
CREATE  INDEX sales_f_funcidx_2 ON sales_f((SYSDATE - time_id));
```

Oracle will decline to create such an index because the use of SYSDATE will cause the index values to change between the time the index is created, and the time you attempt to use it.

FUNCTIONAL INDEXES AND STATISTICS

Functional indexes are an essential technique to avoid disabling indexes when columns are subjected to functions or expressions in the WHERE clause. However, the optimizer often finds it difficult to estimate the number of rows that might be returned by a functional index. For instance, consider the following function that is designed to categorize customers into four generations:

```
CREATE OR REPLACE FUNCTION f_generation (p_yob NUMBER)
    RETURN VARCHAR2 DETERMINISTIC
IS
BEGIN
    RETURN (CASE
                WHEN p_yob < 1950
                    THEN 'Pre-boomer'
                WHEN p_yob < 1965
                    THEN 'Baby Boomer'
                WHEN p_yob < 1990
                    THEN 'Generation X'
                ELSE 'Generation Y'
            END
          );
END;
```

When we use the function in a SQL query, the optimizer tries to estimate the number of rows returned by the function based on some rough rules of thumb:

```
SQL> SELECT AVG (cust_credit_limit), count(*)
  2    FROM customers_fi
  3    WHERE f_generation (cust_year_of_birth) = 'Generation X';


AVG(CUST_CREDIT_LIMIT)    COUNT(*)
---------------------- ----------
            6219.03517       18739


Execution Plan
----------------------------------------------------------
Plan hash value: 2419842198


-----------------------------------------------------------------
| Id  | Operation                      | Name               | Rows  |
-----------------------------------------------------------------
|   0 | SELECT STATEMENT               |                    |     1 |
|   1 |  SORT AGGREGATE                |                    |     1 |
|   2 |   TABLE ACCESS BY INDEX ROWID| CUSTOMERS_FI         |   555 |
|*  3 |    INDEX RANGE SCAN            | CUSTOMERS_FUNCIDX2 |   222 |
-----------------------------------------------------------------
```

The optimizers guess is way off: It estimated 222 rows; we actually get 18,739. This is an example of where 11g extended statistics (discussed in Chapter 7) would be useful. Let's collect statistics for the function expression and retry:

```
SQL>   BEGIN
  2      DBMS_STATS.gather_table_stats
  3        (ownname        => user,
  4         tabname        => 'CUSTOMERS_FI',
  5         method_opt     => 'FOR ALL COLUMNS '||
  6         ' FOR COLUMNS (f_generation(cust_year_of_birth))'
  7        );
  8   END;
  9   /


PL/SQL procedure successfully completed.


SQL> SELECT AVG (cust_credit_limit), count(*)
  2    FROM customers_fi
  3    WHERE f_generation (cust_year_of_birth) = 'Generation X';


AVG(CUST_CREDIT_LIMIT)    COUNT(*)
---------------------- ----------
            6219.03517       18739
```

```
Execution Plan
---------------------------------------------------------------------
Plan hash value: 3123856637


---------------------------------------------------------------------
| Id  | Operation            | Name         | Rows  | Bytes |
---------------------------------------------------------------------
|   0 | SELECT STATEMENT     |              |     1 |    18 |
|   1 |  SORT AGGREGATE      |              |     1 |    18 |
|*  2 |   TABLE ACCESS FULL| CUSTOMERS_FI | 19138 |  336K|
---------------------------------------------------------------------
```

Now that extended statistics have been gathered, Oracle's estimate of 19,138 is within a whisker of the actual 18,739 rows returned. As a result, the optimizer now declines to use the index and instead employs a more-efficient full table scan.

When using functional indexes, consider collecting Oracle 11g extended statistics on the functional index expression. This will allow the optimizer to make better decisions as to whether to use the functional index.

VIRTUAL COLUMNS

An alternative to creating a functional index and extended statistics is to create an Oracle 11g virtual column based on the expression concerned. By creating a virtual column based on our function, the optimizer can create accurate cardinality estimates without the need to collect extended statistics:

```
SQL> ALTER TABLE customers_fi ADD cust_generation GENERATED
  2            ALWAYS AS (f_generation (cust_year_of_birth) );

Table altered.

SQL> BEGIN
  2      DBMS_STATS.gather_table_stats(ownname => USER,
  3            tabname => 'CUSTOMERS_FI');
  4  END;

PL/SQL procedure successfully completed.

SQL> SELECT AVG(cust_credit_limit), COUNT( * )
  2  FROM customers_fi
  3  WHERE cust_generation = 'Generation X';
```

```
AVG(CUST_CREDIT_LIMIT)    COUNT(*)
----------------------    ----------
            6219.03517       18739
```

```
--------------------------------------------------------------
| Id  | Operation         | Name        | Rows  | Bytes  |
--------------------------------------------------------------
|   0 | SELECT STATEMENT  |             |     1 |    20  |
|   1 |  SORT AGGREGATE   |             |     1 |    20  |
|*  2 |   TABLE ACCESS FULL| CUSTOMERS_FI |  13875 |  270K  |
--------------------------------------------------------------
```

> In 11g, an indexed virtual column can be used instead of a functional index. Using a virtual column eliminates the need to collect extended optimizer statistics on the functional index expression.

Of course, to take advantage of an indexed virtual column, you need to rewrite SQLs to reference the virtual column instead of the virtual column's expression. If you can't do this, a functional index with extended statistics is the best approach.

MULTICOLUMN LOOKUPS

So far we have discussed the performance of retrieving rows that match a single column equality condition. When we add conditions that reference additional columns, our options increase. Where there are multiple conditions in the WHERE clause, we can resolve the query by

- ❏ Using a single column index on the most selective column
- ❏ Using a concatenated index that includes two or more of the columns referenced in the WHERE clause.
- ❏ Using more than one index and merging the results
- ❏ Using a full table scan

The inexperienced SQL programmer often uses EXPLAIN PLAN to determine that a full table scan has been avoided. If there is no full table scan, the programmer might conclude that the plan is a good one. In fact, there are usually a wide variety of index-based retrievals possible, and merely ensuring that one of these access plans is used does not mean that the SQL statement is optimized.

Selecting the best of all actual and potential indexes, and ensuring that the indexes are used to their full potential, is at least as important as avoiding a full table scan.

USING CONCATENATED INDEXES

If we are querying against multiple column values in a table, a concatenated index on all those values will usually offer the most-efficient retrieval. We looked at concatenated indexes in detail in Chapter 5, but we briefly recap here.

A concatenated index is optimized if

❏ It contains all columns referenced for that table in the WHERE clause.
❏ The order of columns in the concatenated index supports the widest range of queries.
❏ Index compression has been used when appropriate (see Chapter 5).
❏ If possible, the concatenated index contains the columns in the SELECT list and the columns in the WHERE clause. This might improve query performance by allowing the query to be satisfied from the index lookup alone.

Chapter 5 provides further guidance on optimizing concatenated index lookups.

INDEX MERGES

It's possible for Oracle to resolve a query against multiple columns by using multiple indexes. When performing an index merge, Oracle might convert index entries to bitmaps and then use bitmap operations to merge the results.[1] You can encourage Oracle to perform an index merge using the INDEX _COMBINE hint:

```
SQL> SELECT /*+ INDEX_COMBINE(c, C_LAST_IDX1 , C_FIRST_IDX1 ,C_YOB_IDX1)
*/
  2          cust_id
  3     FROM customers_m c
  4    WHERE cust_last_name = 'Tang'
  5      AND cust_first_name = 'Sydney J'
  6      AND cust_year_of_birth = 1947;
```

---

[1] Bitmap conversion will occur only if you use Oracle Enterprise Edition because other versions are not licensed for bitmap indexing. Index merges still occur in other editions but are less efficient.

```
------------------------------------------------------------------------
| Id  | Operation                        | Name         | Rows | Bytes |
------------------------------------------------------------------------
|   0 | SELECT STATEMENT                 |              |   1  |   24  |
|   1 |  TABLE ACCESS BY INDEX ROWID     | CUSTOMERS_M  |   1  |   24  |
|   2 |   BITMAP CONVERSION TO ROWIDS    |              |      |       |
|   3 |    BITMAP AND                    |              |      |       |
|   4 |     BITMAP CONVERSION FROM ROWIDS|              |      |       |
|*  5 |      INDEX RANGE SCAN            | C_FIRST_IDX1 |      |       |
|   6 |     BITMAP CONVERSION FROM ROWIDS|              |      |       |
|*  7 |      INDEX RANGE SCAN            | C_LAST_IDX1  |      |       |
|   8 |     BITMAP CONVERSION FROM ROWIDS|              |      |       |
|*  9 |      INDEX RANGE SCAN            | C_YOB_IDX1   |      |       |
------------------------------------------------------------------------
```

An index merge will almost always be far less efficient than a concatenated index and might well be less efficient than a full table scan if the columns concerned are not selective (that is, have few distinct values). For nonselective columns, bitmap indexes merge more effectively; although remember (as discussed in Chapter 5) that bitmap indexes incur a significant locking overhead. When merging B*-Tree indexes in Enterprise Edition, Oracle converts them to bitmaps on-the-fly and merges them using the same efficient algorithms as are used for bitmap indexes.

If you can't construct concatenated indexes to suit all your queries you might be able to use index merges. However, be aware that low cardinality B*-Tree indexes cannot be merged efficiently. Bitmap index merges are efficient, but remember than bitmap indexes incur a substantial lock overhead.

See Chapter 5 for a detailed comparison of the performance of bitmap and B*-Tree indexes merges and with concatenated indexes.

UNIQUENESS AND OVER-INDEXING

Sometimes, we want to select only a small number of columns from a table. For instance, in the following example, we know the surname, first name, and email address and want to retrieve the phone number:

```
SELECT cust_main_phone_number
  FROM customers_oi
 WHERE cust_last_name = 'Tang'
   AND cust_first_name = 'Sydney'
   AND cust_email = 'Sydney.Tang@company.com';
```

With an index on the surname, first name, and email, we can satisfy this query effectively. Oracle accesses the head index block, one or two branch index blocks, and the appropriate index leaf block. This leaf block contains the ROWID for the row in question, which will then be retrieved from the table block. A total of four or five block IOs will be required.

```
-------------------------------------------------------------------
| Id  | Operation                  | Name                         |
-------------------------------------------------------------------
|   1 |  TABLE ACCESS BY INDEX ROWID|  CUSTOMERS_OI               |
|*  2 |   INDEX RANGE SCAN         |  CUSTOMERS_OI_NAME_IDX       |
-------------------------------------------------------------------
```

If we are certain that the WHERE clause criteria are unique—that there will never be two people of the same name with the same email—then we can optimize the retrieval slightly by specifying a unique index. When a unique index is used, Oracle can be sure that the first matching row found is the only matching row, and this saves an IO because Oracle can stop scanning the index as soon as a match is found.

Another way to speed up the query is to add the phone number to the index. If we do this, we can resolve the query without having to access the table at all because all the data required is contained in the index. This usually saves a single IO, which is not very noticeable for a single lookup, but a 20 percent to 25 percent savings that can be a significant improvement if the query is being executed frequently (perhaps in an OLTP environment).

```
---------------------------------------------------------------
| Id  | Operation         | Name                              |
---------------------------------------------------------------
|*  1 |  INDEX RANGE SCAN| CUSTOMERS_OI_NAME_PHONE_IDX        |
---------------------------------------------------------------
```

SEARCHING FOR RANGES

We looked at queries that attempt to retrieve rows in which a column value matches an exact value. Let's move on to discuss queries that seek to find rows that match a range of values.

We're going to look at the following types of range scans:

❏ **Unbounded range scan**—This involves getting all rows with a column value greater or less than a particular value.

❏ **Bounded range scan**—This involves getting all rows with column values between two values.

❏ **Range lookup**—Find a row in a table in which one column is less than the specified value and the other column is greater. In other words, the table has a "high" value column and a "low" value column that we use to categorize an input variable.

UNBOUNDED RANGE SCAN

Consider a query that performs an unbounded range scan based on the date of birth of our customers:

```
SQL> SELECT MAX (cust_credit_limit), COUNT (*)
  2    FROM customers_r
  3    WHERE cust_year_of_birth > :yob;

MAX(CUST_CREDIT_LIMIT)    COUNT(*)
----------------------  ----------
                 11000          31
```

Id	Operation	Name	Rows	Bytes
0	SELECT STATEMENT		1	8
1	SORT AGGREGATE		1	8
* 2	TABLE ACCESS FULL	CUSTOMERS_R	**2775**	22200

When a bind variable is provided to a range scan query such as this one, the optimizer will by default assume that 5 percent of rows will be returned (5 percent from 55,500 customers = 2,775). In this case the estimate is quite inaccurate. Only 31 rows actually matched the bind variable, and the decision to use a full table scan was probably unwise.

If a literal is provided, and appropriate object statistics exist, the optimizer correctly decides to use an index:

```
SQL> SELECT MAX (cust_credit_limit), COUNT (*)
  2    FROM customers_r
  3    WHERE cust_year_of_birth > 1989;
```

```
MAX(CUST_CREDIT_LIMIT)    COUNT(*)
--------------------- ----------
                11000        31
```

```
-------------------------------------------------------------------
| Id  | Operation                   | Name            | Rows | Bytes |
-------------------------------------------------------------------
|   0 | SELECT STATEMENT            |                 |    1 |     8 |
|   1 |  SORT AGGREGATE             |                 |    1 |     8 |
|   2 |   TABLE ACCESS BY INDEX ROWID| CUSTOMERS_R    |   15 |   120 |
|*  3 |    INDEX RANGE SCAN         | CUSTOMERS_R_IX1 |   15 |       |
-------------------------------------------------------------------
```

Oracle 10g Bind variable "peeking" and 11g adaptive cursor sharing allows Oracle to examine bind variables and adjust execution plans accordingly. In 10g, you might get an indexed plan depending on the value of the bind variable first provided. In 11g, you might end up with two plans, one that uses the index and one that doesn't. The AUTOTRACE output in SQLPLUS might not reflect these decisions, but if we examine SQL trace output, we can observe the index being used with the bind variable:

```
SELECT MAX (cust_credit_limit), COUNT (*)
  FROM customers_r
 WHERE cust_year_of_birth > :yob

Misses in library cache during parse: 1
Misses in library cache during execute: 1
Optimizer mode: ALL_ROWS
Parsing user id: 88

Rows      Row Source Operation
-------   -------------------------------------------------
      1   SORT AGGREGATE
     31    TABLE ACCESS BY INDEX ROWID CUSTOMERS_R
     31     INDEX RANGE SCAN CUSTOMERS_R_IX1
```

See Chapter 3, "Tools of the Trade," for guidance on using the SQL Trace facility.

In 10g unbounded range scans usually will use an index only if the first "peeked" bind variable suggests a selective plan. You might therefore want to use hints or plan stability in 10g to ensure a consistent outcome. In 11g the optimizer will create multiple "adaptive" plans if appropriate to optimize for selective and unselective bind variables.

In the absence of histogram data, Oracle calculates the cardinality as approximately:

$$Cardinality = NoOfRows \times \frac{(value - lowvalue)}{(highvalue - lowvalue)}$$

So in the case of our example—where CUST_YEAR_OF_BIRTH varies between 1913 and 1990 and our input value is 1989—the cardinality comes out to about 740:

```
SQL> SELECT MAX (cust_credit_limit), COUNT (*)
  2    FROM customers_r
  3    WHERE cust_year_of_birth > 1989;
```

```
-------------------------------------------------------------
| Id  | Operation             | Name         | Rows  |
-------------------------------------------------------------
|   0 | SELECT STATEMENT      |              |     1 |
|   1 |  SORT AGGREGATE       |              |     1 |
|*  2 |   TABLE ACCESS FULL|  CUSTOMERS_R  |   740 |
-------------------------------------------------------------
```

However, customer ages are not uniformly distributed—there are few very young customers—and if we create a histogram the optimizer calculates a more accurate cardinality of 25 (the correct value is 31).

For range scans on data that is not uniformly distributed, the optimizers' decisions will be improved by the presence of a histogram.

BOUNDED RANGE SCANS

A bounded range scan is one in which we provide a maximum and a minimum as in the following example:

```
SQL> SELECT MAX (cust_credit_limit), COUNT (*)
  2    FROM customers_r
  3    WHERE cust_year_of_birth BETWEEN :yob1 AND :yob2;
```

As we might expect, the principles of bounded range scans also apply as to unbounded range scans. The optimizer uses its 5-percent guess as in our previous example, but because there are now two boundaries on the range scan, it estimates that only 0.25 percent of rows will be returned (5 percent of 5 percent = 139):

```
-------------------------------------------------------------
| Id  | Operation             | Name        | Rows  |
-------------------------------------------------------------
|   0 | SELECT STATEMENT      |             |     1 |
|   1 |  SORT AGGREGATE       |             |     1 |
| * 2 |   FILTER              |             |       |
| * 3 |    TABLE ACCESS FULL  | CUSTOMERS_R |   139 |
-------------------------------------------------------------
```

As with unbounded range scans, the use of literals and histograms can help the optimizer make a better choice. As with unbounded range scans, bind variable peeking in 10g might cause the optimizer decisions to appear random, so you might want to use a hint to force the plan you prefer.

RANGE LOOKUPS

In a range lookup, we are trying to find a particular value in a table that is keyed on a low value–high value pair of columns. For instance, suppose the SALESREGION table defines each region in terms of a range of phone numbers that apply to that region. To find the region for any given phone number, you might enter a query like this:

```
SQL> SELECT /*+FIRST_ROWS*/
  2         *
  3     FROM salesregion
  4    WHERE '500000015' BETWEEN lowphoneno AND highphoneno;
```

```
-------------------------------------------------------------------
| Id  | Operation                   | Name         | Rows  |
-------------------------------------------------------------------
|   0 | SELECT STATEMENT            |              | 22356 |
|   1 |  TABLE ACCESS BY INDEX ROWID| SALESREGION  | 22356 |
| * 2 |   INDEX RANGE SCAN          | SALESREGION_I1 | 22356 |
-------------------------------------------------------------------
```

```
Statistics
-------------------------------------------------------------------
          1  recursive calls
          0  db block gets
        177  consistent gets
          0  physical reads
```

The query uses the index, but rather than the 4–5 logical IOs we might expect if the index was resulting in a direct lookup of the matching row, we see a relatively high 177 logical reads. What's going on?

To understand why Oracle's retrieval plan seems so poor, we have to recognize the hidden assumptions we make when formulating our "mental" execution plan. For instance, Oracle does not know that LOWPHONENO is always lower than HIGHPHONENO, whereas we know this intuitively from the names of the columns. Furthermore, we assume that there are no overlaps between rows (that is, that any given phone number matches only a single SALESREGION). Oracle cannot assume this.

Without knowing what we know about the data, the optimizer must perform the following steps:

1. Search the index to find a row where the LOWPHONENO is less than the phone number specified. This will be the first (that is, lowest) matching entry in the index.
2. Check to see if the HIGHPHONENO is greater than the number specified.
3. If it is not, check the next index entry.
4. Continue performing a range scan of this nature until it finds an entry where LOWPHONENO is higher than the phone number provided. The entry just prior to this entry will be the correct entry.

So in essence, the optimizer must perform a range scan across all rows where the low value is less than the value provided. Therefore, on average half of the index will be scanned.

A better solution can be achieved by employing PL/SQL (or another procedural language). By using an index on the "high" value (HIGHPHONENO, in this case), we can position ourselves at the first row in the lookup table that has a high value greater than our search value. If the low value is less than our lookup value, we have found a match. The following PL/SQL function illustrates the technique:

```
CREATE OR REPLACE FUNCTION region_lookup (p_phone_no VARCHAR2)
    RETURN VARCHAR2
IS
    CURSOR salesregion_csr (cp_phone_no VARCHAR2)
    IS
        SELECT    /*+ INDEX(S) */
                  regionname, lowphoneno
            FROM salesregion s
           WHERE cp_phone_no < highphoneno
        ORDER BY highphoneno;

    salesregion_row    salesregion_csr%ROWTYPE;
    v_return_value     salesregion.regionname%TYPE;
BEGIN
    OPEN salesregion_csr (p_phone_no);
```

```
FETCH salesregion_csr
 INTO salesregion_row;

IF salesregion_csr%NOTFOUND
THEN
   -- No match found;
   NULL;
ELSIF salesregion_row.lowphoneno > p_phone_no
THEN
   -- Still no match
   NULL;
ELSE
   -- The row in salesregion_row is the matching row
   v_return_value := salesregion_row.regionname;
END IF;

CLOSE salesregion_csr;

RETURN (v_return_value);
END;
```

Figure 9-6 compares performance of the two approaches. The PL/SQL function requires only a single index lookup to resolve the lookup, whereas the SQL approach must effectively scan half the table (on average).

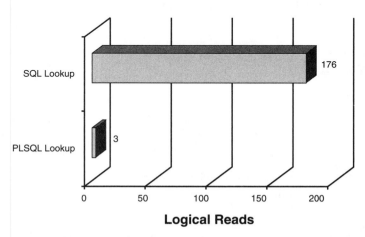

FIGURE 9-6   Range lookup implemented in PLSQL function versus "straight" SQL.

> Range lookups—finding a matching range in a table that contains "high" and "low" values—might fail to optimize successfully with standard SQL. In these cases, a PL/SQL or other procedural approach might be necessary.

USING THE LIKE OPERATOR

You can use the LIKE operator to search for rows and columns that match a wildcard condition. For instance, the following query uses an index to find all customers with a surname that starts with Vaugh.

```
SQL> SELECT MAX (cust_credit_limit),count(*)
  2    FROM customers_l
  3    WHERE cust_last_name LIKE 'Vaugh%';
```

Id	Operation	Name	Rows
0	SELECT STATEMENT		1
1	SORT AGGREGATE		1
2	TABLE ACCESS BY INDEX ROWID	CUSTOMERS_L	61
* 3	INDEX RANGE SCAN	CUSTOMERS_L_IX1	61

This query makes good use of our index on surname and requires only a few IOs to satisfy. However, if we use a wildcard to match the starting portion of a column, we cannot use the index directly. For instance, we can search for all surnames ending in "aughn" using the following query:

```
SQL> SELECT MAX (cust_credit_limit),count(*)
  2    FROM customers_l
  3    WHERE cust_last_name LIKE '%aughn';
```

Id	Operation	Name	Rows
0	SELECT STATEMENT		1
1	SORT AGGREGATE		1
* 2	TABLE ACCESS FULL	CUSTOMERS_L	2775

The optimizer usually resolves the preceding query using a full table or a full index scan. This is because it cannot make effective use of the index unless the first characters of the index key are known.

Oracle can use B*-Tree indexes to efficiently resolve queries involving the LIKE operator only if there is not a leading wildcard (%,_) in the search string.

MULTVALUE SINGLE-COLUMN LOOKUPS

When a query on a single table contains an OR clause on a single column (or the equivalent IN clause), it can be processed in one of the following ways:

❑ Perform a full table scan and check each row against the selection criteria (which shows up as FILTER in the execution plan).
❑ Perform multiple index based lookups of the table.

The cost based optimizer tries to estimate when the cost of performing multiple index lookups will be higher than the cost of a full table scan. If the column values are not evenly distributed, the cost based optimizer's calculations will be improved by the presence of a histogram on the relevant column. For instance, in the following query the optimizer calculates that about 306 rows will satisfy the query and decides to use an index:

```
SQL> SELECT MAX (cust_credit_limit), COUNT (*)
  2     FROM customers_o
  3     WHERE cust_last_name IN ('Baker', 'Bakerman',
  4                     'Bakker', 'Backer', 'Bacer');

MAX(CUST_CREDIT_LIMIT)   COUNT(*)
----------------------  ----------
                 15000         234
```

Id	Operation	Name	Rows
0	SELECT STATEMENT		1
1	SORT AGGREGATE		1
2	**INLIST ITERATOR**		
3	TABLE ACCESS BY INDEX ROWID	CUSTOMERS_O	306
* 4	INDEX RANGE SCAN	CUSTOMERS_O_IX1	306

The INLIST ITERATOR step simply denotes that the steps below will be executed for each value in the IN list or each value in the set of OR conditions.

As the number of values in the IN list increases, the selectivity of the expression reduces, and the likelihood that an index will be effective decreases.

Optimization of multivalue, single column queries is essentially the same as for single-value lookups. We should ensure that the most optimal indexes exist, that a histogram exists if appropriate, and be prepared to override any optimizer decisions that we don't agree with.

OPTIMIZING NECESSARY FULL TABLE SCANS

So far, we have talked mainly about ways to avoid full table scans. Yet all too often using an index is not the fastest way to get the data you need. This is particularly true when you need to access a large proportion of the table's data.

Even if a full table scan is the only practical way of retrieving the required data, there are still options for improving the performance of your query. Techniques for optimizing full table scans include

- ❏ Reducing the number of *logical* block reads required for the scan by making the table smaller
- ❏ Reducing the number of *physical* block reads required for the scan by making database IO more efficient
- ❏ Reducing scan overhead by caching or sampling
- ❏ Assigning more resources to the scan by using the parallel query option
- ❏ Performing a fast full index scan instead of a full table scan
- ❏ Partitioning the table and reading only from selected partitions

In particular, the amount of work required to complete a full table scan is primarily determined by the number of blocks to be scanned. There are a number of ways to reduce this number:

- ❏ Lower the high water mark by rebuilding the table.
- ❏ Squeeze more rows into each block by modifying PCTFREE and/or PCTUSED.
- ❏ Reduce the row length, possibly by moving large, infrequently accessed columns to a separate table.
- ❏ Compress the data in the table.

LOWERING THE HIGH WATER MARK

Oracle does not need to scan every block that is allocated to the table. For instance, when we first create a table with a large storage allocation, Oracle knows that none of the blocks contain data, and a full table scan will be almost instantaneous—no matter how many blocks have been allocated to the table.

When a full table scan is required, Oracle reads every block from the first block allocated to the highest block that has ever contained data. This "highest" block is called the high watermark. For instance, if we insert enough rows into a table to cause 100 blocks to be populated, then a full table scan will perform approximately 100 block reads. Even if we delete every row in the table, the high watermark will still be at 100 blocks, and the table scan will still need to read about 100 blocks.

Automatic Segment Storage Management (ASSM) complicates this algorithm somewhat by keeping track of two high watermarks—one for blocks allocated that have never held data and one for blocks that have held data at some point in the past. However, the general principle of the high watermark remains.

It should, therefore, be apparent that if a table is subject to a large number of deletes, the highwater mark might be higher than it needs to be. The average number of rows per block will decrease, and the IO cost to retrieve each row will increase.

You can rebuild the table if necessary, by using the ALTER TABLE .. MOVE command, which rebuilds the table in another location, or by using the SHRINK SPACE clause, which compacts the table in place. Because SHRINK SPACE causes rows to be moved within the table, you need to enable the ROW MOVEMENT table option before using SHRINK SPACE. So to shrink the space in a table, you might issue both the following commands:

```
ALTER TABLE hwm_test ENABLE ROW MOVEMENT;

ALTER TABLE hwm_test SHRINK SPACE;
```

Figure 9-7 illustrates how important lowering the high water mark can be. After inserting 100,000 rows to a 2,000 row table, we expect full table scan overhead to increase. However, after deleting the same rows, full table scan performance remains unchanged because the high watermark remains at the high point. Only after we issued a SHRINK SPACE command does the full table scan overhead reduce.

Tables that contain substantially fewer rows than they did in the past might require a rebuild or SHRINK SPACE to reset the high watermark. This will reduce the number of blocks read during a full table scan.

OPTIMIZING PCTFREE AND PCTUSED

We first looked at PCTFREE and PCTUSED in Chapter 4, "Logical and Physical Database Design." PCTFREE controls the amount of space reserved in each block for updates that increase the row length. PCTUSED—nearly irrelevant nowadays

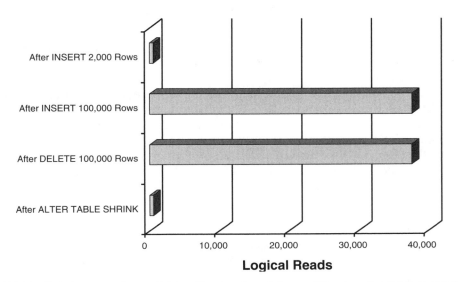

After INSERT 2,000 Rows

After INSERT 100,000 Rows

After DELETE 100,000 Rows

After ALTER TABLE SHRINK

0   10,000   20,000   30,000   40,000

Logical Reads

FIGURE 9-7   Deleting rows from a table will not reduce full scan IO unless the table is rebuilt or "shrunk."

because of the widespread adoption of ASSM—controls when a block becomes re-eligible for inserts after rows are deleted—but only for segments in Manual Segment Storage Management (MSSM) tablespaces. Reducing PCTFREE or increasing PCTUSED can increase the number of rows that fit within a block. This has the effect of reducing the number of blocks required that reduces the overhead of the full table scan.

> If a table is subject to frequent table scans, ensure that PCTFREE is no higher than necessary, especially if the table is not updated. If the tablespace is not using ASSM, also consider increasing PCTUSED.

REDUCING THE ROW LENGTH

If a table is often subjected to a full table scan and contains large, infrequently accessed columns, you might be able to reduce the number of blocks to be scanned by moving these columns to another table. A good example of this technique is moving long VARCHAR2 columns that are only rarely queried to a subtable or using the DISABLE STORAGE IN ROW setting for BLOBs and CLOBs (discussed in more detail in Chapter 4).

For instance, let's imagine that we stored a bitmap thumbnail image of the customer's contract in the CUSTOMERS table, but that we access these bitmaps only infrequently when we perform an index lookup of a single row (perhaps from a "customer details" screen). The average row length of the CUSTOMERS table is only 180 bytes excluding the bitmap. If the bitmap is stored in a 2K VARCHAR, the row length becomes about 12 times longer and hence full table scans will be 12 times more expensive.

The solution to this problem is to move these long columns to a separate table with the same primary key. If you want to retrieve the bitmap together with customer details, you need to perform a join; this might slow the retrieval down somewhat, but the small cost when viewing the bitmap will probably be justified by the large improvement in table scan performance.

If the bitmap is stored in a BLOB or CLOB instead of a VARCHAR2, you can ensure that the BLOB is stored out of line by using the DISABLE STORAGE IN ROW option of the LOB clause. For instance:

```
CREATE TABLE outofline_lob_table
(   id                 number     NOT NULL PRIMARY KEY,
    control_data       char(200) NOT NULL,
    lob_data           blob
)   LOB(lob_data) STORE AS (DISABLE STORAGE IN ROW )
```

Note that LOBs greater than about 4,000 bytes[2] in length will be automatically stored in a separate segment anyway. Note also that in-row LOB storage can be more space-efficient for small LOBs because each LOB stored outside of the row consumes at least one tablespace block of storage.[3]

For Index Organized tables, the PCTTHRESHOLD and INCLUDING clauses define which columns are included in the B*-Tree, and which are specified in the overflow segment. We discussed these considerations in Chapter 5.

For tables in which full table scan performance is critical, consider locating long, infrequently accessed columns in a separate table. For LOBs and CLOBs, consider the DISABLE STORAGE IN ROW clause.

COMPRESSING THE TABLE

We also looked at the COMPRESS option in some detail in Chapter 4. The COMPRESS option allows Oracle to use compression algorithms to reduce the amount of space needed to store table data. Prior to Oracle 11g, table compression could be achieved only when the table was created, rebuilt, or subject to direct load op-

---

[2] The actual threshold is 3964 because of a 36-byte LOB locator.
[3] The CHUNK clause within the LOB storage clauses determine the minimum size of each LOB: CHUNK must be a multiple of the tablespace block size.

erations. However, in 11g, the Advanced Compression option enables data to be compressed when manipulated by standard DML.

As we showed in Chapter 4, compression can result in large improvements in full table scan performance, especially if the full table scan involves a lot of physical IO.

Consider using table compression if a table is expected to generate significant IO from table scans and contains compressible (typically character) data.

In Oracle 11g and forward, we can use OLTP compression, which allows standard DML operations—UPDATE, DELETE, MERGE, and INSERT—to work with and create compressed data. To enable this form of compression, use the COMPRESS FOR ALL OPERATIONS clause of the CREATE TABLE statement.

From Oracle 11.2 forward, we can use *columnar compression* to achieve even higher compression ratios. Standard compression compresses the contents of a table on a row-by-row basis. This means that compression ratios will be higher if there is repeated data *within* a row. However, columnar compression compresses data on a column-by-column basis. This achieves much higher compression ratios, because there is likely to be more repeated data within a column than within a row. The drawback for columnar compression is that it takes a lot longer to create new data, because for each row inserted Oracle has to read all or some of the corresponding column values in other rows.

You can implement columnar compression using the COMPRESS FOR ARCHIVE LEVEL=*compression_level* syntax. *Compression_level* can take a value of 1, 2, or 3. The higher the value, the better the compression but the higher the compression cost. High values should generally be used only for tables that are infrequently updated or where the speed of the update is not important.

Figure 9-8 illustrates the cost benefit ratios for the various forms of compression. Higher levels of compression result in smaller segments that will be quicker to scan. However, at the higher levels of compression, the time it takes to load the tables increases dramatically. The appropriate level for your table depends both on the usage patterns and the type of data; character data will compress better, leading to more benefit. OLTP data will be updated more frequently leading to more overhead.

Oracle 11g Release 2 *columnar compression* allows for much higher compression ratios and consequently smaller tables that can be scanned more quickly. However, the DML overhead for columnar compression is correspondingly very high.

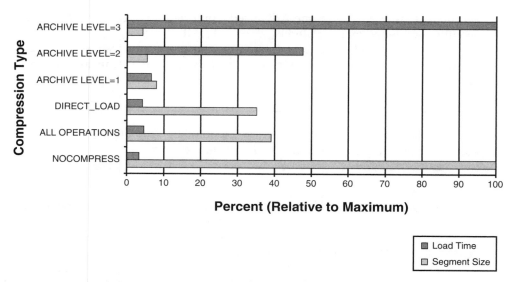

FIGURE 9-8   Cost and benefit of the various compression levels.

MAKING DATABASE IO MORE EFFICIENT

Full table scans typically involve a significant amount of physical disk IO because it's unusual for all of the blocks in a table to be in memory. Index based reads often retrieve relatively recent data that is more likely to still be in cache and consequently usually gets high hit rates. Because full table scans tend to perform more physical IO, table scans are often more sensitive to IO efficiency factors than indexed lookups.

IO optimization has two broad aspects:

❏ Avoiding unnecessary IO by caching data in memory
❏ Ensuring that physical IO is efficient using disk layout optimization, striping, and so on

We devote several chapters to these principles later in the book (see for instance Chapter 18, "Buffer Cache Tuning," on avoiding IO through memory optimization and Chapter 21, "Disk IO Tuning Fundamentals," on physical disk tuning). Therefore, we won't go into great detail on these topics here. However, here are some of the things that can affect the IO efficiency of table scans:

❏ Sizing the buffer cache effectively
❏ Using KEEP and RECYLE pools to further optimize the efficiency of the overall buffer cache
❏ Possibly using the CACHE hint to help keep full table scan blocks in memory if we know that a SQL is going to be frequently executed

❏ Exploiting the 11g client side (Chapter 6, "Application Design and Implementation") or server side result set cache (Chapter 20, "Other Memory Management Topics")

USING THE SAMPLE OPTION

Often when we perform full table scans, we are seeking approximate answers to business questions rather than seeking precise results for quantitative analysis. For instance, questions such as "What are our biggest selling products?" or "What is the average height in America?" probably don't require that we look at every single row in our largest tables. Instead, we might be satisfied with an approximate answer based on a random sample of rows.

The SAMPLE clause enables us to perform such a random sample. Consider the following SQL that lists our top five products and the percent of revenue they have generated:

```
WITH sales_totals AS
    (
        SELECT prod_name,
               ROUND (SUM (amount_sold) * 100
                   / SUM (SUM (amount_sold)) OVER (),2) pct_amount,
               RANK () OVER (ORDER BY SUM (amount_sold) DESC) ranking
          FROM sh.sales JOIN sh.products USING (prod_id)
        GROUP BY prod_name)
SELECT    prod_name, pct_amount
   FROM sales_totals
  WHERE ranking <= 5
ORDER BY pct_amount DESC;
```

If we want a quick answer and are prepared to sacrifice precision, we can use the SAMPLE BLOCK clause to request a 5-percent sample of the potentially large SALES table:

```
WITH sales_totals_sampled AS
    (
        SELECT prod_name,
               ROUND (SUM (amount_sold) * 100
                   / SUM (SUM (amount_sold)) OVER (),2) pct_amount,
               RANK () OVER (ORDER BY SUM (amount_sold) DESC) ranking
          FROM sh.sales SAMPLE BLOCK (5)
          JOIN sh.products USING (prod_id)
        GROUP BY prod_name)
SELECT    prod_name, pct_amount
   FROM sales_totals_sampled
  WHERE ranking <= 5
ORDER BY pct_amount DESC;
```

As you might expect, this massively reduces the amount of IO required, because only 1 in 20 blocks from the SALES table are actually read—the logical reads reduced by approximately 93 percent.

You might wonder how accurate the results from sampling will be. In many cases, they will be very accurate indeed. For instance, the following output shows the data from the sample query compared with that from the full table scan:

```
PROD_NAME                                      Pct (actual) Pct (sampled)
------------------------------------------     ------------ -------------
Envoy Ambassador                                      13.37         12.42
Mini DV Camcorder with 3.5" Swivel LCD                 9.44         10.74
5MP Telephoto Digital Camera                           7.34          7.85
Envoy 256MB - 40GB                                     7.12          8.29
17" LCD w/built-in HDTV Tuner                          6.91           6.9
```

The results vary significantly, but are of the same general magnitude and the top five products are correctly ranked by the sampling approach. Whether the results from sampling are adequate for your requirements depends on your demands for accuracy, the nature of the query, and the distribution of you data.

The SAMPLE BLOCK clause in the preceding example instructs Oracle to randomly sample blocks rather than rows. Randomly sampling rows is more accurate, because there is every chance that rows inside individual blocks were inserted at around the same time and possibly in the same transaction. However, when we sample by row, we get less reduction in IO, because randomly selecting 10 percent of the rows might require that we read 90 percent of the blocks. You rarely see a great reduction in IO overhead when you sample by row, though there might be savings in sorting and other operations.

The SAMPLE clause can be used to get approximate answers to aggregate queries that would normally require a full table scan.

PARALLEL QUERY

One way to significantly improve the performance of any statement that involves a full table scan is to take advantage of the parallel query option. Because of the importance and complexity of this topic, it is addressed in detail in Chapter 13. To briefly summarize, you can get significant improvements in full table scan performance if any or all of the following are true:

❑   There are multiple processors on your host computer.
❑   There is spare CPU capacity. When parallel query is invoked, you consume a greater proportion of the total CPU capacity of the system, so be aware of the possible effect on other sessions.
❑   The data in your table is spread across multiple disk drives.

If these conditions are met, you can expect to get moderate to large improvements in the performance of full table scans through parallel query technology. Refer to Chapter 13 for more details.

THE FAST FULL INDEX SCAN

We've seen a number of examples in which an index alone has been used to resolve a query. Providing all the columns needed to resolve the query are in the index, there is no reason why Oracle can't use the index alone to generate the result set.

However we've also seen that the performance of an index-based lookup degrades as the proportion of rows to be retrieved increases. However, if you are retrieving all or most of the rows in the table and the columns involved all appear in a single index, the *fast full index scan* can be used. The fast full index scan offers some significant advantages:

❏ In an index range scan or full index scan, index blocks are read in key order, one at a time. In a fast full scan, blocks will be read in the order in which they appear on disk, and Oracle will be able to read multiple blocks in each IO operation.

❏ The fast full index scan can be performed in parallel, whereas an index range scan or full index scan can only be processed serially. That is, Oracle can allocate multiple processes to perform a fast full index scan but can only use a single process for traditional index scans.

❏ The index will almost always be smaller than the corresponding table, reducing the number of IOs required for the full scan.

The fast full scan will be invoked automatically by the optimizer if an appropriate index exists and if the optimizer calculates that the fast full scan results in a lower cost. Alternately the fast full scan can be invoked manually by the INDEX_FFS hint.

```
SQL> SELECT   cust_id, SUM (amount_sold)
  2        FROM sales_ffs
  3   GROUP BY cust_id
  4     HAVING SUM (amount_sold) > 350000
  5   ORDER BY 2 DESC;
```

Id	Operation	Name	Rows
0	SELECT STATEMENT		3121
1	SORT ORDER BY		3121
* 2	FILTER		
3	HASH GROUP BY		3121
4	**INDEX FAST FULL SCAN**	SALES_FFS	2476K

The Index fast full scan can take advantage of optimizations normally only available to table scans, such as multiblock read and parallel query. You can use the PARALLEL_INDEX hint to request the fast full scan to be executed in parallel.

The index fast full scan will be more efficient that a full table scan if the index is significantly smaller than the table. Indexes generally have fewer columns than their master table, and index compression (see Chapter 4) can be very effective in reducing the size of the index. On the other hand, the index must include a ROWID (unique row identifier), and for volatile tables, index block splits and row deletes can lead to significant space wastage. So don't assume that an index fast full scan will always outperform a full table scan.

Figure 9-9 illustrates the relative performance. When the table has a long row length, the fast full scan is much more efficient than a table scan. However, when the table row length is shorter—and the difference between index and table size less marked—the difference is minimal.

Take advantage of the fast full index scan for queries that can be resolved by reading all the rows in an index.

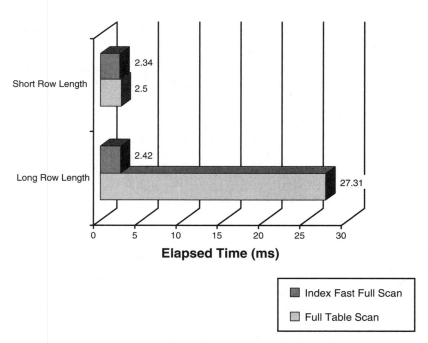

FIGURE 9-9   Index fast full scan performance.

PARTITIONING

As we discussed at the beginning of this chapter, using an index to retrieve rows becomes less effective as the proportion of rows to be retrieved increases. When the percentage of rows to be retrieved is too high to make an index lookup effective, but falls far short of retrieving all the rows in the table, then a partitioned table might give better performance.

For instance, a query such as the following will probably not be optimized by an index lookup unless there are many years of sales data:

```
SELECT SUM (amount_sold)
  FROM sh.sales s
 WHERE time_id > SYSDATE - NUMTOYMINTERVAL (2, 'YEAR')
```

Although an index might be inefficient, it seems a bit extreme to scan the entire table to get a minority of the rows—even if it is a large minority. However, if the table is partitioned by TIME_ID (as indeed is the case for the SALES table in the SH sample schema), we could scan only those partitions that contain relevant data. This process is called *partition elimination*.

We discussed some of the pros and cons of partitioning in Chapter 4. Asides from any other consideration, the partitioning is an extra-cost option of the Enterprise Edition. However when available, partitioning can often provide a middle ground between an index lookup and a full scan.

Figure 9-10 illustrates the advantages of partition elimination. When the proportion of the table accessed was greater than approximately 3 percent, an

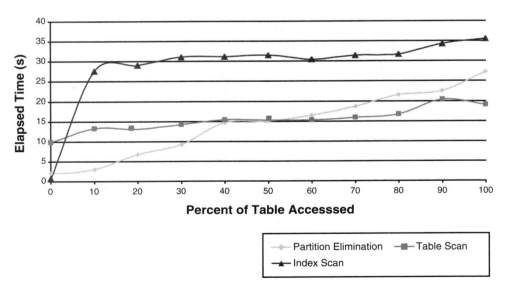

FIGURE 9-10 Performance of partition elimination compared to index and full scan.

index scan was faster than a full table or partition scan. But between 3 percent and 40 percent, partition elimination resulted in better performance than both the index scan and the table scan.

Because partitioned tables involve multiple segments, a full scan is usually slightly more expensive than a scan of an unpartitioned table. The cutoff point depends on the number of partitions, the distribution of data, and the proportion of the table to be processed.

> When the proportion of rows to be processed is too high for an index-based access path, but falls well short of the entire table, a partitioning scheme and partition elimination might provide better performance than either the full scan or an index scan.

SUMMARY

In this chapter, we examined ways to optimize retrieval of data from a single table—a fundamental technique that underlies the construction of more complex SQL queries.

One of the principal decisions to be made when retrieving data from a table is whether to use a full table scan or some form of indexed lookup. Single row lookups work best with indexed methods whereas accessing the entire table is best done through a full table scan. However, between these two extremes there is no magic number that defines the point at which an indexed retrieval becomes less efficient than a full table scan. Object statistics—histograms in particular—can help the optimizer make the best decision.

If an index-based access is required, Oracle's default B*-Tree indexes provide good performance for a wide variety of query types. Under certain circumstances bitmap indexes, hash clusters, or index organized tables might provide a more suitable solution. However, each of these alternative indexing strategies carries a greater risk than the B*-Tree solution and so should be used with care.

Certain types of query operations cannot take advantage of indexes. These operations can lead to unintentional table scans and are a common cause of poor application performance. Some of the things to look out for are

- ❑ Searching for NULL values in a column associated with a B*-Tree index
- ❑ Performing a NOT EQUALS (!=) operation on an indexed column when only a small proportion of rows satisfy the NOT EQUALS operation
- ❑ Using a function on an indexed column where there is no associated *functional* index

Take advantage of concatenated indexes, which are indexes created against more than one column. Creating the best set of concatenated indexes goes a long way toward optimizing table lookups.

If it is impractical to avoid a full table scan, you can optimize table scan performance by

- ❏ Increasing the number of rows stored in each data block by reducing PCTFREE, but not so far as to cause row migration or degrade DML performance
- ❏ Resetting the highwater mark by rebuilding the table or issuing an ALTER TABLE . . . SHRINK after bulk deletes
- ❏ Using compression to reduce the table size
- ❏ Moving large, infrequently queried columns to a separate table
- ❏ Using the parallel query option.
- ❏ Performing a *fast full index scan* of an index that includes all the relevant columns

JOINS AND SUBQUERIES

In this chapter, we discuss ways to improve performance when two or more tables are joined. Most nontrivial SQL statements contain joins, and ensuring that the tables involved are joined in the most effective manner is an important factor when tuning SQL.

The Oracle optimizer will do its best to ensure that the types of joins and the order in which tables are joined is optimal. Sometimes, the optimizer will be unable to determine the best join plan because of limitations in its algorithms and its understanding of your data. It is then up to you to enforce the optimal join approach through hints or other means.

Subqueries are close relatives to joins. Subqueries allow a SQL query to be embedded in another SQL statement and can often achieve similar outcomes to joins but possibly with different efficiency. Subqueries can also be used to express the reverse of a join by retrieving rows from one table that have no match in a second table.

Subqueries can be used to formulate complex queries, and the more complex the query, the greater the likelihood that the optimizer will fail to reach the best solution. In this chapter, we discuss when to use subqueries, which sort of subquery to use, and ways to improve the performance of subqueries.

TYPES OF JOINS

Most joins involve linking rows from tables that have the familiar master-detail relationship. However, there are a wide variety of logical join types, including the following:

❑ The *equi-join* is the most familiar type, in which equality conditions are used to match rows from one table to another.

❑ In a *theta* (or *non-equi*) *join* a join condition that is not an equality condition is specified. Rows can be matched based on a BETWEEN or other range condition operator.

❑ In a *cross join* there is no join condition specified. Every row in one table is joined to every row in the second table. Commonly known as the *Cartesian join*, this type of join leads to a rapid increase in overhead as the tables increase in size.

❑ In an *outer join*, rows in one table that have no match in the other are included in the results. LEFT, RIGHT, and FULL outer joins determine which table's rows are retained in the absence of a matching row in the other.

❑ A *self-join* is a join in which matching rows are sought within the same table.

❑ A *hierarchical join* is a special case of self-join in which parent-child relationships within a table are "exploded" into a hierarchy.

❑ In an *anti-join*, rows from one table that have no matching rows in another table are returned.

❑ In a *semi-join*, rows from one table that have a match in another table are returned. However, only one row from the outer table is returned, regardless of the number of matches in the inner table.

JOIN METHODS

Regardless of the logical category of join, Oracle has three join algorithms at its disposal: the *nested loops join*, the *sort-merge join*, and the *hash join*.

Each join is optimal in different circumstances and whereas the optimizer certainly "understands" these circumstances, you might from time to time need to override optimizer decisions.

NESTED LOOPS JOIN

In a nested loops join, Oracle performs a search of the second (or *inner*) table for each row found in the first (or *outer*) table.

Figure 10-1 illustrates the processing in a nested loops join. Note that the "tables" in the diagram could be actual Oracle tables or could be temporary work tables from previous join operations.

For each row in the outer table, we look for a matching row in the inner table. Because the inner table lookup must occur many times, it had better be efficient: Normally this means that it must be supported by an index lookup. Without an index on the inner table, we might need to scan the inner table once for each row in the outer table; this is the notorious *nested table scan* that can lead to exponential increases in overhead and execution time as the tables grow in size.

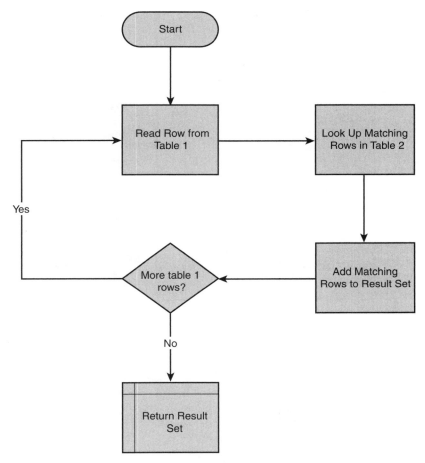

FIGURE 10-1   Nested loops join.

Because nested table scans are so undesirable, the optimizer will usually choose a nested loops operation only if there is an index on the inner table.

Even with an index on the inner table, the nested loops procedure is generally less effective than sort-merge or hash joins if all or most of the inner table data must be accessed.

SORT-MERGE JOIN

When performing a sort-merge join, Oracle must sort each table (or result set) by the value of the join columns. Once sorted, the two sets of data are merged, much as you might merge two sorted piles of numbered pages. Figure 10-2 illustrates the sort-merge algorithm.

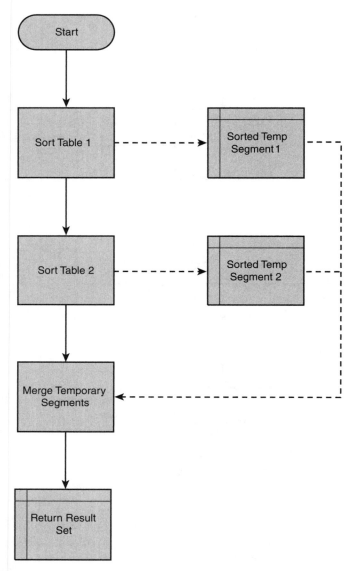

FIGURE 10-2   Sort-merge join.

Sort-merge joins suit joins where most of the data in the tables is to be included or where there is no indexed access available on the inner table. The hash join—which we discuss next—is often more efficient in circumstances where a sort-merge join might be considered. However, sort-merge joins can be employed where hash joins cannot (non-equi joins for instance).

HASH JOIN

When performing a hash join, Oracle builds a hash table for one of the two tables. This hash table is then used to find matching rows in a somewhat similar fashion to the way an index is used in a nested loops join. Figure 10-3 illustrates the hash join algorithm.

The hash join is usually more effective than the sort-merge join in the circumstances in which both are applicable and can be more effective than nested loops where a large proportion of table rows are to be included.

CHOOSING THE RIGHT JOIN METHOD

Most of the time, we can leave the join decision to the optimizer. However, as usual, there are borderline cases when the optimizer might make the wrong call, or where our knowledge of the data allows us to make a better and more informed decision.

SORT-MERGE/HASH VERSUS NESTED LOOPS

In a sense, the sort-merge join and the hash join can be considered as the same "family" of joins—they provide good performance under similar conditions whereas the nested loops join suits a different category of queries. So when determining the optimal join type, you might first decide if a nested loops join is appropriate.

The decision between the hash/sort-merge and nested loops approach should be based on

- ❏ The need for throughput versus the need for response time. Nested loops usually offer better response time, but hash/sort-merge joins can often offer better throughput.
- ❏ The proportion of the tables that are being joined. The larger the subset of rows being processed, the more likely that a sort-merge or hash join will be faster.
- ❏ Indexes available to support the join. A nested loops approach is usually effective only when an index can be used to join the tables.
- ❏ Memory and CPU available for sorting. Large sorts can consume significant resources and can slow execution. Sort-merge involves two sorts, whereas nested loops usually involve no sorting. Hash joins also require memory to build the hash table.
- ❏ Hash joins might get greater benefit from parallel execution and partition-oriented operations—although nested loops and sort-merge joins can also be parallelized.

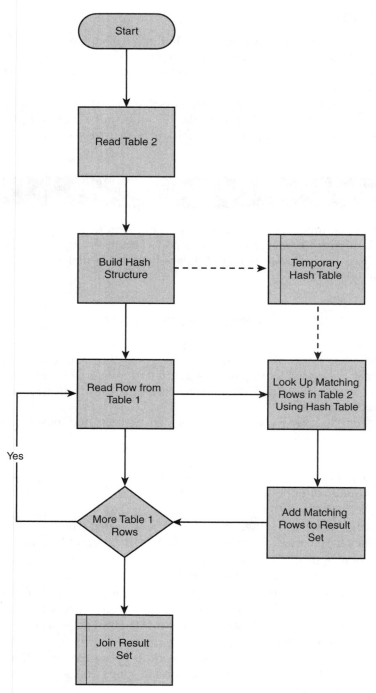

FIGURE 10-3   Hash join algorithm.

Figure 10-4 compares the performance of a hash join with a nested loops join as the amount of data in the join increases. When the join involves only a small subset of table rows, then the nested loops join is the most efficient. However, as the proportion of rows increases, hash join becomes more efficient than the nested loops join.

Table 10-1 provides general guidelines for deciding between the two join techniques. In borderline cases, you could try both methods and use SQL_TRACE or AUTOTRACE to determine which is superior.

The Nested loops join method suits joins involving a relatively small subset of table data and where the join is supported by an index. Sort-merge and hash joins are more suitable when a large proportion of the tables are being joined or if there is no suitable index.

SORT-MERGE VERSUS HASH JOINS

The sort-merge technique has been available since ancient versions of Oracle, whereas the hash join is somewhat more recent. Hash joins can be employed in many, but not all, of the circumstances in which a sort-merge join can be

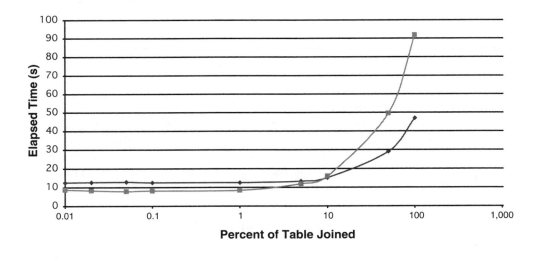

FIGURE 10-4 Hash join and nested loops performance versus join size.

Table 10-1 Determining the Optimal Join Method

WHEN JOINING A TO B (IN THAT ORDER)	CONSIDER SORT-MERGE OR HASH JOIN?	CONSIDER NESTED LOOPS USING AN INDEX ON B?
Both A and B are small.	Yes.	Maybe, depending on the selectivity of the index and the size of the outer table.
Only selecting a small subset of rows from B (and B has an index).	No. Performing a table scan of B will be cost-inefficient.	Yes. The index will reduce the number of IOs on B.
Want the first row as quickly as possible.	No. The first row won't be returned until both A and B are scanned, sorted, and merged or until the hash table has been built.	Yes. Rows can be returned as soon as they are fetched using the index.
Want to get all rows as quickly as possible.	Maybe. Nested loops might still get all rows before sort-merge or hash join if other conditions apply.	Maybe. Nested loops might still get all rows before sort-merge if other conditions apply.
Doing a full table scan of A and want to use parallel query.	Yes.	Yes. Nested loops can be resolved in parallel if the outer (first) table in the join is retrieved via a full table scan.
Memory is limited, especially PGA memory.	Maybe not. Large sorts can have significant overhead, especially if memory for sorts is limited. Hash joins can also require more memory than nested loops.	Yes. The nested loops join avoids sorting and is, therefore, less affected by memory limitations.

performed. When hash join and sort-merge are directly compared, the hash join tends to outperform the sort-merge join.

However, sort-merge join operations have a wider applicability than hash joins. Hash joins can be performed only when the join condition is an equality condition, whereas sort-merge joins can be used to resolve non-equi (or theta) joins. For instance, the following query cannot be resolved by a hash join, and so a sort-merge join is performed:

```
SQL> SELECT max(price_cat) ,max(amount_sold)
  2    FROM sales s JOIN price_cat c
  3      ON (s.amount_sold BETWEEN c.low_price AND c.high_price)

     Execution Plan
     ------------------------------------------------------------
```

```
--------------------------------------------------------------
| Id  | Operation             | Name       | Rows  | Bytes |
--------------------------------------------------------------
|   0 | SELECT STATEMENT      |            |     1 |    30 |
|   1 |  SORT AGGREGATE       |            |     1 |    30 |
|   2 |   MERGE JOIN          |            |  619M |   17G |
|   3 |    SORT JOIN          |            |  100K | 2441K |
|   4 |     TABLE ACCESS FULL | PRICE_CAT  |  100K | 2441K |
| * 5 |     FILTER            |            |       |       |
| * 6 |      SORT JOIN        |            | 2476K |   11M |
|   7 |       TABLE ACCESS FULL| SALES     | 2476K |   11M |
--------------------------------------------------------------
```

> Although the hash join generally out performs the sort-merge join, a hash join cannot
> be used for non-equi or theta joins.

Both hash join and sort-merge join must perform full scans of both input tables. The hash join has the advantage in that it has to create a hash table on only one of the tables, whereas the sort-merge join needs to sort both tables. Consequently, the sort-merge requires more memory to perform efficiently and may use more CPU during the sorts. This advantage of hash joins can be negated if the input data sets are already sorted, or if the output needs to be ordered. In these cases, the gap between sort-merge and hash join decreases.

For example, consider a query such as the following:

```
SQL> SELECT
  2          MAX (data1), MAX (data2)
  3      FROM sorted1 a JOIN sorted2 b USING (sortkey)
  4   ORDER BY sortkey;
```

```
-----------------------------------------------------------------------
| Id  | Operation             | Name     | Rows  | Bytes |TempSpc|
-----------------------------------------------------------------------
|   0 | SELECT STATEMENT      |          |     1 |   210 |       |
|   1 |  SORT AGGREGATE       |          |     1 |   210 |       |
| * 2 |   HASH JOIN           |          |  999K |  200M |  111M |
|   3 |    TABLE ACCESS FULL  | SORTED1  |  999K |  100M |       |
|   4 |    TABLE ACCESS FULL  | SORTED2  |  999K |  100M |       |
-----------------------------------------------------------------------
```

The optimizer decides upon a hash join, but we can force a sort-merge join using the USE_MERGE hint:

```
SQL> SELECT          /*+ ordered use_merge(b) */
  2                MAX (data1), MAX (data2)
  3          FROM sorted1 a JOIN sorted2 b USING (sortkey)
  4    ORDER BY sortkey;
```

```
-----------------------------------------------------------------------
| Id  | Operation               | Name     | Rows  | Bytes |TempSpc|
-----------------------------------------------------------------------
|   0 | SELECT STATEMENT        |          |     1 |   210 |       |
|   1 |  SORT AGGREGATE         |          |     1 |   210 |       |
|   2 |   MERGE JOIN            |          | 999K  | 200M  |       |
|   3 |    SORT JOIN            |          | 999K  | 100M  |  223M |
|   4 |     TABLE ACCESS FULL   | SORTED1  | 999K  | 100M  |       |
| * 5 |    SORT JOIN            |          | 999K  | 100M  |  223M |
|   6 |     TABLE ACCESS FULL   | SORTED2  | 999K  | 100M  |       |
-----------------------------------------------------------------------
```

Although the hash join usually outperforms the sort-merge, if the input data is already sorted, the sort operations will be less expensive and the sort-merge can be more effective. Figure 10-5 illustrates this phenomenon using the preceding queries. When the data in the tables is sorted by the join key, the sort-merge is slightly more efficient than the hash join. However, when the data is in no particular order, the hash join is significantly superior.

> The hash join algorithm usually outperforms the sort-merge algorithm. However, the sort-merge join might outperform a hash join if the input tables (or result sets) are already in sorted order.

OPTIMIZING JOINS

Picking the right join type—or ensuring that Oracle picks the right join type—is a good start but not the end of your join optimization efforts. Each type of join can be further optimized by tuning indexes and/or memory.

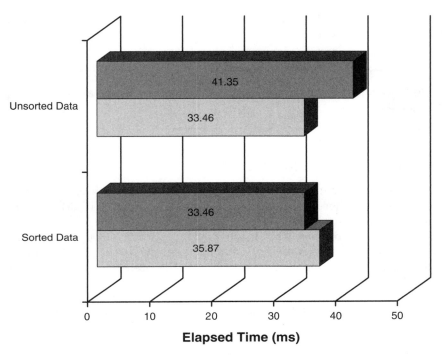

FIGURE 10-5 Sort-merge versus hash join for unsorted and presorted tables.

OPTIMIZING NESTED LOOPS JOIN

The key to optimizing a nested loops join is to ensure that the index lookup on the inner table is efficient. This generally means that we want to ensure that the index is the most selective possible.

We discussed index selectivity in the previous chapter. A selective index is one that returns a small number of rows for each index key value. For instance, consider the following query:

```
SELECT /*+ ORDERED USE_NL(d)    */
      SUM (s.quantity_sold), SUM (d.amount_sold)
  FROM sales_summary s JOIN sales_details d
      USING (prod_id, cust_id, time_id, channel_id, promo_id)
```

There are five columns in the join condition, and optimal performance will be obtained if there is a concatenated index based on all five columns. However, we can still get good performance if there is an index on a single, very selective column—TIME_ID for instance. On the other hand, an index on a single nonselective column such as PROD_ID results in lackluster performance. Figure 10-6 shows how performance varies depending on the index chosen.

Optimizing a nested loops join involves ensuring that a selective index exists on the inner table's join columns.

OPTIMIZING SORT-MERGE AND HASH JOINS

The key to optimizing sort-merge and hash joins is memory; both of these joins degrade significantly if there is insufficient Program Global Area (PGA) memory for the sort, merge, or hash operations to be completed in memory.

We look at sorting in more depth in Chapter 11, "Sorting, Grouping, and Set Operations," and examine PGA memory management in Chapter 19, "Optimizing PGA Memory." But for now, it's worth briefly discussing how memory affects sort and hash operations.

Both sorting and hashing work best if the entire structure can be constructed in memory. A completely in-memory operation is referred to as an *opti-*

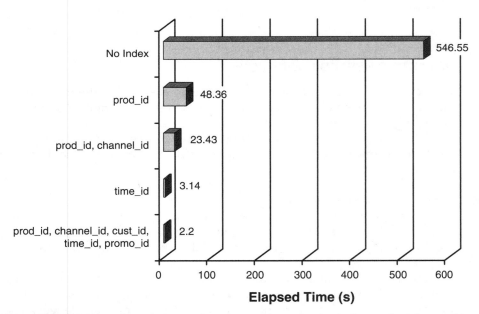

FIGURE 10-6   Nested loop joins perform best with a selective index on the join condition.

mal operation. If the operation cannot complete in memory, one or more temporary work areas will need to be written to and read back from disk. A *one-pass* operation occurs when there is enough memory so that the session needs to write and read only a single temporary disk segment. *Multi-pass* operations need to write and read the data on disk more than once. The more passes the session has to take at the data, the worse the performance. We'll come back to the concepts of optimal, one-pass, and multi-pass operations in Chapter 11.

For a hash join, there is just a single temporary structure—the hash table— that needs to be processed. As a result, hash join performance varies in the same way as a simple sort operation with respect to memory; performance dips suddenly as we go from optimal to one-pass and then gets progressively worse as the number of passes increase.

For a sort-merge operation things are much more complicated. Not only do we have to perform two sort operations, but we also have to merge the results. If we can merge the results in memory, the process will be efficient. However, if we have to merge from disk, performance will degrade substantially. As a result, sort-merge operations perform badly when there's not enough memory to perform the sort and merge operations in memory.

Figure 10-7 illustrates some of these principles. It shows join performance for sort-merge and hash join methods as we vary the amount of memory available.

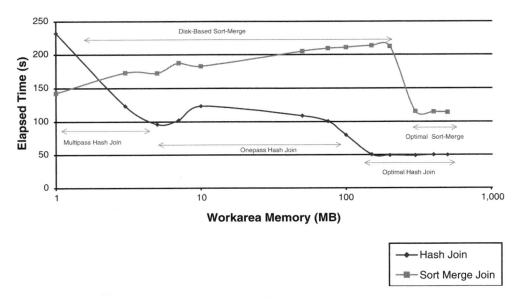

FIGURE 10-7 Join algorithms vary in efficiency depending on available memory.

We can draw the following conclusions from this chart:

❏ Sort-merge tends to require more memory than hash join to reach its optimal performance. Adding memory does not improve sort-merge performance until the optimal level is achieved.[1]

❏ If memory drops below optimal, sort-merge performance degrades abruptly, whereas hash join performance drops off gradually as the memory is reduced.

❏ When memory is very scarce, hash join performance is particularly poor.

Both hash join and sort-merge joins are sensitive to memory. Sort-merge requires more memory for optimal performance, and performance tends to drop off abruptly when the operation cannot complete entirely within memory.

We look in detail at how to measure and optimize sort activity in Chapter 11. To foreshadow though, we can observe disk sorts, and one-pass and multipass operations with the following query:

```
SQL> SELECT NAME, VALUE
  2     FROM v$sysstat
  3    WHERE NAME LIKE 'workarea executions - %'
  4       OR NAME IN ('sorts (memory)', 'sorts (disk)');

NAME                                           VALUE
---------------------------------------- ------------
workarea executions - optimal                247,919
workarea executions - onepass                    962
workarea executions - multipass                  270
sorts (memory)                               320,023
sorts (disk)                                   1,082
```

Memory for sorts and hash joins are controlled by the following parameters:

❏ In Oracle 11g, MEMORY_TARGET controls the total amount of memory to Oracle both for PGA and SGA. Oracle allocates PGA memory to sessions based on demand.

---

[1] Adding memory can result in diminished sort-merge performance if the amount of memory is insufficient to allow the entire join to complete in memory. Jonathan Lewis has also reported this phenomenon (Cost Based Oracle Fundamentals, Apress, 2006, Ch. 13).

❏ In Oracle 10g, or if MEMORY_TARGET is not set, PGA_AGGREGATE_
TARGET controls the amount of PGA memory available for all sessions. Individual PGA memory is made available to sessions based on demand.

❏ If neither MEMORY_TARGET or PGA_AGGREGATE_TARGET are set, the
amount of memory available for sort or hash operations is controlled by the
parameters SORT_AREA_SIZE and HASH_AREA_SIZE.

See Chapter 19 for more guidance on how to optimize PGA memory.

AVOIDING JOINS

Joins are often expensive operations, so it makes sense to avoid them when possible. Some of the ways we might avoid a join include

❏ Maintaining denormalized data from one table in another.
❏ Storing the tables in an index cluster so that rows from two tables with com-
mon keys are stored in the same block.
❏ Creating a materialized view that stores the results of a join operation in a
single segment.
❏ Creating a bitmap join index that is based on the join of two tables.

DENORMALIZATION

Avoiding a join is one of the classic reasons for implementing denormalization.
As discussed in Chapter 4, "Logical and Physical Database Design," denormalizing involves introducing redundancy into our data with the aim of improving
performance.

For instance, the following query joins DEPARTMENTS to EMPLOYEES to
obtain the employees department name:

```
SELECT employee_id, first_name, last_name, department_name
  FROM hr.employees JOIN hr.departments USING (department_id)
```

We could avoid the join by creating a copy of the DEPARTMENT_NAME
column in the EMPLOYEES table. A trigger can be used to maintain the value of
that column:

```
ALTER TABLE employees ADD (department_name VARCHAR2(30));

CREATE OR REPLACE TRIGGER employees_dept_name_trg
   BEFORE INSERT OR UPDATE OF department_id
   ON employees
```

```
    FOR EACH ROW
BEGIN
    IF :NEW.department_id IS NOT NULL
    THEN
        SELECT department_name
          INTO :NEW.department_name
          FROM hr.departments
         WHERE department_id = :NEW.department_id;
    END IF;
END;
/
UPDATE employees /* This will populate DEPARTMENT_NAME */
    SET department_id = department_id;
```

We should also create a trigger on DEPARTMENTS to ensure that updates to the DEPARTMENT_NAME column is denormalized back into the EMPLOYEES table, and a DELETE trigger to nullify the DEPARTMENT_NAME in the event that a department is deleted.

Denormalization of this type can certainly work to avoid join overhead, but you need to exercise care to ensure that the denormalization is correctly maintained. Furthermore, the trigger imposes some overhead on DML operations; see Chapter 12, "Using and Tuning PL/SQL," for details on trigger performance.

Avoiding join overhead is one of the classic reasons for denormalization. Using triggers to automate denormalization is recommended.

INDEX CLUSTERS

We first encountered index clustered tables in Chapter 5, "Indexing and Clustering." In an index cluster, rows from multiple tables that share a common key value—the cluster key—are stored within the same block and can be located via the cluster index.

An index cluster doesn't avoid the join altogether, but it does allow you to retrieve rows from both tables in a single IO operation. This can reduce IO requirements and hence optimize the join.

Figure 10-8 shows performance for various join approaches compared with an index cluster on the two tables for the following statement:

```
SELECT MIN (order_date), MAX (order_date),  SUM (price)
  FROM orders_clu JOIN line_items_clu USING (order_id)
 WHERE customer_id = 12;
```

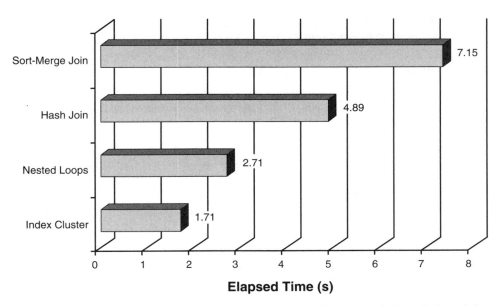

FIGURE 10-8 Under the right circumstances, an index cluster can help optimize a join.

Although there's no doubt that a cluster can be effective in reducing join overhead, the cluster will be truly effective only if the SIZE parameter is set to a value large enough to store all rows for the common key and if all the rows for each key value will fit in a couple of database blocks. Furthermore, clustering in this way optimizes only the join: Full table scans of individual tables in the cluster will probably be significantly degraded. For these reasons, index clusters are rarely used in practice.

An index cluster can help optimize a join but have significant drawbacks that need to be carefully considered.

MATERIALIZED VIEWS

We first looked at materialized views in Chapter 4. Materialized views are a sophisticated mechanism for optimizing data warehousing queries that typically involve aggregate operations and that can leverage *transparent query rewrite* and automatic rebuilds using *materialized view logs*.

Although using a materialized view to avoid a join is a bit like using a sledgehammer to crack a walnut, if you want to avoid join overhead on tables that are infrequently updated it might be worth considering.

For instance, to create a materialized view to support a join between DEPARTMENTS and EMPLOYEES, we could use the following SQL:

```
CREATE MATERIALIZED VIEW  cust_dept_mv
REFRESH COMPLETE
ENABLE QUERY REWRITE
AS
SELECT e.employee_id, e.first_name, e.last_name, department_id,
       d.department_name
  FROM  departments d JOIN  employees e USING (department_id);
```

If the parameter QUERY_WRITE_ENABLED is set to TRUE within a session, then eligible queries can be resolved by accessing the materialized view and avoiding the join:

```
SQL> SELECT e.employee_id, e.first_name, e.last_name,
  2            department_id, d.department_name
  3      FROM departments d JOIN employees e USING (department_id)
```

Id	Operation	Name	Rows
0	SELECT STATEMENT		106
1	MAT_VIEW REWRITE ACCESS FULL	CUST_DEPT_MV	106

The maintenance of materialized views places a significant overhead on DML, and materialized views are more often used in conjunction with *dimensions* in data warehousing environments. The Oracle 11g result set cache might provide greater performance benefits with lower overhead for some queries. See Chapter 20. "Other Memory Management Topics," for more information on the result set cache.

A materialized view, together with query rewrite, can be used to avoid a join.

BITMAP JOIN INDEX

We saw an example of bitmap join indexes in Chapter 5. A bitmap join index is a bitmap index that identifies rows in one table that have values matching a value in a second table. This bitmap index can be used to avoid joining the two tables to resolve the results. We saw an example in Chapter 5 in which a bitmap join index eliminated more than 95 percent of elapsed time for a join.

The normal restrictions on bitmap indexes apply equally to bitmap join indexes. As with all bitmap indexes, you should beware of the increase in lock granularity that usually makes bitmap indexes unacceptable for OLTP style applications.

> For suitable queries, bitmap join indexes can result in significant reductions in join overhead.

JOIN ORDER

Determining the best possible join order can be complex. There are often a large number of potential access methods, join methods, and join orders. For the mathematically inclined, the number of possible join orders is the factorial of the number of tables in the FROM clause. For instance, if there are five tables in the FROM clause, then the number of possible join orders is

$$5! = 5 \times 4 \times 3 \times 2 \times 1 = 120$$

The optimizer attempts to calculate the best of all possible join orders, though it might give up before calculating the cost of every alternative if the number of tables is very large. Generally speaking, you will want to rely on the optimizer here because manually comparing every single join permutation will usually be impractical.

Regardless of the join method and join order, only two tables are ever involved in a single join operation. When joining three or more tables, multiple join operations occur. Each join results in a temporary result set that is then joined to a subsequent table. Reducing the sizes of these intermediate temporary result sets is an important step toward reducing overall join overhead. Figure 10-9 illustrates this concept.

In general, it's best to let the cost based optimizer (CBO) attempt to calculate the optimum join order. You can help the optimizer by ensuring that there are up-to-date statistics and histograms on all join columns. Histograms help the optimizer determine the size of each intermediate result set by identifying column cardinalities, which helps the optimizer compare join order variations.

If you are trying to determine an optimum join order manually, the following rules of thumb might be helpful:

❑ The driving table—the first table in the join order—should be the one that has the most selective and efficient WHERE clause condition.

❑ Eliminate rows from the final result set as early in the join order as possible. In general, we don't want to join rows that will later be discarded, so try to process all filtering conditions early on in the join.

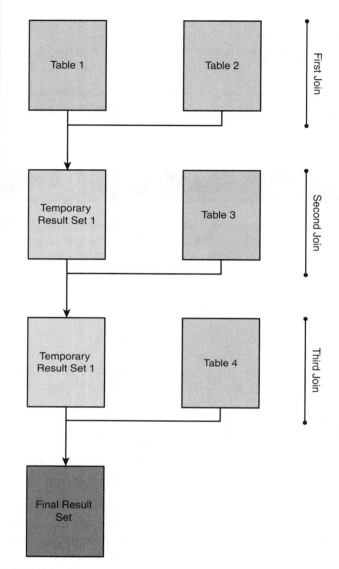

FIGURE 10-9   Oracle joins tables two at a time; each join generates a result set that is then fed into subsequent joins.

❑   If you are joining small subsets of the tables involved, try to use nested loops for each subsequent join providing that there is a supporting index. Otherwise, use hash join in preference to sort-merge.

❑   Make sure the indexes supporting the nested loops join contain all the columns in the WHERE clause for the table being joined and the join columns.

It's generally preferable to let the optimizer choose the join order. If manually choosing the join order, aim to eliminate rows as early as possible in the join.

SPECIAL JOINS

Certain joins have specific optimization approaches or performance profiles. In this section we'll look at

- ❏ *Outer joins*, in which rows missing in one or both of the tables are included in the result set.
- ❏ *Star joins*, in which a large fact table is joined to multiple, smaller dimension tables.
- ❏ *Self-joins*, in which a table is joined to itself. In particular we consider the optimization of *hierarchical self-joins*.

OUTER JOINS

An outer join is one in which a row is returned from one of the tables in a join, even if there is no matching row in the other table. Depending on which table has the missing rows, we might have a LEFT OUTER JOIN or a RIGHT OUTER JOIN. If missing rows from both tables are to be returned, the join is referred to as a FULL OUTER JOIN. A join in which only matching rows from both tables are returned is called an *inner* join.

The performance of a left or right outer join is usually equivalent to that of the corresponding inner join, and all join methods—hash, sort-merge, and nested loops—are available. However, left and right outer joins *do* impose a particular join order. When we perform an outer join, the table that is going to return rows even if there are no matches in the other table must be first in the join order.

For instance, the following outer join will return rows for departments that have no assigned employees:

```
SQL> SELECT /*+ ordered */
  2         first_name, last_name, department_name
  3    FROM employees RIGHT OUTER JOIN departments
  4             USING (department_id)
  5   WHERE department_id IN (99, 40);
```

It doesn't make sense to start with the EMPLOYEES table, because we are going to be including Departments with no employees, and for those departments we'd have nowhere to start. So Oracle ignores the ORDERED hint in the query and resolves the join DEPARTMENTS to EMPLOYEES:

```
-------------------------------------------------------------------
| Id  | Operation                       | Name                    |
-------------------------------------------------------------------
|   0 | SELECT STATEMENT                |                         |
|   1 |  NESTED LOOPS OUTER             |                         |
|   2 |   INLIST ITERATOR               |                         |
|   3 |    TABLE ACCESS BY INDEX ROWID  | DEPARTMENTS             |
| * 4 |     INDEX UNIQUE SCAN           | DEPARTMENTS_PK          |
|   5 |    TABLE ACCESS BY INDEX ROWID  | EMPLOYEES               |
| * 6 |     INDEX RANGE SCAN            | EMPLOYEES_DEPT_IDX      |
-------------------------------------------------------------------
```

> Left and right outer joins will require the optimizer to join tables in a specific order: The table with the missing values will be joined last.

Full outer joins are a different matter, because we are going to return rows missing from both tables. There is a special hash join mode for full outer joins:

```
-----------------------------------------------
| Id  | Operation            | Name           |
-----------------------------------------------
|   0 | SELECT STATEMENT     |                |
| * 1 |  VIEW                | VW_FOJ_0       |
| * 2 |   HASH JOIN FULL OUTER|               |
|   3 |    TABLE ACCESS FULL | DEPARTMENTS    |
|   4 |    TABLE ACCESS FULL | EMPLOYEES      |
-----------------------------------------------
```

If sort-merge or nested loops joins are used instead, then two result sets are generated and the UNION operation used to join the two. Note the presence of both OUTER and ANTI joins (discussed later in this chapter), in this result set:

```
-------------------------------------------------------------------
| Id  | Operation                       | Name                    |
-------------------------------------------------------------------
|   0 | SELECT STATEMENT                |                         |
|   1 |  VIEW                           |                         |
|   2 |   UNION-ALL                     |                         |
| * 3 |    FILTER                       |                         |
|   4 |     NESTED LOOPS OUTER          |                         |
|   5 |      TABLE ACCESS FULL          | EMPLOYEES               |
|   6 |      TABLE ACCESS BY INDEX ROWID| DEPARTMENTS             |
```

```
| *  7 |        INDEX UNIQUE SCAN          | DEPARTMENTS_PK      |
|    8 |      NESTED LOOPS ANTI            |                     |
|    9 |        INLIST ITERATOR           |                     |
|   10 |        TABLE ACCESS BY INDEX ROWID| DEPARTMENTS        |
| * 11 |         INDEX UNIQUE SCAN        | DEPARTMENTS_PK      |
| * 12 |        INDEX RANGE SCAN          | EMPLOYEES_DEPT_IDX  |
 --------------------------------------------------------------
```

Oracle proprietary syntax—in which the (+) operator is used to denote an outer join—cannot be used to properly specify a full outer join and can lead to subtle bugs in left and right outer joins because the (+) operator might need to be applied to non-join WHERE conditions. ANSI syntax, in which joins are specified within the FROM clause rather than the WHERE clause, is arguably preferable for all new code but is particularly superior when it comes to specifying outer joins.

STAR JOINS

We first examined the star schema pattern in Chapter 4. A star schema involves a large *fact* table that contains detail rows and foreign keys to smaller more static *dimension* tables that categorize the fact items in business contexts, typically including time, product, customer, and so on.

Figure 10-10 shows a simplified representation of the star schema that is included in the Oracle sample SH schema. A more complete diagram can be found in Chapter 4.

A join against a star schema is referred to, not surprisingly, as a star join. Here's an example of such a query:

```
SELECT quantity_sold, amount_sold
  FROM sales s JOIN products p USING (prod_id)
       JOIN times USING (time_id)
       JOIN customers c USING (cust_id)
 WHERE week_ending_day = '29-Nov-2008'
   AND prod_name = '1.44MB External 3.5" Diskette'
   AND cust_first_name = 'Hiram'
   AND cust_last_name = 'Abbassi'
   and cust_year_of_birth=1965;
```

Oracle's default approach to this sort of star join is to query all of the dimension tables—PRODUCTS, TIMES, and CUSTOMERS—to retrieve the foreign key values corresponding to the WHERE clause conditions. These results sets are then merged—using a full *Cartesian* join—and the resulting foreign keys are used to identify the fact table rows required. If there are suitable indexes on the foreign key values in the fact table, those can be used to optimize the final step. So in the case of the preceding query, this index would be optimal:

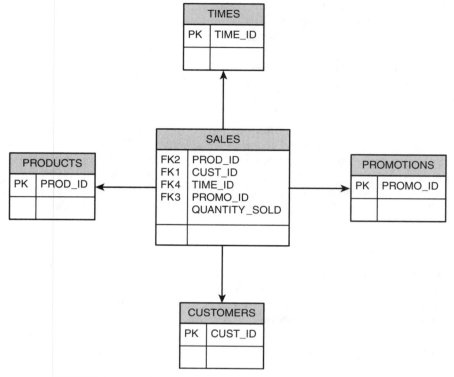

FIGURE 10-10 Star schema (from the Oracle sample schema).

```
CREATE INDEX sales_concat_idx ON
            sales(prod_id,time_id,cust_id);
```

The resulting execution plan looks like this:

```
-------------------------------------------------------------------
| Id  | Operation                       | Name               |
-------------------------------------------------------------------
|  0  | SELECT STATEMENT                |                    |
|  1  |  NESTED LOOPS                   |                    |
|  2  |   NESTED LOOPS                  |                    |
|  3  |    MERGE JOIN CARTESIAN         |                    |
|  4  |     MERGE JOIN CARTESIAN        |                    |
|  5  |      TABLE ACCESS BY INDEX ROWID | CUSTOMERS         |
|* 6  |       INDEX RANGE SCAN          | CUST_NAMEDOB_IDX  |
|  7  |      BUFFER SORT                |                    |
|  8  |       TABLE ACCESS BY INDEX ROWID| PRODUCTS          |
```

```
|*  9 |          INDEX RANGE SCAN          | PROD_NAME_IDX      |
|   10 |        BUFFER SORT                 |                    |
|   11 |        TABLE ACCESS BY INDEX ROWID | TIMES              |
|*  12 |          INDEX RANGE SCAN          | TIMES_WEND_IDX     |
|*  13 |        INDEX RANGE SCAN            | SALES_CONCAT_IDX   |
|   14 |      TABLE ACCESS BY INDEX ROWID   | SALES              |
 ------------------------------------------------------------------
```

The Cartesian merge joins of customers, products, and times (step ID 3 and 4) identify the foreign key values that are then fed into an index lookup on our concatenated index (step ID 13) to retrieve the SALES table rows.

This approach to star join execution is efficient because it reduces access to the large fact table but has one critical drawback: Because there are typically a wide variety of WHERE clause conditions supplied in the data warehousing environments in which the star schema is common, a large number of concatenated indexes would be required to satisfy the full range of queries.

Star Transformation The Cartesian-join approach to STAR queries outlined in the preceding section might fail for more complex schemas or queries. For instance

❑ If the number of matching rows in the dimension tables is large, the Cartesian products might become huge.

❑ Concatenated indexes that support all possible combinations of dimension keys will be required; creating all these indexes might not be practical.

To address these concerns, Oracle provides the *star transformation* optimization. The star transformation uses bitmap indexes on the fact table to produce a superior execution plan for queries where the number of dimension tables is large or where it is not practical to provide concatenated indexes for all possible queries.

In a star transformation, the cost based optimizer will transform the query from a join into a query against the fact table that contains subqueries against each of the dimension tables. For instance, when star transformation is in effect, our query might be rewritten something like this:

```
SELECT quantity_sold, amount_sold
  FROM sales s
 WHERE s.prod_id IN (SELECT prod_id
                       FROM products
                      WHERE prod_name
            = '1.44MB External 3.5" Diskette')
   AND s.time_id IN (SELECT time_id
                       FROM times
                      WHERE week_ending_day = '29-Nov-2008')
```

```
      AND s.cust_id IN (
                SELECT cust_id
                  FROM customers
                 WHERE cust_first_name = 'Hiram'
                       AND cust_last_name = 'Abbassi'
                       and cust_year_of_birth=1965  );
```

To get the star transformation plan, the parameter STAR_TRANSFORMA-TION_ENABLED should be set to TRUE. We can set this parameter using an ALTER SYSTEM or ALTER SESSION statement or, if we want it to be in effect for the query only, by setting it with the OPT_PARAM hint, as here:

```
SELECT /*+ OPT_PARAM('star_transformation_enabled' 'true')
         star_transformation */
      quantity_sold, amount_sold
  FROM sales s JOIN products p USING (prod_id)
      JOIN times USING (time_id)
      JOIN customers c USING (cust_id)
 WHERE week_ending_day = '29-Nov-2008'
   AND prod_name = '1.44MB External 3.5" Diskette'
   AND cust_first_name = 'Hiram'
   AND cust_last_name = 'Abbassi'
   and cust_year_of_birth=1965;
```

The star transformation plan is recognizable by the use of bitmap indexes against the fact table as in the following execution plan:

```
-----------------------------------------------------------------
| Id  | Operation                        | Name                 |
-----------------------------------------------------------------
|   0 | SELECT STATEMENT                 |                      |
|   1 |  TABLE ACCESS BY INDEX ROWID     | SALES                |
|   2 |   BITMAP CONVERSION TO ROWIDS    |                      |
|   3 |    BITMAP AND                    |                      |
|   4 |     BITMAP MERGE                 |                      |
|   5 |      BITMAP KEY ITERATION        |                      |
|   6 |       TABLE ACCESS BY INDEX ROWID| CUSTOMERS            |
| *  7 |        INDEX RANGE SCAN          | CUST_NAMEDOB_IDX     |
| *  8 |       BITMAP INDEX RANGE SCAN    | SALES_CUST_BI        |
|   9 |     BITMAP MERGE                 |                      |
|  10 |      BITMAP KEY ITERATION        |                      |
|  11 |       TABLE ACCESS BY INDEX ROWID| TIMES                |
| * 12 |        INDEX RANGE SCAN          | TIMES_WEND_IDX       |
| * 13 |       BITMAP INDEX RANGE SCAN    | SALES_TIMES_BI       |
```

```
|  14 |         BITMAP MERGE                 |               |
|  15 |          BITMAP KEY ITERATION        |               |
|  16 |           TABLE ACCESS BY INDEX ROWID| PRODUCTS      |
|* 17 |            INDEX RANGE SCAN           | PROD_NAME_IDX |
|* 18 |           BITMAP INDEX RANGE SCAN     | SALES_PROD_BI |
 ---------------------------------------------------------------
```

Note that star transformation performance is *not* better than what you'll get from a concatenated index on the fact table. However, you usually can't create enough concatenated indexes to support all possible queries, whereas with star transformation, you merely need a bitmap index on each foreign key to support all the possible combinations of WHERE clause conditions.

The star transformation optimization, when supported by bitmap indexes, gives good performance and will support the widest range of possible WHERE clause conditions.

Star Transformation with Bitmap Join Indexes In the previous example, we used indexes on the dimension tables to identify the foreign key values in the fact table (for instance, we used PROD_NAME_IDX to get a PROD_ID for a PROD_NAME) and then used a bitmap index on the fact table to retrieve the fact detail rows (for instance, SALES_PROD_BI).

Bitmap join indexes enable us to bypass this two-step process, because a bitmap join index can point directly to rows in the fact table that match values in a dimension table. To get the bitmap join index execution plan, we create bitmap join indexes on each of the predicates in the WHERE clause. For instance, we create the following index to allow us to identify SALES rows that match a specific PROD_NAME:

```
CREATE BITMAP INDEX sales_prod_bjix
   ON sales(products.prod_name)
  FROM sales, products
 WHERE sales.prod_id=products.prod_id;
```

With similar bitmap join indexes in place for TIMES and CUSTOMERS, our execution plan is substantially simplified:

```
 ------------------------------------------------------------
| Id  | Operation                      | Name      |        |
 ------------------------------------------------------------
|   0 | SELECT STATEMENT               |           |        |
|   1 |  TABLE ACCESS BY INDEX ROWID   | SALES     |        |
|   2 |   BITMAP CONVERSION TO ROWIDS  |           |        |
```

```
|   3 |     BITMAP AND                         |                   |
| *  4 |       BITMAP INDEX SINGLE VALUE| SALES_TIME_BJIX |
| *  5 |       BITMAP INDEX SINGLE VALUE| SALES_PROD_BJIX |
| *  6 |       BITMAP INDEX SINGLE VALUE| SALES_CUST_BJIX |
---------------------------------------------------------
```

We now can completely avoid accessing the dimension tables and this significantly improves performance.

Bitmap join indexes often offer the best star join performance by avoiding the need to directly access the dimension tables.

Figure 10-11 illustrates the performance characteristics of each approach. Using some form of indexing on the fact table is essential to getting good performance. A concatenated index on the entire set of join keys results in excellent performance and is usually slightly better than the bitmap star transformation. However, as we noted previously, star transformation usually supports a wider range of queries with a smaller number of indexes. Bitmap join indexes offer the best performance.

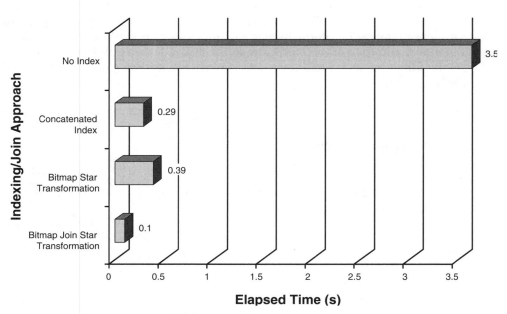

FIGURE 10-11   Star join performance.

Remember that bitmap indexes offer significant lock overhead; you should use bitmap indexes only in low concurrency environments where this lock contention is not an issue. See Chapter 5 for a longer discussion on bitmap indexes.

HIERARCHICAL JOINS

A hierarchical query, sometimes referred to as an "explosion of parts," is a special case of self-join. In the hierarchical query, a column in the table points to the primary key of another row in the same table. This row in turn points to a further row and so on until the head of the hierarchy is reached.

In the Oracle HR sample schema, the MANAGER_ID and EMPLOYEE_ID columns of the EMPLOYEE table form such a hierarchy. The MANAGER_ID column points to the EMPLOYEE_ID of that employee's manager. In the sample schema, EMPLOYEE_ID 100 represents the CEO. So if we want to print the full organizational hierarchy, we can use the following query:

```
SELECT  LPAD (' ', LEVEL) || employee_id,
        first_name, last_name, manager_id
   FROM hr.employees
CONNECT BY PRIOR employee_id = manager_id
  START WITH employee_id = 100
```

In older versions of Oracle (8i, for example), an index on the join column would be necessary for such a query to be efficient. However in modern Oracle, the query can be resolved by a single table scan of the table and without an index:

```
----------------------------------------------------------------
| Id | Operation                                   | Name      |
----------------------------------------------------------------
|  0 | SELECT STATEMENT                            |           |
|* 1 | CONNECT BY NO FILTERING WITH START-WITH     |           |
|  2 |   TABLE ACCESS FULL                         | EMPLOYEES |
----------------------------------------------------------------
```

If an index on the PRIOR column (in this case MANAGER_ID) exists, Oracle can use an indexed access path:

```
---------------------------------------------------------------
| Id | Operation                          | Name           |
---------------------------------------------------------------
|  0 | SELECT STATEMENT                    |                |
|* 1 |  CONNECT BY WITH FILTERING          |                |
|  2 |   TABLE ACCESS BY INDEX ROWID       | EMPLOYEES      |
|* 3 |    INDEX UNIQUE SCAN                 | EMPLOYEES_PK   |
```

```
|   4  |       NESTED LOOPS                    |                  |
|   5  |         CONNECT BY PUMP               |                  |
|   6  |       TABLE ACCESS BY INDEX ROWID|  EMPLOYEES           |
|*  7  |         INDEX RANGE SCAN          |  EMPLOYEE_MGR_ID |
-----------------------------------------------------------------
```

The indexed-based approach is superior when a small subset of the hierarchy is built. The full scan approach is superior when building the entire hierarchy. Figure 10-12 compares the performance of the two approaches when building a full hierarchy and when building a small subset (a manager with only four reports).

In most circumstances, the optimizer makes pretty good decisions when it comes to choosing between full table scans and index scans. However, the normal mechanisms for calculating cardinality don't work for hierarchical queries. The optimizer does not know that EMPLOYEE_ID 100 is the president and that EMPLOYEE_ID 108 is the senior janitor! So the optimizer chooses the same plan for each manager, even though the performance outcomes are very different. If the index is present, the optimizer will usually use it, even if the entire hierarchy is built.

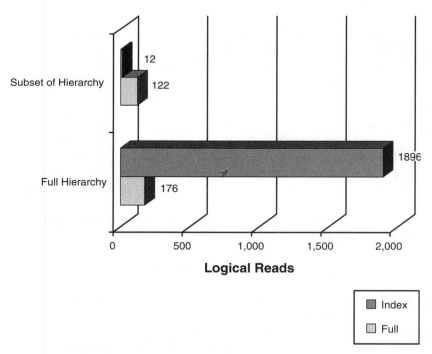

FIGURE 10-12 CONNECT BY performance and indexing.

Therefore, you will sometimes want to force a full scan—using a FULL hint or an outline—when you know that the full hierarchy is being built. If you know a subset of the hierarchy is being constructed, make sure you have an index to support the more efficient indexed plan.

When constructing a full hierarchy, avoid an indexed plan using a hint or outline if necessary. When building a subset of the hierarchy, consider creating an index on the PRIOR column.

SUBQUERIES

A subquery is a SELECT statement contained within another SQL statement. The main SQL statement, sometimes called the outer or parent statement, can be another SELECT statement, a DML statement (DELETE, INSERT, MERGE or UPDATE), or certain DDL statements.

SIMPLE SUBQUERIES

A simple subquery is one that makes no reference to the parent query and that often returns only a single row.

For instance, the following query returns the number of employees who share the honor of having the lowest salary in the firm:

```
SELECT COUNT (*)
  FROM employees
 WHERE salary = (SELECT MIN (salary)
                   FROM employees);
```

The same result could be achieved by executing the parent and the subquery separately:

```
    SELECT MIN (salary)
      INTO :minsal
      FROM employees;

    SELECT COUNT (*)
      FROM employees
     WHERE salary = :minsal;
```

It follows that because each subquery is executed independently, each can be optimized independently. For example, we would optimize the preceding join query by first optimizing the query to find the minimum salary and then optimizing the query to find the count of a given salary. The obvious way to optimize each would be to create an index on the salary column.

The optimization of simple subqueries is, therefore, relatively straightforward: Tune parent and child statements separately.

Although subqueries are often the best or only way to formulate a specific operation within a single SQL statement, they often require more resources than are absolutely necessary. For instance, our example subquery results in the following execution plan:

```
------------------------------------------------
| Id  | Operation              | Name      |
------------------------------------------------
|   0 | SELECT STATEMENT       |           |
|   1 |  SORT AGGREGATE        |           |
| * 2 |   TABLE ACCESS FULL    | EMPLOYEES |
|   3 |    SORT AGGREGATE      |           |
|   4 |     TABLE ACCESS FULL| EMPLOYEES |
------------------------------------------------
```

As we might expect, two full table scans of the EMPLOYEES table are required: one to find the maximum salary and another to get those employees with that salary.

Without adding an index, it's hard to avoid these full table scans using a single SQL statement. However, using PL/SQL, we can query the table only once:

```
DECLARE
    last_salary     hr.employees.salary%TYPE;
    counter         NUMBER:= 0;
BEGIN
    FOR emp_row IN (SELECT    *
                        FROM employees
                    ORDER BY salary)
    LOOP
        -- Exit the loop if the salary is greater
        -- than the previous salary
        EXIT WHEN counter > 0 AND emp_row.salary >
last_salary;
        counter := counter + 1;
        last_salary := emp_row.salary;
    END LOOP;
    DBMS_OUTPUT.put_line (counter ||
' employees have the minimum salary');
END;
```

With this approach, we scan the EMPLOYEES table only once. Furthermore, we stop fetching rows when we hit an employee on more than the minimum wage. This further reduces execution time.

Another possibility in this case is to use one of the *analytic functions*. This SQL performs the same task but requires only a single scan of the EMPLOYEES table:

```
SQL> WITH emp_salary AS
  2          (SELECT salary, MIN (salary) OVER () min_salary
  3              FROM employees)
  4    SELECT SUM (DECODE (salary, min_salary, 1))
  5      FROM emp_salary;
```

```
-----------------------------------------------------------
| Id  | Operation            | Name      | Rows  | Bytes  |
-----------------------------------------------------------
|   0 | SELECT STATEMENT     |           |     1 |     26 |
|   1 |  SORT AGGREGATE      |           |     1 |     26 |
|   2 |   VIEW               |           |   107 |   2782 |
|   3 |    WINDOW BUFFER     |           |   107 |   1391 |
|   4 |     TABLE ACCESS FULL| EMPLOYEES |   107 |   1391 |
-----------------------------------------------------------
```

The MIN(salary) OVER () clause returns the minimum salary that we then compare to each salary and count the number of matches.

> When optimizing SQL with simple subqueries, try optimizing the parent and subquery individually.

CORRELATED SUBQUERIES

A correlated subquery is one in which the subquery refers to values in the parent (outer) query and is logically executed once for each row returned by the parent query. For instance, the following query returns employees who have the maximum salary of all employees within a given department:

```
SELECT employee_id, first_name, last_name, salary
  FROM employees a
 WHERE salary = (SELECT MIN (salary)
                   FROM employees b
                  WHERE b.department_id = a.department_id);
```

Logically, and in older versions of Oracle, the subquery would actually be executed once for every row returned by the parent query. However, in modern

Oracle, a query transformation usually results in the query being executed as some form of join. For instance, the preceding query gets transformed to something like this:

```
SELECT    a.employee_id employee_id, a.first_name first_name,
          a.last_name last_name, a.salary salary
  FROM    (  SELECT   MIN (b.salary) "MIN(SALARY)",
                      b.department_id item_1
               FROM   opsg.employees b
             GROUP BY   b.department_id) vw_sq_2, opsg.employees a
 WHERE    a.salary = vw_sq_2."MIN(SALARY)"
   AND vw_sq_2.item_1 = a.department_id;
```

This transformation enables the query to be resolved by first performing a group by and then joining that result set to the main query using a hash join:

```
----------------------------------------------------------
| Id  | Operation              | Name        | Rows   |
----------------------------------------------------------
|   0 | SELECT STATEMENT       |             |   11   |
|*  1 |   HASH JOIN            |             |   11   |
|   2 |    VIEW               |             |   11   |
|   3 |     HASH GROUP BY      |             |   11   |
|   4 |      TABLE ACCESS FULL| EMPLOYEES   |  107   |
|   5 |      TABLE ACCESS FULL | EMPLOYEES   |  107   |
----------------------------------------------------------
```

The preceding query is clearly still suboptimal because it performs two scans of the EMPLOYEES table. Again, *analytic functions* can provide a possible improvement. In this case, we could use the PARTITION BY feature of analytic functions to calculate the minimum salary for each department and include only EMPLOYEE rows that have that matching salary:

```
SQL> WITH employees_w AS
  2        (SELECT e.*,
  3           MIN(salary) OVER (PARTITION BY department_id)
                AS dept_min_sal
  4         FROM employees e)
  5  SELECT employee_id, first_name, last_name, salary
  6    FROM employees_w
  7   WHERE salary=dept_min_sal;
```

```
---------------------------------------------------------------
| Id  | Operation            | Name      | Rows  | Bytes |
---------------------------------------------------------------
|   0 | SELECT STATEMENT     |           |  107  |  6955 |
|*  1 |  VIEW                |           |  107  |  6955 |
|   2 |   WINDOW SORT        |           |  107  |  2782 |
|   3 |    TABLE ACCESS FULL | EMPLOYEES |  107  |  2782 |
---------------------------------------------------------------
```

Be aware that although analytic functions can often avoid redundant table processing, they might require internal sort operations and be more dependent on available memory. Always benchmark an analytic function-based solution to make sure that it is actually an improvement.

Consider rewriting correlated subqueries as joins, using analytic functions, or in some other way avoid the awkward syntax and sometimes inefficient plans that are often associated with the correlated subquery.

ANTI-JOIN SUBQUERIES

An anti-join is a query that returns rows in one table that *do not* match some set of rows from another table. Because this is effectively the opposite of normal join behavior, the term *anti-join* has been used to describe this operation. Anti-joins are usually expressed using a NOT IN or NOT EXISTS subquery.

Perhaps the most natural and commonly used method for expressing the anti-join is to use the IN operator together with the NOT operator. For instance, the following query counts the number of Google customers who are not Microsoft customers:

```
SELECT COUNT (*)
  FROM google_customers
 WHERE (cust_first_name, cust_last_name)
    NOT IN (SELECT cust_first_name, cust_last_name
              FROM microsoft_customers)
```

The same query can be expressed using a NOT EXISTS subquery, as follows:

```
SELECT  COUNT (*)
  FROM google_customers gc
 WHERE NOT EXISTS (
          SELECT 0
            FROM microsoft_customers mc
           WHERE mc.cust_first_name = gc.cust_first_name
             AND mc.cust_last_name = gc.cust_last_name)
```

Under normal circumstances, Oracle uses the same approach for both queries by employing a formal anti-join operation—usually a HASH JOIN (ANTI) as in the following plan:

```
-------------------------------------------------------------------
| Id  | Operation          | Name                | Rows  |
-------------------------------------------------------------------
|   0 | SELECT STATEMENT   |                     |     1 |
|   1 |  SORT AGGREGATE    |                     |     1 |
| * 2 |   HASH JOIN ANTI   |                     |     1 |
|   3 |    TABLE ACCESS FULL| GOOGLE_CUSTOMERS    | 19999 |
|   4 |    TABLE ACCESS FULL| MICROSOFT_CUSTOMERS | 19999 |
-------------------------------------------------------------------
```

Adding an index to the subquery table might result in a slightly optimized outcome, though usually only because Oracle does a fast full scan of the index, not because it is performing actual index lookups:

```
-------------------------------------------------------------------
| Id  | Operation          | Name                | Rows  |
-------------------------------------------------------------------
|   0 | SELECT STATEMENT   |                     |     1 |
|   1 |  SORT AGGREGATE    |                     |     1 |
| * 2 |   HASH JOIN ANTI   |                     |     1 |
|   3 |    TABLE ACCESS FULL | GOOGLE_CUSTOMERS   | 19999 |
|   4 |    INDEX FAST FULL SCAN| MSFT_CUST_NAMES_I | 19999 |
-------------------------------------------------------------------
```

In modern Oracle, NOT IN and NOT EXISTS result in the same execution plan, and an index is not necessarily required. However, there is at least one circumstance in which the NOT IN anti-join can perform badly: if the columns involved are NULLABLE.

If the join columns in a NOT IN anti-join are NULLABLE, the anti-join method cannot be used. Instead, Oracle transforms the statement into a NOT EXISTS that looks something like this:

```
SELECT   COUNT ( * )
  FROM   google_customers
 WHERE   NOT EXISTS
         (SELECT 0
            FROM microsoft_customers mc
```

```
WHERE LNNVL (mc.cust_first_name <> gc.cust_first_name)
  AND LNNVL (mc.cust_last_name <> gc.cust_last_name))
```

The LNNVL function, which returns TRUE if the condition within would normally return NULL, and the strange use of <> comparisons suppress any index that might otherwise be used to evaluate the NOT EXISTS subquery. Consequently, the only way to resolve the query is to use the following (pseudo-code) plan:

```
FOR each row in GOOGLE_CUSTOMERS:
PERFORM a full scan of MICROSOFT_CUSTOMERS
```

This nested table scan approach to the resolution of the query is not just inefficient, it's also completely unscalable: The time taken to resolve the query rises steeply as the number of rows in each table increases. Figure 10-13 shows how the performance degrades as the number of rows involved increases. Consequently, you should almost never use a NOT IN subquery when any of the columns involved are NULLable.

For this type of query, you either want to define the columns as NOT NULL or add IS NOT NULL clauses to the WHERE clause as in this example:

```
SELECT COUNT (*)
  FROM google_customers
 WHERE cust_first_name IS NOT NULL
   AND cust_last_name  IS NOT NULL
   AND (cust_first_name, cust_last_name) NOT IN (
             SELECT cust_first_name, cust_last_name
               FROM microsoft_customers
              WHERE cust_first_name  IS NOT NULL
                AND cust_last_name IS NOT NULL);
```

Alternatively, the query could be rewritten as a NOT EXISTS subquery: NOT EXISTS subqueries are not vulnerable to the poor performance associated with NULLable columns. Figure 10-13 shows how NOT EXISTS performance remains stable as the size of the tables involved increase.

Don't use NOT IN to perform anti-joins unless the join keys are defined as NOT NULL. If the columns involved are NULLABLE, use a NOT EXISTS anti-join instead.

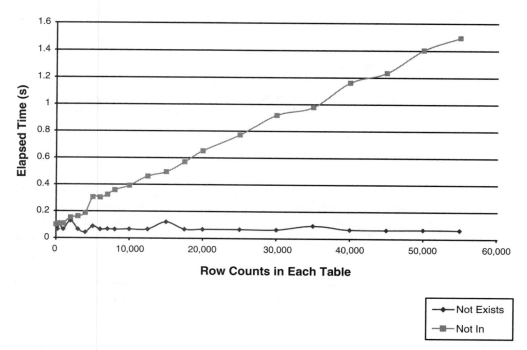

FIGURE 10-13 Performance of a NOT IN subquery degrades rapidly if the columns involved are NULLable.

SEMI-JOIN SUBQUERIES

A semi-join is expressed as a WHERE IN or WHERE EXISTS subquery. For instance, each of these two queries represents a semi-join between MICROSOFT _CUSTOMERS and GOOGLE_CUSTOMERS:

```
SELECT COUNT (*)
  FROM google_customers
 WHERE (cust_first_name, cust_last_name)
    IN (SELECT cust_first_name, cust_last_name
          FROM microsoft_customers);

SELECT COUNT (*)
  FROM google_customers g
 WHERE EXISTS (
         SELECT 0
           FROM microsoft_customers m
          WHERE m.cust_first_name = g.cust_first_name
            AND m.cust_last_name = g.cust_last_name);
```

These are called semi-joins because they return rows from the first table—GOOGLE_CUSTOMERS in this case—only once, even if there is more than one matching row in the second table.

Oracle employs a special semi-join operation to resolve such queries, and these semi-joins can use any of the hash, sort-merge, or nested loop algorithms. Optimization of these subqueries follow the optimization principles for normal joins; for instance, an index to promote nested loops joins might pay off if the subquery is highly selective.

SUMMARY

In this chapter we looked at principles for optimizing SQL statements that join data from two or more tables.

Oracle has three fundamental join algorithms:

❑ Nested loops, in which for each row in one table, a matching row in the other table is sought.
❑ Sort-merge, in which each table is sorted and then the results merged.
❑ Hash join, in which a hash table is constructed from one of the tables and used to join matching rows to the other table.

Nested loops is the optimal method when small subsets of rows are being joined and an index exists to perform the lookup match. Hash join is the preferred mechanisms for larger joins, though sort-merge might be the best option for joins that aren't based on equality lookups.

Optimizing a nested loops join involves ensuring that the best concatenated index exists. The performance of sort-merge and hash-joins is most directly affected by available memory.

Joins are relatively expensive, and you will sometimes be motivated to avoid a join by denormalization, using materialized views or employing bitmap join indexes.

Outer joins are optimized in much the same way as other joins, though for a LEFT or RIGHT outer join, a specific join order will be required.

Star joins, in which a large central fact table is joined to smaller dimension tables, are recognized by the optimizer and subject to different join rules. The star transformation approach, especially in conjunction with bitmap join indexes, should be considered.

Hierarchical joins involving the CONNECT BY operator do not need an index if the full hierarchy is being built. However, when a small subset of the hierarchy is involved, an index on the PRIOR column is useful.

Subqueries are generally transformed to join operations, and the usual optimization principles of joins apply. Anti-join subqueries, in which all rows not matching in the other table are returned, cannot be expressed as a normal join, and Oracle has unique optimization routines for them. Beware of anti-joins using the NOT IN clause on NULLable columns; these queries can exhibit exponential degradation as table sizes grow.

SORTING, GROUPING, AND SET OPERATIONS

In this chapter we look at improving the performance of SQL operations that require Oracle to order or group data and operations that work on complete *sets* of data rather than on individual rows.

Oracle might need to sort data as a result of an explicit request to return data in order (for instance, ORDER BY) or as a result of an internal intermediate operation that requires the data to be in sorted order (for instance, the INTERSECT operation). Sorts can consume significant computer resources—especially memory—and have a substantial effect on query performance. Knowing when Oracle performs sorts, ways of avoiding sorts, and how to optimize sorts is, therefore, important when tuning SQL.

The GROUP BY operator aggregates rows with common values and returns a summary row for each group. GROUP BY uses hashing or sorting of rows to perform its work.

The set operations, UNION, INTERSECT, and MINUS, combine two or more result sets with the same number and types of columns into a single result set. Set operators often involve sorts and are also discussed in this chapter.

SORT OPERATIONS

Sorting is one of the most fundamental operations undertaken by computers, especially in the field of data processing—and Oracle is no exception. The operations that might require Oracle to sort data include

❑ Creating an index
❑ Grouping or aggregating data via the GROUP BY, UNIQUE, or DISTINCT keywords
❑ Returning data in sorted order as a result of the ORDER BY clause
❑ Joining tables or result sets using the sort-merge method
❑ Using the set operators UNION, INTERSECT, or MINUS
❑ Performing certain subqueries

Sorting can require significant resources:

❑ CPU will always be consumed. The amount of CPU required is proportional to the size of the result set to be sorted.
❑ Oracle allocates an area of memory for the sort. This memory is allocated from the Program Global Area (PGA). The total amount of PGA memory available is usually determined by either MEMORY_TARGET or PGA_AGGREGATE_TARGET (see Chapter 19, "Optimizing PGA Memory," for details).
❑ If the area of memory is not sufficient for the sort to complete, Oracle allocates one or more temporary segments within a temporary tablespace. This is known as a *disk sort*. If a disk sort is required, there is the additional overhead of allocating space in the temporary segment and IO to write and read back blocks from the temporary tablespace.

OPTIMAL, ONE-PASS AND MULTI-PASS SORTS

The amount of memory available for performing sort operations is the most important determinate of sort performance. If the amount of memory available for the sort is sufficient to enable the sort to complete in memory, then performance will be most favorable and indeed Oracle refers to these types of sort operations as *optimal sorts*.

When there is not enough memory, Oracle must read and write to temporary segments during the sort operation. In a *one-pass sort*, Oracle needs to write out—and then read back—only a single segment. In a *multi-pass sort*, Oracle needs to write and read back many sort segments. The more passes required, the more IO is involved in the sort and the worse the sort performance will be.

The IO required for a sort grows rapidly as the number of passes increases and eventually becomes the dominant factor in the SQLs performance.

Figure 11-1 shows how the time spent on multi-pass sort IO becomes greater than all other processing time as the amount of memory becomes limited.

The optimization of Oracle memory and IO are the subjects of later chapters in this book. But for now, be aware that sort operations need adequate memory,

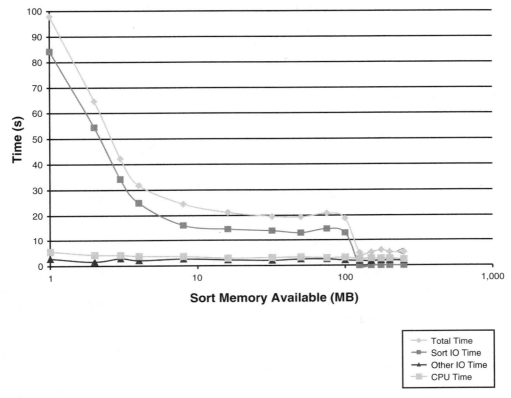

FIGURE 11-1 As sorts become memory constrained, sort IO becomes the dominant response time factor.

and that a failure to provide sufficient sort memory is liable to overwhelm any other factors in optimizing a SQL that performs a large sort.

SQL statements that sort large amounts of data will degrade rapidly if PGA memory is insufficient to allow the sort to complete in memory.

MEASURING SORT ACTIVITY

Let's now look at how we can measure sort activity.

The optimizer calculates the amount of memory it thinks will be required, and you can view this—even before you execute the SQL—by examining the TempSpc column in DBMS_XPLAN:

```
SQL> EXPLAIN PLAN for  SELECT        *
   2    FROM customers
   3      ORDER BY cust_last_name, cust_first_name,
cust_year_of_birth;

SQL>   SELECT *
   2      FROM TABLE (DBMS_XPLAN.display());


---------------------------------------------------
| Id  | Operation           | Name      |TempSpc|
---------------------------------------------------
|   0 | SELECT STATEMENT    |           |       |
|   1 |  SORT ORDER BY      |           |  102M|
|   2 |   TABLE ACCESS FULL| CUSTOMERS |       |
---------------------------------------------------
```

The value generated by DBMS_XPLAN is an approximate value but will give you a rough feel for how much memory might be required.

The V$SQL_WORKAREA view contains detailed statistics relating to memory utilization and sort activity that has occurred in the database. V$SQL_WORKAREA contains one row for each sort operation and for similar operations, such as hash joins and hash grouping operations.

By joining V$SQL_WORKAREA to V$SQL, we can identify the SQLs that have the highest amount of sort activity:

```
SQL> WITH sql_workarea AS
   2        (
   3          SELECT sql_id || '-' || child_number SQL_ID_Child,
   4              operation_type operation ,
   5              last_execution last_exec,
   6              ROUND (active_time / 1000000,
   7                     2) seconds,
   8              optimal_executions || '/'
   9              || onepass_executions || '/'
  10              || multipasses_executions o1m,
  11              '    ' || SUBSTR (sql_text, 1, 155) sql_text,
  12            RANK () OVER (ORDER BY active_time DESC) ranking
  13          FROM v$sql_workarea JOIN v$sql
  14              USING (sql_id, child_number)  )
  15  SELECT     sql_id_child "SQL ID - CHILD",seconds,operation,
  16          last_exec,  o1m "O/1/M",sql_text
  17       FROM sql_workarea
  18      WHERE ranking <= 2
  19  ORDER BY ranking;
```

```
SQL ID - CHILD      SECONDS OPERATION                LAST_EXEC  O/1/M
---------------  --------  -------------------  ---------  ---------
SQL_TEXT
----------------------------------------------------------------------
cfvt4v55huvsn-14   224.03 SORT (v2)                3108 PASSE 0/0/4
    SELECT /*+ FULL(c) */    * FROM customers c                  ORDER
BY cust_last_name, cust_first_name, cust_year_of_birth
----------------------------------------------------------------------
cfvt4v55huvsn-13   141.10 SORT (v2)                1027 PASSE 0/0/4
    SELECT /*+ FULL(c) */    * FROM customers c                  ORDER
BY cust_last_name, cust_first_name, cust_year_of_birth
----------------------------------------------------------------------
```

DBMS_XPLAN.DISPLAY_CURSOR will show statistics relating to sorting and hashing if you request the MEMSTATS option. The *OMem* column reports the amount of memory required for an optimal sort or hash, whereas *1Mem* reports the amount of memory required for a one-pass operation. The *O/1/M* column reports the number of Optimal, 1-pass, and multi-pass operations, respectively. Unfortunately, there appears to be a bug with the O/1/M column, and it is not always included in the output:

```
SQL> SELECT * FROM TABLE (DBMS_XPLAN.display_cursor
  2     (:sql_id,:child_number,'MEMSTATS'));

PLAN_TABLE_OUTPUT
----------------------------------------------------------------------

SQL_ID  0zc69bryyrru9, child number 0
-------------------------------------
select * from ( SELECT    /*+ FULL(c) */  *    FROM customers c   ORDER
BY cust_last_name, cust_first_name, cust_year_of_birth) where rownum=1
```

Id	Operation	Name	OMem	1Mem	O/1/M
0	SELECT STATEMENT				
* 1	COUNT STOPKEY				
2	VIEW				
* 3	SORT ORDER BY STOPKEY		37M	2171K	
4	TABLE ACCESS FULL	CUSTOMERS			

TRACING SORT ACTIVITY

The 10032 trace event can be used to get detailed statistical information about session sorting. To invoke the trace, issue the following command:

```
ALTER SESSION SET EVENTS '10032 trace name context forever, level 1';
```

The resulting tracefile—found in the usual USER_DUMP_DEST location—includes sort parameters and statistics for every sort that occurs during session execution. Here's a partial report from a session that performed a single pass disk sort:

```
---- Sort Parameters ------------------------------
sort_area_size                      1048576
sort_area_retained_size             1048576
sort_multiblock_read_count          2
max intermediate merge width        29

*** 2008-12-09 16:01:22.862
---- Sort Statistics ------------------------------
Initial runs                              4
Number of merges                          1
Input records                             55500
Output records                            55324
Disk blocks 1st pass                      285
Total disk blocks used                    287
Total number of comparisons performed     786566
  Comparisons performed by in-memory sort 723239
  Comparisons performed during merge      63327
Temp segments allocated                   1
Extents allocated                         3
Uses version 1 sort
Uses asynchronous IO
```

Event 10033 can also produce some useful, though somewhat more obscure, output relating to the activity of intermediate sort runs.

USING AN INDEX TO AVOID A SORT

If an index exists with some or all the columns in the ORDER BY clause, Oracle might use the index to fetch the rows in the required order and hence avoid the sort operation.

Oracle can read the rows in sorted order directly from the index providing the index is on the same columns that appear in the ORDER BY clause. However, reading rows in key order requires a block-by-block full scan of index leaf blocks that is incompatible with the *Fast Full Scan* described in Chapter 5, "Indexing and

Clustering." Although the fast full scan is much more efficient than a normal full index scan, the fast full scan does not return rows in index order and cannot be used to avoid the sort operation.

For example, consider the following query:

```
SELECT        *
 FROM customers
  ORDER BY cust_last_name, cust_first_name, cust_year_of_birth;
```

```
------------------------------------------------------------------
| Id  | Operation          | Name      | Rows   | Bytes  |TempSpc|
------------------------------------------------------------------
|   0 | SELECT STATEMENT   |           |   118K |   33M  |       |
|   1 |  SORT ORDER BY     |           |   118K |   33M  |  40M  |
|   2 |   TABLE ACCESS FULL| CUSTOMERS |   118K |   33M  |       |
------------------------------------------------------------------
```

As you might expect, it will normally involve a sort operation. However, if we create an index on the ORDER BY columns and use a FIRST_ROWS hint (or an INDEX hint), Oracle will use the index and avoid the sort:

```
CREATE INDEX cust_namedob_i ON customers (cust_last_name,
cust_first_name, cust_year_of_birth);
```

```
SELECT        *
FROM customers
ORDER BY cust_last_name, cust_first_name, cust_year_of_birth;
```

```
----------------------------------------------------------------
| Id  | Operation                    | Name           | Rows   |
----------------------------------------------------------------
|   0 | SELECT STATEMENT             |                |   118K |
|   1 |  TABLE ACCESS BY INDEX ROWID | CUSTOMERS      |   118K |
|   2 |   INDEX FULL SCAN            | CUST_NAMEDOB_I |   118K |
----------------------------------------------------------------
```

Although the use of an index might eliminate the need to perform a sort, the overhead of reading both the index and the table, and the less efficient block by block index scan, is much less optimal than simply reading the table blocks using a full scan. Often this means that using an index to avoid a sort will actually result in poorer performance. However, using the index should result in a quicker retrieval of the *first row* because as soon as the row is retrieved, it can be returned, whereas the sort approach requires that *all* rows be retrieved, and sorted, before *any* rows are returned. As a result, the optimizer tends to use the index if the optimizer goal is FIRST_ROWS_*N* but chooses a full table scan if the goal is ALL_ROWS.

Figure 11-2 illustrates this phenomenon; using an index to retrieve the first rows far outperforms the full table scan and sort. However, when all rows are to be returned in sorted order, then the index-based plan comes a distant second to the full table scan and sort.

Using an index to avoid a sort can result in better performance when retrieving the first row. However, when retrieving all the rows, a sort will usually outperform an index lookup.

The other scenario in which an index based fetch will outperform a scan and fetch is when memory is extremely limited. If available memory for sorting is constrained, the amount of IO required to read and write temporary sort segments can exceed the additional IO involved in the index and table scan. It would be far better, of course, to arrange for more memory, but if that is not possible, you might want to use the INDEX hint to avoid the sort.

Figure 11-3 illustrates this trade-off. When memory is abundant, the full table scan and sort is approximately 30 times faster than the index-based

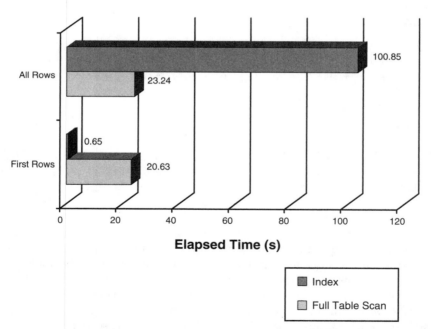

FIGURE 11-2 Using an index to return rows in sorted order optimizes the retrieval of the first rows, but usually degrades retrieval of all rows.

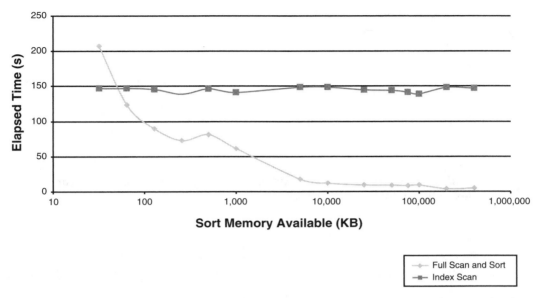

FIGURE 11-3   ORDER BY using a table scan and sort degrades as memory is constrained.

approach. However, as memory is constrained, the sort degrades while the index lookup is unaffected. Eventually the sort overhead exceeds the overhead of the index scan.

Ordering rows using an index requires less memory than a sort; if memory is very constrained, an index lookup might outperform a sort.

GROUPING AND AGGREGATES

Aggregate operations return data based on more than one row: averages, sums, maximums, and minimums, and so on. Grouping allows us to return aggregates for sets of rows each of which share the same GROUP BY values.

AGGREGATE OPERATIONS

Aggregate operations such as SUM and AVERAGE must process every row in the input data. Therefore, they are often associated with a full table scan:

```
SQL> SELECT SUM (quantity_sold)
  2      FROM sales;
```

```
---------------------------------------------
| Id  | Operation         | Name  | Rows   |
---------------------------------------------
|   0 | SELECT STATEMENT  |       |      1 |
|   1 |  SORT AGGREGATE   |       |      1 |
|   2 |   TABLE ACCESS FULL| SALES |  2216K|
---------------------------------------------
```

If an index exists on the columns to be aggregated, a fast full scan on that index will usually be more efficient:

```
----------------------------------------------------------------
| Id  | Operation          | Name                              |
----------------------------------------------------------------
|   0 | SELECT STATEMENT   |                                   |
|   1 |  SORT AGGREGATE    |                                   |
|   2 |   INDEX FAST FULL SCAN| SALES_QUANT_SOLD_I1            |
----------------------------------------------------------------
```

MAXIMUMS AND MINIMUMS

Unlike most other aggregate operations, MAX and MIN operations don't need to read every row if there is an index on the columns concerned. If there's a B*-Tree index, we can examine the first or last index entry to determine the maximum or minimum value, at the cost of only 3–5 logical reads:

```
SQL> SELECT MAX (amount_sold)
  2      FROM sales;
```

```
---------------------------------------------------------------------
| Id  | Operation              | Name                               |
---------------------------------------------------------------------
|   0 | SELECT STATEMENT       |                                    |
|   1 |  SORT AGGREGATE        |                                    |
|   2 |   INDEX FULL SCAN (MIN/MAX)| SALES_AMOUNT_SOLD_I            |
---------------------------------------------------------------------
```

```
Statistics
---------------------------------------------------------------
          0   recursive calls
          0   db block gets
          3   consistent gets
```

However, if we want to find the maximum *and* the minimum, Oracle scans the entire index at a much higher logical read cost (4,706 in this example):

```
SQL> SELECT MAX (amount_sold), MIN (amount_sold)
  2    FROM sales;
```

```
--------------------------------------------------------------
| Id  | Operation            | Name                | Rows  |
--------------------------------------------------------------
|   0 | SELECT STATEMENT     |                     |     1 |
|   1 |  SORT AGGREGATE      |                     |     1 |
|   2 |   INDEX FAST FULL SCAN| SALES_AMOUNT_SOLD_I |  2216K|
--------------------------------------------------------------
```

```
Statistics
--------------------------------------------------------------
         0   recursive calls
         0   db block gets
      4706   consistent gets
```

We'd actually be better issuing separate MAX and MIN queries and then merging the results:

```
SQL> SELECT max_sold, min_sold
  2    FROM (SELECT MAX (amount_sold) max_sold
  3            FROM sales) maxt,
  4         (SELECT MIN (amount_sold) min_sold
  5            FROM sales) mint;
```

```
--------------------------------------------------------------
| Id  | Operation                    | Name                | Rows  |
--------------------------------------------------------------
|   0 | SELECT STATEMENT             |                     |     1 |
|   1 |  NESTED LOOPS                |                     |     1 |
|   2 |   VIEW                       |                     |     1 |
|   3 |    SORT AGGREGATE            |                     |     1 |
|   4 |     INDEX FULL SCAN (MIN/MAX)| SALES_AMOUNT_SOLD_I |  2216K|
|   5 |   VIEW                       |                     |     1 |
|   6 |    SORT AGGREGATE            |                     |     1 |
|   7 |     INDEX FULL SCAN (MIN/MAX)| SALES_AMOUNT_SOLD_I |  2216K|
--------------------------------------------------------------
```

```
Statistics
-----------------------------------------------------
        0   recursive calls
        0   db block gets
        6   consistent gets
```

Oracle can use an index to efficiently obtain a maximum or minimal value. Finding the maximum and minimum might require two subqueries.

THE "TOP N" QUERY

If you are ever unlucky enough to be interviewed by me for a job, pay attention now because I almost always ask candidates how they would get the top 10 rows from a table. For instance, the top 10 sales by dollar value in the SALES table.

The absolute wrong answer is to use ROWNUM to restrict the number of rows returned. This query, for instance, is an incorrect solution:

```
SQL>    SELECT *
  2       FROM sales
  3      WHERE ROWNUM <= 10
  4    ORDER BY amount_sold DESC;
```

This answer is wrong because WHERE is processed *before* ORDER BY. Consequently this query fetches the first 10 rows it finds and then orders them. The result is *not* the top 10.

This answer is better:

```
SQL> SELECT /* top10 subquery */ *
  2     FROM (SELECT cust_id, prod_id, time_id, amount_sold
  3             FROM sales
  4           ORDER BY amount_sold DESC)
  5    WHERE ROWNUM <= 10;
```

In this case, we sort the rows in the subquery and then fetch the first 10. The execution plan looks like this:

Id	Operation	Name	Rows	Bytes	TempSpc
0	SELECT STATEMENT		9	432	
* 1	COUNT STOPKEY				
2	VIEW		2497K	114M	
* 3	SORT ORDER BY STOPKEY		2497K	114M	286M
4	TABLE ACCESS FULL	SALES	2497K	114M	

The SORT ORDER BY STOPKEY indicates that Oracle sorts all the rows but doesn't return them all (STOPKEY). This is therefore a reasonably efficient solution.

I do worry that this query relies on the outputs of a subquery being in sorted order that, by some readings of relational theory, is not guaranteed.[1] However, this is a widely used query pattern, so the chances that it will return the wrong results in some future version of Oracle are quite remote.

The "correct" way to get the top 10, in my opinion of course, is to issue a query that makes use of one of the ranking analytic functions: RANK() and DENSE_RANK().[2] This query returns the top-10 sales:

```
SQL> SELECT /* top10 dense_rank*/ *
  2     FROM (SELECT cust_id, prod_id, time_id, amount_sold,
  3                    DENSE_RANK () OVER (ORDER BY amount_sold DESC)
ranking
  4                 FROM sales)
  5    WHERE ranking <= 10;
```

```
-----------------------------------------------------------------------
| Id  | Operation                 | Name  | Rows  | Bytes |TempSpc|
-----------------------------------------------------------------------
|   0 | SELECT STATEMENT          |       | 2497K |  145M |       |
| * 1 |  VIEW                     |       | 2497K |  145M |       |
| * 2 |   WINDOW SORT PUSHED RANK |       | 2497K |  114M |  286M |
|   3 |    TABLE ACCESS FULL      | SALES | 2497K |  114M |       |
-----------------------------------------------------------------------
```

Despite my reservations regarding the subquery based approach to the top-10 query, it is more efficient. The DENSE_RANK approach consumes more memory and CPU than the sorted subquery. In our example, the subquery based approach took approximately 21 percent of the elapsed time of a RANK() approach: Figure 11-4 compares the performance. RANK() and other analytic functions can have a high CPU and memory overhead, which often makes them less efficient than their alternatives.

---

[1] Not everyone agrees, but *relations* (of which an in-line view is an example) are supposed to have no intrinsic order. In earlier versions of Oracle, ORDER BY was not supported in an in-line view definition for this reason. In Chapter 4 of *The Art of SQL* (O'Reilly, 2006), Stephane Faroult and Peter Robson argue this point in more detail.

[2] The two vary in how they deal with ties. RANK() skips ranks when a tie exists, whereas DENSE_RANK() does not. DENSE_RANK() can therefore return more than 10 rows in our example if there are tied ranks in the first rows returned.

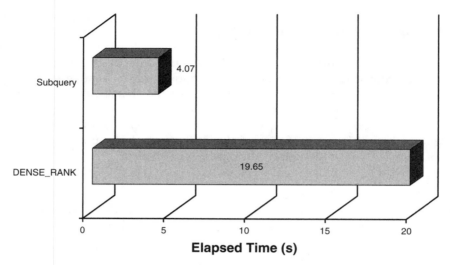

FIGURE 11-4 For a top-10 style query, a subquery is usually more efficient than using RANK or DENSE_RANK.

COUNTING THE ROWS IN A TABLE

Counting the number of rows in a table has been the subject of some of the most consistent "old DBAs tales." From time to time you hear that COUNT(1) is more effective than COUNT(*) or that COUNT(*unique_indexed_column*) is best.

Generally speaking, these suggestions are without merit. Any time you issue a COUNT() operation that resolves to a count of all the rows, Oracle counts the rows using the most effective method, which often involves scanning the smallest index on a NOT NULL column.

For instance, all these SQLs result in the same execution plan:

```
SQL> SELECT COUNT (*) FROM customers;
SQL> SELECT COUNT (1) FROM customers;
SQL> SELECT COUNT (cust_id) FROM customers;
```

```
---------------------------------------------------------------
| Id  | Operation              | Name          | Rows  |
---------------------------------------------------------------
|   0 | SELECT STATEMENT       |               |     1 |
|   1 |  SORT AGGREGATE        |               |     1 |
|   2 |   INDEX FAST FULL SCAN | CUSTOMERS_PK  | 55500 |
---------------------------------------------------------------
```

Using an index to count the exact number of rows in a table is usually the best approach. However, for an inexact count, you can look in NUM_ROWS in

ALL_TAB_STATISTICS or combine COUNT with SAMPLE to get an approxima-
tion of the current number of rows. See Chapter 9, "Tuning Table Access," for a
discussion on the use of the SAMPLE clause.

GROUP BY OPERATIONS

GROUP BY allows a SQL statement to return one row for each distinct value for a
set of columns and to calculate aggregates for each of these groups. For instance,
the following returns the average credit limit for each country code:

```
SELECT country_id, AVG (cust_credit_limit)
   FROM customers
GROUP BY country_id;
```

```
---------------------------------------------------
| Id  | Operation          | Name       | Rows   |
---------------------------------------------------
|   0 | SELECT STATEMENT   |            |     19 |
|   1 |   HASH GROUP BY    |            |     19 |
|   2 |    TABLE ACCESS FULL| CUSTOMERS  |   222K |
---------------------------------------------------
```

Prior to Oracle 10g, GROUP BY was implemented by sorting the rows on
the GROUP BY columns. In 10g forward, the HASH GROUP BY operation avoids
the sort by accumulating aggregates in a hash table as the table is read. The explain output above shows the resulting HASH GROUP BY step.

HASH GROUP BY in theory should be significantly faster and consume less
memory than SORT GROUP BY. However, the initial implementation of HASH
GROUP BY was associated with a number of significant bugs, including wrong
results (!), poor performance, excessive memory consumption, and inaccurate reporting of activity in V$SQL_WORKAREA and related views. These issues ap-
pear to have been resolved with the release of 11.1.0.7 and 10.2.0.4; however, if
you experience issues with the hash group by method, it might be worth experimenting with turning off HASH GROUP BY. This can be achieved by setting the
parameter _GBY_HASH_AGGREGATION_ENABLED to FALSE.[3]

If you combine GROUP BY with an ORDER BY on the same expressions,
the optimizer will usually decide to use the SORT GROUP BY (instead of
HASH GROUP BY) operation because SORT GROUP BY returns rows in sorted
order:

---

[3] Oracle generally advises that "undocumented" parameters such as this should be modified only under the advice of Oracle support.

```
SQL>    SELECT country_id, AVG (cust_credit_limit)
  2         FROM customers
  3   GROUP BY country_id
  4   ORDER BY country_id;
```

```
-----------------------------------------------------------
| Id  | Operation           | Name      | Rows  |
-----------------------------------------------------------
|   0 | SELECT STATEMENT    |           |    19 |
|   1 |   SORT GROUP BY     |           |    19 |
|   2 |    TABLE ACCESS FULL| CUSTOMERS |  222K |
-----------------------------------------------------------
```

In releases of Oracle prior to 10g, the GROUP BY operation would often return rows in sorted order, and the ORDER BY clause was effectively free. However, from 10g forward, ORDER BY suppresses the HASH GROUP BY method and can, therefore, reduce performance.

As with most operations that potentially involve a full scan, creating an index on the columns in question and using the fast full index scan can result in significant optimization. In the preceding examples, an index on COUNTRY_ID and CUST_CREDIT_LIMIT reduced execution time by about 45 percent.

HAVING VERSUS WHERE

The HAVING clause eliminates rows from a GROUP BY after they have been aggregated. For instance, the following query eliminates customers from countries that have less than 10,000 customers:

```
SELECT country_name, AVG (cust_credit_limit), COUNT (*)
    FROM customers join countries using (country_id)
GROUP BY country_name
  HAVING COUNT (*) < 10000
```

This is a valid use of HAVING and merely adds a filter condition after the aggregation. However, you should never use HAVING in place of WHERE. If rows can be eliminated by WHERE, they will be eliminated *before* the aggregation, whereas HAVING eliminates rows *after* the aggregation. The fewer rows to be aggregated the better, so the WHERE clause is generally preferable to the HAVING clause.

For example, the following query eliminates all countries except the USA and New Zealand after the aggregates have been calculated:

```
SQL> SELECT country_name, AVG (cust_credit_limit),
  2           COUNT (*)
  3      FROM customers JOIN countries USING (country_id)
```

```
4   GROUP BY country_name
5     HAVING country_name IN ('United States of America',
                              'New Zealand');
```

```
--------------------------------------------------------
| Id  | Operation              | Name       | Rows  |
--------------------------------------------------------
|   0 | SELECT STATEMENT       |            |    1  |
|*  1 |  FILTER                |            |       |
|   2 |   HASH GROUP BY        |            |    1  |
|*  3 |    HASH JOIN           |            |  222K |
|   4 |     TABLE ACCESS FULL  | COUNTRIES  |   23  |
|   5 |     TABLE ACCESS FULL  | CUSTOMERS  |  222K |
--------------------------------------------------------
Predicate Information (identified by operation id):
--------------------------------------------------------
```

```
   Predicate Information (identified by operation id):
--------------------------------------------------------
```

```
   1 - filter("COUNTRIES"."COUNTRY_NAME"='United States of America' OR
              "COUNTRIES"."COUNTRY_NAME"='New Zealand')
   3 - access("CUSTOMERS"."COUNTRY_ID"="COUNTRIES"."COUNTRY_ID")
```

The preceding predicate information indicates that the filter condition is applied as step (1), *after* the GROUP BY. Next, we apply the filter condition using the WHERE clause:

```
SQL> SELECT country_name, AVG (cust_credit_limit),
  2             COUNT (*)
  3      FROM customers JOIN countries USING (country_id)
  4      WHERE country_name IN ('United States of America', 'New
Zealand')
  5   GROUP BY country_name;
```

```
-------------------------------------------------------
| Id  | Operation              | Name       | Rows   |
-------------------------------------------------------
|   0 | SELECT STATEMENT       |            |     2  |
|   1 |  HASH GROUP BY         |            |     2  |
|*  2 |   HASH JOIN            |            | 23368  |
|*  3 |    TABLE ACCESS FULL   | COUNTRIES  |     2  |
|   4 |    TABLE ACCESS FULL   | CUSTOMERS  |  222K  |
-------------------------------------------------------
```

```
Predicate Information (identified by operation id):
---------------------------------------------------

   2 - access("CUSTOMERS"."COUNTRY_ID"="COUNTRIES"."COUNTRY_ID")
   3 - filter("COUNTRIES"."COUNTRY_NAME"='New Zealand' OR
               "COUNTRIES"."COUNTRY_NAME"='United States of America')
```

In this case, the filter is applied in step (3), before the GROUP BY. For our preceding example, the result is a reduction in elapsed time by almost 50 percent (see Figure 11.5).

Where possible, use the WHERE clause in place of the HAVING clause to eliminate rows before they are grouped. Use the HAVING clause with group functions only.

SET OPERATIONS

The set operators, UNION, MINUS, and INTERSECT, enable multiple result sets with the same number and type of columns to be combined into a single result set.

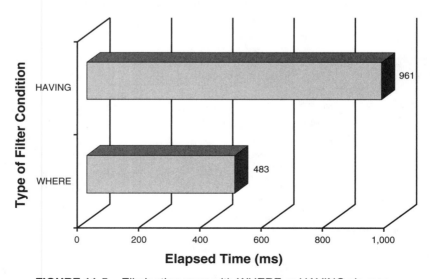

FIGURE 11-5   Eliminating rows with WHERE or HAVING clauses.

UNION VERSUS UNION ALL

The UNION operator is the most commonly used set operation. UNION differs from UNION ALL in that UNION eliminates any duplicate rows across the two results sets, whereas UNION ALL returns all rows, even if duplicated. For instance, the following query returns all Google and Microsoft customers, but if a customer appears in both tables, they will be reported only once:

```
SELECT cust_first_name, cust_last_name, cust_year_of_birth
  FROM microsoft_customers
UNION
SELECT cust_first_name, cust_last_name, cust_year_of_birth
  FROM google_customers;
```

```
----------------------------------------------------------------
| Id | Operation          | Name                 | Rows  |TempSpc |
----------------------------------------------------------------
|  0 | SELECT STATEMENT   |                      | 333K|         |
|  1 |  SORT UNIQUE       |                      | 333K|    20M |
|  2 |   UNION-ALL        |                      |     |         |
|  3 |    TABLE ACCESS FULL| MICROSOFT_CUSTOMERS | 166K|         |
|  4 |    TABLE ACCESS FULL| GOOGLE_CUSTOMERS    | 166K|         |
----------------------------------------------------------------
```

The corresponding UNION ALL query returns the same result set, but if a matching row exists in both GOOGLE_CUSTOMERS and MICROSOFT_CUSTOMERS, it will be reported twice:

```
SELECT cust_first_name cust_first_name, cust_last_name, cust_year_of_birth
  FROM microsoft_customers
UNION ALL
SELECT cust_first_name cust_first_name, cust_last_name, cust_year_of_birth
  FROM google_customers;
```

```
------------------------------------------------------------
| Id | Operation          | Name                 | Rows  | Bytes |
------------------------------------------------------------
|  0 | SELECT STATEMENT   |                      | 333K| 6829K|
|  1 |  UNION-ALL         |                      |     |      |
|  2 |   TABLE ACCESS FULL| MICROSOFT_CUSTOMERS | 166K| 3414K|
|  3 |   TABLE ACCESS FULL| GOOGLE_CUSTOMERS    | 166K| 3414K|
------------------------------------------------------------
```

You might notice that the execution plan for the UNION statement is almost exactly identical to that of the UNION ALL statement, except that the SORT

(UNIQUE) step is absent in the UNION ALL version. Removing the sort from a large UNION can substantially speed up the query. In the preceding example, UNION ALL took only 2.4 seconds, whereas UNION took 5.9 seconds.

> If you don't need to eliminate duplicate rows in a UNION operation, use UNION ALL instead of UNION. This can avoid a potentially expensive sort.

INTERSECT

The INTERSECT operation returns rows that are common to both tables or result sets. For instance, the following INTERSECT statement returns customers common to Google and Microsoft:

```
SELECT cust_first_name, cust_last_name, cust_year_of_birth
  FROM microsoft_customers
INTERSECT
SELECT cust_first_name, cust_last_name, cust_year_of_birth
  FROM google_customers;
```

```
-------------------------------------------------------------------------
| Id  | Operation              | Name                  | Rows  |TempSpc |
-------------------------------------------------------------------------
|  0  | SELECT STATEMENT       |                       | 222K|          |
|  1  |   INTERSECTION         |                       |     |          |
|  2  |    SORT UNIQUE         |                       | 222K|   13M    |
|  3  |     TABLE ACCESS FULL| MICROSOFT_CUSTOMERS    | 222K|          |
|  4  |    SORT UNIQUE         |                       | 222K|   13M    |
|  5  |     TABLE ACCESS FULL| GOOGLE_CUSTOMERS       | 222K|          |
-------------------------------------------------------------------------
```

As you can see, the INTERSECT operation performs two sorts and the INTERSECT operation; it's similar to a sort-merge join algorithm.

You can alternately express an INTERSECT query as a join. If a sort merge join is performed, you can expect the performance to be similar to that of the INTERSECT because Oracle has to perform a sort and merge for both methods. However, using a join allows you to employ the nested loops or hash join methods. Depending on the data being intersected, this can lead to substantial performance improvements.

If one result set is a small subset of an entire table, and the other result set has an index on join columns, the nested loops join might be more effective than the INTERSECT. On the other hand, if the tables are large and/or we scan all rows of the tables, a hash join usually outperforms an INTERSECT. For instance, when our previous INTERSECT example is recoded as follows:

```
SELECT cust_first_name, cust_last_name, cust_year_of_birth
  FROM microsoft_customers JOIN google_customers
       USING (cust_first_name, cust_last_name, cust_year_of_birth);
```

Then Oracle resolves the query using a more efficient hash join:

```
--------------------------------------------------------------------
| Id  | Operation            | Name                 | Rows  |TempSpc |
--------------------------------------------------------------------
|   0 | SELECT STATEMENT     |                      | 222K|          |
|*  1 | HASH JOIN            |                      | 222K|  7160K   |
|   2 |  TABLE ACCESS FULL| MICROSOFT_CUSTOMERS |     | 222K|          |
|   3 |  TABLE ACCESS FULL| GOOGLE_CUSTOMERS    |     | 222K|          |
--------------------------------------------------------------------
```

The elapsed time reduces from 3.51 to 1.55 seconds.

When performing an INTERSECT operation, consider recoding the statement to a join: this will enable a more efficient nested loops or hash join.

MINUS

The MINUS operator returns all rows in the first SELECT list that are not included in the second. For instance, the following returns the Microsoft customers that are not Google customers:

```
SELECT cust_first_name, cust_last_name, cust_year_of_birth
  FROM microsoft_customers
MINUS
SELECT cust_first_name, cust_last_name, cust_year_of_birth
  FROM google_customers;
```

```
--------------------------------------------------------------------
| Id  | Operation            | Name                 | Rows  |TempSpc |
--------------------------------------------------------------------
|   0 | SELECT STATEMENT     |                      | 222K|          |
|   1 |  MINUS               |                      |     |          |
|   2 |   SORT UNIQUE        |                      | 222K|   13M    |
|   3 |    TABLE ACCESS FULL| MICROSOFT_CUSTOMERS |   | 222K|          |
|   4 |   SORT UNIQUE        |                      | 222K|   13M    |
|   5 |    TABLE ACCESS FULL| GOOGLE_CUSTOMERS    |   | 222K|          |
--------------------------------------------------------------------
```

This operation is logically equivalent to an anti-join, but MINUS doesn't use the efficient anti-join algorithms we looked at in the last chapter. Recoding the statement to a NOT IN or NOT EXISTS enables the hash anti-join to be used:

```
SELECT cust_first_name, cust_last_name, cust_year_of_birth
  FROM microsoft_customers WHERE
        (cust_first_name, cust_last_name, cust_year_of_birth) NOT IN
        (SELECT cust_first_name, cust_last_name, cust_year_of_birth
          FROM google_customers);
```

```
-----------------------------------------------------------------------
| Id  | Operation          | Name                | Rows  |TempSpc |
-----------------------------------------------------------------------
|   0 | SELECT STATEMENT   |                     |    1 |        |
|*  1 | HASH JOIN ANTI     |                     |    1 | 7160K  |
|   2 |  TABLE ACCESS FULL| MICROSOFT_CUSTOMERS  | 222K|         |
|   3 |  TABLE ACCESS FULL| GOOGLE_CUSTOMERS     | 222K|         |
-----------------------------------------------------------------------
```

If conditions are right, the hash anti-join can significantly outperform the MINUS operation. In the preceding example, elapsed time reduced from 4.34 seconds to 2.56 seconds.

When performing a MINUS operation, consider recoding the statement into an ANTI-JOIN using a NOT IN or NOT EXISTS subquery.

A MINUS (or an anti-join for that matter) can often be expressed as an outer join in which we select for the NULL values that indicate that the outer table contained no matching rows. For instance, our preceding anti-join can be rewritten as follows:

```
SELECT mc.cust_first_name, mc.cust_last_name,
              mc.cust_year_of_birth
   FROM microsoft_customers mc
   LEFT OUTER JOIN google_customers gc
     ON (   mc.cust_first_name = gc.cust_first_name
        AND mc.cust_last_name = gc.cust_last_name
        AND mc.cust_year_of_birth = gc.cust_year_of_birth)
  WHERE gc.cust_first_name IS NULL
    AND gc.cust_last_name IS NULL
    AND gc.cust_year_of_birth IS NULL;
```

The execution plan resembles that of the anti-join, but instead of a HASH JOIN *ANTI*, we see a HASH JOIN *OUTER*:

```
----------------------------------------------------------------------------
| Id  | Operation              | Name                 | Rows  |TempSpc |
----------------------------------------------------------------------------
|   0 | SELECT STATEMENT       |                      |    1 |         |
|*  1 |  FILTER                |                      |      |         |
|*  2 |   HASH JOIN OUTER      |                      |    1 |  7160K  |
|   3 |    TABLE ACCESS FULL|  MICROSOFT_CUSTOMERS  |  222K|         |
|   4 |    TABLE ACCESS FULL|  GOOGLE_CUSTOMERS     |  222K|         |
----------------------------------------------------------------------------
```

The performance profile of the hash outer join solution is essentially equivalent to the hash anti-join. Although an outer join of this type offers similar advantages to an anti-join, the anti-join syntax is simpler and easier to understand.

SET OPERATIONS AND THEIR ALTERNATIVES

Figure 11.6 shows the performance of the SET operations and their alternatives. UNION ALL can be significantly faster than UNION. In addition, the INTERSECT and MINUS operations are usually faster if implemented using joins or anti-joins, respectively.

UNION ALL and UNION will produce different results if there are duplicate values in the tables being unioned. However, it's just as common for the SQL programmer to code UNION without actually requiring that these duplicates be eliminated, resulting in what is sometimes a far more expensive operation. Use UNION only if you really want duplicates eliminated; otherwise, use UNION ALL.

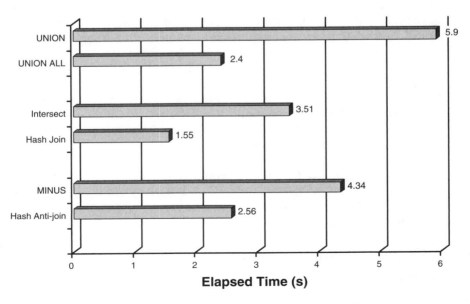

FIGURE 11-6 SET operations and their alternatives.

INTERSECT and MINUS will generate the same result sets—sometimes with cleaner syntax—as their join and anti-join alternatives. However, from a performance view, joins and anti-joins almost always perform better than INTERSECT and MINUS and are, therefore, preferred.

SUMMARY

Many Oracle procedures require sort operations. Sorts can be expensive and avoiding sorting can result in significant improvements to query performance. The most common cause of Oracle sorts are

- ❑ Using the ORDER BY clause to return rows in sorted order
- ❑ Table joins using the sort merge method
- ❑ Set operations such as UNION, MINUS, and INTERSECT

Sort performance is highly dependent on memory. A sort that can complete in memory—an *optimal* sort—is preferable. If there is insufficient memory, one or more temporary segments must be employed. No temporary segments are preferable to one segment, and one is preferable to many. As the number of temporary segments increase, the amount of temporary IO increases quickly, and temporary segment IO can easily be the most expensive operation in the query.

An index can be used to perform an ORDER BY without a sort. This will be effective if you are optimizing for response time, rather than throughput, or when the query can be resolved entirely from the index. Oracle might therefore use indexes to avoid sorts if the optimizer goal is FIRST_ROWS_N. Using indexes to retrieve rows in order also requires less memory than a sort and might be preferred if memory is scarce.

GROUP BY operations no longer require an explicit sort (as of 10g), but the HASH GROUP BY operation is still quite memory-dependent. The use of HAVING to eliminate rows from the resulting groups should only be considered if the use of WHERE is not practical.

The set operators UNION, INTERSECT, and MINUS enable multiple result sets to be combined or compared.

- ❑ The frequently used UNION operator is less efficient than UNION ALL because UNION ALL doesn't require a sort to eliminate duplicates. Use UNION ALL in preference to UNION unless you really need these duplicates eliminated.
- ❑ The set operations INTERSECT and MINUS can almost always be more efficiently implemented as a hash join or anti-join, respectively.

Chapter 12

USING AND TUNING PL/SQL

PL/SQL is a procedural programming language tightly integrated with the Oracle RDBMS, which allows programs to be stored and executed in the database as stored procedures, functions, and triggers. *Anonymous* PL/SQL blocks—which are not stored in the database—might also be directly submitted by an application.

PL/SQL offers a rich and productive environment in which to implement database-centric application logic. Also, PL/SQL can often enhance the performance of problematic queries and can offer significant performance improvements for complex DML.

PL/SQL programs are highly tunable. In addition to the code optimization strategies applicable to all procedural languages, PL/SQL has a number of features specifically designed to improve its performance. We'll look at each of these features and also at ways of measuring and profiling PL/SQL performance, and of identifying PL/SQL programs that might be causing performance problems.

PERFORMANCE ADVANTAGES OF PL/SQL

PL/SQL can often add to program functionality and programmer efficiency, and there are certainly many cases in which a procedural language such as PL/SQL can do things that a nonprocedural language such as SQL cannot. For a number of reasons, a PL/SQL approach might offer performance improvements over a traditional SQL approach.

A PROCEDURAL APPROACH

You might recall from Chapter 3, "Tools of the Trade," that SQL is a nonprocedural language—this means that you don't have to specify how to retrieve data—you only specify what data you want. However, this means that although we can influence the retrieval strategy through hints and other methods, it might be impossible to get the optimizer to process the SQL exactly as we want.

When we think we know how the data should be retrieved but can't get the optimizer to comply, we can sometimes use PL/SQL to force the desired approach. For instance, in Chapter 9, "Tuning Table Access," we used PL/SQL to implement the range lookup algorithm. By procedurally specifying *exactly* the data retrieval algorithm we wanted, we achieved a performance optimization not possible with nonprocedural SQL.

REDUCTION IN NETWORK OVERHEAD

In a traditional SQL-based application, SQL statements and data flow back and forth between the application and the database server. This traffic can cause delays even when both the application and database server are on the same machine. If the application and database are on different machines, the overhead is even higher.

Using PL/SQL stored programs can eliminate much of this overhead. A succinct message is sent from the client to the server (the stored procedure execution request), and a minimal response is sent from the server to the client (perhaps only a return code).

The reduction in network traffic can significantly enhance performance—especially in a client-server environment. We looked at this issue in detail in Chapter 6, "Application Design and Implementation," and showed how moving to a stored procedure-based solution can radically reduce network overhead.

DIVIDE AND CONQUER MASSIVE SQLS

The more complex the SQL statement, the harder it is to optimize. This goes not only for human optimizers, but also for the optimization code in the Oracle kernel. You might have seen massive SQL statements that include multiple subqueries, set operations (UNIONS and such), and complex joins. It's not uncommon for these monster SQL statements to generate pages of explain plan output. Tuning these sorts of SQL statements can be next to impossible for both the human programmer and the software optimizer.

It can be a winning strategy to break these massive SQL statements into smaller individual statements and optimize each individually. For instance, subqueries could be run outside of the SQL statement and the results forwarded to subsequent steps as query parameters or through temporary tables. PL/SQL—or another procedural language—can serve as the glue that combines the multiple steps.

A PL/SQL based solution can offer advantages over "straight" SQL: The procedural approach enables more precise definition of a data access strategy; there can be a reduction in network overhead; and you can divide-and-conquer overly large and complex SQLs.

MEASURING PL/SQL PERFORMANCE

If we are employing PL/SQL to improve performance, or looking to improve performance of existing PL/SQL, we will need to have tools to measure the overhead of our PL/SQL, identify PL/SQL that might need tuning, and find the parts of a PL/SQL package that are contributing most to overhead. Oracle provides tooling for all these needs.

MEASURING PL/SQL OVERHEAD

How much time is PL/SQL execution contributing to our overall database execution time? We can use the V$SYS_TIME_MODEL table to identify this fairly simply:

```
SQL> WITH plsql_times
  2         AS (SELECT SUM (CASE stat_name
  3                              WHEN 'DB time'
  4                              THEN value/1000000 END) AS db_time,
  5                    SUM(CASE stat_name
  6                              WHEN 'PL/SQL execution elapsed time'
  7                              THEN value / 1000000 END) AS plsql_time
  8              FROM v$sys_time_model
  9              WHERE stat_name IN ('DB time',
 10                            'PL/SQL execution elapsed time'))
 11  SELECT ROUND (db_time, 2) db_time_secs,
 12         ROUND (plsql_time, 2) plsql_time_secs,
 13         ROUND (plsql_time * 100 / db_time, 2) pct_plsql_time
 14    FROM plsql_times
 15  /

   DB_TIME_SECS  PLSQL_TIME_SECS  PCT_PLSQL_TIME
   ------------- ---------------- --------------
       8,504.86         1,595.71           18.76
```

This query reports time spent executing PL/SQL statements only: Time spent on SQL statements included within PL/SQL programs is not reported. In this example, PL/SQL contributes approximately 19 percent of the total database elapsed time.

For individual SQL and PL/SQL blocks, we can get a breakdown of PL/SQL and SQL time with a query against V$SQL, in which the PLSQL_ EXEC_TIME column reveals how much time was spent executing PL/SQL code within the SQL statements. The following query lists SQL statements that include PL/SQL execution time and shows how much of the total SQL execution time was PL/SQL, and how much that statement contributed to the database's total PL/SQL overhead:

```
SQL> SELECT sql_id,
  2         SUBSTR (sql_text, 1, 150) AS sql_text,
  3         ROUND (elapsed_time / 1000) AS elapsed_ms,
  4         ROUND (plsql_exec_time / 1000) plsql_ms,
  5         ROUND (plsql_exec_time * 100 / elapsed_time, 2) pct_plsql,
  6         ROUND (plsql_exec_time * 100 /
  7            SUM (plsql_exec_time) OVER (), 2) pct_total_plsql
  8    FROM v$sql
  9   WHERE plsql_exec_time > 0 AND elapsed_time > 0
 10   ORDER BY plsql_exec_time DESC
 11  /
```

SQL_ID	SQL Text	Total time ms	Pct PLSQL	PCT of Tot PLSQL
6gvch1xu9ca3g	DECLARE job BINARY_INTEGER := :job; next_date DATE := :mydate; broken BOOLEAN := FALSE; BEGIN EMD_MAINTENANCE.EXECUTE_EM_DBMS_JOB_PROCS(); :mydate :=	476853	40.36	42.02
b6usrg82hwsa3	call dbms_stats.gather_database_stats_job_proc ( )	497184	20.01	21.72
6mcpb06rctk0x	call dbms_space.auto_space_advisor_job_proc ( )	85620	44.60	8.34

Using these two queries we can determine whether PL/SQL overhead on the database is a tuning priority and identify which SQL and PL/SQL statements are incurring the highest PL/SQL load.

Use V$SQL to identify the PL/SQL overhead of individual SQLs and V$SYS_TIME_MODEL to identify the overhead of PL/SQL in the database as a whole.

USING DBMS_PROFILER

Having identified PL/SQL routines of concerns, where do we start in tuning PL/SQL code?

This chapter contains a wide variety of PL/SQL performance best practices and tuning techniques, but we shouldn't just pick one of these at random! Instead, our first step should be to identify the most resource-intensive lines of PL/SQL code and start by optimizing that code.

To do this, we use the PL/SQL profiler. The profiler is implemented in the package DBMS_PROFILER. When we surround a program call with START_PROFILER and STOP_PROFILER calls, Oracle collates execution statistics on a line-by-line basis. In the following example, we profile a procedure in the NOCOPY_TEST package:

```
DECLARE
    ReturnCode    BINARY_INTEGER;
BEGIN
    ReturnCode    := DBMS_PROFILER.start_profiler ('Profiler Demo 2');

    nocopy_test.test_copy (400, 1);

    ReturnCode    := DBMS_PROFILER.stop_profiler;
    DBMS_OUTPUT.put_line ('Profiler return code=' || ReturnCode);
    COMMIT;
END;
```

The profiling data is stored in a collection of tables prefixed with PLSQL_PROFILER. The following is a query that reports the five most-expensive lines of code (in terms of execution time) in the profiling run:

```
SQL> WITH plsql_qry AS (
  2      SELECT u.unit_name, line#,
  3             ROUND (d.total_time / 1e9) time_ms,
  4             round(d.total_time * 100 / sum(d.total_time) over(),2)
                    pct_time,
  5             d.total_occur as execs,
  6             substr(ltrim(s.text),1,40) as text,
  7             dense_rank() over(order by d.total_time desc) ranking
  8      FROM plsql_profiler_runs r JOIN plsql_profiler_units u
                USING (runid)
  9             JOIN plsql_profiler_data d USING (runid, unit_number)
 10             LEFT OUTER JOIN all_source s
 11             ON (    s.owner = u.unit_owner
 12                 AND s.TYPE = u.unit_type
 13                 AND s.NAME = u.unit_name
```

```
14                   AND s.line = d.line# )
15       WHERE r.run_comment = 'Profiler Demo 2'
16           )
17    select unit_name,line#,time_ms,pct_time,execs,text
18      from plsql_qry
19     where ranking <=5
20    ORDER BY ranking;
```

```
                     Time  Pct of
Unit Name     Line    (ms)   Time    Execs Line text
-----------   -----  ------- ------  ------- ----------------------------
NOCOPY_TEST      83  109424  98.75    89244 x := get_avalue (my_number_ta
NOCOPY_TEST      25     106    .10    89244 l_index := ((p_row - 1) * p_n
NOCOPY_TEST      39      87    .08   400000 l_index := ((p_row - 1) * p_n
NOCOPY_TEST      29      84    .08        0 FUNCTION get_avalue_nv (
NOCOPY_TEST      39      82    .07   400000 l_index := ((p_row - 1) * p_n
```

We can see that for this routine, almost 99 percent of the execution time can be attributed to a single line of code. This line would be the starting point for our tuning efforts.[1]

Use the DBMS_PROFILER package to identify hot spots in your PL/SQL code and to identify starting points for further tuning efforts.

Issuing queries against the profiling tables is certainly acceptable, but it's more usual to use the profiler from within a PL/SQL Integrated Development Environment (IDE). Many commercial IDE's, such as Quest Software's *TOAD* and *SQL Navigator*, offer integrate profiling capabilities. Figure 12-1 shows the profiler integration within Quest Software's *SQL Navigator* PL/SQL development tool.[2]

THE 11G HIERARCHICAL PROFILER

Much of the time identifying the most-expensive lines of code is sufficient to discover hot spots and tuning opportunities. But on other occasions you need to identify expensive subroutines, or identify the calling routine to understand the

---

[1] For this example, the performance issue was related to the NOCOPY parameter option that we discuss later in this chapter.

[2] Full disclosure: At the time of writing, I'm a director of development at Quest Software and involved in the design and development of products such as TOAD and SQL Navigator.

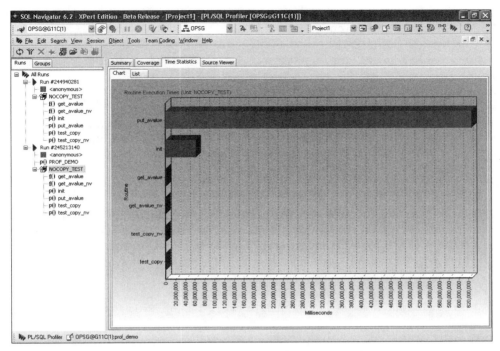

FIGURE 12-1 DBMS_PROFILER support in SQL Navigator.

context in which a line of code is being executed. To help with these scenarios, Oracle introduced the hierarchical profiler in Oracle 11g.

You access this profiler via the DBMS_HPROF package.[3] START_PROFIL-ING and STOP PROFILING procedures commence and terminate the profiling run. The output from the profiling session will be written to the external file identified in the START_PROFILING call. If you want to load this file into database tables for analyses, you can do so by using the ANALYZE procedure.

In this example, we profile the NIGHTLY_BATCH procedure to an external file hprof_trace.trc that is created in the HPROF_DIR directory. We then load the trace file into the profiling tables using the ANALYZE procedure:

```
CREATE OR REPLACE DIRECTORY hprof_dir AS 'C:\\traceFiles';
DECLARE
    runid    NUMBER;
```

---

[3] To use the DBMS_PROF package, you need to grant access to the package from the SYS account and run the dbmshptab.sql script from the rdbms/admin directory. The dbmshptab.sql script creates the tables used by the dbms_hprof.ANALYZE subroutine.

```
BEGIN
   hprof_demo_pkg.init(1000);

dbms_hprof.start_profiling('HPROF_DIR','hprof_trace.trc',max_depth=>10);
   hprof_demo_pkg.nightly_batch();
   dbms_hprof.stop_profiling ();
   runid :=
      dbms_hprof.ANALYZE (LOCATION          => 'HPROF_DIR',
                          filename          => 'hprof_trace.trc',
                          run_comment       => 'Hprof demo 1'
                          );
END;
```

There are two ways to analyze the trace file. First, the plshprof command line utility converts the trace file into an html report. For instance, we could generate a HTML report from the trace file we previously generated by issuing the following command:

```
C:\traceFiles>plshprof -output hprof_report hprof_trace.trc
PLSHPROF: Oracle Database 11g Enterprise Edition Release 11.1.0.7.0 -
Production
[5 symbols processed]
[Report written to 'hprof_report.html']
```

We can view the report by pointing our browser at the hprof_report.html file generated by the preceding command. Figure 12-2 shows the report.

Personally, I find the HTML report a bit hard to interpret and prefer to issue SQL against the profiler tables. In the following example, a hierarchical self-join is issued that exposes the call tree for the profiled NIGHTLY_BATCH routine:

```
SQL> WITH dbmshp AS
  2     (SELECT   module||'.'||function as function,
  3              NVL(pci.calls,f.calls) calls,
  4              NVL(pci.function_elapsed_time,f.function_elapsed_Time)
  5                AS  function_elapsed_Time,
  6              NVL(pci.subtree_elapsed_time,f.subtree_elapsed_time)
  7                AS subtree_elapsed_time,
  8              f.symbolid , pci.parentsymid
  9       FROM    dbmshp_runs r
 10       JOIN    dbmshp_function_info f ON (r.runid = f.runid)
 11       FULL OUTER JOIN dbmshp_parent_child_info pci
 12              ON (pci.runid = r.runid AND pci.childsymid =
f.symbolid)
```

```
13        WHERE  r.run_comment='Hprof demo 2')
14    SELECT    rpad(' ',level)||function as function,calls,
15              function_elapsed_time,
16              subtree_elapsed_time,
17              subtree_elapsed_time-function_elapsed_Time
18                AS subtree_only_time
19      FROM    dbmshp
20    CONNECT BY   PRIOR symbolid = parentsymid
21    START WITH   parentsymid IS NULL;
```

```
Function Call                       Func time Subtree time Subtree only
----------------------------------- --------- ------------ ------------
HPROF_DEMO_PKG.NIGHTLY_BATCH               7        48080        48073
 HPROF_DEMO_PKG.CALC_DISCOUNT          23587        47626        24039
  HPROF_DEMO_PKG.GET_AVALUE_NV         24039        24039            0
  HPROF_DEMO_PKG.CALC_SALESTOTALS        221          447          226
   HPROF_DEMO_PKG.GET_AVALUE_NV          226          226            0
DBMS_HPROF.STOP_PROFILING                  0            0            0
```

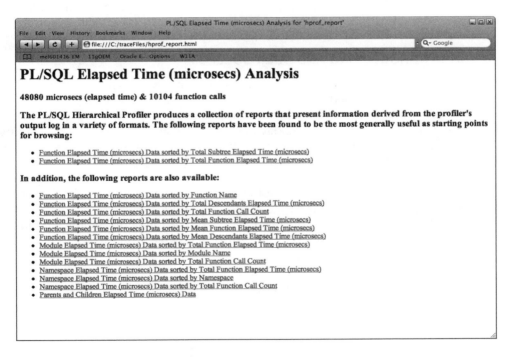

FIGURE 12-2 Hierarchical profiler report generated by the plshprof utility.

The FUNCTION_ELASPED_TIME column shows the amount of time elapsed in the function alone *excluding* all time sent in subroutines. Conversely, SUBTREE_ELAPSED_TIME shows the time spend in the function *and* all its subroutines. So for instance, we can see that the CALC_DISCOUNT routine consumed 47,626 microseconds, 24,039 of which were spent in subroutines such as the GET_AVALUE_NV function. We can also see that the GET_AVALUE_NV routine is most heavily used by CALC_DISCOUNT and not so much by CALC_SALESTOTALS; we should look at the former routine if we want to optimize the use of GET_AVALUE_NV.

As with the DBMS_PROFILER package, DBMS_HPROF is integrated into commercial development environments such as TOAD, and also into Oracle's own SQL Developer tool.

DATA ACCESS OPTIMIZATION

The major factor in the performance of data access routines will be the optimization of the SQL statements concerned. However, the PL/SQL constructs surrounding and controlling these SQL executions can also make the difference between user satisfaction and frustration.

ARRAY PROCESSING AND BULK COLLECT

We first looked at the impact of array processing in Chapter 6. Almost all languages that can embed SQL statements offer an array processing interface that enables multiple rows to be processed in a single API call. For programming languages that run outside the database, such as Java, C#, and so on, array processing reduces network round trips and reduces logical read overhead, CPU overhead, and context switches.

Because PL/SQL runs inside the database, the network round-trip reduction is not a factor. However, the other considerations, such as reduction in logical reads, CPU, and context switches, are still significant.

Prior to Oracle 10g, statements such as the following would *not* employ array processing and would typically perform relatively poorly:

```
BEGIN
    FOR r IN (SELECT   pk, data FROM mytable)
    LOOP
        --Do something with the data
    END LOOP;
END;
```

One can use BULK COLLECT to fetch all the rows concerned in a single batch, as in the following example:

```
DECLARE
   t_pk             dbms_sql.number_table;
   t_data           dbms_sql.varchar2_table;
BEGIN
   SELECT pk, DATA
      BULK COLLECT INTO t_pk, t_DATA
      FROM mytable t;
END;
```

Providing the result set concerned is not massive, this results in good performance. However, if the result set *is* large, the amount of memory required might be excessive. This can cause poor performance both for the PL/SQL program and for other sessions that compete for memory to perform memory-intensive operations such as sorts and hash-joins.

We can get the benefits of the array fetch while keeping memory usage reasonable by using BULK COLLECT with the LIMIT clause. LIMIT restricts the number of rows retrieved in a FETCH call, and we can process the FETCH in a loop to retrieve and process all the rows.

The following code shows a well-constructed BULK COLLECT loop using LIMIT:

```
DECLARE
   CURSOR c1
   IS SELECT   pk, data
        FROM   mytable t;

   t_pk             dbms_sql.number_table;
   t_data           dbms_sql.varchar2_table;
   v_fetch_count    NUMBER := 0;
BEGIN
   OPEN c1;
   LOOP
      FETCH c1 BULK COLLECT INTO t_pk, t_data LIMIT 100;
      EXIT WHEN t_pk.COUNT = 0;
      v_fetch_count := v_fetch_count + 1;
   END LOOP;
   CLOSE c1;
END;
```

From Oracle 10g forward, if PLSQL_OPTIMIZE_LEVEL is set to the default of 2 or higher, Oracle will rewrite simple FOR cursor loops so that they perform a BULK COLLECT with a LIMIT value of 100. In other words, in Oracle 10g and above PL/SQL will automatically use array fetch when you write a cursor FOR loop without a BULK COLLECT, unless PLSQL_OPTIMIZE_LEVEL has a value less than 2.

Figure 12-3 shows the performance of various multirow selects with PLSQL_OPTIMIZE_LEVEL set to 2 or 1. This chart illustrates the following behaviors:

❏ If PLSQL_OPTIMIZE_LEVEL is set to 1 (or in Oracle 9i), a simple FOR loop with no BULK COLLECT performs poorly for large amounts of data.

❏ Regardless of the setting of PLSQL_OPTIMIZE_LEVEL, using a BULK COLLECT with a reasonable LIMIT clause results in the best performance. The optimal value of LIMIT is dependent on the row size and amount of memory available.

❏ Regardless of the setting of PLSQL_OPTIMIZE_LEVEL, using BULK COLLECT without a LIMIT clause for large result sets results in poorer performance due to excessive memory demands.

Although Oracle 10g and above might automatically apply array fetch by default, using BULK COLLECT with a LIMIT clause provides the best performance. Using BULK COLLECT without a LIMIT can lead to poorer performance if the number of rows is high.

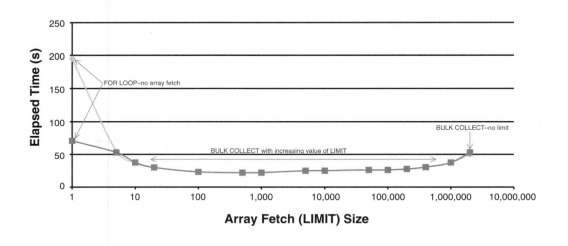

FIGURE 12-3 Array fetch performance for various array sizes and settings for PLSQL_OPTIMIZE_LEVEL.

ARRAY PROCESSING FOR INSERT STATEMENTS

You can use array processing for DML operations as well. Array processing is most commonly used in INSERT statements, though it is possible to perform bulk processing with UPDATEs or DELETEs as well.

Array DML is made possible by the FORALL statement. For instance, say we are inserting rows into a table and that those rows are contained in PL/SQL tables. We might code this—without using array insert—as follows:

```
FOR idx IN t_pk.FIRST .. t_pk.LAST
  LOOP
     INSERT INTO bulk_collect_tab (pk, data)
        VALUES   (t_pk (idx), t_data (idx));
  END LOOP;
```

FORALL uses a similar syntax but performs an array insert. The simplest form of FORALL would look like this:

```
FORALL idx IN t_pk.FIRST .. t_pk.LAST
     INSERT INTO bulk_collect_tab (pk, data)
        VALUES   (t_pk (idx), t_data (idx));
```

The performance advantages of FORALL are significant. Figure 12-4 shows the performance advantages gained by using FORALL for a 100,000 row insert.

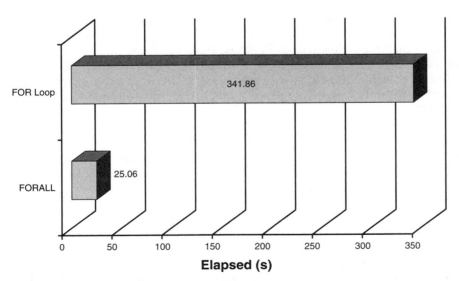

FIGURE 12-4   Performance benefit from employing array insert with the FORALL clause.

We saw in the previous section that Oracle often transparently rewrites query FOR loops so that they use array processing. You should be aware that Oracle performs no such automatic array optimization of INSERT statements: You *must* use the FORALL construct if you want your PL/SQL to perform bulk DML.

Use the FORALL statement to perform bulk inserts, updates, deletes, and merges into tables whenever possible.

Best practice coding with the FORALL statement often requires more sophisticated error handling and collections logic than is included in these simple examples. In particular, make sure you are familiar with the SAVE EXCEPTIONS and INDICES OF clauses of the FORALL statement. See the *PL/SQL Language Reference* or *Oracle PL/SQL Programming* by Steven Feuerstein (O'Reilly, 2009) for more details.

BIND VARIABLES AND DYNAMIC SQL

We looked at the importance of bind variables for application performance in Chapter 6. Bind variables enable SQLs that are essentially identical, differing only in parameter values, to be parsed only once and then executed many times. Using bind variables reduces parse overhead—a CPU-intensive operation—and also reduces contention for latches and mutexes that protect shared SQL structures in the shared pool.

In most programming languages, we have to go to special effort to use bind variables, and sometimes the convoluted code that results can be tedious to write and hard to maintain. However in PL/SQL, bind variables are employed automatically: Every PL/SQL variable inside a SQL statement is effectively a bind variable and, therefore, PL/SQL programs rarely suffer from parse overhead and associated latch/mutex contention issues that are all too common in languages such as PHP, Java, or C#.

However, when we use dynamic SQL in PL/SQL, this automatic binding does not occur: Dynamically constructed SQL in PL/SQL is just as prone to poor use of bind variables as SQL embedded in any other language.

For example, consider the following generic routine, which counts the rows in any table matching a certain condition:[4]

---

[4] This simple example is vulnerable to SQL injection. To be secure, it should validate that p_table_name and p_column_name are valid table and column names, and that p_column_value does not contain any malicious SQL fragments. Using bind variables in dynamic SQL also helps reduce the risk of SQL injection. See http://www.oracle.com/technology/tech/pl_sql/pdf/how_to_write_injection_proof_plsql.pdf for more details.

```
FUNCTION matching_rows (
   p_table_name      VARCHAR2,
   p_column_name     VARCHAR2,
   p_column_value    VARCHAR2
)
   RETURN NUMBER
IS
   v_count    NUMBER := 0;
BEGIN
   EXECUTE IMMEDIATE      'SELECT COUNT (*) FROM '
                      || p_table_name
                      || ' WHERE '
                      || p_column_name
                      || '='
                      || p_column_value
               INTO v_count;

   RETURN v_count;
END;
```

The routine builds up the SQL statement by concatenating the name of the table and the name of the column to be used. This is perfectly reasonable because bind variables can only specify *values*: They cannot be used to supply table or column references. However, the concatenation of P_COLUMN_VALUE is problematic: This value should be specified as a bind variable so that we don't generate a unique SQL every time we count the rows with a specific column value.

Here's a better implementation:

```
FUNCTION matching_rows2 (
      p_table_name      VARCHAR2,
      p_column_name     VARCHAR2,
      p_column_value    VARCHAR2
)
   RETURN NUMBER
IS
   v_count    NUMBER := 0;
BEGIN
   EXECUTE IMMEDIATE      'SELECT COUNT (*) FROM '
                      || p_table_name
                      || ' WHERE '
                      || p_column_name
                      || '=:columnValue'
               INTO v_count
              USING p_column_value;

   RETURN v_count;
END;
```

This implementation defines the bind variable placeholder as *:columnValue* in the dynamic SQL string. The actual value is provided by the USING clause.

Although we still request the parse every time this routine is executed, Oracle will quite possibly find a matching SQL in the shared pool, providing only that the same table and column names have been used in a previous execution. Figure 12-5 shows the performance gains from issuing 100,000 calls like this:

```
matching_rows ('SH.CUSTOMERS',      'CUST_ID',
                ROUND (DBMS_RANDOM.VALUE (1, 100000)) );
```

PL/SQL uses bind variables automatically and transparently in most circumstances. However, when you create dynamic SQL, you should ensure that you employ bind variables where appropriate to reduce parse overhead and latch/mutex contention.

PL/SQL CODE OPTIMIZATION

Usually, we think of PL/SQL as a database access language and concentrate on optimizing the SQL within the PL/SQL program. But as a procedural language, PL/SQL is subject to many of the same principles of optimization as other languages. There are circumstances in which PL/SQL itself, even without any database accesses, can consume excessive CPU or memory.

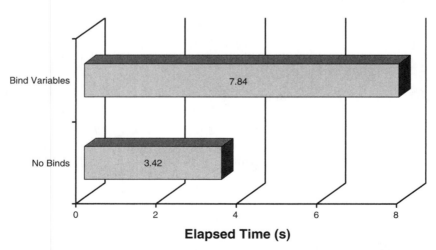

FIGURE 12-5   Improvements gained through bind variables in Dynamic SQL.

TUNE THE SQL FIRST

The vast majority of PL/SQL programs contain SQL statements that access data in the database. And of course, it's usually these SQL statements that consume the bulk of time in the PL/SQL program. Stored programs tend to be used primarily for data intensive applications—not surprising because these routines run inside the database—and data access is inherently more time-consuming than other activities because it can involve physical IO.

When tuning a PL/SQL program, make sure that you don't neglect to tune the SQL that it contains using the techniques outlined in previous chapters. As discussed previously in this chapter, profiling can be used to identify which parts of your PL/SQL code consume the most elapsed time. When these lines represent SQL statements, those SQL statements should be tuned before tuning the PL/SQL code itself.

Before launching into a PL/SQL code optimization effort, make sure that you determine that it is the PL/SQL that needs tuning and not the SQL within the PL/SQL.

PLSQL_OPTIMIZE_LEVEL

Starting with Oracle 10g, the parameter PLSQL_OPTIMIZE_LEVEL controls some automatic optimizations that Oracle can apply to PL/SQL routines. In some cases, these optimizations are equivalent to rewriting of PL/SQL code. The higher the PLSQL_OPTIMIZATION_LEVEL value, the more aggressive the PL/SQL rewrites.

The parameter can take the following values:

0   No optimization
1   Minor optimizations, not much reorganization
2   (the default) Significant reorganization including loop optimizations and automatic bulk collect
3   (11g only) Further optimizations, notably automatic in-lining of subroutines

We discuss the impact of this parameter where appropriate throughout this chapter.

LOOP OPTIMIZATION

The LOOP–END LOOP clauses repeatedly execute statements within a loop. Because statements within a loop are executed many times, they can often consume a high proportion of overall execution time. A badly constructed loop can have a drastic effect on performance.

When optimizing loops

❏ Try to minimize the number of iterations in the loop. Each iteration of the loop consumes CPU, so if you are finished in the loop, use the EXIT statement to move out of the loop.

❏ Make sure that there are no statements inside the loop that are *loop invariant* (do not change with each execution of the loop body) that could be located outside of the loop. If a statement doesn't reference a loop variable, it's possible that it could execute outside the loop—and perhaps execute only once, rather than many times.

The following code illustrates the principle of exiting a loop as early as possible. The code calculates the number of prime numbers less than the number provided as a parameter (P_NUM). It does this by attempting to divide the number by every number smaller than the parameter (line 13). If a match is found the number is clearly not a prime number (line 15).

```
1          i := 2;
2          nprimes := 0;
3
4          <<main_loop>>
5          WHILE (i < p_num)
6          LOOP
7             isprime := 1;
8             j := 2;
9
10            <<divisor_loop>>
11            WHILE (j < i)
12            LOOP
13               IF (MOD (i, j) = 0)
14                 THEN
15                    isprime := 0;
16                    --EXIT divisor_loop;
17                 END IF;
18
19                 j := j + 1;
20            END LOOP;
21
22            IF (isprime = 1)
23            THEN
24               nprimes := nprimes + 1;
25            END IF;
26
27            i := i + 1;
28         END LOOP;
```

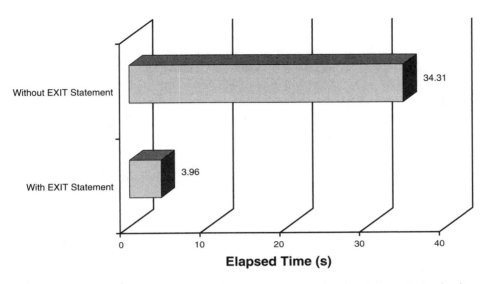

FIGURE 12-6 Improvement gained by adding an EXIT statement to a complex loop.

I originally wrote this code many years ago when comparing Java and PL/SQL performance. In the first version of this code, I omitted to include the EXIT statement included as a comment in line 16. The program worked but performed poorly because it kept looping even after it had already determined that the number was not a prime.

Figure 12-6 shows the performance improvement that was gained by adding the EXIT statement to the code shown in the preceding PL/SQL example. By exiting the loop once the number is determined to be a prime, we avoid unnecessary loop iterations and greatly reduce processing overhead.

Avoid unnecessary loop iterations; use an EXIT statement to leave a loop as soon as all work is done.

Loop invariant expressions are those that don't change with each iteration of the loop. For instance in the following code, the expressions on lines 5 and 7 remain unchanged with each iteration of the loop that begins on line 3. Recalculating these expressions with each iteration of the loop is unnecessary and wastes CPU cycles.

```
1        FOR v_counter1 IN 1 .. 1000
2          LOOP
3              FOR v_counter2 IN 1 .. 4000
```

```
 4              LOOP
 5                 v_modcounter1 := MOD (v_counter1, 10);
 6                 v_modcounter2 := MOD (v_counter2, 10);
 7                 v_sqrt1 := SQRT (v_counter1);
 8                 v_sqrt2 := SQRT (v_counter2);
 9
10                 IF v_modcounter1 = 0
11                 THEN
12                    IF v_modcounter2 = 0
13                    THEN
14                       v_sum1 := v_sum1 + v_sqrt1 + v_sqrt2;
15                    END IF;
16                 END IF;
17              END LOOP;
18           END LOOP;
```

Prior to 10g, this sort of loop coding would result in poor performance. From 10g forward, Oracle will transparently relocate the invariant expressions if PLSQL_OPTIMIZE_LEVEL is set to the default value of 2 or higher.

Figure 12-7 illustrates the performance impact of loop invariant expressions for the previous code. If PLSQL_OPTIMIZE_LEVEL is set to 1 (or prior to Oracle 10g), the loop invariant expressions more than double execution time. Relocating the loop invariants reduces execution time, as does setting PLSQL_OPTIMIZE_LEVEL=2.

This transparent relocation of loop invariant expressions will sometimes enable you to escape the performance penalty of loop invariants, but it's still better to construct efficient loops in the first place—especially if there is any chance that your code might have to run at a PLSQL_OPTIMIZE_LEVEL of less than 2.

Avoid loop invariant expressions in loops. However, from Oracle 10g forward, Oracle transparently relocates such expressions if PLSQL_OPTIMIZE_LEVEL is set to 2 (the default) or higher.

"SHORT CIRCUITING" EXPRESSIONS

You can reduce the overhead of an IF or CASE statement by reducing the number of logical evaluations that need to be performed.

As in many other programming languages, PL/SQL will not evaluate the second argument in a logical expression (typically an expression containing an AND or an OR) if the first argument makes the overall result inevitable.

If the left side of an AND is false, the whole expression is false. If the left side of an OR is true, the whole expression is true. So quite often, Oracle needs to

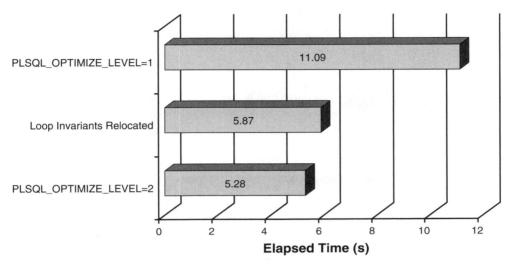

FIGURE 12-7   Effect of relocating loop invariants.

evaluate only part of the expression to determine if it is true or false. Therefore by putting the expressions in a particular order, you can reduce the amount of work Oracle has to do.

For AND conditions, this means that it is more optimal to place the *least* likely expression first. So the following code is suboptimal because almost all sales are greater than $1, but only a small number where placed prior to June 1998:

```
FOR i IN t_time_id.FIRST .. t_time_id.LAST
LOOP
    IF  t_amount_sold (i) > 1 AND t_time_id (i) < '01-JUN-98'
    THEN
       -- do something
    END IF;
END LOOP;
```

If we reverse the order of the expressions, we reduce the PL/SQL processing time by about one-third (see Figure 12-8).

Put the least likely condition first in an AND expression. Oracle doesn't need to evaluate the second expression if the first is FALSE.

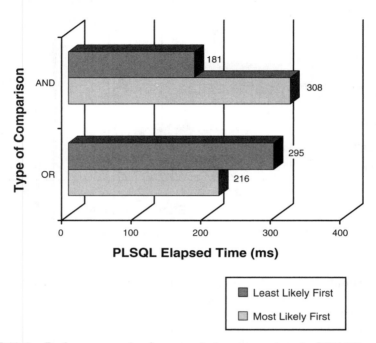

FIGURE 12-8 Performance gains from reordering expressions in OR/AND evaluations.

The opposite order is optimal for OR conditions. In this case performance is improved by placing the most likely condition *first*. So in the following example, the order is not ideal because we almost always have to evaluate the second expression (because the first is almost always false):

```
LOOP
    IF t_time_id (i) < '01-JUN-98' OR t_amount_sold (i) > 1
    THEN
        -- do something
        NULL;
    END IF;
END LOOP;
```

Put the most likely expression first in an OR expression. Oracle does not have to evaluate the second expression if the first is TRUE.

Figure 12-8 illustrates how the order of expressions affects processing time for the preceding code example.

ORDER OF EXPRESSIONS IN IF AND CASE STATEMENTS

Just as the order of arguments within an expression can affect performance, so can the ordering of arguments within an IF or CASE statement. For instance, in the following example, the least likely expression appears first in the IF statement, meaning that both comparisons need to be performed for almost all orders:

```
FOR i IN t_time_id.FIRST .. t_time_id.LAST
LOOP
   IF    t_time_id (i) < '01-JUN-98'   THEN
      v_time_category:=1;
   ELSIF t_time_id(i) < '01-JUN-99' THEN
      v_time_category:=2;
   ELSE
      v_time_category:=3;
   END IF;

END LOOP;
```

If we reorder the expressions as follows, we ensure that for most rows only the first comparison needs to be performed:

```
IF    t_time_id (i) >= '01-JUN-99'   THEN
   v_time_category:=3;
ELSIF t_time_id(i) >= '01-JUN-98' THEN
   v_time_category:=2;
ELSE
   v_time_category:=1;
END IF;
```

Figure 12-9 shows the performance advantage gained by reordering the IF clauses in this manner.

Ordering conditions in an IF or CASE statement from most likely to least likely can reduce the number of comparisons required and help improve performance.

RECURSION

A recursive routine is one that invokes itself. Recursive routines often offer elegant solutions to complex programming problems but tend to consume large amounts of memory and to be less efficient than iterative—loop based—alternatives.

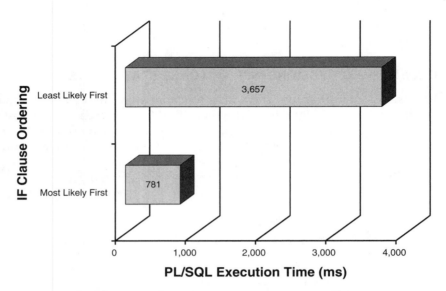

FIGURE 12-9   Effect of reordering clauses in an IF clause.

Many recursive algorithms can be reformulated using nonrecursive iterative techniques. Where possible, you should give preference to the more efficient iterative approach.

For example, the following procedure recursively generates the Fibonacci sequence, in which each element in the sequence is the sum of the previous two numbers:

```
CREATE OR REPLACE PROCEDURE recursive_fibonacci (p_limit NUMBER)
IS
BEGIN
   IF p_limit > 1
   THEN
      recursive_fibonacci (p_limit - 1);
   END IF;

   DBMS_OUTPUT.put_line (p_limit || ' ' || TO_CHAR (p_limit + p_limit -
1));
END;
/
```

The next example generates the same sequence without recursion:

```
CREATE OR REPLACE PROCEDURE nonrecursive_fibonacci (p_limit NUMBER)
IS
```

```
BEGIN
    FOR i IN 1 .. p_limit
    LOOP
        DBMS_OUTPUT.put_line (i || ' ' || TO_CHAR (i + i - 1));
    END LOOP;
END;
/
```

Every time the recursive version invokes itself, it must allocate more memory from the process memory known as the Program Global Area (PGA). Figure 12-10 shows how PGA memory increases steadily as the depth of the recursion increases. The iterative solution shows no similar increase in memory consumption.

Because the total amount of PGA memory available is shared across all sessions,[5] this increase in memory consumption won't just slow your session down—it could also cause degradation to other sessions that want to allocate PGA memory—perhaps for more sensible purposes such as sorting.

> Avoid deeply recursive solutions. Iterative solutions will almost always outperform recursive solutions and will be far more memory-efficient.

THE NOCOPY CLAUSE

Users of other programming languages might be familiar with the concept of passing a parameter *by value* as opposed to *by reference*. When we pass a parameter by value, we create a copy of the parameter for the subroutine to use. When we pass the parameter by reference, the subroutine uses the actual variable passed; any changes made to the variable in the subroutine are visible to the calling routine.

The NOCOPY directive instructs PL/SQL function or procedure to use the parameter variable directly, by reference, rather than making a copy. This is an important optimization when passing large PL/SQL collections into a subroutine because otherwise the process of creating a copy can consume significant resources.

---

[5] In most systems, PGA_AGGREGATE_TARGET sets the target amount of PGA memory that all sessions are expected to share. A single session can usually allocate only a portion of this memory, the exact amount being dependent on the size of PGA_AGGREGATE_TARGET. Chapter 19, "Optimizing PGA Memory," discusses PGA memory management in more detail.

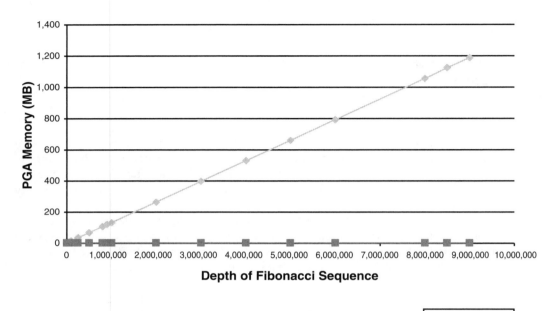

FIGURE 12-10 PGA memory increases steadily as the depth of recursion increases.

Consider the following function. It is used to create a virtual two-dimensional array in a PL/SQL table. You pass in the input table a row and column number, and you are returned the value within the table that corresponds to the row and column specified.

```
FUNCTION get_avalue (
    p_input_table    IN OUT    number_tab_type,
    p_row                      NUMBER,
    p_col                      NUMBER,
    p_num_cols                 NUMBER
)
    RETURN NUMBER
IS
    l_index    NUMBER;
BEGIN
    l_index := ((p_row - 1) * p_num_cols) + p_col;
    RETURN (p_input_table (l_index));
END;
```

Such a routine could be called thousands of times during the execution of its parent program, and every time the PL/SQL table would be copied in and out of the subroutine. Such a function is a definite candidate for the NOCOPY clause.

To use the NOCOPY mode, we simply add the NOCOPY keyword—and IN OUT if not already present—to the parameter declaration:

```
FUNCTION get_avalue_nv (
    p_input_table    IN OUT NOCOPY    number_tab_type,
    p_row                             NUMBER,
    p_col                             NUMBER,
    p_num_cols                        NUMBER
)
```

Figure 12-11 shows the effect of NOCOPY when performing 4,000 lookups against a 4,000-row, 10-column virtual table. As you can see, using NOCOPY makes these lookups virtually instantaneous whereas failing to use NOCOPY results in the lookups being very expensive indeed.

Consider the NOCOPY clause when passing large PL/SQL tables as arguments to functions or procedures.

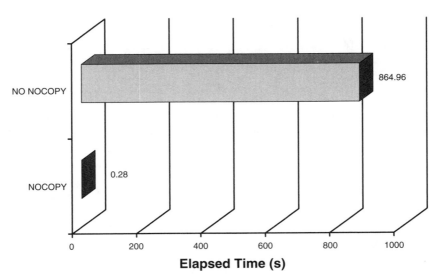

FIGURE 12-11   Performance improvements gained from using the NOCOPY keyword.

Although NOCOPY has performance advantages, it might sometimes lead to less robust code. The parameters must be defined as OUT or IN OUT, and changes made to the parameters within the subroutine will be visible outside of the subroutine. This lack of encapsulation can sometimes lead to subtle bugs.

ASSOCIATIVE ARRAYS

We looked in Chapter 6 at using PL/SQL collections to cache frequently accessed but relatively static data to avoid database lookups. Prior to Oracle 9.2, when seeking a non-numeric value in such a cache, we might use two collections: one of which contained keys and the other which contained values. For instance, in the following example, we scan through the G_CUST_NAMES table looking for a specific customer name and date of birth. If we find a match, we look in the corresponding index of the G_CUST_IDS table to find the CUSTOMER_ID:

```
FUNCTION get_cust_id (p_cust_name_dob VARCHAR2)
   RETURN NUMBER
IS
   v_cust_id   sh.customers.cust_id%TYPE;
BEGIN
   FOR i IN 1 .. g_cust_names_dob.COUNT
   LOOP
      IF g_cust_names_dob (i) = p_cust_name_dob
      THEN
         v_cust_id := g_cust_ids (i);
         EXIT;
      END IF;
   END LOOP;

   RETURN (v_cust_id);
END;
```

On average, we have to scan through half of the G_CUST_NAMES table looking for a match. Associative arrays offer a more efficient solution. An associative array might be indexed by a non-numeric variable; so we can look up the matching customer name directly. And the code is simpler:

```
FUNCTION get_cust_id_assoc (p_cust_name_dob VARCHAR2)
   RETURN NUMBER
IS
   v_cust_id   sh.customers.cust_id%TYPE;
BEGIN
   v_cust_id := g_cust_assoc_array (p_cust_name_dob);
   RETURN (v_cust_id);
END;
```

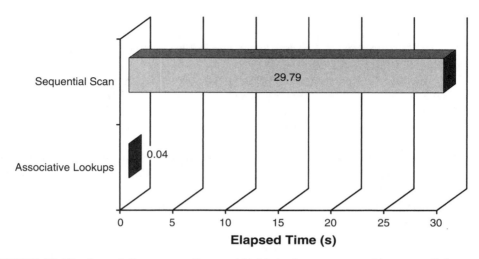

FIGURE 12-12   Associative arrays allow rapid table lookups compared to sequential scans.

For the 55,000-row customer table, the associative array solution is something like 700 times faster. Figure 12-12 shows the relative performance from 10,000 random customer lookups.

OTHER OPTIMIZATIONS

So far, we have looked at how to restructure your PL/SQL code for performance. These optimizations have the greatest potential and generally should be attempted first, especially because it's often hard to change your code after you deploy it to production.

In this section we look at some of the facilities in Oracle that provide for optimization while requiring little or no changes to your PL/SQL code, such as native compilation and in-lining. We also consider the effect of specific data types, Java as an alternative to PL/SQL, and exploiting the Oracle 11g PL/SQL function cache.

NATIVE COMPILATION

PL/SQL is an interpreted language; the PL/SQL code is submitted to an *interpreter* at run time that then invokes the appropriate machine instructions to implement the program logic. In a compiled language, the program code is translated to machine code (native code) by a *compiler* prior to execution. Compiled languages typically outperform interpreted languages for computationally intensive operations (that is, for number crunching).

It's been possible since Oracle 9i to compile a PL/SQL program to native code, but the process has been cumbersome prior to Oracle 11g. Oracle 11g allows native compilation to be requested simply by setting the parameter PLSQL_CODE_TYPE to NATIVE.

Some fairly extreme claims have been made for native compilation; I once heard a claim that performance improvements of 100 times were achievable. Maybe so, in some cases. However, it's relatively unusual for a PL/SQL program to spend the majority of its time performing CPU-intensive operations: Most PL/SQL programs spend the bulk of their time interacting with the database. Furthermore, even when a PL/SQL program is compute-intensive, much of the CPU overhead might be incurred in PL/SQL functions such as POWER, SUM, and so on. These functions already exist in compiled form in the Oracle libraries and get little or no benefit from native compilation.

Consider the following PL/SQL function, which calculates Einstein's $E=MC^2$ formula for various values of M (mass):

```
PROCEDURE emc21
   IS
      c    NUMBER := 299792458;    -- Speed of light m/s
      e    NUMBER;                 -- Energy in Joules
   BEGIN
      FOR m  IN 1 .. g_max_mass
      LOOP
         e := m * c * c;
      END LOOP;
   END;
```

This function performs no database activities and uses no PLSQL built-in functions. It should be a good candidate for native compilation and indeed native compilation results in a 13 percent performance boost.

Now consider this function, which calculates square roots for a range of numbers.

```
   PROCEDURE sqrts
   IS
      v_sqrt_val    NUMBER;
   BEGIN
      FOR i IN 1 .. g_max
      LOOP
         v_sqrt_val := SQRT (i);
      END LOOP;
   END;
```

This function is just as CPU-intensive, but almost all the work is done by the SQRT function that is already compiled code contained within the PL/SQL libraries. Consequently, compiling this function gives us a smaller performance improvement—only about 9 percent.

Finally, let's look at a function that performs the same amount of computation as the first E=MC2 example, but which gets inputs from the database:

```
PROCEDURE emc23
IS
    c       NUMBER := 299792458; -- Speed of light
    e       NUMBER;
BEGIN
    FOR row IN (    SELECT    ROWNUM m
                    FROM      DUAL
                CONNECT BY    ROWNUM < g_max_mass)
    LOOP
        e := row.m * c * c;
    END LOOP;
END;
```

Database access gets no performance advantage from native compilation; therefore, this routine gets the least advantage—only a 6 percent improvement.

Figure 12-13 shows the performance gains by native compilation for each of our three examples for an Oracle 11g database.

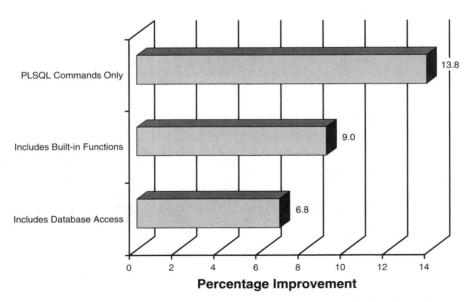

FIGURE 12-13 Performance improvements from native compilation depend on the type of PL/SQL code involved.

Native compilation can result in significant performance improvements for computationally intensive programs. However, native compilation will not improve the performance of built-in functions or of database accesses.

PL/SQL IN-LINING

In-lining is a technique used by many optimizing compilers to improve code performance. In-lining extracts code from subroutines and inserts it, in-line, into the calling code. This reduces the overhead of performing the subroutine call. Oracle 11g introduces in-lining for PL/SQL programs.

For example, consider this PL/SQL fragment:

```
1       FUNCTION mass_to_energy (p_mass NUMBER)
2          RETURN NUMBER
3       IS
4          c    NUMBER := 299792458;           -- Speed of light
5          e    NUMBER;
6       BEGIN
7          e := p_mass * c * c;
8          RETURN (e);
9       END;
10
11      PROCEDURE emc2b
12      IS
13         e    NUMBER;
14      BEGIN
15         FOR m IN 1 .. g_max_mass
16         LOOP
17            e := mass_to_energy (m);
18         END LOOP;
19      END;
```

Einstein's famous equation is encapsulated in the MASS_TO_ENERGY subroutine in lines 1–9; this subroutine is called multiple times from within the EMC2B procedure at line 17. This encapsulation represents good programming practice, especially if Einstein's equation needs to be called from other routines. (Perhaps this package will be utilized in Larry Ellison's upcoming intergalactic yacht.) However, the subroutine calls add overhead, and from a performance point of view, it would probably be better to include the equation directly within the calling routine, like this:

```
PROCEDURE emc2a
   IS
      c    NUMBER := 299792458;                -- Speed of light
```

```
    e    NUMBER;
BEGIN
    FOR m IN 1 .. g_max_mass
    LOOP
        e := m * c * c;
    END LOOP;
END;
```

With 11g in-lining, you can write your code using modularity and encapsulation without paying a performance penalty because Oracle can automatically move relevant subroutines in-line to improve performance. The optimizer will perform some in-lining automatically if PLSQL_OPTIMZE_LEVEL=3. If you want to perform in-lining when PLSQL_OPTIMIZE_LEVEL=2 (the default in Oracle 11g) or you want to increase the likelihood of in-lining when PLSQL_OPTIMIZE_LEVEL=3, you can use PRAGMA INLINE in your subroutine, such as in this example:

```
PROCEDURE emc2c
IS
    e    NUMBER;
BEGIN
    FOR m IN 1 .. g_max_mass
    LOOP
        PRAGMA INLINE (mass_to_energy, 'YES');
        e := mass_to_energy (m);
    END LOOP;
END;
```

Figure 12-14 shows the performance gains gained by in-lining for the preceding example code. For this code either manually in-lining, or using Oracle 11g in-lining, reduces elapsed time by approximately 50 percent. The magnitude of benefit depends on the relative cost of the subroutine and the number of executions. Very small, but frequently executed subroutines are obvious candidates for in-lining.

Consider manually in-lining minor but frequently executed functions or procedures. In Oracle 11g, PRAGMA INLINE or PLSQL_OPTIMIZE_LEVEL=3 might achieve the same results at no cost to the modular structure of your packages.

DATA TYPES

So far, we have used the Oracle NUMBER data type when performing numeric computation. The NUMBER type is extremely flexible and capable of storing both high-precision and high-magnitude numbers. However, this flexibility comes at a cost when performing numeric computations: Certain numeric calculations will be faster if a less flexible data type is chosen.

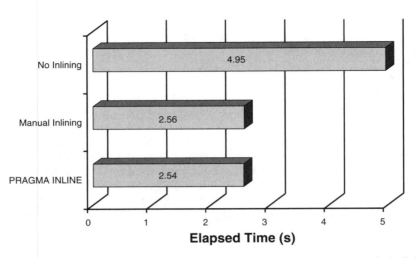

FIGURE 12-14 Performance improvements gained by manual or automatic in-lining.

In particular, the PLS_INTEGER and SIMPLE_INTEGER data types perform faster than the NUMBER type for computation. Both are signed 32 bit integers, which means that they can store numbers between –2,147,483,648 and 2,147,483,648. SIMPLE_INTEGER is the same as PLS_INTEGER but cannot be NULL and overflows (attempts to store numbers larger than 2,147,483,648, for instance) will not cause exceptions to be raised. SIMPLE_INTEGER can offer a performance advantage when the PL/SQL package is compiled to native code.

For instance, consider the following code fragment, which performs some simple but repetitive mathematics:

```
WHILE in_val < g_max_input_value
LOOP
    sq_val := in_val * in_val + in_val;
    in_val := in_val + 1;
END LOOP;
```

If the variables IN_VAL and SQ_VAL are defined as PLS_INTEGER, performance is roughly three times better than if they are defined as NUMBER. The performance of SIMPLE_INTEGER is similar to PLS_INTEGER, except when the code is natively compiled: Then the performance of SIMPLE_INTEGER is ten times greater. Figure 12-15 shows the relative performance for each data type for both native and interpreted PL/SQL code.

Use PLS_INTEGER or SIMPLE_INTEGER when appropriate to optimize PL/SQL integer calculations.

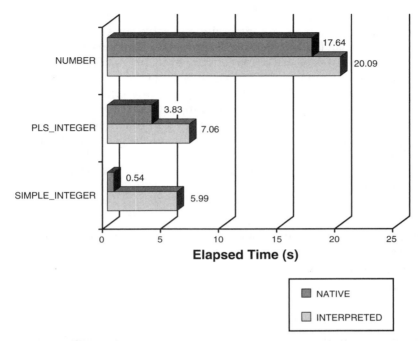

FIGURE 12-15   Effect of data types on PL/SQL number crunching.

For floating point operations, BINARY_FLOAT and BINARY_DOUBLE allow for single-precision and double-precision floating-point operations. The exact limits on these data types depend on whether your system is 32 bit or 64 bit. In either case, these data types provide significant performance advantages over the NUMBER data type.

Regardless of the type of data stored, we want to avoid data type conversions whenever possible. It's sometimes handy to store a number or a date in a VARCHAR2 variable and let Oracle perform implicit data conversions as required. However, these conversions generally result in poorer performance: Best performance can be achieved when every variable is stored in its most natural data type.

USING JAVA FOR COMPUTATION

Oracle enables you to create stored procedures in the Java language. Java-stored procedures can outperform PL/SQL for number crunching, though the advantages of Java for computation have been steadily decreasing with each release of Oracle. When Java was first introduced, performance gains of anywhere between 10 to 100 times were achievable when rewriting computationally intensive PL/SQL routines in Java. However, improvements in PL/SQL language efficiency, including some of the optimizations outlined in this chapter, have closed the gap.

As with all computational optimizations, using Java to optimize number crunching operations is not generally advisable for PL/SQL programs that are database-intensive. Efforts to optimize math operations for a PL/SQL program that does mainly database operations are probably misdirected.

Furthermore, a lot of the advantages that Java had over PL/SQL in previous releases can be overcome in Oracle 11g by using efficient data types, SIMPLE_ INTEGER, for example, and native compilation. Figure 12-16 illustrates this. A Java implementation of the algorithm used in our previous SIMPLE_INTEGER tests outperforms a default implementation of the same algorithm by more than 400 times. However, if we use native compilation for PL/SQL and employ the SIMPLE_INTEGER data type, the performance difference is vastly reduced, though still significant.

Java stored procedures can offer significant advantages over straight PL/SQL for number crunching. However, the advantage is reduced if the PL/SQL uses efficient data types and is natively compiled.

FUNCTION CACHING

Oracle 11g introduced the result set cache, which allows entire result sets to be cached in memory. SQL statements that perform expensive operations on relatively static tables can benefit tremendously from the result set cache.

The function cache is a related facility that can benefit PL/SQL routines or SQL statements that call PL/SQL functions. Oracle 11g can store the results of a

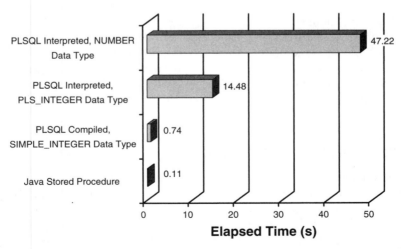

FIGURE 12-16 Java integer arithmetic compared to various PL/SQL alternatives.

PL/SQL function in memory and, if the function is expensive to resolve, can retrieve the results for the function from memory more efficiently than by re-
executing the function.

You might want to use the function cache in the following circumstances:

❏ You have a computationally expensive function that is deterministic: It will
always return the same results given the same inputs.

❏ You have a database access routine encapsulated in a function that accesses
tables that are infrequently updated.

The prime number function we introduced previously in this chapter is a
good example of the first type of function. It is expensive to calculate but will always return the same outputs given the same inputs.

To take advantage of the function cache, we add the RESULT_CACHE
clause to our function definition. For our prime number function, we would add
the clause as follows:

```
CREATE OR REPLACE FUNCTION nprimes1_rc (p_num NUMBER)
    RETURN NUMBER
    RESULT_CACHE IS
```

For SQL statements that access the database, you also will want to include
the RELIES clause. This lets Oracle know that changes to the data in the specified
table invalidate the cached results. For instance, the following function retrieves
sales totals for the last specified number of days:

```
CREATE OR REPLACE FUNCTION time_sales_rc (p_days NUMBER)
    RETURN NUMBER
    RESULT_CACHE RELIES_ON(sh.sales) IS

    v_amount_sold    NUMBER;
BEGIN
    SELECT SUM (amount_sold)
      INTO v_amount_sold
      FROM sh.sales
     WHERE time_id>sysdate-numtodsinterval(p_days,'DAY');
     return(v_amount_sold);
END;
```

The SH.SALES table might be updated infrequently (perhaps overnight),
and caching the function could avoid expensive lookups should the function
be issued with the same arguments between data loads. Figure 12-17 shows the
effect of implementing the function cache on this function for 100 executions with
random date ranges between 1 to 30 days.

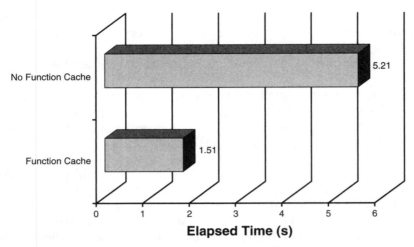

FIGURE 12-17   Example of Oracle 11g function cache performance.

Oracle 11g PL/SQL function cache can result in large improvements for expensive but deterministic functions, or for data access functions on static tables.

The Oracle 11g function cache is part of the more general result set cache that we discuss in detail in Chapter 20, "Other Memory Management Topics."

DML TRIGGER PERFORMANCE

DML Triggers are PL/SQL programs that execute whenever DML operations alter the contents of a table. They can be used to validate data, enforce business rules, or to automatically implement denormalization and nondeclarative referential integrity. Because trigger code can create an overhead on DML statements, it's critical to ensure that the trigger code is executed only when absolutely necessary.

UPDATE OF AND WHEN CLAUSES

The UPDATE OF clause of the CREATE TRIGGER statement allows a FOR UPDATE trigger to fire only when the nominated columns are updated. In a similar way, the WHEN clause can prevent the execution of the trigger unless a logical condition is met.

These clauses help to prevent the trigger from executing unnecessarily and can improve performance of DML operations on the table in which the trigger is based.

For example, the following trigger fires whenever any column in the SALES table is updated, even though it does nothing unless the new AMOUNT_SOLD value is greater than 1500:

```
CREATE OR REPLACE TRIGGER sales_upd
    BEFORE UPDATE OR INSERT
    ON sales
    FOR EACH ROW
DECLARE
    v_adjusted_amount    sales.amount_sold%TYPE;
BEGIN
    v_adjusted_amount := sales_discount (:new.amount_sold);
    IF :new.amount_sold > 1500
    THEN
        :new.amount_sold := v_adjusted_amount;
    END IF;
END;
```

The following trigger is more efficient because it fires only when the AMOUNT_SOLD column is updated and only when the new value of AMOUNT_SOLD is greater than $1,500:

```
CREATE OR REPLACE TRIGGER sales_upd
    BEFORE UPDATE OF amount_sold OR INSERT
    ON sales
    FOR EACH ROW
    WHEN (new.amount_sold > 1500)
DECLARE
    v_adjusted_amount    sales.amount_sold%TYPE;
BEGIN
    v_adjusted_amount := sales_discount (:new.amount_sold);
    IF :new.amount_sold > 1500
    THEN
        :new.amount_sold := v_adjusted_amount;
    END IF;
END;
```

Figure 12-18 shows that for an example workload, the WHEN and UPDATE OF clauses significantly improved performance.

Make use of the OF *columns* and WHEN clauses of the CREATE TRIGGER statement to ensure that your trigger fires only when necessary.

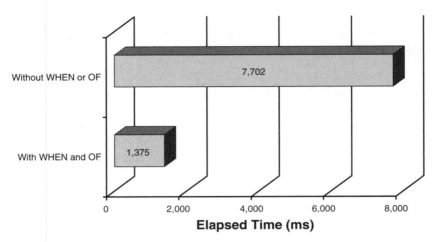

FIGURE 12-18   Using the WHEN and UDATE OF trigger clauses to reduce trigger overhead.

BEFORE AND AFTER ROW TRIGGERS

Sometimes you might be able to implement a trigger so that it fires either BE-FORE or AFTER the row is updated. Unless you have a specific reason to use the BEFORE trigger, use the AFTER trigger in preference. The reason for this recommendation is that the BEFORE trigger locks the row in question before the trigger is executed. If the trigger then decides not to actually change the row in question, this locking will have unnecessarily consumed database resources.

Similarly, avoid FOR EACH ROW triggers if possible. FOR EACH ROW causes the trigger to be executed for each affected row. Unless you need to process each row individually, this option should not be used.

Don't use FOR EACH ROW triggers unnecessarily. If using FOR EACH ROW triggers, use AFTER triggers in preference to BEFORE triggers.

SUMMARY

You can use PL/SQL stored procedures to good effect when optimizing applications. They can reduce network round trips in complex transactions and when performing calculations on large data sets. Additionally, use PL/SQL to optimize certain SQL constructs that resist other techniques and to divide-and-conquer SQL statements that are overly complex.

PL/SQL is a very tunable programming language. Oracle provides two different profilers that help you identify hot spots in PL/SQL code. The second hierarchical profiler was introduced in Oracle 11g. The *time model* views can be used to measure overall PL/SQL overhead, and V$SQL can be used to identify PL/SQL overhead within individual SQL statements.

You can take a number of specific measures to improve the performance of PL/SQL code. In particular

❏ Use traditional code optimization techniques. In particular, avoid unnecessary loops, avoid recursion, and place the more frequently satisfied conditions first in expressions and within IF and CASE statements.

❏ Use the array processing (BULK COLLECT and FORALL) when appropriate. Use the LIMIT clause to optimize the performance of BULK COLLECT.

❏ Consider using the NOCOPY clause when passing large tables as arguments to PL/SQL routines.

❏ Use associative arrays to implement rapid lookups within a PL/SQL collection.

❏ Use bind variables in Native Dynamic SQL.

❏ Use native compilation for computationally expensive operations, especially in 11g in which it's relatively trivial to implement.

❏ Use efficient data types such as PLS_INTEGER and SIMPLE_INTEGER when performing computationally expensive numeric operations.

❏ Exploit the Oracle 11g PL/SQL function result cache, which can result in significant improvements for expensive but deterministic functions, or for functions that query rows from tables more frequently than they are updated.

❏ Exploit Oracle 11g automatic in-lining for subroutines that are simplistic and have very high execution rates.

❏ Optimize trigger code to avoid unnecessary activation and processing.

Chapter 13

PARALLEL SQL

Parallel SQL enables a SQL statement to be processed by multiple threads or processes simultaneously.

Today's widespread use of dual and quad core processors means that even the humblest of modern computers running an Oracle database will contain more than one CPU. Although desktop and laptop computers might have only a single disk device, database server systems typically have database files spread—striped—across multiple, independent disk devices. Without parallel technology—when a SQL statement is processed in *serial*—a session can make use of only one of these CPUs or disk devices at a time. Consequently, serial execution of a SQL statement cannot make use of all the processing power of the computer. Parallel execution enables a single session and SQL statement to harness the power of multiple CPU and disk devices.

Parallel processing can improve the performance of suitable SQL statements to a degree that is often not possible by any other method. Parallel processing is available in Oracle Enterprise Edition only.

In this chapter we look at how Oracle can parallelize SQL statements and how you can use this facility to improve the performance of individual SQLs or the application as a whole.

UNDERSTANDING PARALLEL SQL

In a serial—nonparallel—execution environment, a single process or thread[1] undertakes the operations required to process your SQL statement, and each action must complete before the succeeding action can commence. The single Oracle process might only leverage the power of a single CPU and read from a single disk at any given instant. Because most modern hardware platforms include more than a single CPU and because Oracle data is often spread across multiple disks, serial SQL execution cannot take advantage of all the available processing power.

For instance, consider the following SQL statement:

```
SELECT    *
  FROM    sh.customers
ORDER BY  cust_first_name, cust_last_name, cust_year_of_birth
```

If executing without the parallel query option, a single process would be responsible for fetching all the rows in the CUSTOMERS table. The same process would be responsible for sorting the rows to satisfy the ORDER BY clause. Figure 13-1 illustrates the workflow.

We can request that Oracle execute this statement in parallel by using the PARALLEL hint:

```
SELECT    /*+ parallel(c,2) */ *
  FROM    sh.customers c
ORDER BY  cust_first_name, cust_last_name, cust_year_of_birth
```

If parallel processing is available, the CUSTOMERS table will be scanned by two processes[2] in parallel. A further two processes will be employed to sort the resulting rows. A final process—the session that issued the SQL in the first place—combines the rows and returns the result set. The process that requests and coordinates the parallel processing stream is the *Query coordinator*. Figure 13-2 illustrates this sequence of events.

---

[1] A process is a unit of execution with its own private memory. A thread is also a unit of execution but shares memory with other threads within a process. On UNIX and Linux Oracle servers, tasks are implemented as processes and on Windows as threads.
[2] Because the PARALLEL hint requested a Degree of Parallelism (DOP) of 2.

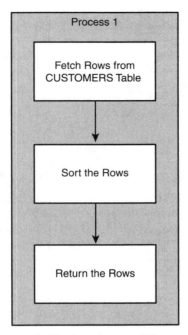

FIGURE 13-1   Serial execution of a SQL statement.

Oracle supports parallel processing for a wide range of operations, including queries, DDL, and DML:

❑ Queries that involve table or index range scans
❑ Bulk insert, update, or delete operations
❑ Table and index creation
❑ The collection of object statistics using DBMS_STATS (see Chapter 7, "Optimizing the Optimizer")
❑ Backup and recovery operations using Recovery Manager (RMAN)

PARALLEL PROCESSES AND THE DEGREE OF PARALLELISM

The Degree of Parallelism (DOP) defines the number of parallel streams of execution that will be created. In the simplest case, this translates to the number of parallel slave processes enlisted to support your SQL's execution. However, the number of parallel processes is more often twice the DOP. This is because each step in a nontrivial execution plan needs to feed data into the subsequent step, so two sets of processes are required to maintain the parallel stream of processing.

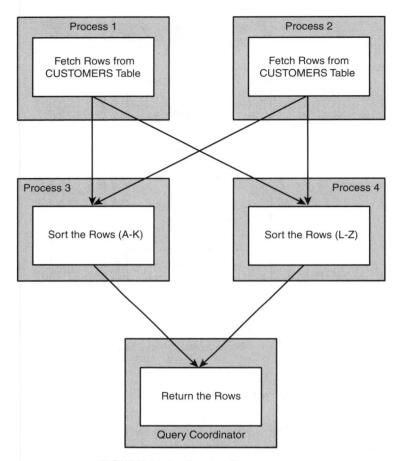

FIGURE 13-2   Parallel Execution.

For instance, if the statement includes a full table scan, an ORDER BY and a GROUP BY, three sets of parallel processes are required: one to scan, one to sort, and one go group. Because Oracle reuses the first set of parallel processes (those that performed the scan) to perform the third operation (the GROUP BY), only two sets of processes are required. As a result of this approach, the number of parallel slaves allocated should never be more than twice the DOP.

Figure 13-3 shows how parallel slaves are allocated for a DOP of 2.

PARALLEL SLAVE POOL

The Oracle server maintains a pool of parallel slave processes available for parallel operations. The database configuration parameters PARALLEL_MIN_ SERVERS

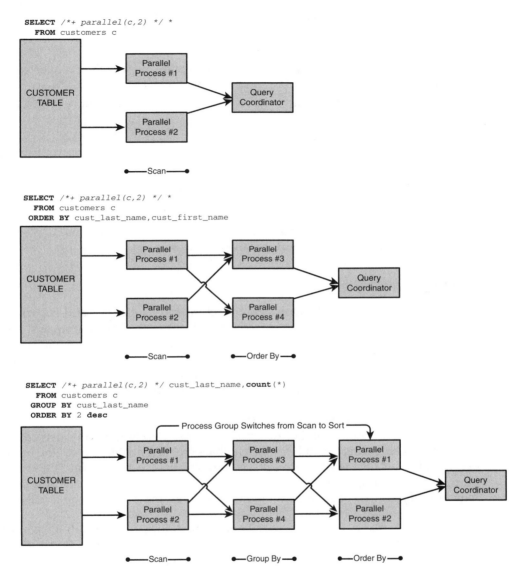

FIGURE 13-3 Parallel process allocation for a DOP of 2.

and PARALLEL_MAX_SERVERS determine the initial and maximum size of the pool. If insufficient slaves are currently active but the pool has not reached its maximum value, Oracle will create more slaves. After a configurable period of inactivity, slave processes will shut down until the pool is again at its minimum size.

If there are insufficient query processes to satisfy the DOP requested by your statement, one of the following outcomes results:

❏ If there are some parallel query slaves available, but less than requested by your SQL statement, your statement might run at a reduced DOP.

❏ If there are no parallel query slaves available, your statement might run serially.

❏ Under specific circumstances, you might get an error. This will only occur if the database parameter PARALLEL_MIN_PERCENT has been set to a value that is higher than the percentage of required slaves that are available.

❏ In Oracle 11g Release 2 and forward, your SQL execution might be delayed until sufficient parallel servers are available.

See the "Parallel Configuration Parameters" section later in this chapter for more information on how to configure these outcomes.

PARALLEL QUERY IO

We discussed in Chapter 2, "Oracle Architecture and Concepts," and elsewhere, how the Oracle buffer cache helps reduce disk IO by buffering frequently accessed data blocks in shared memory. Oracle has an alternate IO mechanism, *direct path* IO, which it can use if it determines that it would be faster to bypass the buffer cache and perform the IO directly. For instance, Oracle uses direct IO when reading and writing temporary segments for sorting and intermediate result sets. In Oracle 11g onward, Oracle sometimes uses direct path IO in preference to the normal buffered IO for serial table access as well.

When performing Parallel query operations, Oracle normally uses direct path IO. By using direct path IO, Oracle avoids creating contention for the buffer cache and allows IO to be more optimally distributed between slaves. Furthermore, for parallel operations that perform full table scans the chance of finding matching data in the buffer cache is fairly low, so the buffer cache adds little value.

In Oracle 10g and earlier, parallel query always uses direct path IO, and serial query will always use buffered IO.[3] In 11g, Oracle can use buffered IO for parallel query (from 11g release 2 forward), and serial queries might use direct path IO. However, it remains true that parallel queries are less likely to use buffered IO and might, therefore, have a higher IO cost than serial queries. The higher IO cost will, of course, be shared amongst all the parallel processes so the overall performance might still be superior.

---

[3] Unless the undocumented parameter serial_direct_read has been set to TRUE.

Direct path and buffered IO are discussed in more detail within Chapter 21, "Disk IO Tuning Fundamentals."

PARALLEL PERFORMANCE GAINS

The performance improvements that you can expect to obtain from parallel SQL depend on the suitability of your host computer, Oracle configuration, and the SQL statement. If all the conditions for parallel processing are met, you can expect to get substantial performance improvements in proportion to the DOP employed.

On many systems, the limit of effective parallelism will be determined by segment spread, not by hardware configuration. For instance, if you have 32 CPUs and 64 independent disk devices, you might hope for effective parallelism up to at least a DOP of 32 or maybe even 64. However, if the table you are querying is spread over only 6 disks, you are likely to see performance improvements reduce as you increase the DOP beyond 6 or so.

Figure 13-4 illustrates the improvements gained when increasing the DOP for a SQL statement that performs a table scan and GROUP BY of a single table.

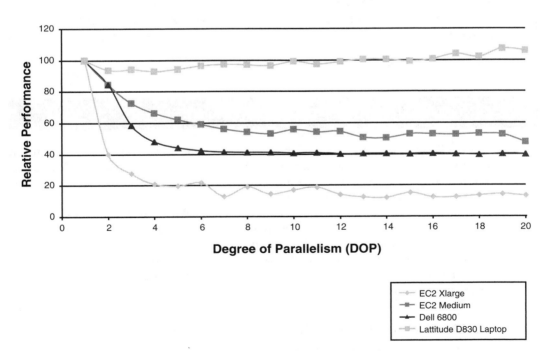

FIGURE 13-4   Improvement gains for various DOPs on various host configurations.

The host configurations shown are

❏ An Amazon CPU-intensive Extra Large EC2 image. This is a virtual server running in Amazon's AWS cloud that has the equivalent of 8 × 2.5-GHz CPUs and has storage on a widely striped SAN.

❏ An Amazon CPU-intensive Medium EC2 image. This is similar to the extra large image, but has only 2 CPUs.

❏ A Dell 6800 4 CPU server with disk storage on a widely striped SAN using ASM.

❏ A Dell latitude D830 laptop (my laptop). It is dual core, but all data files are on a single disk.

In each case, the parallel SQL was the only SQL running.

These examples show that for suitably configured systems, performance gains were greater the more CPUs that were available. However, attempting to use parallel on a host that is unsuitable (as in my laptop) is futile at best and counter-productive at worst.

The performance gains achieved through parallel processing are most dependent on the hardware configuration of the host. To get benefits from parallel processing, the host should possess multiple CPUs and data should be spread across multiple disk devices.

DECIDING WHEN TO USE PARALLEL PROCESSING

A developer once saw me use the parallel hint to get a rapid response to an ad-hoc query. Shortly thereafter, every SQL that developer wrote included the parallel hint, and system performance suffered as the database server became overloaded by excessive parallel processing.

The lesson is obvious: If every concurrent SQL in the system tries to use *all* the resources of the system, parallel makes performance worse, not better. Consequently, we should use parallel only when doing so improves performance without degrading the performance of other concurrent database requests.

The following sections discuss some of the circumstances in which you can effectively use parallel SQL.

YOUR SERVER COMPUTER HAS MULTIPLE CPUS

Parallel processing will usually be most effective if the computer that hosts your Oracle database has multiple CPUs. This is because most operations performed by the Oracle server (accessing the Oracle shared memory, performing sorts, disk accesses) require CPU. If the host computer has only one CPU, the parallel processes might contend for this CPU, and performance might actually decrease.

Almost every modern computer has more than one CPU; dual-core (2 CPUs in a single processor slot) configurations are the minimum found in systems likely to be running an Oracle server including the desktops and laptops running development databases. However, databases running within Virtual machines might be configured with only a single (virtual) CPU.

THE DATA TO BE ACCESSED IS ON MULTIPLE DISK DRIVES

Many SQL statements can be resolved with few or no disk accesses when the necessary data can be found in the Oracle buffer cache. However, full table scans of larger tables—a typical operation to be parallelized—tends to require significant physical disk reads. If the data to be accessed resides on a single disk, the parallel processes line up for this disk, and the advantages of parallel processing might not be realized.

Parallelism will be maximized if the data is spread evenly across the multiple disk devices using some form of striping; we discuss principles of striping in Chapter 21.

THE SQL TO BE PARALLELIZED IS LONG RUNNING OR RESOURCE-INTENSIVE

Parallel SQL suits long running or resource-intensive statements. There is an overhead in activating and coordinating multiple parallel query processes and in co-coordinating the flow of information between these processes. For short-lived SQL statements, this overhead might be greater than the total SQL response time.

Parallel processing is typically used for

- ❏ Long-running reports
- ❏ Bulk updates of large tables
- ❏ Building or rebuilding indexes on large tables
- ❏ Creating temporary tables for analytical processing
- ❏ Rebuilding a table to improve performance or to purge unwanted rows

Parallel processing is not usually suitable for transaction processing environments. In these environments, multiple sessions process transactions concurrently. Full use of available CPUs is already achieved because each concurrent transaction can use a different CPU. Implementing parallel processing might actually degrade overall performance by allowing a single user to monopolize multiple CPUs.

Parallel processing is suitable for long-running operations in low-concurrency environments. Parallel processing is less suitable for OLTP style databases.

THE SQL PERFORMS AT LEAST ONE FULL TABLE, INDEX, OR PARTITION SCAN

Parallel processing is generally restricted to operations that include a scan of a table, index, or partition. However, the SQL might include a mix of operations, only some of which involve scans. For instance, a nested loops join that uses an index to join two tables can be fully parallelized providing that the driving table is accessed by a table scan.

Although queries that are driven from an index lookup are not normally parallelizable, if a query against a partitioned table is based on a local partitioned index, each index scan can be performed in parallel against the table partition corresponding to the index partition. We see an example of this later in the chapter.

THERE IS SPARE CAPACITY ON YOUR HOST

You are unlikely to realize the full gains of parallel processing if your server is at full capacity. Parallel processing works well for a single job on an underutilized, multi-CPU machine. If all CPUs on the machine are busy, your parallel processes will bottleneck on the CPU and performance will be degraded.

Remember that when a session uses parallel query, it requests a greater share of machine resources. If many processes simultaneously attempt to run in parallel, the result will usually be that some fail to run at the requested degree of parallelism whereas others acquire more than their fair share of resources.

THE SQL IS WELL TUNED

Parallelizing a poorly tuned SQL might well reduce its execution time. However, you'll also be magnifying the impact of that SQL on the database server and increasing its impact on other sessions. You should make sure that the SQL is efficient before attempting to grant it access to more of the database server's resources. Parallelizing the SQL is *not* an alternative to tuning the SQL.

CONFIGURING PARALLEL PROCESSING

Oracle tries to automate the configuration of the system to maximize the performance of parallel operations. However, there's still a lot of scope for manually tweaking the database and SQL for optimal parallel performance.

DETERMINING THE DEGREE OF PARALLELISM

An optimal DOP is critical for good parallel performance. Oracle determines the DOP as follows:

❏   If parallel execution is indicated or requested, but no DOP is specified, the default DOP is set to twice the number of CPU cores on the system. For a

RAC system, the DOP will be twice the number of cores in the entire cluster. This default is controlled by the configuration parameter PARALLEL_THREADS_PER_CPU.

❑ From Oracle 11g release 2 forward, If PARALLEL_DEGREE_POLICY is set to AUTO, Oracle will adjust the DOP depending on the nature of the operations to be performed and the sizes of the objects involved.

❑ If PARALLEL_ADAPTIVE_MULTI_USER is set to TRUE, Oracle will adjust the DOP based on the overall load on the system. When the system is more heavily loaded, the DOP will be reduced.

❑ If PARALLEL_IO_CAP is set to TRUE in Oracle 11g or higher, Oracle will limit the DOP to that which the IO subsystem can support. These IO subsystem limits can be calculated by using the procedure DBMS_RESOURCE_MANAGER.CALIBRATE_IO.

❑ A DOP can be specified at the table or index level by using the PARALLEL clause of CREATE TABLE, CREATE INDEX, ALTER TABLE, or ALTER INDEX.

❑ The PARALLEL hint can be used to specify the DOP for a specific table within a query.

❑ Regardless of any other setting, the DOP cannot exceed that which can be supported by PARALLEL_MAX_SERVERS. For most SQL statements, the number of servers required will be twice the requested DOP.

As we saw in Figure 13-4, increasing the DOP beyond an optimal point fails to result in further performance increases. However, increasing the DOP beyond optimal *can* have a significant negative effect on overall system performance. Although the SQL being parallelized might not degrade significantly as the DOP increases, load on the system continues to increase and can cause other SQLs running concurrently to suffer reduced response time.

Figure 13-5 shows how increasing the DOP influences CPU utilization. As we hit the optimal DOP—approximately 8 for this system—the reduction in query-elapsed time flattens out. However, the time other sessions spend waiting for CPU to become available continues to increase. Other sessions wanting to access the CPU will need to wait, resulting in degraded response time.

Increasing the DOP beyond the optimal level might overload the host, degrading the performance of other SQLs.

PARALLEL HINTS

The PARALLEL hint can invoke parallel processing. In its simplest form, the hint takes no argument as in the following example:

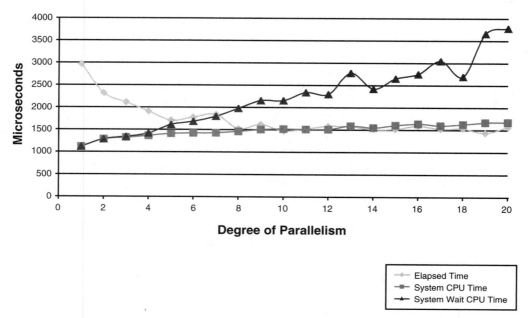

FIGURE 13-5   Increasing the DOP causes increases in system CPU wait times.

```
SELECT /*+ parallel */ *  FROM sh.sales s
```

It's legal, but not always necessary to specify a table name or alias in the hint:

```
SELECT /*+ parallel(s) */  *  FROM sh.sales s
```

The hint can request a specific DOP:

```
SELECT /*+ parallel(s,8) */ * FROM sh.sales s;
```

The NOPARALLEL hint can be used to suppress parallel processing:

```
SELECT  /*+ noparallel */ COUNT ( * ) FROM sales;
```

In 11g release 2, the AUTO option allows you to request that the AUTO setting for PARALLEL_DEGREE_POLICY be used to calculate the DOP:

```
SELECT  /*+ parallel(auto) */ COUNT ( * ) FROM sales;
```

For ad-hoc query execution, you might want to set an explicit DOP. However, for SQL embedded within an application, this might not be a good idea because the SQL will be less able to adapt to changes in machine configuration (more CPUs for instance), workload (more concurrent sessions), or configuration (changes to the number of parallel slaves or the default DOP). For embedded SQL, it's probably better to omit an explicit DOP or to use the AUTO keyword (in Oracle 11g Release 2 and higher).

PARALLEL CONFIGURATION PARAMETERS

Determining the optimal DOP, especially when taking concurrent system activity into account, is a daunting task. Luckily, Oracle has invested significant effort into automating the process. Each release of Oracle has increased the level of intelligent automation of parallel configuration. In general, you should try Oracle's automation before attempting to manually configure automatic processing.

Nevertheless, significant tweaking is possible; the following lists the significant configuration parameters that you can adjust to optimize parallel SQL:

parallel_adaptive_multi_user	When set to TRUE, Oracle will adjust the DOP to account for the load on the system. On a heavily loaded system, Oracle will reduce the DOP from the requested or default degree.
parallel_degree_limit	In Oracle11g Release 2 and higher, places an absolute limit on the DOP that can be achieved. A value of CPU prevents the DOP from exceeding that specified by parallel_threads_per_cpu. A value of IO sets the maximum to the IO limit determined by running DBMS_RESOURCE_MANAGER.CALIBRATE_IO. AUTO allows Oracle to select a value. An integer value corresponding to a specific DOP might also be specified.
parallel_degree_policy	In 11G release 2 and forward, this parameter controls the means by which the DOP will be calculated. MANUAL equates to the behavior in 11.1 and earlier. If AUTO, the DOP will be calculated based on the types of operations in the SQL statement and the sizes of the tables. AUTO also enables parallel queries to fetch data from the buffer cache rather than using direct path IO and will queue parallel processes if the requested DOP execution is not immediately available.
parallel_execution_message_size	Sets the size of buffers for communication between the processes involved in parallel processing.
parallel_force_local	From Oracle 11g Release 2 forward, this parameter, if set to TRUE, suppresses multi-instance parallelism on RAC clusters.
parallel_io_cap_enabled	This 11g parameter if set to TRUE will limit the DOP to that which Oracle thinks the IO subsystem can support. To use the parameter, you should first use DBMS_RESOURCE_MANAGER.CALIBRATE_IO to determine these IO limits.
parallel_max_servers	The maximum number of parallel servers that can be started. This provides an absolute limit on the amount of concurrent parallel operations that can execute.

parallel_min_percent	If set to nonzero, this parameter determines the minimum acceptable DOP for a query. If the DOP requested or determined cannot be provided due to system load or other parallel processes that are using the parallel server pool, the DOP will be reduced only to the value of PARALLEL_MIN_ PERCENT. For instance, if your query requested a DOP of 8 and only 5 were available (5 / 8 = 62%), your query would execute in parallel if PARALLEL_ MIN_PERCENT was below 62. If PARALLEL_MIN_ PERCENT were above 62, your statement will either terminate with an error or, if PARALLEL_DEGREE_ POLICY is set to AUTO, will be queued for later execution.
parallel_min_servers	The minimum number of parallel servers—the number that will be initialized when the database is first started.
parallel_min_time_threshold	Specifies the amount of elapsed time (in seconds) required for a SQL statement to be automatically parallelized. If the estimated elapsed time of a SQL statement exceeds the threshold, Oracle automatically parallelizes the SQL. The default of AUTO results in Oracle automatically calculating a value.
parallel_threads_per_cpu	Sets the number of parallel threads that can be applied per CPU. Oracle generally restricts the DOP so that this limit is not exceeded.

MONITORING PARALLEL SQL

Because multiple processes are involved in parallel execution, explaining, tracing, and monitoring parallel execution can be more complex than for serial SQL.

PARALLEL EXPLAIN PLANS

EXPLAIN PLAN reflects additional steps for a parallelized SQL statement that reflect the additional parallel operations involved in the parallel execution.

For instance, consider this simple SQL statement and explain plan:

```
SQL> EXPLAIN PLAN  FOR
  2     SELECT   * FROM   customers
  3     ORDER BY   cust_last_name;


-----------------------------------------
| Id | Operation            | Name      |
-----------------------------------------
|  0 | SELECT STATEMENT     |           |
|  1 |  SORT ORDER BY       |           |
|  2 |   TABLE ACCESS FULL| CUSTOMERS |
-----------------------------------------
```

The CUSTOMERS table is scanned, and the rows scanned are sorted.

When the statement is parallelized, additional operations are added to the execution plan:

```
SQL> EXPLAIN PLAN  FOR
  2     SELECT /*+ parallel */ *
  3       FROM   customers
  4     ORDER BY   cust_last_name;

SQL> SELECT * FROM table (DBMS_XPLAN.display
  2                    (null,null,'BASIC +PARALLEL'));
```

```
--------------------------------------------------------------------------
|Id  | Operation               | Name      | TQ    |IN-OUT| PQ Distrib  |
--------------------------------------------------------------------------
|  0 | SELECT STATEMENT        |           |       |      |             |
|  1 |  PX COORDINATOR         |           |       |      |             |
|  2 |   PX SEND QC (ORDER)    | :TQ10001  | Q1,01 | P->S | QC (ORDER)  |
|  3 |    SORT ORDER BY        |           | Q1,01 | PCWP |             |
|  4 |     PX RECEIVE          |           | Q1,01 | PCWP |             |
|  5 |      PX SEND RANGE      | :TQ10000  | Q1,00 | P->P | RANGE       |
|  6 |       PX BLOCK ITERATOR |           | Q1,00 | PCWC |             |
|  7 |        TABLE ACCESS FULL| CUSTOMERS | Q1,00 | PCWP |             |
--------------------------------------------------------------------------
```

The new plan contains a variety of PX steps that describe the parallel operations involved. Let's look at each of these steps:

PX BLOCK ITERATOR	This operation is typically the first step in a parallel pipeline. The BLOCK ITERATOR breaks up the table into chunks that are processed by each of the parallel servers involved.
PX SEND	PX SEND operations simply indicate that data is being sent from one parallel process to another.
PX RECEIVE	PX RECEIVE operations indicate the data being received by one parallel process from another.
PX SEND QC	This is a send operation to the parallel query co-coordinator process.
PX COORDINATOR	This step simply indicates that the parallel query co-coordinator is receiving the data from the parallel streams and returning it to the SQL statement.

Figure 13-6 illustrates how these steps relate to parallel processing with a DOP of 2.

PX SEND and PX RECEIVE operations are associated with distribution options—shown in the "PQ Distrib" column of DBMS_XPLAN—which describe how data is sent from one slave to another. In sort operations it's typical to see

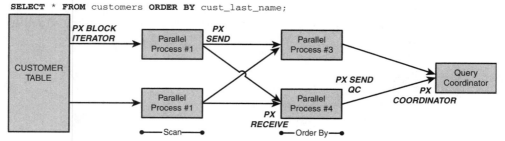

FIGURE 13-6   EXPLAIN PLAN parallel execution steps.

the RANGE option because rows to be sorted are distributed based on the value of the sort columns. For instance when sorting by CUST_FIRST_NAME as in the preceding query, Oracle might send names from A–K to one slave and names from L–Z to the other. Here are the commonly encountered distribution options:

RANGE	Rows are distributed based on ranges of values. This is typical when sort operations are parallelized.
HASH	Rows are distributed to parallel query slaves based on a hash of the value concerned. This is suitable for joins and HASH GROUP BY operations and generally ensures a more even distribution of rows than for RANGE operations.
RANDOM	Rows are randomly assigned to parallel query slaves.
ROUND ROBIN	Rows are distributed one at a time in a circular fashion, just as you would deal cards in a game of poker.

The IN-OUT column of the DBMS_XPLAN output describes how data flows between and within the parallel processes. The column corresponds to the OTHER_TAG column in the PLAN_TABLE table. These columns can contain one of the values shown in Table 13-1.

The presence of a PARALLEL_FROM_SERIAL or S->P tag in the PLAN_TABLE or DBMS_XPLAN output might represent a serial bottleneck in an otherwise parallel execution stream.

TRACING PARALLEL EXECUTION

Using SQL trace to tune our queries becomes somewhat more difficult when the SQL is parallelized. This is because each process involved in the parallel execution has its own trace file. Furthermore, because these processes are shared among all parallelized SQLs and sessions, the trace files contain trace data for other SQLs and sessions in addition to the ones we are interested in.

Table 13-1 Parallel Data Flow Tags

IN-OUT VALUE	OTHER_TAG VALUE	DESCRIPTION
P->P	PARALLEL_TO_PARALLEL	This tag denotes parallel processing that passes results to a second set of parallel processes. For instance, a parallel table scan might have passed results to a parallel sort.
P->S	PARALLEL_TO_SERIAL	This is usually the top level of a parallel query. The results are fed in parallel to the query coordinator.
PCWP PCWC	PARALLEL_COMBINED_ WITH_PARENT PARALLEL_COMBINED_ WITH_CHILD	The step was executed in parallel. Either the parent step or the child step was also executed in parallel by the same process. For instance, in a parallel nested loops join, the parallel query process scanned the driving table and also issued index lookups on the joined table.
S->P	PARALLEL_FROM_SERIAL	A serial operation that passed results to a set of parallel processes. The presence of this tag can indicate a serial bottleneck within a parallel statement because it suggests that parallel processing might wait on serial processing.

However, it is possible, through a somewhat convoluted process, to trace parallel execution. Here are the steps:

1. Set a unique client identifier in your session using DBMS_SESSION.SET_ IDENTIFIER.
2. Enable tracing for that client identifier using DBMS_MONITOR.CLIENT_ ID_TRACE_ENABLE.
3. Run your parallel SQL.
4. Use the *trcsess* utility to create a new trace file that contains only trace entries for your client identifier.
5. Analyze the new trace file as usual.

Here we invoke steps 1, 2, and 3:

```
BEGIN
    DBMS_SESSION.set_identifier ('gh pqo test 27');
    DBMS_MONITOR.client_id_trace_enable
        (client_id => 'gh pqo test 27',
        waits => TRUE);
END;
/
```

```
SELECT /*+ parallel */ prod_name, SUM (amount_sold)
  FROM    products JOIN sales
  USING (prod_id)
GROUP BY    prod_name
ORDER BY    2 DESC;
```

Here we perform steps 4 and 5:

```
$ trcsess clientid='gh pqo test 27' output=pqo_test_27.trc *
$ tkprof pqo_test_27.trc pqo_test_27.prf sort='(prsela,fchela,exeela)'

TKPROF: Release 11.1.0.6.0 - Production on Mon Dec 29 19:40:38 2008
Copyright (c) 1982, 2007, Oracle.  All rights reserved.
```

The merged trace file now accurately reflects not only the activity from our invoking session, but also from all the parallel server processes that were involved in executing the query.

> To trace a parallel execution, set a Client Identifier and use the trcsess utility to extract trace records for that client identifier into a single file.

Advanced tracing of parallel server activity can also be achieved by using the "_px_trace" facility.[4] For instance

```
ALTER SESSION SET "_px_trace"="compilation","execution","messaging";
```

The 10391 event can also be used to dump information about parallel server allocation:

```
ALTER SESSION SET EVENTS '10391 trace name context forever, level 128';
```

Both of these events generate rather cryptic and sometimes voluminous output and should probably be used only if all other techniques fail to shed light on parallel execution.

THE V$PQ_TQSTAT VIEW

Even with EXPLAIN PLAN and SQL trace output, it's hard to work out exactly how a parallel query executed. For instance, what was the actual DOP? How much work did each parallel server process do?

---

[4] See Oracle support note 444164.1

The V$PQ_TQSTAT view contains information about the data transferred between each set of parallel query servers, including the number of rows transmitted and received. Unfortunately, the view is visible only from within the session that issued the parallel query and only for the most recent query executed. This limits its usefulness in a production environment, but it is still invaluable when tuning parallel queries.

For instance, consider this parallel query:

```
SQL>    SELECT /*+ parallel */
  2            prod_id, SUM (amount_sold)
  3        FROM    sales
  4    GROUP BY    prod_id
  5    ORDER BY    2 DESC;
```

Id	Operation	Name	TQ	IN-OUT
0	SELECT STATEMENT			
1	PX COORDINATOR			
2	PX SEND QC (ORDER)	:TQ10002	Q1,02	P->S
3	SORT ORDER BY		Q1,02	PCWP
4	PX RECEIVE		Q1,02	PCWP
5	PX SEND RANGE	:TQ10001	Q1,01	P->P
6	HASH GROUP BY		Q1,01	PCWP
7	PX RECEIVE		Q1,01	PCWP
8	PX SEND HASH	:TQ10000	Q1,00	P->P
9	HASH GROUP BY		Q1,00	PCWP
10	PX BLOCK ITERATOR		Q1,00	PCWC
11	TABLE ACCESS FULL	SALES	Q1,00	PCWP

If we query V$PQ_TQSTAT directly after the query executes[5] we can see the number of rows passed between each of the parallel server sets. Each of the unique TQ_IDs corresponds to one of the interactions between server sets denoted in the execution plan by 'P->P' or 'P->S' values for the IN-OUT column. You can correlate the value of TQ_ID with the TQ column in the EXPLAIN PLAN output.

```
SQL>    SELECT    dfo_number, tq_id, server_Type, MIN (num_rows),
                  MAX (num_rows),count(*) dop
  2        FROM    v$pq_tqstat
```

---

[5] You might need to wait a few seconds to allow parallel server processes to flush their statistics.

```
   3  GROUP BY    dfo_number, tq_id, server_Type
   4  ORDER BY    dfo_number, tq_id, server_type DESC;
```

DFO_NUMBER	TQ_ID	SERVER_TYP	MIN(NUM_ROWS)	MAX(NUM_ROWS)	DOP
1	0	Producer	72	72	2
1	0	Consumer	62	82	2
1	1	Ranger	72	72	1
1	1	Producer	31	41	2
1	1	Consumer	35	37	2
1	2	Producer	35	37	2
1	2	Consumer	72	72	1

For complex parallel SQLs, there might be multiple parallel pipelines that are indicated by different values for the DFO_NUMBER column.

> Use the V$PQ_TQSTAT view to measure the actual DOP and amount of data transferred between parallel servers.

OTHER STATISTICS

We can get a view of parallel execution occurring on the system in real time by examining the V$PX_SESSION view, which shows which parallel slave processes are currently executing SQL. Joining V$PX_SESSION to V$SESSION and V$SQL enables us to identify the sessions and SQLs currently employing parallel processing to see the desired and actual DOP:

```
SQL> WITH px_session AS (SELECT qcsid, qcserial#, MAX (degree) degree,
  2                             MAX (req_degree) req_degree,
  3                             COUNT ( * ) no_of_processes
  4                      FROM v$px_session p
  5                   GROUP BY   qcsid, qcserial#)
  6  SELECT   s.sid, s.username, degree, req_degree, no_of_processes,
  7           sql_text
  8  FROM     v$session s  JOIN px_session p
  9           ON (s.sid = p.qcsid AND s.serial# = p.qcserial#)
 10           JOIN v$sql sql
 11           ON (sql.sql_id = s.sql_id
 12               AND sql.child_number = s.sql_child_number)
 13  /
```

```
       SID USERNAME    DEGREE REQ_DEGREE NO_OF_PROCESSES
---------- -------- ---------- ---------- ---------------
SQL_TEXT
-------------------------------------------------------
       144 OPSG            18         18              36
select   /*+ parallel(sa,18) */ prod_id,sum(quantity_sold)
   , sum(amount_sold)  from sales_archive sa group by prod
_id  order by 3 desc
```

V$SYSSTAT contains some statistics relating to parallel query downgrades that can help us determine how often parallel queries are being downgraded from the requested DOP:

```
SQL> SELECT  name,value, round(value*100/sum(value) over(),2) pct
  2    FROM  v$sysstat
  3   WHERE  name LIKE 'Parallel operations%downgraded%';
```

NAME	VALUE	PCT
Parallel operations not downgraded	109	93.97
Parallel operations downgraded to serial	0	0
Parallel operations downgraded 75 to 99 pct	0	0
Parallel operations downgraded 50 to 75 pct	3	2.59
Parallel operations downgraded 25 to 50 pct	2	1.72
Parallel operations downgraded 1 to 25 pct	2	1.72

OPTIMIZING PARALLEL PERFORMANCE

Now that we have a solid grounding in the theory of parallel execution, and understand how to influence and measure parallel execution, we are in a good position to formulate some guidelines for optimizing parallel execution. Here are the guidelines for getting the most out of parallel execution:

❏ Start with a SQL that is optimized for *serial* execution.
❏ Ensure that the SQL is a suitable SQL for *parallel* execution.
❏ Ensure that the database server host is suitably configured for parallel execution.
❏ Make sure that all parts of the execution plan are parallelized.
❏ Ensure that the requested DOP is realistic.
❏ Monitor the actual versus requested DOP.
❏ Check for skew in data and skew in workload between processes.

Let's now look at each of these guidelines in detail.

START WITH A SQL THAT IS OPTIMIZED FOR SERIAL EXECUTION

An optimal parallel plan might be different from an optimized serial plan. For instance, parallel processing usually starts with a table or index scan, whereas the optimal serial plan might be based on an index lookup. However, you should ensure that your query is optimized for serial execution before parallelizing for these reasons:

❏ The structures and methods of serial tuning—indexing, statistics collections, and such—are often essential for good parallel tuning as well.

❏ If the resources required for parallel execution are not available, your query might be serialized (depending on the settings of PARALLEL_DEGREE_ POLICY and PARALLEL_MIN_PERCENT). In that case, you want to ensure than your parallel query's serial plan is as good as possible.

❏ A SQL that is poorly tuned might become an even worse SQL—at least in terms of its impact on other users—when it is permitted to consume more of the database server's CPU and IO resources.

When optimizing a SQL statement for *parallel* execution, start by optimizing the SQL for *serial* execution.

ENSURE THAT THE SQL IS A SUITABLE SQL FOR PARALLEL EXECUTION

Not every SQL can benefit from parallel execution. Here are a few examples of SQLs that probably should *not* be parallelized:

❏ SQL statements that have a short execution time when executed serially.

❏ SQL statements likely to be run at high rates of concurrency in multiple sessions.

❏ SQL statements based on index lookups. Nonpartitioned index lookups or range scans cannot be parallelized. Index full scans *can* be parallelized, however. Index lookups on partitioned indexes can also be parallelized.

Make sure that the SQL to be parallelized is suitable for parallel execution; OLTP type queries are generally not suitable for parallelization.

ENSURE THAT THE SYSTEM IS SUITABLY CONFIGURED
FOR PARALLEL EXECUTION

Not all SQLs are suitable for parallel execution, and not all database server hosts are suitable either. In today's world, most physical server hosts will meet the minimum requirements: multiple CPUs and data striped across multiple physical drives. However, some virtual machine hosts might fail to meet those minimum requirements and desktop machines, which typically have only a single disk device, are usually not optimized for parallel execution.

> Don't try to use parallel execution on systems that do not meet the minimum requirements (multiple CPUs and data striped across multiple drives).

MAKE SURE THAT ALL PARTS OF THE EXECUTION PLAN ARE PARALLELIZED

In a complex parallel SQL statement, it's important to ensure that all significant steps in the query execution are implemented in parallel. If one of the steps in a complex query is performed in serial, the other parallel steps might have to wait for the serial step to complete, and the advantages of parallelism will be lost. The OTHER_TAG column of the PLAN_TABLE indicates such a step with the PARALLEL_FROM_SERIAL tag and DBMS_XPLAN record S->P in the IN-OUT column.

For instance, in the following example the CUSTOMERS table is parallelized, but the SALES table is not. The join and GROUP BY of the two tables includes many parallelized operations, but the full table scan of SALES is not parallelized and the tell-tale S->P tag shows that SALES rows are fed in serial into subsequent parallel operations:

```
SQL> ALTER TABLE customers PARALLEL(DEGREE 4);

SQL> ALTER TABLE sales NOPARALLEL ;

SQL> EXPLAIN PLAN FOR
  2    SELECT /*+ ordered use_hash(c) */
  3           cust_last_name, SUM (amount_sold)
  4      FROM sales s JOIN customers c
  5           USING (cust_id)
  6     GROUP BY cust_last_name;

SQL> SELECT * FROM table (DBMS_XPLAN.display
(NULL, NULL, 'BASIC +PARALLEL'));
```

Id	Operation	Name	TQ	IN-OUT	PQ Distrib
0	SELECT STATEMENT				
1	PX COORDINATOR				

```
|  2|    PX SEND QC (RANDOM)         |:TQ10002 | Q1,02| P->S |QC (RAND)  |
|  3|     HASH GROUP BY             |         | Q1,02| PCWP |           |
|  4|      PX RECEIVE               |         | Q1,02| PCWP |           |
|  5|       PX SEND HASH            |:TQ10001 | Q1,01| P->P |HASH       |
|  6|        HASH GROUP BY          |         | Q1,01| PCWP |           |
|  7|         HASH JOIN             |         | Q1,01| PCWP |           |
|  8|          BUFFER SORT          |         | Q1,01| PCWC |           |
|  9|           PX RECEIVE          |         | Q1,01| PCWP |           |
| 10|            PX SEND BROADCAST  |:TQ10000 |      | S->P |BROADCAST  |
| 11|             VIEW              |VW_GBC_5 |      |      |           |
| 12|              HASH GROUP BY    |         |      |      |           |
| 13|               TABLE ACCESS FULL| SALES  |      |      |           |
| 14|          PX BLOCK ITERATOR    |         | Q1,01| PCWC |           |
| 15|           TABLE ACCESS FULL   |CUSTOMERS| Q1,01| PCWP |           |
------------------------------------------------------------------------
```

A partially parallelized execution plan, such as the preceding one, can deliver the worst of both worlds: Elapsed time is not improved because the serial operation forms a bottleneck on overall execution. Nevertheless, the SQL ties up parallel server processes and might impact the performance of other concurrently executing SQL.

If we set a default degree of parallelism for the SALES table, the serial bottleneck disappears. The full scan of SALES is now performed in parallel, and the S->P bottleneck is replaced by the fully parallelized P->P operation:

```
------------------------------------------------------------------------
| Id  | Operation                      | Name     |    TQ  |IN-OUT|
------------------------------------------------------------------------
|  0  | SELECT STATEMENT               |          |        |      |
|  1  |  PX COORDINATOR                |          |        |      |
|  2  |   PX SEND QC (RANDOM)          |:TQ10003  | Q1,03  | P->S |
|  3  |    HASH GROUP BY               |          | Q1,03  | PCWP |
|  4  |     PX RECEIVE                 |          | Q1,03  | PCWP |
|  5  |      PX SEND HASH              |:TQ10002  | Q1,02  | P->P |
|  6  |       HASH GROUP BY            |          | Q1,02  | PCWP |
|  7  |        HASH JOIN               |          | Q1,02  | PCWP |
|  8  |         PX RECEIVE             |          | Q1,02  | PCWP |
|  9  |          PX SEND BROADCAST     |:TQ10001  | Q1,01  | P->P |
| 10  |           VIEW                 |VW_GBC_5  | Q1,01  | PCWP |
| 11  |            HASH GROUP BY       |          | Q1,01  | PCWP |
| 12  |             PX RECEIVE         |          | Q1,01  | PCWP |
| 13  |              PX SEND HASH      |:TQ10000  | Q1,00  | P->P |
| 14  |               HASH GROUP BY    |          | Q1,00  | PCWP |
| 15  |                PX BLOCK ITERATOR|         | Q1,00  | PCWC |
```

```
|  16 |                    TABLE ACCESS FULL|  SALES      |  Q1,00 |  PCWP |
|  17 |          PX BLOCK ITERATOR          |             |  Q1,02 |  PCWC |
|  18 |              TABLE ACCESS FULL      |  CUSTOMERS  |  Q1,02 |  PCWP |
---------------------------------------------------------------------------
```

> When optimizing a parallelized execution plan, ensure that all relevant steps are executed in parallel: The S->P tag in DBMS_XPLAN or PARALLEL_FROM_SERIAL in the PLAN_TABLE often indicates a serial bottleneck in an otherwise parallel plan.

ENSURE THAT THE REQUESTED DOP IS REALISTIC

We saw previously (in Figure 13-5, for instance), how increasing the DOP beyond the optimal level can place excessive load on the system without improving performance. In worst case scenarios, increasing the DOP beyond optimal can result in a reduction in query elapsed time as well. Therefore, setting an appropriate DOP is important both for the health of the database as a whole, and for the optimal performance of the query being parallelized.

> Ensure that your requested or expected DOP is realistic; an overly-high DOP can result in excessive load on the database server without improving the SQL's performance.

MONITOR THE ACTUAL DOP

Your requested DOP might be optimal but not always achievable. When multiple parallelized queries contend for finite parallel execution resources, the DOP might be reduced, or the SQL statement might be run in serial mode.

We previously discussed how Oracle decides on the actual DOP; most importantly the parameters PARALLEL_MIN_PERCENT, PARALLEL_DEGREE_POLICY, and PARALLEL_ADAPTIVE_MULTI_USER control how Oracle changes the DOP and whether a statement runs at reduced parallelism, terminates with error, or is deferred for later processing when insufficient resources exist to run the statement at the requested DOP.

Reductions in the DOP can result in disappointing performance for your parallel SQL. You should monitor query execution to see if such reductions in the DOP are actually occurring. We previously saw how we can use V$PQ_TQSTAT to measure the actual DOP and how we can use statistics in V$SYSTAT to measure parallel downgrades overall.

If you determine that downgraded parallelism is leading to disappointing performance, you might want to revisit your system resources (memory, IO bandwidth), scheduling of parallel SQLs, or revisit your server configuration. Possible options include

❏ Rescheduling parallel SQLs so that they do not attempt to run concurrently. Oracle 11g Release 2 can automatically reschedule SQLs if the PARALLEL_DEGREE_POLICY is set to AUTO.

❏ Adjusting parallel configuration parameters to allow greater concurrent parallelism. You can do this by increasing PARALLEL_THREADS_PER_CPU or PARALLEL_MAX_SERVERS. The risk here is that the amount of parallel execution will be greater than your system can support, leading to degraded SQL performance.

❏ Increasing the power of your database server. You can increase the number of CPUs, the number of instances in a RAC cluster, and the number of disks in your disk array.

❏ Adjust PARALLEL_MIN_PERCENT to enable SQLs to run at reduced parallelism rather than signalling an error.

Disappointing parallel performance might be the result of Oracle downgrading the requested DOP due to concurrent load or limits on parallel execution resources.

CHECK FOR SKEW IN DATA AND SKEW IN WORKLOAD BETWEEN PROCESSES

Parallel processing works best when every parallel process in a step has the same amount of work to do. If one slave process has more work than a peer process, the "lazy" slave will wait for the "busy" slave, and we won't get performance improvements in line with the number of processes working on the SQL.

Most of the algorithms that Oracle employs are designed to achieve an even distribution of data; these algorithms include the HASH, ROUND ROBIN, and RANDOM distribution mechanisms. However, when a sort operation is performed, Oracle cannot use these random or pseudo-random mechanisms. Instead, Oracle must distribute data to the slaves based on the sort key columns. We saw an example of this in Figure 13-2 where a parallel process fed rows from A–K to one slave for sorting and rows from L–Z to the other.

If the distribution of data in the sort column is very skewed, this allocation might be uneven. For instance, consider this simple query:

```
SQL> EXPLAIN PLAN
  2      FOR
  3          SELECT /*+ parallel */
  4              cust_last_name, cust_first_name, cust_year_of_birth
  5          FROM    customers
  6      ORDER BY    CUST_LAST_NAME;
```

```
--------------------------------------------------------------------
|Id | Operation             | Name      |  TQ   |IN-OUT| PQ Distrib |
--------------------------------------------------------------------
| 0 | SELECT STATEMENT      |           |       |      |            |
| 1 |  PX COORDINATOR       |           |       |      |            |
| 2 |   PX SEND QC (ORDER)  | :TQ10001  | Q1,01 | P->S | QC (ORDER) |
| 3 |    SORT ORDER BY      |           | Q1,01 | PCWP |            |
| 4 |     PX RECEIVE        |           | Q1,01 | PCWP |            |
| 5 |      PX SEND RANGE    | :TQ10000  | Q1,00 | P->P | RANGE      |
| 6 |       PX BLOCK ITERATOR|          | Q1,00 | PCWC |            |
| 7 |        TABLE ACCESS FULL| CUSTOMERS | Q1,00 | PCWP |         |
--------------------------------------------------------------------
```

In the preceding step 5, Oracle distributes data from one set of slaves to another based on the range of values contained in the sort column. If the data is well distributed, all should be well. However, should the data be heavily skewed (perhaps we have an extra large number of Smiths and Zhangs), the distribution of data to slaves might become uneven. For example, the following V$PQ_TQSTAT output shows such an uneven distribution with twice as many rows directed to one slave than the other (I deliberately skewed customer surnames to achieve this):

```
SQL>   SELECT   dfo_number, tq_id, server_Type, MIN (num_rows),
  2              MAX (num_rows), COUNT ( * ) dop
  3      FROM   v$pq_tqstat
  4  GROUP BY   dfo_number, tq_id, server_Type
  5  ORDER BY   dfo_number, tq_id, server_type DESC;


DFO_NUM     TQ_ID SERVER_TYP MIN(NUM_ROWS) MAX(NUM_ROWS)        DOP
------- ---------- ---------- ------------- ------------- ----------
      1         0 Ranger               182           182          1
      1         0 Producer          158968        174512          2
      1         0 Consumer          103262        230218          2
      1         1 Producer          103262        230218          2
      1         1 Consumer          333480        333480          1
```

Unfortunately, there might be little that can be done about such a data skew. Oracle does not appear to take histogram data into account when distributing rows between parallel slaves. If the distribution of rows seems particularly uneven, you can consider changing the DOP or reviewing whether the SQL is truly suitable for parallelizing.

Effective parallelism depends on the even distribution of processing across the parallel slave processes. V$PQ_TQSTAT enables you to evaluate the efficiency of the load balancing across the parallel slaves.

OTHER PARALLEL TOPICS

Most of what we covered so far applies to all parallel execution but focused mainly on single-instance parallel queries involving table scans. Now let's turn our attention to other parallel scenarios.

PARALLEL EXECUTION IN RAC

In a Real Application Clusters (RAC) database, SQL can be parallelized across the multiple instances that make up the cluster. Indeed, Oracle transparently parallelizes across the entire cluster unless you take specific steps to prevent it.

Using all the instances in the cluster enables Oracle to take advantage of all the CPUs of the host computers that support the cluster database and, therefore, will usually lead to better performance than could be achieved by running the SQL on a single instance. Oracle multiples the default DOP by the number of instances in the cluster to take full advantage of the processing power of the cluster.

To see exactly how the query distributes across the instances within the cluster, we can observe the INSTANCE column in V$PQ_TQSTAT. The following gives a good summary of overall parallelism:

```
SQL> SELECT   dfo_number, tq_id, server_Type, MIN (num_rows) min_rows,
  2           MAX (num_rows) max_rows, COUNT ( * ) dop,
  3           COUNT (DISTINCT instance) no_of_instances
  4    FROM   v$pq_tqstat
  5  GROUP BY dfo_number, tq_id, server_Type
  6  ORDER BY dfo_number, tq_id, server_type DESC;


DFO_NUMBER         TQ_ID SERVER_TYP   MIN_ROWS    MAX_ROWS   DOP INSTANCES
---------- ---------- ---------- ---------- ---------- ----- ---------
         1          0 Producer         842        1617    48         3
         1          0 Consumer        1056        1239    48         3
         1          1 Producer        8779       38187    48         3
         1          1 Consumer       15331       24572    48         3
         1          2 Producer         107         159    48         3
         1          2 Consumer          64         244    48         3
         1          3 Ranger           479         479     1         1
         1          3 Producer           9          10    48         3
         1          3 Consumer           9          55    48         3
         1          4 Producer           9          10    48         3
         1          4 Consumer           9           9     1         1
```

The above output was generated on a 3 instance RAC cluster in which each instance had 8 CPUs available. Oracle applied the default formula of 2 threads per CPU to achieve a DOP of 48 for the 24 CPUs available across the 3 hosts.

Although parallelism in RAC scales well with additional instances, there is an additional overhead in communication when the parallel slave processes reside on different hosts. The RAC cluster's high-speed interconnect might become taxed if the amount of data transferred is high, and the performance of a RAC-parallelized query might not be quite as good as for a locally parallelized query with an equivalent DOP.

From Oracle 11g Release 2 forward, the parameter PARALLEL_FORCE_LOCAL can be set to restrict parallel processing to the current instance only.

We discuss some further aspects of RAC optimization in Chapter 23, "Optimizing RAC."

PARALLEL INDEX LOOKUPS

Index-based queries are not usually parallelizable; however, if the index involved is a locally partitioned index on a partitioned table, a lookup using that index can be parallelized. Each partition lookup can be performed by a separate process, and a DOP as high as the number of partitions can be achieved.

For example, if the SALES table had a local partitioned index on the CUST_ID column like this:

```
CREATE INDEX sales_i1 ON sales(cust_id) LOCAL;
```

We could use the PARALLEL_INDEX hint to parallelize lookups on specific CUST_ID values:

```
SELECT /*+ parallel_index(s) */ *
FROM sales s
WHERE cust_id = 247;
```

```
---------------------------------------------------------------------
| Id | Operation                          | Name     | TQ    |IN-OUT|
---------------------------------------------------------------------
|  0 | SELECT STATEMENT                   |          |       |      |
|  1 |  PX COORDINATOR                    |          |       |      |
|  2 |   PX SEND QC (RANDOM)              | :TQ10000 | Q1,00 | P->S |
|  3 |    PX PARTITION HASH ALL           |          | Q1,00 | PCWC |
|  4 |     TABLE ACCESS BY LOCAL INDEX ROWID| SALES  | Q1,00 | PCWP |
|  5 |      INDEX RANGE SCAN              | SALES_I1 | Q1,00 | PCWP |
---------------------------------------------------------------------
```

PARALLEL DML

Any DML statement that performs a scan operation can be parallelized, at least for that part of the statement that performs the table reads.

For instance, parts of the following UPDATE statement executes in parallel:

```
SQL> EXPLAIN PLAN
  2      FOR     .
  3          UPDATE /*+ parallel(s)  */
  4               sales s
  5          SET   unit_price = amount_sold / quantity_sold;
```

```
-----------------------------------------------------------------------
|Id | Operation            | Name      |   TQ  |IN-OUT| PQ Distrib |
-----------------------------------------------------------------------
|  0 | UPDATE STATEMENT     |           |       |      |            |
|  1 | UPDATE               | SALES     |       |      |            |
|  2 |   PX COORDINATOR     |           |       |      |            |
|  3 |     PX SEND QC (RANDOM)| :TQ10000 | Q1,00 | P->S | QC (RAND)  |
|  4 |      PX BLOCK ITERATOR|           | Q1,00 | PCWC |            |
|  5 |       TABLE ACCESS FULL| SALES    | Q1,00 | PCWP |            |
-----------------------------------------------------------------------
```

The full scan of SALES is parallelized, but note that the UPDATE statement (step 1) is executed outside the parallel processing stream; although the rows to be updated are identified by the parallel processes, the actual updates are performed in serial by the query coordinator.

To perform true parallel DML, you should first enable parallel DML with the following statement:

```
ALTER SESSION ENABLE PARALLEL DML.
```

After we do this, we get a fully parallelized execution plan:

```
SQL> EXPLAIN PLAN
  2      FOR
  3          UPDATE /*+ parallel(s)  */
  4               sales_p s
  5          SET   unit_price = amount_sold / quantity_sold;
```

```
-----------------------------------------------------------------------
|Id | Operation            | Name      |   TQ  |IN-OUT| PQ Distrib |
-----------------------------------------------------------------------
|  0 | UPDATE STATEMENT     |           |       |      |            |
|  1 | PX COORDINATOR       |           |       |      |            |
|  2 |   PX SEND QC (RANDOM)| :TQ10000  | Q1,00 | P->S | QC (RAND)  |
|  3 |     UPDATE           | SALES_P   | Q1,00 | PCWP |            |
|  4 |      PX BLOCK ITERATOR|           | Q1,00 | PCWC |            |
|  5 |       TABLE ACCESS FULL| SALES_P  | Q1,00 | PCWP |            |
-----------------------------------------------------------------------
```

The UPDATE step is now executed by the same parallel server processes that perform the scan of the SALES table. The UPDATE is now fully parallelized.

To fully parallelize a DML statement, issue an ALTER SESSION ENABLE PARALLEL DML statement; otherwise the statement will be only partially parallelized (at best).

Parallel INSERT Inserting rows in parallel is a particularly good use of parallel DML, especially for bulk operations in which the input data is in another table (such as a staging or transaction table). In this scenario, it's important to parallelize both the SELECT and INSERT operations. For instance, here we parallelize the INSERT but not the SELECT that performs the table scan on the SALES_UPDATE table:

```
SQL> EXPLAIN PLAN FOR
  2    INSERT /*+ parallel(s) */
  3      INTO sales s
  4    SELECT * FROM sales_updates;
```

Id	Operation	Name	TQ	IN-OUT	PQ Distrib
0	INSERT STATEMENT				
1	PX COORDINATOR				
2	PX SEND QC (RANDOM)	:TQ10001	Q1,01	P->S	QC (RAND)
3	LOAD AS SELECT	SALES	Q1,01	PCWP	
4	BUFFER SORT		Q1,01	PCWC	
5	PX RECEIVE		Q1,01	PCWP	
6	PX SEND ROUND-ROBIN	:TQ10000		**S->P**	RND-ROBIN
7	**TABLE ACCESS FULL**	**SALES_UPDATES**			

The full table scan of SALES_UPDATE is processed serially, and the S->P tag should raise a red flag, indicating parallel processing waiting on serial processing.

This plan is more perfectly parallelized:

```
SQL> EXPLAIN PLAN FOR
  2    INSERT /*+ parallel(s) */
  3      INTO     sales s
  4    SELECT /*+ parallel(u) */ *
  5      FROM    sales_updates u;
```

```
|Id| Operation              | Name         |  TQ  |IN-OUT| PQ Distrib |
----------------------------------------------------------------------
| 0| INSERT STATEMENT       |              |      |      |            |
| 1|  PX COORDINATOR        |              |      |      |            |
| 2|   PX SEND QC (RANDOM)  |:TQ10000      |Q1,00 | P->S | QC (RAND)  |
| 3|    LOAD AS SELECT      |SALES         |Q1,00 | PCWP |            |
| 4|     PX BLOCK ITERATOR  |              |Q1,00 | PCWC |            |
| 5|      TABLE ACCESS FULL |SALES_UPDATES |Q1,00 | PCWP |            |
----------------------------------------------------------------------
```

> When parallelizing an INSERT from a SELECT, remember to parallelize both the INSERT and SELECT steps, using two hints if necessary.

By default, parallel insert uses the direct load APPEND method, creating new data blocks and appending them directly to the segment, bypassing the buffer cache. We talk about the pros and cons of direct load inserts in Chapter 14, "DML Tuning." However, for now it's enough to note that direct path insert is usually the best choice for parallel insert because otherwise the parallel slaves might contend for latches, free lists, and data buffers. However, if you want to use the conventional insert method—inserting rows into existing data blocks where appropriate and utilizing the buffer cache—you can use the NOAPPEND hint:

```
SQL> EXPLAIN PLAN FOR
  2    INSERT /*+ parallel(s) noappend */
  3      INTO    sales s
  4    SELECT /*+ parallel(u) */ *
  5      FROM    sales_updates u;
```

```
|Id| Operation                | Name        |  TQ  |IN-OUT|PQ Distrib|
----------------------------------------------------------------------
| 0| INSERT STATEMENT         |             |      |      |          |
| 1|  PX COORDINATOR          |             |      |      |          |
| 2|   PX SEND QC (RANDOM)    |:TQ10000     |Q1,00 | P->S |QC (RAND) |
| 3|    LOAD TABLE CONVENTIONAL|SALES        |Q1,00 | PCWP |          |
| 4|     PX BLOCK ITERATOR    |             |Q1,00 | PCWC |          |
| 5|      TABLE ACCESS FULL   |SALES_UPDAT  |Q1,00 | PCWP |          |
----------------------------------------------------------------------
```

Parallel MERGE The MERGE statement combines the functionality of INSERT and UPDATE into a single statement. A MERGE execution plan usually involves an outer join between the target table and the source tables. To optimize the merge, we most truly need to optimize that outer join.

We look more at MERGE optimization in Chapter 14.

Merge statements can be fully parallelized, although you normally want to ensure that both target and source tables are parallelized. For instance, in the following example we supply PARALLEL hints for both the source and target tables:

```
SQL> EXPLAIN PLAN FOR
  2  MERGE /*+ parallel(s) parallel(u) */ INTO sales s
     USING sales_updates u
  3  ON (s.prod_id=u.prod_id AND s.cust_id=u.cust_id
         AND s.time_id=u.time_id
  4         AND s.channel_id=u.channel_id
         AND s.promo_id = u.promo_id)
  5  WHEN MATCHED THEN
  6  UPDATE SET  s.amount_sold  =u.amount_sold,
  7              s.quantity_sold=u.quantity_sold
  8  WHEN NOT MATCHED THEN
  9  INSERT VALUES ( u.prod_id, u.cust_id, u.time_id  ,
 10                  u.channel_id, u.promo_id,
 11                  u.quantity_sold, u.amount_sold);
```

Id	Operation	Name	TQ	IN-OUT
0	MERGE STATEMENT			
1	PX COORDINATOR			
2	PX SEND QC (RANDOM)	:TQ10003	Q1,03	P->S
3	MERGE	SALES	Q1,03	PCWP
4	PX RECEIVE		Q1,03	PCWP
5	PX SEND HYBRID (ROWID PKEY)	:TQ10002	Q1,02	P->P
6	VIEW		Q1,02	PCWP
7	HASH JOIN OUTER BUFFERED		Q1,02	PCWP
8	PX RECEIVE		Q1,02	PCWP
9	PX SEND HASH	:TQ10000	Q1,00	P->P
10	PX BLOCK ITERATOR		Q1,00	PCWC
11	TABLE ACCESS FULL	SALES_UPDATES	Q1,00	PCWP
12	PX RECEIVE		Q1,02	PCWP
13	PX SEND HASH	:TQ10001	Q1,01	P->P
14	PX BLOCK ITERATOR		Q1,01	PCWC
15	TABLE ACCESS FULL	SALES	Q1,01	PCWP

DBMS_PARALLEL_EXECUTE Parallel DML is an incredibly powerful way to speed up bulk DML. However, it has the disadvantage of applying all changes in a single transaction. This results in the generation of long-standing locks, requires large undo segments, and runs the risk of expensive rollback operations should the operation fail.

The DBMS_PARALLEL_EXECUTE package, introduced in Oracle 11g Release 2, helps to resolve this dilemma by enabling you to execute parallel DML in smaller "chunks," each of which is committed individually. The package enables you to restart the job should any of the individual chunked operations fail.

The following code shows an example of DBMS_PARALLEL_EXECUTE in action:

```
1   DECLARE
2       v_dml_sql      VARCHAR2(1000);
3       v_task_name    VARCHAR2(1000)
4                      := 'dbms_parallel_execute demo';
5       v_status       NUMBER;
6   BEGIN
7       DBMS_PARALLEL_EXECUTE.CREATE_TASK(
8           task_name => v_task_name);
9
10      DBMS_PARALLEL_EXECUTE.CREATE_CHUNKS_BY_ROWID(
11          TASK_NAME => v_task_name,
12          TABLE_OWNER => USER, TABLE_NAME => 'SALES',
13          BY_ROW => TRUE, CHUNK_SIZE => 1000);
14
15      v_dml_sql :=
16             'UPDATE sales SET   unit_price = '
17         || '          amount_sold / quantity_sold '
18         || ' WHERE rowid BETWEEN :start_id AND :end_id ';
19
20      DBMS_PARALLEL_EXECUTE.RUN_TASK(TASK_NAME => v_task_name,
21          SQL_STMT => v_dml_sql, LANGUAGE_FLAG => DBMS_SQL.NATIVE,
22          PARALLEL_LEVEL => 2);
23
24      v_status := DBMS_PARALLEL_EXECUTE.TASK_STATUS(
25                  task_name  => v_task_name);
26
27      IF v_status = DBMS_PARALLEL_EXECUTE.FINISHED THEN
28          DBMS_PARALLEL_EXECUTE.DROP_TASK(task_name => v_task_name);
29      ELSE
30      -- could use dbms_parallel_execute.resume_task here to retry
31      -- if required
32          raise_application_error(-2001,
```

```
33              'Task ' || v_task_name || ' abnormal termination: status='
34              || v_status);
35       END IF;
36     END;
```

DBMS_PARALLEL_EXECUTE works in two phases. The first phase, shown on line 10 above, uses one of the CREATE_CHUNK procedures to define the table chunks that are to be processed. There are a number of ways of chunking, including defining chunks using custom SQL. In this example, we use the CREATE_CHUNKS_BY_ROWID procedure that simply creates chunks that have a sequential set of ROWIDS. These rows tend to be in contiguous blocks, and this method will result in a fairly even distribution of rows. The approximate size of each chunk is defined by the CHUNK_SIZE argument (line 13).

The second phase executes a SQL statement to work on the chunks. The SQL statement, shown on lines 15-18 in our example, must define bind variables :START_ID and :END_ID that are used to feed in the ROWID ranges or—if you use a different chunking strategy—column values that define the chunks. The SQL statement is fed into the RUN_TASK procedure that also specifies the DOP to be used in the operation (line 22).

DBMS_PARALLEL_EXECUTE runs the SQL statement against each chunk using the DOP specified. A COMMIT will be executed after each chunk has been processed. This means that if there is an error, only some of the rows in the table will have been processed. If this occurs, you can use the RESUME_TASK procedure to restart the operation on the chunks that have not been processed.

Consider the 11g Release 2 DBMS_PARALLEL_EXECUTE package when you want to issue parallel DML without the drawbacks of performing all the DML in a single transaction.

PARALLEL DDL

The DDL statements CREATE INDEX and CREATE TABLE AS SELECT statements can both be parallelized. The CREATE TABLE AS SELECT statement parallelizes in much the same way as a parallel INSERT. Parallel CREATE INDEX parallelizes the table or index scan necessary to create the index blocks, sorts the rows in parallel, and builds the index leaf and branch blocks in parallel.

In both cases, the DOP is controlled by the PARALLEL clause of the CREATE INDEX or CREATE TABLE statement. That DOP is then set for subsequent query operations that use the index or table.

Here is an example of CREATE INDEX:

```
SQL> EXPLAIN PLAN FOR
  2    CREATE INDEX sales_i ON sales(prod_id,time_id)
            PARALLEL(DEGREE DEFAULT);
```

Id	Operation	Name	TQ	IN-OUT	PQ Distrib
0	CREATE INDEX STATEMENT				
1	PX COORDINATOR				
2	PX SEND QC (ORDER)	:TQ10001	Q1,01	P->S	QC (ORDER)
3	INDEX BUILD NON UNIQUE	SALES_I	Q1,01	PCWP	
4	SORT CREATE INDEX		Q1,01	PCWP	
5	PX RECEIVE		Q1,01	PCWP	
6	PX SEND RANGE	:TQ10000	Q1,00	P->P	RANGE
7	PX BLOCK ITERATOR		Q1,00	PCWC	
8	TABLE ACCESS FULL	SALES	Q1,00	PCWP	

Here is a parallel CREATE TABLE AS SELECT:

```
SQL> EXPLAIN PLAN FOR
  2    CREATE TABLE sales_copy  PARALLEL(DEGREE DEFAULT)
            AS SELECT * FROM sales;
```

Id	Operation	Name	TQ	IN-OUT	PQ Distrib
0	CREATE TABLE STATEMENT				
1	PX COORDINATOR				
2	PX SEND QC (RANDOM)	:TQ10000	Q1,00	P->S	QC (RAND)
3	LOAD AS SELECT	SALES_COPY	Q1,00	PCWP	
4	PX BLOCK ITERATOR		Q1,00	PCWC	
5	TABLE ACCESS FULL	SALES	Q1,00	PCWP	

SUMMARY

In this chapter we looked at the parallel execution facilities provided by the Oracle RDBMS, how to use these to improve SQL performance, and how to optimize the performance of SQL running in parallel.

Parallel processing uses multiple processes or threads to execute a single SQL statement. Providing that the system is suitably configured, parallel processing can result in big improvements in SQL throughput, though at the cost of an increased load on the system.

The Degree of Parallelism (DOP) defines the amount of parallelism that is applied to your SQLs. For simple SQLs the DOP equates to the number of parallel processes, but in most nontrivial statements, twice as many processes will be required to achieve a pipeline of parallel processing.

Parallel processing might be indicated if

❏ The database server has multiple CPUs.
❏ The data is distributed across multiple disk devices.
❏ The SQL is long running or resource-intensive.
❏ Free resources are available on the system to support the additional overhead associated with parallel processing.
❏ The SQL involves a full table or index scan, or locally partitioned index lookups.

You can use EXPLAIN PLAN and DBMS_XPLAN to determine the parallel execution plan and V$PQ_TQSTAT to determine the actual DOP achieved.

The key principles for optimizing parallel SQL are

❏ Starting with an SQL that is optimized for serial execution
❏ Ensuring that the SQL is suitable for parallel execution
❏ Determining that that the database server host is suitably configured for parallel execution
❏ Ensuring that all the steps in the SQL are parallelized
❏ Configuring a realistic DOP
❏ Monitoring the actual DOP and determining the approach when that DOP cannot be achieved (downgrade, defer, or fail)
❏ Checking for skew in data and in workload between processes

You can apply parallel processing across instances in a RAC cluster, making full use of all the resources of the entire cluster database. You can also apply parallel processing to DML or DDL statements.

DML TUNING

In this chapter, we look at issues relating to the performance of Data Manipulation Language (DML) statements. These statements (INSERT, UPDATE, MERGE, and DELETE) alter the information contained within your Oracle database.

Even in transaction processing environments, most database activity is related to data retrieval. You need to find data to change or delete it, and even inserts often have a query component. However, there are many DML-specific optimizations available, and we cover these in this chapter.

One of the key features of relational databases is the ability to group multiple DML statements into a group of statements that must succeed or fail as a unit. These groups of statements are known as transactions. COMMIT statements mark the successful termination of transactions and are associated with specific performance issues and tuning opportunities.

DML PERFORMANCE FUNDAMENTALS

The overhead of all DML statements are directly affected by the following fundamental factors:

❑ The efficiency of any WHERE clause included in the DML.
❑ The amount of index maintenance that must be performed.
❑ Overheads involved in enforcing referential integrity constraints.
❑ Trigger execution overhead.

WHERE CLAUSE OPTIMIZATION

Much of the overhead involved in modifying and removing rows is incurred locating the rows to be processed. DELETE and UPDATE statements usually contain a WHERE clause that defines the rows to be deleted or updated. INSERT, MERGE, and UPDATE statements can contain subqueries, which define either the data to be inserted or the updated row values. The obvious first step in optimizing the performance of these statements is to optimize these WHERE clauses or subqueries.

Subqueries and WHERE clauses in DML can be optimized using the principles discussed in previous chapters. For instance

❏ Creating indexes on columns in the WHERE clause
❏ Ensuring that the appropriate statistics (including histograms) have been collected and that statistics are up to date

---

If a DML statement contains a WHERE clause or a subquery, ensure that the subquery or WHERE clause is optimized using standard query optimization principles.

INDEX OVERHEAD

In previous chapters, we made extensive use of indexes to improve the performance of queries. Usually, when we could improve query performance by adding an index, we have done so. Although indexes can considerably improve query performance, they do impact the performance of DML. All of a table's indexes must be updated when a row is inserted or deleted, and an index must also be amended when an update changes any column that appears in the index.

It is, therefore, important that all our indexes contribute to query performance[1] because these indexes otherwise needlessly degrade DML performance. In particular, you should be especially careful when creating indexes on frequently updated columns. A row can be inserted or deleted only once but can be updated many times. Indexes on heavily updated columns or on tables that have a high insert/delete rate can, therefore, exact a particularly high cost.

Indexes always add to the overhead of INSERT and DELETE statements and might add to the overhead of UPDATE statements. Avoid over-indexing, especially on columns that are frequently updated.

---

[1] An exception can be made for foreign key indexes, which reduce lock contention, and for unique constraint indexes. We might want to keep these even if they don't contribute to query performance.

We looked in Chapter 5, "Indexing and Clustering," at the overhead of indexes, and it's worth briefly revisiting the overhead here. Figure 14-1 shows the overhead of each additional index on a 1,000 row delete. Each index adds substantial overhead to the delete because all matching index entries must be found and removed when removing the row. The overhead of deleting the indexes is, therefore, often greater than that of deleting the row itself.

Chapter 5 includes guidelines on identifying indexes that are not used in queries and that might, therefore, be candidates for removal. Remember that unique and foreign key indexes might be enforcing referential and data integrity; removing these in an attempt to improve DML throughput could jeopardize database integrity.

TRIGGER OVERHEAD

Triggers are PL/SQL blocks that execute when specified DML operations occur. The overhead of executing the PL/SQL is going to depend on the contents of the trigger and the rate of DML on the table involved, but there will always be some overhead.

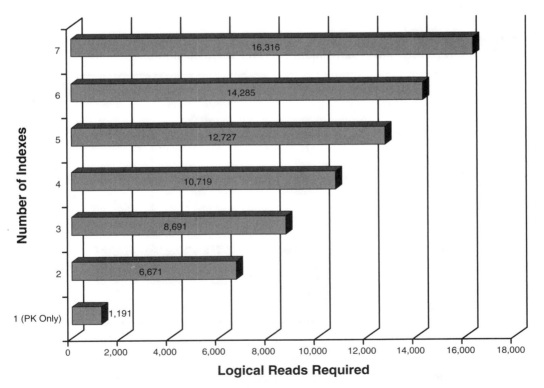

FIGURE 14-1 Overhead of indexes on DELETES.

Consider the following trigger, which maintains a UNIT_PRICE column that we might add to the SALES table:

```
CREATE TRIGGER sales_iu_trg
   BEFORE INSERT OR UPDATE
   ON sales
   FOR EACH ROW
   WHEN   (new.quantity_sold>0)
BEGIN
   :new.unit_price := :new.amount_sold/:new.quantity_sold;
END;
```

This is about as simple as a trigger gets, and yet it still creates a significant overhead on inserts and updates into the SALES table.

Figure 14-2 compares the performance of a 2.5 million row insert with and without the trigger. When the trigger was not present, the UNIT_PRICE column needed to be maintained within each SQL statement that INSERTED or UPDATED the SALES table. However, while the trigger automated this maintenance, the degradation in INSERT time was extremely significant.

Even the simplest trigger creates a significant overhead on DML. Using triggers to maintain derived columns is convenient but not always efficient.

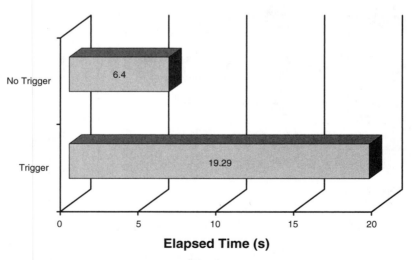

FIGURE 14-2   Overhead of a trigger on INSERT performance.

In Oracle 11g, we can create *virtual columns* defined by expressions on other columns within the table. Virtual columns can be used to implement some categories of denormalization and can do so with a lower overhead and greater reliability than triggers.

For instance, in 11g we can avoid creating a trigger and instead create a virtual column UNIT_PRICE defined as follows:

```
ALTER TABLE sales  ADD unit_price GENERATED ALWAYS AS (
     CASE WHEN quantity_sold > 0 THEN
          ROUND(amount_sold/quantity_sold,2)
     END );
```

> In Oracle 11g virtual columns can be used to create and maintain some derived columns without the overhead of trigger processing.

REFERENTIAL INTEGRITY

Referential integrity constraints prevent foreign key columns from referring to nonexistent primary key values. For instance, the following constraint prevents the CUST_ID column in SALES from referring to a nonexistent customer:

```
ALTER TABLE sales
     ADD CONSTRAINT fk1_sales FOREIGN KEY (cust_id)
          REFERENCES customers (cust_id)
```

The presence of the foreign key constraint forces Oracle to check the CUSTOMER table for every row inserted into the SALES table. Not surprisingly, this slows down inserts into SALES (see Figure 14-3). Similar overheads are involved during UPDATES and DELETEs.

> Using referential integrity constraints helps ensure self-consistency within your database and is generally recommended. However, be aware of the impact during INSERTs (and UPDATEs of foreign keys).

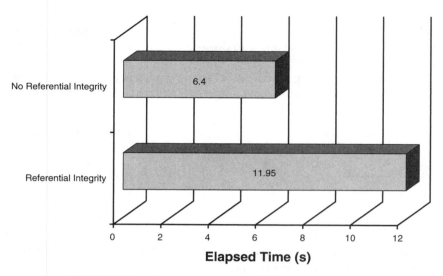

FIGURE 14-3 Overhead of referential integrity on inserts.

INSERT SPECIFIC OPTIMIZATIONS

Oracle provides quite a few optimizations designed to speed up inserts, especially when you want to insert multiple rows.

- ❏ Array processing enables multiple rows to be inserted in a single operation.
- ❏ Direct path inserts perform insert IO directly against the database files, bypassing the buffer cache.
- ❏ Multi-table inserts enable multiple tables to be involved in a single insert SQL statement.
- ❏ In Manual Segment Storage Management (MSSM) tablespaces, multiple free-lists help avoid contention for the data blocks that are to receive the inserts.
- ❏ Parallel DML—although available for all DML statements—is most often used with bulk insert operations.

ARRAY PROCESSING

We first looked at array processing in Chapter 6, "Application Design and Implementation," in which we discussed the use of array fetch and array insert. Array processing enables a single SQL to fetch or modify multiple rows in a single database call.

Array processing can be applied to all DML statements, but it's most valuable during insert. INSERTs add new rows into empty or nearly empty Oracle blocks, and it's almost as easy to add many rows to a block as to add a single row. Array insert also reduces the number of round trips between the application and the database that can be particularly important if you insert the rows across the network.

In many environments, array processing is provided transparently, whereas in others you need to employ specific programming techniques. Chapter 6 provides an overview of the techniques used in Java and PL/SQL.

Array processing can have a dramatic effect on insert performance. Figure 14-4 shows the effect of varying the array size on the performance of a bulk insert.

> Use the array INSERT facility whenever possible to improve bulk insert performance.

DIRECT PATH INSERTS

In a default, or *conventional mode,* insert, Oracle tries to insert rows into existing blocks that have spare capacity before creating new blocks. The new blocks and modified blocks will be processed in memory (in the buffer cache) and written out to disk later by the database writer process.

Direct path insert bypasses the buffer cache and writes directly to the database files on disk, bypassing the buffer cache. Only new blocks are used, so existing free space in the table is not reused. Only minimal redo log entries are generated when using direct path inserts. Figure 14-5 compares conventional mode insert with direct path insert.

In some, but certainly not all, circumstances direct path inserts can improve performance by reducing the overhead associated by buffer cache management (latches, free buffer waits, and so on) and in redo log IO.

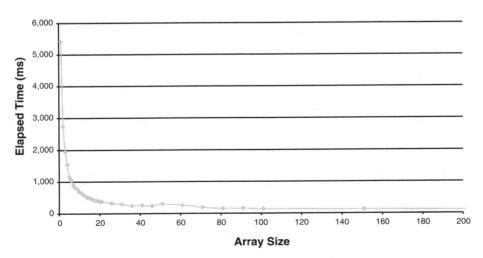

FIGURE 14-4   Performance of array insert.

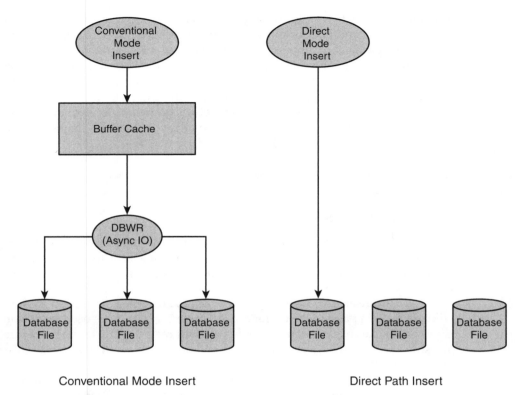

Conventional Mode Insert   Direct Path Insert

FIGURE 14-5   Direct path insert compared with conventional mode insert.

Direct IO can be invoked by using the APPEND hint, is performed by default in parallel inserts, and is also available when using SQL*LOADER to load data from files.

Direct path inserts are subject to a range of restrictions: for instance, the table cannot be clustered or contain object types, and after the direct path insert completes, no other SQL can read or modify the table within the same transaction: a COMMIT must be issued before any further SQLs can be issued against the table. Furthermore, a direct path insert places a table level lock on the table in question that blocks concurrent DML requests from other sessions.

If your buffer cache is subject to heavy concurrent activity, or redo log IO is a concern, direct path inserts are probably faster than conventional path, might result in less buffer cache contention between sessions, and result in better overall buffer cache efficiency.

However, direct mode IO will not always be faster. Remember that with conventional path inserts the application inserts the data into memory, whereas in direct path IO the data is written directly to disk. Memory *is* faster than disk,

so if memory is free and your disks are slow or busy, the disk IO overhead dominates and direct IO might actually be slower.

Furthermore, direct path inserts require a full table or partition lock on the
object in question. This lock blocks any concurrent DML execution, so direct path
inserts should not be attempted if other DML might be issued against the table at
the same time. We look at direct path insert and locking again in Chapter 15,
"Lock Contention."

Figure 14-6 compares direct and conventional mode IO on two database
hosts. One host has a fast IO subsystem, whereas the other has a single relatively
slow disk drive. For the system with the slow disk subsystem, direct path insert is
actually slower than conventional path, whereas for the system with faster disks,
the opposite is true.

Direct path IO can reduce redo log and buffer cache overhead or contention and might
be faster than conventional mode. However, if disk IO is the limiting factor, direct mode
insert might actually be slower than conventional mode.

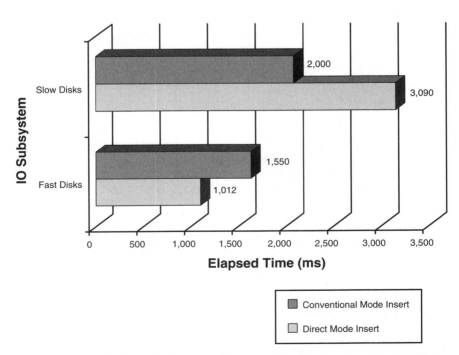

FIGURE 14-6 Direct mode insert can be slower than conventional inserts if the
disk subsystem is slow or overloaded.

Direct path insert is most commonly associated with CREATE TABLE AS SELECT and INSERT from SELECT statements. However, you can also use direct path insert when doing bulk inserts in PL/SQL, as in this example:

```
FORALL i IN 1 .. g_prods.LAST
    INSERT /*+ append */
        INTO SALES(PROD_ID, CUST_ID, TIME_ID,
                   CHANNEL_ID, PROMO_ID,
                   QUANTITY_SOLD, AMOUNT_SOLD)
    VALUES (g_prods(i), g_custs(i), g_times(i), g_channels(i),
            g_promos(i), g_quantities(i), g_amounts(i));
```

A direct path insert is indicated in EXPLAIN PLAN by the LOAD AS SELECT step. If the rows are inserted by an array insert, the child operation is BULK BIND GETS:

Id	Operation	Name	Rows	Cost (%CPU)	Time
0	INSERT STATEMENT		1	1 (0)	00:00:01
1	**LOAD AS SELECT**	SALES			
2	**BULK BINDS GET**				

In an INSERT from SELECT statement, the LOAD AS SELECT is followed by the execution plan for the SELECT statement:

Id	Operation	Name	Rows
0	INSERT STATEMENT		99999
1	**LOAD AS SELECT**	SALES	
2	**TABLE ACCESS FULL**	SALES_UPDATES	99999

Because direct path inserts cannot reuse free space within existing blocks, a table that is populated exclusively by direct path inserts tends to use more blocks, which make full table scans more expensive. Consequently, you might be motivated to rebuild tables populated by direct path inserts more frequently.

MULTI-TABLE INSERT

A single INSERT statement can insert rows into more than one table. This comes in handy if we have a source table containing new data that needs to be applied to multiple target tables.

For instance, say we receive the sales updates for the US and EMEA (Europe, Middle East, and Africa) in a single staging table but that each region has its own SALES fact table. Our first thought might be to issue multiple INSERT statements:

```
INSERT INTO sales_emea
        (PROD_ID, CUST_ID, TIME_ID, CHANNEL_ID,
         PROMO_ID, QUANTITY_SOLD, AMOUNT_SOLD)
    SELECT PROD_ID, CUST_ID, TIME_ID, CHANNEL_ID,
         PROMO_ID, QUANTITY_SOLD, AMOUNT_SOLD
    FROM sales_updates
    WHERE region = 'EMEA';

INSERT INTO sales_us
        (PROD_ID, CUST_ID, TIME_ID, CHANNEL_ID,
         PROMO_ID, QUANTITY_SOLD, AMOUNT_SOLD)
    SELECT PROD_ID, CUST_ID, TIME_ID, CHANNEL_ID,
         PROMO_ID, QUANTITY_SOLD, AMOUNT_SOLD
    FROM sales_updates
    WHERE region = 'US';
```

Alternatively, we can use a single INSERT, like this:

```
SQL> INSERT ALL
  2    WHEN region = 'EMEA' THEN INTO sales_emea
  3            (PROD_ID, CUST_ID, TIME_ID, CHANNEL_ID, PROMO_ID,
  4             QUANTITY_SOLD, AMOUNT_SOLD)
  5      VALUES (PROD_ID, CUST_ID, TIME_ID, CHANNEL_ID, PROMO_ID,
  6             QUANTITY_SOLD, AMOUNT_SOLD)
  7    WHEN region = 'US' THEN INTO sales_us
  8            (PROD_ID, CUST_ID, TIME_ID, CHANNEL_ID, PROMO_ID,
  9             QUANTITY_SOLD, AMOUNT_SOLD)
 10      VALUES (PROD_ID, CUST_ID, TIME_ID, CHANNEL_ID, PROMO_ID,
 11             QUANTITY_SOLD, AMOUNT_SOLD)
 12  SELECT * FROM sales_updates;
```

Id	Operation	Name	Rows
0	INSERT STATEMENT		1061K
1	**MULTI-TABLE INSERT**		
2	INTO	SALES_EMEA	
3	INTO	SALES_US	
4	TABLE ACCESS FULL	SALES_UPDATES	1061K

The multi-table insert outperforms the individual inserts because it needs to only do a single pass through the source table. Figure 14-7 illustrates the performance gain for our preceding example.

A multi-table INSERT statement might outperform multiple individual INSERT statements.

MANUAL SEGMENT STORAGE MANAGEMENT (MSSM) AND FREELISTS

We first discussed the role of freelists and Manual Segment Storage Management (ASSM) in Chapter 4, "Logical and Physical Database Design."

When MSSM is employed—relatively rarely in modern Oracle deployments—each table is associated with one or more *freelists*, which keep track of blocks that have free space and that are therefore eligible to be the target of INSERT operations. When multiple processes concurrently insert into tables with an insufficient number of freelists, contention can result, usually showing up as "buffer busy" waits. The solution is simply to add more freelists using an ALTER TABLE statement.

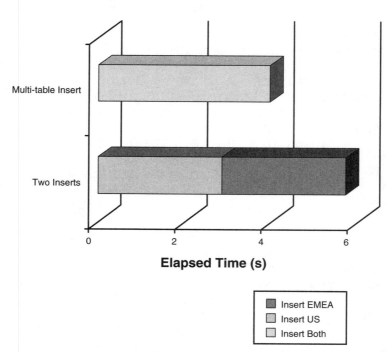

FIGURE 14-7 A multi-table INSERT can outperform multiple single-table inserts.

However, when using the default Automatic Segment Storage Management (ASSM) mechanisms, it is not necessary to manually configure freelists; Oracle automatically manages free space as to avoid this sort of contention.

If you use Manual Segment Storage Management (MSSM), make sure tables have sufficient freelists to support concurrent insert activities.

PARALLEL DML

We first looked at parallel DML in Chapter 13, "Parallel SQL." Although most bulk DML can exploit parallel DML, its most frequently used to optimize INSERT operations. Parallel DML is well-suited for bulk inserts using both NOLOGGING and Direct path inserts. (Parallel inserts use direct path inserts by default.) Remember that an ALTER SESSION ENABLE PARALLEL DML statement should be executed before issuing parallel DML. See Chapter 13 for more information on parallel DML.

DELETE OPERATIONS

It might not be intuitively obvious, but the deletion of a row is often the single-most expensive operation that the database ever performs upon the row. During a DELETE, some or all of the following must occur:

- ❏ Finding the row to be deleted (from the WHERE clause of the DELETE, if specified)
- ❏ Removing the row from the data block
- ❏ Finding and removing every entry in every index that refers to that row
- ❏ Checking referential integrity and, if a CASCADE DELETE constraint exists, removing all child rows
- ❏ Processing any ON DELETE triggers than might be defined against the table
- ❏ Creating ROLLBACK (undo) entries for all the above

Index lookups during delete can be particularly expensive because for a nonunique index, Oracle might need to scan many leaf blocks looking for matching entries.

Consequently, we have a strong motivation to optimize DELETE operations, and the most common approach to optimizing DELETEs is actually to avoid the delete all together by using TRUNCATE, dropping a partition, or sometimes even rebuilding the table from scratch.

TRUNCATE

The TRUNCATE TABLE command allows *all* rows to be removed from a table with minimal overhead. Rather than removing rows one at a time—generating rollback segment and redo information for each row—all the rows associated with the table are removed in a single irreversible action. Using TRUNCATE can also reset the table's high water mark that improves subsequent full table scans (see Chapter 9, "Tuning Table Access").

Strictly speaking, the TRUNCATE command is a Data Definition Language (DDL) statement rather than a Data Manipulation Language (DML) statement. This means that it cannot be rolled back, and it issues an implicit COMMIT (so any preceding statements will be committed and also will become permanent).

Remember that TRUNCATE can be used only to remove *all* rows from a table.

When removing all the rows of a table, consider using TRUNCATE rather than DELETE.

PARTITIONS

One of the most powerful incentives for implementing partitions is the ability to purge unneeded rows from a table by dropping a partition rather than by issuing DELETE statements.

For instance in Oracle's SH sample schema, the SALES table is partitioned by the value of TIME_ID. If we want to purge old SALES data, we can drop the relevant partition rather than having to DELETE them. By simply dropping the partition, we can remove all these rows almost immediately. Alternately, issuing a DELETE statement requires a large amount of IO, both to identify and remove the rows and to identify and remove the index entries.

If deleting stale rows from large tables is a significant overhead, consider creating a table that is range or interval partitioned on the date column that identifies the rows to be purged. You can then remove these rows by dropping the partition in question.

CREATE TABLE AS SELECT

INSERTs and DELETEs will be significantly slower for tables with a large number of indexes. If you regularly insert large numbers of rows into such a table during a batch window that has no associated query activity, it might be worth dropping the indexes before the data load and re-creating them later. In fact, you could re-create the table using CREATE TABLE AS SELECT only including the rows that are to be kept.

This will be especially effective if you use NOLOGGING and PARALLEL clauses when re-creating the table and its indexes. NOLOGGING is discussed later in this chapter and parallel options in Chapter 13. CREATE TABLE AS SELECT also automatically uses the direct path insert mode discussed earlier in this chapter.

To reduce the overhead of deleting from heavily indexed tables, you could consider "logically" deleting the rows using a status column. Queries against the table would have a WHERE clause condition that eliminates the "logically" deleted rows. During a regular batch window the rows could either be deleted, or the table could be rebuilt without the unwanted rows.

> If you need to delete a large proportion of rows from a table, it might be more efficient to rebuild the table without the unneeded rows using CREATE TABLE AS SELECT.

UPDATE AND MERGE OPERATIONS

UPDATE changes the values of existing rows in a table. MERGE updates rows if they exist, and inserts new rows where there is no match.

CORRELATED UPDATES

A correlated update is an UPDATE statement in which both the rows to be updated and the new values for those rows are defined by identical or similar SELECT statements. This might occur, for instance, when a staging table contains batch updates to be applied to a fact table.

The obvious way to approach this (and maybe the only way in older versions of Oracle) is to repeat the subquery in both the SET and WHERE clauses. In this example, SALES_UPDATES contains changes to be applied to the SALES table:

```
SQL> UPDATE sales s
  2  SET
  3      (amount_sold,
  4      quantity_sold
  5      ) =
  6          (SELECT amount_sold, quantity_sold
  7           FROM sales_updates u
  8           WHERE     u.prod_id = s.prod_id
  9                 AND u.cust_id = s.cust_id
 10                 AND u.time_id = s.time_id
 11                 AND u.channel_id = s.channel_id)
 12  WHERE EXISTS
 13          (SELECT 0
 14           FROM sales_updates u
```

```
15                WHERE      u.prod_id = s.prod_id
16                    AND u.cust_id = s.cust_id
17                    AND u.time_id = s.time_id
18                    AND u.channel_id = s.channel_id);
```

Id	Operation	Name	Rows
0	UPDATE STATEMENT		1072K
1	UPDATE	SALES	
* 2	HASH JOIN RIGHT SEMI		1072K
3	INDEX FAST FULL SCAN	SALES_UPDATES_PK	999K
4	TABLE ACCESS FULL	SALES	2476K
5	TABLE ACCESS BY INDEX ROWID	SALES_UPDATES	1
* 6	INDEX RANGE SCAN	SALES_UPDATES_PK	1

This approach is inefficient because the SALES_UPDATE table is queried twice. A more efficient approach is to update a "joined" version of both tables, by issuing an UPDATE against an in-line view that references both tables:

```
SQL> UPDATE (SELECT s.amount_sold,
  2                 s.quantity_sold,
  3                 u.amount_sold new_amount_sold,
  4                 u.quantity_sold new_quantity_sold
  5         FROM    sales s
  6                 JOIN
  7                 sales_updates u
  8                 USING (prod_id, cust_id, time_id,
  9                        channel_id, promo_id))
 10  SET amount_sold = new_amount_sold,
 11      quantity_sold = new_quantity_sold;
```

Id	Operation	Name	Rows
0	UPDATE STATEMENT		1021K
1	UPDATE	SALES	
* 2	HASH JOIN		1021K
3	TABLE ACCESS FULL	SALES_UPDATES	999K
4	TABLE ACCESS FULL	SALES	2476K

Although this technique employs a somewhat awkward syntax, it eliminates the duplicate accesses of the update table and results in optimal performance.

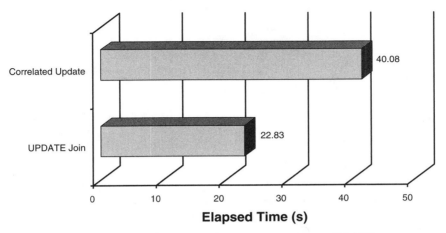

FIGURE 14-8 UPDATE join versus Correlated UPDATE.

To use this UPDATE join technique, there must be a unique index on the join columns in the source table (SALES_UPDATES in our case) so that Oracle can verify that there is no more than one row for each row in the target table (SALES in this example).

The performance advantages gained by the UPDATE join for the preceding examples are shown in Figure 14-8.

Consider using the UPDATE join technique in preference to correlated UPDATES that include redundant SET and WHERE subqueries.

OPTIMIZING MERGE

The MERGE statement processes rows in a source table, and applies either IN-SERTS or UPDATES to a target table depending on whether there are matching rows in that target table. Such operations are common in data warehousing environments where a staging table might contain both new and updated rows to be applied to a fact table.

Without the MERGE statement, we need to issue both an INSERT and an UPDATE. For example, if we had a SALES_UPDATES table that contained both new SALES rows and updates to existing rows, we might apply those changes using an UPDATE and INSERT statement as follows:

```
UPDATE (SELECT s.amount_sold, s.quantity_sold,
               u.amount_sold new_amount_sold,
               u.quantity_sold new_quantity_sold
```

```
    FROM    sales s
            JOIN sales_updates u
            USING (prod_id, cust_id, time_id, channel_id, promo_id))
    SET amount_sold = new_amount_sold,
        quantity_sold = new_quantity_sold;

INSERT INTO sales s
    SELECT *
    FROM sales_updates u
    WHERE NOT EXISTS
            (SELECT 0
             FROM sales s
             WHERE      s.prod_id = u.prod_id
                    AND s.cust_id = u.cust_id
                    AND s.time_id = u.time_id
                    AND s.channel_id = u.channel_id
                    AND s.promo_id = u.promo_id);
```

The MERGE statement enables us to perform the operation with a single statement:

```
MERGE INTO sales s USING sales_updates u
    ON (s.prod_id=u.prod_id      AND s.cust_id=u.cust_id
        AND s.time_id=u.time_id AND s.channel_id=u.channel_id
        AND s.promo_id = u.promo_id)
    WHEN MATCHED THEN
UPDATE SET  s.amount_sold  =u.amount_sold,
            s.quantity_sold=u.quantity_sold
WHEN NOT MATCHED THEN
INSERT VALUES ( u.prod_id, u.cust_id, u.time_id ,
                u.channel_id, u.promo_id,
                u.quantity_sold, u.amount_sold);
```

Not only does this allow us to simplify our application logic, but it is also usually much more efficient. Figure 14-9 compares the performance of MERGE with that of the combined UPDATE and INSERT statement approach.

A single MERGE statement usually significantly outperforms the combination of UP-DATE and INSERT statements.

The MERGE statement performs an outer join between the target and source tables. This outer join identifies new rows and updated rows in a single

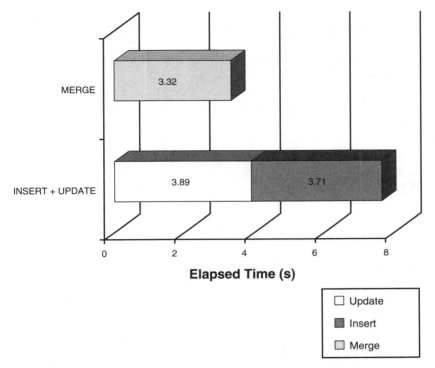

FIGURE 14-9 MERGE statement performance compared with INSERT and UPDATE.

operation. Optimizing the performance of the outer join is, therefore, critical to the performance of the MERGE. If no suitable index exists, a standard hash outer join is used:

```
-------------------------------------------------------------
| Id  | Operation           | Name          | Rows  |
-------------------------------------------------------------
|  0  | MERGE STATEMENT     |               | 19998 |
|  1  |  MERGE              | SALES         |       |
|  2  |   VIEW              |               |       |
|* 3  |    HASH JOIN OUTER  |               | 19998 |
|  4  |     TABLE ACCESS FULL| SALES_UPDATES | 19998 |
|  5  |     TABLE ACCESS FULL| SALES        | 2476K |
-------------------------------------------------------------
```

If there is an index on the join keys in the source or target table, the index can be used to optimize the outer join. As with all joins, an index-based approach might or might not be optimal, depending on the size of the tables and the

number of matching rows. You might also need to use an INDEX hint or use
other means to persuade the optimizer to use the index:

```
SQL> MERGE /*+    index(s) */ INTO sales s USING sales_updates u
  2      ON (s.prod_id=u.prod_id AND s.cust_id=u.cust_id
            AND s.time_id=u.time_id
  3            AND s.channel_id=u.channel_id AND s.promo_id = u.promo_id)
  4      WHEN MATCHED THEN
  5  UPDATE SET    s.amount_sold  =u.amount_sold,
  6                s.quantity_sold=u.quantity_sold
  7  WHEN NOT MATCHED THEN
  8  INSERT VALUES ( u.prod_id, u.cust_id, u.time_id  ,
  9                  u.channel_id, u.promo_id,
 10                  u.quantity_sold, u.amount_sold);
```

```
-----------------------------------------------------------------
| Id  | Operation                      | Name          | Rows  |
-----------------------------------------------------------------
|   0 | MERGE STATEMENT                |               | 19998 |
|   1 |  MERGE                         | SALES         |       |
|   2 |   VIEW                         |               |       |
|   3 |    NESTED LOOPS OUTER          |               | 19998 |
|   4 |     TABLE ACCESS FULL          | SALES_UPDATES | 19998 |
|   5 |     TABLE ACCESS BY INDEX ROWID| SALES         |     1 |
|*  6 |      INDEX UNIQUE SCAN         | SALES_PK      |     1 |
-----------------------------------------------------------------
```

In our example, the index-based Nested Loops outer join significantly outperformed the Hash outer join. Figure 14-10 shows how the two compared for
our example MERGE statement.

> The performance of a MERGE statement is dependent on the performance of the
> OUTER JOIN that is performed to identify rows for INSERT and UPDATE. Optimize
> this join to optimize the MERGE by determining the optimal join type—usually Hash
> outer join or Nested Loops.

COMMIT OPTIMIZATION

A transaction is a set of DML statements that will succeed or fail as a unit. In Oracle (and in the ANSI standard), a transaction implicitly commences when a DML
statement is issued and completes with a COMMIT or ROLLBACK statement or
when a program terminates.

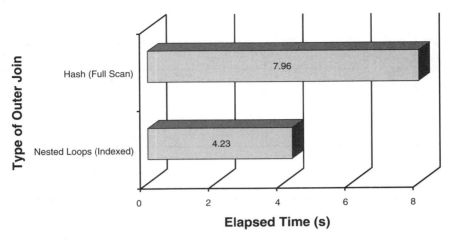

FIGURE 14-10 MERGE performance for indexed and nonindexed outer join.

A COMMIT always requires a write to disk (with some exceptions that we will consider soon). This is so your transaction is not lost if the system should crash and information in memory is lost. Because COMMIT involves physical disk IO, it is an important factor in DML performance.

COMMIT FREQUENCY

Because a COMMIT always requires some disk IO, it follows that the more frequently a program commits, the more IO overhead it incurs.

Usually, the determination of when to COMMIT a transaction is driven by application design or user requirements rather than by performance considerations. For instance, if users press a SAVE button in an on-line application, they have a reasonable expectation that the transaction is now saved—and this would require a COMMIT. You should never place performance ahead of transactional integrity by avoiding a commit that is required by application logic.

On the other hand, when coding bulk load or batch jobs, you might have some options as to how often to COMMIT. Committing less frequently can improve batch throughput. Figure 14-11 shows elapsed times for various COMMIT frequencies. By reducing the COMMIT frequency, we reduced elapsed times for this example job by more than 75 percent.

Because committing a transaction involves an I/O overhead, COMMIT infrequently during bulk updates if the application logic permits it.

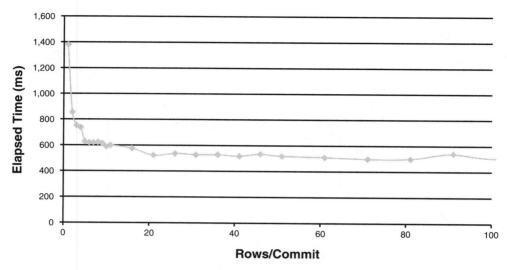

FIGURE 14-11 Commit frequency and batch throughput.

BATCH AND NOWAIT COMMIT

By default, a COMMIT requires Oracle to immediately write redo log entries to disk. This ensures that a transaction can be recovered in the event of a database failure, and this behavior ensures the Durable characteristic of ACID (Atomic-Consistent-Independent-Durable) transactions.

However, Oracle enables you to modify this behavior to reduce commit overhead. You should consider this only if you are prepared to accept the reduction in transactional integrity that will result: It's a core assumption of most applications that when committed, a transaction cannot be lost: If you take advantage of some of the options we are about to discuss, this assumption might be violated.

The COMMIT statement can be associated with the NOWAIT clause. Normally, when a COMMIT is issued, control does not return to the calling application until the IO to the redo log completes. When the NOWAIT clause is in effect, control returns to the calling application immediately, and the IO to the redo log occurs in the background. There's a small chance with NOWAIT that the IO might fail, even though the COMMIT appears to have succeeded.

The BATCH clause of the COMMIT statement delays processing even further than the NOWAIT clause. With NOWAIT, the IO to the redo log occurs immediately, even though the COMMIT statement does not wait for the IO to complete. With the BATCH option, the IO to the redo log might occur sometime later, when a batch of redo log entries is ready to be written. This reduces the IO rate to the redo log because more redo entries will be written in each IO. However, the chance that a committed transaction might not be written to disk will be higher.

In Oracle 11g, the COMMIT_LOGGING parameter can be set to BATCH, which will force the COMMIT BATCH behavior on all sessions, unless they override it with a COMMIT IMMEDIATE statement or with an ALTER SESSION clause.

The Oracle 11g COMMIT_WAIT parameter, if set to NOWAIT, can apply the COMMIT NOWAIT behavior to all sessions, unless they override it with an ALTER SESSION statement or a COMMIT WAIT statement.

The 11g COMMIT_WAIT parameter can also be set to FORCE_WAIT. This causes transactions in all sessions to wait for the redo log IO to complete and overrides the use of NOWAIT in COMMIT statements or a setting of NOWAIT in an ALTER SESSION statement.

In Oracle 10g, both the NOWAIT and BATCH behaviors are controlled by the COMMIT_WRITE parameter that can accept a comma-separated string containing various combinations of WAIT, NOWAIT, BATCH, and IMMEDIATE.

Confused? Table 14-1 summarizes the various settings and behaviors.

The performance effect of both NOWAIT and BATCH is to reduce the application overhead of issuing a COMMIT. The performance improvement is similar to that gained by reducing the commit frequency. NOWAIT in particular can provide a best of both worlds alternative to very low commit frequencies because rows can be committed frequently, but the application can continue to process without waiting for the redo log IO. However, there is still the chance that a committed transaction could be lost in the event of database failure.

BATCH has a similar effect on application performance but can also increase the amount of concurrent throughput on the system because the overall

Table 14-1 COMMIT BATCH and NOWAIT Options

BEHAVIOR	COMMIT CLAUSE	10g PARAMETERS	11g PARAMETERS
COMMIT statement completes only when the redo log entry is written to the redo log.	COMMIT [WAIT] [IMMEDIATE]	COMMIT_WRITE = 'IMMEDIATE,WAIT'	COMMIT_WAIT = WAIT
			COMMIT_LOGGING = IMMEDIATE
When a COMMIT is issued, redo is written to disk immediately, but control can return to the application before that IO completes.	COMMIT NOWAIT	COMMIT_WRITE = 'IMMEDIATE, NOWAIT'	COMMIT_WAIT = NOWAIT
			COMMIT_LOGGING = IMMEDIATE
When a COMMIT is issued, redo is held in memory and later written to disk in batches.	COMMIT NOWAIT BATCH	COMMIT_WRITE = 'BATCH, NOWAIT'	COMMIT_WAIT = NOWAIT
			COMMIT_LOGGING = BATCH

number of redo log IOs are reduced; more redo log entries are written in each IO, reducing the number of IOs required. We look more at redo log IO in Chapter 21, "Disk IO Tuning Fundamentals."

Figure 14-12 compares the effect of NOWAIT and BATCH options on transaction throughput. Both NOWAIT and BATCH increase transaction throughput, especially when the commit frequency is high.

The NOWAIT and BATCH COMMIT capabilities can reduce the overhead of COMMIT and the overall amount of redo log IO. However, both violate some long established expectations as to the reliability of committed transactions and should be used with extreme care.

NOLOGGING

Finally, let's look at using the NOLOGGING keyword to reduce the amount of redo generated by DML.

In the previous section we saw how redo log IO, as a consequence of commit processing, can impact the performance of DML statements and transactions. Reducing COMMIT frequency, using COMMIT NOWAIT, and utilizing direct path insert all have the effect of either reducing the amount of redo IO, or reducing the application wait for that IO.

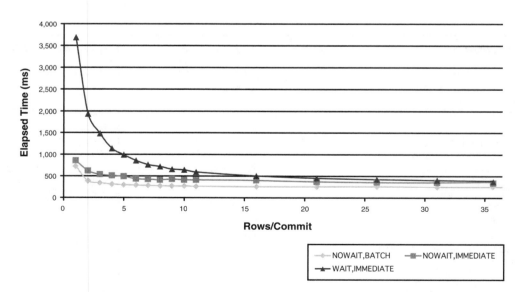

FIGURE 14-12   Effect of NOWAIT and BATCH COMMIT options.

The NOLOGGING option takes the reduction of redo log overhead even further, by directly eliminating most of the redo generation that occurs when DML is issued. However, because redo log entries are essential to recovering an object in the event of a database restore, this option should be used only for tables that contain short term or noncritical information that you are prepared to lose in the event that you need to recover the database from backup.

The NOLOGGING option can apply to the following commands and operations:

❏ **Create Table as Select:** In which a table is created and populated from the results of a SELECT statement.

❏ **Create index:** An index can always be rebuilt from table data, so there's no risk of data loss when you create an index with the NOLOGGING option.

❏ **Direct path inserts:** Either as a result of a parallel operation, APPEND hint, or from SQL*Loader. Direct path inserts that occur after an object has been created with the NOLOGGING option will not be logged.

Because the data inserted with the NOLOGGING mode can't be restored from redo logs, you're not likely to use this facility for your critical application data. You might use the NOLOGGING feature in the following circumstances:

❏ Loading a temporary table for intermediate processing in a long running batch job
❏ Quickly building a dispensable summary or aggregate table

Also note that because redo log writes are performed asynchronously by the redo log writer, you might not obtain a noticeable performance improvement for many operations. However, you will see an improvement in commit times and might see a general system-wide performance improvement when redo log activity is a bottleneck.

You can use NOLOGGING to reduce the redo log overhead for INSERT operations. But be aware that these objects will not be recoverable in the event of a database failure.

SUMMARY

In this chapter we looked at how to optimize DML statements: INSERT, UPDATE, DELETE, and MERGE.

Many DML statements include a query component—to identify the rows to be processed or to gather the new rows to be inserted. Optimizing this query aspect—tuning the DML WHERE clause for instance—is usually the first step in DML tuning.

Indexes exist mainly to optimize query performance, but this benefit comes at significant cost for DML statements. Index maintenance is often the single biggest component of DML performance. Therefore, make sure that all indexes are needed. Referential integrity and triggers create an overhead on DML as well.

Inserts can be optimized by using the array interface—inserting multiple rows in a single call—and by using direct path inserts, which bypass the buffer cache. Direct path insert is not always indicated however, and might not always be faster.

DELETEs are often the most-expensive DML operation; you can sometimes avoid deletes by range partitioning the table and dropping partitions containing old data rather than issuing deletes. In some cases it might actually be quicker to rebuild a table rather than to delete a large number of rows.

UPDATEs that include a subquery in both the SET and WHERE clauses, sometimes called correlated UPDATEs, can often be optimized by performing an UPDATE join.

Using a MERGE is often faster than issuing separate UPDATE and INSERT statements. MERGE statements use an outer join to distinguish between rows to be inserted and those to be updated. Optimize this outer join, possibly by creating an appropriate index.

In transactions you can increase throughput by reducing commit frequency. You should do this only if your application transaction logic allows, however. Likewise, COMMIT NOWAIT or COMMIT BATCH can increase throughput, though the effect on transactional integrity will often be unacceptable.

For temporary tables or tables that do not need to be recovered in the event of failure, the NOLOGGING option, which reduces redo log generation, might be a useful optimization.

Parallel DML, discussed in depth in Chapter 13, can also increase DML performance, though at a possible cost to system load and concurrency.

Lock Contention

This chapter is the first of several that deal with the various types of contention that commonly inflict Oracle databases.

As we discussed in Chapter 1, "Oracle Performance Tuning: A Methodical Approach," contention occurs when two or more sessions attempt to simultaneously utilize limited or serialized resources. Contention limits the amount of work that the database can get done because sessions queue up for the limited resources concerned.

We introduced the concepts of transactions and locking in Chapter 4, "Logical and Physical Database Design." The ACID (Atomic-Consistent-Independent-Durable) properties of transactions, especially the consistency characteristic, require that Oracle limit concurrent changes to table data. Locks are the mechanism by which Oracle implements these constraints.

Most locks are row level locks that prevent two sessions from changing the same row. And most of these row level locks occur as a result of DML issued by the application. Therefore, application design has a big impact on locking. We first introduced the essential locking minimization design patterns in Chapter 6, "Application Design and Implementation," and we revisit and expand upon those principles in this chapter.

There are some circumstances in which low contention row level locking can break down into locks that apply to multiple rows: possibly all rows in a block or even all rows in a table. We look at how to diagnose and prevent these row level locking failures in this chapter.

The locking that results from application DML is not the only locking that you observe in a busy oracle database. Oracle uses locks to synchronize some internal activities such as modifications to the data dictionary. Sometimes contention for these internal locks can cause issues, so we examine these locks as well.

LOCK TYPES AND MODES

Oracle categorizes locks using a two character code. The code, lock names, and descriptions can be found in the table V$LOCK_TYPE:

```
SQL> SELECT TYPE, name, description
  2    FROM v$lock_type
  3    ORDER BY TYPE;
TYPE NAME                   DESCRIPTION
---- --------------------   -------------------------------------------------
AD   ASM Disk AU Lock       Synchronizes accesses to a specific ASM disk AU
AE   Edition Lock           Prevent Dropping an edition in use
AF   Advisor Framework      This enqueue is used to serialize access to an
                            advisor task
AG   Analytic Workspace     Synchronizes generation use of a particular
     Generation             workspace
AK   GES Deadlock Test      Lock used for internal testing
AM   ASM Enqueue            ASM instance general-purpose enqueue
     . . .                      . . .
```

There are almost 200 lock types, most of which are internal and rarely seen. For most applications and databases, the locks we see most often are the TM (DML) and TX (transaction) locks. You will often see the combination of TM and TX locks when a DML statement is issued against an object. You can observe all the locks that are currently held in the view V$LOCK—more on that view later.

Locks can be held in a variety of modes. First, locks can be held in exclusive mode or shared mode. Shared mode locks prevent exclusive mode locks of the same type but not other shared mode locks. So you can take out a shared mode lock if you want to prevent anyone else getting an exclusive mode lock.

Locks can be held at the table level or the row level. The combination of shared/exclusive and table/row accxounts for four of the five lock modes. There's also a fifth mode—shared row exclusive—that Oracle can take out on your behalf in some circumstances. Table 15-1 lists the Oracle lock modes.

Let's look at some of these simple locks in action. The V_MY_LOCKS view is created if you install the utility packages available at this book's Web site; it has the following definition:

Table 15-1   Oracle Lock Modes

LMODE VALUE (IN V$LOCK)	CODE[1]	DESCRIPTION
1	NULL	No Lock
2	SS or RS	Shared row lock
3	SX or RX	Exclusive row lock
4	S	Shared table lock
5	SSX or SRX	Shared row exclusive lock
6	X	Exclusive table lock

```
SELECT TYPE,name,
       lock_mode(lmode) lock_mode , id1, id2, lmode,
       DECODE(TYPE, 'TM',(SELECT object_name
                          FROM dba_objects
                          WHERE object_id = id1))
           table_name
 FROM v$lock JOIN v$lock_type USING (type)
WHERE sid = (SELECT sid
             FROM v$session
             WHERE audsid = USERENV('sessionid'))
   and type <> 'AE'
```

First, let's issue a simple SQL that updates a row:

```
SQL> UPDATE customers
  2    SET cust_valid = 'Y'
  3    WHERE cust_id = 49671;

SQL> SELECT TYPE, name, lock_mode, table_name FROM v_my_locks;
TYPE NAME              LOCK_MODE               TABLE_NAME
---- ----------------  ----------------------- -----------
TM   DML               Row-Exclusive (RX)      CUSTOMERS
TX   Transaction       Exclusive (X)
```

We see two locks. The TM lock is associated with the table, but the lock mode of RX tells us that the locks applied are actually exclusive row level locks. The locks prevent anyone else from updating the same row at the same time. The TX lock is taken out whenever a transaction is in progress.

---

[1] The Oracle documentation set is inconsistent in its use of codes, sometimes referring to Row share as RX, sometimes as SX. The same inconsistencies apply to the other lock mode codes.

We can get the same lock profile by querying the row with the FOR UP-
DATE clause:

```
SQL> SELECT *
  2  FROM customers
  3  WHERE cust_id = 49671
  4  FOR UPDATE;

SQL> SELECT TYPE, name, lock_mode, table_name FROM v_my_locks;
TYPE NAME             LOCK_MODE                TABLE_NAME
---- --------------- ------------------------ ---------------

TM   DML              Row-Exclusive (RX)       CUSTOMERS
TX   Transaction      Exclusive (X)
```

In a simple transaction, you will obtain a single TX lock and one TM lock for
each table involved. Only one TM lock will be acquired, even if multiple rows in
the table are locked:

```
SQL> UPDATE customers
  2     SET cust_valid = 'Y'
  3  WHERE cust_id = 100667;
1 row updated.

SQL> UPDATE sales
  2     SET channel_id = 2
  3  WHERE cust_id = 100667;
5 rows updated.

SQL> SELECT TYPE, name, lock_mode, table_name FROM v_my_locks;
TYPE NAME             LOCK_MODE                TABLE_NAME
---- --------------- ------------------------ ---------------

TM   DML              Row-Exclusive (RX)       CUSTOMERS
TM   DML              Row-Exclusive (RX)       SALES
TX   Transaction      Exclusive (X)
```

We can lock entire tables if we want using the LOCK TABLE keyword, and
we can specify a lock mode as well:

```
SQL> LOCK TABLE customers IN EXCLUSIVE MODE;
Table(s) Locked.
SQL>
SQL> SELECT TYPE, name, lock_mode, table_name FROM v_my_locks;
TYPE NAME             LOCK_MODE                TABLE_NAME
---- --------------- ------------------------ ---------------

TM   DML              Exclusive (X)            CUSTOMERS
```

Normal application level locking usually results in lock entries similar to those previously shown. Although a wide variety of internal lock situations can arise in Oracle, and also a variety of blocking scenarios, the simple row level locks as previously shown are the most common types of locks you'll see acquired in most databases.

WAITING FOR LOCKS

By default, a session that requests a lock held by another session must wait until the lock is released, which occurs when the holding session issues a COMMIT or ROLLBACK. These waits are our primary concern from a performance point of view because they represent database sessions that cannot do their work and result in increased response times.

Applications can, however, attempt to obtain locks and, if the lock is not immediately available, exit from the attempt with an error. The session can attempt to gain a lock with the FOR UPDATE clause, using the NOWAIT clause. If the lock is not available, an error will be raised as in this example:

```
SQL> SELECT *
  2  FROM customers
  3  WHERE cust_id = 49671
  4  FOR  UPDATE NOWAIT ;
FROM customers
     *
ERROR at line 2:
ORA-00054: resource busy and acquire with NOWAIT specified
or timeout expired
```

The session can also indicate a willingness to wait for a specified number of seconds, as in this example:

```
SQL> SELECT *
  2  FROM customers
  3  WHERE cust_id = 49671
  4  FOR UPDATE WAIT 2;
FROM customers
     *
ERROR at line 2:
ORA-30006: resource busy; acquire with WAIT timeout expired
```

You can use the SKIPPED LOCKED clause to skip those rows that are already locked. By using this clause you can implement concurrent threads of execution that process eligible rows for processing, without waiting on each other.

For instance, in the following example, there are nine rows with the 'X' code for CUST_VALID, but another session has five of the rows locked. By using SKIP LOCKED we can fetch the unlocked rows only:

```
SQL> SELECT COUNT( * )
  2  FROM customers
  3  WHERE cust_valid = 'X';
  COUNT(*)
----------
         9
SQL>
SQL> SELECT cust_id
  2  FROM customers
  3  WHERE cust_valid = 'X'
  4  FOR UPDATE SKIP LOCKED;
  CUST_ID
----------
      3602
     32237
     12108
    103435
```

The FOR UPDATE clause enables us to preemptively lock rows; SKIP LOCKED, NOWAIT, and WAIT clauses enable us to modify the behavior of the clause when locks are already held.

A *deadlock* occurs when two transactions are each waiting for the other to release a lock; they each block each other, and neither can proceed. For instance, consider the situation in which one transaction attempts to transfer $100 from account #2 to account #1. Simultaneously, another transaction attempts to transfer $300 from account #1 to account #2. If the timing of the two transactions is sufficiently unfortunate, each might end up waiting for the other to release a lock, resulting in a stalemate that never ends.

Luckily Oracle *does* intervene to eliminate deadlocks by terminating one of the transactions:

```
SQL> update accounts set balance=balance-100 where account_id=1;
update accounts set balance=balance-100 where account_id=1
        *
ERROR at line 1:
ORA-00060: deadlock detected while waiting for resource
```

Deadlocks can occur in any database system, but in a row level locking database such as Oracle, the possibility of a deadlock is usually low. You can further reduce the frequency of deadlocks by locking rows or tables in a consistent order and by keeping your transactions as short as possible.

If you are building an application in which deadlocks seem likely to occur, and you cannot reorganize your transactions to avoid them, you can add logic to your programs to handle deadlocks and retry the transaction.

MONITORING AND ANALYZING LOCKS

Oracle collects a lot of data about locks and locking. Despite the extensive array of information available, it can still be difficult to completely identify the causes of and solutions for lock contention. We need information that can help us answer the key questions:

- ❏ Is there a locking problem?
- ❏ What are the SQLs, sessions, and objects involved?
- ❏ Who is holding the locks, and who is waiting on them?

LOCK WAIT STATISTICS

It's the time spent waiting for locks that primarily concerns us: It is these lock waits that throttle throughput and increase response time.

Whenever an Oracle session needs to stop processing and wait for a lock, or for any other resource for that matter, it will record the wait in the various "wait interface" tables such as V$SYSTEM_EVENT. We can interrogate these views to measure the extent of lock waits and hence to determine if we have a high level lock wait problem.

Lock waits—sometimes referred to as enqueue waits[2]—are identified by the *enq:* prefix, which is then followed by the two character lock code. As we previously saw, the two-character lock codes are defined in the V$LOCK_TYPE table. The wait identifier also includes a brief description of the wait, and there can be more than one wait type for a particular lock code. For instance, here are the varieties of waits that are associated with the TX (transaction) lock wait type:

---

[2] Lock waits are referred to as enqueues because you wait in a queue to obtain the lock. This is in contrast to some other waits, latches in particular, for which there is no ordered queue.

```
SQL> SELECT name
  2  FROM v$event_name
  3  WHERE name LIKE 'enq: TX%';
NAME
---------------------------------------------
enq: TX - row lock contention
enq: TX - allocate ITL entry
enq: TX - index contention
enq: TX - contention
```

This next query breaks out the lock waits and compares them to other high-level wait categories and to CPU time. This query reveals the amount of time spent waiting for locks relative to other activities:

```
SQL> WITH system_event AS
  2    (SELECT CASE WHEN event LIKE 'enq:%'
  3               THEN event  ELSE wait_class
  4           END wait_type, e.*
  5       FROM v$system_event e)
  6  SELECT wait_type,SUM(total_waits) total_waits,
  7          round(SUM(time_waited_micro)/1000000,2)
  8          time_waited_seconds, ROUND(  SUM(time_waited_micro)
  9              * 100
 10              / SUM(SUM(time_waited_micro)) OVER (), 2) pct
 11  FROM (SELECT  wait_type, event, total_waits, time_waited_micro
 12         FROM     system_event e
 13         UNION
 14         SELECT   'CPU', stat_name, NULL, VALUE
 15         FROM v$sys_time_model
 16         WHERE stat_name IN ('background cpu time', 'DB CPU')) l
 17  WHERE wait_type <> 'Idle'
 18  GROUP BY wait_type
 19  ORDER BY 4 DESC
 20  /
WAIT_TYPE                        TOTAL_WAITS TIME_WAITED_SECONDS    PCT
------------------------------- ------------ ------------------- ------
User I/O                           4,140,679           11,987.46  33.56
System I/O                         3,726,628            9,749.85  27.30
CPU                                                     8,084.14  22.63
Other                                 69,987            1,380.59   3.87
Commit                               684,784            1,327.28   3.72
enq: TX - row lock contention             13            1,218.91   3.41
enq: TM - contention                       6              751.16   2.10
Concurrency                           29,350              486.48   1.36
Configuration                         40,486              428.82   1.20
```

> Times spent waiting for events prefixed by *enq:* in the wait interface tables, such as V$SYSTEM_EVENT, are the best measures of overall lock contention.

Of course, these numbers represent totals because the database was last started and hence are of limited use for a database that has been running for some time or just experienced a change in workload. If you install the utility scripts that are available on this book's Web site, you can use the LOCK_DELTA_VIEW to retrieve timing for a sample period. Each time you query from the view within a session, it reports only the statistics for the period since your last query. So if we run the following query twice within a minute, we get short-term statistics showing how lock waits compare to other lock times:

```
SQL> SELECT wait_type, time_waited_ms, pct_time, sample_seconds
  2     FROM lock_delta_view
  3     WHERE pct_time > 1;
WAIT_TYPE                         TIME_WAITED_MS   PCT_TIME SAMPLE_SECONDS
-------------------------------   --------------   -------- --------------
CPU                                   130127.864         80             51
enq: TX - row lock contention          18463.13         11             51
Scheduler                               6382.076          4             51
User I/O                                5727.745          4             51
```

In this case, we see that lock waits accounted for approximately 11 percent of total wait time over the past 51 seconds.

Oracle Enterprise Manager (OEM) can display a near real-time summary of waits, and these can be used to detect lock contention issues. You will need to be licensed for the diagnostic pack to use this capability, however.

Figure 15-1 shows Enterprise Manager plotting activity times by high-level category. In this database, most of the elapsed time is CPU. The other significant category is Application, which includes waits for TX and TM locks and other locks that are typically the result of application behavior. Other—system—locks are included in the Concurrency category.

High wait times for the Application wait class are usually the result of row level lock waits; you can confirm this by clicking on the *Application* hyperlink next to the chart. Figure 15-2 shows the display that results when we do this: The Application waits category indeed mainly consists of row lock waits (*enq: TX— row lock contention*).

FINDING THE RESPONSIBLE SQL

The wait interface enables us to measure the overall magnitude of lock contention and to identify which specific locks are most associated with contention. However, to identify the probable causes and solutions for our locking issues—at least for

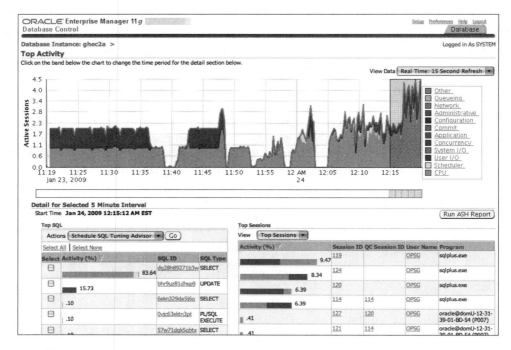

FIGURE 15-1   Oracle Enterprise manager Top Activity showing Application waits.

application locking issues—we want to identify the parts of the application most responsible for lock waits.

If you are licensed for the Oracle Diagnostic pack, you can examine Active Session History (ASH) and Active Workload Repository (AWR) tables to identify the SQLs concerned or use the appropriate parts of Oracle Enterprise Manager. For instance, in Figure 15-2 clicking on the hyperlink in the SQL ID column of the Top SQL table can identify the SQLs most associated with the row level locks during the period selected.

You can also, providing you have a license for the diagnostic pack, query the ASH or AWR tables directly. The following query shows the SQLs and objects contributing to lock waits in the Active Session History (typically including information for the last hour or so):

```
SQL> WITH ash_query AS (
  2       SELECT substr(event,6,2) lock_type,program,
  3              h.module, h.action,   object_name,
  4              SUM(time_waited)/1000 time_ms, COUNT( * ) waits,
  5              username, sql_text,
  6              RANK() OVER (ORDER BY SUM(time_waited) DESC)
                     AS time_rank,
```

```
 7                    ROUND(SUM(time_waited) * 100 / SUM(SUM(time_waited))
 8                       OVER (), 2)              pct_of_time
 9          FROM   v$active_session_history h
10          JOIN   dba_users u  USING (user_id)
11          LEFT OUTER JOIN dba_objects o
12                 ON (o.object_id = h.current_obj#)
13          LEFT OUTER JOIN v$sql s USING (sql_id)
14          WHERE event LIKE 'enq: %'
15          GROUP BY substr(event,6,2) ,program, h.module, h.action,
16                object_name,  sql_text, username)
17     SELECT lock_type,module, username,  object_name, time_ms,
18                pct_of_time, sql_text
19     FROM ash_query
20     WHERE time_rank < 11
21     ORDER BY time_rank;
LOCK MODULE            USERNAME OBJECT_NAME          TIME_MS PCT_OF_TIME
---- ------------      -------- -----------      ------------- -----------

SQL_TEXT
-----------------------------------------------------------------------

TX   SQL*Plus         OPSG     CUSTOMERS            16,961       48.97
UPDATE CUSTOMERS SET CUST_VALID = 'I' WHERE CUST_ID = :B1
KO   SQL*Plus         OPSG                          12,370       35.71
SELECT /*+ full(s) parallel(s) */ DISTINCT CUST_ID FROM SALES S WHERE
AMOUNT_SOLD > 10
KO   SQL*Plus         OPSG     CUSTOMERS             5,306       15.32
SELECT /*+ full(s) parallel(s) */ DISTINCT CUST_ID FROM SALES S WHERE
AMOUNT_SOLD > 10
```

Substituting DBA_HIST_ACTIVE_SESS_HISTORY for V$ACTIVE_SESSION
_HISTORY in the preceding query will use the longer term data held in the Active Workload Repository and will allow you to view lock waits across a period typically spanning days or weeks rather than hours.

If you have a diagnostic pack license, you can use ASH or AWR to identify the tables and SQLs most strongly associated with lock waits.

If you are not licensed for the diagnostic pack, these views are officially off limits, but you can still get a good idea about the source of lock waits from other views. V$SQL includes a column APPLICATION_WAIT_TIME, which records the amount of time spent waiting for events in the Application wait class. This wait

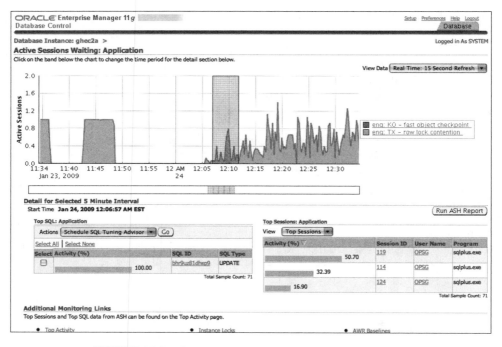

FIGURE 15-2   Oracle Enterprise manager Application wait details.

class includes TX, TM, and other locks resulting from normal application DML, and it's a good bet that you can find your culprit SQLs by using this column.

For instance, the following query retrieves the top 10 SQLs in terms of APPLICATION_WAIT_TIME. We can see that the first SQL (a FOR UPDATE statement), accounts for 57 percent of the application wait time of all the SQLs currently cached. This statement spends virtually all (99.99 percent) of its elapsed time in application waits, probably waiting for the requested row lock to become available.

```
SQL> WITH sql_app_waits AS
  2      (SELECT sql_id, SUBSTR(sql_text, 1, 80) sql_text,
  3              application_wait_time/1000 app_time_ms,
  4              elapsed_time,
  5              ROUND(application_wait_time * 100 /
  6                  elapsed_time, 2) app_time_pct,
  7              ROUND(application_wait_time * 100 /
  8                  SUM(application_wait_time) OVER (), 2)
                      pct_of_app_time,
  9              RANK() OVER (ORDER BY application_wait_Time DESC)
                      ranking
 10          FROM v$sql
```

```
11          WHERE elapsed_time > 0 AND application_wait_time>0)
12   SELECT sql_text, app_time_ms, app_time_pct,
13          pct_of_app_time
14   FROM sql_app_waits
15   WHERE ranking <= 10
16   ORDER BY ranking   ;
```

SQL Text	AppTime(ms)	SQL App Time%	% Tot App Time
SELECT CUST_ID FROM CUSTOMERS WHERE CUST _ID = :B1 FOR UPDATE	16,028,591	99.99	57.40
UPDATE CUSTOMERS SET CUST_VALID = 'I' WHERE CUST_ID = :B1	3,856,750	99.79	13.81
lock table customers in exclusive mode	1,953,773	100.00	7.00
UPDATE sales SET channel_id = 2 WHERE cust_id = 100667	1,821,471	99.92	6.52

In V$SQL, times in the APPLICATION_WAIT_TIME category usually represent time spent waiting for locks. The SQLs with the highest APPLICATION_WAIT_TIMEs are lock contention suspects.

The V$SEGEMENT_STATISTICS table can also be useful in identifying the tables involved in lock waits. V$SEGEMENT_STATISTICS includes counts, though not times, of row level locks against individual segments (tables, partitions, indexes). The following query identifies the objects in the database that have been subject to the most row level lock waits:

```
SQL> SELECT object_name, VALUE row_lock_waits,
  2          ROUND(VALUE * 100 / SUM(VALUE) OVER (), 2) pct
  3     FROM v$segment_statistics
  4     WHERE statistic_name = 'row lock waits' AND VALUE > 0
  5     ORDER BY VALUE DESC;
```

OBJECT_NAME	ROW_LOCK_WAITS	PCT
CUSTOMERS	2611	98.49
SALES	30	1.13
MGMT_METRICS_1HOUR_PK	6	.23
WRH$_SEG_STAT_PK	2	.08
MGMT_JOB_EXECUTION	1	.04
WRI$_ADV_MESSAGE_GROUPS_PK	1	.04

MEASURING LOCK CONTENTION FOR SPECIFIC TRANSACTIONS

Because row level locking is a result of application design, it is often restricted to specific transactions. Measuring lock contention in the database as a whole might indicate little or no lock contention. However, lock contention could still be severe for critical transactions.

Therefore you often want to test for lock contention in specific transactions. There are a few ways to do this.

If the transaction identifies itself using the MODULE and ACTION identifiers (as set by DBMS_APPLICATION_INFO) and you are licensed for the Oracle Diagnostic pack, you can use the ASH and AWR tables to determine lock waits and other performance metrics for SQLs that match that MODULE and ACTION. Minor variations on the ASH and AWR queries shown in the previous section could achieve this.

If your transaction uses the MODULE and ACTION but you are not licensed for the diagnostic pack, you can identify the SQLs for the MODULE or ACTION by querying V$SQL. For instance, the following SQL would indicate how much time a specific module ('OPSG' in this case) is spending in application waits (which are usually lock waits):

```
SELECT COUNT( * ), SUM(elapsed_time) elapsed_Time,
       SUM(application_wait_time) application_time,
       ROUND(SUM(elapsed_time) * 100 /
             SUM(application_wait_time), 2)
             pct_application_time
  FROM v$sql
 WHERE module = 'OPSG'
```

If the transaction does not identify itself using the MODULE or ACTION identifiers, you might be able to get some insight by looking at wait times on a username basis. If the transaction uses a dedicated and specific Oracle account, you can use V$SESSION_EVENT and VSESS_TIME_MODEL to accumulate waits only for sessions logged on to those accounts. In this case we examine waits for sessions logged on as 'OPSG':

```
SQL> WITH session_event AS
  2    (SELECT CASE WHEN event LIKE 'enq:%'
  3                 THEN event  ELSE wait_class
  4            END wait_type, e.*
  5       FROM v$session_event e   )
  6  SELECT    wait_type, SUM(total_waits) total_waits,
  7         round(SUM(time_waited_micro)/1000000,2) time_waited_seconds,
  8         ROUND(  SUM(time_waited_micro)
  9                 * 100
 10                 / SUM(SUM(time_waited_micro)) OVER (), 2) pct
```

```
11    FROM (SELECT  e.sid, wait_type, event, total_waits, time_waited_micro
12         FROM     session_event e
13         UNION
14         SELECT  sid, 'CPU', stat_name, NULL, VALUE
15         FROM v$sess_time_model
16         WHERE stat_name IN ('background cpu time', 'DB CPU')) l
17    WHERE wait_type <> 'Idle'
18      and sid in (select sid from v$session where username='OPSG')
19    GROUP BY wait_type
20    ORDER BY 4 DESC
21    /
```

WAIT_TYPE	TOTAL_WAITS	TIME_WAITED_SECONDS	PCT
enq: TX - row lock contention	703	795.79	88.30
CPU		76.17	8.45
User I/O	1,839	12.86	1.43
Application	41	11.72	1.30

Note that the preceding query only reports data for sessions currently connected: The information in these views is lost when a session disconnects.

TRACING LOCK ACTIVITY

Probably the best way to examine lock activity at the session or transaction level is to use the SQL trace facility. We looked in detail at how to use SQL trace in Chapter 3, "Tools of the Trade." In particular, remember that you can use DBMS_MONITOR to invoke SQL trace whenever a session registers as a specific MODULE, and you can merge the contents of multiple trace files using the *trcsess* utility. This enables you to use SQL Trace to record and analyze wait times for specific sessions and modules and to determine the exact degree and source of any lock waits that might be experienced. Analyzing the trace file with the tkprof *waits=yes* option causes lock and other wait times to be included in the tkprof report.

Here is a sample of trace output including wait timings for a specific SQL:

```
**********************************************************************
SQL ID : 9x404cp2kdhr1
SELECT *
FROM
 CUSTOMERS WHERE CUST_ID = :B1 FOR UPDATE WAIT 1
call     count       cpu    elapsed       disk      query    current       rows
-------  ------  --------  ---------- ---------- ---------- ---------- --------
Parse      228      0.00       0.00          0          0          0          0
Execute  55499      2.33     230.63          0     175913     166102          0
```

Fetch	110542	0.60	0.57	0	0	0	55271
-------	------	--------	----------	----------	----------	----------	--------
total	166269	2.93	**231.21**	0	175913	166102	55271

Misses in library cache during parse: 0
Optimizer mode: ALL_ROWS
Parsing user id: 88   (recursive depth: 1)

```
Rows      Row Source Operation
-------   -------------------------------------------------
      0   FOR UPDATE  (cr=0 pr=0 pw=0 time=0 us)
      1    TABLE ACCESS BY INDEX ROWID CUSTOMERS (cr=43 pr=0 pw=0 time=0 us
      1     INDEX UNIQUE SCAN SYS_C0026051 (cr=2 pr=0 pw=0 time=0 us cost=1
```

Elapsed times include waiting on following events:

Event waited on	Times Waited	Max. Wait	Total Waited
--------------------------------------	----------	----------	-----------
enq: TX - row lock contention	230	1.03	227.90
enq: TX - contention	1	0.05	0.05

As usual, the trace file output shows us the essential information we need to tune the SQL, but more importantly in this case, it tells us that for more than 55,000 executions, we had to wait only 230 times for locks. However, those 230 waits added up to 228 out of 231 seconds of execution—more than 98 percent of the elapsed time.

Lock contention is often restricted to individual transactions. It's therefore important to test for lock contention on a transaction by transaction basis, using SQL trace and other means.

BLOCKERS AND WAITERS

Most of the time lock waits are of short duration, and it's not helpful to try to examine the waits in real time. However, from time to time locking conundrums can occur in which a single long-held lock might bring the entire database, or at least some aspect of application processing, to a halt.

If you want to find lock blockers and lock waiters in real time, you have a few options. If you're licensed for the Oracle Diagnostic pack, you can use the Blocking Sessions page in Oracle Enterprise Manager (OEM) to show who is waiting and who is blocking, and you can drill into individual sessions to see SQLs and wait details. Figure 15-3 shows the OEM Blocking Sessions page.

---

[3] Full disclosure: I designed large parts of Spotlight on Oracle while working at Quest Software.

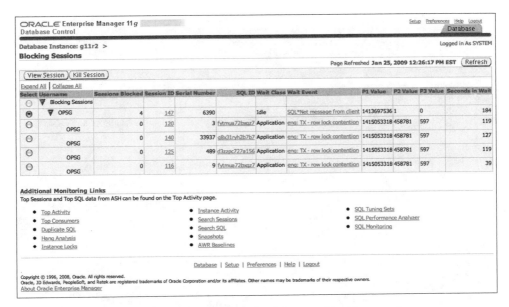

FIGURE 15-3 Oracle Enterprise Manager blocking sessions.

Third-party products such as Quest Software's Spotlight on Oracle product can also display this information, in some cases providing additional information. Figure 15-4 shows the Spotlight blocking lock display.[3]

If you don't have a diagnostic pack license or a third-party tool, you can still query V$LOCK to identify the holders of locks and the sessions that are waiting to obtain those locks. V$LOCK includes details of both of the locks that are held, and locks that are requested; by matching between requests and holds, we can determine who is waiting and who is holding:

```
SQL> WITH sessions AS
  2       (SELECT /*+ materialize*/ username,sid,sql_id
  3           FROM v$session),
  4      locks AS
  5        (SELECT /*+ materialize */ *
  6           FROM v$lock)
  7  SELECT l2.type,s1.username blocking_user, s1.sid blocking_sid,
  8         s2.username blocked_user, s2.sid blocked_sid, sq.sql_text
  9    FROM locks l1
 10    JOIN locks l2 USING (id1, id2)
 11    JOIN sessions s1 ON (s1.sid = l1.sid)
 12    JOIN sessions s2 ON (s2.sid = l2.sid)
 13    LEFT OUTER JOIN  v$sql sq
 14         ON (sq.sql_id = s2.sql_id)
 15   WHERE l1.BLOCK = 1 AND l2.request > 0;
```

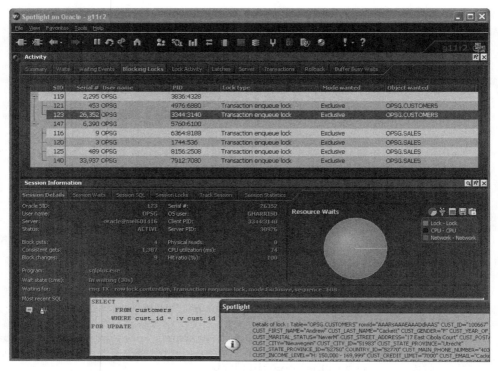

FIGURE 15-4   Quest Software's Spotlight on Oracle blocking lock display.

```
Lock Blocking Blocking Blocked  Blocked
Type user          SID user         SID SQL text
---- -------- -------- -------- ------- ------------------------------------
TX   OPSG          120 OPSG          140 SELECT * FROM SALES WHERE CUST_ID =
                                             100667 FOR UPDATE
TX   OPSG          117 OPSG          129 select * from customers where cust_
                                             id=:v_cust_id for update
TX   OPSG          117 OPSG          126 select * from customers where cust_
                                             id=:v_cust_id for update
```

A few notes about this query:

❏   Locks are held for a short period of time and V$ tables do not support read
    consistency. Therefore there's a nontrivial chance that the data in the view
    will change while we're reading it. To reduce that chance, we take a single
    "snapshot" of the table into a temporary table by using the MATERIALIZE
    hint.

❑ On systems with many sessions and locks, it might be that the queries against V$LOCK, V$SESSION, and V$SQL can be quite time-consuming. So don't expect this query to run quickly and don't run it too frequently.

Another view of lock waits can be obtained by examining the V$SESSION view. V$SESSION includes the current wait state of the session, and can identify how long the session has waited and the identity of any row level locks being sought. The following shows two sessions waiting on row level locks, both are blocked by session #133:

```
SQL> SELECT sid, event, wait_time_micro / 1000 time_ms,
           blocking_session,
  2        object_type || ': ' || object_name object, sql_text
  3    FROM v$session s
  4    LEFT OUTER JOIN v$sql
  5        USING (sql_id)
  6    LEFT OUTER JOIN dba_objects
  7        ON (object_id = row_wait_obj#)
  8  WHERE event LIKE 'enq: %';
Blocked                                                    MS Blocking
    SID Wait event                               Waited       SID
------- --------------------------------- ---------- --------
Object Type: name
------------------------------------------
SQL Text
-------------------------------------------------------------------
    126 enq: TX - row lock contention        142,486.60        133
TABLE: SALES
UPDATE sales   SET channel_id = 2  WHERE cust_id = 100667
    125 enq: TX - row lock contention          1,316.48        133
TABLE: SALES
SELECT * FROM SALES WHERE CUST_ID = 100667 FOR UPDATE
```

When long-held locks start to create long queues of waiting processes, it can sometimes be useful to build up a *lock tree* showing the sometimes complex relationships between waiting sessions. We can build up a simple lock tree, at least for row level locks, by linking the BLOCKING_SESSION and SID columns in V$SESSION. Here is a simple lock tree generated in this fashion:

```
SQL> WITH sessions AS
  2      (SELECT /*+materialize*/
  3              sid, blocking_session, row_wait_obj#, sql_id
  4        FROM v$session)
  5  SELECT LPAD(' ', LEVEL ) || sid sid, object_name,
```

```
 6          substr(sql_text,1,40) sql_text
 7    FROM sessions s
 8    LEFT OUTER JOIN dba_objects
 9          ON (object_id = row_wait_obj#)
10    LEFT OUTER JOIN v$sql
11          USING (sql_id)
12    WHERE sid IN (SELECT blocking_session FROM sessions)
13       OR blocking_session IS NOT NULL
14    CONNECT BY PRIOR sid = blocking_session
15    START WITH blocking_session IS NULL;
SID        OBJECT_NAME      SQL_TEXT
--------   ---------------  ----------------------------------------
  127      SALES
  117      SALES            UPDATE sales SET quantity_sold=:v_qs WHE
  118      SALES            UPDATE sales SET quantity_sold=:v_qs WHE
   130     CUSTOMERS        UPDATE customers SET country_id = :v_cou
   137     CUSTOMERS        UPDATE customers SET country_id = :v_cou
```

The output shows that session 127 is at the top of the lock tree. Although sessions 130 and 137 are blocked on session 118, session 118 is in turn blocked on session 127. Persuading session 127 to relinquish its locks—possibly using ALTER SYSTEM KILL SESSION—will probably resolve the locking issue.

In Oracle 11g, the V$WAIT_CHAINS views provides a more direct way to build up the lock tree that might be more efficient. This query, which is valid only for Oracle 11g, uses that view:

```
SQL> SELECT RPAD('+', LEVEL ,'-') || sid||' '||
             sess.module session_detail,
 2           blocker_sid,  wait_event_text,
 3           object_name,RPAD(' ', LEVEL )||sql_text sql_text
 4    FROM         v$wait_chains c
 5             LEFT OUTER JOIN
 6                dba_objects o
 7             ON (row_wait_obj# = object_id)
 8          JOIN
 9             v$session sess
10          USING (sid)
11       LEFT OUTER JOIN
12          v$sql sql
13       ON (sql.sql_id = sess.sql_id
14          AND sql.child_number = sess.sql_child_number)
15    CONNECT BY    PRIOR sid = blocker_sid
```

```
16                AND PRIOR sess_serial# = blocker_sess_serial#
17                AND PRIOR INSTANCE = blocker_instance
18   START WITH blocker_is_valid = 'FALSE';
                 Blkd
Sid and module        by Wait event                      Object
--------------  -----  ----------------------------  ------------------
current sql
---------------------------------------------------------------------
+124 SQL*Plus          SQL*Net message from client
+-118 SQL*Plus    124  enq: TX - row lock contention CUSTOMERS
  select cust_id from customers where cust_id=1 for update wait 500
+---119 SQL*Plus  118  enq: TX - row lock contention CUSTOMERS
    select cust_id from customers where cust_id=6 for update wait 500
+-120 SQL*Plus    124  enq: TX - row lock contention CUSTOMERS
  select cust_id from customers where cust_id=1 for update wait 500
+-140 SQL*Plus    124  enq: TX - row lock contention CUSTOMERS
  select cust_id from customers where cust_id=2 for update wait 500
+--141 SQL*Plus   140  enq: TX - row lock contention CUSTOMERS
    select cust_id from customers where cust_id=3 for update wait 500
```

> The Oracle Diagnostic pack and some third-party products can build up a lock tree showing you who is waiting and who is holding various locks. If these are not available, a query against V$LOCK, V$SESSION, or V$WAIT_CHAINS can reveal most of the critical information.

APPLICATION LOCKING STRATEGIES

Row level locks for application tables are usually a necessary consequence of transactional integrity and some degree of row level lock contention is to be expected. However, it's definitely an objective of application design to keep the amount of time spent waiting for locks to a minimum. We discussed the principles of application design for lock management in some detail in Chapter 6. Let's briefly review those principles.

The essential principles of application lock management are

❑ To place or acquire locks only when necessary
❑ To minimize the amount of time the locks are held

The techniques for adhering to these principles can vary from application to application. However, two common patterns of lock management can have a fundamental impact on lock contention: the *optimistic* and *pessimistic* locking strategies.

The pessimistic locking strategy is based on the assumption that it is quite possible that a row will be updated by another user between the time you fetch it and the time you update it. To avoid any contention, the pessimistic locking strategy requires that you lock the rows as they are retrieved. The application is therefore assured that no changes will be made to the row between the time the row is retrieved and the time it is updated.

The optimistic locking strategy is based on the assumption that it is unlikely that an update will be applied to a row between the time it is retrieved and the time it is modified. Based on this assumption, the optimistic locking strategy does not require that the row be locked when fetched. However, to cope with the situation in which the row *is* updated between retrieval and modification, it is necessary to check that the row has not been changed by another session before finally issuing the change.

The optimistic locking strategy tends to result in less lock contention than the pessimistic strategy because locks are held for a briefer period of time. However, should the optimism be misplaced, the optimistic strategy will require that failed transactions be retried, possibly resulting in an increase in overall transaction rates.

Carefully choose your application locking strategy to minimize row level lock contention. In particular, consider an optimistic locking strategy if at all possible. See Chapter 6 for more details.

It's hard to relieve lock contention that is a result of application design without re-architecting the application. However, it is also often true that poorly tuned SQL will increase the duration of transactional SQL and hence can increase the amount of time in which locks are held. For this reason, it's usually best to ensure that your application SQL is adequately tuned before attempting any changes to locking strategy.

Poorly tuned SQL can increase transaction duration and hence increase lock wait times. Make sure that all SQL in critical transactions are fine-tuned to reduce lock durations.

WHEN ROW LEVEL LOCKING FAILS

When determining an application locking strategy, it is fair to assume that Oracle's row level locking strategy will result in locks being applied only to the rows that are updated, and not to entire tables or blocks of rows. However, there are well-known circumstances in which Oracle's row level locking mechanisms can break down to block level or table level locks. You should always try to avoid these row level locking failures.

UNINDEXED FOREIGN KEYS

We discussed in Chapter 5, "Indexing and Clustering," how un-indexed foreign key constraints can result in table level locks being applied to the child table when a parent table row is deleted or has an update to a primary key.

These table locks are held for the duration of the statement, not the transaction in which the statement occurs, so they are generally of short duration. However, because they apply to an entire table, they might significantly affect throughput. These locks can be hard to diagnose as well, because they are not identified as foreign key related lock waits in any way. The only clue as to their origin is that the lock waits will show up as TM locks, rather than as the TX locks that you will usually see during row lock contention. For instance, in the following output, the TM - contention enqueue waits are the result of concurrently updating the CUSTOMERS and SALES tables without indexing the foreign key that associates them:

WAIT_TYPE	TOTAL_WAITS	TIME_WAITED_SECONDS	PCT
User I/O	98,956	824.33	45.41
System I/O	23,988	308.64	17.00
CPU		305.27	16.82
enq: TM - contention	317	201.46	11.10
Configuration	565	137.95	7.60

Unindexed foreign keys can cause short-term table level locks to be created on the child table. Waits for the TM enqueue—rather than the normal TX waits associated with row level locks—might be a sign that this is occurring.

ITL WAITS

Oracle's row level locking implementation achieves a high-degree of scalability by maintaining lists of row level locks in each data block rather than in some centralized data structure. This list is called the *Interested Transaction List* (ITL). To request a row level lock, you need to obtain an entry in the ITL in the block that contains the row.

The ITL approach works well except when there is no room for new entries in the ITL. Normally this won't happen unless there is a massive amount of concurrent demand for a small number of rows, in which case the full ITL will be the least of your problems.

However, you can accidentally create a situation in which the ITL has no room to grow by setting poor values for the parameters INITRANS, MAXTRANS, or PCTFREE. INITRANS controls the number of entries that will be available in each block when first created. PCTFREE keeps some room in the block free for rows to grow when updated and also for the ITL to grow. If you set PCTFREE very low (which you might do to get very high row densities), the ITL might not have room to grow as row level lock requests increase. Setting a very low value for MAXTRANS will have the same effect.

These issues are uniquely identified by the "allocate ITL entry" wait on the TX enqueue. The following query against V$SESSION identifies a session that is waiting on an ITL entry:

```
SQL> SELECT sid, event, wait_time_micro/1000 time_ms,
  2         blocking_session, sql_text
  3    FROM v$session
  4    LEFT OUTER JOIN v$sql
  5         USING (sql_id)
  6   WHERE event LIKE 'enq: %';
Blocked                                              Time  Blocking
    SID Wait event                                   (ms)       SID
------- -------------------------------------- ---------- ---------
SQL Text
--------------------------------------------------------------------
    132 enq: TX - allocate ITL entry          272,682.95       134
UPDATE itl_lock_demo SET data = :tdata WHERE id = :tid
```

The query is waiting on an entry to become vacant in the ITL, even though the row it wants to update is not currently locked. When the ITL fills in a block, locks on any row in that block effectively lock all rows in the block. Unfortunately, the only practical solution at this point might be to rebuild the table with higher values for PCTFREE or INITRANS.

> Lock waits on "allocate ITL entry" might be a sign that there is insufficient free space in blocks for new row level locks. Rebuilding the table with higher values for MAXTRANS or PCTFREE might be required.

BITMAP INDEXES

We examined bitmap indexes in Chapter 5. Bitmap indexes provide a lot of query optimization advantages, particularly in data warehousing environments. However, they have a significant downside when DML is involved. Indeed, the presence of bitmap indexes can cause row level locking to break down.

If a bitmap index exists on a column being updated, Oracle locks all the other rows in the same bitmap index fragment. Because bitmap entries are very small, this can result in a lot of rows being locked. Therefore row level locking might be ineffective for tables with bitmap indexes, although a bitmap index might be okay for columns that are rarely updated.

Bitmap index lock contention will appear to be row level lock contention except that the object being waited for will be the relevant bitmap index. The following output illustrates the phenomenon: The lock appears to be a row level lock but the object required is the bitmap index, not the table:

```
SQL> SELECT sid, event, wait_time_micro / 1000 time_ms,
            blocking_session,
  2         object_type || ': ' || object_name object, sql_text
  3    FROM v$session s
  4    LEFT OUTER JOIN v$sql
  5         USING (sql_id)
  6    LEFT OUTER JOIN dba_objects
  7         ON (object_id = row_wait_obj#)
  8   WHERE event LIKE 'enq: %';
Blocked                                               Time Blocking
    SID Wait event                                    (ms)      SID
------- ----------------------------------- ----------- --------
Object Type: name
-----------------------------------------
SQL Text
----------------------------------------------------------------
    123 enq: TX - row lock contention         8,329.01      137
INDEX: MY_BITMAPPED_INDEX2
UPDATE bitmapped_index_table SET y = :yval WHERE x = :xval
```

Bitmap indexes lock at the bitmap fragment level, not the row level. Row level locking breaks down if you update a column that is included in a bitmap index.

DIRECT PATH INSERTS

We looked at direct path inserts in Chapter 14, "DML Tuning"; they can sometimes improve insert performance by avoiding buffer cache contention and writing directly to the database files. However, direct path inserts require a full table (or partition) lock on the table or partition. If you are performing concurrent direct path inserts or trying to perform direct path inserts while performing other DML, you will see heavy lock contention.

For example, if we run direct path inserts concurrently in two separate sessions, one of the sessions will always be waiting. Here's a trace file from one of the sessions that illustrates the effect:

```
INSERT /*+ APPEND */ INTO SALES_STAGE(PROD_ID, CUST_ID, TIME_ID,
  CHANNEL_ID, PROMO_ID, QUANTITY_SOLD, AMOUNT_SOLD)
VALUES
 (:B1 , :B2 , :B3 , :B4 , :B5 , :B6 , :B7 )
call      count        cpu      elapsed       query     current       rows
-------  ------   --------  ----------  ----------  ----------   --------
Parse        1      0.00        0.00           0           0          0
Execute    100     14.46       31.91         368       51174   10000000
Fetch        0      0.00        0.00           0           0          0
-------  ------   --------  ----------  ----------  ----------   --------
total      101     14.46       31.91         368       51174   10000000
Rows      Row Source Operation
-------  --------------------------------------------------------
       1  LOAD AS SELECT   (cr=49 pr=0 pw=481 time=0 us)
  100000  BULK BINDS GET   (cr=0 pr=0 pw=0 time=0 us)

Elapsed times include waiting on following events:
   Event waited on                      Times    Max. Wait   Total Waited
   ---------------------------          Waited   ----------  ------------
   enq: TM - contention                   100         0.23         16.32
   control file sequential read           500         0.00          0.20
   direct path write                      275         0.03          1.83
   latch: enqueue hash chains               9         0.00          0.00
```

The session spent about half its time waiting for a table lock. When *this* session wasn't waiting, the *other* session was blocked. It would have been more effective to use a single session, possibly exploiting parallel DML.

Direct path inserts require full table locks on the table or partition concerned. Attempting to run other DML on the table while the direct path insert is running will result in heavy lock contention.

SYSTEM LOCKS

So far, we looked at locks that occur as a result of application DML. Most of these will be standard row level locks, though we've also looked at how application row level locking can break down to block or table level locks.

Although most locking is application-generated, the Oracle database is a complex system and many internal operations also involve locks. For the most part, these system locks should rarely impact on application performance and many can be ignored. However, other system locks might create contention that limits application throughput, and these should be investigated and resolved.

In this section we consider some of the more commonly encountered system locks. Be aware that contention for these locks will generally arise under fairly unusual circumstances and not all of them can be reproduced on demand. Contention for Oracle internal locks might also be associated with issues in the Oracle software and might be corrected in a subsequent release or a patch.

THE HIGH WATER MARK (HW) ENQUEUE

The High Water Mark (HW) enqueue is required to change the High Water Mark for a table. The Highwater mark represents the highest block number in the table that has ever held data. We first discussed the High Water Mark in Chapter 9, "Tuning Table Access."

As we add rows to a table from time to time we will want to increase its High Water Mark and this lock ensures that only one session can do this at a time.

If concurrent insert activity is very high, there might be occasional waits on this lock. In particular, when inserting LOBs or very long rows into tables with relatively small extents, we might need to increase the High Water Mark frequently. Automatic Segment Storage Management (ASSM) generally employs relatively small uniform extent sizes, and in some extreme cases almost every LOB insert into such a table can result in the HW lock being acquired.

In this worst-case scenario, every LOB insert requires the HW lock, so only one session can insert a LOB at any one time. To avoid this situation you might need to increase the extent size for the segment or, in the case of ASSM, the tablespace as a whole.

You might also try using the ALLOCATE EXTENT clause to push up the High Water Mark prior to the insert operations. You should also avoid reducing the High Water Mark using the SHRINK SPACE option.

Contention for the HW (High Water Mark) lock can occur when concurrently inserting LOBs or very long rows into ASSM tables. Increasing the High Water Mark and extent size might reduce this contention.

THE SPACE TRANSACTION (ST) ENQUEUE

The space transaction (ST) enqueue is required in a dictionary managed tablespace whenever a space operation, such as allocating an extent, occurs. The lock effectively protects two sessions from concurrently modifying the free space and extent information held in the data dictionary.

Contention for the ST enqueue was quite prevalent prior to the introduction of Locally Managed Tablespaces (LMT), and reducing contention for the ST enqueue is one of the definite advantages of using LMTs. ST enqueue contention is rarely seen nowadays, but if you do have Dictionary Managed Tablespaces and you are encountering ST lock contention, you should either

❑ Migrate the tables to a Locally Managed Tablespace.
❑ Reduce the frequency of space transactions, perhaps by increasing the segment extent size (so that extents don't have to be allocated quite so often).

THE SEQUENCE CACHE (SQ) ENQUEUE

The sequence cache (SQ) enqueue prevents multiple sessions from concurrently updating the sequence cache. Oracle sequence generators enable Oracle to provide unique identifiers with minimal contention by caching number ranges in shared memory. Where the numbers in shared memory are exhausted, the cache is refreshed, and this lock prevents two sessions from attempting to do so simultaneously.

High waits for this enqueue are generally the result of setting a small value for the CACHE clause in the CREATE SEQUENCE statement. The default value of 30 is arguably far too small given the rate of sequence number generation in a high throughput application.

The following shows the impact of the SQ lock during a simple benchmark during which two sessions acquired sequence numbers at a high rate from a default sequence:

```
SQL> SELECT wait_type, time_waited_ms, pct_time, sample_seconds
  2      FROM lock_delta_view
  3      WHERE pct_time > 1;
WAIT_TYPE                     TIME_WAITED_MS   PCT_TIME SAMPLE_SECONDS
----------------------------- -------------- ---------- --------------
CPU                               104501.041         67             48
System I/O                         23635.058         15             48
enq: SQ - contention               22527.525         14             48
Concurrency                         3413.318          2             48
```

High waits for the SQ lock probably indicate that the cache size of the sequence should be increased. That will reduce the frequency with which the SQ lock will be required. However be aware that this will also mean that a larger number of sequence numbers will be "lost" should the database be restarted.

Contention on the Sequence Cache (SQ) enqueue is usually an indication that there are sequences that need to be rebuilt with a higher CACHE setting.

THE USER LOCK (UL) ENQUEUE

Waits for locks created by the DBMS_LOCK package will show up as waits on the User Lock (UL) enqueue. DBMS_LOCK enables you to create named locks and to acquire these locks using the same locking behaviors as for predefined Oracle locks and for locks on tables.

User Locks are by definition totally under application control. If you experience significant UL enqueue waits, review your use of the DBMS_LOCK package. In some cases, sessions wait on the UL lock deliberately as part of some multisession synchronized application processing. Long waits on the UL enqueue can be quite acceptable in these scenarios.

OTHER SYSTEM LOCKS

As we noted in the beginning of the chapter, there are almost 200 defined lock types, and many of them have no performance impact on typical applications. You can find brief descriptions of each lock in V$LOCK_TYPE and, if you find a lock not mentioned here is accounting for significant wait time, you can always investigate the lock on Oracle support or elsewhere on the Internet.

Table 15-2 lists a few of the other internal locks that you might encounter.

Table 15-2 More Oracle Internal Locks

CODE	NAME	DESCRIPTION
CF	Controlfile Transaction	Synchronizes accesses to the controlfile. This contention mostly affects processes that are involved in checkpointing operations such as the log writer (LGWR), Database writer (DBWR), recovery writer (RVWR), and archive writer (ARCH). Queries that need to get at controlfile data, such as queries on certain V$ views, might also block on this lock.
FB	Format Block	This lock serializes the formatting of new blocks for Automatic Segment Storage Management (ASSM) tablespaces. Waits usually occur only when other contention issues (free buffer, recovery writer, log buffer) form a bottleneck on database writes.
FU	Feature Usage	This lock controls access to the Feature usage and High Water Mark statistics that Oracle maintains, mainly for license auditing purposes. User sessions should not normally be affected.
JQ	Job Queue	This lock is required when a job queue process executes a job. You might see mild contention between instances in a RAC cluster.
RO	Multiple/Fast Object Reuse	Involved in the recycling of segments after DROP and TRUNCATE operations. Involved in several bugs posted on Oracle support.
SS	Sort Segment	Serializes accesses to sort segments. Probably will not be seen if true temporary tablespaces are employed.
TS	Temporary Segment	Serializes accesses to temp segments. Probably will not be seen if true temporary tablespaces are employed.
TT	Tablespace	Required for ALTER TABLESPACE operations. For instance, when a datafile is being added to a tablespace or a segment is being added or removed from the tablespace.
WF	AWR Flush	An internal lock that appears to be taken out by the Memory Manager (MMAN) and Manageability Manager (MMON) only. It sometimes shows up with relatively high wait times, but it's unlikely that an application session would ever be blocked on it.

SUMMARY

Locks support Oracle's transactional capabilities by preventing two sessions from concurrently modifying table data in a way that would violate the transactions' consistency requirements. Oracle implements a high-concurrency row level locking mechanism. Row level locks are acquired when rows are updated, deleted, or inserted, or when the application specifically requests a lock with the FOR UP-DATE clause.

When a lock cannot be immediately acquired, a wait is recorded in the wait interface tables such as V$SYSTEM_EVENT. The relative amount of time waiting for locks is the best measure of lock contention. The Oracle Diagnostic pack allows SQLs and sessions associated with lock waits to be identified. If the diagnostic pack is not available, we can get good insight using data in V$SQL and V$SEGEMENT_STATISTICS.

For real-time evaluation of locks, both V$LOCK and V$SESSION can help identify what is waiting on a lock release and what is holding the lock concerned.

The most important factor in lock minimization is application design. We looked at lock management principles in Chapter 6. In essence, minimize the duration and number of row level locks, in particular by making an informed choice between optimistic and pessimistic locking strategies.

Row level locking sometimes breaks down to table or block level locking; unindexed foreign keys, Interested Transaction List (ITL) waits, and bitmap indexes are often involved. Direct path insert operations also take out full table locks.

In addition to application locks, Oracle takes out locks to manage internal operations. Sometimes these locks can impact on application performance. Such locks include the Sequence Cache (SQ) lock and the HW (High Water Mark) lock.

LATCH AND MUTEX CONTENTION

In the last chapter we examined Oracle locking mechanisms that exist primarily to prevent two sessions from simultaneously and inconsistently modifying the same data in a table. Latches and mutexes perform a similar function, except that instead of protecting data in *tables*, they protect data in *shared memory*.

You remember from Chapter 2, "Oracle Architecture and Concepts"—and elsewhere—that Oracle sessions share information in the buffer cache, shared pool, and in other sections of the shared memory known as the System Global Area (SGA). It's essential that the integrity of SGA memory is maintained, so Oracle needs a way to prevent two sessions from trying to change the same piece of shared memory at the same time. Latches and mutexes serve this purpose.

Prior to Oracle 10g release 2, Oracle used latches for all shared memory synchronization. In 10g release 2, mutexes—a sort of lightweight variation on the latch concept—replaced some latches. We examine both latches and mutexes in detail in this chapter, but from this point on we may use the term *latch* to refer to both unless otherwise indicated.

The very nature of latches and mutexes creates the potential for contention. If one session is holding a latch that is required by another session, the sessions concerned are necessarily contending for the latch. Latch contention is consequently one of the most prevalent forms of Oracle contention.

OVERVIEW OF LATCH AND MUTEX ARCHITECTURE

Let's spend a little time going over the latch and mutex implementation in Oracle before looking at specific contention scenarios.

Latches are serialization mechanisms that protect areas of Oracle's shared memory (the SGA). In simple terms latches prevent two processes from simultaneously updating—and possibly corrupting—the same area of the SGA.

Oracle sessions need to update or read from the SGA for almost all database operations. For example:

❏ When a session reads from a database file, it normally stores the block into the *buffer cache* in the SGA. A latch is required to add the new block.

❏ If a block of data exists in the buffer cache, a session will read it directly from there, rather than reading from disk. Latches are used to "lock" the buffers for a very short time while being accessed.

❏ When a new SQL statement is parsed, it will be added to the library cache within the SGA. A latch or mutex prevents two sessions from adding or changing the same SQL.

❏ As modifications are made to data blocks, entries are placed in a redo buffer before being written to the redo log. Access to the redo buffers are protected by latches.

Latches and mutexes prevent any of these operations—and many others—from interfering with each other and possibly corrupting the SGA.

Latches typically protect small groups of memory objects. For instance, each *cache buffers chains* latch protects a group of blocks in the buffer cache—a few dozen perhaps. However, unlike locks, latches almost always span rows or SQL statements; a single latch or mutex might protect hundreds or thousands of table rows or dozens of SQL statements.

GETS, SPINS, AND SLEEPS

Because the duration of operations against memory is small (typically in the order of nanoseconds) and the frequency of memory requests potentially high, the latching mechanism needs to be very lightweight. On most systems, a single machine instruction called *test and set* is used to see whether the latch or mutex is taken (by looking at a specific memory address) and if not, acquires it (by changing the value in the memory address). However, there can be hundreds of lines of Oracle code surrounding this single machine instruction.

If the latch or mutex is already in use, Oracle assumes that it will not be in use for long, so rather than go into a passive wait (relinquishing the CPU and going to sleep), Oracle retries the operation a number of times before giving up and sleeping. This algorithm is called acquiring a *spinlock*, and the number of requests (*spins*) before sleeping is controlled by the (hidden) Oracle initialization parameter _SPIN_COUNT. Each attempt to obtain the latch is referred to as a *latch get*, each failure is a *latch miss*, and sleeping after spinning on the latch is a *latch sleep*.

A session can awaken from a sleep in one or two ways. Either the session awakens automatically after a period of time (a timer sleep), or it can awake when the latch becomes available.

In the case where a session uses the timer sleep approach, an *exponential back off* algorithm might be employed. The first time the session sleeps, it will attempt to awaken after a millisecond or so. Subsequent waits will increase in duration and in extreme circumstances might reach 100s of milliseconds.

The alternative to the timer sleep is called *latch wait posting*. The session that waits places itself on the *latch wait list*. When another session relinquishes the latch in question, it looks in the latch wait list and sends a signal to the sleeping session indicating that the latch is now available. The sleeping session immediately wakes up and tries to obtain the latch.

Both types of wait have an impact on performance. The active *spinning* waits consume CPU but are of short duration and won't noticeably increase the execution time of SQL requests. The passive *sleeping* waits consume no CPU—though they occur only after CPU has already been consumed by spinning—but they are of much longer duration and typically have a greater effect on response time.

MUTEXES

Mutexes are similar to latches in concept but are implemented in more fundamental operating system calls that have an even lower memory and CPU overhead than a latch. The primary advantage of mutexes is that there can be more of them, which allows each mutex to protect a smaller number of objects.

In Oracle 10g release 2 (10gR2) and in 11g, mutexes protect cached SQL statements in the library cache within the shared pool. Prior to 10gR2, latches were used for this purpose, and each latch would typically protect a much larger number of SQL statements.

Unlike latches, mutexes support a *shared mode* get. A latch is binary—you either have it or you do not. However, a mutex can be held in shared or exclusive mode. When held in shared mode, no other session can acquire the mutex in exclusive mode. However, many sessions can hold the mutex in shared mode concurrently.

Like latches, mutexes use a spinlock algorithm; if the mutex is not immediately available, Oracle attempts to acquire the mutex repeatedly and if unsuccessful goes to sleep.

MEASURING AND DIAGNOSING LATCH/MUTEX CONTENTION

As with most contention scenarios, the wait interface and time model provide the best way to determine the extent of any contention that might exist. Time spent in latch or mutex sleeps will be recorded in V$SYSTEM_EVENT and similar tables and will usually be the primary indication that a problem exists.

However, be aware that the wait interface records only latch *sleeps*; latch *misses* do not result in a wait being recorded, even though they do consume CPU and should be considered to be a lesser but still important aspect of latch contention.

Prior to Oracle 10g, a single *latch free* wait event was recorded for all latch sleeps. From 10g forward, certain latches now have their own event, such as *latch: cache buffers chains*. Not all latches have their own event though, and those that do not continue to be included in the *latch free* wait.

Mutex waits are represented by waits such as *library cache: mutex X*, which represents a wait on an exclusive library cache mutex.

To break out mutex and latch waits and compare them to other high-level wait categories, we can issue a query such as this:

```
SQL> WITH system_event AS
  2    (SELECT CASE WHEN (event LIKE '%latch%'  or event
  3                       LIKE '%mutex%' or event like 'cursor:%')
  4              THEN event   ELSE wait_class
  5              END wait_type, e.*
  6      FROM v$system_event e)
  7  SELECT wait_type, SUM(total_waits) total_waits,
  8         round(SUM(time_waited_micro)/1000000,2)
              time_waited_seconds,
  9         ROUND(  SUM(time_waited_micro)
 10               * 100
 11               / SUM(SUM(time_waited_micro)) OVER (), 2) pct
 12  FROM (SELECT  wait_type, event, total_waits, time_waited_micro
 13        FROM    system_event e
 14        UNION
 15        SELECT  'CPU', stat_name, NULL, VALUE
 16        FROM '$sys_time_model
 17        WHERE stat_name IN ('background cpu time', 'DB CPU')) 1
 18  WHERE wait_type <> 'Idle'
 19  GROUP BY wait_type
 20  ORDER BY 4 DESC
 21  /
```

WAIT_TYPE	TOTAL_WAITS	TIME_WAITED_SECONDS	PCT
CPU		1,494.63	69.26
latch: shared pool	1,066,478	426.20	19.75
latch free	93,672	115.66	5.36
wait list latch free	336	58.91	2.73
User I/O	9,380	27.28	1.26
latch: cache buffers chains	2,058	8.74	.40
Other	50	7.26	.34
System I/O	6,166	6.37	.30
cursor: pin S	235	3.05	.14
Concurrency	60	3.11	.14
library cache: mutex X	257,469	2.52	.12

Of course, this reports all waits since the database first started. If you've installed this book's packages and views available from the book's Web site, you can use the view LATCH_DELTA_VIEW to show waits over a shorter period of time. Each time you query the view within a session, it will report the times spent in the various wait categories since the last query:

```
SQL> SELECT wait_type, time_waited_ms, pct_time, sample_seconds
  2    FROM latch_delta_view
  3    WHERE pct_time > .01;
```

WAIT_TYPE	TIME_WAITED_MS	PCT_TIME	SAMPLE_SECONDS
CPU	1421123.76	96.44	123
wait list latch free	45333.013	3.08	123
System I/O	3370.432	.23	123
cursor: pin S	1533.455	.10	123
Commit	1520.581	.10	123
Concurrency	461.696	.03	123
Application	246.298	.02	123

> Times spent waiting for events including the term latch or mutex in the wait interface tables, such as V$SYSTEM_EVENT, are the best measure of overall latch/mutex contention.

IDENTIFYING INDIVIDUAL LATCHES

If we're lucky, the latch that is responsible for whatever latch contention exists will be identified by its specific wait event; *latch: cache buffers chains*, for instance. However, this won't always be the case; some latches are included within the general purpose *latch free* wait and some might be recorded against the event *wait list latch free*.

The *wait list latch free* event relates to the latch wait posting algorithm discussed earlier. Oracle implements a latch wait list that enables sessions sleep on a latch to be woken when the latch becomes available. When a session sleeps on a latch, it sometimes places itself on the latch wait list to be awoken by the session that releases the latch. The wait interface might then show a wait for *wait list latch free*.

If the specific latch waits are being obscured by these general purpose latch free events, you might need to examine V$LATCH that includes latch statistics for each specific latch. The V$LATCH view records the number of gets, misses, sleeps, and wait times for each latch. The following query interrogates this view to identify the latches with the most sleeps and wait times:

```
SQL> WITH latch AS (
  2        SELECT name,
  3        ROUND(gets * 100 / SUM(gets) OVER (), 2) pct_of_gets,
  4              ROUND(misses * 100 / SUM(misses) OVER (), 2)
pct_of_misses,
  5              ROUND(sleeps * 100 / SUM(sleeps) OVER (), 2)
pct_of_sleeps,
  6           ROUND(wait_time * 100 / SUM(wait_time) OVER (), 2)
  7                   pct_of_wait_time
  8        FROM v$latch)
  9  SELECT *
 10  FROM latch
 11  WHERE pct_of_wait_time > .1 OR pct_of_sleeps > .1
 12  ORDER BY pct_of_wait_time DESC;
                                 Pct of Pct of Pct of   Pct of
NAME                             Gets Misses Sleeps Wait Time
------------------------------   ------ ------ ------ ---------
cache buffers chains             99.59  99.91  70.59     89.75
shared pool                        .07    .03  16.69      7.78
session allocation                 .18    .05  11.39      1.88
row cache objects                  .07    .00    .78       .24
simulator lru latch                .01    .00    .31       .18
parameter table management         .00    .00    .08       .14
channel operations parent latc     .00    .00    .16       .02
```

V$LATCH can identify the latches that are responsible for waits on the generic latch events such as *latch free* and *wait list latch free*.

FINDING SQLS AND SEGMENTS ASSOCIATED WITH LATCH WAITS

Determining the latches associated with contention is usually not enough to identify the root cause of the contention. We most likely need to identify the SQLs and segments involved.

If you have an Oracle Diagnostic pack license, you can query the Active Session History (ASH) and/or Active Workload Repository (AWR) tables to identify the SQLs and segments associated with particular wait conditions. We used this technique in Chapter 15, "Lock Contention," when diagnosing lock contention. The following query identifies entries in the ASH table associated with latch contention:

```
SQL> WITH ash_query AS (
  2       SELECT event, program,
  3              h.module, h.action,    object_name,
  4              SUM(time_waited)/1000 time_ms, COUNT( * ) waits,
  5              username, sql_text,
  6              RANK() OVER (ORDER BY SUM(time_waited) DESC)
                    AS time_rank,
  7              ROUND(SUM(time_waited) * 100 / SUM(SUM(time_waited))
  8                 OVER (), 2)               pct_of_time
  9         FROM  v$active_session_history h
 10         JOIN  dba_users u  USING (user_id)
 11         LEFT OUTER JOIN dba_objects o
 12              ON (o.object_id = h.current_obj#)
 13         LEFT OUTER JOIN v$sql s USING (sql_id)
 14       WHERE event LIKE '%latch%' or event like '%mutex%'
 15       GROUP BY event,program, h.module, h.action,
 16            object_name,  sql_text, username)
 17  SELECT event,module, username,      object_name, time_ms,
 18         pct_of_time,  sql_text
 19  FROM ash_query
 20  WHERE time_rank < 11
 21  ORDER BY time_rank;
EVENT                   MODULE    USERNAME OBJECT_NAME    TIME_MS PCT_O
---------------------   --------  -------- -----------  ---------- -----
SQL_TEXT
-------------------------------------------------------------------------
wait list latch free SQL*Plus      OPSG     LOG_DATA      71,990 99.69
select max(data) from log_data where id<:id
latch: cache buffers SQL*Plus      OPSG     LOG_DATA         221   .31
 chains
select max(data) from log_data where id<:id
```

If you don't have an Oracle Diagnostic pack license, we can indirectly identify the SQLs by focusing on those SQLs with the highest concurrency wait times. The concurrency wait class includes most commonly encountered latch and mutex waits, although it also includes some internal locks and buffer waits. However, if you're encountering high rates of latch contention, it's a fair bet that the SQLs with the highest concurrency waits are the ones you need to look at.

The following SQL pulls out the SQLs with the highest concurrency waits:

```
SQL> WITH sql_conc_waits AS
  2       (SELECT sql_id, SUBSTR(sql_text, 1, 80) sql_text,
  3              concurrency_wait_time/1000 con_time_ms,
  4              elapsed_time,
```

```
5              ROUND(concurrency_wait_Time * 100 /
6                  elapsed_time, 2) con_time_pct,
7              ROUND(concurrency_wait_Time* 100 /
8                  SUM(concurrency_wait_Time) OVER (), 2)
                     pct_of_con_time,
9              RANK() OVER (ORDER BY concurrency_wait_Time DESC)
                     ranking
10          FROM v$sql
11         WHERE elapsed_time > 0)
12    SELECT sql_text, con_time_ms, con_time_pct,
13          pct_of_con_time
14    FROM sql_conc_waits
15    WHERE ranking <= 10
16    ORDER BY ranking  ;
```

SQL Text	Conc (ms)	SQL Conc Time%	% Tot ConcTime
DECLARE job BINARY_INTEGER := :job; next _date DATE := :mydate; broken BOOLEAN :	899	18.41	44.21
select max(data) from log_data where id< :id	472	.01	23.18
begin query_loops (run_seconds=>120 , hi_val =>1000 , use_	464	.01	22.80
update sys.aud$ set action#=:2, returnco de=:3, logoff$time=cast(SYS_EXTRACT_UTC(	143	75.46	7.02

As expected the SQL that generated the latch waits is found; the second and third entries are from the job I ran to generate the latch waits. However other SQLs associated with waits for certain internal Oracle locks are also shown. You'll need to exercise judgment to determine which SQLs are most likely associated with latch waits.

If you have an Oracle Diagnostic pack license, use ASH or AWR queries to identify the SQLs associated with latch waits. If you don't have a diagnostic pack license, the CONCURRENCY_WAIT_TIME column in V$SQL can help identify suspect SQLs.

SPECIFIC LATCH/MUTEX SCENARIOS

In addition to these generic methods of associating latch waits with SQLs and segments, there are diagnostic techniques specific to certain types of latch contention. We look at these as we discuss specific latch/mutex waits scenarios next.

LIBRARY CACHE MUTEX WAITS

The library cache is the part of the shared pool in which cached definitions of SQL, PL/SQL, and Java classes are held. Modifications to the library cache are protected by library cache mutexes. Prior to 10g release 2, they were protected by library cache latches.

The most common reason to acquire a library cache mutex in exclusive mode is to add a new entry to the cache. This happens, for instance, when we parse a new SQL statement. Oracle looks for a matching entry in the cache, and if one is not found (a *miss*), it acquires the relevant mutex and inserts the new entry.

The most common type of miss is for new SQL statements, although PL/SQL blocks might also be involved. You can determine which type of object is responsible for the most cache misses—and therefore probably the most mutex waits—by running the following query:

```
SQL> SELECT namespace, gets, gethits,
  2             ROUND(CASE gets WHEN 0 THEN NULL
  3                  ELSE gethits * 100 / gets END, 2) hitratio,
  4          ROUND(gets * 100 / SUM(gets) OVER (), 2) pct_gets,
  5          ROUND((gets - gethits) * 100 /
  6               SUM(gets - gethits) OVER (), 2) pct_misses
  7  FROM v$librarycache;
```

NAMESPACE	GETS	GETHITS	HITRATIO	PCT_GETS	PCT_MISSES
SQL AREA	18,450,309	12,906,044	69.95	63.66	99.59
TABLE/PROCEDURE	10,272,904	10,252,057	99.8	35.44	.37
BODY	118,314	117,269	99.12	.41	.02
TRIGGER	127,485	127,202	99.78	.44	.01
INDEX	3,544	3,208	90.52	.01	.01
CLUSTER	10,759	10,720	99.64	.04	.00
OBJECT	0	0		.00	.00
PIPE	0	0		.00	.00
JAVA SOURCE	0	0		.00	.00
JAVA RESOURCE	0	0		.00	.00
JAVA DATA	178	175	98.31	.00	.00

As is usually the case, SQL statement misses comprised the fast majority of all misses—more than 99 percent.

In the vast majority of cases, the cause of library cache mutex contention is excessive hard parsing as a consequence of a failure to use bind variables within the application. We looked at bind variables and parsing in quite some detail in Chapter 6, "Application Design and Implementation." When an application uses literals rather than bind variables, almost every SQL statement execution requires a new SQL parse. Consequently, every SQL execution requires a mutex acquisition, and mutex contention becomes almost inevitable. This typically shows up as high waits on the *library cache: mutex X* event.

> The most common cause of library cache mutex contention is excessive hard parsing caused by a failure to use bind variables in application code.

To identify the SQLs that are causing the most hard parses, we need to find those SQLs that are identical other than for the values of literals. These SQLs will show up in V$SQL as SQLs with the same value for FORCE_MATCHING_SIGNATURE. As we saw in Chapter 6, we can use a query like this to identify those SQLs:

```
SQL> WITH force_matches AS
  2          (SELECT force_matching_signature,
  3                  COUNT( * )  matches,
  4                  MAX(sql_id || child_number) max_sql_child,
  5                  DENSE_RANK() OVER (ORDER BY COUNT( * ) DESC)
  6                      ranking
  7           FROM v$sql
  8           WHERE force_matching_signature <> 0
  9             AND parsing_schema_name <> 'SYS'
 10           GROUP BY force_matching_signature
 11           HAVING COUNT( * ) > 5)
 12  SELECT sql_id,     matches, parsing_schema_name schema, sql_text
 13    FROM        v$sql JOIN force_matches
 14      ON (sql_id || child_number = max_sql_child)
 15  WHERE ranking <= 10
 16  ORDER BY matches DESC;
SQL_ID              MATCHES SCHEMA
------------- ---------- --------------------

SQL_TEXT
-------------------------------------------------------------------
gzxu5hs6sk4s9        13911 OPSG
select max(data) from log_data where id=717.91
```

Ideally, applications should make use of bind variables whenever possible; we discussed this in detail in Chapter 6.

However, it's not always easy or possible to rewrite an application to use bind variables. Therefore, Oracle provides a mechanism for imposing bind variables transparently; when the parameter CURSOR_SHARING is set to FORCE or SIMILAR, Oracle can replace a statement such as this:

```
SELECT MAX(data) FROM log_data WHERE id=99
```

with a statement like this:

```
SELECT MAX(data) FROM log_data WHERE id=:"SYS_B_0"
```

Oracle then substitutes the appropriate values into the system generated bind variables (a value of 99 would be assigned in the preceding example), and the library cache miss can be avoided. As we saw in Chapter 6, this reduces parse overhead because Oracle can retrieve the already parsed version from the shared pool and also reduces mutex contention, because Oracle doesn't have to acquire the mutex in exclusive mode if the matching SQL is found.

Setting the parameter CURSOR_SHARING to FORCE or SIMILAR can reduce or eliminate library cache mutex contention.

LIBRARY CACHE PIN

The library cache pin is not strictly a latch or mutex but often shows up in similar circumstances. A library cache pin is required whenever an object in the library cache is to be parsed or reparsed. This can happen, for instance, if the execution plan for a SQL statement needs to be changed or a PL/SQL package is modified or recompiled.

The session wanting to modify the object will attempt to acquire the library cache pin in exclusive mode; sessions executing the object will be holding a shared library cache pin.

Waits on the library cache pin will often be caused by a session trying to modify or compile a PL/SQL program that is simultaneously being executed by another session.

SHARED POOL LATCH

The primary purpose of shared pool latches is to control access to the shared pool memory map. Sessions that look for free space in the shared pool for a new SQL statement or PL/SQL package need to acquire shared pool latches, and many Oracle internal operations (resizing the shared pool, for instance) also acquire these latches.

Excessive hard parsing, which is the primary cause of library cache mutex contention, generally results in shared pool latch contention as well, because the constant allocation of one off SQL statements fragment the shared pool and requires continual de-allocation of old statements.

Shared pool latch contention is often a side effect of high hard parse rates and can also indicate the need to use bind variables or adjust the CURSOR_SHARING parameter.

Shared pool fragmentation has other deleterious side effects, including ORA-4031 errors and excessive shared pool memory consumption. Over the years, we've seen a variety of techniques employed to combat this fragmentation:

❑ Some sites flush the shared pool periodically using the ALTER SYSTEM FLUSH SHARED POOL command.

❑ Using automatic SGA memory management, which we look at in detail in Chapter 20, "Other Memory Management Topics," can exacerbate fragmentation issues because the memory management algorithms cannot always predict or measure the degree of fragmentation that results. Setting a minimum value for the shared pool, as discussed in Chapter 20, might be indicated. In 11g release 1, the MMAN process might hold shared pool latches for extended periods of time when automatic memory management is in effect. Reverting to manual memory management might alleviate the problem.

❑ Pinning large but infrequently executed PL/SQL packages in the shared pool, using DBMS_SHARED_POOL, might help reduce fragmentation by preventing large objects from moving in and out of memory.

CACHE BUFFERS CHAINS LATCH

When a session needs to access a block from the buffer cache, it must acquire a *cache buffers chains* latch on the *buffer chain* that controls that buffer. A chain is a small number of blocks that hash to a common value; each cache buffers chains latch protects a number of chains.

The amount of time it takes to access a block in memory is small, and there are a large number of cache buffers chains latches. Nevertheless, cache buffers chains latch contention can become significant on systems with high logical read rates, especially if these logical reads concentrate on a small number of blocks.

Ironically, cache buffers chains latch contention often occurs on systems that have been almost perfectly optimized in every other respect: To get the high logical read rates necessary to induce cache buffers chains contention, the system typically needs to minimize all other forms of contention and waits, such as IO, parsing, locking, and so on.

High logical read rates and the resulting cache buffers chains latch contention can, however, be the result of poorly tuned SQL. For example, a nested loops join that uses an unselective index might scan the same set of blocks on the inner table many times over. These blocks then become "hot" and can be the subject of latch contention. Tuning the SQL by creating a more selective index will reduce the redundant logical reads and reduce the latch contention, and improve the performance of the SQL concerned.

> Cache buffers chains latch contention is associated with high logical read rates, often
> against a relatively small number of blocks. Reducing logical read rates by tuning SQL
> is a sensible first step in reducing the latch contention.

The mapping of cache buffers to cache buffers chains latches is based on an Oracle hashing algorithm, and the number of blocks per latch can vary significantly. If you want to examine the configuration of your cache buffers chains latches the following query, which you must run as SYS, reveals the latch to buffer ratios:

```
SQL> SELECT COUNT(DISTINCT l.addr) cbc_latches,
  2            SUM(COUNT( * )) buffers,
  3            MIN(COUNT( * )) min_buffer_per_latch,
  4            MAX(COUNT( * )) max_buffer_per_latch,
  5            ROUND(AVG(COUNT( * ))) avg_buffer_per_latch
  6   FROM       v$latch_children l
  7       JOIN
  8          x$bh b
  9       ON (l.addr = b.hladdr)
 10   WHERE name = 'cache buffers chains'
 11   GROUP BY l.addr;
```

CBC Latch Count	Buffer Cache Buffers	Min Buffer Per Latch	Max Buffer Per Latch	Avg Buffer Per Latch
8192	89386	3	46	11

So on this database, an average of 11 blocks was associated with each latch, but some latches protected as few as 3 or as many as 46 blocks.

The chance that contention for a cache buffers chains latch is a result of two hot blocks being mapped to the same latch is small, and although you can attempt to change the number of latches using undocumented Oracle parameters, the chances that you'll relieve latch contention by doing so is low.

Each latch exposes its individual statistics into the view V$LATCH_CHILDREN. You can link these latches to the buffers they protect by examining the view X$BH, which, unfortunately, you can do only as the SYS user. This query joins the two tables to identify the segments that are most heavily associated with cache buffers chains latch sleeps:

```
SQL> WITH cbc_latches AS
  2       (SELECT addr, name, sleeps,
  3               rank() over(order by sleeps desc) ranking
```

```
 4              FROM v$latch_children
 5            WHERE name = 'cache buffers chains')
 6   SELECT owner, object_name,object_type,
 7          COUNT(distinct l.addr) latches,
 8          SUM(tch) touches
 9     FROM cbc_latches l JOIN x$bh b
10          ON (l.addr = b.hladdr)
11     JOIN dba_objects o
12          ON (b.obj = o.object_id)
13    WHERE l.ranking <=100
14    GROUP BY owner, object_name,object_type
15    ORDER BY sum(tch) DESC;
OWNER          OBJECT_NAME          OBJECT_TYP    LATCHES      TOUCHES
------------   --------------------  ----------    ----------   ------------
OPSG           LOG_DATA             TABLE            103         1,149
```

This query shows that the top 100 cache buffers chains latches are all associated with the LOG_DATA table and that it is probably the high rates of logical IO against this table that are the root cause of the cache buffers chains latch contention we are experiencing.

Finding the segment involved in cache buffers chains contention is a good first step, but where do we go from here? There are a couple of possibilities:

❏ If the cache buffers chains contention is associated with an index, you could consider reimplementing the table as a hash cluster and use a hash key lookup rather that a B*-Tree index lookup. B*-Tree indexes often become associated with cache buffers chains contention, because index root and branch blocks tend to be accessed more frequently than index leaf blocks or table blocks. If we use a hash cluster lookup instead, this potential for cache buffers chains latch contention is eliminated.

❏ At the risk of belaboring the point, is there any way to reduce the logical IO rate? Review and tune the SQL that accesses the table. Perhaps Oracle 11g client side caching (see Chapter 6) or the Oracle 11g server-side result set cache (see Chapter 20) could be used to reduce the logical IO rate.

❏ If there are multiple hot rows within the same hot block, explore options for splitting these rows across multiple blocks. Partitioning the table and its indexes can be an attractive option, especially because it requires no changes to application code.

> To reduce cache buffers chains latch contention, try reducing logical reads against the hot object by changing indexing options, partitioning the object concerned, or by tuning SQL against the object.

ROW CACHE OBJECTS LATCH

The row cache objects latch protects the contents of the row cache: The section of the shared pool that caches data dictionary information. High rates of DDL can cause contention for this latch, and often this DDL is associated with recursive SQL that maintains internal Oracle information (such as space management, undo management, and so on).

The potential causes of row cache object contention are many and varied, but each is relatively rare. Identifying the SQL concerned using the techniques discussed previously in this chapter might suggest the root cause.

You can also identify the specific areas of the row cache associated with the row cache object latch contention. The following SYS-only query shows the row cache objects associated with the highest number of sleeps. Note that some latches protect more than one row cache object. In this example DC_OBJECTS and DC_OBJECT_GRANTS are both on child latch #9.

```
SQL> SELECT kqrsttxt namespace,  child#, misses, sleeps,wait_time,
  2          ROUND(wait_time*100/sum(wait_time) over(),2) pct_wait_Time
  3     FROM v$latch_children
  4     JOIN (SELECT DISTINCT kqrsttxt, kqrstcln FROM x$kqrst) kqrst
  5          ON (kqrstcln = child#)
  6    WHERE name = 'row cache objects'  AND wait_Time > 0
  7    ORDER BY  wait_time DESC;
```

NAMESPACE	Latch Child#	Misses	Sleeps	Wait Time	Pct of Wait
dc_tablespaces	5	11020892	2741416	17640736	100
dc_objects	9	73	8	151	0
dc_object_grants	9	73	8	151	0
dc_histogram_data	14	86	14	149	0
dc_histogram_defs	14	86	14	149	0
global database name	32	14	5	61	0
dc_users	8	167	5	53	0
dc_rollback_segments	1	12	2	8	0

OTHER LATCH SCENARIOS

Cache buffers chains latches and library cache mutexes are the most commonly encountered forms of latch/mutex contention. However, other forms of latch contention arise from time to time. Here are some of the other latches that you might encounter:

❑ The **cache buffers lru chain latch** controls access to the LRU (Least Recently Used) list in the buffer cache. Buffers "move" up and down this list as they are accessed and, when they reach the end of the list, are eventually flushed out of the pool. Contention for this latch is generally associated with cache buffers chains latch contention and will generally respond to a similar resolution. However, although the cache buffers chains latch is most sensitive to *hot* blocks, the cache buffers lru chains latch is more heavily utilized when *new* blocks are introduced into the buffer cache.

❏ The **simulator lru latch** controls access to the "virtual" LRU list that Oracle uses to work out the effect of increasing or decreasing the size of the buffer cache. This information is used to populate the DB_CACHE_ADVICE tables and to perform the automatic memory management that we look at in detail in Chapter 20. Contention for this latch can occur under similar circumstances as for the cache buffers chains and cache buffers lru chains latches, and might mask contention for those latches. Setting DB_CACHE_ADVICE to OFF usually eliminates this contention but might merely shift the contention to the cache buffers chains latch. Note also that contention on this latch was associated with some bugs in early versions of Oracle 11g.

❏ The **redo allocation latch** serializes entries to the redo log buffers and private *strands*, both of which buffer IO to the redo logs. This latch and the related redo copy latch were often implicated in latch contention issues in earlier versions of Oracle. However, Oracle made significant changes to redo handling in 9i and 10g, parallelizing redo generation, creating multiple independent buffers, and introducing private buffer strands. As a result redo related latch contention issues are rarely reported as issues today. You might see some contention for the redo allocation latch when there are high levels of concurrent DML activity. However, it's unlikely to dominate overall performance because these levels of DML generally create substantial IO related waits.

❏ The **session allocation** and **process allocation latches** are often involved during the creation of a new session and the associated server process. Contention on these latches will often be seen if there is a high rate of logon/ logoff to the database. Oracle is not really optimized for sessions that connect, issue a single SQL, and then disconnect; performance is usually better when sessions stay connected to issue multiple SQLs. Using application server connection pools might be indicated if you see this sort of contention, and you might see some relief if you configure the database for multi-threaded server connections rather than dedicated server connections.

❏ The **kks stats latch** seems to be associated with mutex operations; we might speculate that it is involved in maintaining mutex sleep statistics. Some contention on this latch seems to be associated with other mutex contention scenarios. If you see this latch in conjunction with mutex waits, you should probably try resolving the mutex issue first in the hope of curing contention for this latch as well.

❏ The **in memory undo latch** is associated with Oracle's relatively new *in memory undo* (IMU) structures in which information formerly maintained in rollback (undo) segments is held in memory. Some contention for the in memory undo latch might be the cost you have to pay for the reduction in redo generation and undo segment IO that the new algorithm provides. However, some users have suggested turning in memory undo off by adjusting the undocumented parameter _IN_MEMORY_UNDO or increasing the value of the PROCESSES parameter, which indirectly controls the default number of IMU latches.

❏ The **Result Cache: RC Latch** (11g release 2) or the **Result Cache: Latch** (11g release 1) controls the creation and deletion of result sets in the Oracle 11g Result set cache. Contention for the latch occurs if multiple sessions attempt to simultaneously create cached result sets. We discuss this issue again in Chapter 20; result sets in the result set cache should generally be restricted to a relatively small number of infrequently executing SQLs.

IS LATCH CONTENTION INEVITABLE?

We often see latch contention, especially cache buffers chains latch contention, in the most highly tuned, high-powered databases.

This makes sense if you think about it. If we create a database configuration in which all other constraints are removed on database performance, such as locking, IO, memory, and CPU, database sessions will essentially be competing for access to shared memory alone. In that scenario, latch contention inevitably becomes the limiting factor.

So it might be that some degree of latch contention, especially on the cache buffers chains latch, must be accepted in high throughput systems running on premium hardware.

WHAT ABOUT CHANGING _SPIN_COUNT?

As noted earlier, when an Oracle session cannot immediately obtain a latch, it *spins* until the latch becomes available or until the value of the internal parameter _SPIN _COUNT is reached. After that, it relinquishes the CPU and sleep.

Prior to Oracle 8i, the spin count parameter (SPIN_COUNT or LATCH _SPIN_COUNT) was a documented parameter, and many DBAs attempted to adjust it to resolve latch contention. However, ever since Oracle8i the parameter has been "undocumented": It does not appear in V$PARAMETER and is not documented in the Oracle reference manual. Why did Oracle do this?

The official Oracle Corporate explanation is that the value of SPIN_COUNT is correct for almost all systems and that adjusting it can degrade performance. For instance, Oracle support note 30832.1 states that "If a system is not tight on CPU resource, SPIN_COUNT can be left at higher values, but anything above 2000 is unlikely to be of any benefit."

However, I believe that higher values of SPIN_COUNT can relieve latch contention in circumstances in which no other solution is practical.

Oracle set the default value of SPIN_COUNT to 2000 in Oracle 7. Almost 15 years later, CPUs are capable of processing instructions at more than 50 times the rate that was current when the original value of SPIN_COUNT was determined. This means that Oracle databases are spending a decreasing amount of time spinning whereas the latch sleep time has remained essentially constant. So even if the value of SPIN_COUNT was optimal in all circumstances in the Oracle7 time frame, the optimal value should have increased over the years in line with increasing processer speeds.

SPIN COUNT, LATCH CONTENTION, AND THROUGHPUT

In this section we review the results of some experiments conducted into the effect of adjusting _SPIN_COUNT on a database suffering from heavy latch contention.

In these tests, _SPIN_COUNT was adjusted programmatically across a wide range of values, and the impact on database throughput, latch waits, and CPU utilization recorded. Figure 16-1 summarizes the relationship between database throughput (as measured by the number of SQL statement executions per second), the amount of time spent in latch waits, and the CPU utilization of the system (as measured by the CPU run queue).

The data indicates that as _SPIN_COUNT increased, waits for latches reduced as CPU utilization increased. As CPU utilization saturated (an average run queue per processor of one or more), further improvements in throughput and reduction in latch free time were not observed.

Note that the optimal value for _SPIN_COUNT in this simulation was somewhere in the vicinity of 10,000: five times the default value provided by Oracle. Throughput had increased by approximately 80 percent at this value.

The results indicate that at least in some circumstances, manipulating the value of _SPIN_COUNT can result in significant reductions in latch free waits and improve the throughput of latch constrained applications. Because it is an undocumented parameter, some DBAs are reluctant to manipulate _SPIN _COUNT. However, if faced with intractable latch contention, particularly for cache buffers chains latches, manipulating _SPIN_COUNT might be the only option available for improving database throughput.

_SPIN_COUNT should be adjusted only when there are available CPU resources on the system. Specifically, if the average CPU Queue length is approaching or greater than 1, increasing _SPIN_COUNT is unlikely to be effective.

When absolutely all else fails, intractable latch contention can sometimes be relieved by adjusting the undocumented, and hence At Your Own Risk, parameter _SPIN_ COUNT.

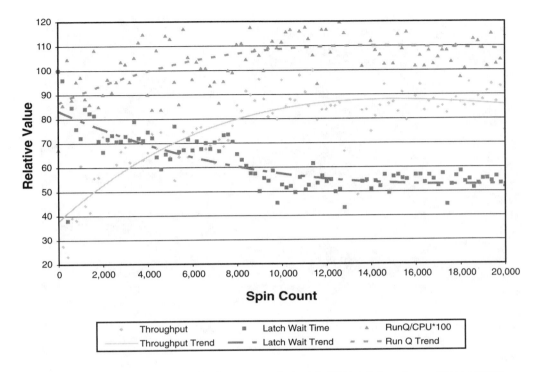

FIGURE 16-1 Relationship between spin count, CPU, latch waits, and throughput.

The value of _SPIN_COUNT can be changed on the running system by issuing an ALTER SYSTEM command such as the following:

```
SQL> ALTER SYSTEM SET "_SPIN_COUNT"=5000 SCOPE=BOTH;
System altered.
```

Quest Software's Spotlight on Oracle[1] includes a latch tuning module that attempts to establish the optimal value of _SPIN_COUNT for a database. It varies the value of _SPIN_COUNT across a configurable range while monitoring the effect on CPU, throughput, and latch wait times. It then recommends an appropriate value. Figure 16-2 shows the Spotlight latch tuning facility in action.

---

[1] Full disclosure: I participated in the design of Spotlight's latch tuning module while working at Quest Software.

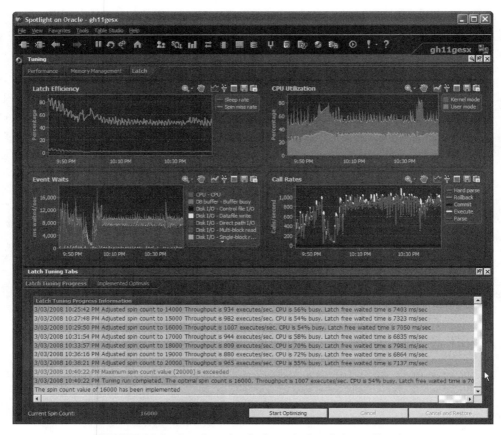

FIGURE 16-2   Latch tuning in Quest's Spotlight on Oracle.

SETTING SPIN COUNT FOR INDIVIDUAL LATCHES

You can change the spin count for individual latches by assigning a latch to a latch class and then setting a new value for that class. So if we want to change the spin count for the cache buffers chains latch only, we use the following commands:

```
SQL> SELECT latch#
  2  FROM v$latch
  3  WHERE name = 'cache buffers chains';
    LATCH#
----------
       141
```

```
SQL>
SQL> ALTER SYSTEM SET "_latch_classes" = "141:1" SCOPE=SPFILE;
System altered.
SQL> ALTER SYSTEM SET "_latch_class_1"=10000 SCOPE=SPFILE;
System altered.
```

In the first statement, we obtain the latch number for the cache buffers chains latch. We then assign that latch number to class 1 by changing the _LATCH_CLASSES parameter. Finally, we assign a spin count of 10,000 to latch class 1 by changing the _LATCH_CLASS_1 parameter.

Unfortunately, we need to restart the database to adjust the spin count for individual latches in this manner. We can then see the nondefault spin values assigned to latches with the following query, which must be run as SYS:

```
SQL> SELECT kslltnam latch_name, class_ksllt latch_class,
  2         c.spin class_spin_count
  3     FROM x$kslltr r JOIN x$ksllclass c
  4       ON (c.indx = r.class_ksllt)
  5     WHERE r.class_ksllt > 0;
LATCH_NAME                     LATCH_CLASS CLASS_SPIN_COUNT
------------------------------ ----------- ----------------
process allocation                       2             5000
cache buffers chains                     1            10000
```

SUMMARY

Latches and mutexes protect areas of Oracle's shared memory, preventing corruption or inconsistencies that might arise if multiple sessions were to try to change the same area of shared memory at the same time.

Latches and mutexes are light-weight mechanisms, designed to support high rates of concurrency and to be held for short periods of time. When a latch is not immediately available, the session *spins* on the latch, repeatedly trying to acquire it, and sleeps (relinquishes the CPU) only after a certain number of spins have been unsuccessful. These latch sleeps are recorded in the wait interface and are the best indication of a latch contention problem.

Waits for the library cache mutex occur most frequently when sessions try to concurrently add new SQLs to the SQL area. This is almost always caused by a failure to employ bind variables within the application and can almost always be solved by implementing bind variables, or by setting the CURSOR_SHARING parameter.

Waits for the cache buffers chains latch occur when high logical read rates against a relatively small number of hot blocks occurs. Tuning the SQLs that are generating the high logical read rates is a sensible first step. Partitioning the object concerned or changing the indexing strategy might also be warranted.

The library cache mutex and cache buffers chains latch are responsible for most of the latch/mutex contention seen in modern versions of Oracle. Contention for other latches might arise under more unusual circumstances and might be associated with Oracle bugs.

When all else fails it is possible, though strictly speaking unsupported by Oracle, to change the number of spins that occur when Oracle attempts to obtain a latch. Doing this might reduce the number of latch sleeps, at the expense of higher CPU consumption while spinning on the latch.

SHARED MEMORY CONTENTION

Oracle uses shared memory in the System Global Area (SGA) to improve performance by caching frequently accessed data in the *buffer cache*, reducing the amount of disk IO required to access that data. Oracle maintains other caches in the SGA as well, such as the *redo log buffer*, which buffers IO to the redo log files. Chapter 2, "Oracle Architecture and Concepts," provides a review of the components and architecture of the SGA.

We look at how to configure these areas of memory to optimize performance in Chapter 18, "Buffer Cache Tuning," and Chapter 20, "Other Memory Management Topics." In this chapter we look at how *contention* for shared memory, the buffer cache in particular, can restrict SQL processing and negatively impact performance.

The sharing of memory creates the potential for contention and requires that Oracle serialize—restrict concurrent access—to some areas of shared memory to prevent corruption. Oracle manages some of this serialization using the latching mechanisms discussed in 16, "Latch and Mutex Contention." However, contention for shared memory goes beyond latches because sessions might need to wait for free buffers in memory when inserting new blocks, or for other sessions to finish processing blocks already in memory.

BUFFER CACHE ARCHITECTURE

Oracle maintains multiple buffer cache areas called *pools*. As well as the default cache, the following pools might also exist:

❏ The keep pool, intended to cache small tables subject to frequent full table scans.

❏ The recycle pool, intended for caching larger tables subject to infrequent scans.

❏ Up to four pools that cache data blocks of a nondefault block size. These pools can have a block sizes of 2, 4, 8, 16, or 32K.

The use of multiple buffer pools can have a big effect on buffer cache and IO effectiveness, and we discuss this in Chapter 18. However, from the point of view of contention, these different pools aren't all that important. For now, we can consider the buffer cache as a single area of memory containing data blocks.

When a session wants to access a block of data from a table or index, it first looks for that block in the buffer cache. Oracle implements a complex algorithm for working out which blocks should be kept in memory. From a simplistic point of view, the longer it has been since the block has been accessed, the more likely it is to be removed from the cache to make room for other blocks. This modified *Least Recently Used (LRU)* algorithm is implemented by the *LRU list*; if a block is accessed it might be moved *up* the list (metaphorically speaking). If blocks are not accessed, they might move *down* the list and eventually will be removed from memory.

When a DML statement changes the contents of a block, the changes are made to a copy of the block in memory. The changed *dirty* block will not immediately be written to disk. The database writer (DBWR) background process will write the dirty blocks out to database files at a later time. This deferred writing of changed blocks is generically known as a *lazy write*, and the principle is used by most databases and buffered filesystems such as Linux EXT2 or Windows NTFS.

A dirty block cannot be flushed from the cache: The dirty block can be removed from the cache only after the database writer has written the change to disk.

If the database is in flashback mode, the unchanged version of the block (the before image) must also be written to the flashback logs by the recovery writer (RVWR).

Figure 17-1 illustrates the essential flows of data blocks into, and out of, the buffer cache.

The essential things to remember are

❏ User sessions, or at least the server processes that work on their behalf, read blocks from disk and place them in the buffer cache.

❏ Old blocks, or Least Recently Used (LRU) blocks, make way for new blocks.

❏ If a block is changed, it can't be removed from the cache until the database writer has written the changed block to disk.

❏ Some reads and writes—the direct path operations—bypass the buffer cache.

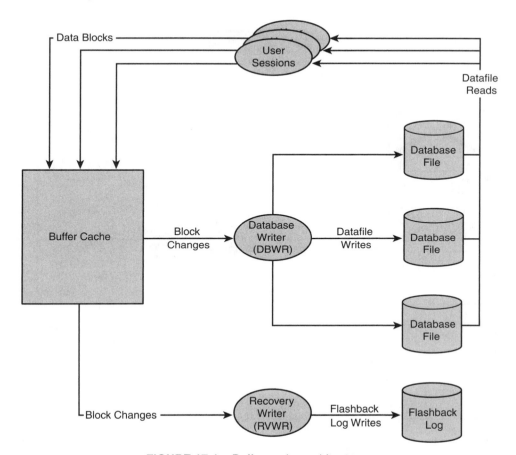

FIGURE 17-1 Buffer cache architecture.

FREE BUFFER WAITS

As noted in the previous section, dirty (modified) blocks cannot be removed from the cache until the database writer has written the changed blocks to disk. If all the blocks in the buffer cache are dirty, sessions that want to bring new blocks into the cache will have to wait. These waits are called *free buffer waits* and are a frequently encountered form of buffer cache contention.

Figure 17-2 illustrates this phenomenon. All the blocks in the buffer cache are modified, and sessions cannot introduce new buffers until the database writer writes some modified blocks to disk.

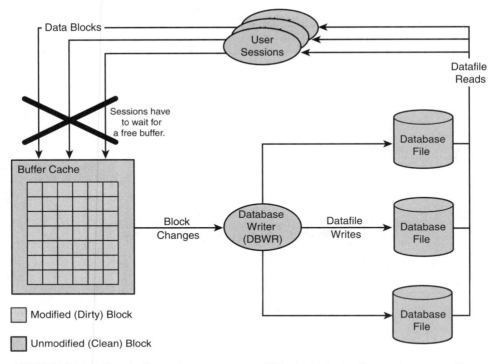

FIGURE 17-2 Free buffer waits occur when all blocks in the buffer cache are modified.

Free buffer waits occur when the buffer cache fills up with modified blocks, blocking sessions that want to introduce new blocks into the buffer cache.

Free buffer waits generally occur when heavy DML activity causes a large number of blocks to be modified while at the same time blocks are being read into the buffer cache from disk. If the rate of change in the buffer cache exceeds the capability of the database writer to write the modified blocks to disk, free buffer waits might result.

For example, consider a transaction in which data is read from one table and inserted into a second table. This activity creates a need to read data into the cache, while at the same time creating new blocks or modifying existing blocks that need to be written out to the database files.

Below is some SQL trace output from a transaction of this type. This transaction was one of four executing simultaneously. Because of the inability of the database writer to keep up with the block modifications, free buffer waits accounted for more than half the elapsed time of the SQL:

```
**********************************************************************
insert /*+ noappend */ into opsg2_log_data d
select  * from log_etlfile_117

call      count    elapsed       disk       query     current        rows
-------  ------   --------  ----------  ----------  ----------  ----------
Parse        1      0.00           0           2           0           0
Execute      1    210.65      147290      417574     1252637      999999
Fetch        0      0.00           0           0           0           0
-------  ------   --------  ----------  ----------  ----------  ----------
total        2    210.65      147290      417576     1252637      999999

Rows     Row Source Operation
-------  -------------------------------------------------------
      0  LOAD TABLE CONVENTIONAL  (cr=418875 pr=147290 pw=0 time=0 us)
 999999    TABLE ACCESS FULL LOG_ETLFILE_117 (cr=142895 pr=142838 pw=0

Elapsed times include waiting on following events:
  Event waited on                    Times    Max. Wait  Total Waited
  ---------------------------       Waited    ----------  ------------
  db file scattered read             1193          0.30         48.48
  db file sequential read            4453          0.01          0.11
  log file switch completion           17          0.37          1.48
  free buffer waits                 51787          0.99        127.70
  latch: cache buffers lru chain      174          0.02          0.26
  buffer busy waits                  1831          0.36          2.74
```

Free buffer waits occur when the database writer process (DBWR) cannot keep up with the rate of changed blocks in the buffer cache. But why would the DBWR fall behind? Shouldn't it be able to keep up? Actually, the database writer is at a significant disadvantage compared to user sessions and can fall behind quite easily. Here are a few of the factors working against the database writer:

❏ There is only one database writer process responsible for writing the dirty blocks to disk, whereas there can be hundreds or thousands of user sessions modifying blocks. Even with Asynchronous IO allowing the DBWR to write to multiple disks in parallel (more on that later), the DBWR can easily be overwhelmed by user session activity.

❏ Writing a modified block to disk requires a real disk IO, whereas modifying a block involves changing only data in memory. Memory is faster than disk, so it will always be faster to change a block than to write out a block.

DBWR DIRECT AND ASYNCHRONOUS IO

Asynchronous IO enables a process to write to multiple disk devices simultaneously. Without asynchronous IO, a process must wait for each IO to complete before requesting the next IO. Asynchronous IO is tremendously important for the

DBWR because otherwise it will almost certainly fall behind when multiple user sessions modify blocks concurrently.

When datafiles are on filesystems—as opposed to Automatic Storage Management (ASM) or raw devices—asynchronous IO is controlled by the parameter FILESYSTEMIO_OPTIONS. For ASM, asynchronous IO is enabled by default.

In addition, filesystems usually have their own buffer cache that reduces disk IO in a similar way to Oracle's buffer cache. Sometimes the combination of Oracle's buffer cache and the filesystem buffer cache can work in your favor. However, for the DBWR the filesystem buffer cache just gets in the way because the DBWR has to *write through* the cache to ensure that the IO makes it to disk. Filesystem direct IO allows the DBWR and other Oracle processes to bypass the filesystem buffer cache.

Both asynchronous IO and filesystem direct IO tend to help reduce free buffer waits. There's no real drawback to asynchronous IO, but filesystem direct IO might have the effect of increasing disk read waits. This is because the filesystem buffer cache sometimes reduces IO read times by keeping some filesystem blocks in memory.

Figure 17-3 shows how the various settings of FILESYSTEMIO_OPTIONS affected the free buffer wait times experienced by our earlier example. Both asynchronous IO and filesystem direct IO were effective in reducing free buffer waits. However note that enabling filesystem direct IO reduced free buffer waits but also increased data file read time. In this example the net effect was positive; in other situations the increase in disk read time might be more costly than the reduction in free buffer waits.

To enable asynchronous IO, you should ensure that the value of DISK_ASYNCH_IO is set to TRUE and the value of FILESYSTEMIO_OPTIONS is set to ASYNCH or SETALL.

To enable filesystem direct IO, the value of FILESYSTEMIO_OPTIONS should be set to DIRECTIO or SETALL.

If free buffer waits are an issue, ensure that asynchronous IO is enabled and consider filesystem direct IO. For filesystem based datafiles, try FILESYSTEMIO_OPTIONS= SETALL.

On older versions of Oracle and the OS, asynchronous IO might be unavailable or inefficient.[1] If so, the DBWR_IO_SLAVES can be used to create multiple database writer processes that simulate asynchronous IO. It's conceivable that

---

[1] See, for instance, Oracle support notes 279069.1, 414673.1.

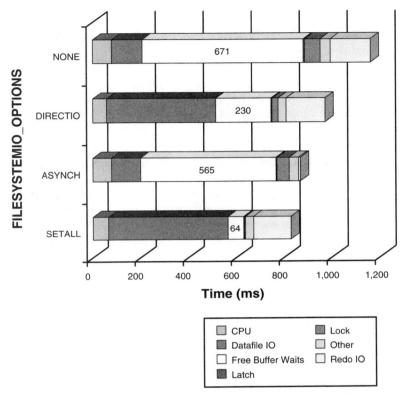

FIGURE 17-3 Effect of asynchronous IO and filesystem Direct IO on free buffer waits.

employing both asynchronous IO and multiple slaves together might give better performance in cases where free buffer waits are extreme.

In Oracle 11g, the table V$IOSTAT_FILE can be used to check that asynchronous IO is enabled; the following query shows that all data files have asynchronous IO enabled:

```
SQL> SELECT asynch_io, COUNT( * )
  2   FROM v$iostat_file
  3   WHERE filetype_name in ( 'Data File', Temp File')
  4   GROUP BY asynch_io
  5   /
ASYNCH_IO   COUNT(*)
---------   ----------
ASYNC_ON          5
```

OTHER REMEDIES FOR FREE BUFFER WAITS

After implementing asynchronous and filesystem direct IO, you can consider these measures to reduce free buffer waits:

❏ Direct path inserts, as described in Chapter 14, "DML Tuning," bypass the buffer cache and so do not contribute to free buffer waits. Of course, only one process can perform direct path inserts on a given table at any time, but you can use parallel DML, as discussed in Chapter 13, "Parallel SQL," to improve insert throughput.

❏ Direct path disk reads are usually utilized when Oracle performs parallel query and in Oracle 11g might also be used when performing serial full table scans. Because blocks read in this manner are not introduced to the buffer cache, they will not contribute to, or suffer from, free buffer waits. See Chapter 18 for more information on direct path IO.

❏ The capability of the DBWR to write blocks to the datafiles is ultimately limited by the speed and the bandwidth of the disks that support those datafiles. Providing datafiles are well striped, adding disks to the volume might increase bandwidth; see Chapter 21, "Disk IO Tuning Fundamentals," for a more detailed discussion.

❏ RAID 5 and similar parity-based redundancy schemes (RAID4, RAID3, and such) impose a heavy penalty on IO write times. Imposing RAID 5 or similar on Oracle data files is a perfect recipe for creating free buffer wait contention.

❏ Increasing the buffer cache size can reduce free buffer waits by enabling the DBWR more time to catch up between IO write peaks. Figure 17-4 illustrates the reduction in free buffer waits when the relevant database cache (KEEP cache, in this example) was increased from 50M to 400M.

Free buffer waits might indicate a need to increase IO bandwidth on data file volumes, potentially by adding additional disks to the stripe. Also consider increasing the size of the buffer cache or using direct path IO.

RECOVERY WRITER (RVWR) WAITS

The Flashback Database feature enables the database to be rolled back to a prior state if a problem occurs. This can reduce the recovery time compared to the traditional approach of restoring datafiles from backup and rolling forward from archived redo logs.

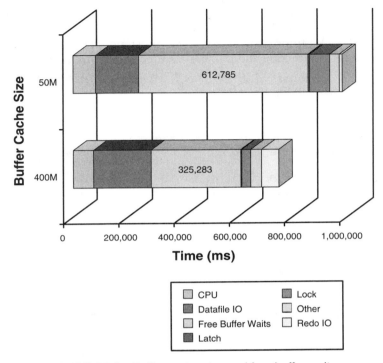

FIGURE 17-4   Buffer cache size and free buffer waits.

Although a useful feature, the Flashback Database feature can result in contention for buffers in the SGA.

If Flashback Database is enabled, whenever a block is modified, a *before image* of the affected data needs to be written to *flashback logs*. These before image records are written first to an area of the SGA called the *flashback buffer*. This area is dynamically sized and usually only 4MB to 16MB in size. You can view the size of the buffer with the following query:

```
SQL> SELECT pool,name,round(bytes/1048576,2) mb
  2  FROM v$sgastat
  3  WHERE name LIKE 'flashback generation buff';
POOL           NAME                        MB
------------   ------------------------    ----------
shared pool    flashback generation buff      3.8
```

The recovery writer process (RVWR) is responsible for writing the contents of the flashback buffer to disk. If the RVWR can't keep up, sessions will need to wait for space in the buffer to be freed before completing their block modification. In this event a *flashback buf free by RVWR* wait, which we might refer to as a *flashback buffer wait*, occurs.

Flashback buffer waits occur in circumstances similar to free buffer waits. Indeed, after optimizing the database writer in our previous example, enabling the flashback log feature immediately resulted in flashback buffer waits, as shown in the following trace file:

```
*************************************************************************
insert /*+ noappend */ into opsg2_log_data d
select  * from log_etlfile_117

call     count      elapsed       disk      query    current       rows
-------  ------  ----------  ---------  ---------  ---------  ----------
Parse        1        0.00          0          2          0           0
Execute      1      790.29     196722     402288    1342106      999999
Fetch        0        0.00          0          0          0           0
-------  ------  ----------  ---------  ---------  ---------  ----------
total        2      790.29     196722     402290    1342106      999999

Rows     Row Source Operation
-------  -------------------------------------------------
      0  LOAD TABLE CONVENTIONAL  (cr=411486 pr=196758 pw=0 time=0 us)
 999999    TABLE ACCESS FULL LOG_ETLFILE_117 (cr=142895 pr=57274 pw=0

Elapsed times include waiting on following events:
  Event waited on              Times   Max. Wait  Total Waited
  -------------------------    Waited  ----------  ------------
  db file scattered read          488       0.24         12.59
  enq: FB - contention            434       0.25         12.15
  db file sequential read      139448       0.54        614.78
  enq: TX - contention            101       0.15          2.03
  enq: HW - contention            125       0.04          0.24
  buffer busy waits              1250       1.00          3.59
  read by other session           242       0.03          0.29
  log buffer space                 10       1.00          6.83
  log file switch completion       17       0.26          1.37
  flashback buf free by RVWR      938       0.99        108.64
  flashback free VI log             4       0.05          0.16
```

IMPROVING FLASHBACK LOG IO

We have fewer options for relieving flashback buffer waits than we do for free buffer waits. Increasing the buffer cache itself is unlikely to help, and the FILESYSTEMIO_OPTIONS parameter does not directly influence recovery writer IO. The most effective course of action is to ensure that the RVWR has adequate

IO bandwidth: The IO system needs to support a sustained write rate sufficient to ensure that the flashback buffer does not fill up. This might involve

❏ Placing the Flashback Recovery Area (FRA)—the area on disk that hosts flashback logs—on dedicated devices. It's common to co-locate archived logs and flashback logs in the FRA; you might consider moving each to its own dedicated volume on independent disks. The FRA should generally not be co-located with the disk volumes supporting database files or redo logs.

❏ Increasing the number of disk devices supporting the FRA. Although flashback IO is sequential, the maximum write rate increases if you extend the FRA across multiple disk drives and use fine-grained striping. See Chapter 21 for more guidance on optimizing disk layouts.

❏ Performing other IO optimizations as outlined in Chapters 21 and 22, "Advanced IO Techniques."

Figure 17-5 shows how placing archive logs and flashback logs on separate devices can reduce flashback buffer waits. Changing the archive destination from

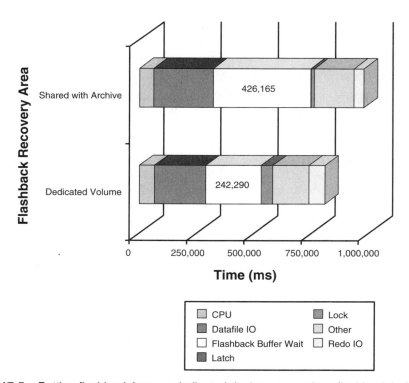

FIGURE 17-5   Putting flashback logs on dedicated devices can reduce flashback buffer waits.

the FRA (USE_DB_RECOVERY_FILE_DEST) to a dedicated destination supported by independent disks reduced flashback buffer waits by almost 45 percent.

To relieve flashback buffer waits (***flashback buf free by RVWR***), optimize the IO layout of the Flashback Recovery Area by placing it on dedicated, fine-grained striped disk devices.

INCREASING THE SIZE OF THE FLASHBACK LOG BUFFER

Increasing the size of the flashback log buffer might help relieve flashback buffer waits.

The size of the flashback buffer is limited to one SGA *granule*. An SGA granule is usually either 4M or 16M, depending upon the size of the SGA. Furthermore the hidden parameter _FLASHBACK_GENERATION_BUFFER_SIZE limits the size of the flashback buffer to 8MB. To maximize the flashback buffer size, both need to be adjusted. Here are the steps to create a 16M flashback buffer:

1. Increase your SGA granule size to 16M, either by setting the SGA size greater than 1GB or by setting the hidden parameter _KSMG_GRANULE_SIZE (not recommended on a production system).
2. Set the parameter _FLASHBACK_GENERATION_BUFFER_SIZE to 16777216.
3. Turn flashback off to clear the existing logs and then turn it back on. This is necessary because the existing logs will be sized to the old flashback buffer size. You need to clear them out, or flashback log switch waits might occur.
4. You might also want to set _FLASHBACK_LOG_SIZE: The default setting is 1,000 database blocks. You can probably benefit from setting _FLASHBACK_LOG_SIZE to match your new _FLASHBACK_GENERATION_BUFFER_SIZE unless you use a large block size.

After following the preceding steps, you should now have a 16MB flashback buffer and 16MB flashback log files. Depending on your workload, this might reduce or eliminate flashback buffer waits. For the sample workload used earlier in this chapter, increasing the flashback buffer to 16M reduced flashback buffer waits by approximately 40 percent. Figure 17-6 illustrates the improvement.

Increasing the size of the flashback buffer can involve the use of undocumented and hence unsupported parameters but might be effective in reducing flashback buffer waits.

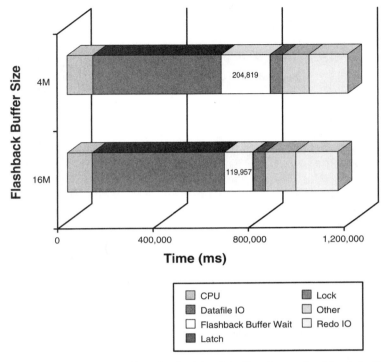

FIGURE 17-6 Effect of increasing the flashback buffer size on flashback buffer waits.

BUFFER BUSY WAITS

Buffer busy waits occur when a session wants to perform an operation on a buffer, but the buffer is operated on by another session.

Traditionally, the buffer busy waits event has been a catch all for any situation in which a session can obtain the relevant buffer cache latch but has to wait for another session to complete an operation on the buffer.

MEASURING BUFFER BUSY

The *buffer busy waits* event will be recorded whenever a buffer busy situation occurs. It is included in the *Concurrency* wait class. High levels of buffer busy waits will, therefore, show up in Enterprise Manager in the *Concurrency* category.

The analysis of buffer busy waits can depend on the type of buffer involved. We can ascertain those by examining V$WAITSTAT:

```
SQL> SELECT class, COUNT, time,
  2          ROUND(time * 100 / SUM(time) OVER (), 2) pct
  3  FROM v$waitstat
  4  ORDER BY time DESC
  5  /
CLASS                                  COUNT        TIME     PCT
-------------------------------   ---------   ---------   -------
data block                               138         185   60.66
undo header                              327         114   37.38
file header block                          6           6    1.97
save undo header                           0           0     .00
```

For waits against blocks from segments (tables, indexes, and so on) we can identify the segments involved in buffer busy waits by examining the V$SEGMENT_STATISTICS table:

```
SQL> SELECT owner, object_name, SUM(VALUE) buffer_busy_count ,
  2          round(sum(value) * 100/sum(sum(value)) over(),2) pct
  3   FROM v$segment_statistics
  4  WHERE statistic_name IN ('gc buffer busy', 'buffer busy waits')
  5    AND VALUE > 0
  6  GROUP BY owner, object_name
  7  ORDER BY SUM(VALUE) DESC
  8  /
OWNER              OBJECT_NAME           BUFFER_BUSY_COUNT     PCT
----------------   -------------------   -----------------   -------
OPSG               LOG_DATA_PK                         114   83.82
SYS                SEG$                                  4    2.94
SYSMAN             MGMT_JOB_EXECUTION                    4    2.94
SYS                JOB$                                  4    2.94
SYS                I_JOB_NEXT                            3    2.21
```

TRADITIONAL CAUSES OF BUFFER BUSY WAITS

Many of the historical causes of buffer busy wait contention have been alleviated in recent releases of Oracle or have been recategorized to make the diagnosis easier. The three most common causes of buffer busy wait prior to Oracle 10g were

❑ Buffer busy waits on data blocks caused by insufficient freelists. In Manual Segment Storage Management (MSSM) (see Chapter 4, "Logical and Physical Database Design"), when sessions want to insert rows into a table, they first inspect the freelist to identify blocks that might have free space. If there is only one freelist, all sessions attempting to insert will be directed to the same blocks, and buffer busy waits against that block will result. In Automatic Segment Storage Management (ASSM), multiple freelists are automatically configured as required and this form of buffer busy waits is minimized.

❑ Buffer busy waits occurring as a result of simultaneous reads of a block that is not in the buffer cache. When two sessions want to read the same block that is not in the cache, one session reads the block into the buffer cache while the other session waits until the block is loaded. Prior to Oracle 10g, the wait was recorded as *buffer busy*. From 10g forward, this form of wait is recorded as *read by other session*. High levels of this wait are often associated with concurrent full table scans of a single table and do not generally represent a cause for concern. However, segments that experience this wait might be candidates for cache optimization by using the CACHE hint or the KEEP pool (see Chapter 18).

❑ Buffer busy waits against undo header block classes might indicate that the number of undo (rollback) segments is insufficient for the number of concurrent transactions. Adding more undo segments might be indicated. With automatic undo management, this scenario should rarely occur.

Many of the traditional causes of buffer busy waits, such as freelists, read by other session, and undo header waits, should be rare in Oracle 10g and 11g.

BUFFER BUSY AND HOT BLOCKS

With the traditional causes of buffer busy eliminated or recategorized, modern buffer busy waits are generally the result of high rates of normal activity against specific buffers: hot blocks.

Most of the time, the contention is for multiple rows within a single block, not contention for specific rows. If multiple sessions want to modify different rows in the same block, buffer busy waits can occur.

For instance, the following trace output shows a SQL statement that updates rows in a fairly small table, only a couple of blocks of data in total. When multiple sessions run this workload concurrently, they will experience lock waits when they try to update the same row. When they try to update different rows within the same block, buffer busy waits can result:

```
UPDATE BB_DATA SET DATETIME = :B3 , NVAL = :B2
WHERE
 ID=:B1
```

call	count	elapsed	disk	query	current	rows
Parse	1	0.00	0	0	0	0
Execute	125332	96.02	0	305168	364142	125332
Fetch	0	0.00	0	0	0	0
total	125333	96.02	0	305168	364142	125332

Rows	Row Source Operation
1	UPDATE BB_DATA (cr=2 pr=0 pw=0 time=0 us)
1	INDEX UNIQUE SCAN BB_DATA_PK (cr=2 pr=0 pw=0 time=0 us

```
Elapsed times include waiting on following events:
```

Event waited on	Times Waited	Max. Wait	Total Waited
latch: In memory undo latch	2162	0.35	4.77
latch: enqueue hash chains	72	0.04	0.24
latch: cache buffers chains	18	0.08	0.15
enq: TX - row lock contention	1466	0.31	14.14
buffer busy waits	3143	0.26	16.45
resmgr:cpu quantum	363	0.12	4.82
latch free	5	0.00	0.00
. . .	. . .	. . .	. . .

```
****************************************************************************
```

If buffer busy waits are caused by contention for rows within the same block, logically the solution might be to try to arrange for those rows to be stored in separate blocks.

Partitioning the table is an effective way to split up rows; if you hash partition the table, rows that would normally be stored together will be stored in separate blocks within different partitions. Although partitioning is an effective strategy, it might not be available to you if you have not licensed the partitioning option.

Another way to split up the blocks, not requiring any special licensing, is to reduce the number of rows that are stored in each block. This can increase the storage requirements for the table, but if the table is small we probably don't care too much. Unfortunately, we have only an indirect mechanism for adjusting the rows per block by adjusting PCTFREE. PCTFREE determines the amount of free space reserved for row updates; if we set it high, the number of rows in each block will be low.

We can calculate the appropriate value of PCTFREE by looking at the row length statistics for the table. For instance, this query suggests that each row is approximately 3 percent of block size. Setting PCTFREE to 97 would, therefore, usually result in only a single row in each block.

```
SQL> SELECT block_size, avg_row_len,
  2           ROUND(avg_row_len * 100 / block_size, 2)
  3              row_pct_of_block
  4      FROM user_tablespaces
  5      JOIN user_tables
  6      USING (tablespace_name)
  7   WHERE table_name = 'BB_DATA';
BLOCK_SIZE AVG_ROW_LEN ROW_PCT_OF_BLOCK
---------- ----------- ----------------
      8192         234             2.86
```

Figure 17-7 shows the effect of rebuilding the table with a higher PCTFREE; buffer busy waits were practically eliminated.

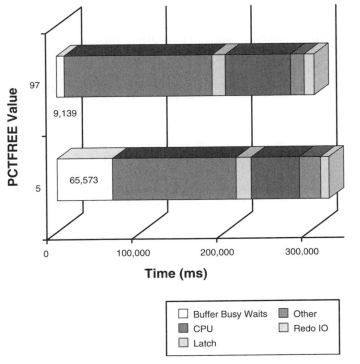

FIGURE 17-7   Increasing PCTFREE to reduce buffer busy contention.

Another way to split up rows across blocks is to use a hash cluster as discussed in Chapter 6, "Application Design and Implementation." The hash value of the primary key determines in which block a row will be stored, and the SIZE and HASHKEYS parameters effectively determine how many rows will be stored in each block.

Buffer busy waits can result for contention for different rows within the same block. Storing these rows into separate blocks might be the best solution using partitioning, high values for PCTFREE, or hash clustering.

REDO LOG BUFFER WAITS

DML operations make entries either to the shared redo *log buffer* or to private redo log *strands*. Theses entries are written to the redo logs periodically or when a commit occurs. If the in-memory entries can't be written to the redo log fast enough, the session must wait for space to be cleared and *log buffer space* waits will result.

Here is trace file output showing a DML operation in which log buffer space accounted for a little more than 50 percent of the total elapsed time:

```
SQL ID: 6k8x7wtwzkz1t
Plan Hash: 0
INSERT INTO OPSG_LOG_DATA(ID, DATETIME, DATA)
VALUES
 (:B1 , :B2 , :B3 )

call      count    elapsed        disk       query     current        rows
------- ------  --------- ---------- ---------- ---------- ----------
Parse         1     0.00           0           0           0           0
Execute    1000    61.41           1      227832     1075182     1000000
Fetch         0     0.00           0           0           0           0
------- ------  --------- ---------- ---------- ---------- ---------
total      1001    61.41           1      227832     1075182     1000000

Rows     Row Source Operation
------- ---------------------------------------------------
      0  LOAD TABLE CONVENTIONAL   (cr=558 pr=1 pw=0 time=0 us)

Elapsed times include waiting on following events:
  Event waited on                   Times   Max. Wait  Total Waited
  ------------------------------    Waited  ---------- ------------
  log buffer space                    341       0.35        32.07
```

Clearly, using UNLOGGED DML (see Chapter 14) can reduce the amount of redo generation, but this will not be acceptable in most circumstances because the changes made will be unrecoverable in the event we need to recover from backup.

Direct mode insert operations, which we looked at earlier in this chapter and in Chapter 14, significantly reduce the amount of redo generation and can be effective when log buffer space waits are a concern. Of course, direct mode insert is not applicable in all circumstances; in particular, direct mode insert locks the table in question, blocking other concurrent DML.

Figure 17-8 shows how using direct path inserts almost totally eliminated log buffer waits for a sample workload. However, some of the gain came at the cost of increased wait time for direct path IO.

The log buffer is generally fairly small and increasing it (by altering the LOG_BUFFER parameter) is not always going to reduce space waits. If the redo generation is consistently high, and the redo log writer cannot clear the log as fast as entries are generated, a bigger buffer is unlikely to help. On the other hand, if your redo generation occurs in bursts, having a larger redo log buffer might help because the redo log writer can empty the buffer between bursts.

Figure 17-9 shows how increasing the log buffer from 5m to 20m had a small but significant effect for such a workload that exhibited bursts of redo generation.

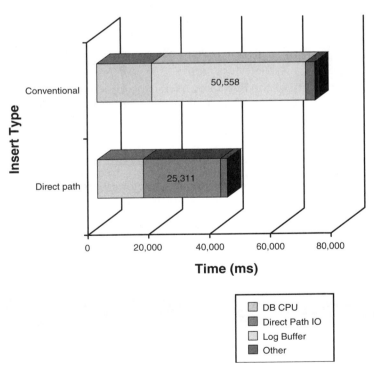

FIGURE 17-8 Direct path inserts can reduce redo log buffer waits.

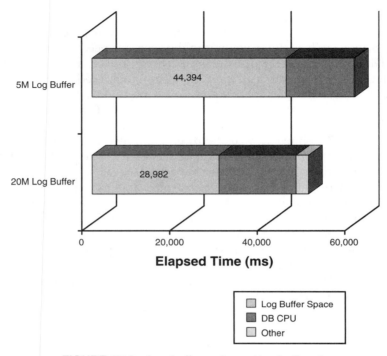

FIGURE 17-9   Log buffer waits and log buffer size.

The capability of the Redo Log Writer process to clear the redo log buffer is limited by the IO bandwidth available. Consequently, redo log space waits will almost always occur if the redo logs are placed on slow or unoptimized disk volumes. We discuss redo log IO optimization in detail in Chapter 21.

> Redo log buffer space waits can occur during heavy redo generation. Reducing redo generation by using direct path inserts can help reduce these waits, and increasing the log buffer might help during bursts of redo generation. Ultimately, optimizing redo log IO is critical to avoiding log buffer waits.

SUMMARY

In this chapter we looked at contention for shared memory. Oracle uses shared memory to cache data blocks and to reduce IO delays when writing log records to the redo and flashback logs.

Free buffer waits occur when a session wants to introduce a new block into the buffer cache, but all blocks are modified (or dirty). This occurs when the database writer (DBWR) cannot write the blocks out to disk as fast as they are being modified. Optimizing data file IO is usually indicated, particularly asynchronous and filesystem direct IO. Increasing the size of the buffer cache might also relieve the contention if the DBWR is falling behind only sporadically. Direct path read-and-write operations bypass the buffer cache and will not suffer from, or contribute to, free buffer waits.

The recovery writer (RVWR) process writes before image records of changed blocks to the flashback logs when the database is operating in flashback database mode. Flashback buffer waits—*flashback buf free by RVWR*—occur if the small flashback buffer cannot be cleared fast enough. Ensuring the flashback logs are on fast dedicated devices can help. Increasing the size of the flashback buffer is an unsupported procedure that might, however, reduce flashback waits.

Buffer busy waits occur when there is contention for rows in the same block. Splitting rows across multiple blocks might relieve the contention. Possible options include partitioning, hash clustering, or setting high values for PCTFREE.

The redo log buffer is used to accumulate redo log entries that will eventually be written to the redo log. Sessions experience *log buffer space* waits if they want to generate redo but the buffer is full. Asides from optimizing redo log IO, you can explore the use of unlogged and direct path inserts that generate reduced redo entries. Increasing the size of the log buffer can relieve short-term log buffer space waits.

Chapter 18

BUFFER CACHE TUNING

In the preceding chapters, we discussed how to reduce the demand placed on the Oracle database through application design and SQL tuning. We then proceeded to eliminate contention preventing Oracle from processing that demand. Our objective has been to minimize the logical IO demand that is sent from the application to Oracle and remove any obstacles that block that demand.

If we've done a good job so far, we have achieved a logical IO rate that is at a realistic level for the tasks that the application must perform. Now it's time to try to prevent as much as possible of that logical IO from turning into physical IO. Remember, no matter how much you optimize your IO subsystem, disk IO will still be orders of magnitude, at least a hundred times, slower than IO requests that can be satisfied in memory.[1] We therefore want to ensure that the amount of logical IO (*fast* IO) that turns into physical IO (*slow* IO) is as small as possible.

In this chapter we look at how to optimize buffer cache memory to reduce disk IO for datafile IO operations. The buffer cache exists primarily to cache frequently accessed data blocks in memory so that the application doesn't need to read them from disk. Buffer cache tuning is, therefore, critical in preventing logical IO from turning into physical IO.

In each release of Oracle since 9i, Oracle has increasingly automated the allocation of memory to the various caches and pools. In 10g, Oracle introduced

---

[1] A raw memory access is easily 1,000s of times faster than a disk read. However, because of the complex nature of Oracle memory accesses, things like latches and mutexes, a logical read might "only" be 100s of times faster.

Automatic Shared Memory Management (ASMM) that allows Oracle to allocate memory within the SGA dynamically based on workload demand. In 11g Automatic Memory Management (AMM) enables memory to be moved between the SGA and PGA automatically.

AMM is a Very Good Thing and will usually result in a more than adequate outcome with a minimum of effort. However, as is often the case with automation, moving from adequate to optimal might require human intervention. This is definitely true for buffer cache tuning; configuring multiple buffer pools and setting minimum sizes for specific pools is often required to get the best outcome.

BUFFER CACHE PRINCIPLES

The buffer cache consists of one or more shared memory regions within that overall area of shared memory known as the System Global Area (SGA). Chapter 2, "Oracle Architecture and Concepts," provides a high-level description of the SGA and its various components and the other memory regions used by Oracle.

When a SQL statement executes, it identifies the blocks of data that are needed to satisfy the request, mostly index and table blocks. Most of the time, the query first looks for these blocks in the buffer cache; if the blocks are not present, the server process reads the blocks from the data files and inserts them into the buffer cache.

Of course, the buffer cache can hold only so many blocks, and the introduction of new blocks into the cache implies that some older blocks need to be eliminated from the cache. If all blocks are dirty (modified) and cannot be eliminated from the cache, a *free buffer wait* occurs as Oracle waits for the database writer to write the dirty blocks to disk. This is discussed in Chapter 17, "Shared Memory Contention."

THE LRU LIST

To determine which blocks should be kept in the buffer cache, and which should be freed to make way for new blocks, Oracle maintains a list of cached blocks that indicates roughly how frequently the blocks have been accessed. Oracle documentation and Oracle specialists often refer to this as the *Least Recently Used (LRU) list* and the *LRU algorithm*, although Oracle has not used a strict implementation of an LRU algorithm since at least version 8i.

The exact implementation of the LRU list is complex and only partially documented. However, the basics of the algorithm are straightforward. Blocks on the list are either "warm" (recently accessed) or "cold" (not recently accessed). Blocks are warmed as they are accessed and cool if they have not been accessed recently. The coldest blocks will be removed from the cache first to make way for new blocks. We often describe the coldest blocks as being at the LRU end of the LRU list, and the hottest blocks as being at the Most Recently Used (MRU) end. Of course, these movements are somewhat metaphorical: Blocks are not actually moving in the cache.

When a block is first introduced into the cache, it will be located around the middle of the list and will not be warmed until a short timeout period has expired. This is so that blocks that are accessed from within the same transaction do not get inappropriately warmed. Subsequent accesses to a block tend to warm the block and tend to prevent it from being removed from the cache.

TABLE SCAN HANDLING

Oracle treats blocks introduced from large table scans[2] differently from blocks introduced by index lookups. The chance that blocks from a large table scan will be accessed again are low, and there's a risk that by putting all the blocks from that table scan into cache that they will flush out blocks that are likely to be accessed again soon. Consequently, Oracle tries to avoid filling the buffer cache with blocks from a large full table scan.

Oracle has two options to prevent these blocks from flooding the cache:

❑ Putting the blocks at the LRU end of the list, so that they will be flushed almost immediately.
❑ Using direct path IO, which bypasses the buffer cache. Blocks read in this way will not enter the buffer cache at all.

By default, the first approach, moving table scan blocks to the LRU end of the list, is the approach employed by Oracle in 10g whereas the direct path option, bypassing the buffer cache, is the approach favored by Oracle 11g.

Blocks from large table scans will generally not be included in the buffer cache at all (11g) or will be quickly flushed out of the buffer cache (10g).

THE CACHE PROPERTY

The CACHE table property, which can be set in the CREATE TABLE or ALTER TABLE statements and by the CACHE hint, instructs Oracle to treat blocks read from a table scan equally to blocks read by index lookup. When the CACHE setting is in effect, blocks from a full table scan are inserted into the middle of the LRU list rather than at the LRU end of the list.

---

[2] A large table scan is one that involves more blocks than the value of the hidden parameter "_SMALL_TABLE_THRESHOLD".

The CACHE property or hint will have no effect if the table is being read using direct path IO because the blocks will not enter the buffer cache at all.

We looked at using the CACHE property to optimize table scans in Chapter 6, "Application Design and Implementation."

The CACHE hint or table property can be used to encourage caching of table scan blocks. It will be less effective in Oracle 11g because the table might have been read using direct path reads.

DIRECT PATH IO

The *adaptive direct read* algorithm introduced in Oracle 11g enables Oracle to choose direct path IO when it determines that there would be little benefit from introducing buffers into the buffer cache. The algorithm appears to take into account the size of the buffer cache, the number of table blocks to be read, the number of blocks already in cache, the type of access (index versus table scan), and certain undocumented parameters. Prior to Oracle 11g these direct path reads would usually be used only by parallel queries.

The advantage of the direct read approach is that Oracle can avoid introducing useless blocks into the buffer cache and also assists in avoiding the contention for cache buffers chains latches (see Chapter 16, "Latch and Mutex Contention") and in avoiding the other buffer contention issues as discussed in Chapter 17.

These virtues aside, it can be frustrating when Oracle decides to use direct path IO in circumstances in which you want to minimize IO by exploiting the buffer cache. Adjusting various undocumented parameters to avoid these direct reads might not be effective and is not generally recommended. However, if you really want to discourage direct path reads for serial table scans, increasing the value of _SMALL_TABLE_THRESHOLD to a value greater than the table in question seems to be effective.

Make sure that you don't confuse direct IO that arises from temporary segment IO—resulting from sorts and hash joins where PGA memory is insufficient—with direct IO arising from datafile reads. Direct IO from temporary segments cannot and should not use the buffer cache, whereas direct IO against permanent segments *might* perform better if buffered in the buffer cache.

You can see how the IO breaks down by issuing the following query:

```
SQL> WITH sysstat AS
  2       (SELECT name, VALUE,
  3               SUM(DECODE(name, 'physical reads', VALUE)) OVER ()
  4               total_phys_reads,
  5               SUM(DECODE(name, 'physical reads direct', VALUE))
  6                 OVER ()
```

```
 7                          tot_direct_reads
 8            FROM v$sysstat
 9            WHERE name IN
10                  ('physical reads',
11                   'physical reads direct',
12                   'physical reads direct temporary tablespace'))
13  SELECT name, VALUE,
14         ROUND(VALUE * 100 / total_phys_reads, 2) pct_of_physical,
15         decode(name,'physical reads',0,
16         ROUND(VALUE * 100 / tot_direct_reads, 2)) pct_of_direct
17  FROM sysstat
18  /
```

| | | Pct of | Pct of |
NAME	Count	Phys Rds	Direct Rds
physical reads	43,486,570	100.00	.00
physical reads direct	34,987,037	80.45	100.00
physical reads direct temporary	181,061	.42	.52
tablespace			

In this example, direct path reads account for just more than 80 percent of overall physical reads. No matter how perfectly we size or configure the buffer cache, we can reduce the physical read load only by 20 percent. Only a very small amount of the direct path reads are the result of temporary tablespace IO, so it's unlikely in this case that we could reduce the IO through PGA memory management either.

> Direct path IO bypasses the buffer cache and cannot be reduced through buffer cache configuration. Direct path reads to the temporary tablespace are best addressed through PGA memory configuration.

BUFFER CACHE CONFIGURATION AND TUNING

Let's now turn our attention to optimizing the configuration of the buffer cache with an aim to minimizing physical IO.

MONITORING THE BUFFER CACHE

The contents of the buffer cache can be examined in the view V$BH, which contains one row for each block in the buffer cache. We can use this view to see which segments are currently in the buffer cache and how many blocks for each segment are cached.

```
SQL> SELECT s.buffer_pool, o.owner || '.' || o.object_name segment,
  2            COUNT( * ) cached_blocks, s.blocks seg_blocks,
  3            ROUND(COUNT( * ) * 100 / s.blocks, 2) pct_cached,
  4            SUM(DECODE(dirty, 'Y', 1, 0)) dirty_blocks
  5     FROM v$bh
  6     JOIN dba_objects o   ON (object_id = objd)
  7     JOIN dba_segments s
  8       ON (o.owner = s.owner AND object_name = segment_name)
  9   GROUP BY s.buffer_pool, s.blocks, o.owner, o.object_name
 10   HAVING COUNT( * ) > 100
 11   ORDER BY COUNT( * ) DESC;
```

Buffer		Cached	Segment	Pct	Dirty
Pool	Segment	Blocks	blocks	Cached	blocks
DEFAULT	OPSG.TXN_DATA	57,242	3,737,632	1.53	0
KEEP	OPSG.TXN_SUMMARY	8,233	9,216	89.33	0
DEFAULT	OPSG.TXN_DATA_PK	2,548	92,160	2.76	0
DEFAULT	SYS.C_OBJ#	1,277	1,280	99.77	0
DEFAULT	SYS.OBJ$	868	896	96.88	0
DEFAULT	SYS.C_FILE#_BLOCK#	211	256	82.42	0

Note that the percentage of blocks cached as shown by this query can actually exceed 100 percent. For tables that are updated frequently, previous "versions" of data blocks can still be in memory to support consistent read, so it is possible for a table or index to have more blocks in cache than exist on disk. The STATUS column in V$BH will differentiate between the current blocks (xcur) and those maintained for consistent read (cr).

THE BUFFER CACHE HIT RATE

Of all the metrics, ratios, and indicators put forward in the name of Oracle performance tuning, none has a longer or more controversial history than the notorious Buffer Cache Hit Ratio.

The Buffer Cache Hit Ratio represents the proportion of block requests that are satisfied by the buffer cache without requiring a disk read. Each *hit*—when a block is found in memory—is a Good Thing because it avoids a time consuming disk IO. It therefore seems intuitively obvious that a high Buffer Cache Hit Ratio is also a Good Thing. Since time immemorial, or at least since the 1980s, Oracle DBAs have therefore attempted to tune their Oracle databases by achieving an increase in the Buffer Cache Hit Ratio.

Unfortunately, while the Buffer Cache Hit Ratio clearly measures *something*, it's not necessarily or even usually true that a high Buffer Cache Hit Ratio is indicative of a well-tuned database. In particular, poorly tuned SQL often reads the same data blocks over and over again; these blocks are almost certainly in memory, so the most grossly inefficient SQLs ironically tend to generate very high Buffer Cache Hit Ratios. Indeed, Connor McDonald famously created a script that could generate any desired hit ratio, essentially by uselessly reading the same blocks over and over again (www.oracledba.co.uk/tips/choose.htm). Connor's script performs no useful work but can achieve an almost perfect hit ratio.

> There is no "correct" value for the Buffer Cache Hit Ratio; high values are just as likely to be the result of poorly tuned SQL as the result of well-tuned memory configuration.

The Buffer Cache Hit Ratio isn't necessarily irrelevant in all circumstances, however. For a constant workload and execution environment, an increase in the Buffer Cache Hit Ratio represents a decrease in the amount of physical IO, which will be desirable. However, outside of an automated benchmark, it's rare to observe a truly constant workload running within a static execution environment. However as we see later, attempting to increase the Buffer Cache Hit Ratio for a specific SQL can still be a valid goal.

If you want to calculate it, the *Oracle Performance Guide* suggests using the V$BUFFER_POOL_STATISTICS view to calculate the hit ratio. This has the advantage of allowing us to calculate the statistic for each buffer pool:

```
SELECT name, physical_reads, db_block_gets, consistent_gets,
       1 - (physical_reads / (db_block_gets + consistent_gets))
          AS "Hit Ratio"
    FROM v$buffer_pool_statistics;
```

However, this calculation ignores the effect of direct path IO and, therefore, might lead to an overly favorable calculation of the Buffer Cache Hit Ratio. You could argue that because direct path reads bypass the buffer cache, they should not be taken into account when calculating a Buffer Cache Hit Ratio. However it's also arguably true that you can't know the effectiveness of the buffer cache without taking into account the IO that bypasses it.

The following query calculates the Buffer Cache Hit Ratio and shows the underlying logical and physical read values for combined IO, direct IO, and nondirect IO:

```
SQL> WITH sysstats AS
  2      (SELECT CASE WHEN name LIKE '%direct' THEN 'Direct'
  3                   WHEN name LIKE '%cache' THEN 'Cache'
  4                   ELSE 'All' END AS category,
```

```
 5                    CASE WHEN name LIKE 'consistent%' THEN 'Consistent'
 6                      WHEN name LIKE 'db block%' THEN 'db block'
 7                      ELSE 'physical' END AS TYPE, VALUE
 8             FROM v$sysstat
 9             WHERE name IN ('consistent gets','consistent gets direct',
10                              'consistent gets from cache',
                               'db block gets',
11                             'db block gets direct',
                               'db block gets from cache',
12                             'physical reads', 'physical reads cache',
13                             'physical reads direct'))
14    SELECT category, db_block, consistent, physical,
15           ROUND(DECODE(category,'Direct', NULL,
16                 ((db_block + consistent) - physical)* 100
17                      / (db_block + consistent)), 2) AS hit_rate
18    FROM (SELECT category, SUM(DECODE(TYPE, 'db block', VALUE))
                 db_block,
19                SUM(DECODE(TYPE, 'Consistent', VALUE)) consistent,
20                SUM(DECODE(TYPE, 'physical', VALUE)) physical
21           FROM sysstats
22           GROUP BY category)
23    ORDER BY category DESC
24    /
                  DB Block    Consistent      Physical      Hit
Category             Gets          Gets          Gets     Rate
------------ ----------- ----------- ----------- ------
Direct         3,244,911   3,801,362   6,679,827
Cache         53,267,961  87,396,756   1,609,176   98.86
All           56,512,872  91,198,118   8,289,004   94.39
```

This query above calculates hit rates since database start-up. If you want to calculate the hit ratio over a shorter period of time, and you have installed the PL/SQL packages available at this book's Web site, you can issue the following query, which calculates the IO rates and hit ratio since the last time the query was run in the same session:

```
SQL> SELECT * FROM hit_rate_delta_view ;
 Sample             DB Block    Consistent     Physical     Hit
Seconds Category        Gets          Gets         Gets    Rate
------- ------------ ----------- ----------- ----------- ------
    311 Direct                0     100,034     100,717
    311 Cache             2,116     113,064      34,189   70.32
    311 All               2,116     213,098     134,906   37.32
```

Note the discrepancy between the two hit rates when calculated over the past 311 seconds: For reads that are eligible to utilize the buffer cache, approximately 70 percent were resolved without a physical IO. However, when we take direct reads into account, we see that the buffer cache was successful in reducing the overall read IO rate by only 37 percent.

The key insight here is that when direct path reads contribute to a significant proportion of overall IO, tuning the buffer cache might offer limited benefit: You might be better off trying to convert the direct IO to buffered IO or proceed directly to tuning the disk IO subsystem.

> On some databases, direct path reads might be a significant or dominant component of overall IO. In these cases, attempting to increase the Buffer Cache Hit Ratio will be partly or wholly futile.

MULTIPLE BUFFER CACHES

Oracle enables you to configure up to seven buffer caches. In addition to the default cache, you can specify two other caches named KEEP and RECYCLE and four caches with specific block sizes: 2, 4, 8, 16, and 32K. Only four of these block size-specific caches can be created because you cannot create one that has the database default block size: This block size is managed by the default cache.

The block size-specific caches only cache blocks from tablespaces with the equivalent nondefault block size. You might create such tablespaces when you want to align the block size with workload characteristics and segment sizes. The caches also support the scenario in which a transportable tablespace is installed that has a block size that is different from the database default.

The KEEP and RECYCLE pools enable you to optimize buffer cache effectiveness by segregating the objects within separate caches. Oracle has two main scenarios in mind for these caches as suggested by the cache names:

❏ Smaller segments that are typically accessed via frequent full table scans can be placed in the KEEP pool. This helps prevent them from being prematurely aged out of the buffer cache by the table scan caching algorithms discussed previously.

❏ Larger segments that are accessed by full table scan can be placed in the RECYCLE pool. This stops their blocks from being added to the default pool and possibly displacing more useful blocks.

These scenarios might have motivated the original implementation and the naming of the caches, but need not restrict the uses to which we put the caches today. In particular, the adaptive direct path algorithms of 11g generally prevents large table scan blocks from entering the cache at all, so assigning these tables to the RECYCLE pool is unlikely to achieve much. The KEEP cache scenario is still generally applicable, however.

Let's consider an example in which we take advantage of multiple buffer pools. Suppose our application processing is primarily based on two transactions. The first runs an OLTP style query that runs thousands of times per second and performs indexed lookups against a huge transaction table:

```
SELECT * FROM TXN_DATA WHERE TXN_ID = :B1
```

The second transaction is just as critical but runs at a much lower frequency. Among other things, it needs to read data from a much smaller summary table using the following query:

```
SELECT  TXN_TYPE, TIMESTAMP, SUM_SALES FROM TXN_SUMMARY TS
```

We want good performance for both of these queries, but when we examine their performance; we find that the summary query has a high miss rate and poor response time:

```
SQL> SELECT buffer_gets, disk_reads,
  2            ROUND(disk_reads * 100 / buffer_gets, 2) miss_rate,
  3            ROUND(user_io_wait_time * 100 / elapsed_time, 2) pct_io_time,
  4            ROUND(elapsed_time / executions / 1000, 2) avg_ms, sql_text
  5  FROM v$sql
  6  WHERE        sql_text NOT LIKE '%V$SQL%'
  7       AND buffer_gets > 0
  8       AND executions > 0
  9       AND sql_text LIKE '%FROM TXN_%'
 10  ORDER BY (buffer_gets) DESC
 11  /
    BUFFER_GETS        DISK_READS MISS_RATE PCT_IO_TIME     AVG_MS
--------------- ----------------- --------- ----------- ----------
SQL_TEXT
-------------------------------------------------------------------
     56,111,344         8,268,899     14.74       92.39        .34
SELECT * FROM TXN_DATA WHERE TXN_ID = :B1
        243,275           186,259     76.56       61.50    1035.43
SELECT  TXN_TYPE, TIMESTAMP, SUM_SALES FROM TXN_SUMMARY TS
```

Although the summary table is easily small enough to fit into cache, its blocks are being flushed out by the blocks introduced to cache by the OLTP query. We can use the CACHE hint to attempt to improve the caching of this small table scan, but that won't help if the sheer volume of the OLTP query pushes out summary table blocks between each execution.

Moving the TXN_SUMMARY table to the KEEP pool provides an ideal solution. We can achieve an almost perfect hit ratio for the summary query without sacrificing efficiency for the OLTP query. After doing this, we achieve the following execution profile:

```
   BUFFER_GETS      DISK_READS MISS_RATE PCT_IO_TIME      AVG_MS
---------------- ----------------- --------- ----------- ----------
SQL_TEXT
------------------------------------------------------------------
   648,871,297      94,531,395     14.57       91.19         .29
SELECT * FROM TXN_DATA WHERE TXN_ID = :B1
     2,861,836           8,105       .28         .70      349.71
SELECT TXN_TYPE, TIMESTAMP, SUM_SALES FROM TXN_SUMMARY TS
```

Average execution time for the summary query is reduced by more than 65 percent. Performance of the OLTP query is unaffected or even slightly improved. Figure 18-1 illustrates the performance gain.

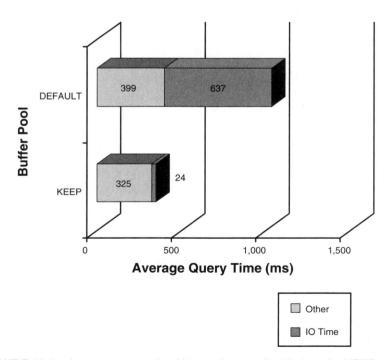

FIGURE 18-1   Improvement gained by moving small table into the KEEP pool.

Consider using multiple buffer caches to optimize the performance of infrequently executed SQLs that are achieving a poor Buffer Cache Hit Ratio.

We can examine the size and configuration of the various buffer pools by
examining the view V$BUFFER_POOL:

```
SQL> SELECT name, block_size / 1024 block_size_kb, current_ size,
  2          target_size,prev_size
  3  FROM v$buffer_pool;
                    Block      Current      Target        Prev
NAME                Size K          MB          MB          MB
------------------- ------ ----------- ----------- -----------
KEEP                    8          112         112           0
DEFAULT                 8          560         560         336
DEFAULT                 2           64          64           0
```

The V$BUFFER_POOL_STATISTICS view shows IO and other statistics for
each buffer pool:

```
SQL> SELECT name, block_size / 1024 block_size_kb,
  2          ROUND(db_block_change / 1000) db_change,
  3          ROUND(db_block_gets / 1000) db_gets,
  4          ROUND(consistent_gets / 1000) con_gets,
  5          ROUND(physical_reads / 1000) phys_rds
  6  FROM v$buffer_pool_statistics;
            Block      DB Block     DB Block   Consistent      Physical
NAME        Size K    Chg /1000   Gets /1000  gets /1000   Reads /1000
------- ------ ------------ ----------- ----------- -----------
KEEP          8            0           0       4,811            16
DEFAULT       8        8,850      16,177   1,391,797       339,738
```

SIZING THE BUFFER CACHE

The relationship between the size of the buffer cache and the amount of physical
IO is heavily dependent on the nature of the application workload. Sometimes,
increasing the buffer cache results in an immediate reduction in physical IO, but
in other circumstances the result is negligible. It depends on how frequently the
application reads the specific data blocks, the gap in time between accesses of
specific blocks, the size of the segments, and so on. It's difficult to determine how
effective additional buffer cache memory can be from theory alone.

Luckily Oracle provides us with a powerful tool for sizing the buffer cache: the buffer cache advisories. Buffer cache advisories provide accurate estimates of the increase or reduction in physical IO that would occur if the buffer cache were changed in size.

The mechanism Oracle uses to create these estimates is simple but powerful. Oracle essentially maintains an LRU list that contains twice as many blocks as actually exist within the cache. When a block is removed from the cache, it is not removed from the list, and if the block is requested later, Oracle can determine that the block *would* have been available *had* the buffer cache been larger. Oracle can therefore calculate with great accuracy the IOs that could have been avoided had the cache been bigger. A similar algorithm is used to determine the additional IOs that would have been incurred had the cache been smaller.

This advice is available in the table V$DB_CACHE_ADVICE. For each buffer pool, this view shows the estimated amount of IO that would have resulted had the cache been larger or smaller, from one-tenth to double the current size. The following query shows the effect of changing the size of a 500MB default buffer cache:

```
SQL> SELECT size_for_estimate, size_factor * 100 size_factor_pct,
  2          estd_physical_read_factor * 100
                estd_physical_read_factor_pct,
  3          estd_physical_reads, estd_physical_read_time,
  4          estd_pct_of_db_time_for_reads
  5   FROM v$db_cache_advice
  6   WHERE name = 'DEFAULT' AND block_size=8192
  7   ORDER BY size_for_estimate;
```

Cache Size	Relative Size pct	Relative Phys Rds Pct	Estimated Phys Rds	Estimated Read Time	Estimated Phys Reads Pct of DB Time
48	9.60	253.110	400,789,743	188,004	208.80
96	19.20	206.230	326,555,008	153,167	170.10
144	28.80	191.020	302,473,869	141,866	157.60
192	38.40	178.090	281,998,007	132,257	146.90
240	48.00	165.510	262,086,569	122,913	136.50
288	57.60	153.190	242,567,499	113,753	126.30
336	67.20	140.950	223,192,595	104,660	116.20
384	76.80	128.770	203,900,600	95,607	106.20
432	86.40	116.730	184,838,315	86,661	96.20
480	96.00	104.850	166,034,155	77,837	86.40
500	100.00	100.000	158,348,848	74,230	82.40
528	105.60	93.270	147,694,301	69,230	76.90
576	115.20	81.940	129,746,874	60,808	67.50

624	124.80	70.960	112,358,106	52,648	58.50
672	134.40	60.770	96,229,180	45,078	50.10
720	144.00	51.770	81,978,077	38,391	42.60
768	153.60	43.440	68,785,115	32,199	35.80
816	163.20	35.800	56,683,950	26,521	29.50
864	172.80	28.950	45,841,193	21,432	23.80
912	182.40	22.960	36,363,344	16,984	18.90
960	192.00	17.880	28,310,046	13,205	14.70

Increasing the size of the buffer cache from 500MB to 960MB is estimated to reduce IO, or at least the IO going through the buffer cache, by approximately 82 percent. So increasing the buffer cache size, if we have available free memory, would definitely be worthwhile.

> Use the buffer cache advisories, V$DB_CACHE_ADVICE, to determine the likely impact of resizing the buffer pools.

Here's a variant on that query that provides some graphical insight into the effect of changing memory:

```
SQL> SELECT size_for_estimate size_mb,
  2            ROUND(estd_physical_read_factor * 100, 2)
estd_factor_pct,
  3            RPAD(' ',
  4            ROUND(estd_physical_reads /
MAX(estd_physical_reads) OVER () * 60),
  5            DECODE(size_factor, 1, '-', '*'))
  6                histogram
  7    FROM v$db_cache_advice
  8    WHERE name = 'DEFAULT' and block_size='8192'
  9    ORDER BY 1 DESC
 10    /
Size HISTOGRAM
----- -------------------------------------------------------------
  800 *******
  760 ********
  720 ********
  680 *********
  640 *********
  600 **********
```

```
560  * * * * * * * * * *
520  * * * * * * * * * * *
480  * * * * * * * * * * *
440  * * * * * * * * * * * *
424  – – – – – – – – – – –
400  * * * * * * * * * * * *
360  * * * * * * * * * * * * *
320  * * * * * * * * * * * * * *
280  * * * * * * * * * * * * * * * *
240  * * * * * * * * * * * * * * * * * * *
200  * * * * * * * * * * * * * * * * * * * * * * * *
160  * * * * * * * * * * * * * * * * * * * * * * * * * * * * *
120  * * * * * * * * * * * * * * * * * * * * * * * * * * * * * * * * * * * *
 80  * * * * * * * * * * * * * * * * * * * * * * * * * * * * * * * * * * * * * * * * * * *
 40  * * * * * * * * * * * * * * * * * * * * * * * * * * * * * * * * * * * * * * * * * * * * * * * * * * * * * *
```

We can also see a graphical representation of the advisory information in Enterprise Manager. In Figure 18-2 Enterprise Manger charts the relationship between buffer cache size and physical reads.

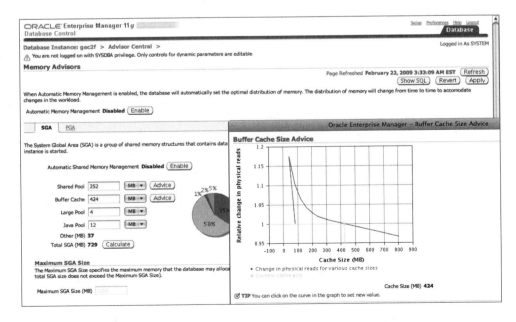

FIGURE 18-2   V$DB_CACHE_ADVICE in Enterprise Manager.

AUTOMATIC SHARED MEMORY MANAGEMENT (ASMM)

From Oracle 10g forward, Oracle has supported Automatic Shared Memory Management (ASMM) that allows some of the components of Oracle shared memory (the SGA) to be automatically sized. The SGA includes all the various buffer pools, and the shared pool, log buffer, large pool, and other areas of memory shared between server processes. See Chapter 2 for a description of the various regions in the SGA.

When ASMM is enabled, the parameter SGA_TARGET specifies the desired total size of all shared memory regions. Oracle will then dynamically change the various pool sizes based on the output from the buffer cache advisories, and from similar advisories generated for the shared pool and other pools.

In Oracle 11g, Automatic Memory Management (AMM) performs global allocation of memory for both the SGA and PGA. We discuss this in Chapter 20, "Other Memory Management Topics." The following discussion assumes that AMM is turned off, by setting the 11g MEMORY_TARGET parameter to 0.

IMPLEMENTING ASMM

ASMM is generally configured as follows:

1. For Oracle 11g, turn off AMM by setting MEMORY_TARGET to 0.
2. Set the value of SGA_MAX_TARGET to the maximum amount of memory you intend to allocate to the SGA. Changing this parameter requires a database restart, and your host must have at least this much shared memory available for Oracle.
3. Set a value for SGA_TARGET. The view V$SGA_TARGET_ADVICE can provide guidance as to an effective overall value.
4. Optionally, set values for various dynamic SGA areas, such as DB_CACHE _SIZE, SHARED_POOL_SIZE, and LARGE_POOL_SIZE. These parameters specify *minimum* sizes for these pools when ASMM is in effect.

You can also enable ASMM from within Enterprise Manager. The *Memory Advisors* section of *Advisor Central* provides controls to enable and disable ASMM and to monitor the allocation of memory to the various pools (see Figure 18-3).

MONITORING RESIZE OPERATIONS

We can observe resize operations by querying the V$SGA_RESIZE_OPS view. The following query shows the resize operations that have occurred in the past 24 hours:

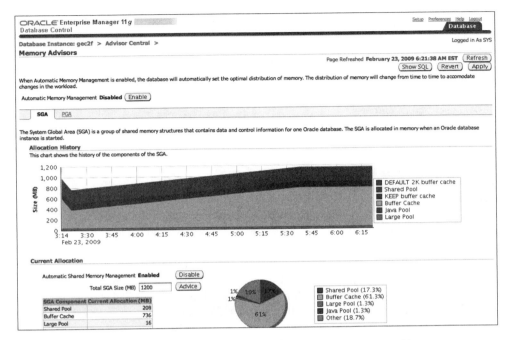

FIGURE 18-3 Enabling and monitoring ASMM from Enterprise Manager.

```
SQL> SELECT TO_CHAR(end_time, 'HH24:MI') end_time, component,
  2         oper_type, oper_mode,
  3         ROUND(initial_size / 1048576) initial_mb,
  4         ROUND(final_size / 1048576) final_mb, status
  5    FROM v$sga_resize_ops o
  6   WHERE end_time > SYSDATE - NUMTODSINTERVAL(24, 'HOUR')
  7   ORDER BY end_time DESC;

                                               Init  Final
                                                 MB     MB STATUS
END_T COMPONENT            OPER_TYPE OPER_MODE
----- -------------------- --------- --------- ----- ----- ------
01:27 DEFAULT buffer cache SHRINK    DEFERRED    444   424 COMPLETE
01:27 shared pool          GROW      DEFERRED    460   480 COMPLETE
```

We can view the current configuration of all resizable objects by looking at V$SGA_DYNAMIC_COMPONENTS:

```
SQL> SELECT component, ROUND(current_size / 1048576) current_mb,
  2         ROUND(min_size / 1048576) minimum_mb,
  3         ROUND(user_specified_size / 1048576) specified_mb
  4    FROM v$sga_dynamic_components sdc;
```

COMPONENT	CURRENT_MB	MINIMUM_MB	SPECIFIED_MB
shared pool	480	460	460
large pool	76	72	72
java pool	4	4	4
streams pool	0	0	0
DEFAULT buffer cache	424	416	400
KEEP buffer cache	32	32	32
RECYCLE buffer cache	0	0	0
DEFAULT 2K buffer cache	0	0	0
DEFAULT 4K buffer cache	0	0	0
DEFAULT 8K buffer cache	0	0	0
DEFAULT 16K buffer cache	0	0	0
DEFAULT 32K buffer cache	0	0	0
Shared IO Pool	0	0	0
ASM Buffer Cache	0	0	400

We can also monitor most of this information from within Enterprise Manager. The same Enterprise Manager screen that allows ASMM administration actions also displays variations in memory allocation over time. Refer to Figure 18-3 for an example.

TUNING ASMM

ASMM and 11g Automatic Memory Management represent a legitimate and significant improvement in Oracle memory management. The effort involved in continuously monitoring and adjusting memory to reduce IO and other memory-related waits is prohibitive for most Oracle DBAs and by performing these tasks automatically, performance will be improved for many or most databases.

However ASMM is not suitable for all application workloads and usually benefits from some tweaking in the circumstances for which it is suitable.

Setting Minimum Sizes   You can give ASMM free reign to adjust shared memory regions by setting the values for the relevant pools to 0. For instance, the following gives ASMM complete control over the allocations to the buffer pool, shared pool, and large pool within a one-gigabyte SGA:

```
ALTER SYSTEM SET sga_target=1024M  SCOPE=BOTH;
ALTER SYSTEM SET db_cache_size=0 SCOPE=BOTH;
ALTER SYSTEM SET large_pool_size=0 SCOPE=BOTH;
ALTER SYSTEM SET shared_pool_size=0 SCOPE=BOTH;
```

However, even when ASMM is in effect, we can still specify values for the various pools. If we do, these values will become the minimum sizes for those pools.

Next we set an overall SGA size of 1GB, and 200M minimums for the buffer cache, large pool, and shared pools. ASMM can allocate the remaining 400M as it sees fit, subject to fixed and static allocations such as the log buffer, but should not reduce any of the specified buffers below 200M:

```
ALTER SYSTEM SET sga_target=1024M  SCOPE=BOTH;
ALTER SYSTEM SET db_cache_size=200M SCOPE=BOTH;
ALTER SYSTEM SET large_pool_size=200M SCOPE=BOTH;
ALTER SYSTEM SET shared_pool_size=200M SCOPE=BOTH;
```

As we'll see in a moment, specifying minimum values for a selected pool can help refine ASMM allocations. In particular, it will prevent ASMM from inadvertently shrinking a pool too far in response to short-term changes in workload demand.

Consider setting minimums for selected pools within the SGA: This helps prevent ASMM from overreacting to transitory peaks and troughs of activity.

NONDEFAULT POOLS

ASMM does not manage all the memory areas in the SGA. The main redo log buffer, which we discussed in Chapter 17, is a static area of memory that can be adjusted only by restarting the instance. The KEEP, RECYCLE, and block-size specific caches can be adjusted dynamically but will not be adjusted on-the-fly by ASMM.

The redo log buffer is small and isn't of much concern for automatic adjustment of other memory areas. However, the nondefault buffer pools could be quite large, and because ASMM will not adjust them, it's up to you to ensure that their memory allocations are worthwhile. You don't want ASMM to take memory away from a busy default buffer cache while memory in the nondefault pools is underutilized and hence wasted.

Here's an example of what you *don't* want to see:

```
SQL> SELECT b.name, b.block_size / 1024 block_size_kb,
  2          current_size, prev_size,
  3          ROUND(db_block_gets / 1000) db_gets,
  4          ROUND(consistent_gets / 1000) con_gets,
  5          ROUND(physical_reads / 1000) phys_rds
  6    FROM v$buffer_pool_statistics s
  7    JOIN v$buffer_pool b
  8      ON (b.name = s.name AND b.block_size = s.block_size);
```

NAME	Block Size K	Current MB	Prev MB	DB Block Gets /1000	Consistent gets /1000	Physical Reads /1000
DEFAULT	2	**64**	0	0	0	0
KEEP	8	**112**	0	0	0	0
DEFAULT	8	16	32	68	2,258	482

Memory pressure, on the large pool in this case, has resulted in ASMM shrinking the DEFAULT cache to only 16M, despite the relatively high ratio of physical reads incurred by queries using blocks in the cache. Meanwhile the KEEP and 2K pools are unused but still consuming 176M of memory, 10 times the current size of the default pool.

> If you use nondefault buffer pools, such as KEEP, RECYCLE, DB_*n*K_cache, with ASMM, you should regularly monitor the size and utilization of these caches to ensure that they are used effectively. ASSM will *not* manage the size of these caches.

MEMORY THRASHING

ASMM works best for relatively static workloads or workloads that change gradually. It's not quite so good at responding to the workloads that are changing frequently. ASMM essentially keeps tabs on advisory data and adjusts memory periodically if the advisory data suggests that an adjustment might be warranted. However, if the workload is constantly fluctuating, ASMM might be continually adjusting memory to suit the conditions that have just passed, rather than for current load.

ASMM memory thrashing can be recognized by frequent large changes in the sizes of the various pools. For instance, in Figure 18-4 we see ASMM shifting large amounts of memory between the large pool and the buffer cache every 5 to 10 minutes or so.

Not only does this thrashing suggest that ASMM is operating in an overly reactive mode and probably failing to keep up with workload changes, but it also exacts an overhead cost on the database. Sessions that are accessing shared memory might have to wait for ASMM to complete its memory adjustments, leading to delays that can be identified by waits such as *SGA: allocation forcing component growth*, as shown in the following query:

```
SQL> WITH wait_times AS (SELECT event, total_waits, time_waited_micro,
  2                             ROUND( time_waited_micro * 100
  3                             /SUM(time_waited_micro) OVER(),2) AS pct
```

```
4                         FROM v$system_event
5                        WHERE wait_class <> 'Idle')
6   SELECT *
7     FROM wait_times
8    WHERE pct > 1
9    ORDER BY pct DESC;
EVENT                             WAITS TIME_WAITED_MICRO        PCT
------------------------------- ------- ----------------- ----------
db file sequential read          128618       1161461294      53.07
SGA: allocation forcing compon    27388        698712427      31.92
ent growth
PX qref latch                    290748         96601540       4.41
db file scattered read             7484         74222258       3.39
control file sequential read      11932         51862197       2.37
direct path read                   4086         39741910       1.82
```

If you observe excessive ASMM thrashing, you might want to disable ASMM altogether or to set minimum values for ASMM components.

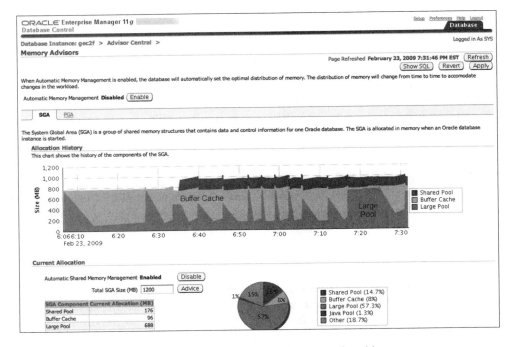

FIGURE 18-4   ASMM shared memory thrashing.

Dynamically changing workloads can result in ASMM rapidly and frequently moving memory between shared memory areas. This thrashing might indicate a need to disable ASMM or to set minimum values for selected pools.

Buffer Cache Starvation Poorly crafted application code can result in large memory allocation demands against the large or shared pools. For instance, when shared servers are in use, global PL/SQL variables will be stored in the large pool or, if no large pool is configured, the shared pool. The following SQL, when run in a PL/SQL block, will create in-memory collections containing the entire SALES table. In a shared server configuration, these collections need to be stored in either the shared or large pool:

```
SELECT prod_id, cust_id, time_id, channel_id,
       promo_id, quantity_sold, amount_sold
  BULK COLLECT
  INTO g_prod_id, g_cust_id, g_time_id, g_channel_id, g_promo_id,
       g_quantity_sold, g_amount_sold
  FROM sh.sales;
```

The creation of unusually large collections might result in sudden and excessive demand for large or shared pool memory. With ASMM in effect, this results in the pool in question growing, possibly at the expense of the buffer cache. In some circumstances, we would rather that the PL/SQL fail with a memory allocation error (typically ORA-04031) than to allow this single session to eliminate most of the memory in the buffer cache!

Figure 18-5 illustrates this scenario: the large pool suddenly expands as a single PL/SQL block running in a shared server session creates a large collection. The buffer cache shrinks to make way for the large pool, resulting in an increase in IO as transactions that previously found blocks in the buffer cache must read them from disk. You might also see other side effects from the smaller buffer cache such as free buffer waits.

Buffer pool starvation can also occur if poor cursor management leads to a perpetual increase in the size of the shared pool.

You can avoid this scenario either by turning off ASMM or by setting minimum values for the buffer cache. Unfortunately, although you can set minimum values in ASMM, you cannot set maximums. So in this case we can set a minimum value for the buffer cache, but we cannot set a maximum large pool size.

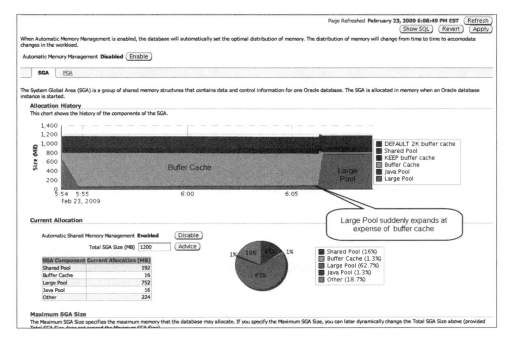

FIGURE 18-5   Buffer pool starvation as a result of large pool growth.

ASMM can sometimes lead to starvation of the buffer cache when large memory allocations are made in the large or shared pool. Set minimum values for the buffer cache to avoid this starvation.

SUMMARY

The buffer cache is the area of memory that caches data blocks. Sessions can find data blocks in the buffer cache, thereby avoiding a disk IO. The buffer cache in this manner reduces the amount of logical IO that must translate into physical IO.

Blocks in the buffer cache are managed using a LRU-like (Least Recently Used) algorithm: Blocks that have not been accessed recently can be flushed out of the cache to make way for new blocks.

You can have multiple buffer pools within the buffer cache: a separate KEEP and RECYCLE pool, and up to four caches for nondefault block sizes. The

nondefault block size pools cache objects in tablespaces that implement a nondefault block size, so you won't use these often. However, using the KEEP pool to
cache infrequently accessed small table scans can be a significant optimization for
key transactions.

The Buffer Cache Hit Ratio describes the ratio in which blocks are found in
cache and therefore are accessed without a disk read. The Buffer Cache Hit Ratio
has probably caused more harm and wasted effort than benefit, and you should
be particularly aware that a high hit ratio is just as likely to be caused by poorly
tuned SQL as anything else.

Oracle provides a precise tool for determining the impact of resizing the
buffer caches: The V$DB_CACHE_ADVICE view shows the impact of changing a
buffer cache in terms of IO that would have been avoided or incurred in the past
had the buffer cache been differently sized.

Oracle can automatically manage the size of the certain SGA memory components in Oracle 10g and can manage overall memory allocations, both PGA
and SGA, in 11g. This Automatic Shared Memory Management (ASMM) is a
Good Thing for most databases, but you might avoid problems if you set minimum values for key memory areas—especially the buffer cache.

Optimizing **PGA** Memory

The System Global Area (SGA) is an area of *shared* memory; all Oracle sessions can read and write from this common memory space. In contrast, the Program Global Area (PGA) represents *private* memory that each server process uses for maintaining temporary work areas, program stack, and variables.

The SGA includes the buffer cache, which serves to reduce disk IO by caching data blocks in memory. Sessions can avoid reading from disk if the required data block is present in the cache. The PGA serves an equally important, though possibly less recognized, role in reducing IO. Most nontrivial SQL processing employs temporary work areas to support intermediate result sets, hash join areas, and sorts. We looked at these operations in Chapter 11, "Sorting, Grouping, and Set Operations." PGA memory enables these operations to complete in memory. If there's insufficient PGA memory, temporary segments must be read from and written to disk—incurring disk IO overhead.

Correctly configuring PGA can, therefore, be just as critical to minimizing IO as SGA optimization.

IO AND PGA MEMORY

We first looked at the relationship between memory and sort/hash performance in Chapter 11. If sufficient memory is available for a sort or hash operation to complete in memory, performance is considered *optimal*. As memory reduces, sessions must write and read data to temporary segments on disk. A *single pass* disk operation is bad enough, but if memory is short, data might need to be read from and written to disk more than once—a *multi-pass* operation. With each pass, IO increases and performance degrades.

As a result of the historical emphasis on the Buffer Cache Hit Ratio as a means of reducing IO, and the lack of temporary segment IO visibility in earlier versions of Oracle, tuning temporary segment IO has been underemphasized. However, temporary segment IO can easily exceed data file IO if PGA memory is in short supply.

Figure 19-1 shows IO wait times for a query that performs a full table scan and sort. If PGA memory is abundant, the response time consists primarily of table scan IO together with CPU time required to perform the sort. However, as PGA memory is restricted, IO for sorting rapidly dominates the execution time.

> Temporary segment IO can be as significant an IO burden on your database as Table/Index IO. PGA memory can be just as significant in reducing IO as buffer cache memory.

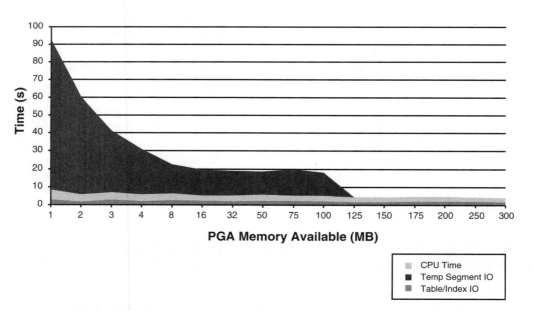

FIGURE 19-1   Temporary segment IO can exceed table or index IO if PGA memory is in short supply.

PGA MEMORY MANAGEMENT

PGA memory consists of private memory used by the Oracle shared or dedicated server processes. It consists only of memory regions that are specific to the process; memory that is specific to the session are held in the User Global Areas (UGA) contained within a dedicated server process or, in the case of shared servers, in the shared or large pools.

PGA_AGGREGATE_TARGET

Prior to Oracle 9i, server processes managed their PGA memory independently. Each process was free to allocate as much memory as it saw fit, up to the limits imposed by the parameters SORT_AREA_SIZE and HASH_AREA_SIZE. From 9i forward, the total amount of PGA memory can be managed to the value of PGA_AGGREGATE_TARGET. If the parameter WORKAREA_SIZE_POLICY is set to AUTO, Oracle will attempt to keep the sum of all PGAs within the bounds of PGA_AGGREGATE_TARGET (attempt, but not always succeed!).

In Oracle 11g, Automatic Memory Management (AMM) allows Oracle to manage both PGA and SGA memory automatically. When AMM is enabled, Oracle effectively adjusts the value of PGA_AGGREGATE_TARGET from time to time based on workload demands. We look at AMM in Chapter 20, "Other Memory Management Topics." For the purposes of this chapter, assume AMM is not enabled.

It's not always possible for server processes to respect the limits imposed by PGA_AGGREGATE_TARGET. Certain operations require a minimum amount of physical memory, and if PGA_AGGREGATE_TARGET is set too low, server processes have no choice but to exceed the unrealistic restrictions; these are called *overallocations*.

SESSION PGA LIMITS

Individual processes are generally not at liberty to expand to use all the PGA_AGGREGATE_TARGET either. If the PGA_AGGREGATE_TARGET is below 1GB, each process is limited to a PGA of 200MB. Above 1GB, each process can allocate 20 percent of the PGA_AGGREGATE_TARGET. This limit leads to some apparently strange behavior. If your sort activity is limited to a small number of sessions, you'll see performance improve as you increase the PGA_AGGREGATE_TARGET. However, as you exceed a PGA_AGGREGATE_TARGET of 200M, no further improvements will be observed until you exceed 1GB, after which individual PGA allocations will again be free to increase.

PGA_AGGREGATE_TARGETs lower than 200M are rare, but targets under 1GB are common enough. If your PGA_AGGREGATE_TARGET is under 1GB, you might find that increasing PGA_AGGREGATE_TARGET is ineffective in improving the performance of an individual sort that is already using 200MB of PGA memory. Only when you increase the PGA Aggregate Target above 1GB will the 200MB per process limit be relaxed.

> Increasing PGA_AGGREGATE_TARGET to values less than 1GB does not necessarily increase the amount of memory available to individual processes, which normally are restricted to 200MB until the PGA Aggregate Target exceeds 1GB.

The situation is further complicated by a distinction between the total PGA for a process and the size of a single work area. Most nontrivial SQLs will use multiple work areas, although a simple SELECT from a single table with an ORDER BY needs only one. Oracle limits the size of a single work area to 20 percent of the PGA Aggregate Target when the PGA Aggregate Target is under 512MB and then to half of the session PGA limit.

An additional limitation exists for parallel SQL; Oracle applies a limit of 50 percent of the PGA Aggregate Target for all the processes working on a single SQL statement. If you perform a sort using a Degree of Parallelism (DOP) of 8, each process will be restricted to 6.25 percent of the PGA Aggregate Target (50 percent of the PGA Aggregate Target divided among 8 processes: 50 /8 = 6.25).

Figure 19-2 plots these limits against various values of PGA Aggregate Target. Note that all these limits can apply simultaneously. A single parallel process must respect the process PGA maximum and the work area maximum; in addition the work areas of all the processes combining to process the SQL in parallel cannot exceed the parallel work area limitation.

We can see the limitations in place by running the following query (as SYS), which displays the values of the various hidden parameters that control these settings:

```
SQL> SELECT ksppinm name, ksppdesc description,
  2          CASE WHEN ksppinm LIKE '_smm%' THEN ksppstvl/1024
  3               ELSE ksppstvl/1048576 END as MB
  4     FROM sys.x$ksppi JOIN sys.x$ksppcv
  5          USING (indx)
  6    WHERE ksppinm IN
  7              ('pga_aggregate_target',
  8               '_pga_max_size',
  9               '_smm_max_size',
 10               '_smm_px_max_size','_ _pga_aggregate_target'
 11               );
```

```
NAME                    DESCRIPTION                                    MB
--------------------    ----------------------------------------     -------
pga_aggregate_target    Target size for the aggregate PGA memory       1,000
                        consumed by the instance

__pga_aggregate_target  Current target size for the aggregate          1,792
                        PGA memory consumed

_pga_max_size           Maximum size of the PGA memory for one           200
                        process

_smm_max_size           maximum work area size in auto mode              100
                        (serial)

_smm_px_max_size        maximum work area size in auto mode              500
                        (global)
```

The preceding undocumented parameters, _PGA_MAX_SIZE, _SMM_MAX_SIZE, and _SMM_PX_MAX_SIZE, can be changed—but definitely at your own risk—if you want to adjust the amount of memory that can be consumed by individual processes.

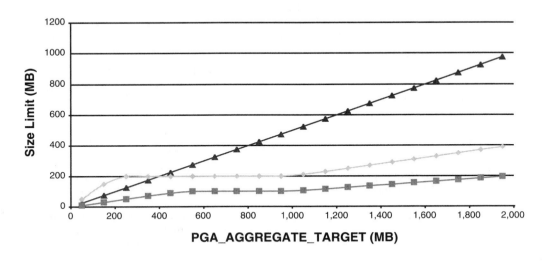

FIGURE 19-2 Default PGA limits versus PGA aggregate target.

MEASURING PGA USAGE AND EFFICIENCY

We have a variety of options for monitoring PGA configuration and status. Overall PGA memory allocation status is best examined through the view V$PGASTAT, which presents various PGA related statistics.

```
SQL> SELECT * FROM v$pgastat;

NAME                                                  VALUE UNIT
----------------------------------------- --------------- -----
aggregate PGA target parameter                   69,999,616 bytes
aggregate PGA auto target                         4,374,528 bytes
global memory bound                                 638,976 bytes
total PGA inuse                                   70,206,464 bytes
total PGA allocated                             124,704,768 bytes
maximum PGA allocated                           855,141,376 bytes
total freeable PGA memory                        15,204,352 bytes
process count                                            48
max processes count                                      53
PGA memory freed back to OS                  24,026,415,104 bytes
total PGA used for auto workareas                 3,126,272 bytes
maximum PGA used for auto workareas              40,306,688 bytes
total PGA used for manual workareas                       0 bytes
maximum PGA used for manual workareas                     0 bytes
over allocation count                                 2,058
bytes processed                             103,338,357,760 bytes
extra bytes read/written                      9,842,753,536 bytes
cache hit percentage                                     91 percent
recompute count (total)                             156,576
```

Here are a few of the more significant statistics explained:

aggregate PGA target parameter	This is the value of PGA_AGGREGATE_TARGET.
aggregate PGA auto target	This is the amount of PGA memory that is available for work areas (sorts and hash operations), as opposed to PL/SQL and Java variables and program stacks. If a PL/SQL routine creates a large collection, that memory is not usually available for work areas, resulting in this value becoming less than the total aggregate PGA target.
total PGA inuse	This is the amount of memory allocated to work area operations.
total PGA allocated	This is the amount of PGA allocated for all purposes.
total freeable PGA memory	This is the amount of memory that could be released from the PGA if necessary to meet other demands for memory.

over allocation count	Overallocations occur when Oracle has no choice but to expand a work area beyond that which would normally be indicated by the PGA Aggregate Target. High values can indicate that the PGA Aggregate Target is too small for the concurrent workload demands.
bytes processed	The amount of bytes processed in work area operations such as sorts and hash joins.
extra bytes read/written	The amount of bytes processed in single and multi-pass operations. This normally represents the amount of data that needs to be written to and read from temporary segments when an operation cannot fit in memory.
cache hit percentage	Relative effectiveness of the PGA. A value of 100 percent means that all operations were processed in memory. It is calculated as

$$\frac{bytes\_processed * 100}{(bytes\_processed + extra\_bytes\_read/written)}$$

SESSION PGA UTILIZATION

We can see the utilization of PGA on a per-session basis by looking at the session statistics 'session pga memory' and 'session pga memory max'. The following query uses those statistics to show the top five consumers of PGA memory and their currently executing SQLs:

```
SQL> WITH pga AS
  2       (SELECT sid,
  3               ROUND(SUM(CASE name WHEN 'session pga memory'
  4                   THEN VALUE / 1048576 END),2)
                      pga_memory_mb,
  5               ROUND(SUM(CASE name WHEN 'session pga memory max'
  6                   THEN VALUE / 1048576  END),2)
                      max_pga_memory_mb
  7         FROM v$sesstat
  8         JOIN v$statname  USING (statistic#)
  9        WHERE name IN ('session pga memory',
                      'session pga memory max' )
 10        GROUP BY sid)
 11  SELECT sid, username,s.module,
 12         pga_memory_mb,
 13         max_pga_memory_mb, substr(sql_text,1,70) sql_text
 14    FROM v$session s
 15    JOIN (SELECT sid, pga_memory_mb, max_pga_memory_mb,
 16                 RANK() OVER (ORDER BY pga_memory_mb DESC)
                      pga_ranking
 17           FROM pga)
```

```
18    USING (sid)
19    LEFT OUTER JOIN v$sql sql
20      ON  (s.sql_id=sql.sql_id
               AND s.sql_child_number=sql.child_number)
21    WHERE pga_ranking <=5
22    ORDER BY  pga_ranking
23   /
```

| | | | | PGA MAX |
SID USERNAME	MODULE		PGA MB	MB
Currently executing SQL				

```
    155 SYSMAN       OEM.CacheModeWaitPool              703.29    703.29
SELECT EXECUTION_ID, STATUS, STATUS_DETAIL FROM MGMT_JOB_EXEC_SUMMARY

    120 OPSG         SQL*Plus                            80.98    107.86
SELECT * FROM TXN_DATA WHERE ROWNUM < :B1 ORDER BY TDATA, DATETIME

    109 OPSG         SQL*Plus                            53.66     99.29
SELECT /*+ parallel(d,2) */ * FROM TXN_DATA D ORDER BY TDATA, DATETIME

    114 OPSG         SQL*Plus                            29.30    107.86
SELECT * FROM TXN_DATA WHERE ROWNUM < :B1 ORDER BY TDATA, DATETIME

    147 OPSG         SQL*Plus                            28.36     40.86
SELECT * FROM SH.SALES JOIN SH.CUSTOMERS USING (CUST_ID) JOIN SH.PRODU
```

MEASURING TEMPORARY IO WAIT TIME

Our primary interest in allocating PGA memory effectively is to avoid the IO to temporary segments that occurs when there is insufficient PGA to perform work area operations in memory. This impact can be observed by comparing temporary direct IO with other activities.

The following query splits out direct path IO to temporary segments and compares it to the time spent in other activities (other IO, CPU, and so on):

```
SQL> WITH system_event AS
  2    (SELECT CASE WHEN event LIKE       'direct path%temp'
  3                 THEN event  ELSE wait_class
  4             END wait_type, e.*
  5        FROM v$system_event e)
  6  SELECT wait_type,SUM(total_waits) total_waits,
  7           round(SUM(time_waited_micro)/1000000,2)
                time_waited_seconds,
```

```
 8              ROUND(  SUM(time_waited_micro)
 9                 * 100
10                 / SUM(SUM(time_waited_micro)) OVER (), 2) pct
11  FROM (SELECT   wait_type, event, total_waits, time_waited_micro
12         FROM    system_event e
13         UNION
14         SELECT   'CPU', stat_name, NULL, VALUE
15         FROM v$sys_time_model
16         WHERE stat_name IN ('background cpu time', 'DB CPU')) l
17  WHERE wait_type <> 'Idle'
18  GROUP BY wait_type
19  ORDER BY 4 DESC;
```

WAIT_TYPE	TOTAL_WAITS	TIME_WAITED_SECONDS	PCT
CPU		178,371.45	45.38
User I/O	14,256,100	127,106.90	32.34
direct path read temp	3,026,548	40,393.56	10.28
System I/O	6,860,830	17,493.11	4.45
Other	13,786,339	11,750.53	2.99
Application	39,348	8,145.53	2.07

Of course, you might want to measure your direct path IO during a specific period. If you've installed the packages available on this book's Web site, you can query the view DIRECT_IO_DELTA_VIEW, which provides the same information calculated since the time period between each execution. Here we see that over the past 66 seconds temporary segment IO accounts for approximately 49 percent of total database time:

```
SQL> SELECT * FROM direct_io_delta_view;
```

WAIT_TYPE	TOTAL_WAITS	TIME_WAITED_MS	PCT_TIME	Sample Secs
CPU		262,259.02	50.00	66
direct path read temp	15,137	254,594.02	49.00	66
System I/O	207	3,633.23	1.00	66
direct path write temp	396	2,870.15	1.00	66

---

direct path read temp and *direct path write temp* events measure the time spent performing IO to temporary segments and are a direct indication of the IO cost of sort and hash operations. If these are high, increasing PGA Aggregate Target may be effective.

Oracle categorizes all direct path IO, temporary or otherwise, as *User I/O*, which makes it difficult to observe in Enterprise Manager because high-level performance charts simply indicate a certain amount of IO occurring. However, in the IO drill down of the performance page, you might see high levels of direct IO if the PGA Aggregate Target is too low, as shown in Figure 19-3.

Note, however, that not all direct IO will necessarily be temporary segment IO.

Alternatively, by drilling into the User I/O category on the Enterprise Manager Performance page, you can break the User I/O waits down to low level wait categories. In Figure 19-4 we see that most of the User I/O waits are 'direct path read temp', suggesting that we have insufficient PGA for the activity we are attempting.

Note that the preceding two Enterprise Manager screens are only available if you have licensed the Oracle Diagnostic pack.

MEASURING WORK AREA ACTIVITY

We looked in detail at how to measure work area activities, sort and hash operations, in Chapter 11 when we discussed optimizing SQL statements that performed sorts and similar operations.

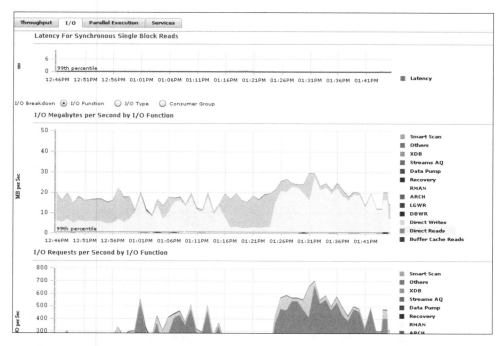

FIGURE 19-3 IO Performance tab in Enterprise Manager showing high direct read activity.

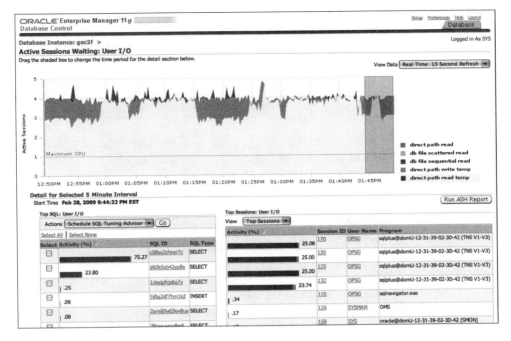

FIGURE 19-4   Enterprise Manager User I/O breakdown.

Our two main tools for measurement are EXPLAIN PLAN and the
V$SQL_WORKAREA view.

EXPLAIN PLAN and DBMS_XPLAN can be used to determine the expected
or actual demand for PGA memory. For a SQL that we have not yet executed, we
can use EXPLAIN PLAN to obtain an estimate of the expected optimal memory
size (in the *TempSpc* column):

```
SQL> EXPLAIN PLAN FOR
  2  SELECT * FROM sh.sales ORDER BY cust_id,prod_id,time_id;

SQL> select * from table(dbms_xplan.display());
```

Id	Operation	Name	Rows	**TempSpc**	Cost	(%CPU)
0	SELECT STATEMENT		918K		7824	(1)
1	SORT ORDER BY		918K	**84M**	7824	(1)
2	PARTITION RANGE ALL		918K		494	(3)
3	TABLE ACCESS FULL	SALES	918K		494	(3)

The estimate of temporary space suggests that this SQL will require a work area of about 84MB to complete in memory.

Actual execution statistics can be obtained from the V$SQL_WORKAREA view. This view shows statistics for work area operations from SQL statements that are still cached in memory:

```
SQL> WITH sql_workarea AS
  2        (
  3          SELECT sql_id || '-' || child_number SQL_ID_Child,
  4              operation_type operation ,
  5              last_execution last_exec,
  6              ROUND (active_time / 1000000,
  7                         2) seconds,
  8              optimal_executions || '/'
  9              || onepass_executions || '/'
 10              || multipasses_executions o1m,
 11              '   ' || SUBSTR (sql_text, 1, 155) sql_text,
 12            RANK () OVER (ORDER BY active_time DESC) ranking
 13          FROM v$sql_workarea JOIN v$sql
 14              USING (sql_id, child_number)   )
 15   SELECT      sql_id_child "SQL ID - CHILD",seconds,operation,
 16          last_exec,  o1m "O/1/M",sql_text
 17      FROM sql_workarea
 18     WHERE ranking <= 2
 19   ORDER BY ranking;


SQL ID - CHILD       SECONDS OPERATION LAST_EXEC  O/1/M
---------------- ---------- --------- ---------- --------


------------------------------------------------------------------
c58yy2chnyr7c-0   12,099.30 SORT (v2) 10112 PASS 0/0/6
    SELECT * FROM TXN_DATA WHERE ROWNUM < :B1 ORDER BY TDATA, DATE
TIME
------------------------------------------------------------------
d60k5sb42yp8x-0      126.90 HASH-JOIN OPTIMAL    1/0/0
    SELECT * FROM SH.SALES JOIN SH.CUSTOMERS USING (CUST_ID) JOIN
SH.PRODUCTS USING (PROD_ID) LEFT OUTER JOIN SH.CHANNELS USING
(CHANNEL_ID) JOIN SH.TIMES USIN
------------------------------------------------------------------
```

These views help you determine how much PGA memory would be optimal for individual SQL statements. However, they don't offer much advice when it comes to optimizing memory for the aggregate demand from all SQLs.

EXPLAIN PLAN and V$SQL_WORKAREA can be used to determine the optimal amount of PGA memory for individual SQLs.

SIZING THE PGA WITH V$PGA_TARGET_ADVICE

The view V$PGA_TARGET_ADVICE provides advice as to the probable impact of adjusting the PGA_AGGREGATE_TARGET. When Oracle performs a work-area operation such as a sort or hash join, it can accurately determine the amount of memory that would have been required for an optimal operation (completely in memory) or for a one-pass disk operation. These statistics are used to create an estimate of the amount of temporary segment IO that would have been avoided had more memory been available. Of course, the estimates assume that the concurrent demand in the future will be similar to the demand in the past.

This query displays the raw V$PGA_AGGREATE_ADVICE data:

```
SQL> SELECT ROUND(pga_target_for_estimate / 1048576) pga_target_mb,
  2         pga_target_factor * 100 pga_target_factor_pct, estd_time,
  3         ROUND(estd_extra_bytes_rw / 1048576) estd_extra_mb_rw,
  4         estd_pga_cache_hit_percentage, estd_overalloc_count
  5  FROM v$pga_target_advice
  6  ORDER BY pga_target_factor;
```

Pga MB	Pga Size Pct	Estimated Time (s)	Estd extra MB	Estd PGA Hit Pct	Estd Overalloc
128	13	28,921,729	465,639	33.00	1,408
256	25	26,754,027	413,203	36.00	1,305
512	50	24,323,023	354,399	40.00	1,148
768	75	24,316,904	354,251	40.00	943
1,024	100	16,411,411	163,023	59.00	634
1,229	120	16,182,999	157,498	60.00	423
1,434	140	15,921,625	151,176	61.00	201
1,638	160	15,643,430	144,446	62.00	0
1,843	180	14,447,749	115,524	67.00	0
2,048	200	14,447,749	115,524	67.00	0
3,072	300	14,447,749	115,524	67.00	0
4,096	400	14,447,749	115,524	67.00	0
6,144	600	14,447,749	115,524	67.00	0
8,192	800	14,447,749	115,524	67.00	0

Here are some of the key columns in V$PGA_AGGREGATE_TARGET:

PGA_TARGET_FOR_ESTIMATE	PGA target for the estimate.
PGA_TARGET_FACTOR	PGA target for estimate relative to the current PGA Aggregate Target.
BYTES_PROCESSED	The amount of bytes processed in work area operations such as sorts and hash joins.
ESTD_TIME	Estimated time in seconds required to process the BYTES_PROCESSED.
ESTD_EXTRA_BYTES_RW	The amount of bytes processed in single and multi-pass operations. This normally represents the amount of data that needs to be written to and read from temporary segments when an operation cannot fit in memory.
ESTD_PGA_CACHE_HIT _PERCENTAGE	Estimated cache hit rate, defined as $$\frac{bytes\_processed * 100}{(bytes\_processed + extra\_bytes\_read / written)}$$
ESTD_OVERALLOC_COUNT	Estimated number of overallocations for this PGA target value. Overallocations occur when Oracle has no choice but to expand a work area beyond that which would normally be specified by PGA Aggregate Target. High values might indicate that the estimated PGA Aggregate Target will be too small for the concurrent workload demands.

Here's an alternative query for V$PGA_AGGREGATE_TARGET that presents the advice in a more visually intuitive fashion. The histogram for each estimated PGA Aggregate Target shows the relative value for ESTD_EXTRA _BYTES_RW. Estimates where over-allocations exist are indicated as x; otherwise they are shown as *.

```
SQL> SELECT ROUND(PGA_TARGET_FOR_ESTIMATE / 1048576) size_mb,
  2         ROUND(PGA_TARGET_FACTOR * 100, 2) estd_target_pct,
  3         RPAD(' ',
  4         ROUND(ESTD_EXTRA_BYTES_RW / MAX(ESTD_EXTRA_BYTES_RW)
                  OVER () * 60),
  5         DECODE(PGA_TARGET_FACTOR,
  6                1, '=',
  7                   DECODE(SIGN(estd_overalloc_count), 1, 'x', '*')))
  8            extra_bytes_histogram
  9  FROM v$pga_target_advice
 10  ORDER BY 1 DESC;
```

```
Size
   MB Relative Extra Bytes RW
------- --------------------------------------------------------------
8,192 **************
6,144 **************
4,096 *************
3,072 *************
2,048 *************
1,843 **************
1,638 ****************
1,434 xxxxxxxxxxxxxxxxx
1,229 xxxxxxxxxxxxxxxxx
1,024 ===================
  768 xxxxxxxxxxxxxxxxxxxxxxxxxxxxxxxxxxxxxxxxxxx
  512 xxxxxxxxxxxxxxxxxxxxxxxxxxxxxxxxxxxxxxxxxxx
  256 xxxxxxxxxxxxxxxxxxxxxxxxxxxxxxxxxxxxxxxxxxxxxxxxxx
  128 xxxxxxxxxxxxxxxxxxxxxxxxxxxxxxxxxxxxxxxxxxxxxxxxxxxxxxxxxxxx
```

Looking at this output, it's apparent that performance will degrade fairly significantly if we reduce PGA Aggregate Target. Modest reductions in overhead can be achieved by increasing PGA Aggregate Target from 1GB to 1.8GB, though no further improvements are predicted beyond this point. However, over-allocations are estimated to occur even at the current target of 1GB, and PGA Aggregate Target should be set to at least 1.6GB to avoid these.

> Use V$PGA_TARGET_ADVICE to determine an optimal setting for PGA Aggregate Target. Avoid setting the PGA Aggregate Target to values for which over-allocations are estimated.

Enterprise Manager also displays this data, in the *Memory Advisors* section of *Advisory Central*. Figure 19-5 shows Enterprise Manager graphing the PGA hit percent value from V$PGA_TARGET_ADVICE and highlighting estimated over-allocations.

OVER-RIDING PGA AGGREGATE TARGET

Allowing Oracle to allocate available PGA memory across sessions using the PGA Aggregate Target is generally a Good Thing. Prior to the PGA Aggregate Target mechanism, each Oracle session was free to specify its own memory limit

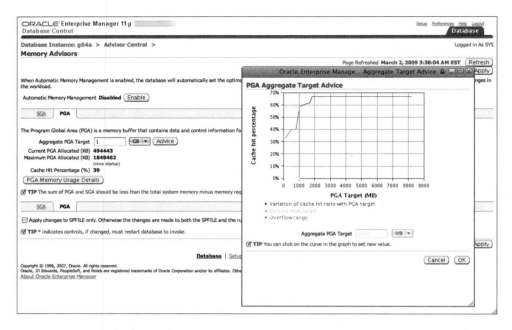

FIGURE 19-5   PGA Target Advice in Enterprise Manager.

that often led to excessive PGA memory consumption, excessive temporary segment IO, or both.

However, from time to time it might make sense for a session to control its own PGA memory allocation. This is particularly true when the number of concurrent sessions is low or where a single session is going to perform a high-priority sort operation. In these cases, the session can opt out of the PGA Aggregate Target mechanism and set its own PGA size.

To opt out of PGA Aggregate Target, you must set the parameter WORKAREA_SIZE_POLICY to MANUAL and then set specific values for the parameters SORT_AREA_SIZE and HASH_AREA_SIZE. For instance, to acquire a 500M area for sorting, we can issue the following commands:[1]

```
ALTER SESSION SET workarea_size_policy = manual;
ALTER SESSION SET sort_area_size = 524288000;
ALTER SESSION SET sort_area_size = 524288000;
```

For instance, let's say that we have a 1GB PGA Aggregate Target and are about to perform a million row ORDER BY. We know that we are doing the only

---

[1] Jonathan Lewis discovered that these settings don't always take effect immediately and recommends setting them twice to ensure that they take effect; see http://jonathanlewis. wordpress.com/2008/11/25/sas-bug/.

significant sort within the Oracle instance, so we'd like to use a significant amount of the PGA Aggregate Target. However, the sizing policies previously outlined in this chapter result in us only being allocated about 100MB of PGA so that we will, therefore, perform an expensive multipass sort.

If we set WORKAREA_SIZE_POLICY to MANUAL and specify a SORT_AREA_SIZE of 800M—80 percent of the PGA Aggregate Target—we only need to perform a one-pass sort. Consequently, our ORDER BY completes more quickly and generates less temporary IO. After the ORDER BY completes, we can revert to automatic work-area sizing:

```
ALTER SESSION SET workarea_size_policy = auto;
```

Figure 19-6 shows the improvement achieved by this technique. In addition to a reduction in sort IO, we also saw reduced time for table scan IO; this is because the IO required for sorting was competing for the same disk volumes as the IO for the table scan. Of course, our session used more memory than it otherwise would have, so you will want to ensure that the system has sufficient free RAM to accommodate this short-term increase in memory utilization.

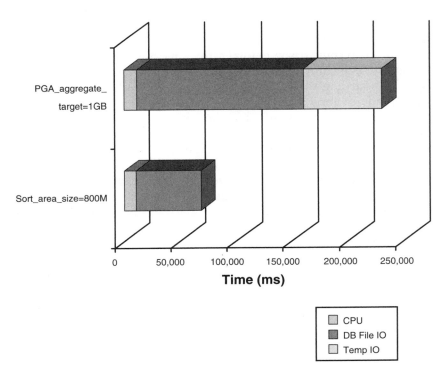

FIGURE 19-6 Advantages gained by overriding PGA_AGGREGATE_TARGET for a single big sort.

If a single session or SQL needs a particularly large amount of work area memory, consider temporarily setting WORKAREA_SIZE_POLICY to MANUAL and directly controlling SORT_AREA_SIZE and/or HASH_AREA_SIZE.

SUMMARY

Every server process maintains an area in memory known as the PGA (Program Global Area) that is used as a work area for temporary result sets and to sort and hash data. When these work area operations cannot complete in memory, Oracle must write to and read from temporary segments, resulting in significant IO overhead.

The total amount of PGA memory available for all sessions is normally controlled by the parameter PGA_AGGREGATE_TARGET. The value is truly a "target" and sometimes sessions will have to exceed the setting. Furthermore, individual sessions cannot use all the PGA Aggregate Target; typically only 20 percent will be available to a single session.

The overall overhead of temporary disk IO can be measured by observing the times spent in *direct path read temp* and *direct path write temp* wait events. The higher these waits are in comparison to total active time, the higher our incentive to reduce temporary segment IO, possibly by increasing PGA Aggregate Target.

The effect of adjusting the PGA Aggregate Target can be accurately estimated using the advice in V$PGA_TARGET_ADVICE. This view shows the change in the amount of IO that would have occurred in the past had the PGA Aggregate Target been set to a different size. This view is your primary tool in determining whether extra PGA memory would be effective in reducing temporary segment IO.

Because a single session is normally prevented from using more than a fraction of the PGA Aggregate Target, you might want to temporarily "opt out" of the PGA Aggregate Target mechanism when you need to do a particularly large high-priority sort or hash operation.

OTHER MEMORY MANAGEMENT TOPICS

In the past two chapters, we've seen how to analyze the memory allocated to the PGA and the buffer cache and how to optimize each memory area for greatest effectiveness. Maximizing the memory *within* each of these areas is important, but getting the most out of your overall memory is impossible unless you allocate effectively *between* the two regions. In 11g, Oracle can manage the allocation of memory within the two regions automatically, whereas in 10g it's up to you to determine the relative size of each region. Even in 11g, you might want to manually allocate memory to optimize for a specific workload rather than to allow Oracle to adjust memory continuously. We cover both techniques in this chapter.

In this chapter we also examine the 11g result set cache, which can store entire result sets in memory. This is a special form of caching that can provide significant optimization for specific SQL statements. We also discuss optimization of other memory areas such as the shared pool, large pool, and redo buffer.

OPTIMIZING OVERALL ORACLE MEMORY

Both the PGA and buffer cache memory have significant roles in reducing IO. PGA memory reduces IO by avoiding temporary segment IO, whereas the buffer cache reduces IO by keeping frequently accessed table and index blocks in memory. Deciding how much memory to allocate to each area is probably the most important memory optimization decision of all.

In Oracle 11g, Automatic Memory Management (AMM) relieves us of the responsibility for this important decision. We simply tell Oracle how much memory to use, and Oracle decides how much should be in the buffer cache and other SGA pools and how much should be in the PGA. AMM is a significant advance and generally results in improved memory configuration. However, just as Automatic Shared Memory Management (ASMM) sometimes needs to be disabled or adjusted to get the most out of SGA memory, you will sometimes find that AMM doesn't provide the best of all possible configurations, and you will need to adjust or override it.

In Oracle 10g AMM is unavailable so it's your responsibility to determine how much of your available memory should be SGA and how much PGA.

IO WAIT TIMES AND MEMORY OPTIMIZATION

Most of our memory optimization efforts are intended to reduce IO. So it makes sense to examine our IO first; some types of IO can be reduced by PGA manipulation and some by changing buffer cache sizing. Other types of IO are unaffected by either.

Here are the main categories of IO that we need to be concerned with for now:

❑ **Buffered datafile IO**—*db file sequential read* and *db file scattered read* occur when a session reads blocks of data into the buffer cache from a data file. Increasing the size of the buffer cache might be successful in reducing this type of IO.

❑ **Temporary segment IO waits**—*direct path read temp* and *direct path write temp* occur when a work area operation such as a sort runs out of PGA memory and needs to overflow to temporary segments on disk. This sort of IO might be reduced by changing PGA memory configuration.

❑ **Direct path reads**—Other than those from temporary segments—occur when Oracle bypasses the buffer cache. This sort of IO is generally unaffected by memory configuration.

❑ **System IO**—Such as writes to redo logs and database files, are conducted by Oracle background processes and generally are not directly affected by memory optimization.

The following query generates a high-level breakdown of IO times as compared to other components of database time:

```
SQL> WITH system_event AS
  2       (SELECT CASE
  3                 WHEN event LIKE 'direct path%temp' THEN
  4                   'direct path read/write temp'
```

```
 5                    WHEN event LIKE 'direct path%' THEN
 6                       'direct path read/write non-temp'
 7                    WHEN wait_class = 'User I/O' THEN
 8                       event
 9                    ELSE  wait_class
10                    END AS  wait_type, e.*
11               FROM v$system_event e)
12  SELECT wait_type, SUM(total_waits) total_waits,
13         ROUND(SUM(time_waited_micro) / 1000000, 2)
                   time_waited_seconds,
14         ROUND(  SUM(time_waited_micro)
15                 * 100
16                 / SUM(SUM(time_waited_micro)) OVER (), 2)
17            pct
18  FROM (SELECT wait_type, event, total_waits, time_waited_micro
19         FROM system_event e
20         UNION
21         SELECT 'CPU', stat_name, NULL, VALUE
22         FROM v$sys_time_model
23         WHERE stat_name IN ('background cpu time', 'DB CPU')) l
24  WHERE wait_type <> 'Idle'
25  GROUP BY wait_type
26  ORDER BY 4 DESC
27  /
```

WAIT_TYPE	TOTAL_WAITS	TIME_WAITED_SECONDS	PCT
direct path read/write non-temp	1,606,382	188,318.38	40.16
direct path read/write temp	36,688,005	172,095.46	36.70
db file sequential read	10,315,473	69,515.42	14.83
System I/O	830,540	15,386.04	3.28
Concurrency	71,397	10,365.80	2.21
CPU		6,403.38	1.37

The preceding output indicates that the largest proportion—approximately 40 percent—of IO time is taken up by direct path IO from permanent segments. This IO is not directly amenable to buffer cache or PGA memory optimization. However, 37 percent of time relates to temporary segment IO and 15 percent to buffered IO. It might be possible to reduce these categories of IO waits through PGA or SGA configuration.

If temporary IO is greater than buffered IO, or vice versa, it might be an indication of which memory area should be increased first. However, remember that increasing memory does not always reduce IO; you should look at the relevant advisories to determine if a memory increase is likely to pay off with a performance improvement.

The more time spent in temporary segment IO—*direct path . . . temp waits*—the greater the potential for improving performance by increasing PGA Aggregate Target. Likewise, the greater the amount of time spent in buffered IO—*db file sequential read* in particular—the greater the chance that increasing the size of buffer caches will improve performance.

The report above shows totals since the database was started. If you have an Oracle Diagnostic pack license, you can drill into the User I/O category within the Enterprise Manager *Active Sessions Waiting* chart. You can then see the low level events associated with the User I/O wait category, as shown in Figure 20-1.

Alternatively, if you install the scripts and packages available from this book's Web site, you can use the IO_TIME_DELTA_VIEW view to show IO waits over a specific interval. Each time you query the view from within a session, it will show the amount of time spent in the various wait categories since the last

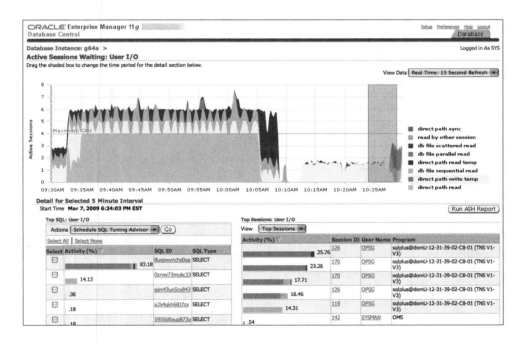

FIGURE 20-1   Enterprise manager user I/O details.

time you issued the query. Below we see that over the past 8 minutes or so (531 seconds), approximately 46 percent of database time was spent in temporary segment IO:

```
SQL> SELECT sample_seconds, wait_type, total_waits, time_waited_seconds, pct
  2  FROM io_time_delta_view
  3  ORDER BY pct DESC;
```

Sample Seconds	Wait Category	Total Waits	Time Waited Seconds	Time Pct
531	**direct path read/write temp**	35,403	996.43	**46.50**
531	db file sequential read	36,743	654.75	30.55
531	read by other session	7,839	342.88	16.00
531	System I/O	3,778	148.25	6.92
531	Network	1,018	.63	.03

USING ADVISORIES TO DISTRIBUTE PGA/BUFFER CACHE MEMORY

IO wait times can often point us in the right memory tuning direction: For instance, if all our wait times are for buffered IO, increasing the PGA is unlikely to help. However, if both temporary segment waits and buffered IO waits are significant, the best course of action might not be obvious.

In the past two chapters we looked at the PGA and database cache advisories: V$PGA_TARGET_ADVICE and V$DB_CACHE_ADVICE. These advisories allow us to determine the likely effect of increasing or decreasing cache or PGA size. We can use these advisories to determine how best to allocate memory between PGA and SGA.

In Oracle 10g, the procedure is made more complicated than one might like because the PGA advisory does not include estimates for elapsed time. In Oracle 10g the procedure is essentially the following:

1. Determine the average time and block counts for temporary segment direct IO operations.
2. Use those averages to convert the byte counts in V$PGA_TARGET_ADVICE to elapsed times.
3. Combine these PGA elapsed times with the buffer cache advisory elapsed times in V$DB_CACHE_ADVICE to determine which combination of targets results in the greatest reduction in overall elapsed times.

For Oracle 11g, it's unnecessary to perform the first two steps because elapsed time estimates are included in the V$PGA_TARGET_ADVICE view.

Determining Temporary Segment IO Times in Oracle 10g In Oracle 10g, V$PGA_TARGET_ADVICE reports IO savings in terms of bytes read and written to temporary segments. To work out the savings relative to other IO, we need to convert these byte counts to IO elapsed times. To do that, we need to know the average number of blocks in a temporary segment IO and the average time for a temporary segment IO.

One way to get this data is to use trace file information. As outlined in Chapter 3, "Tools of the Trade," we can create a SQL trace file that also includes details of each wait event. If we create a trace for a session that performs typical temporary segment IO, we can determine the block sizes and elapsed times for temporary segment IO.

The following perl code analyzes the temporary segment IO recorded in SQL trace output. Note that it assumes an 8K block size:[1] You should change the first line if you are using a different block size:

```
$blocksize=8192;
while (<>) {
        if ($_=~/WAIT #(.*) nam='direct
path(.*)temp'(.*)ela=(.*)file(.*)cnt=(.*)obj#=(.*)/)
        {
                $count++;
                $ela+=$4;
                $blocks+=$6;
        }
}
printf("%-20s %10d\n","Total temp IO waits",$count);
printf("%-20s %10d\n","Elasped Microseconds",$ela);
printf("%-20s %10d\n","Total blocks",$blocks);
printf("%-20s %10d\n","Average blocks",$blocks/$count);
printf("%-20s %10d\n","Microseconds/block",$ela/$blocks);
printf("%-20s %10.4f\n","Microseconds/byteRW",$ela/$blocks/$blocksize);

print "\nNB: assuming blocksize of $blocksize\n";
```

Most UNIX and Linux distributions have a copy of perl available, and you can easily install perl on Windows. However, you can also use the version of perl that is shipped with Oracle. On Windows, you can find perl.exe in a directory named something like this:

```
%ORACLE_HOME%\perl\5.8.3\bin\MSWin32-x86-multi-thread.
```

Running the perl script prints details of the direct path temp IOs recorded in the trace file:

---

[1] You can query DBA_TABLESPACES to find the block size for the temporary tablespace.

```
>perl trc_tempio_stat.pl <g10a_ora_27060.trc
Total temp IO waits          7593
Elasped Microseconds    115996220
Total blocks               111979
Average blocks                 14
Microseconds/block           1035
Microseconds/byteRW        0.1279
```

```
NB: assuming blocksize of 8192
```

Calculating PGA Advisory Elapsed Times (10g) The Microseconds/ byteRW from our perl output is a magic number we are going to use in subsequent calculations. It represents the average time cost for each byte of temporary file IO. If we plug this value into V$PGA_TARGET_ADVICE, we can estimate relative changes in IO times for various changes in the PGA target:

```
SQL> SELECT current_size / 1048576 current_size_mb,
  2          pga_target_for_estimate / 1048576 pga_target_mb,
  3          (estd_extra_bytes_rw - current_extra_bytes_rw)
  4              * 0.1279 / 1000000 AS estd_seconds_delta,
  5          estd_extra_bytes_rw / 1048576 estd_extra_mb_rw
  6  FROM v$pga_target_advice,
  7      (SELECT pga_target_for_estimate current_size,
  8              estd_extra_bytes_rw current_extra_bytes_rw
  9       FROM v$pga_target_advice
 10       WHERE pga_target_factor = 1);
```

Current MB	Target MB	Estimated time delta (s)	Estimated extra MB
500	63	75,206.67	867,971
500	125	8,230.72	368,571
500	250	972.50	314,451
500	375	721.38	312,578
500	500	.00	307,199
500	600	-1.10	307,191
500	700	-1.10	307,191
500	800	-1.10	307,191

Calculating the time cost for IOs in V$DB_CACHE_ADVICE is far simpler because V$DB_CACHE_ADVICE already provides time estimates:

```
SQL> SELECT current_size, size_for_estimate,
  2          (estd_physical_read_time - current_time)
```

```
 3                estd_io_seconds_delta,
 4            estd_physical_reads - current_reads
 5              physical_reads_delta
 6  FROM v$db_cache_advice,
 7        (SELECT size_for_estimate current_size,
 8                estd_physical_read_time current_time,
 9                estd_physical_reads current_reads
10         FROM v$db_cache_advice
11         WHERE size_factor = 1 AND name = 'DEFAULT'
12            AND block_size = 8192)
13  WHERE name = 'DEFAULT' AND block_size = 8192;
```

Current MB	Estimate MB	Est IO Time Delta (s)	Phys Reads Delta
404	40	1,202,966	76,149,733
404	80	999,489	63,269,307
...	...	...	...
404	280	228,083	14,438,021
404	320	127,328	8,060,085
404	360	50,139	3,173,861
404	400	3,318	210,066
404	404	0	0
404	440	-29,661	-1,877,597
404	480	-36,936	-2,338,118
404	520	-38,058	-2,409,108
...	...	...	...
404	760	-41,040	-2,597,909
404	800	-41,043	-2,598,103

Combining the PGA and Buffer Cache Advisories in 10g   If we combine the two advisories together, we can see if any combinations of buffer cache and PGA memory appear to be more effective than the configuration we are currently using. Here's the query that outputs possible improvements in memory distribution between the PGA and the default buffer cache:

```
SQL> WITH db_cache_times AS
 2      (SELECT current_size current_cache_mb,
 3              size_for_estimate target_cache_mb,
 4              (estd_physical_read_time - current_time)
 5                cache_secs_delta
 6       FROM v$db_cache_advice,
 7              (SELECT size_for_estimate current_size,
 8                      estd_physical_read_time current_time
```

```
 9                        FROM v$db_cache_advice
10                     WHERE  size_factor = 1
11                        AND name = 'DEFAULT' AND block_size = 8192)
12           WHERE name = 'DEFAULT' AND block_size = 8192),
13    pga_times AS
14       (SELECT current_size / 1048576 current_pga_mb,
15               pga_target_for_estimate / 1048576 target_pga_mb,
16               ROUND((estd_extra_bytes_rw - current_extra_bytes_rw)
17                 * 0.1279 / 1000000,2)   pga_secs_delta
18         FROM v$pga_target_advice,
19              (SELECT pga_target_for_estimate current_size,
20                      estd_extra_bytes_rw current_extra_bytes_rw
21                FROM v$pga_target_advice
22               WHERE pga_target_factor = 1))
23    SELECT current_cache_mb||'MB->'||target_cache_mb||'MB'
               Buffer_cache,
24            current_pga_mb||'->'||target_pga_mb||'MB' PGA,
25            pga_secs_delta,cache_secs_delta,
26            (pga_secs_delta+cache_secs_delta) total_secs_delta
27      FROM db_cache_times d,pga_times p
28     WHERE (target_pga_mb+target_cache_mb)
29              <=(current_pga_mb+current_cache_mb)
30       AND (pga_secs_delta+cache_secs_delta) <0
31     ORDER BY (pga_secs_delta+cache_secs_delta);
```

Buffer Cache Change	PGA Change	Pga Time Delta (s)	Cache Time Delta (s)	Total Time Delta (s)
444MB->880MB	702->175.5MB	3,565	-40,303	-36,738
444MB->880MB	702->87.75MB	3,565	-40,303	-36,738
444MB->836MB	702->175.5MB	3,565	-36,066	-32,501
444MB->836MB	702->87.75MB	3,565	-36,066	-32,501
444MB->792MB	702->175.5MB	3,565	-31,828	-28,263
444MB->792MB	702->87.75MB	3,565	-31,828	-28,263
444MB->792MB	702->351MB	3,565	-31,828	-28,263

This query is a bit longer than most we've used so far, but is relatively simple in concept:

❏ Lines 1–12 define a view into V$DB_CACHE_ADVICE that shows changes in elapsed times for various buffer cache sizes.

❏ Lines 13–22 do the same for V$PGA_TARGET_ADVICE: an in-line view that reports the effect on elapsed times for changes in PGA Aggregate Target (using the time per byte value of 0.1279 that we calculated earlier).

❑ Lines 23–31 perform a Cartesian join of both views: Every row in V$DB_CACHE_ADVICE is joined with every row in V$PGA_TARGET _ADVICE. However, we eliminate rows in which the elapsed time or total amount of memory allocated is greater than for the current memory allocations (line 30).

The analyses suggest that if memory is moved from the PGA into the buffer cache, an overall reduction in IO time results. A reduction in the PGA Aggregate Target from 702M to 175M results in an increase in IO time of 3,565 seconds, whereas the same memory in the buffer cache results in a reduction of 40,303 seconds of IO time—a significant overall improvement.

Performing Advisory Calculations in 11g In Oracle 11g, the procedure is less complicated. It's not necessary to calculate average direct IO times or convert the PGA advisory data from bytes to elapsed time because the V$PGA_ TARGET_ADVICE view already includes elapsed time estimates. Therefore, we can simply—well at least more simply than for 10g—issue a query that directly compares the two advisories:

```
SQL> WITH db_cache_times AS
  2       (SELECT current_size current_cache_mb,
  3               size_for_estimate target_cache_mb,
  4               (estd_physical_read_time - current_time)
  5                 cache_secs_delta
  6          FROM v$db_cache_advice,
  7               (SELECT size_for_estimate current_size,
  8                       estd_physical_read_time current_time
  9                  FROM v$db_cache_advice
 10                 WHERE  size_factor = 1
 11                   AND name = 'DEFAULT' AND block_size = 8192)
 12          WHERE name = 'DEFAULT' AND block_size = 8192),
 13     pga_times AS
 14       (SELECT current_size / 1048576 current_pga_mb,
 15               pga_target_for_estimate / 1048576 target_pga_mb,
 16               estd_time-base_time pga_secs_delta
 17          FROM v$pga_target_advice ,
 18               (SELECT pga_target_for_estimate current_size,
 19                       estd_time base_time
 20                  FROM v$pga_target_advice
 21                 WHERE pga_target_factor = 1))
 22  SELECT current_cache_mb||'MB->'||target_cache_mb||'MB' Buffer_cache,
 23         current_pga_mb||'->'||target_pga_mb||'MB' PGA,
 24         pga_secs_delta,cache_secs_delta,
 25         (pga_secs_delta+cache_secs_delta) total_secs_delta
 26    FROM db_cache_times d,pga_times p
```

```
27    WHERE (target_pga_mb+target_cache_mb)
28          <=(current_pga_mb+current_cache_mb)
29      AND (pga_secs_delta+cache_secs_delta) <0
30    ORDER BY (pga_secs_delta+cache_secs_delta);
```

Buffer Cache Change	PGA Change	Pga Time Delta (s)	Cache Time Delta (s)	Total Time Delta (s)
1024MB->1280MB	1792->896MB	0	-2,783	-2,783
1024MB->1280MB	1792->1344MB	0	-2,783	-2,783
1024MB->1216MB	1792->896MB	0	-2,152	-2,152
1024MB->1216MB	1792->1344MB	0	-2,152	-2,152
1024MB->1152MB	1792->1344MB	0	-1,475	-1,475
1024MB->1152MB	1792->896MB	0	-1,475	-1,475
1024MB->1088MB	1792->1344MB	0	-798	-798
1024MB->1088MB	1792->896MB	0	-798	-798

In this example, the advisory information suggests that a modest decrease in time can be achieved by moving memory from the PGA to the SGA: Increasing the buffer cache by 256M results in a savings of 2,783 seconds, while PGA can be reduced by this amount without penalty.

These recommendations are only as good as the data provided by Oracle's advisories, and in the case of Oracle 10g, our calculations of temporary segment IO average block size and times.

There are also some circumstances in which the advisory information is reset; for instance, by changing the value of the configuration parameter DB_CACHE_ADVICE. If only one of the advisories has been reset, each might be generating advice for a different time period and the combined analyses might be misleading. If in doubt, you should analyze advisory information following a database restart.

Although this analysis serves as a good basis for trialing changes in memory distribution, you should definitely monitor performance following the change.

To manually determine the correct distribution of memory between PGA and the buffer cache, convert V$PGA_TARGET_ADVICE estimates to elapsed time (Oracle 10g only) and compare with the time estimates from V$DB_CACHE_ADVICE.

Estimating optimal memory configuration becomes significantly more complex if you attempt to factor in the advisories for the nondefault buffer caches (KEEP, RECYCLE, and the block size specific caches). Although you can apply the same general procedures to determine the best distribution, the complexity might become excessive.

Quest Software's Spotlight on Oracle[2] automates the procedures we've just outlined and incorporates many significant optimizations on the algorithms. It can recommend optimal memory configurations (including minimum values for individual caches) for 10g and 11g databases. Figure 20-2 shows Spotlight's memory management capability.

ORACLE 11G AUTOMATIC MEMORY MANAGEMENT (AMM)

If the procedure just outlined seems a little too complicated, take heart. In Oracle 11g you can assign the responsibility for computing relative trade-offs between the PGA, the buffer cache, and other areas of the SGA to Oracle. Oracle will determine the optimum trade-off between the various memory areas and periodically adjusts memory allocations. This facility is known as Automatic Memory Management (AMM).

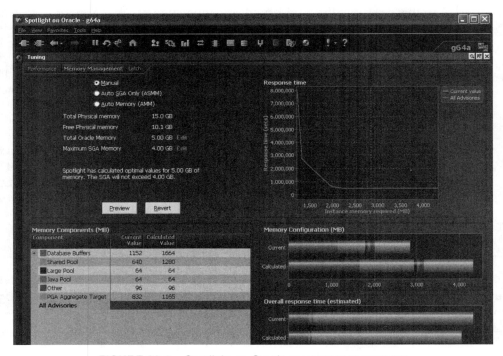

FIGURE 20-2   Spotlight on Oracle memory management.

---

[2] Full disclosure: I was heavily involved in the design and construction of Spotlight's memory management facilities while working at Quest Software.

AMM is a welcome innovation: Prior to AMM, DBAs were forced to determine the optimum memory configuration using something akin to the time-consuming manual procedure outlined in the previous section or, more often, by trial and error. Because the division of memory between PGA and SGA is so crucial to reducing IO overhead, suboptimal distribution of this memory was and is a major cause of diminished database performance.

However much AMM improves upon trial-and-error memory management; it is not perfect, and you might need to invest some time configuring and monitoring AMM operation for best results.

Enabling AMM   You can enable AMM in Enterprise Manager or by directly setting appropriate parameters. To manually enable AMM:

1. Set a value for MEMORY_MAX_TARGET, which determines the maximum possible value for MEMORY_TARGET. You will need sufficient operating system memory to support the value you set: On Linux this requires configuring /dev/shm to at least the size of MEMORY_MAX_TARGET. You must restart the database to allow the new value to take effect.

2. Optionally set SGA_TARGET, PGA_AGGREGATE_TARGET, and other memory configuration parameters (such as SHARED_POOL_SIZE) to 0. If any of these parameters have nonzero values while AMM is in effect, the parameter values define *minimum* sizes for the specified memory region.

3. Set MEMORY_TARGET to the total amount of memory you want to share between SGA and PGA.

In Enterprise Manager, you can enable AMM from the AdvisorCentral > MemoryAdvisors page. Figure 20-3 shows us enabling AMM with a total memory target of 4G, within an absolute maximum (MEMORY_MAX_TARGET) of 6G.

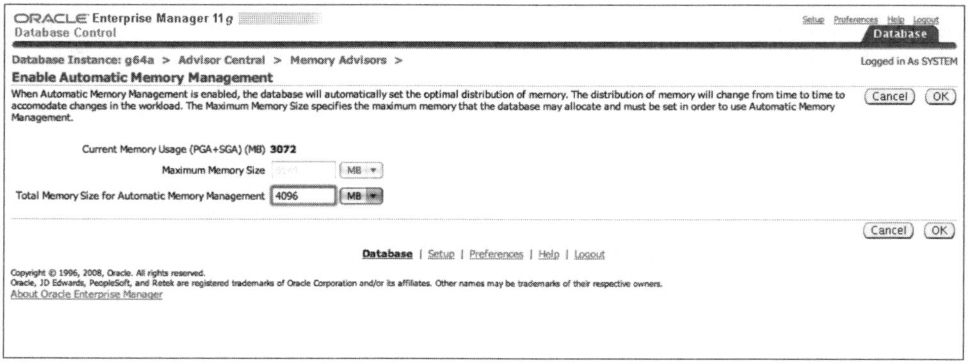

FIGURE 20-3   Enabling AMM in Enterprise Manager.

Monitoring Memory Allocations The current sizes for all memory areas, together with minimum and maximum values, last resize operation, and user-specified minimum values can be obtained from the view V$MEMORY_ DYNAMIC_COMPONENTS:

```
SQL> BREAK ON REPORT
SQL> COMPUTE SUM LABEL TOTAL OF current_mb ON REPORT
SQL>
SQL> SELECT component, ROUND(current_size / 1048576) current_mb,
  2         ROUND(min_size / 1045876) min_mb,
  3         ROUND(max_size / 1045876) max_mb,
  4         ROUND(user_specified_size / 1048576) user_spec_mb,
  5         last_oper_type
  6  FROM V$MEMORY_DYNAMIC_COMPONENTS;
```

COMPONENT	Current MB	Min MB	Max MB	User set MB	Last Resize
shared pool	704	321	706	0	SHRINK
large pool	256	64	257	256	GROW
java pool	64	64	64	0	STATIC
streams pool	0	0	0	0	STATIC
SGA Target	1,856	1861	3657	0	SHRINK
DEFAULT buffer cache	512	513	2759	0	SHRINK
KEEP buffer cache	256	0	257	256	GROW
RECYCLE buffer cache	0	0	0	0	STATIC
DEFAULT 2K buffer cache	0	0	0	0	STATIC
DEFAULT 4K buffer cache	0	0	0	0	STATIC
DEFAULT 8K buffer cache	0	0	0	0	STATIC
DEFAULT 16K buffer cache	0	0	0	0	STATIC
DEFAULT 32K buffer cache	0	0	0	0	STATIC
Shared IO Pool	0	0	0	0	STATIC
PGA Target	2,240	64	2502	0	GROW
ASM Buffer Cache	0	0	0	0	STATIC

TOTAL	5,888				

You can monitor resize operations from the view V$MEMORY_RESIZE _OPS. The following query shows the resize operations that have occurred over the past hour:

```
SQL> SELECT component, oper_type,
  2         initial_size / 1048576 initial_mb,
  3         target_size / 1048576 target_mb,
  4         to_char(end_time,'HH24:MI') end_time
```

```
5  FROM v$memory_resize_ops
6  WHERE end_time > SYSDATE - NUMTODSINTERVAL(1, 'HOUR')
7  ORDER BY start_time DESC;
```

COMPONENT	OPER_TYPE	INITIAL_MB	TARGET_MB	End Time
DEFAULT buffer cache	SHRINK	384	320	20:30
PGA Target	GROW	2,368	2,432	20:29
SGA Target	SHRINK	1,728	1,664	20:30
DEFAULT buffer cache	SHRINK	448	384	20:26
SGA Target	SHRINK	1,792	1,728	20:26
PGA Target	GROW	2,304	2,368	20:26
DEFAULT buffer cache	SHRINK	512	448	20:23
PGA Target	GROW	2,240	2,304	20:23
SGA Target	SHRINK	1,856	1,792	20:23
large pool	GROW	64	256	20:22
DEFAULT buffer cache	SHRINK	704	512	20:22
DEFAULT buffer cache	SHRINK	768	704	20:20
SGA Target	SHRINK	1,920	1,856	20:20
PGA Target	GROW	2,176	2,240	20:20
shared pool	SHRINK	704	640	20:19

You can also monitor high-level memory allocations from Enterprise Manager in the Advisor Central > Memory Advisors page (see Figure 20-4).

The Memory Target Advisory   V$MEMORY_TARGET_ADVICE provides estimates of the effect on performance that would result from adjusting the MEMORY_TARGET parameter. In the following example, it looks like a relatively small increase in MEMORY_TARGET (to 5760M) could result in a significant reduction in DB time. On the other hand, the advisory suggests that reducing memory to 62 percent of the current value (3200M) might not harm performance:

```
SQL> SELECT memory_size, memory_size_factor * 100
memory_size_pct,
  2          estd_db_time_factor * 100 estd_db_time_pct,
  3          estd_db_time
  4  FROM v$memory_target_advice a
  5  ORDER BY memory_size_factor
  6  /
```

Memory Size MB	Memory Pct of Current	Relative DB Time	Estimated DB Time
2,560	50.00	114.65	1,002,341
3,200	62.50	100.00	874,262

4,480	87.50	100.00	874,262
5,120	100.00	100.00	874,262
5,760	112.50	83.02	725,812
6,400	125.00	83.02	725,812
7,040	137.50	83.02	725,812
7,680	150.00	83.02	725,812
8,320	162.50	83.02	725,812
8,960	175.00	83.02	725,812
9,600	187.50	83.02	725,812
10,240	200.00	83.02	725,812

You can obtain a graphical representation of this information by clicking the Advice button on the Memory advisor page as shown in Figure 20-5.

The chart shown in Figure 20-5 suggests that increasing the MEMORY _TARGET to approximately 4.5G would result in a 15 percent improvement in DB Time. Further increases are unlikely to result in any improvement.

V$MEMORY_TARGET_ADVICE can give you some idea as to the benefit or cost of changing the overall memory target.

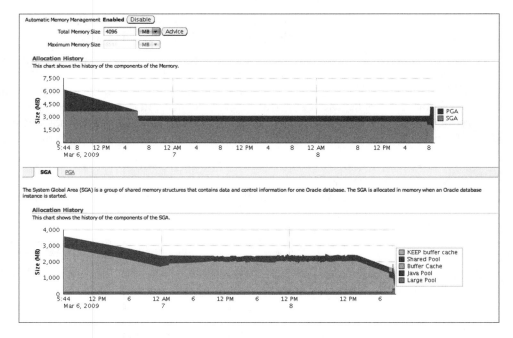

FIGURE 20-4   Monitoring memory allocations in Enterprise Manager.

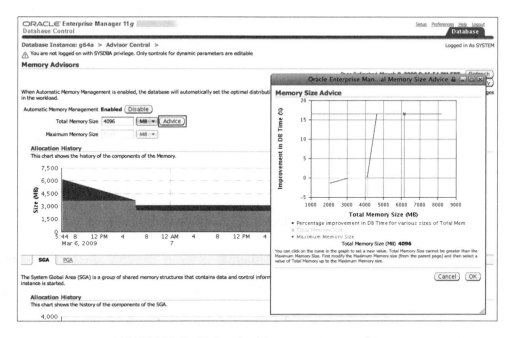

FIGURE 20-5 Enterprise Manager memory advice.

V$MEMORY_TARGET_ADVICE is a bit obscure about exactly what it thinks would happen if memory was increased: It doesn't indicate which areas of memory, if any, would be increased. You can get more detail by going directly against the X$ table—X$KMSGSBSMEMADV—which underlies V$MEMORY _TARGET_ADVICE. It shows what values of PGA and SGA are used for each estimate provided by V$MEMORY_TARGET_ADVICE. Unfortunately, you can only run this query as SYS:

```
SQL> SELECT memsz memory_size, ROUND(memsz * 100 / base_memsz)
            memory_size_pct,
  2        sga_sz sga_size, pga_sz pga_size, dbtime estd_db_time,
  3        ROUND(dbtime * 100 / base_estd_dbtime) db_time_pct,
  4        sgatime estd_sga_time, pgatime estd_pga_time
  5  FROM x$kmgsbsmemadv
  6  ORDER BY memsz;
```

Memory Size	Memory Pct	SGA Size	PGA Size	Est. DB Time	Est. SGA Time	Est. PGA Time
2,560	50.00	1,216	448	199,678,450	541,340	199,137,110
3,840	75.00	1,216	1,792	199,029,009	541,340	198,487,669

4,480	88.00	1,792	1,792	198,867,521	379,852	198,487,669
5,120	100.00	2,432	1,792	198,799,483	311,814	198,487,669
5,760	113.00	3,008	1,792	198,785,950	298,281	198,487,669
6,400	125.00	3,648	1,792	198,780,868	293,199	198,487,669
7,040	138.00	3,648	2,496	198,780,868	293,199	198,487,669
7,680	150.00	5,440	1,344	198,775,473	287,804	198,487,669
8,320	163.00	4,864	2,496	198,775,473	287,804	198,487,669
8,960	175.00	4,864	3,200	198,775,473	287,804	198,487,669
9,600	188.00	5,440	3,200	198,775,473	287,804	198,487,669
######	200.00	6,016	3,200	198,775,473	287,804	198,487,669

This query shows the exact values of PGA and SGA that are used to create each row in V$MEMORY_TARGET_ADVICE. For instance, the first line of output tells us that the memory target of 2560M is based on the combination of a 1216M SGA and a 448M PGA.[3]

Setting Minimum Sizes Although you can give AMM complete control over the sizes of all the memory components, it's often preferable to set minimum values for certain memory areas. When you do this, AMM automatically resizes as usual, but avoids shrinking any area to a size less than the minimum you have specified. You can set minimum sizes by setting a value for SGA_TARGET and PGA_AGGREGATE_TARGET together with a value for MEMORY_TARGET. You can also continue to specify minimum sizes for various components of the SGA such as the shared pool. (See Chapter 18, "Buffer Cache Tuning," for an example of using this technique with ASMM.)

The following query shows parameter settings for a database with AMM enabled that also has minimum values set for the db cache, KEEP cache, large pool, and shared pool:

```
SQL> SELECT name, display_value, description
  2  FROM v$parameter
  3  WHERE name IN
  4               ('sga_target',
  5                'memory_target',
  6                'memory_max_target',
  7                'pga_aggregate_target',
  8                'shared_pool_size',
  9                'large_pool_size',
 10                'java_pool_size')
 11        OR name LIKE 'db%cache_size'
 12  ORDER BY name
 13  /
```

---

[3] It doesn't quite add up, presumably because Oracle makes allowance for fixed overheads and nondynamic memory areas.

```
NAME                     Value   DESCRIPTION
--------------------     ------  -------------------------------------
db_16k_cache_size        0       Size of cache for 16K buffers
db_2k_cache_size         0       Size of cache for 2K buffers
db_32k_cache_size        0       Size of cache for 32K buffers
db_4k_cache_size         0       Size of cache for 4K buffers
db_8k_cache_size         0       Size of cache for 8K buffers
db_cache_size            256M    Size of DEFAULT buffer pool for standard
                                   block size buffers

db_keep_cache_size       64M     Size of KEEP buffer pool for standard
                                 block size buffers

db_recycle_cache_size    0       Size of RECYCLE buffer pool for standard
                                   block size buffers

java_pool_size           0       size in bytes of java pool
large_pool_size          128M    size in bytes of large pool
memory_max_target        6G      Max size for Memory Target
memory_target            5G      Target size of Oracle SGA and PGA memory
pga_aggregate_target     0       Target size for the aggregate PGA memory
                                   consumed by the instance

sga_target               0       Target size of SGA
shared_pool_size         512M    size in bytes of shared pool
```

AMM Issues and Considerations   The potential performance gains from AMM are significant; however, the algorithm can fall short under certain circumstances. AMM is subject to many of the issues that affect ASMM, namely

- ❏ Thrashing can occur if workloads oscillate or change frequently. For instance, a workload that periodically alternates between sort-intensive and read-intensive operations might cause memory to shift frequently between PGA and SGA. The result might be that the memory is constantly configured for the workload that just finished, rather than the workload currently executing.
- ❏ Memory Starvation can occur if a single session acquires a huge amount of memory. For instance, we saw in Chapter 18 how a PL/SQL routine that creates large PL/SQL tables while running in shared server mode can cause memory from the buffer pool to be eliminated in favor of large pool memory. The same issue can occur when AMM is enabled.
- ❏ Not all memory regions are automatically resized. The same regions that are excluded from ASMM—most significantly the nondefault buffer pools—are also out of scope of AMM. For instance, if you create a KEEP or

RECYLE pool, you need to make sure that these pool sizes are sufficient but not excessive because they will not be adjusted by AMM.

❏ AMM is incompatible with Linux HugePages. Linux HugePages provide access to memory pages larger than the 4K or 16K default sizes available on 32-bit and 64-bit Linux. HugePages provide substantial advantages when dealing with large memory address spaces. However, HugePages and AMM are incompatible.

❏ You can't lock the SGA when using AMM. In rare circumstances, it might be advantageous to prevent SGA memory from being "paged out" to disk. However, the memory model used by AMM is inconsistent with the LOCK_SGA option that Oracle provides for this purpose.

Some of these issues can be avoided by setting minimum sizes for specific components. In particular, setting a minimum size for the buffer cache can prevent excessive thrashing and alleviate starvation. In other cases, you might be better off calculating an optimal static distribution using the techniques outlined earlier in this chapter and disabling AMM.

Set minimum values for key memory areas to avoid starvation of, or excessive thrashing between, memory areas.

RESULT SET CACHE

The 11g result set cache stores entire result sets in shared memory.[4] If a SQL query is executed and its result set is in the cache, almost the entire overhead of the SQL execution is avoided: This includes parse time, logical reads, physical reads, and any cache contention overhead (latches for instance) that might normally be incurred.

Sounds good, right? You might be thinking that the result set cache is better than the buffer cache; however, the reality is that the result set cache will be effective only in a small number of situations. This is because

❏ Multiple SQLs that have overlapping data will store that data redundantly in the cache. So the result set that summarizes data for customers from California will duplicate some of the data in the cached result set that summarizes all of North America. Therefore, the result set cache is not always as memory-efficient as the buffer cache.

---

[4] This is similar to, but independent of, the client result cache that we discussed in Chapter 6.

❑ Any change to a dependent object—to any table referenced in the query—invalidates the entire cached result set. The result set cache is most suitable for tables that are read only or nearly read only.

❑ Big result sets will either be too small to fit in the result set cache or will force all the existing entries in the cache out; this is similar to the issue of full table scans and the buffer cache that we looked at in Chapter 18. To prevent this from happening, we need to restrict the result set cache to smaller result sets only.

❑ Rapid concurrent creation of result sets in the cache can result in latch contention for the Result Cache Latch. The contents of the result set cache, therefore, need to change relatively slowly.

The result set cache can be effective in reducing the overhead of IO intensive queries on static tables that return limited results. For instance, the following query returns only a single row but must scan large proportions of the SALES _ARCHIVE table to do so:

```
SELECT SUM(amount_sold)
  FROM sales_archive
 WHERE cust_id = :cust_id;
```

If SALES_ARCHIVE is infrequently updated, and this query executed regularly, the result cache could result in significant improvements. For instance, for 1,000 executions of the preceding query, with 500 possible values for the CUST _ID variable, we experienced an 88 percent reduction in elapsed time when using a default result set cache. Figure 20-6 illustrates the performance improvement.

You might like to think of cached result sets as on-the-fly, in-memory materialized views. The same sorts of queries that lead you to consider materialized views—queries on large, static tables producing small aggregate result sets—might make effective use of Result Set caching.

ENABLING AND CONFIGURING THE RESULT SET CACHE

The result set cache is controlled by the following parameters:

RESULT_CACHE_MODE   The operating mode for the result cache:

❑ OFF: disable.

❑ MANUAL: Only queries that use the RESULT_CACHE hint or queries that access tables with the "RESULT_CACHE(MODE FORCE)" attribute will be cached.

❑ FORCE: All eligible queries will be cached.

RESULT_CACHE_MAX_SIZE	Size of the Result set cache. The default is 1% of shared pool size.
RESULT_CACHE_MAX_RESULT	The maximum percentage of the cache that can be consumed by any single result set. Result sets bigger than this will not be cached.

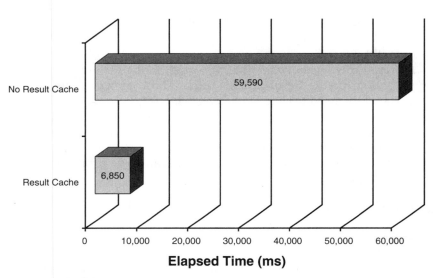

FIGURE 20-6   Benefits gained by using the result set cache.

Unless you set RESULT_CACHE_MODE to FORCE, only queries that use the RESULT_CACHE hint, or access a table with the RESULT_CACHE table property enabled, will be eligible for the result set cache. As we will see, setting RESULT_CACHE_MODE to FORCE produces a high risk of significant latch contention and is not recommended. The RESULT_CACHE table property was introduced in Oracle 11g Release 2.

RESULT CACHE STATISTICS

Oracle provides only indirect indications of result cache effectiveness. The V$RESULT_CACHE_STATISTICS view shows summary statistics for the result set cache:

```
SQL> SELECT name,value FROM v$result_cache_statistics;

NAME                                     VALUE
-------------------------------- ----------------
Block Size (Bytes)                       1,024
Block Count Maximum                      1,536
Block Count Current                        736
```

```
Result Size Maximum (Blocks)              1,536
Create Count Success                        670
Create Count Failure                          0
Find Count                           24,019,888
Invalidation Count                            0
Delete Count Invalid                          0
Delete Count Valid                            0
```

From an efficiency point of view, the key statistics are

❏ **Create Count Success**—The number of result set caches created.

❏ **Find Count**—The number of queries that found a result set in the cache.

❏ **Invalidation Count**—The number of result set caches that were invalidated when DML changed the contents of a dependent object.

❏ **Delete Count Valid**—The number of valid result sets removed to make way for new result sets. (Result sets are aged out using a Least Recently Used algorithm.)

These statistics can give us only a rough indication as to result set cache efficiency: If the Find Count is low relative to creations, invalidations, and deletes, the result sets created are generally not useful. So we would hope to see a Find count many times higher than the Create count. The following query calculates some interesting ratios from V$RESULT_CACHE_STATISTICS:

```
SQL> WITH execs AS (SELECT VALUE executions
  2                   FROM v$sysstat
  3                   WHERE name = 'execute count'),
  4        rscache AS
  5         (SELECT SUM(DECODE(name, 'Create Count Success',
  6                       VALUE)) created,
  7                 SUM(DECODE(name, 'Find Count', VALUE)) find_count
  8          FROM v$result_cache_statistics),
  9        rscounts AS (SELECT COUNT( * ) resultSets,
 10                         COUNT(DISTINCT cache_id) statements
 11                   FROM v$result_cache_objects
 12                   WHERE TYPE = 'Result')
 13   SELECT resultSets, statements, created,
 14          find_count / 1000 find_count1000,
 15          ROUND(find_count * 100 / created, 2) find_created_pct,
 16          executions / 1000 execs1000,
 17          ROUND(find_count * 100 / executions, 2) find_exec_pct
 18   FROM   rscache CROSS JOIN  execs
 19          CROSS JOIN  rscounts;
```

Current	Unique	Sets	Sets Found	Find/Created	Executions	Find/Exec
sets	SQL	Created	/1000	PCT	/1000	PCT
1,512	2	9,503	24	255.26	300	8.09

A Find/Create ratio less than 100 percent means that most cached result sets are not used even once and might suggest a review of the use of the RE-SULT_CACHE hint or overall result set cache configuration.

However, it could be that while *most* result sets are not efficient, a few are *extremely* efficient and more than make up for those that get flushed out unused. We can examine the efficiency of individual result sets by looking at statistics for SQLs in the cache that include the RESULT CACHE operation in their plan. The following query does that:

```
SQL> WITH result_cache AS (SELECT cache_id,
  2                               COUNT( * ) cached_result_sets,
  3                               SUM(scan_count) hits
  4                          FROM v$result_cache_objects
  5                          GROUP BY cache_id)
  6  SELECT /*+ ordered */
  7         s.sql_id, s.executions, o.cached_result_sets,
  8         o.hits cache_hits,
  9         ROUND(s.rows_processed / executions) avg_rows,
 10         buffer_gets,
 11         ROUND(buffer_gets / (executions - o.hits))
 12            avg_gets_nocache,
 13         round((buffer_gets / (executions - o.hits))
 14            *o.hits) estd_saved_gets,
 15         s.sql_text
 16  FROM      v$sql_plan p
 17         JOIN
 18            result_cache o
 19         ON (p.object_name = o.cache_id)
 20      JOIN
 21         v$sql s
 22      ON (s.sql_id = p.sql_id AND s.child_number = p.child_number)
 23  WHERE operation = 'RESULT CACHE'
 24    order by 7 desc ;
```

Execs	Cached Results	Cache Hits	Buffer Gets	Avg Gets w/o Cache	Estd. Saved Buffer gets /1000
4,388	494	3,894	150,279	304	1,184,588

```
Sql Text
SELECT /*+ RESULT_CACHE */ PROD_NAME, SUM(AMOUNT_SOLD) FROM SALES JOIN
PRODUCTS USING (PROD_ID) JOIN CUSTOMERS USING (CUST_ID) WHERE CUST_ID
= :B2 AND TIME_ID > :B1 GROUP BY PROD_NAME
```

Execs	Cached Results	Cache Hits	Buffer Gets	Avg Gets w/o Cache	Estd. Saved Buffer gets /1000
14,187	3,128	11,059	9,389	3	33,195

```
SELECT /*+ RESULT_CACHE */ SUM(AMOUNT_SOLD) FROM SALES_ARCHIVE JOIN PR
ODUCTS USING (PROD_ID) JOIN CUSTOMERS USING (CUST_ID) WHERE PROD_ID =
:B2 AND CUST_ID = :B1
```

Note that both of the preceding SQL statements generated more than one cached result set. Indeed 494 and 3,128 cached result sets were created for the two SQLs. The result set cache can create a unique cached result set for each distinct combination of bind variables provided for each statement.

For suitable SQL statements, substantial savings in overhead can be achieved. The two statements illustrated showed reductions in overhead of between 80 percent and 90 percent. Not all the result sets will be reused, and some might have been flushed out of memory before being reused. Nevertheless, we can see that for the two preceding statements, cache hits were a significant majority of the overall execution count.

> The result cache can be effective for expensive queries on relatively static tables that return small result sets.

RESULT CACHE DEPENDENCIES

Cached result sets will be eliminated from cache when DML alters any of the dependent tables involved in the query.

You can list the queries in the cache and the dependent objects by using the following query:

```
SQL> SELECT /*+ ordered */ max(co.name) cached_object,
  2          count(*) result_sets_cached, do.cache_id dependency
  3  FROM        v$result_cache_dependency d
  4      JOIN
  5          v$result_cache_objects do
  6      ON (d.depend_id = do.id)
  7      JOIN
```

```
 8            v$result_cache_objects co
 9       ON (d.result_id = co.id)
10   group by do.cache_id, co.cache_id
11   order by cached_object;
```

```
                                                No of   Dependent
CACHED_OBJECT                                 Result Sets   Object
----------------------------------------      -----------   ------------------
SELECT /*+ RESULT_CACHE */ PROD_NAME, SU          194   OPSG.CUSTOMERS
M(AMOUNT_SOLD) FROM SALES JOIN PRODUCTS
USING (PROD_ID) JOIN CUSTOMERS USING (CU
ST_ID) W


                                                        OPSG.SALES
                                                        OPSG.PRODUCTS


SELECT /*+ RESULT_CACHE */ SUM(AMOUNT_SO        1,319   OPSG.PRODUCTS
LD) FROM SALES_ARCHIVE JOIN PRODUCTS
USING (PROD_ID) JOIN CUSTOMERS USING (CUST_
ID) WHER


                                                        OPSG.SALES_ARCHIVE
                                                        OPSG.CUSTOMERS
```

RESULT CACHE LATCHES

The *Result Cache: RC Latch* (Oracle 11g Release 2) or the *Result Cache: Latch* (Oracle 11g Release 1) controls the creation and deletion of result sets in the Result set cache. Contention for this latch occurs if multiple sessions attempt to simultaneously create cached result sets. This sort of contention will not normally occur if long-running expensive queries are cached because the rate at which new entries are loaded will be low. However, if you attempt to cache all SQLs, or those that run at high frequencies, this latch contention might dominate response time.

The Result Cache latch does not have its own wait event. Contention for the latch shows up under the general purpose *latch free* wait event:

```
SQL> select * from latch_delta_view;
```

WAIT_TYPE	TOTAL_WAITS	TIME_WAITED_MS	PCT_TIME	SAMPLE_SEC
CPU		97098.449	91.7	31
latch free	**365**	**3403.802**	**3.21**	**31**
latch: cache buffers chains	35	1822.472	1.72	31
User I/O	40	1455.908	1.37	31
latch: row cache objects	16	1133.492	1.07	31

To determine whether it is the Result Cache latch, query V$LATCH to determine the latch that has the most sleeps:

```
SQL> WITH latch AS (
  2         SELECT name,
  3                ROUND(gets * 100 / SUM(gets) OVER (), 2)
  4                     pct_of_gets,
                 ROUND(misses * 100 / SUM(misses) OVER (), 2)
                      pct_of_misses,
  5                ROUND(sleeps * 100 / SUM(sleeps) OVER (), 2)
                      pct_of_sleeps,
  6                ROUND(wait_time * 100 / SUM(wait_time) OVER (), 2)
  7                      pct_of_wait_time
  8         FROM v$latch)
  9   SELECT *
 10   FROM latch
 11   WHERE pct_of_wait_time > .1 OR pct_of_sleeps > .1
 12   ORDER BY pct_of_wait_time DESC;
```

NAME	Pct of Gets	Pct of Misses	Pct of Sleeps	Pct of Wait Time
Result Cache: RC Latch	**1.46**	**4.61**	**11.09**	**34.56**
cache buffers chains	34.97	6.34	1.89	33.46
enqueues	2.66	.84	1.22	9.20
process queue reference	13.35	86.89	52.16	8.90
row cache objects	1.41	.08	.51	6.81
enqueue hash chains	2.69	.67	.72	5.17
shared pool	.37	.05	1.13	.83
SQL memory manager workarea list latch	.67	.00	.04	.38

Setting RESULT_CACHE_MODE to FORCE or setting the RESULT _CACHE table to FORCE for a popular table creates the possibility of Result Cache latch contention because almost every query result—or every query result involving the table—could become eligible for caching. Forcing all SQLs to use the Result cache is probably a dubious idea to begin with, but the latch contention issue renders it impractical in almost all circumstances.

Setting the RESULT_CACHE attribute at the table level is obviously less dangerous than setting it for all SQLs but still could affect a wide range of queries including some that might have high execution frequencies.

> The Result Cache latch limits the rate at which new results can be introduced to the result cache. For this reason, you should almost never set RESULT_CACHE_MODE to FORCE. Also be cautious when setting the table property RESULT_CACHE.

PL/SQL FUNCTION CACHE

PL/SQL functions can be stored in the result cache if their results are deterministic—always returning the same outputs when supplied with the same inputs—and if the RELIES_ON clause identifies table dependencies. Functions in the result cache are otherwise treated similarly to SQL statements. We looked at the PL/SQL function cache in some detail in Chapter 12, "Using and Tuning PL/SQL."

OTHER MEMORY OPTIMIZATIONS

The PGA and buffer cache are typically the most important performance-related memory areas. However, configuration of other memory areas in the SGA can also have a significant impact.

SIZING THE SHARED POOL

A primary objective of the shared pool is to cache SQL statements, PL/SQL objects, and data dictionary information. Caching SQL and PL/SQL statements avoids the need to parse or compile the object with each execution and, therefore, affords significant performance gains. We talked about this in detail in Chapter 6, "Application Design and Implementation."

However, unlike the buffer cache and the PGA, the performance gains afforded by the shared pool don't usually increase as you enlarge the pool. In a well-designed application, the use of sharable SQL ensures that the number of SQLs that need to be cached is fairly limited. It takes only a small amount of memory to cache a parsed SQL statement, and a moderately sized shared pool is usually sufficient to cache all the SQLs for a well-designed application. On the other hand, if the application is not using bind variables, we can expect every SQL statement to be almost unique. In this case even a huge shared pool is unlikely to help.

> A moderately sized shared pool is usually sufficient if the application is using bind variables; if the application is not using bind variables, increasing the shared pool provides minor and probably temporary relief only.

Oracle provides an advisory that reports on the change in parse and library cache load times if the shared pool was of a different size. Oracle estimates the amount of parse time that has been avoided as a result of finding SQLs and other objects in the shared pool and the amount of parse time that would be incurred were the shared pool of a different size. This information can be obtained from the V$SHARED_POOL_ADVICE view:

```
SQL> SELECT shared_pool_size_for_estimate,
  2         shared_pool_size_factor * 100 size_pct,
  3         estd_lc_time_saved,
  4         estd_lc_time_saved_factor * 100 saved_pct,
  5         estd_lc_load_time,
  6         estd_lc_load_time_factor * 100 load_pct
  7  FROM v$shared_pool_advice
  8  ORDER BY shared_pool_size_for_estimate;
```

Shared Pool MB	Size Pct Current	Time Saved (s)	Relative Time Saved(%)	Load/Parse Time (s)	Relative Time (%)
128	20	123,735,056	100.00	5,110	134.72
192	30	123,735,376	100.00	4,790	126.29
256	40	123,735,757	100.00	4,409	116.24
320	50	123,735,964	100.00	4,202	110.78
384	60	123,736,125	100.00	4,041	106.54
448	70	123,736,227	100.00	3,939	103.85
512	80	123,736,291	100.00	3,875	102.16
576	90	123,736,338	100.00	3,828	100.92
640	100	123,736,373	100.00	3,793	100
704	110	123,736,418	100.00	3,748	98.81
768	120	123,736,465	100.00	3,701	97.57
832	130	123,736,509	100.00	3,657	96.41
896	140	123,736,551	100.00	3,615	95.31
960	150	123,736,587	100.00	3,579	94.36
1,024	160	123,736,622	100.00	3,544	93.44
1,088	170	123,736,657	100.00	3,509	92.51
1,152	180	123,736,693	100.00	3,473	91.56
1,216	190	123,736,728	100.00	3,438	90.64
1,280	200	123,736,763	100.00	3,403	89.72

The above output shows a fairly typical pattern, at least for an application that employs bind variables. The amount of time saved by even the smallest shared pool is massive compared to the amount of time currently spent parsing. Although small reductions in parse time can be obtained by increasing the size of the shared pool, the relative change in time saved will be negligible.

Nevertheless, when an application fails to use bind variables, the memory allocation algorithms of AMM and ASMM might result in the shared pool increasing in size in a—usually futile—attempt to reduce the high parse overhead that results. For instance, in Figure 20-7 the introduction of a workload that does not use bind variables (on March 12th) results in the shared pool growing to 2GB. This sort of increase in the size of a shared pool might indicate that employing bind variables—or setting CURSOR_SHARING=FORCE or SIMILAR—should be a priority.

Failure to use bind variables might result in AMM or ASMM creating a large shared pool. This shared pool growth is a symptom, not a solution: Using bind variables or setting CURSOR_SHARING might be indicated.

LARGE POOL SIZING

We introduced the large pool in Chapter 2, "Oracle Architecture and Concepts." The large pool is an optional area of the SGA that serves a number of purposes, such as

❑ Reducing shared pool fragmentation by providing an area for large memory allocations
❑ Providing an area for local session variables when using shared servers
❑ Affording an area for messaging between parallel slave processes

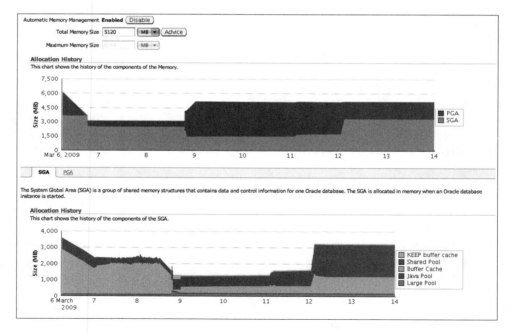

FIGURE 20-7   Oracle might increase the size of the shared pool when bind variables are not used.

The first two uses are not strictly performance-related, though reducing shared pool fragmentation can reduce shared pool latch contention (see Chapter 16, "Latch and Mutex Contention").

As we noted in Chapter 18, when shared servers are used with AMM or ASMM, it's possible that Oracle will "steal" buffer cache memory to populate the large pool. You should guard against that, probably by setting minimum values for the buffer cache and other SGA regions.

The memory region used for parallel slave messaging is known as the PX msg pool. The optimal sizing depends on the number of parallel slaves, amount of concurrent parallel execution, and the complexity of the parallel data flows.[5] However, the amount of memory required is typically in the order of 10M or so; therefore, any decently sized large pool probably has enough memory for parallel message buffers.

REDO LOG BUFFER

The redo log buffer is a relatively small area in memory that buffers write to the redo log. Oracle has optimized the log buffer significantly in recent releases, adding private buffer *strands* and partitioning the main buffer into multiple segments to reduce contention. As a result, performance problems relating to the redo log buffer are less frequent today than in the past.

However, as we saw in Chapter 17, "Shared Memory Contention," log buffer space waits can occur when the buffer is full. If these waits are associated with bursts of redo generation, increasing the log buffer might reduce the severity of these waits. Chapter 17 provides an example of this technique.

LOCKING THE SGA

Virtual memory enables the operating system to address shortages of memory by writing idle memory to disk. If the memory is needed later, it can be *paged in* from disk.

It's extremely undesirable for a database server to be overcommitted for memory in this way. You generally should configure hardware and memory so that paging of memory does not occur. However, certain application processing patterns—especially if you are not using Automatic PGA management—can result in server processes acquiring large amount of memory and not releasing that memory. In this circumstance it can make sense to allow the operating system to page out this memory to make memory available for other sessions.

However, it doesn't make sense to allow SGA memory to be paged in this manner. SGA memory is largely caching data on disk anyway, and if the cache is paged out, it is worse than useless. For this reason, Oracle enables you to lock the

---

[5] The *Oracle Data Warehousing Guide* includes the official formula in the "Using Parallel Execution" section.

SGA in memory and prevent it from being paged out. By setting LOCK_SGA to TRUE, you force Oracle to keep all SGA in real memory

You might need to increase the system limit on locked memory. On Linux this might involve editing the memlock limits defined in the /etc/security/limits.conf or issuing an ulimit –l command.

As we noted earlier, locking the SGA in memory is incompatible with AMM.

SUMMARY

Optimizing memory configurations *within* the SGA and *within* the PGA is critical, but arguably the most important memory configuration decision you make is the distribution *between* the two areas. SGA—buffer cache—memory reduces the amount of physical IO that results from reading table and index blocks, whereas PGA memory reduces the amount of physical IO that results from sorting and hash operations. Minimizing total physical IO therefore requires that memory be distributed between the PGA and SGA correctly.

Examining the waits recorded for various types of IO—*db file* waits and *direct path read/write temp* waits—provides some indication as to which type of IO is most prevalent and where memory might most profitably be allocated. However, it is only the memory advisories—V$PGA_TARGET_ADVICE and V$SGA_TARGET_ADVICE—that can indicate how much IO would actually be avoided if memory configurations changed. We saw in this chapter how to use those views in 10g and 11g to determine optimal PGA/SGA allocations.

In 11g you can use Oracle Automatic Memory Management (AMM) to move memory between the PGA and SGA dynamically based on workload demands. AMM is a significant advance and often provides improved performance. However in some cases its decisions might be overly reactive or might conflict with business priorities (prioritizing sorts at the expense of index lookups, for instance). Setting minimum values for key memory areas can often lead to a more optimal outcome.

In this chapter we also looked at the result set cache: A new Oracle 11g feature that enables complete result sets to be stored in memory. If a result set can be reused, almost all the overhead of SQL execution can be avoided. The result set cache best suits small result sets from expensive queries on tables that are infrequently updated. Applying the result set cache to all SQLs or to all SQLs for a specific table is unlikely to be effective and can lead to significant latch contention.

DISK IO TUNING FUNDAMENTALS

Most of the techniques we looked at in preceding chapters have been aimed at avoiding or minimizing disk IO. Tuning our SQL and PL/SQL reduces the workload demand—largely logical IO—on our database. Minimizing contention attacks the bottlenecks that might be preventing that workload demand from being processed. Optimizing memory reduces the amount of workload that translates into disk activity. If you applied the practices in the previous chapters, your physical disk demand has been minimized: now it's time to optimize the disk subsystem to meet that demand.

Reducing IO *demand* should almost always come before disk tuning. Disk tuning is often expensive in terms of time, money, and database availability. It might involve buying expensive new disk devices and performing time-consuming data reorganizations that result in temporary reductions in availability and performance. If you attempt these undertakings before tuning workload, contention, and memory, you might be unnecessarily optimizing the disks for an unrealistic demand.

Disk IO tuning is simultaneously the easiest and most-difficult aspect of database tuning. It's easy in the sense that disk devices are predictable, and it's relatively straightforward to specify a hardware configuration to meet a particular demand. At the same time it's often difficult to persuade management that you need to buy sufficient disks to meet IO requirements: IT management expects to buy disks by the gigabyte, not the IO per second.

DISK IO CONCEPTS

In this section we briefly review the performance characteristics of conventional disk devices. The emergence of Solid State Disk (SSD) and in-memory databases (such as Oracle TimesTen) might well signify that the dominance of the spinning magnetic disk is coming to an end, and we cover some of those new technologies in the next chapter. However, today most Oracle databases still use conventional magnetic disk devices, and this chapter focuses on those traditional technologies.

SERVICE TIME AND THROUGHPUT

Disk devices have two fundamental characteristics that concern us from a performance point of view: *service time* (or *latency*) and *throughput* (or *bandwidth*).

Service time describes the time it takes to retrieve a single item of information from the disk. For a spinning disk drive, this is the time it takes to rotate the disk platter into the correct position (rotational latency), plus the time it takes to move the read/write head into position (seek time), plus the time it takes to transfer the data from the disk to the server. Seek time is the most important determinate of service time for most disks and, being a mechanical rather than an electronic operation, is much slower than any of the other operations (CPU, network, and memory) conducted by a database server. Service time is typically measured in milliseconds (ms).

IO bandwidth or *throughput* describes the number of IOs that can be performed by the disk devices in a given unit of time. For a single disk device performing random reads (where each data request can be on a "random" location on the disk), the throughput is determined by the combination of seek time and rotational latency: If my average seek time is 10ms, I can logically expect to do only 100 random IOs per second. (Each second contains 100 10ms intervals.) When the IOs are sequential—each block of data is next to the preceding block—then rotational latency is relatively more important than seek time and much higher IO rates are possible. Throughput is generally expressed in terms of IO operations Per Second, often abbreviated as *IOPS*.

In most database servers data is stored on multiple disk devices and "striped" across the disks concerned. In this case, IO bandwidth is a function of the types of IO operations (random versus sequential), service time, and the number of disks. For instance, a perfectly striped disk array containing 10 disks with 10ms service times might have a random IO bandwidth of approximately 1,000 IOPS (100 IOPS for each disk times 10 disks).

QUEUING

The service time for disk devices remains fairly predictable when the disk is idle and awaiting requests. The service time varies somewhat depending on the disk's internal cache and the distance that the read/write head needs to move to acquire the relevant data. But in general the response time will be within the range quoted by the disk manufacturer.

However, as the number of requests increase, some requests will have to wait while other requests are serviced. The disk controller employs an *elevator algorithm*, sequencing the servicing of requests to minimize the movement of the read/write head, but as the request rate increases, eventually a queue forms. Just as in a busy supermarket, you soon find you spend more time in the queue than actually being serviced.

Because of queuing, disk service time increases sharply as a disk system approaches full capacity. When the disk becomes 100 percent busy, any additional requests simply increase the length of the queue, and service time increases without any consequent increase in throughput.

DISK DRIVES: SLOW AND GETTING SLOWER

Most aspects of computer technology are subject to continuous and rapid performance improvements. Most notably, George Moore's famous *Moore's law* postulated that the number of transistors that can be placed on an integrated circuit increases exponentially, doubling every 1 to 2 years. Moore's law directly impacts increases in CPU processing power, and similar increases are observed with respect to memory capacity and other digital technologies. Disk drive storage capacity is also growing exponentially, with the size of standard disk drives typically doubling every 12 to 18 months.

Although CPU, memory, and magnetic storage generally follow Moore's law, disk latency and throughput are limited by mechanical factors, not digital electronics. Consequently, disk speeds are not increasing in accordance with Moore's law, and whereas average disk capacity has increased roughly 20 times over the past 10 years, disk service times have barely halved.

Although disks are slowly getting faster, the rapid increase in the average size of a disk means that the average IO per MB is actually decreasing. In 2001 disk drives would typically be between 20GB and 40GB in size and provide services times of approximately 4ms. Today, the average disk is 400GB to 1000GB with a service time virtually unchanged.[1] In 2001, a 1TB database would need to be hosted on a disk array composed of dozens of disks with a combined throughput capacity of thousands of IOs per second. Today, the same database could be theoretically hosted on just a couple of disks with less than one-tenth of the IO bandwidth. Therefore, it's essential—and getting more important as time passes—not to acquire disks simply to match storage requirements: You must acquire enough disks to match your IO requirements.

---

[1] In 2009, the Seagate Cheetah NS.2 is a 450GB drive with 3.8ms seek time; in 2001 the Seagate Cheetah X1536LP was a 36GB drive with 3.6ms seek time.

Purchase and configure disk devices that are sufficient to meet your IO requirements, not just your storage requirements.

DISK CAPACITY AND DATA PLACEMENT

A further consideration for disk IO performance is the effect of "disk fill" on service times. Service times actually degrade as the percentage of disk capacity is increased. When a disk is only partially filled and the data is packed together, the range of disk head movement required to seek to any location is reduced. Furthermore, the outer regions of the disk are moving underneath the read/write head at a greater velocity because the circumference of the disk is greater the further we get from the center. As a result, both throughput and latency are optimized when data is packed in the outer sections of the disk.

Simple mathematics (remember πr^2?) tells us that we can store more data on the outside of the disk, where the circumference is higher, than on the inside of the disk. It turns out that the outer third of a typical disk can hold about one-half of the total disk capacity, while reducing the average seek time significantly.

Disk seek time tends to increase as disk capacity is fully utilized. Disks that are half full will typically have significantly reduced latency and significantly improved throughput.

ORACLE IO ARCHITECTURE

We've encountered many varieties of Oracle IO in previous chapters, as we've sought to find ways to avoid various types of IO. Now that we are attacking IO directly, we need to have a clear and precise understanding of the various forms Oracle IO can take.

Figure 21-1 shows the major types of Oracle IO, the processes that participate, and the associated wait events.

DATAFILE SINGLE BLOCK READ

A single block read occurs when Oracle needs to retrieve a single block of information from a data file. This operation is recorded by the wait interface as *db file sequential read.*[2]

---

[2] This is an incredibly badly named wait because from the disk perspective, what occurs is not a sequential read but a random read.

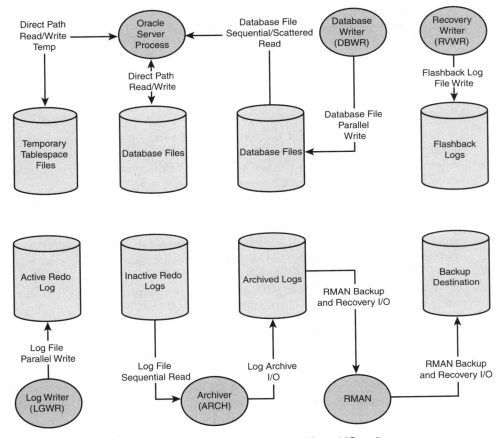

FIGURE 21-1   Overview of Oracle IO and IO waits.

Single block reads are most obviously associated with index lookups; Oracle performs a series of single block reads while navigating the index structure (see Chapter 5, "Indexing and Clustering,") that eventually supplies the address of the required table blocks on disk that are then also retrieved by single block reads.

MULTI BLOCK READ

In a multi-block read, Oracle retrieves multiple blocks of data in a single operation. This is recorded by the wait interface as *db file scattered read*. Despite the inference provided by the term *scattered*, multiblock reads involve a set of contiguous blocks and are used when Oracle scans consecutive blocks typically during a full table scan or an index scan.

The maximum number of blocks that can be read in a single operation is defined by the parameter DB_FILE_MULTIBLOCK_READ_COUNT. The default value for this parameter is operating system- and block size-specific and is usually set to a value that aligns with the maximum operating system IO size, typically 512K or 1M.

DIRECT PATH READS

Db file sequential reads and db file scattered read operations are both *buffer cached* reads. The blocks are read-only if they are not found in the buffer cache and once read are added to the buffer cache. We discussed the operation of the buffer cache in some depth in Chapter 18, "Buffer Cache Tuning."

Direct path read operations do not involve the buffer cache. The Oracle server process instead reads blocks directly from the data files into server process private memory (the PGA). Direct path reads avoid some of the overhead and contention involved with buffer cache management but, unlike in a buffer cache read, the data read is unavailable to other processes. If another process happens to need the same blocks, they will need to be reread from disk.

We also discussed direct path operations in Chapter 18. Oracle uses direct path reads in the following circumstances:

❑ Always when performing temporary segment IO.
❑ Usually when performing parallel query. In Oracle 10g, Oracle uses direct path reads by default for all parallel operations. In Oracle 11g, Oracle can use buffer cache IO during parallel execution if the optimizer calculates an advantage.
❑ In 11g, Oracle sometimes uses direct path reads during serial queries when it calculates an advantage in doing so. We discussed the circumstances in which this might occur in Chapter 17, "Shared Memory Contention."

Direct path reads can be single block or multiblock. However, direct path reads are more often utilized when scan operations are performed: Oracle favors buffered IO when performing indexed single-block reads because the probability of the block being reused in the near future is high. Consequently direct path reads are most often multiblock in nature.

TEMPORARY DIRECT PATH IO

We discussed the nature of temporary segment IO in several earlier chapters: in Chapter 11, "Sorting, Grouping, and Set Operations," while optimizing sorting and in Chapter 19, "Optimizing PGA Memory," when optimizing PGA memory. When a sort, hash join, or other operation requires memory workspace and insufficient PGA memory is available, data must be written to and read from temporary segments. Oracle uses direct path IO for this purpose to avoid creating buffer cache contention.

Oracle identifies direct path IO to temporary segments through the wait events *direct path read temp* and *direct path write temp*.

DATA FILE WRITE IO

By default, DML operations, INSERT, UPDATE, DELETE, and MERGE, modify blocks of data in the buffer cache. The dirty blocks are written to disk by the Database Writer (DBWR) process at some later time. Should the DBWR fail to keep up with the modifications, *free buffer waits* may result; we discussed these in Chapter 17.

As we also noted in Chapter 17, the DBWR should ideally use *asynchronous IO*, which allows the DBWR to send write requests to disk without having to wait for each individual write to complete. Only if asynchronous IO is enabled will the DBWR be able to keep the buffer cache "clean" in DML-intensive environments.

DBWR IO is recorded as *db file parallel write*. However, the interpretation of this wait event can be difficult because the asynchronous IO mechanism results in many IO operations proceeding without the DBWR actively waiting.

DIRECT PATH WRITES

Although the DBWR is generally responsible for writing data blocks from the buffer cache to disk, the Oracle server processes will sometimes write directly to the datafiles. The most common circumstance is when writing temporary segment data to the temporary tablespace; these writes always use direct path operations and are always performed by the session itself, not the DBWR.

The other common direct path write scenario is when a session performs a direct path *append* insert. We looked at direct path insert in Chapter 14, "DML Tuning." When using direct path insert, the Oracle session inserts new blocks directly into the datafile—possibly in parallel—and bypasses the buffer cache.

Direct path write operations are visible as *direct path write* waits.

REDO LOG IO

Redo logs record transaction information sufficient to recover the database if a database failure occurs. When a session issues a DML statement, it makes entries to a redo log buffer (or *strand*) in the SGA. For the transaction to be recovered if a failure occurs, these redo log entries need to be written to disk when the transaction commits. However, you can configure Oracle to defer or batch these writes using COMMIT_WAIT and COMMIT_LOGGING parameters (Oracle 11g) or the COMMIT_WRITE parameter (Oracle 10g) (see Chapter 14).

Redo log IO consists of intensive *sequential* writes. Each write follows the proceeding write that means if the redo log is on an exclusive single disk device, the disk read/write head does not need to move when each successive write is issued. Disk seek time can, therefore, be very low for redo log write operations.

Most redo log IO is recorded as *log file parallel write*; *log file single write* and *log file sequential read* waits are observed when the redo log writer initializes a new log file.

When a session commits, it might experience a *log file sync* wait while the redo log writer flushes redo log records from memory to disk. Although a log file sync is not strictly an IO wait, it represents the user's experience of redo log IO and, unlike log file parallel writes, does contribute to SQL response time and throughput.

ARCHIVE LOG IO

When the database is running in Archivelog mode, Oracle copies inactive redo logs to archived logs that can be used to recover the database following a restore from backup.

The Archiver process (ARCH) reads from inactive redo logs and writes to archived logs. The reads from the redo log are visible as *log file sequential read*, whereas the writes to the archived log are recorded as *Log archive I/O*. Both operations are sequential in nature.

FLASHBACK IO

Flashback logs contain rollback or undo records that can be used to undo changes to the database if some sort of logical corruption occurs. This can reduce time to recover compared to restoring from backup and then rolling the database forward using archived logs.

The Recovery Writer process (RVWR) is responsible for writing flashback log records from the flashback buffer to the flashback logs. We looked at the flashback buffer in Chapter 17.

The Recover Writer records *flashback log file write* waits as it writes to the flashback logs.[3]

User sessions might experience *flashback log file sync* waits while waiting for flashback log records to be flushed to disk or *flashback buf free by RVWR* when waiting for the RVWR to free up space in the flashback buffer.

CONTROL FILE IO

Control files are relatively small files that contain essential data regarding database file locations and status. The control file records not only the location of the various files, but also their status. For data files, the checkpoint number, which can be used to determine which transactions have been written to the file, is stored in the control file. Checkpoint information is updated fairly regularly, in

---

[3] This wait might not be visible in versions of Oracle prior to 11g release 2.

particular by the Redo Log Writer (LGWR) and the Checkpoint process (CKPT). Other background processes read from the control files from time to time to determine database status and configuration.

User sessions generally do not perform control file IO except when issuing queries against certain system views, V$ views in particular. Monitoring programs that access these views, such as the Enterprise Manager agent, will therefore perform control file IO.

Control file IO results in the waits *control file parallel write* and *control file sequential read*.

MEASURING AND MONITORING ORACLE IO

We've reviewed the types of IO that Oracle databases perform, so let's consider how we can measure and monitor this IO.

IO WAIT TIMES

IO is usually a *blocking* operation—a session needs to wait for an IO to complete. When using asynchronous IO, the session issues a set of IOs and then waits for them all to complete. Time spent blocked in either fashion will be recorded in the wait interface, such as in V$SYSTEM_EVENT. We looked at the wait events associated with each type of IO earlier in this chapter.

The best high-level summary of IO times can be obtained by querying the IO-related wait categories. This query retrieves the IO categories and compares them to other wait times and to active CPU:

```
SQL> WITH system_event AS
  2       (SELECT CASE
  3                   WHEN wait_class IN ('User I/O', 'System I/O')
  4                   THEN event ELSE wait_class
  5                   END  wait_type, e.*
  6          FROM v$system_event e)
  7  SELECT wait_type, SUM(total_waits) / 1000 waits_1000,
  8         ROUND(SUM(time_waited_micro) / 1000000 / 3600, 2)
  9                time_waited_hours,
 10         ROUND(SUM(time_waited_micro) / SUM(total_waits) / 1000, 2)
 11                avg_wait_ms,
 12         ROUND(  SUM(time_waited_micro)
 13                * 100
 14                / SUM(SUM(time_waited_micro)) OVER (), 2)
 15                pct
 16    FROM (SELECT wait_type, event, total_waits, time_waited_micro
```

```
17        FROM system_event e
18        UNION
19        SELECT 'CPU', stat_name, NULL, VALUE
20        FROM v$sys_time_model
21        WHERE stat_name IN ('background cpu time', 'DB CPU')) 1
22  WHERE wait_type <> 'Idle'
23  GROUP BY wait_type
24  ORDER BY SUM(time_waited_micro) DESC
25  /
```

Wait Type	Waits \1000	Time Hours	Avg Wait Ms	Pct
Concurrency	2,329,851	956.92	1.48	51.42
CPU		470.36		25.27
direct path write temp	**21,344**	**112.40**	**18.96**	**6.04**
db file sequential read	**469,684**	**107.62**	**.82**	**5.78**
Other	137,624	75.79	1.98	4.07
direct path read	**1,585**	**52.67**	**119.66**	**2.83**
direct path read temp	**1,080,998**	**47.41**	**.16**	**2.55**
log file parallel write	9,223	28.69	11.20	1.54

The preceding query totals all IO since the database was started. To look at the IO over a shorter period of time, you can use the IO_TIME_DELTA_VIEW view that is included with the packages available from this book's Web site. This query reports IO wait information since the time the query was last run in the same session:

```
SQL> SELECT sample_seconds, wait_type, total_waits,
            time_waited_seconds,
  2         avg_time_ms, pct
  3    FROM io_time_delta_view
  4   WHERE pct > .1
  5   ORDER BY time_waited_seconds DESC;
```

Sample Secs	Wait Type	Total Waits	time Waited (s)	Avg (ms)	Pct
117	CPU		213.65		41.48
117	**direct path read temp**	**8,164**	**111.83**	**13.70**	**21.71**
117	**RMAN backup & recovery I/O**	**2,064**	**109.96**	**53.27**	**21.35**
117	**db file sequential read**	**3,003**	**67.70**	**22.55**	**13.15**
117	**control file sequential read**	**603**	**9.96**	**16.51**	**1.93**
117	control file parallel write	47	1.54	32.79	.30

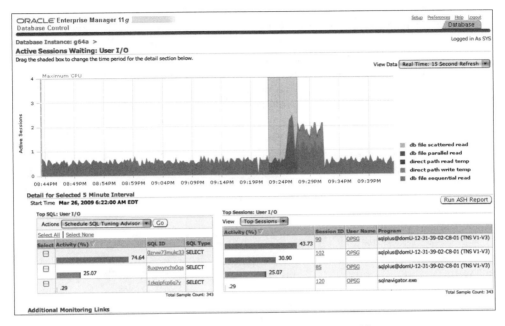

FIGURE 21-2   User IO breakdown in Enterprise Manager.

If you are licensed for the Oracle Diagnostic pack, you can drill into the 'User IO' category in the main Performance page to see a breakdown of IO times over time, such as in Figure 21-2.

In Oracle 11g, the V$IOSTAT_FILE and V$IOSTAT_FUNCTION views can provide enhanced insight into the types of IO that are being performed. V$IO-STAT_FILE records the sizes and request times for IOs that occur against each file or file type in the database. For instance, if we want to summarize IO by file type, we can issue a query such as this:

```
SQL> WITH iostat_file AS
  2     (SELECT filetype_name,SUM(large_read_reqs) large_read_reqs,
  3             SUM(large_read_servicetime) large_read_servicetime,
  4             SUM(large_write_reqs) large_write_reqs,
  5             SUM(large_write_servicetime) large_write_servicetime,
  6             SUM(small_read_reqs) small_read_reqs,
  7             SUM(small_read_servicetime) small_read_servicetime,
  8             SUM(small_sync_read_latency) small_sync_read_latency,
  9             SUM(small_sync_read_reqs) small_sync_read_reqs,
 10             SUM(small_write_reqs) small_write_reqs,
 11             SUM(small_write_servicetime) small_write_servicetime
 12      FROM sys.v_$iostat_file
```

```
13        GROUP BY filetype_name)
14   SELECT filetype_name, small_read_reqs + large_read_reqs reads,
15        large_write_reqs + small_write_reqs writes,
16        ROUND((small_read_servicetime +
17          large_read_servicetime)/1000) read_time_sec,
18        ROUND((small_write_servicetime
19          + large_write_servicetime)/1000) write_time_sec,
20        CASE WHEN small_sync_read_reqs > 0 THEN
21          ROUND(small_sync_read_latency / small_sync_read_reqs, 2)
22        END avg_sync_read_ms,
23        ROUND((  small_read_servicetime+large_read_servicetime
24            + small_write_servicetime + large_write_servicetime)
25            / 1000, 2)  total_io_seconds
26     FROM iostat_file
27     ORDER BY 7 DESC;
```

File Type	Reads	Writes	Read sec	Write sec	Avg Sync Read ms	Total IO sec
Data File	228,267	148,457	7,072	11,879	22.17	18,951
Temp File	247,600	46,554	3,727	2,808	15.51	6,535
Control File	24,005	11,946	680	493	27.60	1,172
Archive Log	0	494	0	115		115
Flashback Log	221	4,011	0	72	.10	72
Log File	501	152,165	7	50	2.29	57
Other	798	1,330	0	1	.67	1

`.  .  .            .  .  .  .  .  .          .  .  .        .  .        .  .  .`

V$IOSTAT_FUNCTION shows similar statistics for high-level IO functions such as buffer cache IO, direct IO, and IO from the various background processes:

```
SQL> SELECT function_name, small_read_reqs + large_read_reqs reads,
  2            small_write_reqs + large_write_reqs writes,
  3            wait_time/1000 wait_time_sec,
  4            CASE WHEN number_of_waits > 0 THEN
  5              ROUND(wait_time / number_of_waits, 2)
  6            END avg_wait_ms
  7     FROM v$iostat_function
  8     ORDER BY wait_time DESC;
```

File Type	Reads	Writes	Wait Time Sec	Avg Wait ms
Buffer Cache Reads	59,989,617	0	699,906	11.70
Direct Reads	74,454,865	50	609,061	8.18

LGWR	8,726	14,538,242	192,377	13.25
Direct Writes	0	2,731,126	83,317	30.51
Others	1,630,061	2,372,176	35,630	14.57
DBWR	798	482,611	7,136	25.00
Streams AQ	7,426	0	168	22.64
. . .	. . .	. . .	. . .	

The information displayed in V$IOSTAT_FUNCTION and V$IOSTAT_FILE can be observed graphically in Enterprise Manager, providing you are licensed for the Oracle Diagnostic pack. The information is shown in the IO tab of the Performance page. Figure 21-3 shows example output.

MONITORING DATAFILE IO

In Oracle 11g, file-level statistics are included in V$IOSTAT_FILE. For 10g and earlier, similar—though less fine-grained—file level statistics are available in the views V$FILESTAT and V$TEMPSTAT. We can merge these two views to get insight into IO at the tablespace or datafile level:

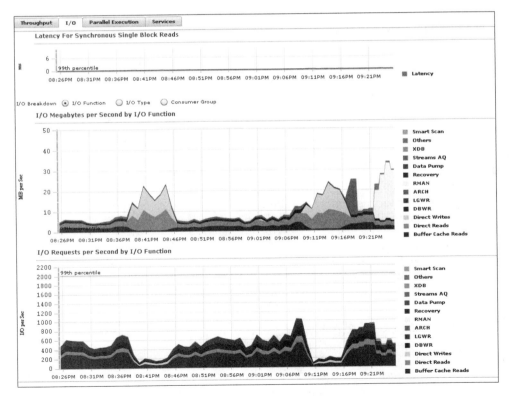

FIGURE 21-3   Enterprise Manager IO tab.

```
SQL> with filestat as
  2    (SELECT tablespace_name, phyrds, phywrts, phyblkrd, phyblkwrt,
  3              singleblkrds, readtim, writetim, singleblkrdtim
  4       FROM v$tempstat JOIN dba_temp_files
  5         ON (file# = file_id)
  6      UNION
  7     SELECT tablespace_name, phyrds, phywrts, phyblkrd, phyblkwrt,
  8              singleblkrds, readtim, writetim, singleblkrdtim
  9       FROM v$filestat  JOIN dba_data_files
 10         ON (file# = file_id))
 11   SELECT tablespace_name, ROUND(SUM(phyrds) / 1000) phyrds_1000,
 12          ROUND(SUM(phyblkrd) / SUM(phyrds), 2) avg_blk_reads,
 13          ROUND((SUM(readtim) + SUM(writetim)) / 100 / 3600, 2)
 14             iotime_hrs,
          ROUND(SUM(phyrds + phywrts) * 100 /
             SUM(SUM(phyrds + phywrts))
 15            OVER (), 2) pct_io, ROUND(SUM(phywrts) / 1000)
             phywrts_1000,
 16          ROUND(SUM(singleblkrdtim) * 10 / SUM(singleblkrds), 2)
 17            single_rd_avg_time
 18    FROM filestat
 19    GROUP BY tablespace_name
 20    ORDER BY (SUM(readtim) + SUM(writetim)) DESC;
```

| | Reads | IO Time | Pct | Writes | Single Blk |
Tablespace Name	\1000	(hrs)	IO Time	\1000	Rd Avg (ms)
USERS	509,566	195	47.27	278	1.10
TEMP	543,740	126	52.41	21,640	.19
SYSAUX	1,245	2	.17	538	2.79
SYSTEM	1,316	1	.13	51	3.00
UNDOTBS1	11	0	.03	282	1.93
EXAMPLE	5	0	.00	0	4.33

Shorter term statistics can be obtained from the V$FILEMETRIC view. This view contains file IO statistics for the past 10 minutes:

```
SQL> SELECT tablespace_name, intsize_csec / 100 sample_time,
  2         ROUND(AVG(average_read_time) * 10, 2) avg_read_time_ms,
  3         ROUND(AVG(average_write_time) * 10, 2) avg_write_time_ms,
  4         SUM(physical_reads) physical_reads,
  5         SUM(physical_writes) physical_writes,
  6         ROUND((SUM(physical_reads) + SUM(physical_writes)) * 100 /
  7           SUM(SUM(physical_reads) + SUM(physical_writes))
  8             OVER (), 2) pct_io,
  9         CASE
 10           WHEN SUM(physical_reads) > 0 THEN
 11             ROUND(SUM(physical_block_reads)
```

```
                         /SUM(physical_reads),2)
12          END  blks_per_read
13      FROM v$filemetric JOIN dba_data_files
14          USING (file_id)
15   GROUP BY tablespace_name, file_id, end_time, intsize_csec
16   ORDER BY 7 DESC;
```

Tablespace Name	Avg Rd (ms)	Avg Wrt (ms)	Phys Reads	Phys Writes	Pct IO	Blks \Rd
USERS	6.02	8.00	95,696	5	97.54	1.00
SYSAUX	.62	9.83	1,727	516	2.29	1.05
SYSTEM	.73	3.53	96	17	.12	9.90
UNDOTBS1	.00	2.78	4	54	.06	1.00
EXAMPLE	.00	.00	2	1	.00	1.00

Average IO times are a useful metric, but to understand service time completely, it's often best to view the distribution of IO. V$FILE_HISTOGRAM shows the number of IOs that fall into various time buckets. This query plots the distributions:

```
SQL> SELECT LAG(singleblkrdtim_milli, 1)
  2          OVER (ORDER BY singleblkrdtim_milli)
  3          || '<' || singleblkrdtim_milli read_time,
  4       SUM(singleblkrds) reads,
  5       RPAD(' ', ROUND(SUM(singleblkrds) * 50 /
  6          MAX(SUM(singleblkrds)) OVER ()), '*')  histogram
  7   FROM v$file_histogram
  8   GROUP BY singleblkrdtim_milli
  9   ORDER BY singleblkrdtim_milli;
```

Read Time (ms)	Reads	
<1	180,590	**
1<2	22,681	*****
2<4	32,806	*******
4<8	91,464	************************
8<16	63,814	*****************
16<32	17,237	****
32<64	1,919	
64<128	164	
128<256	83	
256<512	163	
512<1024	1,191	
1024<2048	7	

CALIBRATING IO

Oracle 11g provides a utility, DBMS_RESOURCE_MANAGER.CALIBRATE_IO, to measure the IO capabilities of your disk subsystem. The utility generates an IO-intensive workload composed of small random IOs performed across the datafiles in your database. It then reports on the IO rate that can be sustained without exceeding a maximum latency.

When using CALIBRATE_IO, you provide a maximum disk service level (which must be at least 10ms) and the number of physical disks that underlie the disk volume.

The CALIBRATE_IO workload consists of random IOs so it is more applicable to an OLTP workload than to a data warehouse. Furthermore, the simplistic workload might differ significantly from the workload generated by your application. Nevertheless, CALIBRATE_IO does give you a quick and reasonably accurate measure of the IO capabilities of your disk subsystem.

In this example, CALIBRATE_IO reports that the disk subsystem can support approximately 300 IO/sec while maintaining a 10 ms response time:

```
SQL> DECLARE
   2      v_max_iops           NUMBER;
   3      v_max_mbps           NUMBER;
   4      v_actual_latency     NUMBER;
   5   BEGIN
   6      DBMS_RESOURCE_MANAGER.calibrate_io(
   7          num_physical_disks => 4,
   8          max_latency => 10,
   9          max_iops => v_max_iops,
  10          max_mbps => v_max_mbps,
  11          actual_latency => v_actual_latency);
  12
  13      DBMS_OUTPUT.put_line('Max IOPS=' || v_max_iops);
  14      DBMS_OUTPUT.put_line('Max MBps=' || v_max_mbps);
  15      DBMS_OUTPUT.put_line('Latency =' || v_actual_latency);
  16
  17   END;
  18   /
Max IOPS=299
Max MBps=87
Latency =9
```

Asynchronous IO must be enabled on your datafiles for the DBMS_RESOURCE_MANAGER.CALIBRATE_IO package to generate its workload. For datafiles on "cooked" filesystems (that is, not on ASM or raw devices), this means that the FILESYSTEMIO_OPTIONS parameter should be set to SETALL or

ASYNCH. You should also make sure that the job runs when the database is otherwise idle: Any concurrent activity might interfere with the benchmark.

The most recent results from DBMS_RESOURCE_MANAGER.CALIBRATE _IO can be seen in the view DBA_RSRC_IO_CALIBRATE. This view also reports in the MAX_PMBPS column, the maximum MB/sec achievable by a single process. So the following output indicates that while the IO subsystem can support up to 80MB/second from multiple concurrent processes, a single process can achieve only 11MB/sec:

```
SQL> SELECT max_iops, max_mbps, max_pmbps, latency,
  2            num_physical_disks
  3     FROM dba_rsrc_io_calibrate;
```

Max IO/Sec	Max MB/Sec	Max MB/Sec Single Proc	Latency ms	Num of Phys Disks
263	80	11	10	8

The single process limit simply reflects that the disk array can process multiple requests in parallel, but that a single-threaded process can action only one read request at a time.

DBMS_RESOURCE_MANAGER.CALIBRATE_IO can obtain a rough estimate of the throughput capacity of your IO subsystem.

OPTIMIZING DATAFILE IO

For most Oracle databases, the vast majority of IO-related waits are related to datafile IO. We've spent most of the book so far trying to reduce the amount of this IO. Now we should try to optimize the IO that must occur. We do this by minimizing IO latency and maximizing IO throughput.

MINIMIZING IO LATENCY

Latency or *service time* reflects the delay that occurs when retrieving data from a disk. Disk latency is often a large part of SQL and application response time, so managing latency can be critical to providing acceptable service levels.

As we previously discussed, the minimum latency for a conventional disk device is predictable and determined primarily by the rotational latency and seek time—time to move the read/write head into position. Remember that a partially full disk usually has a significantly lower latency than a fully packed disk: Keeping disks about half full is a good rule of thumb when trying to minimize latency.

On a busy disk, the service time is determined not only by the disk latency but also by any wait time that occurs when a session waits for the disk to complete any outstanding requests. This time is referred to as *queue time*. Any significant amount of concurrent disk-oriented activity is likely to create some queuing. For instance, when a disk is lightly loaded (say 20-percent busy), 20 percent of the time you will need to wait for another IO to complete before your IO can be processed. The average service time for the disk therefore increases by a significant amount.[4]

As we increase the rate of requests sent to the disk, we get an increase in the amount of throughput but—because of queuing—an increase in latency as well. Figure 21-4 illustrates the typical relationship between throughput and latency: Increasing throughput is usually associated with increasing latency. As we increase the request rate, we eventually reach a point at which no more throughput can be achieved; after this point any increase in the request rate simply increases the queue for the disk and consequently increases latency without increasing throughput.

Latency and throughput are correlated: Increasing the throughput or demand on disk devices usually results in an increase in latency. To minimize latency, it might be necessary to run disks at less than full capacity, say 50 percent to 75 percent.

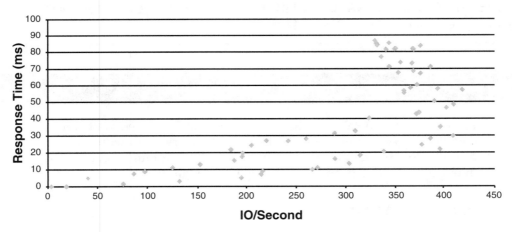

FIGURE 21-4   Disk throughput versus service time.

---

[4] There's a branch of mathematics devoted to estimating these effects called, not surprisingly, queuing theory. Carey Milsap's *Optimizing Oracle* (O'Reilly, 2003) provides the most-extensive coverage of queuing theory for the Oracle performance practitioner.

Asides from replacing your disk devices with faster devices (possibly Solid State Disk as discussed in the next chapter), the key principles for minimizing latency are therefore

❑ Keep disk devices sparsely populated, 50 percent full as a rule of thumb.
❑ Don't overload the disks: Disks that are above 50 percent to 75 percent of maximum throughput capacity are unlikely to provide good service time.

MAXIMIZING IO THROUGHPUT

If an individual disk can do only so many IOs per second, achieving a higher IO throughput rate will require deploying more physical disks. Unlike latency calculations, which are governed by the relatively complex queuing theory calculations, the calculation for the number of disk devices required is simple. If an individual disk can perform 100 IOPS while delivering acceptable latency and we believe we need to deliver 500 IOPS, we are likely to need at least five disk devices.

The throughput of an IO system is primarily determined by the number of physical disk devices it contains. To increase datafile IO throughput, increase the number of physical disks in disk volumes.

However, it's not always possible to determine the "comfortable" IO rate—the IO rate that delivers acceptable service time—for a disk device. Disk vendors specify the minimum latency, which can be achieved with no contention for the disk, and the maximum throughput, which can be achieved while ignoring service time constraints. Almost by definition, the quoted throughput for a disk device is the throughput that can be achieved when the disk is 100-percent busy. To determine the IO rate that can be achieved while obtaining service times that are near the minimum, you will want to aim for an IO rate lower than those quoted by the vendors. The exact variance depends on how you balance response time versus throughput in your application. However, throughputs more than 50 percent to 70 percent of the vendor's quoted maximum usually result in response times several times higher than the vendor's published minimums.

The DBMS_RESOURCE_MANAGER.CALIBRATE_IO enables you to specify a desired latency and determines the maximum throughput that can be achieved without sacrificing service time. We looked at the CALIBRATE_IO procedure previously in this chapter.

STRIPING STRATEGIES

Adding disks to an IO subsystem increases throughput and, by avoiding queuing, reduces latency. However, these benefits can be obtained only when the IO is spread evenly across the disk devices. We achieve this even distribution of IO by *striping* the data files across the disks.

Striping datafiles across disk devices can be achieved in a number of ways:

❏ Hardware striping is the most commonly employed technique for production Oracle databases. Data is evenly distributed across the physical devices by the storage subsystem hardware. The resulting set of disks is then presented to the operating system as a larger logical disk device.

❏ Software striping achieves the same outcome but is performed at the operating system software level. Disks are connected to the host as usual, and the operating system ensures that data is transparently distributed across the devices.

❏ Oracle's Automatic Storage Management (ASM) layer can implement software striping on top of any kind of disk devices or volumes.

❏ Manual (Oracle) striping involves manually distributing datafiles across multiple disk devices in such a way as to achieve an even spread of data. This is the least effective and least common way of striping data. If you do stripe using this technique, either use Automatic Segment Storage Management (ASSM) or manually configure segments so that there are many uniformly sized extents. Then ensure that each tablespace has at least as many data files as you have disks and distribute these data files across the available disks.

RAID ARRAYS

RAID (Redundant Array of Independent Disks) arrays[5] includes a variety of striping and redundancy schemes. The term RAID array typically refers to a storage device composing a number of physical disk devices that can be attached to a server and accessed as one or more logical devices.

There are three levels of RAID commonly provided by storage vendors:

❏ RAID 0 is referred to as disk *striping*. In this configuration, a logical disk is constructed from multiple physical disks. The data contained on the logical disk is spread evenly across the physical disk, and hence random IOs are also likely to be spread evenly. There is no redundancy built in to this con-

---

[5] Originally an acronym for Redundant Array of *Inexpensive* Disks. Changed later by disk vendors to Redundant Array of *Independent* Disks because RAID systems are usually anything but inexpensive.

figuration, so if a disk fails, the files that depend on it need to be recovered from a backup.

❏ RAID 1 is referred to as disk *mirroring*. In this configuration, a logical disk is composed of two physical disks. If one physical disk fails, processing can continue using the other physical disk. Each disk contains identical data and writes are processed in parallel, so there should be little or no negative effects on write performance. Reads can occur from either of the disk pairs, so read throughput should be increased.

❏ In RAID 5, a logical disk is composed of multiple physical disks. Data is arranged across the physical devices in a similar way to disk striping (RAID 0). However, a certain proportion of the data on the physical devices is parity data. This parity data contains enough information to derive data on other disks should a single physical device fail.

❏ Lower RAID levels (2–4) have similar characteristics to RAID 5 but are rarely encountered in practice. RAID 6 is similar to RAID 5 but has more redundancy: Two disks can fail simultaneously without data loss.

It's common to combine RAID 0 and RAID 1 (usually called RAID 10 or RAID 0+1). Such striped and mirrored configurations offer protection against hardware failure together with the benefits of IO striping. Figure 21-5 illustrates the various RAID levels.

The RAID5 Write Penalty   RAID5 provides the most economical architecture for delivering fault tolerant storage with IO distributed across multiple physical disks. Consequently it's popular both among storage vendors and MIS departments. However, it's a questionable configuration for database servers.

Both RAID 0 and RAID 5 improve the performance of concurrent random reads by spreading the load across multiple devices. However, RAID 5 tends to degrade write IO because during a write, both the source block and the parity block must be read and then updated: four IOs in total. This degradation becomes even more extreme if a disk fails because all disks must be accessed to rebuild a logical view of the failed disk.

From a performance point of view, RAID5 offers few advantages and significant drawbacks. The write penalty incurred by RAID5 generally degrades performance for the database writer, for temporary segments writes, and for redo/flashback log operations. RAID5 should be considered only for datafiles that are predominantly read-only. Even for a read-insensitive database such as a data warehouse, RAID5 can still result in disastrous performance when large sort or join operations are performed: The temporary segment writes will be degraded and even apparently read-only performance severely diminished.[6]

---

[6] For a more comprehensive—and humorous—coverage of the evils of RAID5, visit the Battle Against Any Raid Five Web site: http://www.baarf.com.

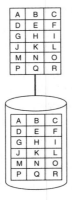

1. A normal disk without any RAID level

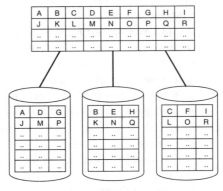

2. RAID level 0, or striping. Data are evenly distributed across multiple disks, but there is no redunancy.

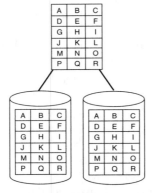

3. RAID 1. Data are replicated on two disks but there is no spread of data.

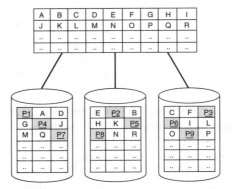

4. RAID 5. Data are spread across multiple devices. Parity information (P1, P2, etc.) can be used to reconstruct data if any single disk fails.

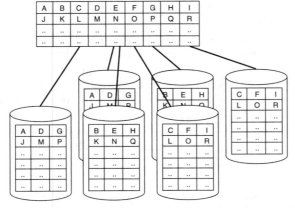

5. RAID 0 + 1 can be combined to provide both spreading of data and redundancy.

FIGURE 21-5 RAID levels.

> The write penalty of RAID5 renders it unsuitable for most databases. Even apparently read-only databases can be degraded by RAID5 when temporary segment IO occurs.

Non-Volatile Caches in RAID5 Devices   The write penalty associated with RAID5 devices can be reduced by the use of a nonvolatile cache. The nonvolatile cache is a memory store with a battery backup, which ensures that the data in the cache is not lost if a power failure occurs. Because the data in the cache is protected against loss, it is allowable for the disk device to report that the data has been written to disk as soon as it is stored into the cache. The data can be written down to the physical disk at a later point in time.

Battery-backed caches can improve the performance of writes immensely, especially when the application requests confirmation that the data written has actually been committed to disk, which Oracle always does. Such caches are common in RAID devices, partially because they help to alleviate the overhead of disk writes in a RAID5 configuration. With a large enough cache, the RAID5 writes overhead can be practically eliminated for *bursts* of write activity. However, if the write activity is sustained over time, the cache will fill up with modified data and array performance will then reduce to that of the underlying disks, and a substantial and sudden drop in performance might occur. The effect is quite remarkable—an abrupt and drastic reduction in disk throughput and massive degradation in service times.

> If considering a RAID5-based solution, give preference to RAID arrays that are configured with a nonvolatile cache. Such a cache can reduce the write IO overhead associated with RAID5 but only for short bursts of write activity.

ISOLATING DATAFILE IO

Striping *all* Oracle files across *all* available disk devices can be a valid strategy. However, it is generally preferable to isolate redo and archive logs to separate disks because of the different types of IO and the different impact each type of IO has on performance. We talk about how best to layout redo and archive logs in a subsequent section.

In addition to isolating log IO, you might also want to consider isolating specific tablespaces to specific disk volumes. The main motivation for isolating datafiles to specific devices is to maintain predictable response time for different types of IO requests. For instance, the temporary tablespace might be subject to sudden bursts of activity when large sort operations occur, whereas the primary datafiles might be subject to high rates of index based lookups for response time critical transactions. If the temporary tablespace shares disk devices with the permanent tablespaces, a single large sort operation might disturb the response time for the OLTP-style queries.

The motivation for separating redo devices from tablespaces is similar. When a log file switches, it usually triggers a redo log archive operation that can be IO-intensive. IO-intensive backup operations also occur from time to time, and these might affect datafile response times if not isolated to dedicated devices. As we will soon see, the flow of data from online redo to offline redo and then to archived logs introduces some unique considerations.

> It's usually desirable to isolate datafiles from redo log devices. You might also want to isolate specific tablespaces: in particular you should consider isolating busy temporary tablespaces to dedicated devices.

REDO AND ARCHIVE OPTIMIZATION

As already discussed, it's generally best to separate redo, flashback, and archived logs from datafiles. The type of IO performed on these files is qualitatively different from datafile IO, and the bursts of IO that occurs during backup and archiving can be disruptive to ongoing datafile IO.

There are then two common ways to configure the redo log, archive logs, and flashback areas:

❑ Alternate redo logs across two disk volumes and place the archive destination on a separate volume.

❑ Put all these files in a single location. For instance, use a single striped volume for all non-datafiles or at least for archive logs and flashback logs.

ALTERNATING AND DISTRIBUTING LOGS

Placing all log files on a single volume is the more administratively easy choice and—if the volume is backed by enough disk devices and well striped—might offer effective performance. The alternative configuration is somewhat more complicated but is designed to enable each IO operation to have exclusive access to the disk device involved.

Because the redo Log Writer (LGWR) performs sequential writes to a specific redo log while the Archiver (ARCH) performs sequential reads from a separate log, if we alternate logs across two devices, the chances are good that the LGWR will be writing to one device while ARCH will be reading from the other. Each process will have virtually exclusive access to the devices concerned.

Because of the sequential nature of redo log IO, write time is minimized if the LGWR has exclusive access to the disk holding the online log. The disk head will always be in the correct position, so seek time will be minimal.

Figure 21-6 illustrates this configuration. Odd sequence numbered redo logs are on one device and even numbered on the other. Consequently, the LGWR has exclusive write access to one of the devices while the ARCH process has exclusive read access to the other.

The redo log devices might be either striped volumes or single disks (preferably mirrored even if not striped). The LGWR and ARCH will not contend for these disks under normal circumstances, so a single disk device will provide close to the maximum possible throughput. However, the archive log destination disk should be striped because it will be subject to concurrent activity when archived logs are periodically copied to backup media.

REDO AND ARCHIVE FINE-GRAINED STRIPING

Alternating and distributing redo logs as described in the previous section is an adequate solution up until the point at which the sustained write capacity of a single disk or disk volume is exceeded. At that point you might want to consider placing the redo logs on a fine-grained stripe.

The sequential write activity performed by the LGWR is not the sort of IO that is normally optimized by striping: the LGWR is writing sequentially to a file, so most of the time will be writing to a single disk only. Striping that file simply causes the LGWR to alternate sequentially between the disks in the stripe with no performance advantage.

However, striping might improve redo log writes if either of the following is true:

❏ The stripe size is significantly smaller than the average redo log write size. If this is true, then a single redo log write operation might be spread among multiple devices and result in increased throughput. Unfortunately, in an OLTP environment, redo log writes will be small and frequent (because of

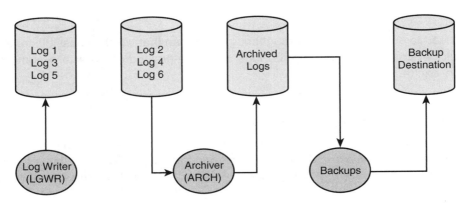

FIGURE 21-6   Alternating redo log devices.

the high COMMIT rate) and too small to span disks in a single operation. However, if the LGWR is flushing a large amount of data (say one-third of a 512M LOG_BUFFER), the capability to write to multiple devices in parallel might reduce the time taken for the write. Using the BATCH COMMIT option (see Chapter 14) tends to increase the average redo IO size that in turn might make fine-grained striping more effective.

❑ The stripe is on a RAID array with a nonvolatile cache. If the LGWR is writing to the cache, and the RAID array is following up with parallel writes to multiple striped disks, both latency and throughput will be optimized.

If the average redo log write is small, and your disk array does not have a nonvolatile memory cache, striping might not be of much use. To determine the average redo log write size, you can use the following query (11g only):

```
SQL> SELECT (small_write_megabytes + large_write_megabytes) total_mb,
  2            (small_write_reqs + large_write_reqs) total_requests,
  3             ROUND((small_write_megabytes + large_write_megabytes)
  4          *  1024
  5          / (small_write_reqs + large_write_reqs),2)
  6             avg_write_kb
  7  FROM v$iostat_function
  8  WHERE function_name = 'LGWR';

   TOTAL_MB   TOTAL_REQUESTS AVG_WRITE_KB
------------ ---------------- ------------
      5,378          143,145        38.47
```

In this case, striping would be unlikely to improve throughput unless a nonvolatile cache is available because the average write size is too small in comparison to the stripe size: Even fine grained stripes will be greater than the 38KB average redo entries shown here.

If you need to achieve redo log throughput greater than that which is possible for a single disk device, consider placing the logs on a fine-grained stripe with a nonvolatile memory cache.

JUST SAY NO TO RAID5 FOR REDO!

Using RAID5 for any database file is questionable, but using RAID5 for redo logs is almost certainly a bad idea. Because redo logs are subject to sustained write activity and because the delay caused by those writes is typically a limiting factor on database processing, the write penalty exacted by RAID5 is almost always unacceptable. You would be better advised to alternate your disk devices as outlined in the previous section than to organize them as RAID5.

RAID5 should almost never be used to host redo log devices. The write penalty of RAID5 will severely limit the transactional capacity of your database.

REDO LOG SIZING

Unless you use one of the NOWAIT or BATCH options for redo log processing—both of which involve a serious compromise in transactional integrity and which we discussed in Chapter 14—redo log IO will often be the limiting factor on transactional throughput. In addition to this somewhat unavoidable limitation, redo log-related waits can occur while redo logs are switched, archived, or check-pointed. These waits *are* avoidable and can be minimized by configuring the size and number of redo logs.

Non-IO related redo log waits can occur under the following circumstances:

❑ Whenever Oracle switches to a new redo log, there is a short wait while the new log file is initialized.

❑ If the database is in archive log mode and the log file that is due to be reused has not yet been archived, the log switch cannot complete until the log is archived. Sessions wanting to write redo (for example, to perform DML) need to wait.

❑ Before a log file can be reused, all the changes corresponding to redo entries in the log must have been written to the appropriate datafile on disk. A *checkpoint*, which initiates such a write to disk, occurs when the log switches. If all entries have not already been written to disk, the log switch will be delayed while the checkpoint completes.

These waits can be a result of poor IO configuration—placing the redo log destination on a slow device, for instance—but are more often the result of having too few or insufficiently large redo logs. It's inevitable, in fact it's *intended*, that the Archiver (ARCH) or Database Writer (DBWR) will fall behind the Log Writer (LGWR) from time to time. If the redo logs are large and numerous, the DBWR and ARCH will have plenty of time to catch up. However, if the logs are small and few, the chances are good that a checkpoint or archive wait will occur. These waits are recorded as *log file switch (archiving needed)* or *log file switch (checkpoint incomplete)*. Furthermore, small logs need to be switched frequently, leading to *log file switch completion* waits.

This query compares the log file related waits, including log switch waits, to other high-level categories:

```
SQL> WITH system_event AS
  2       (SELECT CASE
  3                 WHEN event LIKE 'log file%'
  4                 THEN event ELSE wait_class
  5              END  wait_type, e.*
  6           FROM v$system_event e)
  7  SELECT wait_type, SUM(total_waits) / 1000 waits_1000,
  8         ROUND(SUM(time_waited_micro) / 1000000 / 3600, 2)
  9             time_waited_hours,
 10         ROUND(SUM(time_waited_micro) / SUM(total_waits) / 1000, 2)
 11             avg_wait_ms,
 12         ROUND(  SUM(time_waited_micro)
 13             * 100
 14             / SUM(SUM(time_waited_micro)) OVER (), 2)
 15           pct
 16  FROM (SELECT wait_type, event, total_waits, time_waited_micro
 17          FROM system_event e
 18          UNION
 19          SELECT 'CPU', stat_name, NULL, VALUE
 20          FROM v$sys_time_model
 21          WHERE stat_name IN ('background cpu time', 'DB CPU')) l
 22  WHERE wait_type <> 'Idle'
 23  GROUP BY wait_type
 24  ORDER BY SUM(time_waited_micro) DESC
 25  /
```

Wait Type	Waits \1000	Time Hours	Avg Wait Ms	Pct
User I/O	130	.48	13.18	50.60
Application	0	.19	5,037.76	19.90
System I/O	46	.12	9.38	12.83
CPU		.05		4.97
log file switch (checkpoint incomplete)	0	.03	328.04	**2.87**
log file parallel write	54	.03	1.80	2.86
log file switch completion	0	.02	393.51	**2.40**
Other	1	.02	65.20	1.93
log file sequential read	2	.01	19.55	1.14

If you are licensed for the Oracle Diagnostic pack, you can see log file switch waits showing up under the Configuration category in the Average Active Sessions chart. Figure 21-7 shows a system that is suffering from severe log switch contention.

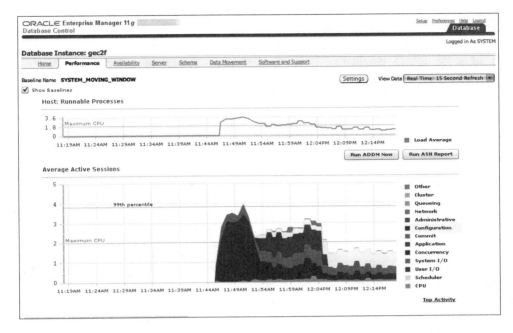

FIGURE 21-7 Log switch waits show up as "configuration" in Enterprise Manager.

Drilling into the Configuration category will show the wait details; in Figure 21-8, we see that the Configuration waits are overwhelmingly log file switch waits.

The optimal size for your redo logs will depend on your transaction rate. You will want to size the logs so that log switches do not occur too rapidly. If you allocate dedicated devices for redo logs, there is likely to be substantial disk capacity available for logs, so it's often easiest to over-configure the log size and number initially. Log sizes of 512M to 1GB are not uncommon. Configuring as many as 10 or 20 redo logs is also not unusual.

The following query reports the average, maximum, and minimum times between log switches over the past 24 hours. Average times under 5 minutes or so might suggest a need to increase the size of the logs:

```
SQL> WITH log_history AS
  2        (SELECT thread#, first_time,
  3              LAG(first_time) OVER (ORDER BY thread#, sequence#)
  4                  last_first_time,
  5              (first_time
  6              - LAG(first_time) OVER (ORDER BY thread#, sequence#))
  7                  * 24* 60   last_log_time_minutes,
```

```
 8                LAG(thread#) OVER (ORDER BY thread#, sequence#)
 9                    last_thread#
10         FROM v$log_history)
11    SELECT ROUND(MIN(last_log_time_minutes), 2) min_minutes,
12           ROUND(MAX(last_log_time_minutes), 2) max_minutes,
13           ROUND(AVG(last_log_time_minutes), 2) avg_minutes
14    FROM log_history
15    WHERE         last_first_time IS NOT NULL
16        AND last_thread# = thread#
17        AND first_time > SYSDATE - 1;


MIN_MINUTES MAX_MINUTES AVG_MINUTES
----------- ----------- -----------
       4.52       39.78       34.79
```

The *log file switch* waits are usually a sign that your redo logs are too small and per-haps not numerous enough. Consider increasing the number and sizes of your redo logs and increasing your archive destination IO bandwidth.

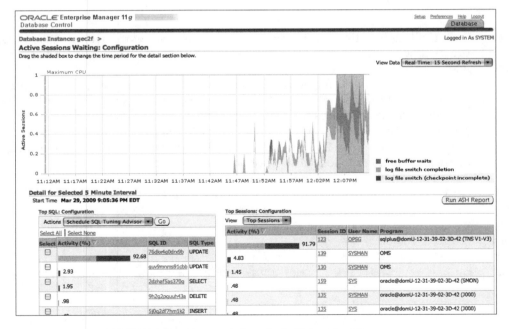

FIGURE 21-8   Log switch waits in Enterprise Manager.

FLASHBACK LOGS

Flashback logs are subject to similar IO activity as redo logs—sequential writes to a single file at any given time. However, flashback logs are not subject to archiving, cannot easily be resized, and do not have a "flush on commit" behavior.

It's often suggested that flashback logs and archive logs be stored together in the flashback recovery area. If you plan to place your redo logs on a single wide-grained stripe, this might be an acceptable solution. Contention between the flashback writer (RVWR) and Log Writer (LGWR) is certainly a possibility because both will become busy during the same sorts of load. However, if the stripe is wide, the chance that each will be writing to the same physical disk at the same time is minimal.

Nonetheless, if both redo and flashback IO appears to be slower than expected, providing each with dedicated IO channels is worth a try. We saw in Chapter 17 an example in which doing so reduced flashback IO waits by almost 45 percent.

Placing flashback logs and redo or archive logs on the same disk devices might introduce contention. Consider placing the flashback logs on a dedicated disk volume.

Flashback IO operations are generally small and so a fine-grained striping strategy is preferred. The following query shows that the average IO for the flashback writer was about 400K:

```
SQL> SELECT (small_write_megabytes + large_write_megabytes)
                total_write_mb,
  2         (small_write_reqs + large_write_reqs) total_write_reqs,
  3         ROUND( (small_write_megabytes + large_write_megabytes)
  4            * 1024
  5            / (small_write_reqs + large_write_reqs), 2)
  6         avg_write_kb
  7  FROM v$iostat_file f
  8  WHERE filetype_name = 'Flashback Log';


TOTAL_WRITE_MB TOTAL_WRITE_REQS AVG_WRITE_KB
-------------- ---------------- ------------
        25,359           62,714       414.06
```

A stripe size of 128K would allow an average IO to be spread across four spindles that might improve performance; although remember that many devices can process a 414K write in about the same time as a 128K write. The advantages might therefore be marginal unless a nonvolatile cache is present, allowing the write to complete at memory speed and be written out later to multiple devices in parallel.

As we saw in Chapter 17, the size of the flashback buffer is determined by the size of the SGA; it's 16M when the SGA is greater than 1GB and 4M otherwise. The size of the average IO might increase in proportion to the size of the flashback buffer, so if flashback IO is a concern, an SGA greater than 1GB might help. You can increase the flashback buffer to 16M if you are prepared to adjust some undocumented parameters; Chapter 17 outlines the procedure.

SUMMARY

After you make all reasonable efforts to avoid physical IO by reducing workload and optimizing memory, it's time to configure the IO subsystem so that it can meet the resulting IO demand.

Disk devices provide lower latency when they are only partially filled with data and when they are producing only a fraction of maximum possible throughput. Keeping disks less than 50-percent full and at less than 50 percent to 75 percent of maximum throughput is a possible rule of thumb for optimizing service time.

Throughput is generally achieved by using multiple disk drives and striping data across the devices. Throughput goals can be achieved only if you acquire enough disks to meet the aggregate IO demand.

The two most popular ways to spread data across Oracle datafiles are RAID5 and striping (RAID0, RAID10, RAID 0+1). RAID5 imposes a heavy penalty on write performance and is not recommended even for primarily read-only databases unless there is no temporary segment IO. Striping is the technique of choice on performance grounds.

Because temporary segment IO and permanent segment IO have such different IO characteristics and diverse service-level expectations, it can often be a good idea to separate temporary tablespace datafiles on their own disk volumes.

For redo and archive logs, RAID5 is even more undesirable and should generally not be used unless performance is not important. Redo logs do not always benefit from striping in any case: Alternating redo logs across two devices and placing the archive destination on a striped volume is often the high-performance solution.

Flashback logs can be stored together with archive logs on a fine-grained striped device, although better performance will often be obtained by allocating the flashback recovery area its own dedicated disk volume.

Advanced IO Techniques

In this chapter we build on the IO tuning fundamentals of the last chapter and consider some specific technologies and IO optimizations.

Oracle's Automatic Storage Management (ASM) provides a storage management layer tightly integrated with the Oracle software stack. DBAs can use ASM to implement striping, mirroring, and load balancing on top of directly attached vanilla disks or on logical disks exposed by a storage array. ASM can be used to implement many of the optimizations discussed in the previous chapter, and offers unique monitoring and tuning opportunities.

Spinning magnetic disk devices continue to be the basis for the vast majority of database storage. However, Solid State Disk (SSD) is becoming increasingly attractive as a means of overcoming the unavoidable latency that is a consequence of the mechanics of magnetic disk.

Although SSD offers a way to mitigate latency limitations, throughput generated by large disk arrays can overload the channels and processing capabilities of the database server. The Oracle/HP Exadata storage server mitigates these limitations by implementing some database operations directly in the storage unit.

Finally, we discuss the possibility of optimizing IO through changes to the Oracle block size (and generally advise against it).

AUTOMATIC STORAGE MANAGEMENT (ASM)

Automatic Storage Management (ASM) was introduced in Oracle 10g to provide cluster-ready storage management facilities tightly integrated with the Oracle software stack. ASM provides a storage virtualization layer that automates many file level database administration tasks and which provides striping, redundancy, load balancing, and other services to an Oracle database. From Oracle 11g release 2 forward, ASM can provide clustered filesystem capabilities as well: the ASM Cluster File System (ACFS).

ASM can provide storage services across a cluster and is ideally suited to providing the shared disk storage subsystem required by Real Application Clusters (RAC); consequently, ASM is particularly popular in conjunction with RAC. However, the services and benefits of ASM are equally valid for a single instance Oracle database.

ASM services can be enabled on top of directly attached disk devices (Just a Bunch Of Disks [JBOD]) or on top of Logical Units (LUNs) exposed by a storage array or volume manager. In either case, the disks are exposed to the Oracle database as a small number of Disk Groups, each of which can contain any number of logical disks.

When using ASM, DDL operations that formally specified file locations need to specify only an ASM Disk Group: ASM determines the optimal location for the files on disk.

ASM ARCHITECTURE

ASM is implemented by a stripped-down Oracle instance. This instance supports no datafiles or database sessions. The purpose of the ASM instance is to maintain and determine the mapping between the database objects and the blocks on disk that store the data for that object. ASM determines the physical placement based on the redundancy (for example, mirroring) and striping characteristics of the file. ASM distributes data evenly across the disks in the disk group and rebalances the data should a disk be added or removed or if a rebalance operation is requested.

Figure 22-1 provides a high-level overview of the ASM and RDBMS interactions. From the RDBMS point of view, segments have extents that are stored on datafiles. These datafiles are stored in an ASM Disk Group. Asides from the Disk Group and logical ASM filename, the RDBMS maintains no information about the physical layout of the data file on disk.

Although ASM determines where each data block should be stored on disk, it's the RDBMS that actually does the reading and writing. When a new block is created, ASM advises the RDBMS where on disk to write that block. When the RDBMS wants to read a logical block, it asks ASM for the physical location. The RDBMS remains responsible for all the physical IOs; ASM simply advises the RDBMS where to direct those IOs.

ASM MONITORING

All the IO monitoring techniques outlined in the previous chapter are relevant for ASM. However, ASM can provide additional insight into IO at the ASM disk

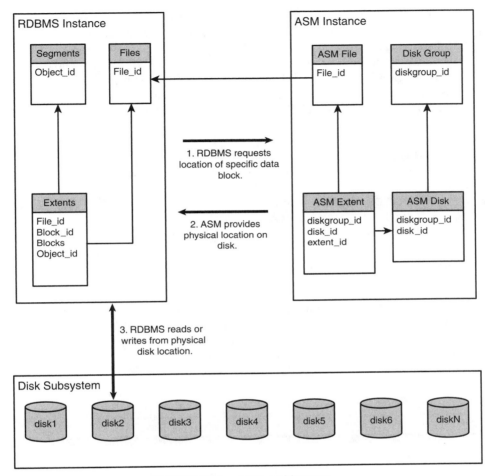

FIGURE 22-1   ASM architecture.

group and device level. In a single instance database, these metrics can help you fine-tune your ASM configuration. In a multi-instance database (for example, in RAC), the statistics become even more important because they enable you to aggregate IO metrics from all the instances in the cluster that are using the shared ASM disks.

   Connecting to the ASM Instance   An Oracle instance can be associated with at most one ASM instance. If so associated, some ASM statistics will be visible in views such as V$ASM_DISKGROUP and V$ASM_DISK_STAT from within the RDBMS instance. However, these views will be missing information: Not all columns are populated within the RDBMS instance, and columns that are populated reflect only the activity generated by the current RDBMS and not activity from other databases that might be connected to the same ASM storage. For this reason, it is usually necessary to connect to the ASM instance to obtain meaningful statistics.

Connections to the ASM instance can be made only by invoking the SYSDBA, SYSOPER, or SYSASM privilege. Typically this requires a SYS connection. In addition, a remote SQL*Net connection in Oracle 10g might need to include the UR=A clause in the TNS definition for the connection. For instance

```
my_asm=
  (DESCRIPTION =
    (ADDRESS = (PROTOCOL = TCP)(HOST = hostname)(PORT = 1521))
    (CONNECT_DATA =
     (SERVICE_NAME = +ASM1)
      (INSTANCE_NAME = +ASM1)
      (UR = A)
    )
  )
```

Accessing ASM from Enterprise Manager might require that you configure the ASM Instance as an Enterprise Manager target. You can do this from the Agents section of the Enterprise Manager Setup page. Figure 22-2 shows us specifying the connection properties for the ASM instance.

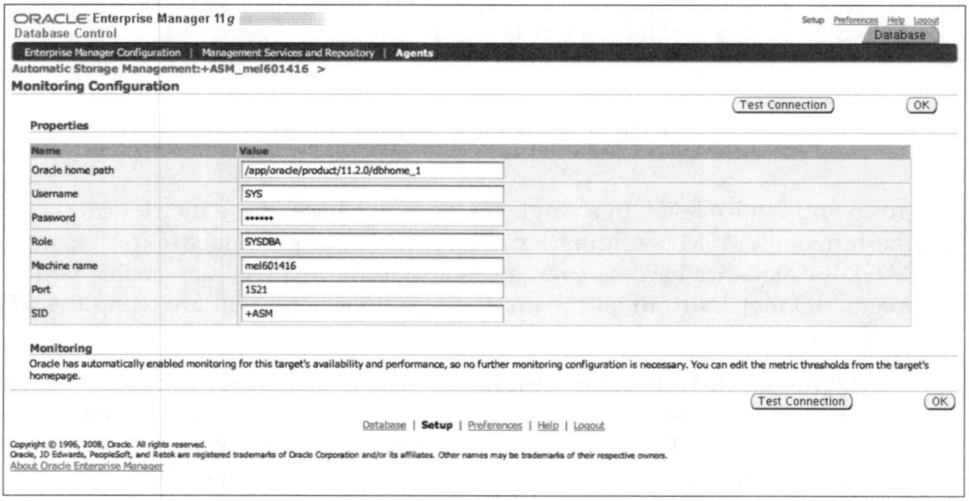

FIGURE 22-2   Configuring the ASM instance as an Enterprise Manager target.

Measuring Disk Group Performance To observe Disk Group activity, we can use the views V$ASM_DISKGROUP_STAT and V$ASM_DISK_STAT. If the ASM storage is clustered (as in a RAC database), we should use *GV*$ASM_DISK_STAT to accumulate statistics from all the hosts sharing the ASM disks; *V*$ASM_DISK_STAT reflects only the IO that occurred on the host to which you are connected. Here we use GV$ASM_DISK_STAT to show disk group IO statistics:

```
SQL> SELECT name, ROUND(total_mb / 1024) total_gb, active_disks,
  2            reads / 1000 reads1k, writes / 1000 writes1k,
  3            ROUND(read_time) read_time, ROUND(write_time) write_time,
  4            ROUND(read_time * 1000 / reads, 2) avg_read_ms
  5  FROM        v$asm_diskgroup_stat dg
  6      JOIN
  7          (SELECT group_number, COUNT(DISTINCT disk_number)
                        active_disks,
  8                  SUM(reads) reads, SUM(writes) writes,
  9                  SUM(read_time) read_time, SUM(write_time)
                        write_time
 10           FROM gv$asm_disk_stat
 11           WHERE mount_status = 'CACHED'
 12           GROUP BY group_number) ds
 13      ON (ds.group_number = dg.group_number)
 14  ORDER BY dg.group_number;
```

Diskgroup Name	Size GB	Active Disks	Reads /1000	Writes /1000	Read Time Secs	Write Time Secs	Avg Read ms
DATA01_WIDE	155	3	13,178	1,007	68,032	27,080	5.16
DATA02_WIDE	94	2	62,913	921	132,546	6,574	2.11
DATA03_SLOW	47	5	155	168	2,443	2,426	15.78
DATA04_MIXED	72	7	890	141	13,011	3,571	14.62

One of our main reasons for looking at Disk Group statistics is to determine if the Disk Group is configured adequately for the IO demands we are placing on it. If there are too few disk devices allocated to the Disk Group, we will probably see high average service times. In the preceding example, there are indications that the final two disk groups are experiencing higher service times and might need more disk devices.

High service times for a disk group might be a sign that the disk group needs more disks.

Disk Level Statistics   Examining IO at the ASM disk level can help determine if there are imbalances within the group. ASM distributes data evenly across all the disks in the Disk Group, but IO imbalances can still occur. For instance, the following query shows a disk group in which the disk devices are of different sizes. ASM allocates blocks across disk proportionally to their sizes, and as a result the bigger disks are serving a higher number of IOs and deliver degraded response times. Note how disk /dev/raw/raw12 is responsible for 63 percent of all IOs and how its response time is correspondingly degraded:

```
SQL> SELECT d.PATH disk_path, d.total_mb,
  2          ROUND(ds.read_secs * 1000 / ds.reads, 2) avg_read_ms,
  3          ds.reads/1000 +  ds.writes/1000 io_1k,
  4          ds.read_secs +ds.write_secs io_secs,
  5          ROUND((d.reads + d.writes) * 100 /
  6              SUM(d.reads + d.writes) OVER (),2) pct_io,
  7          ROUND((ds.read_secs +ds.write_secs)*100/
  8              SUM(ds.read_secs +ds.write_secs) OVER (),2) pct_time
  9   FROM v$asm_diskgroup_stat dg
 10   JOIN v$asm_disk_stat d ON (d.group_number = dg.group_number)
 11      JOIN (SELECT group_number, disk_number disk_number,
                      SUM(reads) reads,
 12              SUM(writes) writes, ROUND(SUM(read_time), 2)
                      read_secs,
 13              ROUND(SUM(write_time), 2) write_secs
 14          FROM gv$asm_disk_stat
 15         WHERE mount_status = 'CACHED'
 16         GROUP BY group_number, disk_number) ds
 17        ON (ds.group_number = d.group_number
 18            AND ds.disk_number = d.disk_number)
 19   WHERE dg.name = '&diskgroup_name'
 20      AND d.mount_status = 'CACHED'
 21   ORDER BY d.PATH;
Enter value for diskgroup_name: DATA04_MIXED
```

Disk Path	MB	Avg Read (ms)	IO /1000	IO seconds	Pct IO	Pct Time
/dev/raw/raw101	2,000	10.80	34	494	2.98	2.28
/dev/raw/raw102	500	6.15	13	113	1.11	.52
/dev/raw/raw103	1,000	8.73	21	247	1.80	1.14
/dev/raw/raw104	3,000	8.35	69	812	6.07	3.75
/dev/raw/raw12	**47,873**	**16.11**	**727**	**14,392**	**63.65**	**66.36**
/dev/raw/raw25	9,538	14.21	138	2,533	12.03	11.68
/dev/raw/raw26	9,538	14.82	141	3,095	12.36	14.27

Monitoring ASM Rebalance Operations When ASM rebalances a Disk Group or when a disk is added or removed from a Disk Group, ASM transparently moves data within the Disk Group to achieve a balanced distribution of data. The Disk Group remains fully available during this operation, though response times can be affected. The progress of these operations is recorded in the view V$ASM_OPERATION. The following query shows a rebalance operation in progress:

```
SQL> SELECT dg.NAME,   d.operation, d.state, d.POWER, d.actual,
  2          est_work ,
  3          d.sofar*100/d.est_work pct_done, d.est_rate, d.est_minutes
  4     FROM v$asm_diskgroup dg LEFT OUTER JOIN gv$asm_operation d
  5          ON (d.group_number = dg.group_number);
```

Disk Group	Operation	State	Power Reqtd	Power Actual	Estd Work	Pct Done	Rate \Min	Estd Min
DATA01_WIDE								
DATA02_WIDE	REBAL	RUN	1	1	8,480	9.91	857	8
DATA03_SLOW								
DATA04_MIXED								

We look at rebalance operations in more detail later in the chapter.

File Level Statistics The V$ASM_FILE view shows information about each file in an ASM Disk Group. This view is primarily useful for determining how space within a Disk Group is allocated. However, from Oracle 11g Release 2 forward, this view also includes information about hot and cold IOs. These are the IOs associated with the Optimal Disk Placement feature of Oracle 11g Release 2 that we discuss later in the chapter.

Getting useful information from V$ASM_FILE requires a join to V$ASM_ALIAS. The following query reports on file configuration and IO[1]:

```
SQL> SELECT rootname,d.name diskgroup_name,f.TYPE, a.name filename,
  2          space / 1048576 allocated_mb, primary_region, striped,
  3          round((hot_reads + hot_writes)/1000,2) hot_ios1k,
  4          round((cold_reads + cold_writes)/1000,2) cold_ios1k
  5     FROM (SELECT CONNECT_BY_ISLEAF, group_number, file_number, name,
  6                  CONNECT_BY_ROOT name rootname, reference_index,
  7                  parent_index
  8           FROM v$asm_alias a
```

---

[1] Some of the columns in this query were introduced in Oracle 11g Release 2: A 10g-compatible version of the query can be obtained from this book's Web site.

```
 9              CONNECT BY PRIOR reference_index = parent_index) a
10      JOIN (SELECT DISTINCT name
11              FROM v$asm_alias
12       /* top 8 bits of the parent_index is the group_number, so
13           the following selects aliases whose parent is the group
14           itself - eg top level directories within the disk group*/
15           WHERE parent_index = group_number * POWER(2, 24)) b
16              ON (a.rootname = b.name)
17      JOIN v$asm_file f
18          ON (a.group_number = f.group_number
19            AND a.file_number = f.file_number)
20      JOIN v$asm_diskgroup d
21          ON (f.group_number = d.group_number)
22      WHERE a.CONNECT_BY_ISLEAF = 1
23      ORDER BY (cold_reads+cold_writes+hot_reads+hot_writes) DESC;
```

File Type	File Name	MB	Primary Region	Stripe Type	Hot IO /1000	ColdIO /1000
DATAFILE	ASM_TS.257.683122375	2,050	COLD	COARSE	0	11,101
DATAFILE	ASM_TS.256.683111957	2,050	COLD	COARSE	0	4,500
DATAFILE	HOT_STUFF.258.683401	265	HOT	FINE	105	0
FLASHBACK	log_21.278.683135803	24	COLD	FINE	0	0

Enterprise Manager and Other Tools   If you have an Oracle Diagnostic pack license, you can use Enterprise Manager to show high-level Disk Group level performance statistics. Figure 22-3 shows Disk Group level statistics reported by Enterprise Manager.

Unfortunately, Enterprise Manager shows only basic Disk Group level statistics. More detailed statistics, including disk level statistics, rebalance operations, and file/segment mappings are available in Quest Software's Spotlight on Oracle and Spotlight on Oracle RAC.[2] Figure 22-4 shows Spotlight drilling down into real-time, disk-level performance for a specific Disk Group.

ASM TUNING

Getting good performance out of ASM depends primarily on following the guidelines outlined in the previous chapter. This can involve

❑   Optimizing latency by ensuring that physical disks are sparsely packed and running below maximum throughput capacity

---

[2] Full disclosure: I was heavily involved in the design and development of Spotlight while working at Quest Software.

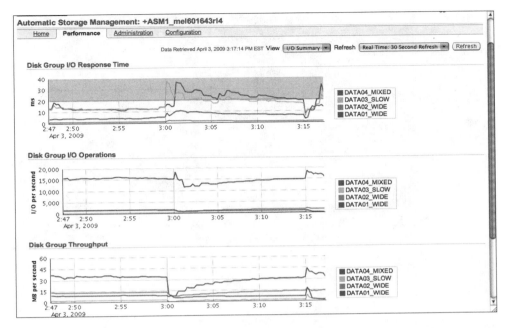

FIGURE 22-3 ASM performance statistics as shown in Enterprise Manager.

❑ Providing enough physical devices to support the desired throughput
❑ Avoiding RAID5 for any files subject to nontrivial write IOs
❑ Isolating redo, flashback, and archive log IO from datafile IO and possibly isolating temporary datafile IO from permanent datafile IO

ASM makes it relatively easy to achieve the above guidelines, whether you use JBOD (Just a Bunch of Disks) or a storage array.

Disk Group Strategy   Isolation of IO is easy to achieve when using ASM. By placing files that have different IO characteristics and service-level requirements on different disk groups, we can ensure that IOs to each Disk Group do not interfere with each other, and we can configure each group with the appropriate number and type of physical disks.

The simplest and most commonly implemented isolation is to create two disk groups: one for datafiles and online redo (usually called DATA) and one for backup related files such as flashback logs and archived logs (usually called FRA). This is sometimes described as a "best practice" for ASM.[3] As a means of reducing complexity, this two disk group configuration has merit. However, as

---

[3]See for instance, http://www.oracle.com/technology/products/database/asm/pdf/asm_10gr2_bestpractices%2009-07.pdf.

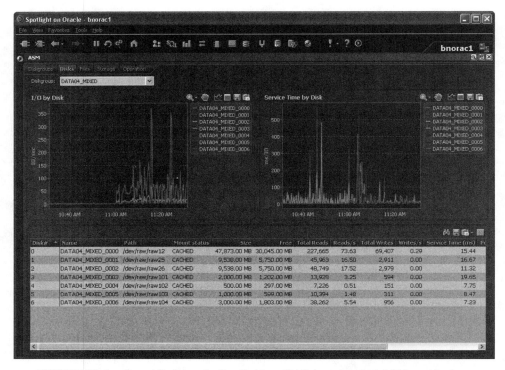

FIGURE 22-4 Quest Software's Spotlight on RAC has detailed ASM monitoring.

we have seen many times in previous chapters, isolating various types of IO can sometimes be critical in reducing performance bottlenecks. For instance, we saw increases in performance for certain queries when temporary tablespaces were separated from permanent data files and when flashback logs were allocated independent storage.

Create disk groups to support your IO isolation strategy. The "best practice" two disk group policy should be regarded as a minimum configuration: More disk groups can be required to isolate temporary, flashback, and other IO.

Redundancy ASM redundancy can be specified at the disk group or file level and can be set to NORMAL, HIGH, or EXTERNAL. Both NORMAL and HIGH instruct ASM to mirror file extents so that processing can continue if a disk failure occurs. External redundancy advises ASM not to implement redundancy, which is assumed to be provided by the underlying storage layer.

If ASM is implemented on top of a storage array that implements mirroring or (sigh) RAID5 redundancy, best performance will usually be achieved if you choose EXTERNAL redundancy. Management of redundancy is normally more efficient if implemented close to the underlying hardware and storage arrays such as those provided by EMC or Hitachi that have mature mirroring facilities. Implementing ASM redundancy on top of storage array redundancy will add unnecessary overhead at best and significant degradation at worst. Multiple mirroring quadruples storage requirements and—if the two mirroring schemes are not synchronized—might offer no additional protection.

However, it's all too common for the hardware level redundancy to be implemented as RAID5 or similar, possibly even without the DBAs explicit knowledge or consent. RAID5 remains a questionable choice for redundancy regardless at which level. If relying on external redundancy, make sure you know what type of redundancy is being provided: Storage administrators and vendors often implement RAID5 or similar as a matter of course. You might need to specifically request mirroring.

ASM redundancy is implemented at the extent level rather than at the disk level: Each extent has a mirrored copy on another disk, but disks themselves are not specifically mirrored.

High redundancy differs from normal redundancy in that two copies of each extent are maintained, allowing for the failure of two disks without resulting in an outage or loss of data.

ASM does not provide any sort of parity-based redundancy such as RAID 5 (yay!).

Both from a performance and availability point of view, it is critical to ensure that each ASM disk is truly independent. If two ASM disks are mapped to the same physical spindle in the underlying disk array, ASM redundancy can lead to both a performance overhead and a loss of data if spindle fails. This is another excellent reason for using external redundancy.

If you have implemented ASM on top of a storage array that provides mirroring, best performance is usually provided by selecting EXTERNAL redundancy when creating disk groups.

Striping Striping is intrinsic to an ASM disk group. Data will always be striped across the disks in the disk group, and there's no way to request storage on a specific disk.

ASM stripes data across all the disks in the Disk Group using either *course-grained* or *fine-grained* striping. Course-grained striping uses a stripe size equal to the allocation unit for the Disk Group: 1MB by default. Fine-grained striping uses a stripe size of 128K.

Course-grained striping is probably the best configuration for database files, whereas fine-grained striping might be more suitable for redo, flashback, and archive logs because it might allow for smaller IOs to be parallelized across multiple devices. However, you should review the discussion in the previous chapter regarding optimal layout for redo logs: Striping might not be the best IO configuration for redo and flashback logs. Because redo and flashback logs are subject to small sequential write operations, IO might be most optimized by allocating dedicated devices. Furthermore, writes less than 1MB in size might complete faster as a single operation to a single disk, rather than as a set of IOs distributed across multiple disks. However, when redo and flashback log IO is not critical, fine-grained striping will probably be adequate.

If you're implementing on top of a storage array, you might end up with double-striping: ASM striping on top of storage array striping. Providing the storage array is not implementing RAID5, this won't normally be a concern. Setting the storage array stripe size to the ASM stripe size (normally to 1MB) might avoid the scenario in which *split-stripes* generate more IOs than are strictly necessary.

The most significant factor in getting good striping performance is to use equivalent disks in the disk group. If ASM disks are JBOD, all disks should be of the same configuration. If disks are Logical Units (LUNs) exposed by a storage array, each LUN should be of the same size and have the same underlying physical characteristics (for example, be striped across the same number of disks).

ASM automatically applies coarse-grained striping to datafiles and fine-grained striping to redo, flashback, and archive logs. These behaviors are controlled by the default ASM templates. You can alter this by adding and applying your own templates or modifying the system default templates. We discuss templates in detail a bit later in the chapter.

Balance and Rebalance   Intuitively, you might think of balance as being achieved when each disk has the same amount of IO. However, ASM distributes data across disks relative to their size. This means that if one disk is twice as large as the rest, it will have twice the amount of data and, all things being equal, be subject to twice as many IOs.

If each ASM disk represents a real physical disk, this strategy will probably result in poor IO balance because the IO capacity of a larger disk is not greater than the IO capacity of a small disk.

If each ASM disk represents a real physical disk, each disk in the Disk Group should be the same size to achieve IO balance.

If, however, each ASM disk is a LUN that is exposed by a storage array, the size of the disk is not as important as the number of physical disks that underlie the LUN. The IO capacity of a LUN is proportional to the number of physical disks in the underlying storage, so it's important that every LUN in a disk group be backed by the same number of physical disks.

If each ASM disk represents a Logical Unit (LUN) from an underlying disk array, each LUN in a disk group should be backed by the same number of physical disk devices.

ASM rebalances the data in the disk group whenever a disk is added or removed or when a REBALANCE operation is requested by an ALTER DISK-GROUP command.

Rebalance operations have a "power" attribute that determines how aggressively ASM will pursue the rebalance. A low power operation will take the longest time but have the least impact on performance while it runs. A high power level will proceed more quickly but with a more disruptive effect on performance. The default power is defined by the parameter ASM_POWER_LIMIT: A nondefault value can be set in the ALTER DISKGROUP command.

Rebalance operations should not be performed capriciously; even at the lowest power level a rebalance can significantly affect response time. Figure 22-5 (from Quest Software's Spotlight on Oracle) shows the impact of a rebalance operation that resulted from removing a disk from the disk group; even at the lowest power level, the service time provided by the disk group was significantly degraded.

Despite occasional claims to the contrary, ASM rebalance operations will generally be disruptive to disk group performance and should be undertaken during off-peak periods.

ASM Optimal Disk Placement In the previous chapter, we discussed how the outermost tracks of a spinning disk offer higher throughput.[4] Oracle 11g release 2 ASM enables you to take advantage of this by specifying files that should be stored in this hot region.

---

[4] The number of blocks passing under the read/write head per unit time is higher as you move out from the center of the disk simply because the circumference of the disk increases while the rotational frequency is constant.

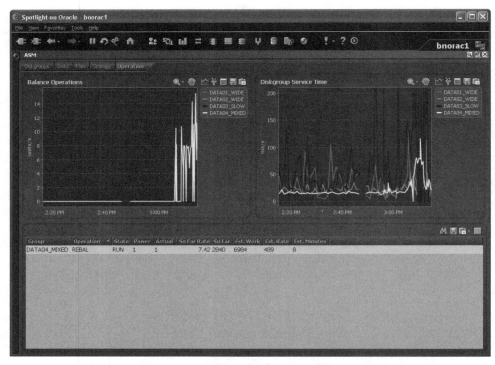

FIGURE 22-5   Impact of an ASM rebalance on service time.

Disk controllers will generally place data first in these outer regions any-way, so if your disk is sparsely populated, as is recommended for performance reasons, using disk placement might have little effect. Furthermore, if the disk de-vice is actually a LUN exposed by a storage array, ASM will be unable to specify an actual physical location for the data and therefore will be unable to implement Optimal Disk placement.

Optimal Disk placement is specified by associating a file with an ASM tem-plate in which the Primary Extent Zone is set to HOT.

Setting ASM File Characteristics with Templates   When a new file is added to an ASM Disk Group, its redundancy, striping, and disk placement char-acteristics are controlled by a template associated with the file. The default tem-plate is determined by the file type. You can list all templates by querying the V$ASM_TEMPLATE view:

```
SQL> SELECT t.name template_name, t.SYSTEM, t.redundancy,
  2          t.stripe, t.primary_region
  3     FROM v$asm_template t
  4     JOIN v$asm_diskgroup d
```

```
  5       ON (d.group_number = t.group_number)
  6    WHERE d.name = 'DATA'
  7    ORDER BY t.name;
```

Template Name	Sy Te	Redundancy	Stripe type	Primary Region
ARCHIVELOG	Y	UNPROT	COARSE	COLD
ASMPARAMETERFILE	Y	UNPROT	COARSE	COLD
ASM_STALE	Y	UNPROT	COARSE	COLD
AUTOBACKUP	Y	UNPROT	COARSE	COLD
BACKUPSET	Y	UNPROT	COARSE	COLD
CHANGETRACKING	Y	UNPROT	COARSE	COLD
CONTROLFILE	Y	UNPROT	FINE	COLD
DATAFILE	Y	UNPROT	COARSE	COLD
DATAGUARDCONFIG	Y	UNPROT	COARSE	COLD
DUMPSET	Y	UNPROT	COARSE	COLD
FLASHBACK	Y	UNPROT	FINE	COLD
HOT_DATAFILE	N	UNPROT	FINE	HOT
OCRBACKUP	Y	UNPROT	COARSE	COLD
OCRFILE	Y	UNPROT	COARSE	COLD
ONLINELOG	Y	UNPROT	FINE	COLD
PARAMETERFILE	Y	UNPROT	COARSE	COLD
TEMPFILE	Y	UNPROT	COARSE	COLD
XTRANSPORT	Y	UNPROT	COARSE	COLD

Note that the default template for DATAFILE specifies COURSE striping while the default for ONLINELOG and FLASHBACK specifies FINE striping.

To change these defaults we can either modify the default system templates or create our own template. Templates are disk group-specific and are controlled by the ALTER DISKGROUP command. For instance, in the following code, we create a template that specifies FINE grained striping and HOT optimal disk placement. We then specify the template name when adding a new datafile:

```
ALTER DISKGROUP data
   ADD TEMPLATE hot_datafile
ATTRIBUTES (UNPROTECTED FINE HOT );

CREATE TABLESPACE hot_stuff
   DATAFILE '+DATA(HOT_DATAFILE)' SIZE 256 M;
```

You can also set ASM template characteristics using ASMCA utility in Oracle 11g release 2 or with the DBCA utility in previous releases. Figure 22-6 shows the Manage Templates dialogue from ASMCA.

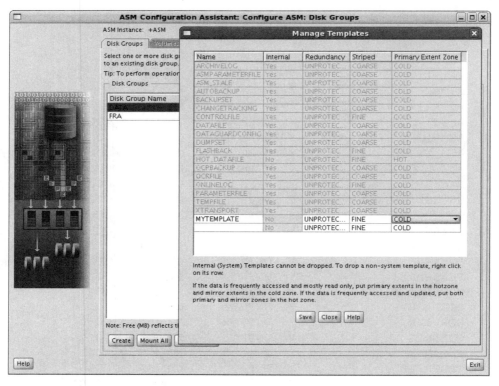

FIGURE 22-6   Managing ASM templates with the ASMCA utility.

SOLID STATE DISK (SSD)

As we discussed in the previous chapter, most computer technologies increase in performance exponentially, doubling in capabilities every 1–2 years. However, the technologies underlying magnetic disk are mechanical rather than electronic in nature and have increased in performance only marginally in the past decade. Although magnetic disks are getting *bigger*, they are not getting much *faster*.

A lot of the techniques we employed so far has had the aim of reducing IO; SQL tuning reduces the logical IO demand, and memory optimization reduces the amount of logical IO that becomes physical. However, some disk IOs are inevitable, and the poor latency of the spinning magnetic disk cannot always be avoided.

Although the fast majority of databases still use magnetic disk for persistent storage, we are definitely entering an era in which alternative technologies will gain in popularity. In particular Solid State Disk (SSD) offers a more high performance, though undoubtedly more expensive, storage solution.

SSD is an umbrella term for any persistent storage device that does not employ spinning magnetic disk or other moving parts. In practice SSD uses one or both of Flash RAM or DDR RAM as the primary storage technologies.

FLASH-BASED SSD

Flash (NAND)-based SSD uses the familiar flash technology that underlies the ubiquitous USB drives that have replaced floppy disks for small portable data storage. Flash RAM is cheap, provides permanent storage without battery backup, and so has low power consumption. It's perhaps 20–30 times faster than magnetic disk for normal reads, though not as fast for writes because data needs to be erased prior to write.

Flash memory cannot be written to indefinitely: Most flash drives can support approximately 100,000 write/erase operations to each block before the block becomes unreliable. However, commercial flash SSD vendors employ sophisticated algorithms to ensure that this write endurance limit is avoided. *Wear leveling* algorithms migrate data from hot spots on the drive before the write limit is reached.

The write performance of flash disks provides the biggest concern for database performance. By default, a flash write involves erasing and reconstructing the block of data concerned. This overhead results in fairly poor performance for writes—potentially worse than equivalent magnetic disk performance. Various techniques mitigate this drawback, such as completing the erase part of the write operation asynchronously. Nevertheless, write performance remains problematic for flash drives.

DDR RAM-BASED SSD

DDR (or SD) RAM-based SSD uses memory modules that are not that different in nature from those that provide core memory for a server. This RAM is backed by nonvolatile storage (disk or flash RAM) and internal batteries. If a power failure occurs, the batteries provide enough power to write the RAM memory to the nonvolatile storage.

DDR RAM is more expensive (per GB) and has a higher power utilization. The bus architecture of a DDR RAM SSD means that the reads are not quite as fast as those from main memory, but latencies in the 15 microsecond range can be achieved.

DDR RAM has no write penalty and provides excellent performance for all IO operations. However, compared with Flash-based SSD, it is more expensive, consumes more power, and generates more heat.

HYBRID SSD

Hybrid SSDs employ both Flash and DDR-RAM technologies. DDR-RAM is effectively used as a nonvolatile cache, providing low latencies for the majority of operations and buffering for write operations. Conceptually, this architecture is similar to the nonvolatile cache that is commonly implemented in storage arrays.

The performance characteristics of this sort of device are somewhat reminiscent of a RAID5 device with a nonvolatile cache. The cache will hide the write penalty of the Flash drives for short bursts of write activity but should a sustained write-intensive workload occur, the device drops to the throughput provided by the flash drives.

Figure 22-7 compares the performance of magnetic disk with DDR-based and flash-based SSD.

USING SSD FOR ORACLE DATABASES

It's probably not yet cost-effective in most cases to place every part of a large database on SSD, though you can certainly find SSD vendors who will disagree! Although the price of SSD storage is dropping rapidly, the size of the average database is also increasing. It's not clear that SSD will become economically viable as the solitary storage technology for databases in the immediate future, especially because the more economical technology (Flash SSD) has such significant write overheads. However, SSD is certainly a viable option for optimizing database performance by selectively deploying SSD for the most IO critical files. We can create a high-performance database implemented over a hierarchy of storage technologies:

❏ Very hot and write-intensive files can be stored on a DDR-based SSD. This might include redo logs and temporary tablespaces.
❏ Warm files that are read less frequently but that are still latency sensitive could be stored on Flash-based or hybrid SSD.
❏ Cold files, tablespaces containing older data, can be stored on magnetic disk.

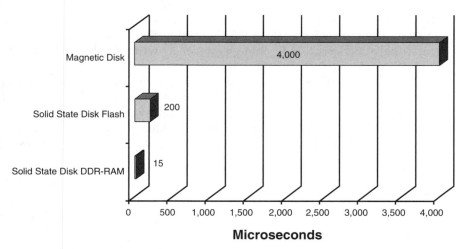

FIGURE 22-7   Read latency for SSD compared with magnetic disk.

Table partitioning can organize data into the three categories. The partition containing current data can be stored on a datafile hosted on DDR-RAM, medium term data partitioned to Flash-based disks, and older data archived to magnetic disk.

When physical disk latency becomes the limiting factor, deploying SSD offers a significant decrease in latency for a significant increase in price. When write latency is at issue, DDR-RAM is preferred over Flash-based SSD.

THE EXADATA STORAGE SERVER

Although the latency of the magnetic disk cannot be completely avoided without abandoning the technology in favor of new technologies such as SSD, getting more throughput out of magnetic disk devices is relatively straightforward: We just use more of them.

However, as the number of disk devices increase, the channel between the disks and the database server host, and the capacity of the database server itself, can become the limiting factor. The Oracle/HP Exadata storage server is a hardware/software solution that addresses this issue by leveraging existing technologies and best practices together with some unique features.

The Exadata storage server includes embedded Oracle database code that is capable of performing limited filtering and projections for a data request. For instance, in a normal full table scan every block in the table is transferred from the storage medium into Oracle address space. Blocks that do not match various WHERE criteria and columns that do not match the SELECT list are then eliminated. With Exadata, at least some of this processing can occur in the storage server; rows and columns not matching the SELECT and WHERE clause are eliminated *before* being shipped across the channel to the database server.

Exadata employs other more conventional techniques to provide optimal performance:

❑ High bandwidth InfiniBand interconnect between the storage and the database servers.
❑ Hot storage utilizing the outer 55 percent of each disk. The Inner 45 percent is used for cold storage.
❑ Parallel query processing within the storage server.
❑ ASM-based mirroring and striping.

Oracle and HP offer a database appliance—the HP Oracle Database Machine—which combines Exadata storage servers and a RAC cluster database in the same physical rack.

A predictable but somewhat misplaced debate has arisen over the competing virtues of Solid State Disk storage versus the Oracle Exadata solution. However, the key technical advantage of SSD is reduced *latency* whereas the key technical advantage of the Exadata storage is increased *throughput*. It's conceivable that SSD technologies and the technologies of Exadata will merge in some future release. For now, they provide solutions for different objectives and database applications.

DATABASE BLOCK SIZE

Certain performance debates seem to polarize the Oracle community. One of the most polarizing has been the issue of changing the Oracle block size to improve performance.

Oracle blocks are the fundamental unit of storage for Oracle: Every IO reads or writes at least one complete block, and it is blocks, not rows or extents, that are held in the buffer cache. Block size is therefore a fundamental characteristic that will impact on logical and physical IO.

Advocates of changing the default block size argue one or more of the following:

❑ Increasing the block size will reduce the number of physical IOs required to perform table or index scans. If the block size is higher, the number of blocks that must be read will be lower and hence the number of IOs required will be less. However, Oracle's multiblock read capability often achieves the same result by reading multiple smaller blocks in a single operating system operation.

❑ A higher block size will make B*-Tree indexes less deep. Because each root and branch block can contain more entries, a smaller number of levels will be required. However, this applies only for a narrow range of table sizes, and the maximum improvement might be marginal. That having been said, it is true that for a small number of indexes, a higher block size *will* reduce the depth of the B*-Tree.

❑ Decreasing the block size will increase the selectivity of blocks in the buffer cache: The bigger the block size, the more wasted rows will be cached. This is definitely theoretically true: If each block contained only one row (that is, if the block size was the size of a single row), every block in the cache would represent a row that had actually been requested, and the buffer cache would be more efficient. This argument is often provided as a reason for *not increasing* your block size.

❑ Decreasing the block size for bitmap indexes can reduce the number of rows that are locked on DML. For a bitmap index, the number of rows locked on DML is block size–dependent; the lower the block size, the fewer rows that will be locked.

❏ Decreasing the block size will reduce block-oriented contention such as cache buffers chains latch contention and buffer busy waits. The more rows we pack into each block, the greater the chance that the block will become hot and be the focus of contention.

❏ Block-oriented contention is particularly prevalent in RAC because hot blocks might become a major cause of excessive interconnect traffic. Furthermore, larger blocks might require a larger number of network transmissions. So a larger block size that might be useful in a single instance database could degrade a RAC database.

All these arguments have at least theoretical merit, and it's easy enough to create a test case that shows either optimization or degradation following a change in block size.

The possibility of slightly improving index structure following a block size increase needs to be balanced against the lower selectivity of the buffer cache that also results. So for instance, if you increase the block size to 16K, you might find that a few of your indexes are shallower, and you therefore need to perform fewer IOs to find the table block you want. However, by making blocks larger, you have fewer of them in the buffer cache, so the chance that your table row is in cache has been reduced. You might save an IO on index lookup but gain an IO because the table block was not in memory.

The reverse situation is just as likely: If you reduce the block size hoping for some increase in buffer cache selectivity or a reduction in block-oriented contention, you might inadvertently increase the depth of some key B*-Tree index and suffer from a reduction in index lookup performance.

The default 8K block size is obviously not the single perfect block size for all circumstances; although it is the block size used in most performance benchmarks and Oracle's internal optimizations might work best with that default size. There might well be situations in which it's worth experimenting with altering the block size for selected tables or indexes. However, you should not in general expect changing the block size to result in a "silver bullet" performance improvement.

Altering the Oracle default block size might change index depth, buffer cache selectivity, and—less often—physical IO requirements. However, changing the block size is not a "silver bullet": A change in the block size will have both positive and negative effects on performance that are hard to predict.

If you do want to try a different block size, it might be less risky to set up a tablespace with the new block size and move selected objects to that tablespace rather than rebuilding the entire database with the new block size. If you do this, make sure you configure a buffer pool for the new block size, following the guidelines introduced in Chapter 18, "Buffer Cache Tuning."

SUMMARY

In this chapter we considered some specific technologies and techniques for IO optimization.

Oracle Automatic Storage Management (ASM) is a storage management layer integrated with the Oracle software stack. ASM allows mirroring, striping, and other IO optimizations to be controlled directly by the DBA and implemented with anything from Just A Bunch Of Disks (JBOD) to Logical Units (LUNs) exposed by a high-end storage array. ASM is implemented by a stripped-down Oracle instance that maintains a mapping between physical locations on disk and logical locations of file extents.

Solid State Disk (SSD) is becoming an increasingly popular alternative to magnetic disk, especially for hot datafiles. The two types of SSD, DDR-RAM and Flash, have very different performance and cost factors. Flash RAM in particular can have high write penalties depending on the implementation: Be sure you understand the write characteristics of the SSD device before implementing it for a write-intensive file.

The Oracle/HP Exadata storage server improves the throughput profile of its disks by performing some row and column elimination within the storage server itself. For databases where the sheer volume of data transferred from disk is overwhelming the database server, Exadata might deliver significant performance improvements.

Changing the Oracle block size is sometimes claimed to provide "silver bullet" improvements to Oracle IO. However, any change to the block size has both positive and negative effects and is a risky and time-consuming optimization that is not recommended under normal circumstances.

Chapter 23

OPTIMIZING RAC

In this chapter we consider performance tuning techniques that are specific to Real Application Clusters (RAC) databases.

Almost all the tuning measures considered so far are as relevant to a RAC database as to a single-instance (that is, non-RAC) database. Tuning SQL, eliminating contention, memory, and IO optimization are common techniques that are relatively independent of the cluster status of the database. However, RAC does present certain unique performance opportunities and challenges, and we look at these in this chapter.

The key principles in RAC performance management are

❏ Maintaining high-speed communications between the instances in the cluster

❏ Eliminating unnecessary inter-instance traffic

❏ Balancing workload between the instances in the cluster

RAC OVERVIEW

RAC is a *shared disk* clustered database: Every instance in the cluster has equal access to the database's data on disk. This is in contrast to the *shared nothing* architecture employed by other RDBMS clusters. In a *shared nothing* architecture, each instance is responsible for a certain subset of data. Whenever a session needs that data, the appropriate instance must be involved in serving up the data.

Shared nothing database clusters have their advantages, but transparent and rapid scalability is not one of them. The shared nothing architecture requires that data be distributed across the instances in the cluster. When a new instance is added to the cluster, data needs to be redistributed across the cluster to maintain a reasonable balance of load. In contrast, a new instance can be added to a RAC cluster without any data rebalancing required: The new instance has immediate and independent access to all the data in the database.

It is this capability to rapidly add or remove instances from RAC clusters that justifies the "G for Grid" in the Oracle 10g and 11g naming convention: RAC has the capability to rapidly scale database clusters by adding or removing instances: That capability is required (but perhaps not sufficient) to create a truly grid-enabled database.

The main challenge in the shared disk architecture is to establish a global memory cache across all the instances in the cluster: Otherwise the clustered database becomes IO bound. Oracle establishes this shared cache via a high-speed private network referred to as the *cluster interconnect*.

All the instances in a RAC cluster share access to datafiles on shared disk, though each have private redo logs and undo segments. Each instance has its own SGA and background processes, and each session that connects to the cluster database connects to a specific instance in the cluster. Figure 23-1 provides a high-level summary of the RAC architecture.

GLOBAL CACHE REQUESTS

Understanding how instances in the cluster communicate is critical to understanding RAC performance. As with single-instance Oracle, we want to avoid disk IO whenever possible—primarily by keeping frequently accessed data in memory. In a RAC configuration, the data we want might be in the memory of one of the other instances. Therefore, RAC uses the interconnect to request the required data from another instance that has it in memory, rather than by reading it from disk. Each request across the interconnect is referred to as a *Global Cache* (GC) request.

To coordinate these interinstance block transfers, Oracle assigns each block to a master instance. This instance is essentially responsible for keeping track of which instance has last accessed a particular block of data.

Whenever an Oracle instance wants a block of data that is not in its buffer cache, it asks the master instance for the block. If the master instance has the data concerned, it sends it back across the interconnect: This is recorded as a *2-way* wait and is referred to as a *2-way get*.

If the master instance does not have the block in memory, but has a record of another instance accessing the block, it forwards the block request to this third instance. The third instance then returns the block to the requesting instance: This is recorded as a *3-way* wait and is referred to as a *3-way get*.

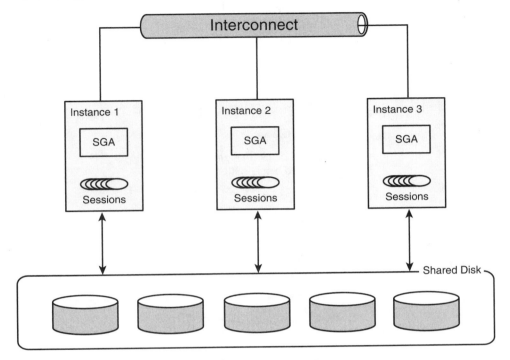

FIGURE 23-1 RAC architecture.

If no instance has the block in memory, the master advises the requesting instance to retrieve the block from disk: This is recorded as a *grant*.

Regardless of which instance wants the block, which instance has the block, and which instance is mastering the block, the number of instances involved in the transfer will never be more than three. This means that the performance penalty as additional instances are added is minimized. However, as we increase the number of instances, the ratio of 3-way waits to 2-way waits will increase, and some reduction in Global Cache performance should be expected.

Figure 23-2 illustrates the sequence of events in 2-way gets, 3-way gets, and grants.

The key background process in these scenarios is the LMS (Global Cache Service[1]) process. One or more of these are initiated at startup, depending on the parameter GCS_SERVER_PROCESSES.

Block requests can either be made for the *current* copy of the block or for a *consistent read* copy. Consistent read blocks are required when performing query processing so that all blocks are consistent as at the start of the query or a read-only transaction. Most query blocks will be consistent read blocks. Current blocks are more often associated with DML operations.

---

[1] Previously known as the Lock Management Service; hence the abbreviation.

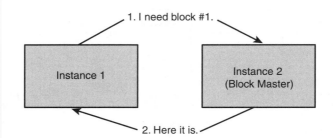

In a 2-way get, the block master instance
has the required block in memory.

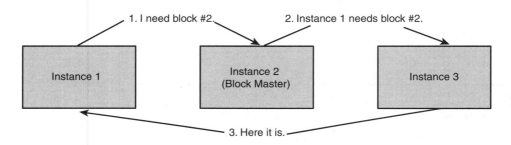

In a 3-way get, a third instance has the required block in memory.

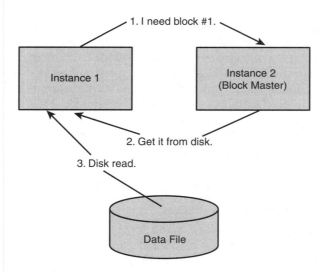

In a grant, the master tells the instance to
read the block from disk.

FIGURE 23-2   Two-way gets, three-way gets, and grants.

RAC TUNING PRINCIPLES

The RAC architecture outlined in the previous section leads directly to the general principles of RAC performance. RAC performs well, and scales well, if the following are true:

❏ The time taken to request a block across the interconnect (*Global Cache* requests) is much lower—say ten times less—than the time to retrieve a block from the disk. Global Cache requests are intended to avoid the necessity of a disk read, and sometimes the disk read must occur even after the Global Cache request. If the Global Cache request time is anywhere near the time it takes to read from disk, the approach backfires. Luckily, properly optimized Global Cache requests are quick—typically ten times less than disk read time.

❏ The cluster is well balanced, or at least there are no overloaded instances in the cluster. Because so many RAC operations involve two or three instances, an overloaded instance might cause problems for its neighbors and itself. Indeed, an overloaded CPU on a remote instance is one of the most common causes for long Global Cache wait times on an otherwise idle local instance.

❏ The overhead incurred through cluster activities is a small proportion of the total database time. We want our RAC database to be a database first and a cluster second. If the proportion of time spent performing Global Cache activities is high in proportion to other activities, we might need to look at ways to reduce the Global Cache traffic.

Three key principles of RAC performance are

❏ Global Cache lookups should be much quicker than disk reads.

❏ Instances in the cluster should have a well-balanced workload.

❏ Time spent performing cluster-related activities should not dominate active database time.

SINGLE INSTANCE TUNING AND RAC

Oracle makes a point of emphasizing that applications that don't scale well on single instance Oracle will probably not scale well on RAC. Although this is generally true, the switch from single instance to RAC tends to magnify some issues while alleviating others.

Performance issues that relate to contention for specific hot data blocks tend to be magnified in RAC because these contentions now also take on a cross-instance overhead. For instance, buffer busy waits can occur for a buffer that is on another instance: Because of the interconnect overhead, the average time spent waiting for the buffer busy wait to complete might increase. Specific types of contention that *increase* in a RAC database follow:

- ❑ **Buffer busy waits**—The sort of operations that cause buffer busy in single-instance will also cause buffer busy in RAC, but the wait will be amplified by the need to transfer the block across the cluster when it is free.

- ❑ **Cache buffer chains latch contention**—Actual contention for this latch experienced in a single instance database will probably reduce in RAC because latches are not acquired across instances. However, for every relatively short latch free wait avoided, you will probably experience a much longer Global Cache wait when transferring the block concerned across the interconnect.

- ❑ **Sequence number generation**—If there are SQ enqueue waits (see Chapter 15, "Lock Contention"), these will likely spread and magnify across instances in a RAC environment.

However, it's also true that some single-instance contention issues can be reduced under RAC. RAC divides up the SGA and sessions across each instance in the cluster, effectively allowing some operations to experience an increase in concurrency. In particular, shared pool related latch and mutex waits might reduce because the activity will be distributed across the multiple shared pools in the cluster.

Contention for data and index blocks in a single instance database will probably magnify in a RAC environment. However, other contention points, such as library cache mutexes, for instance, might be reduced.

MEASURING CLUSTER OVERHEAD

Asides from anything else, we want to make sure that a RAC cluster can perform database activities without being impeded by cluster-related overheads. In a healthy cluster, the time spent in cluster-related activities is mainly determined by the average time to make a Global Cache request (Global Cache latency) multiplied by the number of Global Cache requests that must be made.

$$ClusterTime = AvgGCLatency \times GC\,Requests$$

It therefore follows that reducing cluster overhead is mainly a process of minimizing the Global Cache latency and eliminating any unnecessary Global

Cache requests. The importance of those optimizations depend upon the relative time spent in cluster-related activities.

We can see the overall contribution of cluster-related waits in comparison to other high-level time categories in the following query:

```
SQL> SELECT wait_class time_cat ,ROUND ( (time_secs), 2) time_secs,
  2           ROUND ((time_secs) * 100 / SUM(time_secs) OVER (),2) pct
  3      FROM (SELECT  wait_class wait_class,
  4                    sum(time_waited_micro) / 1000000 time_secs
  5              FROM gv$system_event
  6             WHERE   wait_class <> 'Idle'
  7               AND time_waited > 0
  8             GROUP BY wait_class
  9             UNION
 10             SELECT 'CPU',
 11                    ROUND((SUM(VALUE) / 1000000),2) time_secs
 12               FROM gv$sys_time_model
 13              WHERE stat_name IN ('background cpu time', 'DB CPU'))
 14    ORDER BY time_secs DESC;
```

Time category	TIME_SECS	PCT
CPU	21554.33	43.45
Cluster	**7838.82**	**15.80**
Other	6322.23	12.75
Application	5077.09	10.24
System I/O	3387.06	6.83
User I/O	3302.49	6.66
Commit	1557	3.14
Concurrency	371.5	.75
Network	142.06	.29
Configuration	49.59	.10

As a rule of thumb, we might expect that cluster-related waits comprise less than 10 percent of total database time. Waits above 20 percent certainly warrant investigation.

Cluster waits times greater than 10-20% of total database time probably warrant investigation.

Although cluster waits will usually be composed mainly of straightforward Global Cache request waits, it's not uncommon for more "sinister" Global Cache waits to emerge: lost blocks, congestion, Global Cache buffer busy waits. Drilling down into the low level wait events will often reveal these conditions. The following query breaks out the cluster wait times:

```
SQL> WITH system_event AS
  2       (SELECT CASE
  3                  WHEN wait_class = 'Cluster' THEN event
  4                  ELSE wait_class
  5                END  wait_type, e.*
  6          FROM gv$system_event e)
  7  SELECT wait_type,  ROUND(total_waits/1000,2) waits_1000 ,
  8         ROUND(time_waited_micro/1000000/3600,2) time_waited_hours,
  9         ROUND(time_waited_micro/1000/total_waits,2) avg_wait_ms  ,
 10         ROUND(time_waited_micro*100
 11            /SUM(time_waited_micro) OVER(),2) pct_time
 12  FROM (SELECT wait_type, SUM(total_waits) total_waits,
 13               SUM(time_waited_micro) time_waited_micro
 14          FROM system_event e
 15         GROUP BY wait_type
 16         UNION
 17        SELECT 'CPU',   NULL, SUM(VALUE)
 18          FROM gv$sys_time_model
 19         WHERE stat_name IN ('background cpu time', 'DB CPU'))
 20  WHERE wait_type <> 'Idle'
 21  ORDER BY  time_waited_micro  DESC;
```

Wait Type	Waits \1000	Time Hours	Avg Wait Ms	Pct of Time
CPU		6.15		43.62
Other	38,291	1.76	.17	12.50
Application	32	1.41	157.35	10.00
User I/O	822	.97	4.25	6.88
System I/O	995	.96	3.46	6.78
gc current multi block request	**9,709**	**.87**	**.32**	**6.15**
gc cr multi block request	**16,210**	**.48**	**.11**	**3.37**
Commit	300	.44	5.31	3.13
gc current block 2-way	**5,046**	**.37**	**.26**	**2.59**
gc current block 3-way	**2,294**	**.28**	**.43**	**1.97**
gc cr block busy	**984**	**.16**	**.58**	**1.11**

To get wait times over a shorter time period, you can use the RAC_WAIT_DELTA_VIEW view that is installed with the packages available from this book's Web site. Each time you run it within a session, it reports on the waits since its last execution within the session:

```
SQL> SELECT * FROM rac_wait_delta_view ;
```

Secs	Wait Type	Waits /Sec	Ms /Sec	Avg Ms	Pct Time
37	User I/O	206.51	1,149.81	5.57	50.25
37	**gc current block 2-way**	**783.35**	**264.91**	**.34**	**11.58**
37	**gc current block 3-way**	**376.84**	**231.24**	**.61**	**10.11**
37	System I/O	28.41	166.37	5.86	7.27
37	Concurrency	28.32	135.00	4.77	5.90
37	**gc cr multi block request**	**1,028.97**	**121.00**	**.12**	**5.29**
37	Other	2,367.57	72.65	.03	3.17
37	**gc cr grant 2-way**	**141.27**	**56.89**	**.40**	**2.49**
37	Commit	3.78	55.71	14.72	2.43
37	**gc cr block 2-way**	**13.59**	**8.01**	**.59**	**.35**
37	Network	24.11	7.44	.31	.33
37	Configuration	468.84	7.32	.02	.32
37	**gc cr block 3-way**	**6.43**	**6.90**	**1.07**	**.30**
37	gc current grant busy	2.97	2.83	.95	.12

Here are descriptions for some of the more important Global Cache wait events:

gc cr/current block 2-way	These are waits for Global Cache block requests involving only 2 instances. As outlined at the beginning of the chapter, these occur when the block master instance can forward a block directly to the requesting instance.
gc cr/current block 3-way	These waits occur when the block master does not have the block concerned and forwards the request to a third instance.
gc cr/current multi block request	A wait that occurs when requesting multiple blocks in a single request. This is typically associated with full table or index scans.
gc cr/current grant 2-way	The block master informs the requesting instance that the requested block is not available from another instance. The requesting instance will then perform a disk IO to retrieve the block.
gc cr/current block busy	The requesting instance must wait for the instance that holds the block to complete some other operation before the block can be forwarded. This can happen in the same circumstances as for single instance buffer busy (see Chapter 17, "Shared Memory Contention") or because the requesting instance must flush redo records to the redo log before shipping a consistent copy.

gc cr/current block congested   This wait can be reported when CPU or memory pressure prevents the LMS process from keeping up with requests. Prior to Oracle 10.2, you could manually set LMS to run at a higher than default OS priority to alleviate this situation. From 10.2, LMS runs at a higher priority by default. Changing the number of LMS processes might mask the symptom; however, preventing instances from overloading is a more effective overall solution.

gc cr/current block lost   Lost block waits occur when a block that has been transmitted is not received. If using UDP, which is an **unreliable** protocol in the sense that a network operation does not require an acknowledgment, some small number of lost blocks are to be expected. Moderate rates might suggest that the interconnect is overloaded. High rates probably indicate network hardware issues. We look closer at lost blocks later in the chapter.

REDUCING GLOBAL CACHE LATENCY

The RAC architecture requires and expects that instances will fetch data blocks across the interconnect as an alternative to reading those blocks from disk. The performance of RAC is therefore going to be sensitive to the time it takes to retrieve a block from the Global Cache; which we will call *Global Cache latency*.

Some documents or presentations suggest that Global Cache latency is primarily or exclusively *Interconnect latency*: The time it takes to send the block across the interconnect network. Interconnect latency is certainly an important part of overall Global Cache latency, but it's not the only part. Oracle processes such as the Global Cache Service (LMS) have to perform a significant amount of CPU-intensive processing each time a block is transferred, and this CPU time is usually at least as significant as any other factor in overall Global Cache latency. In certain circumstances non-CPU operations, such as flushing redo entries to disk, will also contribute to Global Cache latency.

Interconnect latency is an important factor in Global Cache latency; however, Oracle CPU and IO are also important contributors.

MEASURING GLOBAL CACHE LATENCY

To measure Global Cache latency, we use the wait interface as exposed by GV$SYSTEM_EVENT.[2] The following query reports on average times for each of the Global Cache request types and single-block read times (for comparison):

---

[2] The V$ views report data for the current instance: GV$ views report data across the entire cluster.

```
SQL> SELECT event, SUM(total_waits) total_waits,
  2          ROUND(SUM(time_waited_micro) / 1000000, 2)
  3             time_waited_secs,
  4          ROUND(SUM(time_waited_micro)/1000 /
  5             SUM(total_waits), 2) avg_ms
  6  FROM gv$system_event
  7  WHERE wait_class <> 'Idle'
  8        AND(   event LIKE 'gc%block%way'
  9            OR event LIKE 'gc%multi%'
 10            or event like 'gc%grant%'
 11            OR event = 'db file sequential read')
 12  GROUP BY event
 13  HAVING SUM(total_waits) > 0
 14  ORDER BY event;
```

Wait event	Total Waits	Time (secs)	Avg Wait (ms)
db file sequential read	283,192	1,978	6.99
gc cr block 2-way	356,193	396	1.11
gc cr block 3-way	162,158	214	1.32
gc cr grant 2-way	141,016	25	.18
gc cr multi block request	503,265	242	.48
gc current block 2-way	325,065	227	.70
gc current block 3-way	117,913	93	.79
gc current grant 2-way	45,580	20	.44
gc current grant busy	168,459	296	1.76
gc current multi block request	91,690	42	.46

This example output provides reason for concern. The average wait for Global Cache consistent read requests (as shown by *gc cr block 2-way* and *gc cr block 3-way*) is more than 1 millisecond and more than 1/10th of the time for a db file sequential read. Although the Global Cache is still faster than disk, it's taking longer than we'd expect if the interconnect and RAC were fully optimized.

The preceding query reports on statistics because each instance in the cluster was started. If you install the packages available from this book's Web site, you can issue the following query that reports the statistics in the interval since the query was last run (in the current session):

```
SQL> SELECT ROUND((end_timestamp - start_timestamp) * 24 * 3600)
  2             sample_seconds,
  3         stat_name, round(waits_per_second,2) waits_per_second,
  4         ROUND(microseconds_per_second/1000/waits_per_second,2)
             avg_ms
```

```
 5   FROM table(opsg_pkg.rac_wait_time_report())
 6   WHERE  (  stat_name LIKE 'gc%block%way'
 7          OR stat_name LIKE 'gc%multi%'
 8          OR stat_name LIKE 'gc%grant%'
 9          OR stat_name = 'db file sequential read')
10   and waits_per_second >0
11   ORDER BY stat_name ;
```

Sample Secs	Wait Type	Waits \sec	Avg ms
354	db file sequential read	97.38	3.86
354	gc cr block 2-way	14.39	.45
354	gc cr block 3-way	7.05	.59
354	gc cr grant 2-way	.12	2.53
354	gc cr multi block request	1,186.21	.10
354	gc current block 2-way	827.98	.26
354	gc current block 3-way	413.89	.46
354	gc current grant 2-way	.21	.78
354	gc current grant busy	.94	2.06
354	gc current multi block request	.06	.18

At least over the past 5 minutes or so, latency on the high volume Global Cache requests has been low. For instance, the average latency for *gc cr block 2-way* is only 0.45 ms.

If you have an Oracle Diagnostics pack license you can view Global Cache latency within Enterprise Manager Performance tab: Figure 23-3 provides an example.

EXAMINING THE INTERCONNECT

When Global Cache waits are high, we should first determine if the latency is primarily the result of interconnect network waits.

The best way to determine the interconnect contribution to overall performance is to use the ping utility to measure latency independently of the Oracle stack. Ping packet handling is not identical to RAC packet handling, but if ping latency is high, you can confidently assume that network responsiveness is an issue.

In Oracle 10g the view X$KSXPIA shows the private and public IP addresses being used by the current instance. In Oracle 11g this information is available in the view GV$CLUSTER_INTERCONNECTS. The following query shows us the private interconnect IP address plus other identifying information for the current instance (this query must be run as SYS):

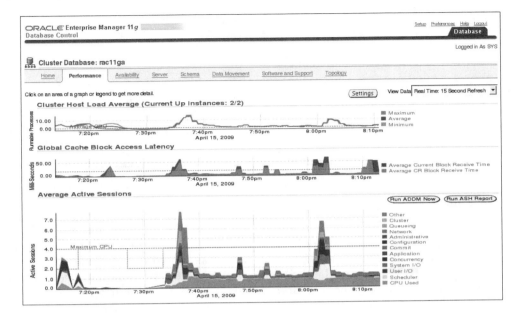

FIGURE 23-3 Enterprise Manager showing Global Cache latency.

```
SQL> SELECT instance_number, host_name, instance_name,
  2         name_ksxpia network_interface, ip_ksxpia private_ip
  3  FROM       x$ksxpia
  4    CROSS JOIN
  5        v$instance
  6  WHERE pub_ksxpia = 'N';
```

```
Inst Host                                               Net   Private
   # Name                          INSTANCE_NAME        IFace IP
---- ------------------------      -------------        ------- -----------
   3 melclul32.melquest.dev.me     MELRAC3              eth1  192.168.0.12
     l.au.qsft
```

We can then ping the IP address from another node in the cluster to determine average latency. On a Linux system, we can use the –s 8192 flag to set an 8K packet size to align with the block size of this Oracle database. On Windows the equivalent flag is -l:

```
$ ping -c 5 -s 8192 192.168.0.12
PING 192.168.0.12 (192.168.0.12) 8192(8220) bytes of data.
8200 bytes from 192.168.0.12: icmp_seq=0 ttl=64 time=0.251 ms
8200 bytes from 192.168.0.12: icmp_seq=1 ttl=64 time=0.263 ms
8200 bytes from 192.168.0.12: icmp_seq=2 ttl=64 time=0.260 ms
```

```
8200 bytes from 192.168.0.12: icmp_seq=3 ttl=64 time=0.265 ms
8200 bytes from 192.168.0.12: icmp_seq=4 ttl=64 time=0.260 ms

--- 192.168.0.12 ping statistics ---
5 packets transmitted, 5 received, 0% packet loss, time 3999ms
rtt min/avg/max/mdev = 0.251/0.259/0.265/0.020 ms, pipe 2
```

The preceding ping output indicates low latency—about .25 ms across the interconnect.

Use the ping utility to measure the interconnect latency independently of the Oracle software stack.

Quest Software's Spotlight on RAC presents both ping latencies and Global Cache latencies for each instance side by side, as shown in Figure 23-4.[3]

Very high network latencies might indicate the need to tune the interconnect as outlined in the next section. However, probably the number one "newbie" error is to inadvertently configure RAC to use the *public* LAN network rather than the *private* interconnect network. Before tuning the private interconnect, make absolutely sure that you didn't accidentally configure RAC to use the public LAN as the interconnect network. Use the X$KSXPIA or V$CLUSTER_ INTERCONNECTS view to double-check the IP addresses are those associated with the interface that is connected to the switch that implements the private network.

It's a common mistake to configure RAC to use the public network, rather than the private network, for the interconnect. Before tuning the interconnect, make absolutely sure that the interconnect is private and that RAC is configured to use the correct network.

FIGURE 23-4   Global Cache and ping latencies in Quest's Spotlight on RAC.

---

[3] Full disclosure: I was heavily involved in the design and development of Spotlight on RAC while working for Quest Software.

SIGNS OF INTERCONNECT PROBLEMS

In addition to high latencies, as exposed by the ping command, interconnect issues can show up as "lost" or congested blocks.

Lost blocks occur when a block is transmitted but never received. The following query shows the number of blocks lost compared to the number sent and received:

```
SQL> SELECT name, SUM(VALUE)
  2  FROM gv$sysstat
  3  WHERE        name LIKE 'gc%lost'
  4          OR name LIKE 'gc%received'
  5          OR name LIKE 'gc%served'
  6  GROUP BY name
  7  ORDER BY name;


NAME                                             SUM(VALUE)
------------------------------------------------ ----------
gc blocks lost                                           99
gc claim blocks lost                                      0
gc cr blocks received                             14207701
gc cr blocks served                               14207721
gc current blocks received                        14471301
gc current blocks served                          14471393
```

Time spent waiting for lost block retransmission is recorded in the wait events *gc cr request retry*, *gc cr block lost*, and *gc current block lost*. The times associated with these waits should be low: typically less than 1 percent of total when compared to the total number of blocks recorded in the *gc cr/current blocks received/served* statistics.

If there are high lost block counts (relative to blocks received) or if the time associated with lost blocks becomes significant compared to total database time, the most likely cause is a network hardware issue. This can be as simple as a poorly mounted network card, crimped networking cables, or faulty network components.

Moderate lost block counts—especially if associated with very high levels of activity—might indicate an overloaded interconnect. The network optimizations below might alleviate the problem, or you might need to increase the throughput of the interconnect hardware (upgrading to 10 Gigabit Ethernet, or InfiniBand for instance).

Global Cache lost blocks can be indicative of an overloaded or miss-configured interconnect or at high levels faulty network hardware.

OPTIMIZING THE INTERCONNECT

If the interconnect is identified as a problem, or even if we just want to optimize it to squeeze the Global Cache latencies down as far as possible, we have a few networking options we can try.

NETWORK HARDWARE AND PROTOCOLS

It's possible to use dual Network Interconnect Cards (NICs) to reduce points of failure in the overall RAC architecture. If so, you should use NIC *bonding* (also known as *link aggregation*) to present the two NICs to Oracle as a single logical interface. This allows for the aggregate network bandwidth of both cards to be fully utilized.

The two most commonly used link and transport protocol combinations for the RAC interconnect are

❑ Gigabit Ethernet (GBe) or 10 Gigabit Ethernet (10GBe) in combination with UDP
❑ InfiniBand in combination with either Reliable Datagram Sockets (RDS) or Internet Protocol (IP)

The GBe/UDP option has the advantage of using standards-based commodity hardware and is supported across a wide set of hardware and operating systems. InfiniBand offers superior throughput and latency but at greater cost and administration effort. Note that Oracle and HP use InfiniBand/RDS inside their Database Machine both to connect the RAC instances and to attach the database nodes to the storage nodes: It's clearly the highest performance solution.

However Gigabit Ethernet can sustain high bandwidth, somewhere in the vicinity of 5,000–10,000 Global Cache transfers per second. Most RAC databases—especially those with an OLTP style workload—are unlikely to overload a GBe or 10GBe interconnect.

Many RAC databases—especially OLTP style—will be adequately served by a Gigabit Ethernet interconnect. However, InfiniBand offers superior throughput and scalability.

ETHERNET JUMBO FRAMES

By default, the maximum-sized packet that can be transmitted across an Ethernet network is only 1500 bytes. This is specified as the Maximum Transmission Unit (MTU). Because Oracle's default block size is 8K, most Global Cache transfers will have to be made in multiple Ethernet packets. The multiple packets will increase network load and possibly overload the interconnect. If any one of the packets that represent a block is lost, Oracle needs to retransmit the lot.

Jumbo frames enables you to set a MTU of up to 9000—large enough for a single default size Oracle block to transmit in a single packet. However, to increase the MTU you might need to apply changes at the switch, the network card, and the operating system level. Setting jumbo frames at the operating system level but failing to do so in the switch is a common mistake. Note too, that not all switches support jumbo frames.

To set jumbo frames at the host level, you use a utility such as ifconfig. On Linux, you can use the ifconfig command to check the MTU size:

```
#ifconfig eth0
eth0        Link encap:Ethernet  HWaddr 00:0D:56:18:2C:60
            inet addr:10.20.12.154  Bcast:10.20.12.255  Mask:255.255.255.0
            inet6 addr: fe80::20d:56ff:fe18:2c60/64 Scope:Link
            UP BROADCAST RUNNING MULTICAST  MTU:1500  Metric:1
            RX packets:951407 errors:0 dropped:0 overruns:0 frame:0
            TX packets:544283 errors:0 dropped:0 overruns:0 carrier:0
            collisions:0 txqueuelen:100
            RX bytes:119973568 (114.4 MiB)  TX bytes:124883921 (119.0 MiB)
            Base address:0xdf40 Memory:feae0000-feb00000
```

The MTU is at the default of 1500. To set it—at the operating system level—to 9000, we again use the ifconfig command:

```
# ifconfig eth0 mtu 9000
# ifconfig eth0
eth0        Link encap:Ethernet  HWaddr 00:0D:56:18:2C:60
            inet addr:10.20.12.154  Bcast:10.20.12.255  Mask:255.255.255.0
            inet6 addr: fe80::20d:56ff:fe18:2c60/64 Scope:Link
            UP BROADCAST RUNNING MULTICAST  MTU:9000  Metric:1
            RX packets:951649 errors:0 dropped:0 overruns:0 frame:0
            TX packets:544386 errors:0 dropped:0 overruns:0 carrier:0
            collisions:0 txqueuelen:100
            RX bytes:119996835 (114.4 MiB)  TX bytes:124902029 (119.1 MiB)
            Base address:0xdf40 Memory:feae0000-feb00000
```

Setting jumbo frames at the OS level will achieve nothing if the NICs or switches are not configured to support an MTU of 9000; you might need to consult with your MIS department or consult the hardware documentation. You also need to make sure that *every* host in the cluster has the same MTU setting.

When enabling Jumbo Frames, be certain that you enable it on all hosts in the cluster and also at the hardware level (switches and NICs).

Each OS supports a different mechanism for enabling Jumbo Frames. On Solaris, you need to edit the interface configuration file (/kernel/drv/e1000g .conf for instance).[4]

If your interconnect is configured using Ethernet (GBe or 10GBe), enabling Jumbo Frames will reduce the packet rate, increasing reliability and throughput.

UDP BUFFER SIZE

When a RAC host receives a network packet over the interconnect, the packet is held in a small memory buffer until the operating system gets around to processing the buffer. If the system is particularly busy or the interconnect is overloaded, packets might be lost. Increasing the UDP receive buffer size can help.

The OS default value for the UDP receive buffer is generally in the vicinity of 128K to 256K, which can be inadequate for the bursts of load that can occur across the interconnect. If the buffer is too small, various network errors might be reported by utilities such as netstat or ifconfig. These symptoms will include dropped packages, overflows, fragmentation, or reassembly errors.

Oracle installation prerequisites require that the value be increased, typically to approximately 4M.

In Linux, the kernel parameter net.core.rmem_max controls the receive buffer size. The sysctl command can be used to obtain the current value:

```
# sysctl -n net.core.rmem_max
4194304
```

Ensure that your UDP receive buffer size is set above the default value, probably to the OS maximum.

LMS WAITS

Interconnect performance is at the heart of Global Cache latency, but high Global Cache latencies are often the result of delays in the Oracle software layers. The LMS service on the remote instances contributes most of the non-network latency

---

[4] See Oracle support note *Recommendation for the Real Application Cluster Interconnect and Jumbo Frames* (341788.1) for more information.

to Global Cache requests; it is responsible for constructing and returning the requested blocks. The following query shows LMS latencies for each instance for current and consistent read requests:

```
SQL> WITH sysstats AS (
  2       SELECT instance_name,
  3              SUM(CASE WHEN name LIKE 'gc cr%time'
  4                       THEN VALUE END) cr_time,
  5              SUM(CASE WHEN name LIKE 'gc current%time'
  6                       THEN VALUE END) current_time,
  7              SUM(CASE WHEN name LIKE 'gc current blocks served'
  8                       THEN VALUE END) current_blocks_served,
  9              SUM(CASE WHEN name LIKE 'gc cr blocks served'
 10                       THEN VALUE END) cr_blocks_served
 11         FROM gv$sysstat JOIN gv$instance
 12         USING (inst_id)
 13        WHERE name IN
 14                   ('gc cr block build time',
 15                    'gc cr block flush time',
 16                    'gc cr block send time',
 17                    'gc current block pin time',
 18                    'gc current block flush time',
 19                    'gc current block send time',
 20                    'gc cr blocks served',
 21                    'gc current blocks served')
 22        GROUP BY instance_name)
 23   SELECT instance_name , current_blocks_served,
 24          ROUND(current_time*10/current_blocks_served,2)
 25                avg_current_ms,
 26          cr_blocks_served,
 27          ROUND(cr_time*10/cr_blocks_served,2) avg_cr_ms
 27     FROM sysstats;
```

Instance	Current Blks Served	Avg CU ms	CR Blks Served	Avg Cr ms
MELRAC1	7,342,829	.03	7,647,581	.05
MELRAC2	7,330,661	.03	7,418,901	.04
MELRAC3	7,310,866	.03	12,696,127	.08

If the network is responsive and fast, but LMS latency is high, one of the following might be implicated:

❏ An overloaded instance cannot respond fast enough to Global Cache requests. In particular, the LMS processes might be overloaded with requests or starved for CPU.

❏ IO bottlenecks, particularly in redo log IO, are slowing down the response to Global Cache requests.

In the first case, the LMS process on the remote instance is simply too busy to process the Global Cache request. This can be due to an excessive volume of requests or because CPU load on the host is making it impossible for the LMS to obtain CPU. The later situation is less common from Oracle 10.2 forward because Oracle now runs the LMS processes at an elevated priority. Severe memory pressure might also lead to a lack of LMS responsiveness.

The too-busy phenomenon is probably a result of an imbalanced cluster: If any instance in the cluster is significantly overloaded, Global Cache response times on the idle instances will suffer. The best solution is to try to achieve a better cluster balance; see the following section on Cluster Balance.

High Global Cache latencies can occur when one or more instances in the cluster become overloaded. Balancing the workload across the cluster may be indicated.

The other typical cause of high latencies is when the LMS process must flush uncommitted changes to the redo log prior to sending the block to the requesting instance. If the application design is such that uncommitted blocks are often in demand across instances in the cluster, these redo log flushes might become common. If there are bottlenecks in the redo log devices, the IO waits will be magnified.

We can measure the impact on LMS response time by leveraging the timing information in GV$SYSTAT and the FLUSHES statistic in GV$CR_BLOCK_SERVER. Putting the two together we can calculate the proportion of block transfers that required a redo log flush and the proportion of LMS time spent performing the flush:

```
SQL> WITH sysstat AS (
  2       SELECT SUM(CASE WHEN name LIKE '%time'
  3                       THEN VALUE END) total_time,
  4              SUM(CASE WHEN name LIKE '%flush time'
  5                       THEN VALUE END) flush_time,
  6              SUM(CASE WHEN name LIKE '%served'
  7                       THEN VALUE END) blocks_served
  8       FROM gv$sysstat
  9       WHERE name IN
```

```
10                          ('gc cr block build time',
11                           'gc cr block flush time',
12                           'gc cr block send time',
13                           'gc current block pin time',
14                           'gc current block flush time',
15                           'gc current block send time',
16                           'gc cr blocks served',
17                           'gc current blocks served')),
18       cr_block_server as (
19       SELECT SUM(flushes) flushes, SUM(data_requests) data_requests
20       FROM gv$cr_block_server      )
21    SELECT ROUND(flushes*100/blocks_served,2) pct_blocks_flushed,
22           ROUND(flush_time*100/total_time,2) pct_lms_flush_time
23       FROM sysstat CROSS JOIN cr_block_server;


PCT_BLOCKS_FLUSHED PCT_LMS_FLUSH_TIME
------------------ ------------------
              .25               36.03
```

Note how even a very small proportion of block flushes (.25%) can still account for a large proportion of total LMS time (36.03%). Tuning the redo log IO layout, as described in Chapter 21, "Disk IO Tuning Fundamentals," might be indicated.

The LMS sometimes needs to flush redo entries to disk before returning a block. Redo log IO can therefore be a critical factor in Global Cache latency.

CLUSTER BALANCE

Achieving balance in a RAC configuration is important for scalability, manageability, and performance. Although some variation in workload across the cluster is to be expected, in an unbalanced cluster, the following undesirable situations can arise:

❑ Sessions on busy instances get poor service time. Even though there might be spare capacity in the cluster as a whole, sessions on busy instances cannot utilize that capacity and experience poor performance.

❑ Sessions on idle instances wait for blocks from busy instances. Because a lot of operations result in requests to remote instances, an over-loaded instance can cause performance problems across the entire cluster. A session on an idle instance might experience high Global Cache wait times waiting on blocks from the busy instance.

❏ Benefits of adding new instances might not be realized. If some of the instances in the cluster are subject to a higher workload, these instances might become bottlenecks to overall database throughput. As instances are added to the cluster, expected performance improvements might be unattainable.

❏ Tuning is harder because each instance has different symptoms. In an unbalanced cluster, sessions on busy instances might experience high CPU waits whereas sessions on less busy instances experience high Global Cache waits. Troubleshooting performance problems on an unbalanced cluster can therefore be more challenging because of the inconsistent symptoms.

ASSESSING CLUSTER BALANCE

We can assess cluster balance fairly easily: The following query reports on CPU, DB time, and logical reads on each instance within the cluster since startup:

```
SQL> WITH sys_time AS (
  2       SELECT inst_id, SUM(CASE stat_name WHEN 'DB time'
  3                            THEN VALUE END) db_time,
  4            SUM(CASE WHEN stat_name IN
                          ('DB CPU','background cpu time')
  5                THEN  VALUE  END) cpu_time
  6         FROM gv$sys_time_model
  7         GROUP BY inst_id                    )
  8  SELECT instance_name,
  9         ROUND(db_time/1000000,2) db_time_secs,
 10         ROUND(db_time*100/SUM(db_time) over(),2) db_time_pct,
 11         ROUND(cpu_time/1000000,2) cpu_time_secs,
 12         ROUND(cpu_time*100/SUM(cpu_time) over(),2)  cpu_time_pct
 13      FROM     sys_time
 14      JOIN gv$instance USING (inst_id);
```

Instance Name	DB Time (secs)	Pct of DB Time	CPU Time (secs)	Pct of CPU Time
MELRAC3	3,705.30	24.48	1,119.99	17.03
MELRAC2	6,278.23	41.48	4,010.85	61.00
MELRAC1	5,150.96	34.03	1,444.06	21.96

In this example it is clear that MELRAC2 is being subjected to a disproportionate level of CPU load: If this is not addressed, increasing cluster workload will almost certainly lead to performance degradation as MELRAC2 becomes the bottleneck for the entire cluster.

The preceding query summarizes performance since the instances in the cluster were started. Of course, instances in a cluster can start and stop independent of the cluster as a whole, which might result in different totals even if the cluster is experiencing a balanced workload. If you want to assess balance over specific periods—and you've installed this book's packages—you could run the following query that reports on CPU and DB time rates across the cluster since the last time the query was run in the current session:

```
SQL> WITH cluster_delta as (
  2      SELECT instance_name, start_timestamp,end_timestamp,
  3        round((end_timestamp-start_Timestamp)*24*3600,2)
             elapsed_seconds,
  4          SUM(CASE WHEN stat_name = 'DB CPU'
  5                 THEN VALUE/1000 END) cpu_ms,
  6          SUM(CASE WHEN stat_name = 'DB time'
  7                 THEN VALUE/1000 END) db_ms
  8      FROM table(opsg_pkg.service_stat_report())
  9      JOIN gv$instance using (inst_id)
 10      GROUP BY instance_name,start_timestamp,end_timestamp
 11  )
 12  SELECT instance_name, elapsed_seconds,
 13         ROUND(cpu_ms / elapsed_seconds, 2) cpu_ms_ps,
 14         ROUND(cpu_ms / elapsed_seconds, 2) db_ms_ps
 15  FROM cluster_delta
 16  ORDER BY instance_name;
```

Instance name	ELAPSED_SECONDS	CPU ms p.s.	DB time ms p.s.
MELRAC1	96	124.19	124.19
MELRAC2	96	840.53	840.53
MELRAC3	96	120.67	120.67

Alternatively, if you have an Oracle Diagnostics pack license, you can look at the instance load averages display within the database control, as shown in Figure 23-5.

Quest Software's Spotlight on RAC probably has the most advanced RAC balance monitoring. Spotlight on RAC displays cluster balance from a number of perspectives and performs a statistical analysis to determine if the imbalance is systematic or due to short-term random fluctuations. Figure 23-6 shows one of the balance analysis screens from Spotlight on RAC.

An imbalance in RAC load can be due to a single session, or just a few sessions, placing heavy load on specific instances. These imbalances might be unavoidable although parallelizing these jobs across the cluster—as discussed in Chapter 13, "Parallel SQL"—might be an option. Other possible causes include

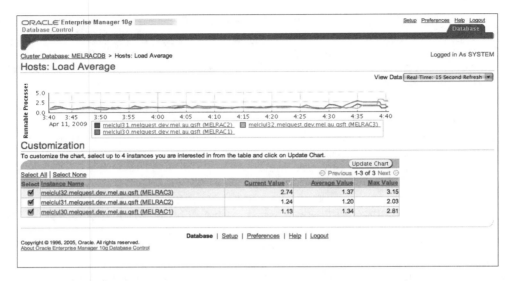

FIGURE 23-5 Monitoring Instance load averages in the database control.

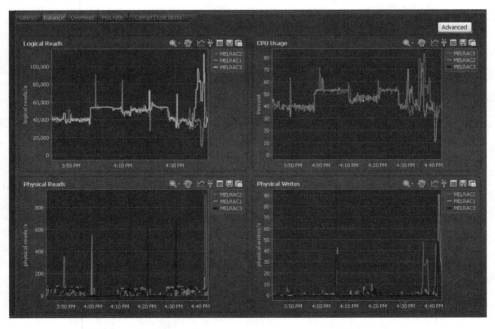

FIGURE 23-6 RAC balance display in Quest's Spotlight on RAC.

❏   Sessions directly connecting to individual instances in the cluster. This might happen if the TNSNAMES.ORA file contains entries for individual instances and cluster entries.

❏   Out of date TNSNAMES.ORA files on clients or on the servers that are causing RAC load balancing to fail: See the next section for more details.

❏   Unbalanced services configuration resulting in specific services placing excessive load on a subset of the instances in the cluster. We discuss services in detail in the next section.

Balancing load across the instances in the cluster is essential for optimal RAC performance. In particular, ensure that no single instance becomes overloaded. An overloaded instance can lead to high Global Cache waits, inconsistent service times, and poor scalability.

CLUSTER BALANCE AND SERVICES

Services enable you to allocate workloads to specific instances within a cluster. Instances within the cluster can be associated with specific services and connection requests for those services will then be directed to those instances. Each service will have one or more preferred instances and optionally one or more available instances. Requests for a service will be directed to preferred instances initially; if none of the preferred instances are available, the request will be sent to an available instance.

After installation, each RAC database will have a few default services: one for each instance, one for the cluster as a whole, and special or internal services (SYS$BACKGROUND, SYS$USERS, the XDB service, and such).

Additional services can be configured and managed by the DBMS_SERVICES package, the srvctl command line utility, through the Database Configuration Assistant (DBCA) in Oracle 10g, or through Enterprise Manager in Oracle 11g. In Figure 23-7 we use Enterprise Manager 11g to add a service (BATCHJOBS) that runs on instance rac11ga1 by default, can be run on instance rac11ga2 if rac11ga1 is not available, but will not run on instance rac11ga3.

Database sessions request a specific service when connecting. For instance, the following TNSNAMES alias requests a connection to the BATCHJOBS service; if we arrange for batch jobs to specify the BATCHJOBS TNS alias, we can be assured that they connect to the appropriate service and hence be allocated to the desired instances:

```
BATCHJOBS=
  (DESCRIPTION =
    (ADDRESS = (PROTOCOL = TCP)(HOST = host1-vip)(PORT = 1521))
```

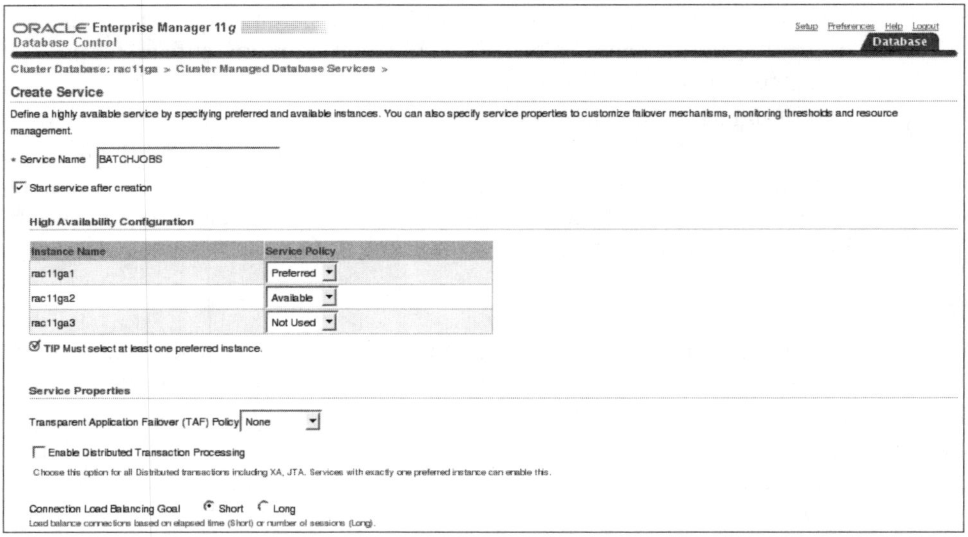

FIGURE 23-7 Configuring services using Enterprise Manager.

```
(ADDRESS = (PROTOCOL = TCP)(HOST = host2-vip)(PORT = 1521))
(ADDRESS = (PROTOCOL = TCP)(HOST = host3-vip)(PORT = 1521))
(LOAD_BALANCE = YES)
(CONNECT_DATA =
  (SERVER = DEDICATED)
  (SERVICE_NAME = batchjobs)
)
)
```

Services serve two main purposes in RAC:

❑ By partitioning certain types of workload to certain instances, services can reduce the amount of Global Cache traffic because similar workloads are most likely to utilize similar data blocks.

❑ Services can help you share a RAC cluster across multiple applications, some of which might have different service level objectives. By allocating more instances in the cluster to a specific service, we effectively allocate the service a bigger share of cluster resources.

When we make use of services, we are deliberately manipulating the workloads on each instance, so we're unlikely to see the perfect balance that we might aspire to when every instance in the cluster is subject to the same workload.

However, avoiding an overloaded instance within the cluster is still critically important when using services.

We can view service workload through the GV$SERVICE_STATS view, which shows various workload statistics for each service. This query breaks down service CPU across the cluster, showing the percentage of total CPU that is consumed by the service on the instance, and how the service workload is distributed across the cluster:

```
SQL> BREAK ON instance_name skip 1
SQL> COMPUTE SUM OF cpu_time ON instance_name
SQL>
SQL> WITH service_cpu AS (SELECT instance_name, service_name,
  2                              round(SUM(VALUE)/1000000,2) cpu_time
  3                      FROM    gv$service_stats
  4                              JOIN
  5                                 gv$instance
  6                              USING (inst_id)
  7                      WHERE stat_name IN ('DB CPU',
                                            'background cpu time')
  8                      GROUP BY  instance_name, service_name )
  9  SELECT instance_name, service_name, cpu_time,
 10         ROUND(cpu_time * 100 / SUM(cpu_time)
 11             OVER (PARTITION BY instance_name), 2) pct_instance,
 12         ROUND(  cpu_time
 13             * 100
 14             / SUM(cpu_time) OVER (PARTITION BY service_name), 2)
 15             pct_service
 16  FROM service_cpu
 17  WHERE cpu_time > 0
 18  ORDER BY instance_name, service_name;
```

Instance Name	Service Name	Cpu secs	Pct Of Instance	Pct of Service
MELRAC1	MELRACDB	4,292	51.50	34.70
	MEL_SRV3	619	7.42	100.00
	MEL_SRV4	621	7.45	53.29
	SYS$BACKGROUND	0	.00	42.86
	SYS$USERS	2,802	33.62	1.32
********		-----------		
sum		8,334		
MELRAC2	MELRACDB	3,834	1.78	31.00
	MEL_SRV1	990	.46	100.00
	MEL_SRV4	544	.25	46.71
	MEL_SRV5	1,228	.57	100.00
	SYS$BACKGROUND	0	.00	28.57

	SYS$USERS	208,954	96.94	98.32
********		-----------		
sum		215,551		
MELRAC3	MELRACDB	4,241	71.87	34.29
	MEL_SRV2	385	6.52	100.00
	MEL_SRV6	507	8.60	100.00
	SYS$BACKGROUND	0	.00	28.57
	SYS$USERS	768	13.01	.36
********		-----------		
sum		5,901		

To view service activity over shorter intervals, the RAC_SERVICE_DELTA view, installed with the packages available at this book's Web site, shows the CPU consumption between successive executions of the script.

Other views, such as GV$SERVICE_EVENT, provide additional performance data aggregated to the instance and service level.

Quest's Spotlight on RAC provides very extensive real-time services monitoring capabilities: It can show how services are utilizing various resources across instances and how the load on each instance is driven by the various services. It also enables you to view wait time and session information for specific services. Figure 23-8 shows one of Spotlight's services management screens.

Getting acceptable cluster balance and avoiding overloaded instances when services are deployed requires fairly careful monitoring and adjustment of service configuration. But in general, you achieve better balance by making instances that are under-utilized available to more services and moving services off over-utilized instances.

When using cluster services to distribute workload, ensure that no instances are overloaded, while also avoiding under-utilization of instances.

RAC LOAD BALANCING FACILITIES

By default, RAC uses client-side, round-robin load-balancing: Each request from a client connects to a different instance in the cluster, and the overall result is that each instance receives approximately the same number of connections.

The client-side load balancing is enabled within the TNSNAMES definition for the cluster database service. Unless the LOAD_BALANCE clause is set to OFF, round robin load balancing will be enabled across all the hosts listed in the TNS entry. So for instance the following TNSNAMES definition results in connection requests being alternated between the hosts *host1-vip*, *host2-vip*, and *host3-vip*:

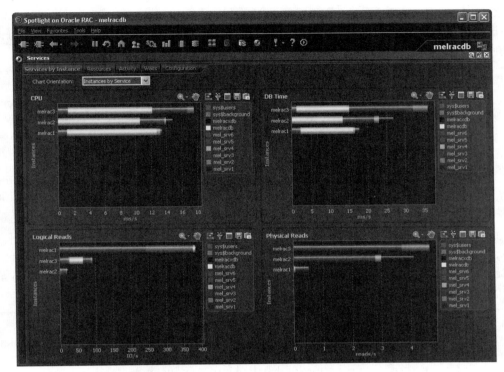

FIGURE 23-8   Spotlight on RAC services monitoring.

```
racdb =
  (DESCRIPTION =
    (ADDRESS = (PROTOCOL = TCP)(HOST = host1-vip)(PORT = 1521))
    (ADDRESS = (PROTOCOL = TCP)(HOST = host2-vip)(PORT = 1521))
    (ADDRESS = (PROTOCOL = TCP)(HOST = host3-vip)(PORT = 1521))
    (LOAD_BALANCE = YES)
    (CONNECT_DATA =
      (SERVER = DEDICATED)
      (SERVICE_NAME = racdb)
    )
  )
```

For client-side load balancing to work properly, all TNSNAMES definitions should be kept up to date. For instance, if you add a new instance to the cluster but fail to update TNSNAMES.ORA files on the clients, the new instance might not pick up its share of the load (although server-side load balancing will probably save the day).

> To keep client-side load balancing current, it is advisable to keep all TNSNAMES entries up to date when instances are added or removed from a cluster.

If you fail to update the TNSNAMES files on all the clients, load balancing should still occur providing that server-side load balancing is enabled. Server-side load balancing works at the listener level. Listeners on each node direct connection requests to the instance or node that is currently least heavily loaded.

Server-side load balancing requires that the REMOTE_LISTENER parameter in each instance be set to the name of a TNSNAMES entry that defines the listeners on all the nodes in the cluster. When adding or removing an instance, you should update the TNSNAMES entries on all hosts in the cluster to ensure that the remote listener definitions are up to date.

> Server-side load balancing requires that the LOCAL_LISTENER parameter point to a TNSNAMES entry that defines all the listeners in the database cluster.

Advanced load balancing capabilities are available within the Oracle client libraries, such as JDBC and ODP.NET. Applications that take advantage of these interfaces can obtain better load balancing—for instance, load balancing at the transaction level rather than at the connection level. Oracle's Fast Application Notification (FAN) and Load Balancing Advisories can optimize client workload to match service goals (throughput or response time) and connection duration (long-lived or short-lived session durations). See the *Oracle RAC Administration and Deployment Guide* for more details.

MINIMIZING GLOBAL CACHE REQUESTS

As we saw earlier, Global Cache requests are integral to RAC and represent both the "cost" of the RAC architecture and the basis of its scalability. Avoiding a disk read by fetching a needed block from another instance prevents RAC databases from becoming IO bound. However, each Global Cache request adds overhead: It's far better to find the data you want in the local buffer cache than to retrieve it from another instance.

Very high Global Cache request rates generally result in a poorly performing RAC cluster. The overhead of the Global Cache activity probably means that response time for the RAC database will be higher than for its single-instance equivalent and might suggest that scalability problems will emerge as more instances are added.

CAUSES OF HIGH GLOBAL CACHE REQUEST RATES

High Global Cache request rates are generally the result of application processing patterns:

- ❏ Hot rows or blocks that are needed by every instance and every transaction. For example, a table-based sequence number generator might contain a single row that has the next order sequence number. This block will be required every time an order is created on any instance and will, therefore, be constantly circulating across the cluster.

- ❏ Other hot blocks. These are the same sorts of blocks that might have caused cache buffers chains latch contention in a single instance database (see Chapter 16, "Latch and Mutex Contention"). The cures for cache buffers chains latch contention (reducing rows per block or partitioning) might also be effective in the RAC environment.

- ❏ Full table scans that retrieve large numbers of blocks across the interconnect. SQL statements that involve full table scans on large tables might request large numbers of blocks from many or all the other instances in the cluster.

MEASURING GLOBAL CACHE REQUEST RATES

To determine how often the database needs to make Global Cache requests, we can compare the number of blocks fetched across the interconnect with the total number of block accessed (that is, the number of logical reads). The following query performs that calculation and determines the ratio of physical to logical reads (yes, the notorious Buffer Cache Hit Ratio):

```
SQL> WITH sysstats AS (
  2       SELECT inst_id,
  3              SUM(CASE WHEN name LIKE 'gc%received'
  4                       THEN VALUE END) gc_blocks_received,
  5              SUM(CASE WHEN name = 'session logical reads'
  6                       THEN VALUE END) logical_reads,
  7              SUM(CASE WHEN name = 'physical reads'
  8                       THEN VALUE END) physical_reads
  9       FROM gv$sysstat
 10       GROUP BY inst_id)
 11   SELECT instance_name, logical_reads, gc_blocks_received,
                physical_reads,
 12          ROUND(physical_reads*100/logical_reads,2)
                phys_to_logical_pct,
 13          ROUND(gc_blocks_received*100/logical_reads,2)
                gc_to_logical_pct
```

```
14     FROM sysstats JOIN gv$instance
15   USING (inst_id);
```

```
Instance    Logical  GC Blocks    Physical Phys/Logical GC/Logical
name          Reads   Received       Reads          Pct        Pct
--------  ----------  ---------  ----------- ------------ ----------
MELRAC3   15,353,311  1,730,818       23,099          .15      11.27
MELRAC2  148,903,331  1,756,882      438,531          .29       1.18
MELRAC1   21,792,614  1,730,366       39,471          .18       7.94
```

Note how in the preceding example it's the least busy instances (in terms of logical reads) that have the highest Global Cache/Logical request ratio: The less busy an instance is, the more likely that the blocks it needs are in the memory of another, busier, instance.

As is typical in general with hit or miss ratios, one should be cautious about forming too many conclusions because the ratio will vary widely depending on workload patterns. However, the higher the percentage of blocks that result in a Global Cache request, the more likely it is that we might achieve performance improvements by reducing either Global Cache latency or Global Cache traffic.

To determine which segments are resulting in the highest rates of Global Cache activity, we can exploit the GV$SEGMENT_STATISTICS view. The following query lists the segments that are associated with the highest number of Global Cache blocks received:

```
SQL> WITH segment_misses AS
  2           (SELECT owner || '.' || object_name segment_name,
  3                  SUM(VALUE) gc_blocks_received,
  4                  ROUND(  SUM(VALUE) * 100
  5                        / SUM(SUM(VALUE)) OVER (), 2) pct
  6           FROM gv$segment_statistics
  7           WHERE statistic_name LIKE 'gc%received' AND VALUE > 0
  8           GROUP BY owner || '.' || object_name)
  9  SELECT segment_name,gc_blocks_received,pct
 10    FROM segment_misses
 11   WHERE pct > 1
 12   ORDER BY pct DESC;
```

```
SEGMENT_NAME                                     GC_BLOCKS_RECEIVED    PCT
----------------------------------------------- -------------------- ------
TRANSIM.GH_SALES_TOTALS                                   1,641,395  79.31
TRANSIM.G_CART_PK                                           104,014   5.03
TRANSIM.G_CART                                               86,185   4.16
SYS.ALERT_QT                                                 39,476   1.91
SYS.SYS_IOT_TOP_8797                                         22,895   1.11
```

TECHNIQUES FOR REDUCING GLOBAL CACHE REQUESTS

The hot-row scenario—for instance, an order number generated from a sequence table—is hard to correct without application changes. If many transactions frequently access a specific row, that row is inevitably going to circulate at high rates throughout the cluster. If this overhead is unacceptable, you probably want to isolate the workloads concerned to specific instances in the cluster, perhaps by using services. Alternatively, you can avoid these single-row contention points by changing your application design (perhaps using an Oracle sequence generator rather than a sequence table).

For instance, let's say we are trying to reduce the interconnect load caused by the GH_SALES_TOTALS table from the preceding example output. We could create a service that is associated with a single instance of the cluster and then allocate all sessions that access GH_SALES_TOTALS to that service. The result would be that all SQLs that access GH_SALES_TOTALS would execute on a specific instance, and the interconnect activity would be eliminated.

In the more general case where blocks or specific segments are associated with heavy Global Cache activity, we can attempt to reduce the amount of interinstance traffic through one of the following techniques:

❏ Isolating workloads to a particular instance or groups of instances. We can do this through services configuration as previously discussed. If transactions and queries that access specific segments or blocks are isolated to a smaller number of instances, the amount of Global Cache traffic will be reduced. However this does make balancing the cluster more difficult.

❏ Isolating sessions that are likely to work on the same data. This is similar to isolating workloads, but instead of isolating specific transaction types, we isolate sessions that are likely to work on the same sets of data. For instance, we might allocate sessions from the East Coast to one set of instances and West Coast to another. Again, this raises concerns about balance: in the East Coast/West Coast scenarios we imbalance the cluster because of the differences in the number of users in each region and the time zones that correspond to peak processing. Nevertheless, this sort of partitioning results in a reduction in Global Cache traffic and—if we are careful with our services configuration—we can still achieve an acceptable distribution of work across the cluster.

❏ Partitioning the segments with the highest levels of Global Cache activity. Hash partitioning can split up the hot blocks, hopefully reducing Global Cache contention for those blocks.

❏ Range or list partitioning the segments with isolation of user populations. In addition to creating services to support geographical regions (East Coast/West Coast for instance), we could also consider partitioning key tables and indexes on the same geographic basis. Partitions specific to a particular region naturally tend to become cached (and mastered) on the instances to which those users connect, resulting in fewer Global Cache requests.

❑ Reverse key indexes. Reverse key indexes can help relieve Global Cache contention for hot index leaf and branch blocks. When a segment has an ascending numeric primary key, all new rows require an update to the leading edge of the index. Freelist management distributes the new table rows across the cluster, but the leading leaf and branch blocks of the index will be in contention by all instances in the cluster. Reverse key indexes distribute new entries across all the leaf blocks, relieving the contention. However, be aware that reverse key indexes cannot be used for index range scans (though you don't often need to perform range scans on primary keys).

❑ Freelists groups for Manual Segment Storage Management (MSSM) tablespaces. If you have legacy tablespaces that don't use Automatic Segment Storage Management (ASSM), you must make sure that you use multiple freelist groups on tables that have nontrivial insert rates. Otherwise all new rows will be directed to the same new blocks, creating Global Cache contention for that block.

Very high Global Cache request rates can limit RAC performance and scalability. Global Cache activity can be reduced by adjusting application design, isolating workloads or sessions using services, reverse key primary indexes, and by partitioning segments.

Inter-instance parallel query, discussed in some detail in Chapter 13, can improve parallel SQL performance but can also increase Global Cache traffic. Restricting parallel execution to a single instance or smaller set of instances will sometimes be indicated. The Oracle 10g INSTANCE_GROUP parameter or the Oracle 11g PARALLEL_INSTANCE_GROUP parameter can control the instances that are involved in a parallel SQL.

SUMMARY

Real Application Clusters (RAC) is a shared disk clustered database in which each instance in the cluster has equivalent access to data held on a shared disk system and which implements a logical Global Cache through a high-speed private network called the interconnect.

Most of the performance optimization techniques discussed in earlier chapters are equally applicable to RAC databases. In particular, before moving to a RAC architecture, make sure you have eliminated any hot block forms of contention such as buffer busy or cache buffers chains latch contention as these tend to magnify in RAC.

The most significant difference in a RAC database is the use of Global Cache requests to fetch blocks from other instances in the cluster rather than to read them from disk. RAC will scale and perform well, providing that

❏ Global Cache latency is much less than disk read latency. Achieving this involves both optimizing the interconnect network and making sure that no instances get too busy to respond to Global Cache requests in a timely manner.

❏ The cluster is reasonably well balanced. In particular, no instance should be overloaded: An overloaded instance is likely to cause performance problems both for itself and other instances in the cluster.

❏ The rate of Global Cache requests is reasonable. In particular, hot blocks that are in constant contention across the cluster should be minimized. Partitioning, reverse key indexes, and workload isolation using services can all be useful in minimizing this traffic.

BIBLIOGRAPHY

This book attempted to strike a sensible balance between breadth—covering most aspects of Oracle performance—and depth. However, no book of this size can hope to cover all topics. The resources in this bibliography go beyond the scope of this book and also document some of the sources that contributed to this book's content.

THE ORACLE DOCUMENTATION SET

A lot of people make the mistake of shopping for a commercial Oracle book or searching through blogs for answers but forget to check out the Oracle documentation set. Oracle's documentation set is voluminous, relatively comprehensive, and generally accurate. The documentation set can be downloaded as HTML or PDF and provides a powerful (online) search capability. You can get the online documentation set at http://www.oracle.com/technology/documentation/database.html.

In particular, I recommend you keep the following handy:

- ❏ *Concepts Manual*
- ❏ *Performance Tuning Guide*
- ❏ *Data Warehousing Guide*
- ❏ *Reference Manual*
- ❏ *SQL Language Manual*

BOOKS

Here are my favorite Oracle performance books:

❏ Antognini, Christian. *Troubleshooting Oracle Performance*. New York: Apress, 2008.
   A relatively recent addition, this book is well written and covers many 11g concepts. It emphasizes an application design approach to performance.

❏ Debes, Nobert. *Secrets of the Oracle Database*. New York: Apress, 2009.
   Originally a self-published "Lulu" book, now published by Apress. This book contains a collection of undocumented Oracle features, many of which are performance-related. The sections on raw SQL trace format and on PGA memory allocations are particularly relevant.

❏ Dyke, Julian, and Steve Shaw. *Pro Oracle Database 10g RAC on Linux*. New York: Apress, 2006.
   Excellent coverage of RAC administration and tuning. The Linux-only perspective results in a deeper level of coverage in many cases because a lot of RAC networking is OS-specific.

❏ Feuerstein, Steven, and Bill Pribyl. *Oracle PL/SQL Programming, 4th Edition*. California: O'Reilly, 2005.
   Probably the best book—by far the most popular book—on the PL/SQL language. Steven is a truly gifted author, and this book is a pleasure to read. The book covers many aspects of PL/SQL performance. A fifth edition might have been published by the time you read this.

❏ Gopalakrishnan, K. *Oracle Database 10g Real Application Clusters Handbook*. California: Oracle Press. 2006.
   A solid coverage of RAC installation and management.

❏ Kyte, Thomas. *Expert Oracle Database Architecture: 9i and 10g Programming Techniques and Solutions*. New York: Apress, 2005.
   Tom Kyte is probably the best "explainer" in the Oracle community. This book is superbly organized and delivers the essential details of the Oracle architecture.

❏ Lewis, Jonathan. *Cost-Based Oracle Fundamentals*. New York: Apress, 2005 (reissued in 2009).
   Jonathan Lewis is one of the most respected independent Oracle experts in the world. This book is an outstanding work of research in which the operations of the Oracle optimizer are thoroughly investigated and described.

❏ Millsap, Cary, and Jeffrey Holt. *Optimizing Oracle Performance*. California: O'Reilly, 2003.
   Carey Millsap is one of the pioneers of empirical Oracle performance management. This book is somewhat dated technically (Oracle 9i era), but his

approach to performance optimization still stands. The section on queuing theory is a must if you want to dive into that advanced topic.

❏ Scalzo, Bert. *Oracle DBA Guide to Data Warehousing and Star Schemas*. Upper Saddle River, NJ: Prentice Hall, 2003.
A thorough but concise coverage of data warehouse star schema implementation in Oracle.

❏ Shallahamer, Craig. *Oracle Performance Firefighting*. OraPub, 2009.
I got hold of *Oracle Performance Firefighting* only after my book was in final production. Craig Shallahamer is another pioneer of Oracle performance management. This book concentrates on contention-related performance issues and expands on some of the ideas covered in Chapters 16 through 17 of this book. It's a great read if you want to to take a deep dive into Oracle internals.

❏ Shee, Richmond, Kirtikumar Deshpande, and K. Gopalakrishnan. *Oracle Wait Interface: A Practical Guide to Performance Diagnostics & Tuning*. California: Oracle Press, 2004.
The Oracle wait interface provides the best insight to many aspects of Oracle performance. This book works through many of the most significant wait categories and explains in detail why they occur. However, it's slightly dated—covers first release of 10g only.

❏ Vengurlekar, Nitin, Murali Vallath, and Rich Long. *Oracle Automatic Storage Management*. California: Oracle Press, 2007.
ASM is a complete technology in its own right, and this book does a very good job of covering the technology. The foreword in which the creator of ASM describes its objectives and history is well worth reading.

INTERNET SITES AND BLOGS

The wealth of Oracle performance information available on the Internet is truly amazing, especially for someone like me who remembers the scarcity of available information in the earlier days of Oracle's history. Those who freely share their expertise, wisdom, and experience to the benefit of the whole community deserve much praise, and they certainly have my gratitude.

Here are the blogs and private Web sites that I find most useful:

❏ Ask Tom, http://asktom.oracle.com.
Chances are if you've ever had a question about Oracle, someone has "asked Tom" (Kyte). Threads on this site go back for years, and there's some incredible long-running and evolving discussions. Tom Kyte has a gift for explaining complex topics accurately and effectively.

❏ Doug's Oracle Blog, http://oracledoug.com/serendipity/.
A lot of good performance related material on this blog.

❏ Foote, Richard. Oracle Blog, http://richardfoote.wordpress.com/. Richard Foote focuses on indexing issues. Each blog posting contains unique and practical insights into Oracle indexing technology and application. Each blog posting is associated with a song title that I constantly struggle to associate with the posting content!

❏ Inside the Oracle Optimizer, http://optimizermagic.blogspot.com/ The blog of the Oracle optimizer team.

❏ Julian Dyke, http://www.juliandyke.com/. Julian Dyke has lots of great general presentations on his site. There is a lot of information on Oracle internals here that is hard to find elsewhere.

❏ Kevin Closson's Oracle Blog, http://kevinclosson.wordpress.com/. Kevin Closson is closely associated with the Oracle ExaData storage device. A lot of material about ExaData here, and broader IO and storage-related topics.

❏ Lewis, Johathan. Oracle Scratchpad, http://jonathanlewis.wordpress.com/. Jonathan Lewis blogs frequently and authoritatively on Oracle performance, internals, and the optimizer.

❏ Tanel Poder's blog, http://blog.tanelpoder.com/. Tanel Poder is one of the most active Oracle hackers around today. A lot of internals and advanced performance optimization techniques can be found on his blog.

INDEX

N

W

Y

 FREE Online Edition

Your purchase of **Oracle® Performance Survival Guide** includes access to a free online edition for 45 days through the Safari Books Online subscription service. Nearly every Cisco Press book is available online through Safari Books Online, along with more than 5,000 other technical books and videos from publishers such as Addison-Wesley Professional, Exam Cram, IBM Press, O'Reilly, Prentice Hall, Que, and Sams.

SAFARI BOOKS ONLINE allows you to search for a specific answer, cut and paste code, download chapters, and stay current with emerging technologies.

Activate your FREE Online Edition at
www.informit.com/safarifree

> **STEP 1:** Enter the coupon code: MDKCIWH.

> **STEP 2:** New Safari users, complete the brief registration form.
> Safari subscribers, just log in.

If you have difficulty registering on Safari or accessing the online edition, please e-mail customer-service@safaribooksonline.com